# ZAGAT®

# Los Angeles
# So. California
# Restaurants
# 2009

D0503326

**LA EDITORS**
Elizabeth Hurchalla, Grace Jidoun and Helen Sillett

**ORANGE COUNTY EDITOR**
Gretchen Kurz

**SENIOR CONSULTING EDITOR**
Merrill Shindler

**STAFF EDITORS**
Michelle Golden and Karen Hudes

Published and distributed by
Zagat Survey, LLC
4 Columbus Circle
New York, NY 10019
T: 212.977.6000
E: losangeles@zagat.com
www.zagat.com

## ACKNOWLEDGMENTS

We thank Kristin Viola (contributor), Kathy Aaronson, Robert Buscemi, Sarah Hadley, Kent Hayward, Merri Howard, Eva Ingvarson, Alec Rubinstein and Sarah Shindler, as well as the following members of our staff: Caitlin Eichelberger (assistant editor), Stacey Slate (editorial assistant), Sean Beachell, Maryanne Bertollo, Jane Chang, Sandy Cheng, Reni Chin, Larry Cohn, Deirdre Donovan, Alison Flick, Jeff Freier, Sharon Gintzler, Justin Hartung, Roy Jacob, Natalie Lebert, Mike Liao, Christina Livadiotis, Allison Lynn, Dave Makulec, Andre Pilette, Kimberly Rosado, Becky Ruthenburg, Troy Segal, Aleksandra Shander, Liz Borod Wright, Sharon Yates, Anna Zappia and Kyle Zolner.

# Contents

# Ratings & Symbols

| Zagat Top Spot | Name | Symbols | | Cuisine | Zagat Ratings | | | |
|---|---|---|---|---|---|---|---|---|
| | | | | | FOOD | DECOR | SERVICE | COST |

| Area, Address & Contact | ⚡ **Tim & Nina's** ◗ *Asian* |
|---|---|
| | Hollywood \| 346 Sunset Blvd. (1st St.) \| 213-555-2570 \| www.zagat.com |

▽ 23 | 9 | 13 | $15

| Review, surveyor comments in quotes | "Trend"-spotters hail this "high-concept" production on Sunset offering "fantastic" Asian-deli fare that includes "tantalizing tongue sushi" slathered in "to-die-for hijiki coleslaw"; decor that "hasn't changed since Cecil B. DeMille" was a regular and "reeeal New Yawk-style" service doesn't seem to deter "agents", "stars" and "working gals" hooked on the "delicious sake-celery soda-tinis." |
|---|---|

**Ratings**

**Food, Decor** and **Service** are rated on the Zagat 0 to 30 scale.

| 0 | – | 9 | poor to fair |
|---|---|---|---|
| 10 | – | 15 | fair to good |
| 16 | – | 19 | good to very good |
| 20 | – | 25 | very good to excellent |
| 26 | – | 30 | extraordinary to perfection |
| ▽ | | | low response \| less reliable |

**Cost**

Reflects our surveyors' average estimate of the price of a dinner with one drink and tip and is a benchmark only. Lunch is usually 25% less. Costs for prix fixe–only places reflect the lowest-priced menu plus 30%. For **newcomers** or survey **write-ins** listed without ratings, the price range is indicated as follows:

| I | $25 and below |
|---|---|
| M | $26 to $40 |
| E | $41 to $65 |
| VE | $66 or more |

**Symbols**

| ⚡ | Zagat Top Spot (highest ratings, popularity and importance) |
|---|---|
| ◗ | serves after 11 PM |
| Ⓢ | closed on Sunday |
| Ⓜ | closed on Monday |
| ⊄ | no credit cards accepted |

**Maps**

Index maps show restaurants with the highest Food ratings in those areas.

# About This Survey

Here are the results of our **2009 Los Angeles/ So. California Restaurants Survey,** covering 1,980 eateries in the greater Los Angeles area and in Orange County, Palm Springs and Santa Barbara as well. Like all of our guides, this one is based on the collective opinions of thousands of local consumers.

**WHO PARTICIPATED:** Extensive input from 9,873 frequent diners forms the basis for the ratings and reviews in this guide (their comments are shown in quotation marks within the reviews). Of these surveyors, 47% are women, 53% men; the breakdown by age is 8% in their 20s; 22%, 30s; 22%, 40s; 23%, 50s; and 25%, 60s or above. Collectively they bring roughly 1.9 million annual meals worth of experience to this Survey.

**HELPFUL LISTS:** Our top lists and indexes can help you find exactly the right place for any occasion. See Most Popular (page 7), LA's Key Newcomers (page 9), Top Ratings (pages 10–16) and Best Buys (page 17) as well as Top Ratings for Orange County (page 308), Palm Springs (page 320) and Santa Barbara (page 333). For additional Orange County coverage, see our companion Orange County pocket guide, available this fall.

**OUR EDITORS:** Special thanks go to our local editors, Elizabeth Hurchalla, who writes about food and entertaining for Evite.com; Grace Jidoun, a freelance food writer; Gretchen Kurz, a Zagat editor for 14 years, who covers OC dining for publications including *Orange Coast* magazine; Merrill Shindler, a CBS radio commentator and columnist, food writer, critic and a Zagat editor for more than 20 years; and Helen Sillett, who edits and writes for numerous travel publications.

**ABOUT ZAGAT:** This marks our 29th year reporting on the shared experiences of consumers like you. Today we have over 350,000 surveyors and now cover airlines, bars, dining, entertaining, fast food, golf, hotels, movies, music, resorts, shopping, spas, theater and tourist attractions worldwide.

**VOTE AND COMMENT:** We invite you to join any of our upcoming surveys at **ZAGAT.com.** There you can rate and review establishments year-round. In exchange for participating you will receive a free copy of the resulting guide when published.

**AVAILABILITY:** Zagat guides are available in all major bookstores as well as on **ZAGAT.com,** the award-winning **ZAGAT.mobi** (for web-enabled mobile phones) and **ZAGAT TO GO** (for smartphones). These products also enable you to reserve with just one click.

**FEEDBACK:** There is always room for improvement, thus we invite your comments and suggestions about any aspect of our performance. Just contact us at **losangeles@zagat.com.**

New York, NY
September 25, 2008

Nina and Tim Zagat

# What's New

**IS LA THE NEW LAS VEGAS?** Last year, we were wondering if LA was the new NY thanks to debuts by Big Apple chefs like Mario Batali and Tom Colicchio. But this year's wave of imports is far more geographically diverse, beginning with arrivals from Boston's Todd English (**Beso**), DC's Michel Richard (**Citrus at Social**) and London's **Gordon Ramsay.** Looking ahead, San Francisco's Michael Mina is prepping his **XIV** on the Sunset Strip for fall and DC-based toque José Andrés will unveil an avant-garde Spaniard, **The Bazaar,** in the new SLS Hotel on La Cienega come winter.

**YOU SAY BISTRO, I SAY BRASSERIE:** It's been a bumper season for French cuisine, which for years has played third banana to spaghetti and sushi in LA. Thanks to high-profile Gallics like Santa Monica's **Anisette Brasserie** (with chef Alain Giraud – fresh off **Bastide** on Melrose) and WeHo's bustling **Comme Ça** by David Myers and glammed-up **Foxtail,** we're rediscovering the joys of côte de boeuf and pommes frites – with a Lipitor chaser.

**LET THEM EAT BURGERS:** LA has always been a good burger town (just ask the permanent crowds at the **Apple Pan** and **In-N-Out**), but the past year has seen our patty consciousness go way up, from the launch of Govind Armstrong's **8 oz.** on Melrose to the new **Father's Office** spin-off in Culver City, to the South Bay opening of a branch of the popular **Five Guys** chain. Is it possible that burgers are the new maki?

**ECO-MANIA:** The trend toward eating green continues to gain momentum with 71% of our surveyors (up from 61% last year) saying it's important that the food they eat is locally grown. More and more restaurants are trumpeting their eco-friendly practices, from the hemp aprons worn by the servers at **Akasha** in Culver City, to solar panels on the roof at **The Lobster** in Santa Monica, to chefs like **Grace's** Neal Fraser converting his Mercedes' engine to run on used cooking oil. Marina del Rey's **Cafe Del Rey** takes responsible eating to a new level by offering line-caught fish and listing the boat's captain on the menu, while Glendale's **Palate Food + Wine** and Santa Monica's **Wilshire** are among those to banish bottled water, leaving us to ponder: could corporate $H_2O$ follow the trail of trans fats into illicit territory?

**IT'S A GAS:** Keen as Angelenos are on going green, it seems little can keep them away from the pump. In fact, 70% say high gas prices haven't affected where they dine, and 87% are willing to drive a half-hour or more (one-way) for a good dinner.

**CHECK, PLEASE!** LA continues to be a relative bargain for diners, with the average meal clocking in at $34.38, considerably less than San Francisco ($38.70), New York ($39.46) and Las Vegas ($44.44). No wonder 80% of surveyors say they're eating out as often as or more than they did two years ago.

Los Angeles, CA
September 25, 2008

Merrill Shindler

# Most Popular

## LOS ANGELES

These places are plotted on the map at the back of the book.

1. Spago | *Californian*
2. Mélisse | *American/French*
3. Café Bizou | *Californian/French*
4. Pizzeria Mozza* | *Pizza*
5. A.O.C. | *Californian/French*
6. Lucques | *Californian/Med.*
7. Fraîche | *French/Mediterranean*
8. Ruth's Chris | *Steak*
9. Cheesecake Factory | *American*
10. Campanile | *Californian/Med.*
11. Mastro's Steak | *Steak*
12. Osteria Mozza | *Italian*
13. Water Grill* | *Seafood*
14. Angelini Osteria | *Italian*
15. In-N-Out | *Burgers*
16. Joe's | *Californian/French*
17. Providence | *American/Seafood*
18. Houston's | *American*
19. Parkway Grill | *Californian*
20. Brent's Deli | *Deli*
21. CUT | *Steak*
22. JiRaffe | *American/French*
23. Lawry's Prime Rib | *Steak*
24. Crustacean | *Asian Fusion/Viet.*
25. Matsuhisa* | *Japanese*
26. Katsu-ya | *Japanese*
27. Katsuya | *Japanese*
28. Arnie Morton's | *Steak*
29. Hotel Bel-Air | *Cal./French*
30. Chinois on Main | *Asian/French*
31. Roy's* | *Asian Fusion/Hawaiian*
32. Valentino | *Italian*
33. Patina | *American/Californian*
34. Grace | *American*
35. Josie | *American*
36. Fleming's Steak | *Steak*
37. Sona* | *French*
38. Hatfield's | *American*
39. Craft | *American*
40. La Cachette | *French*

It's obvious that many of the above restaurants are among the Los Angeles area's most expensive, but if popularity were calibrated to price, we suspect that a number of other restaurants would join their ranks. Thus, we have added two lists comprised of 80 Best Buys on page 17.

## ORANGE COUNTY

1. Napa Rose | *Californian*
2. Marché Moderne | *French*
3. Five Crowns | *Continental*
4. 230 Forest Ave. | *Californian*
5. Cheesecake Factory | *American*
6. Mastro's Steak | *Steak*
7. French 75 | *French*
8. In-N-Out | *Burgers*
9. Mastro's Ocean | *Seafood/Steak*
10. Sapphire Laguna | *Eclectic*

## PALM SPRINGS

1. Le Vallauris | *French/Med.*
2. Cuistot | *Californian/French*
3. Johannes | *Eclectic*
4. Jillian's | *Continental*
5. Roy's | *Asian Fusion/Hawaiian*

## SANTA BARBARA

1. Downey's | *Californian/French*
2. La Super-Rica | *Mexican*
3. Bouchon | *Californian/French*
4. Wine Cask | *Californian*
5. Ca' Dario | *Italian*

* Indicates a tie with restaurant above

Santa Clarita
Glendale
Burbank
Bashan
Los Angeles
Downey
Compton
Long Beach
Inglewood
RED→
DETAIL AT LEFT
San Fernando
sugarFISH
El Segundo
Torrance
Hermosa Beach
Rancho Palos Verdes
Santa Monica
Il Carpaccio
Malibu
Thousand Oaks
Simi Valley
Val Verde Park
Piru
Moorpark
Somis
Camarillo
Fillmore
Westlake Village
PACIFIC OCEAN

S. Pasadena
Alhambra
Monterey Park
E. Los Angeles
EAGLE ROCK
Glendale
Burbank
Palate Food + Wine
Lot 1
LAMILL Coffee Boutique
Medusa Lounge
Little Dom's
Beso
Delancey
Waffle
Citrus at Social
HOLLYWOOD
Downtown
Kress
Loteria Grill
Nobu LA
Kitchen 24
8 oz.
STK
Animal
Comme Ça
BEVERLY HILLS
Jian Korean BBQ
Crudo Bar & Ristorante
BLT Steak
Gordon Ramsay
Paperfish
Foxtail
Wolfgang's Steakhouse
Luckyfish
Katsu Sushi
Bond St.
RockSugar
Blvd 16
Rush Street
Akasha
Gyenari Korean BBQ
NORTH HOLLYWOOD
STUDIO CITY
WEST HOLLYWOOD
BEL AIR
CENTURY CITY
Culver City
View Park
Windsor Hills
SHERMAN OAKS
Anisette Brasserie
VENICE
Santa Monica
Santa Monica Bay
Third & Olive

# LA Key Newcomers

Our editors' take on the year's top arrivals. See page 291 for a full list.

| | |
|---|---|
| Akasha | *American* | Kitchen 24 | *American* |
| Animal | *American* | Kress | *Pan-Asian* |
| Anisette Brasserie | *French* | LAMILL Coffee | *Californian* |
| Bashan | *American* | Little Dom's | *Italian* |
| Beso | *Spanish* | Lotería! | *Mexican* |
| BLT Steak | *Steak* | Lot 1 | *American* |
| Blvd 16 | *American* | Luckyfish | *Japanese* |
| Bond Street | *Japanese* | Medusa Lounge | *Eclectic* |
| Citrus at Social | *Eclectic/French* | Nobu LA | *Japanese* |
| Comme Ça | *French* | Palate Food + Wine | *American* |
| Crudo | *Italian* | Paperfish | *Seafood* |
| Delancey Hollywood | *Italian* | RED | *Steak* |
| 8 oz. | *Burgers* | RockSugar | *Pan-Asian* |
| Foxtail | *French* | Rush Street | *American* |
| Gordon Ramsay | *Continental* | STK | *Steak* |
| Gyenari | *Korean* | sugarFISH | *Japanese* |
| Il Carpaccio | *Italian* | Third & Olive | *Californian/French* |
| Jian Korean BBQ | *Korean* | Waffle | *American* |
| Katsu Sushi | *Japanese* | Wolfgang's Steak | *Steak* |

So far, 2008 has been a blockbuster year for dining in Los Angeles, and more is still to come. Expect to see a bevy of new places Downtown (further proof that the neighborhood is on its way back), starting with **Drago Centro,** the largest enterprise by the brothers Drago, and the new Pan-Latin **Rivera** by local legend John Sedlar (of the fabled St. Estephe, among others). On the horizon, the much-missed **Cole's** – an LA landmark since 1908 – will finally reopen after a two-year hiatus with a new look from nightlife impresario Cedd Moses and a spruced-up American menu by Grace's Neal Fraser, while the Katsuya empire will bring sushi and robata to the LA Live complex. Also hotly anticipated are **Street,** Susan Feniger's upcoming Hollywood venture showcasing global nibbles, and Suzanne Goin's latest in Brentwood.

In 2009, the openings continue apace, as José Andrés unveils **The Bazaar** on La Cienega and Thomas Keller debuts his latest outpost of **Bouchon** in Beverly Hills. And rumors continue to swirl that double-platinum names like Jean-Georges Vongerichten and Ming Tsai are coming to town; in LA, when you're hot, you're hot.

# Top Food Ratings

Excludes places with low votes.

<u>28</u> Mélisse | *American/French*
Asanebo | *Japanese*

<u>27</u> Lucques | *Cal./Med.*
Nobu Malibu | *Japanese*
Shiro | *French/Japanese*
Derek's | *Californian/French*
Matsuhisa | *Japanese*
Bastide | *French*
Leila's | *Californian*
Mori Sushi | *Japanese*
Water Grill | *Seafood*
Katsu-ya | *Japanese*
Sona | *French*
Angelini Osteria | *Italian*
Hatfield's | *American*
Spago | *Californian*
Piccolo | *Italian*
Brandywine | *Continental*
La Cachette | *French*

<u>26</u> Saddle Peak | *American*

Chinois on Main | *Asian/French*
Nobu LA | *Japanese*
Gina Lee's Bistro | *Asian/Cal.*
A.O.C. | *Californian/French*
Sushi Sasabune | *Japanese*
Sushi Nozawa | *Japanese*
Christine | *Med./Pacific Rim*
Pizzeria Mozza | *Pizza*
Josie | *American*
Capo | *Italian*
Sam's by the Beach | *Cal./Med.*
Via Veneto | *Italian*
Bistro 45 | *Californian*
Providence | *American/Seafood*
Mako | *Asian Fusion*
Parkway Grill | *Californian*
Langham Huntington | *Cal.*
Orris | *French/Japanese*
Hamasaku | *Japanese*
JiRaffe | *American/French*

## BY CUISINE

### AMERICAN (NEW)

<u>27</u> Hatfield's
<u>26</u> Saddle Peak
Josie
Providence
JiRaffe

### AMERICAN (TRAD.)

<u>24</u> Grill on Alley
<u>23</u> Lasher's
Original Pancake
Auntie Em's Kitchen
Marston's

### ASIAN/ASIAN FUSION

<u>26</u> Chinois on Main
Gina Lee's Bistro
Mako
<u>24</u> Max
Chaya Brasserie

### BAKERIES

<u>25</u> Jin Patisserie
<u>24</u> Porto's Bakery
<u>23</u> Sweet Lady Jane
Clementine
Joan's on Third

### BARBECUE

<u>25</u> Phillips BBQ
<u>23</u> Baby Blues BBQ
<u>22</u> Lucille's BBQ
Dr. Hogly Wogly's
Johnny Rebs'

### BURGERS

<u>24</u> Father's Office
<u>23</u> In-N-Out
<u>22</u> Apple Pan
Tommy's
<u>21</u> Counter

### CALIFORNIAN

<u>27</u> Lucques
Derek's
Leila's
Spago
<u>26</u> Gina Lee's Bistro

### CARIBBEAN/CUBAN

<u>22</u> Prado
<u>21</u> Cha Cha Chicken
Versailles
<u>20</u> Bamboo
Cha Cha Cha

## CHINESE

25 Din Tai Fung
   Yujean Kang's
24 Sea Harbour
23 Bamboo Cuisine
22 Yang Chow

## COFFEE SHOP/DINER

23 Original Pancake
21 Uncle Bill's Pancake
   Cora's Coffee
19 Pie 'N Burger
18 Rae's

## CONTINENTAL

27 Brandywine
25 Dal Rae
24 Café 14
22 Fins
   Polo Lounge

## DELIS

26 Brent's Deli
25 Langer's Deli
20 Barney Greengrass
   Nate 'n Al
18 Canter's

## DIM SUM

24 Sea Harbour
21 Triumphal Palace
   Ocean Star
20 Mission 261
   Ocean Seafood

## ECLECTIC

25 Chez Mélange
24 Nook Bistro
   Depot
23 Lou
   Vertical Wine Bistro

## FRENCH

28 Mélisse
27 Shiro
   Derek's
   Bastide
   Sona

## FRENCH (BISTRO)

26 Frenchy's Bistro
25 Mistral
   Julienne
23 Bistro Provence
   La Creperie Cafe

## GREEK

24 Petros
22 Papa Cristo's
   George's Greek
21 Papadakis Taverna
   Ulysses Voyage

## INDIAN

26 Addi's Tandoor
24 Surya India
23 Tanzore
   Bombay Cafe
22 All India Café

## ITALIAN

27 Angelini Osteria
   Piccolo
26 Pizzeria Mozza
   Capo
   Via Veneto

## JAPANESE

28 Asanebo
27 Nobu Malibu
   Shiro
   Matsuhisa
   Mori Sushi

## KOREAN

23 ChoSun Galbee
   Soot Bull Jeep
22 Woo Lae Oak
20 Tofu-Ya
19 BCD Tofu

## MEDITERRANEAN

26 Christine
   Sam's by the Beach
   Campanile
24 Fraîche
   Upstairs 2

## MEXICAN

26 Babita
24 El Tepeyac
   La Cabanita
   Chichen Itza
   Lotería!

## MIDDLE EASTERN

24 Sunnin
23 Spitz
22 Carnival
   Carousel
21 Shaherzad

## PIZZA

26 Pizzeria Mozza
23 Village Pizzeria
Casa Bianca
Mulberry St. Pizzeria
22 Abbot's Pizza

## SEAFOOD

27 Water Grill
26 Providence
24 Hungry Cat
23 Paperfish
Ocean Ave.

## SMALL PLATES

26 A.O.C.
Mako
Orris
25 Izaka-Ya
24 Musha

## SOUL FOOD/SOUTHERN

23 Les Sisters
Baby Blues BBQ
22 Lucille's BBQ
Johnny Rebs'
20 Roscoe's

## SOUTH AMERICAN

25 Mario's Peruvian
24 Fogo de Chão

23 Carlitos Gardel
21 Green Field
Picanha

## STEAKHOUSES

26 Mastro's Steak
CUT
Ruth's Chris
25 Jar
Arroyo Chop Hse.

## THAI

26 Jitlada
24 Cholada
Chadaka
23 Saladang
Talesai

## VEGETARIAN

22 Native Foods
21 Real Food Daily
M Café de Chaya
20 Urth Caffé
Inn of Seventh Ray

## VIETNAMESE

24 Benley Vietnamese
Crustacean
23 Golden Deli
21 Gingergrass
Pho Café

# BY SPECIAL FEATURE

## BREAKFAST

24 Lotería!
23 Sweet Lady Jane
Asia de Cuba
Boa
Auntie Em's Kitchen

## BRUNCH

26 Saddle Peak
Campanile
Joe's
25 Hotel Bel-Air
Belvedere

## BUSINESS DINING

28 Mélisse
27 Water Grill
Hatfield's
Spago
La Cachette

## GARDEN DINING

27 Bastide
25 Jin Patisserie
Belvedere
24 Raymond
Michael's

## HOTEL DINING

26 Langham Huntington
CUT (Beverly Wilshire)
25 Hotel Bel-Air
Belvedere (Peninsula Hotel)
24 Noé (Omni Los Angeles)

## LATE DINING

26 Pizzeria Mozza
Osteria Mozza
25 Iroha
24 Katsuya
Hungry Cat

## LUNCH

28 Asanebo
27 Lucques
Matsuhisa
Mori Sushi
Water Grill

## NEWCOMERS (RATED)

26 Nobu LA
Bashan
23 Il Carpaccio
Paperfish
LAMILL Coffee

## PEOPLE-WATCHING

27 Spago
26 A.O.C.
Mastro's Steak
25 Craft
24 Grill on Alley

## POWER SCENES

27 Matsuhisa
Bastide
Sona
Angelini Osteria
26 CUT

## TRENDY

27 Sona
26 Nobu LA
Pizzeria Mozza
Osteria Mozza
25 Jar

## WINNING WINE LISTS

28 Mélisse
27 Lucques
Bastide
Sona
26 Valentino

## WORTH A TRIP

27 Nobu Malibu
Malibu
Leila's
Oak Park
26 Saddle Peak
Calabasas
Christine
Torrance
Babita
San Gabriel

# BY LOCATION

## BEVERLY BOULEVARD

27 Angelini Osteria
Hatfield's
25 Jar
Hirozen
Grace

## BEVERLY HILLS

27 Matsuhisa
Spago
26 Mako
Mastro's Steak
CUT

## BRENTWOOD

26 Vincenti
24 Katsuya
Takao
Osteria Latini
23 Pizzicotto

## CHINATOWN

22 Yang Chow
21 Philippe the Original
Empress Pavilion
20 Ocean Seafood
Hop Li

## DOWNTOWN

27 Water Grill
26 R23
25 Patina
Arnie Morton's
Langer's Deli

## FAIRFAX

24 Lotería!
22 Chameau
21 Monsieur Marcel
Nyala Ethiopian
Ulysses Voyage*

## HOLLYWOOD

26 Pizzeria Mozza
Providence
Osteria Mozza
25 Mario's Peruvian
24 Katsuya

## LA BREA

26 Campanile
22 cube
Sonora Cafe
Ca'Brea
Susina

## LONG BEACH

| | |
|---|---|
| 26 | Frenchy's Bistro |
| 24 | Benley Vietnamese |
| | 555 East |
| | Sunnin |
| 23 | Tracht's |

## LOS FELIZ/
## SILVER LAKE

| | |
|---|---|
| 25 | Aroma |
| 24 | Blair's |
| 23 | LAMILL Coffee |
| 22 | Farfalla Trattoria |
| 21 | Rambutan Thai |

## MALIBU

| | |
|---|---|
| 27 | Nobu Malibu |
| 24 | Cholada |
| 22 | Malibu Seafood |
| | Tra Di Noi |
| 21 | Geoffrey's |

## MELROSE

| | |
|---|---|
| 25 | All' Angelo |
| | Osteria La Buca |
| 23 | Sweet Lady Jane |
| | Carlitos Gardel |
| | Angeli Caffe |

## PASADENA/
## SOUTH PASADENA

| | |
|---|---|
| 27 | Shiro |
| | Derek's |
| 26 | Bistro 45 |
| | Parkway Grill |
| | Langham Huntington |

## SAN FERNANDO
## VALLEY

| | |
|---|---|
| 28 | Asanebo |
| 27 | Katsu-ya |
| | Brandywine |
| 26 | Saddle Peak |
| | Sushi Nozawa |

## SAN GABRIEL VALLEY

| | |
|---|---|
| 26 | Babita |
| 23 | Golden Deli |

| | |
|---|---|
| 20 | Mission 261 |
| | Sam Woo |

## SANTA MONICA

| | |
|---|---|
| 28 | Mélisse |
| 26 | Chinois on Main |
| | Josie |
| | Capo |
| | Sam's by the Beach |

## SOUTH BAY

| | |
|---|---|
| 26 | Gina Lee's Bistro |
| | Christine |
| | Addi's Tandoor |
| 25 | Chez Mélange |
| | Phillips BBQ |

## THIRD STREET

| | |
|---|---|
| 26 | A.O.C. |
| 25 | Izaka-Ya |
| | Ortolan |
| 24 | Locanda Veneta |
| | Surya India |

## VENICE

| | |
|---|---|
| 27 | Piccolo |
| 26 | Joe's |
| 25 | Jin Patisserie |
| 23 | Baby Blues BBQ |
| 22 | Chaya |

## WEST HOLLYWOOD

| | |
|---|---|
| 27 | Lucques |
| | Bastide |
| | Sona |
| 26 | Nobu LA |
| 25 | Vivoli Café |

## WEST LA

| | |
|---|---|
| 27 | Mori Sushi |
| 26 | Sushi Sasabune |
| | Orris |
| | Hamasaku |
| | Sushi Masu |

# Top Decor Ratings

| | |
|---|---|
| __29]__ Hotel Bel-Air | Inn of Seventh Ray |
| __28]__ Takami | Il Cielo |
| __27]__ Gonpachi | __25]__ Gardens |
| Langham Huntington | Polo Lounge |
| Geoffrey's | Geisha House |
| Saddle Peak | Getty Center |
| Yamashiro | Sky Room |
| Madison | Sir Winston's |
| Murano | Crustacean |
| Hampton's | Mélisse |
| Bastide | Blue Velvet |
| Cicada | Dar Maghreb |
| __26]__ La Boheme | Craft |
| Cliff's Edge | Catch |
| Penthouse | Koi |
| Bistro Gdn./Coldwater | Asia de Cuba |
| Tanzore | Michael's |
| Belvedere | Thousand Cranes |
| Little Door | Vertical Wine Bistro* |
| One Pico | Firefly |

## OUTDOORS

| | |
|---|---|
| Bastide | Inn of Seventh Ray |
| Belvedere | Jin Patisserie |
| Chateau Marmont | Langham Huntington |
| Gardens | Lucques |
| Hotel Bel-Air | Michael's |
| Il Cielo | Raymond |

## ROMANCE

| | |
|---|---|
| Anisette Brasserie | Little Door |
| Brentwood | Mélisse |
| Capo | Penthouse |
| Getty Center | Saddle Peak |
| Grace | Spago |
| Il Cielo | Valentino |

## STARGAZING

| | |
|---|---|
| Anisette Brasserie | Ivy |
| Arnie Morton's | Katsuya |
| Brentwood | Koi |
| Comme Ça | Matsuhisa |
| Fogo de Chão | Mr. Chow |
| Grace | Patina |
| Il Sole | Spago |

## VIEWS

| | |
|---|---|
| Asia de Cuba | Moonshadows |
| Blue Velvet | Noé |
| Cafe Del Rey | Penthouse |
| Geoffrey's | Saddle Peak |
| Getty Center | West |
| Lobster | Yamashiro |

# Top Service Ratings

**27** Bastide
Mélisse
Hotel Bel-Air
Belvedere
Brandywine
Sona

**26** Providence
Sam's by the Beach
Saddle Peak
Hampton's
Papadakis Taverna
Langham Huntington
Shiro
Derek's

**25** Valentino
La Cachette
Gardens
Mistral
Lucques
Hatfield's

Dal Rae
Spago
Water Grill
Grace
Bashan
Larchmont Grill
Parkway Grill
Maison Akira

**24** Leila's
Patina
Lawry's Prime Rib
CUT
Bistro 45
Polo Lounge*
Vivoli Café*
Piccolo
JiRaffe
Josie
Tuscany
Sky Room

# Best Buys

In order of Bang for the Buck rating.

1. In-N-Out
2. Spitz
3. Tommy's
4. Noah's NY Bagels
5. Carney's Express
6. Porto's Bakery
7. Astro Burger
8. Portillo's Hot Dogs
9. Pink's Chili Dogs
10. Local Place
11. Philippe the Original
12. Chipotle
13. Lamonica's NY Pizza
14. Apple Pan
15. Poquito Más
16. Jody Maroni's
17. Asahi Ramen
18. El Tepeyac
19. Cha Cha Chicken
20. Rae's
21. Pho Café
22. Golden Deli
23. Sharky's Mexican
24. Baja Fresh Mexican
25. Reddi Chick BBQ
26. Uncle Bill's Pancake
27. California Chicken
28. Susina
29. Stand
30. Village Pizzeria
31. Joe's Pizza
32. Veggie Grill
33. Original Pancake
34. Artisan Cheese
35. Oinkster
36. Abbot's Pizza
37. Sandbag Sandwiches
38. Zankou Chicken
39. Chabuya Tokyo
40. French Crêpe Co.

## OTHER GOOD VALUES

Absolutely Phobulous
A Cow Jumped
Agra Cafe
Alcove
Alejo's
Angelique Café
Antonio's
Auntie Em's Kitchen
Baby Blues BBQ
Back Home
BCD Tofu
Benley Vietnamese
Best Fish Taco
Bloom Café
Blossom
BLT Steak
Blue Hen
Breadbar
Brent's Deli
Cali. Pizza Kitchen
Casa Bianca
Doña Rosa
Griddle Cafe
Gumbo Pot
Indochine Vien
Jinky's
Jin Patisserie
Jitlada
Johnny Reb's
John O'Groats
JR's BBQ
Kansas City BBQ
Kitchen
Koo Koo Roo
Lemon Moon
Mandarin Deli
Papa Cristo's
Ragin' Cajun
Shack
Sunnin

# LOS ANGELES RESTAURANT DIRECTORY

| | FOOD | DECOR | SERVICE | COST |
|---|---|---|---|---|

### Abbey, The ● *American*  14 | 22 | 14 | $29

**West Hollywood** | 692 N. Robertson Blvd. (Santa Monica Blvd.) |
310-289-8410 | www.abbeyfoodandbar.com

A "polyglot scensters" – "gays, lesbians, straights" – "drink their
way to happiness" at this WeHo "sloshfest" in "the heart of Boystown"
where the modern American menu is dubbed "decent" enough, but
perhaps not as "delicious" as the "underwear-model" servers; the
"chic" atmosphere includes "lounge-bed" seating perfect for "reclin-
ing" with a "pastel cocktail" while the "huge" courtyard is made for
"mixing and mingling" and also plays host to "sunny" "open-air"
brunches on weekends.

### Abbot's Pizza  *Pizza*  22 | 6 | 12 | $12

**Santa Monica** | 1811 Pico Blvd. (18th St.) | 310-314-2777
**Venice** | 1407 Abbot Kinney Blvd. (California Ave.) | 310-396-7334

"Former New Yorkers" sing the praises of these "divey" pie palaces in
Santa Monica and Venice featuring "unique" bagel-crusted pizzas
with "clever topping combinations" as well as "crave-worthy"
"cracker-thin" slices; less appealing is the "attitude" from counter
staff and somewhat "depressing" settings – "if atmosphere counts,
definitely take out."

### ABC Seafood  *Chinese/Seafood*  19 | 9 | 14 | $23

**Chinatown** | 205 Ord St. (New High St.) | 213-680-2887

"Hordes" of diners flock to this "hectic" Chinatown "icon" hustling
"authentic" dim sum in a "noisy" cavernous interior, while dinner is a
quieter affair where "fresh" Cantonese seafood is the star; though it's
always "crowded", some patrons pan "spotty" quality, unpredictable
service ("nonexistent" vs. "too pushy") and "tired" decor.

### Absolutely Phobulous  *Vietnamese*  17 | 9 | 15 | $15

**West Hollywood** | 350 N. La Cienega Blvd. (Beverly Blvd.) |
310-360-3930
**NEW** **Encino** | 15928 Ventura Blvd., Ste. 101 (Gaivota Ave.) |
818-788-3560 | www.abpho.com 🗺

WeHo denizens say this "hole-in-the-wall" "keeps pho cravings under
control" with "flavorful" bowls of noodle soup (including a low-carb
version for waist-watchers) plus a "limited" lineup of other
Vietnamese dishes like summer rolls and papaya salad; though it may
not be as "authentic" as the "places in Westminster", slurpers say it's
one of the "best choices" on the Westside; N.B. it recently spun off a
new branch in Encino.

### A Cow Jumped Over the Moon  *French*  ▽ 20 | 11 | 21 | $24

**Beverly Hills** | Rodeo Collection | 421 N. Rodeo Dr. (bet. Brighton Way &
Little Santa Monica Blvd.) | 310-274-4269 |
www.acowjumpedoverthemoon.com

Like a "Parisian kosher cafe", this modestly priced Beverly Hills
French delivers "delish" dairy dishes like French sandwiches, salads
and crêpes in an orange-and-chrome bedecked space "in an underground parking lot", albeit a Rodeo Drive one with a stone fountain;
those who prefer to get it to-go can also pick up picnic supplies like
wines, cheeses and chocolates at the attached gourmet shop;
N.B. closed Saturdays.

| | FOOD | DECOR | SERVICE | COST |
|---|---|---|---|---|

### Adagio ⓜ *Italian* — 23 | 15 | 22 | $36

**Woodland Hills** | 22841 Ventura Blvd. (Fallbrook Ave.) | 818-225-0533
Owner Claudio Gontier "always greets customers with a warm smile" at this "wonderful" Northern Italian stalwart in Woodland Hills where "old-school charm" abounds thanks to an "exceptional" staff that coddles the regulars with "simple", "well-prepared" fare, including a Caesar salad made tableside; the casual space decorated with plants and oil paintings "may not be much to look at", but considering it "never disappoints" and prices are "reasonable" too, many say they "never miss a chance to go."

### ⓩ Addi's Tandoor *Indian* — 26 | 17 | 23 | $29

**Redondo Beach** | 800 Torrance Blvd. (bet. PCH & Prospect Ave.) | 310-540-1616 | www.addistandoor.com
"It's so good, my friend named her baby Addi" gushes one groupie of this incredibly "popular" Redondo Beach Indian that "can't be beat" for "sublime" Goan-style dishes "scrupulously" seasoned to the diners' tastes ("toddler mild" or "smokin' hot"); "authentic" decor is "nothing to rave about", but it remains at the top of fans' "go-back-soon list" nonetheless; P.S. "make reservations on weekends."

### Admiral Risty *Seafood* — 20 | 19 | 20 | $45

**Rancho Palos Verdes** | 31250 Palos Verdes Dr. W. (Hawthorne Blvd.) | 310-377-0050 | www.admiral-risty.com
"Going strong" after more than 40 years, this "old-style" Rancho Palos Verdes "fish house" continues to "hold its own" with "dependable" platters of steaks and seafood that get a lift from "marvelous ocean views"; yet while it remains a "local institution", a number of foes find fault with "uninspired" eats and hit-or-miss service and attest it's ultimately "too expensive for what you get."

### Adobe Cantina *BBQ/Mexican* — 15 | 15 | 15 | $22

**Agoura Hills** | 29100 Agoura Rd. (Kanan Rd.) | 818-991-3474
A "very pleasant" patio "buzzing with activity" makes this well-priced Agoura Hills cantina "the place to be" on "a lazy summer afternoon" with a "fabulous" "margarita in hand"; on the downside are only "average" BBQ and Mexican fare and "personality-challenged" staff, but the "idyllic" outdoor setting redeems it for most.

### Ago *Italian* — 22 | 19 | 20 | $58

**West Hollywood** | 8478 Melrose Ave. (N. La Cienega Blvd.) | 323-655-6333 | www.agorestaurant.com
"Beautiful young starlets", "suits", "hangers-on" and "serious foodies" convene at this pricey "see-and-be-seen" Tuscan trattoria in West Hollywood where the "exquisite" steaks "cooked in their wood-burning oven" generate as much buzz as backer Bob De Niro himself; though service is "always pleasant", expect long waits "even with a reservation", and know that the "electric atmosphere" sometimes comes with "unbearable noise."

### Agra Cafe *Indian* — ▽ 21 | 11 | 16 | $22

**Silver Lake** | 4325 Sunset Blvd. (Fountain Ave.) | 323-665-7818
Though "hidden" in a "seedy strip mall", this BYO Indian draws a steady stream of Silver Lakers for both traditional and "unusual" South

|  | FOOD | DECOR | SERVICE | COST |
|---|---|---|---|---|

Asian dishes, though regulars warn "not every one is a standout"; as for the "just ok" service and bare-bones burgundy-hued decor, most "don't mind" either because tabs are so "cheap", especially the bargain lunch buffet; N.B. they also deliver.

### Ahi Sushi  *Japanese*
| 20 | 15 | 18 | $38 |
|---|---|---|---|

**Studio City** | 12915 Ventura Blvd. (Coldwater Canyon Ave.) | 818-981-0277 | www.ahisushi.com

"Put yourself in the chef's hands" advise enthusiasts who are "hooked" on this "midrange" Japanese "find" on Studio City's sushi row turning out "really fresh" fish and "well-prepared" Asian fusion plates matched with inventive cocktails; the less-impressed say it's "nothing special", though service is "efficient" and the Zen-inspired patio with a trickling fountain is certainly a plus.

### Aioli  *Mediterranean/Spanish*
| 18 | 18 | 18 | $33 |
|---|---|---|---|

**Torrance** | 1261 Cabrillo Ave. (Torrance Blvd.) | 310-320-9200

"Tasty tapas" and a lengthy list of wines by the glass win over the "happy-hour" crowd at this "upscale" spot in Old Town Torrance also turning out "solid" Spanish-Med entrees; though some suggest the "fancy" slate-and-granite decor is "stuck in the early 1980s" at least the "quiet atmosphere" is appealing.

### NEW Akasha  *American*
| 22 | 25 | 23 | $43 |
|---|---|---|---|

**Culver City** | 9543 Culver Blvd. (W. Washington Blvd.) | 310-845-1700 | www.akasharestaurant.com

The "eco-conscious" vibe "shows in every detail" from the servers' hemp-and-cotton uniforms to the energy-efficient light fixtures at this "chic" green newcomer from Akasha Richmond in Culver City luring "vegans and carnivores" for an "amazingly original", mostly organic New American menu plus "delectable" pastries and fair-trade coffee at the in-house bakery counter; factor in a "knowledgeable" staff and a "stunning", "industrial" setting and its no wonder locals are lauding it as a "fabulous addition to the area dining scene", albeit a "pricey" one.

### Akbar Cuisine of India  *Indian*
| 22 | 15 | 19 | $26 |
|---|---|---|---|

**Marina del Rey** | 3115 Washington Blvd. (Yale Ave.) | 310-574-0666
**Santa Monica** | 2627 Wilshire Blvd. (26th St.) | 310-586-7469
**Hermosa Beach** | 1101 Aviation Blvd. (Prospect Ave.) | 310-937-3800
**Pasadena** | 44 N. Fair Oaks Ave. (Union St.) | 626-577-9916
www.akbarcuisineofindia.com

"Refined" takes on traditional fare head up the "modern" menu at this quartet of "upscale" Indians where the "uniquely spiced" cuisine is complemented by a "stash of surprisingly outstanding wines"; service varies from "doting" to "sullen", depending on location, as does decor, though all thrive in "quiet", "unpretentious" environs; P.S. the Hermosa branch features a "reasonable" lunch buffet.

### Alcove  *American*
| 21 | 21 | 15 | $19 |
|---|---|---|---|

**Los Feliz** | 1929 Hillhurst Ave. (Franklin Ave.) | 323-644-0100 | www.alcovecafe.com

"Neighborhood hipsters" (and their dogs) pack the "tree-lined patio" of this "adorable" converted bungalow in Los Feliz for "updated versions" of American "cafe classics" like "huge salads", "trendy sand-

| | FOOD | DECOR | SERVICE | COST |
|---|---|---|---|---|

wiches" and "sinful" desserts worth the "sugar coma"; it's often "a pleasant place to linger", but "unless you like standing on line", avoid "peak hours" – like brunch – when it turns into a "zoo" and the "clumsy" "walk-up" ordering system becomes especially "frustrating."

### Alegria *Nuevo Latino*    19 | 19 | 18 | $31

**Long Beach** | 115 Pine Ave. (bet. B'way & 1st St.) | 562-436-3388 | www.alegriacocinalatina.com

Long Beach locals and "conventiongoers" "get their sangria on" at this "raucous" mosaic-tiled "hot spot" where the Nuevo Latino eats take a backseat to the festive atmosphere with flamenco dancing and live jazz most nights; those in search of a bargain should take note of happy-hour specials daily (9–11 PM) and the "good value" lunch buffet offered the last Friday of every month.

### Alegria on Sunset ⌧⌤ *Mexican*    21 | 11 | 18 | $20

**Silver Lake** | Sunset Plaza | 3510 W. Sunset Blvd. (Golden Gate Ave.) | 323-913-1422 | www.alegriaonsunset.com

Silver Lakers sing the praises of the "Mexican home cooking" at this much-"loved" "hole-in-the-wall" sending out "fresh", "almost healthy" south-of-the-border dishes like "excellent" mole and some of "the best huevos rancheros" around; comfort-hounds criticize the somewhat "cramped" strip-mall digs, but "no attitude" from the "friendly" staff is a plus, and the BYO policy makes for budget-friendly tabs.

### Alejo's *Italian*    19 | 7 | 16 | $19

**Marina del Rey** | 4002 Lincoln Blvd. (Washington Blvd.) | 310-822-0095
**Westchester** | 8343 Lincoln Blvd. (84th St.) | 310-670-6677

"Garlicky old-school Italian fare" comes in "unfathomable portions" at these "family-style", "red-checkered-tablecloth" twins now under separate ownership in Marina del Rey and Westchester; "upscale, they ain't", but devotees are willing to overlook the "lack of decor" and oft-"packed" environs because of the "bargain" prices; P.S. some opt to "get it to go", especially at the BYO branch in MdR.

### Alessio Ristorante Italiano *Italian*    21 | 20 | 20 | $32

**Northridge** | 9725 Reseda Blvd. (Superior St.) | 818-709-8393
**West Hills** | Platt Vill. | 6428 Platt Ave. (Victory Blvd.) | 818-710-0270
🆕 **Simi Valley** | 2892 Cochran St. (Sycamore Dr.) | 805-522-2204
**Westlake Village** | 3731 E. Thousand Oaks Blvd. (Marmon Ave.) | 805-557-0565
www.alessiorestaurant.com

"Solid Italian" pulls patrons into this "busy" quartet of trattorias in the valley where a "huge menu" of "surprisingly sophisticated" options and "effective" service mean most "always enjoy dining here"; dark woods, textured walls and live music on most nights create an "upscale" (some say "generic") atmosphere, though a few demur on tabs they deem "on the pricey side."

### All' Angelo ⌧ *Italian*    25 | 19 | 23 | $62

**Melrose** | 7166 Melrose Ave. (bet. Formosa Ave. & N. Detroit St.) | 323-933-9540 | www.allangelo.com

Chef Mirko Paderno's "simply fantastic" Venetian cuisine is so "authentic" it "made my grandmama cry" avers one acolyte of this "Italian experience" on Melrose, complete with a full lineup of cicchetti (snacks) and an "extensive wine list" that boasts hard-to-find Tuscan reds; a "caring" staff helps make up for "noisy", "cramped" quarters and "expense-account" tabs.

**Allegria**  *Italian*                              20 | 16 | 19 | $37

**Malibu** | 22821 PCH (south of Malibu Pier) | 310-456-3132 | www.allegriamalibu.com

Malibu denizens hail this "dependable" well-priced Italian that "still pleases after all these years" for a "no-fuss" "midweek" meal served by a "friendly" staff; though there's "no ocean view", there's star-gazing aplenty in the "noisy" wood-appointed space, and outside sports a pretty patio that overlooks the garden.

**All India Café**  *Indian*                        22 | 13 | 17 | $22

**West LA** | Santa Monica Plaza | 12113 Santa Monica Blvd. (Bundy Dr.) | 310-442-5250
**Pasadena** | 39 S. Fair Oaks Ave. (bet. Colorado Blvd. & Green St.) | 626-440-0309
www.allindiacafe.com

"Amazing aromas greet you" at these "totally reliable" subcontinentals delivering "spot-on" Indian standards plus "interesting" "regional" dishes requiring "several visits to examine the full repertoire"; customers claim the "price is right" too, though service can be "erratic" and the traditional decor with outdoor seating at all locations is "not fancy, but acceptable."

**Amalfi**  *Italian*                               21 | 19 | 19 | $37

**La Brea** | 143 N. La Brea Ave. (bet. Beverly Blvd. & 1st St.) | 323-938-2504 | www.room5lounge.com

"A table by the fireplace is lovely" at this "low-key" La Brea "date spot" co-owned by radio host Adam Carolla and offering "fancy-ish" fare like pastas and designer pizzas at prices that "won't drain your bank account"; those who find the food only "so-so" forgo the high-ceilinged dining room and head for the upstairs lounge featuring comedy and live music.

**NEW Amaranta Cocina Mexicana**  *Mexican*   ▽ 20 | 21 | 17 | $29

**Canoga Park** | Westfield Shoppingtown Topanga | 6600 Topanga Canyon Blvd. (Victory Blvd.) | 818-610-3599 | www.amarantarestaurant.com

Weary shoppers select this "gourmet" Mexican tucked inside Westfield Topanga for modern south-of-the-border fare that's surprisingly "sophisticated" "for a mall restaurant"; though spendthrifts say it's "a little expensive", most don't mind in light of the "knowledgeable" staff and "exotic" decor with hand-blown glass light fixtures, and pebble-lined floors adding to the overall "classy" vibe; P.S. tipplers should take note of the "tremendous" 400-bottle tequila bar.

**NEW Amarone Kitchen & Wine** ⑤ *Italian*    ▽ 27 | 19 | 28 | $38

**West Hollywood** | 8868 W. Sunset Blvd. (N. San Vincente Blvd.) | 310-652-2233 | www.amarone-la.com

Glasses of "complimentary Prosecco" while you wait set a promising tone at this "tiny" midpriced newcomer "on a nondescript block" of West Hollywood turning out "true Italian" dishes from the Emilia-Romagna region complemented by a "great selection" of from-The-Boot vintages; the "cozy" quarters foster a "warm" atmosphere furthered by hosts who "treat their patrons right" leading most boosters to bet this "nice find" is bound to "stay around."

## American Girl Place Cafe  *American*    ▽ 11 | 25 | 23 | $29

**Fairfax** | Grove at Farmers Mkt. | 189 The Grove Dr. (bet. Fairfax Ave. & 3rd St.) | 877-247-5223 | www.americangirlplace.com

"Ecstatic little girls" flock to this American cafe inside The Grove that "couldn't be cuter" since the namesake "dolls have their own booster seat and placesetting at the table"; the "beautifully decorated" hot-pink interior and "cheerful" staff make the whole experience a "real treat" for kids, so who cares if the "bland" fare tastes as "plastic" as the toys – just "lift your teacup, take your photos and eat later."

## Amici  *Italian*    21 | 18 | 20 | $40

**Beverly Hills** | Beverly Terrace Hotel | 469 N. Doheny Dr. (Santa Monica Blvd.) | 310-858-0271 | www.tamici.com
**Brentwood** | 2538 San Vicente Blvd. (26th St.) | 310-260-4900

"Refreshingly unpretentious" considering their tony addresses, these now separately owned Italians offer "solid" "no-fuss" fare that's hard-to-beat" for a "relaxed" meal; "classy" service lies in store at both, but only the Beverly Terrace Hotel branch sports a "delightful" patio while Brentwood cultivates a more "romantic" vibe with a "candlelit" setting "perfect for canoodling."

## Ammo  *Californian*    22 | 19 | 19 | $41

**Hollywood** | 1155 N. Highland Ave. (bet. Fountain Ave. & Santa Monica Blvd.) | 323-871-2666 | www.ammocafe.com

"Industry" types hail the "healthy", "market-fresh menu" of Californian "comfort food" and "creative cocktails" at this Hollywood hang, a "no-brainer" for "business lunches" set in a "modern" "minimalist" space done up in blond wood with green booths and terrace seating; despite a few quibbles about "high" prices, it draws a "loyal following", though even the "cool" crowd detects a little "too much attitude" from servers.

## NEW Andiamo  *Italian*    - | - | - | I

**Silver Lake** | 2815 W. Sunset Blvd. (Silver Lake Blvd.) | 213-483-7070 | www.andiamotogo.com

The dining-in options are minimal at this delivery-oriented eco-minded pizzeria in Silver Lake that sends its organic pies out packed in compostable containers via Vespa scooters; besides pies with exotic toppings, it offers a selection of panini, pasta and the like; N.B. it's BYO for now.

## Angeli Caffe  Ⓜ *Italian*    23 | 15 | 20 | $34

**Melrose** | 7274 Melrose Ave. (Poinsettia Pl.) | 323-936-9086 | www.angelicaffe.com

"Still wonderful" say those smitten with this "inviting" Melrose Italian helmed by LA "icon" Evan Kleiman that remains "a solid choice" for "inventive" seasonal specials, "sublime" pastas and "handmade bread" straight from the red-brick oven ("diet tomorrow, it's worth every calorie"); it cultivates a "family-centric" vibe with "affordable" tabs and "drab" but "comfortable" quarters, though vets warn that when the crowds hit, the usually "gracious" service "slows to a crawl."

| | FOOD | DECOR | SERVICE | COST |
|---|---|---|---|---|

### ☑ Angelini Osteria Ⓜ *Italian* — 27 | 16 | 22 | $51

**Beverly Boulevard** | 7313 Beverly Blvd. (Poinsettia Pl.) | 323-297-0070 | www.angeliniosteria.com

The "perfect" "neighborhood trattoria" assert champions of "phenomenal chef" Gino Angelini's Beverly Boulevard "gem" that "always gets it right" with "lusty" Italian dishes that "straddle the line between elegance and rusticity" and a "thoughtful" selection of regional vintages that's "terrific" too; "dreamy" waiters "with thick accents" always "try their best" to "please", so even if the "sardine" seating means you'll "literally be rubbing elbows" with neighbors, that's all part of the "charm"; P.S. be sure to "reserve well in advance."

### Angelique Café *French* — 19 | 13 | 15 | $19

**Downtown** | 840 S. Spring St. (bet. 8th & 9th Sts.) | 213-623-8698 | www.angeliquecafe.com

Customers cheer this "darling" "little" daytime bistro that's a "nice respite" from the "hustle and bustle" of Downtown thanks to a "pleasant" shaded patio and a "charming" cafe-style interior done up in sunny yellows and cool blues; though its "affordable" French fare draws "weekday lunch crowds", a chorus of critics cite "disappointing execution" and "lack of attention" from servers, and wonder if it's "lost its sparkle."

### 🆕 Animal *American* — - | - | - | M

**Fairfax** | 435 N. Fairfax Ave. (Oakwood Ave.) | 323-782-9225

Opened by Jon Shook and Vinny Dotolo of the Food Network's *2 Dudes Catering*, this midpriced New American arrival in the heart of Fairfax Avenue's Glatt Gulch features beef, innards and especially pork (chocolate bars coated with bacon, anyone?) along with seasonal organic produce; the minimalist room, its walls simply adorned with bare lightbulbs, offers a counterpoint to the wild creations on the menu.

### 🆕 Anisette Brasserie *French* — - | - | - | E

**Santa Monica** | 225 Santa Monica Blvd. (3rd St. Promenade) | 310-395-3200 | www.anisettebrasserie.com

This hotly anticipated French arrival on the ground floor of Santa Monica's historic Clock Tower Building provides a dramatic backdrop for the return of chef Alain Giraud (last seen at Bastide), who's now serving authentic, steeply priced brasserie fare; located just a few feet from the Third Street Promenade, the multilevel space boasts high ceilings, gleaming tiles and an open kitchen.

### Anna's *Italian* — 15 | 13 | 18 | $24

**West LA** | 10929 W. Pico Blvd. (bet. Veteran Ave. & Westwood Blvd.) | 310-474-0102 | www.annaitalian.com

"Families" frequent this "old-timey" Italian "joint" in West LA for "large portions" of "red-sauce" Roman staples and thin-crust pizzas all at prices that add up to a "good deal"; though plenty of patrons find the fare "dull", it remains an "institution" thanks to its "neighborhoody" vibe; meanwhile, like the menu, the "kitschy" "Chianti-bottle ambiance" and "veteran" staff have all remained "remarkably untouched" since 1969.

|  | FOOD | DECOR | SERVICE | COST |
|---|---|---|---|---|

### Antica Pizzeria  *Pizza*  `20` `15` `16` `$25`

**Marina del Rey** | Villa Marina Mktpl. | 13455 Maxella Ave. (Lincoln Blvd.) | 310-577-8182 | www.anticapizzeria.net

Purists praise this "traditional" Marina del Rey Italian crafting "rustic", "Neapolitan-style" pies baked in an "old-world" wood-burning oven; "inexpensive" prices are a plus, but less appealing are sometimes "slow" service and the "cold" ambiance of the "strip-mall" setting, though patio seating provides a respite.

### Antonio's  Ⓜ *Mexican*  ▽ `19` `15` `21` `$29`

**Melrose** | 7470 Melrose Ave. (bet. Fairfax & La Brea Aves.) | 323-658-9060 | www.antoniosonmelrose.com

Antonio himself "greets you like an old friend" at the door of this long-time Melrose "haunt" that channels "old Hollywood" with "dark" time-worn decor and photos of John Wayne adorning the walls; even if some diners deem the "basic" lineup of Mexican specialties "underwhelming", regulars get a kick out of the "big, delicious" margaritas and say the modest prices and live mariachi give it an appealingly "relaxed" vibe.

### ☒ A.O.C.  *Californian/French*  `26` `22` `23` `$55`

**Third Street** | 8022 W. Third St. (bet. S. Crescent Heights Blvd. & S. Fairfax Ave.) | 323-653-6359 | www.aocwinebar.com

Devotees find "nirvana" in the "exquisite" "little morsels" at this "foodie favorite" on Third Street from Suzanne Goin (Lucques) – a pioneer in the "small-plates revolution" – featuring a "marvelous" Cal-French menu with "wonderful cheeses", housemade charcuterie and 50 wines by the glass; add in "expert" servers and an "energetic" "star-studded" room and it's easy to see why so many "swear by it", even if all that "grazing" can "add up to a big bill."

### Apple Pan  ◑Ⓜ⇗ *American/Burgers*  `22` `10` `18` `$13`

**West LA** | 10801 W. Pico Blvd. (Glendon Ave.) | 310-475-3585

"Step back in time" at this family-owned West LA American "fixture" where locals have been lauding the "amazing" hickory burgers, "crispy fries" and "fresh" pies (the "banana cream is delish") for more than 60 years; a wraparound counter and paper plates add to the "greasy spoon" "charm", and though "waits are daunting", the "always fast-moving line" is helped along by "efficient" servers – "if they seem a bit rude, it's just their shtick."

### ☒ Arnie Morton's The Steakhouse  *Steak*  `25` `21` `24` `$64`

**Downtown** | 735 S. Figueroa St. (bet. 7th & 8th Sts.) | 213-553-4566
**Beverly Hills** | 435 S. La Cienega Blvd. (bet. San Vicente & Wilshire Blvds.) | 310-246-1501
**Burbank** | The Pinnacle | 3400 W. Olive Ave. (Lima St.) | 818-238-0424
**NEW** **Woodland Hills** | Warner Ctr. | 6250 Canoga Ave., Ste. 111 (Erwin St.) | 818-703-7272
www.mortons.com

Meat lovers find "paradise" at these "classy" "carnivoriums" (part of the national Morton's chain) where "hearty portions" of "perfectly prepared" prime steaks are delivered by "courteous" waiters who do a "terrific" raw meat "show and tell" before the meal; decked out in "dark woods", the "elegant" atmosphere attracts a "power-lunch" crowd that isn't fazed by the large tabs – if you don't have an "expense account", just "bring your first-born."

|  | FOOD | DECOR | SERVICE | COST |
|---|---|---|---|---|

### Aroma ☒ *Italian*
|  | 25 | 15 | 22 | $36 |

**Silver Lake** | 2903 W. Sunset Blvd. (bet. Reno St. & Silver Lake Blvd.) | 323-644-2833 | www.aromaatsunset.com

"Good things come in small packages" attest enthusiasts of this "intimate" Silver Lake destination squeezed between "a liquor store and a nail salon", where the "fabulous" Italian dishes are "made with love" by "masterful" chef Edin Marroquin (ex Valentino); insiders appreciate the "warm service" and "reasonable prices", but say that now that this "gem" has "been discovered", reservations are highly recommended.

### Arroyo Chop House *Steak*
|  | 25 | 23 | 23 | $60 |

**Pasadena** | 536 S. Arroyo Pkwy. (bet. California & Del Mar Blvds.) | 626-577-7463 | www.arroyochophouse.com

"Power-lunchers" and "dinner dates" convene at this "heavy-hitting" Pasadena steakhouse from the Smith brothers (Parkway Grill, Smitty's Grill) to clink martini glasses over "melt-in-your-mouth" beef tendered by an "accommodating" staff that won't "rush" you; white tablecloths, "warm decor" and a retro bar create a "clubby atmosphere" that can be as "noisy as a 747", so some find the enclosed patio with brick fireplace a "quieter" option; P.S. "reservations are a must."

### Artisan Cheese Gallery *Cheese/Sandwiches*
|  | 26 | 14 | 18 | $16 |

**Studio City** | 12023 Ventura Blvd. (Laurel Canyon Blvd.) | 818-505-0207 | www.artisancheesegallery.com

*Fromage* fanatics "rejoice" over the "fantastic" stash of 300 imported and domestic cheeses, "irresistible" panini and other gourmet "goodies" like olive oil, vinegars and pickles at this sunny-yellow Studio City shop where the "knowledgeable staff" offers "individual attention", and they're "not shy with samples" either; since it's favored mostly for takeout, prices are manageable, though some say they "love it so much", it's "easy to drop $50 on a visit."

### Art's Deli *Deli*
|  | 20 | 12 | 18 | $21 |

**Studio City** | 12224 Ventura Blvd. (bet. Laurelgrove & Vantage Aves.) | 818-762-1221 | www.artsdeli.com

"The meat's the thing" at this family-owned Jewish deli in Studio City – an "institution" for more than 50 years – where connoisseurs chow down on "heavenly rye-bread" creations "piled high" with "lean" corned beef and matched with "all the right sides" like "wonderful soups" and "standout blintzes"; most overlook "high" prices and occasionally "mediocre" quality since it's "one of the last" of its genre with a "bustling, noisy" environment, "snappy" servers and owner Art still making an appearance on a regular basis.

### Asahi Ramen ⊅ *Japanese*
|  | 20 | 8 | 19 | $12 |

**West LA** | 2027 Sawtelle Blvd. (bet. La Grange & Mississippi Aves.) | 310-479-2231 | www.asahiramen.com

"Basic" ramen is the name of the game at this "no-nonsense" noodle shop on Little Osaka's Restaurant Row where the "huge bowls of soup" leave surveyors "feeling satisfied"; though detractors declare it's "no *Tampopo*", "cheap" tabs keep it "packed" – especially during "peak eat hours" – though "prompt" service keeps the lines moving.

|  | FOOD | DECOR | SERVICE | COST |

### Asaka *Japanese*
▽ 18 | 14 | 18 | $29

**Rancho Palos Verdes** | Golden Cove Shopping Ctr. | 31208 Palos Verdes Dr. W. (Hawthorne Blvd.) | 310-377-5999 | www.asakausa.com

Considering the few Japanese options on the Peninsula, "locals" are "grateful" for this "casual" Rancho Palos Verdes sushi specialist serving up "traditional" nigiri and maki at gentle prices; though "aficionados" attest it's "nothing special", neighborhood "families" find the convenient location with a "wonderful patio" "overlooking the Pacific" "compensates" for the somewhat "uninspiring" fare.

### Asakuma *Japanese*
20 | 15 | 19 | $33

**Beverly Hills** | 141 S. Robertson Blvd. (bet. Charleville & Wilshire Blvds.) | 310-659-1092
**Venice** | Hoyt Plaza | 2805 Abbot Kinney Blvd. (Washington Blvd.) | 310-577-7999
**West LA** | Brentwood Shopping Ctr. | 11701 Wilshire Blvd. (Barrington Ave.) | 310-826-0013
**West LA** | 11769 Santa Monica Blvd. (bet. Granville & Stoner Aves.) | 310-473-8990
www.asakuma.com

A "solid performer" sum up surveyors of this Japanese mini-chain "mainstay" doing a "mostly take-out" business supplying "attractively priced" "staples" like "addictive" miso-glazed black cod, spicy tuna salad and "innovative" maki; while "delivery is fast and reliable", those seeking a "sit-down" meal should head to the separately owned Wilshire Boulevard branch, where the "polite" staff and "pleasant" art-filled dining room creates an experience that's a "cut above" the others.

### Ⓩ Asanebo Ⓜ *Japanese*
28 | 15 | 24 | $63

**Studio City** | 11941 Ventura Blvd. (bet. Carpenter & Radford Aves.) | 818-760-3348

Loyalists liken the "incredible" fish dishes to works of "art" (should you "look at it or eat it"?) at this Japanese in Studio City, where chef Tetsuya Nakao sends out "impressive" displays of "stellar" sushi and sashimi and "immaculately seasoned" daily specials that require a big appetite as well as a "big wallet"; given the "tiny" space jammed with "studio heads and industry players", "reservations" are recommended and insiders assert the bar seating is the way to go.

### Asia de Cuba ❶ *Asian Fusion/Cuban*
23 | 25 | 21 | $61

**West Hollywood** | Mondrian Hotel | 8440 Sunset Blvd. (bet. La Cienega Blvd. & Olive Dr.) | 323-848-6000 | www.chinagrillmanagement.com

This Asian-Cuban hot spot in West Hollywood's Mondrian Hotel is "bigger than life", laying out "huge" "family-style" portions" of "lovely, imaginative" food that comes with equally huge price tags; the "breathtaking" view from the "chic" "white-on-white" dining room and terrace is rivaled by an "over-the-top" array of "fabulous" people (and "tons of tourists" too), making for a "cooler than cool" experience.

### Astro Burger ⊟ *Burgers*
19 | 9 | 15 | $10

**Hollywood** | 5601 Melrose Ave. (Gower St.) | 323-469-1924 ❶
**West Hollywood** | 7475 Santa Monica Blvd. (bet. Fairfax & La Brea Aves.) | 323-874-8041 ❶

*(continued)*

*(continued)*

**Astro Burger**

**Montebello** | 3421 W. Beverly Blvd. (Bradshawe St.) | 323-724-3995 |
www.astroburger.com

"Juicy" burgers and "amazing onion rings" share the menu with "vegetarian" dishes and "healthier" renditions of Greek diner "classics" at this "retro" chainlet whose other "astronomical achievements" include "affordable" prices and "quick" service; though by day it's filled with "families", it's also a "reliable" pick "after a night out on the town" when the "magical" eats have the ability to "minimize hangovers" too; N.B. the WeHo branch is open till 4 AM on weekends.

**Asuka** *Japanese*                                  19 | 12 | 18 | $33

**Westwood** | 1266 Westwood Blvd. (Wilshire Blvd.) | 310-474-7412 |
www.asukasushi.com

"When you're in a rush" this Westwood Japanese meets the need for "pre-theater" meals and "last-minute" family outings since the "friendly" staff accommodates "special orders" for little ones, and adults savor "solid" sushi and "not too pricey" tabs; given its standing as a "nice little" "neighborhood" joint since 1974, most don't mind the total "non-scene", even if the no-frills pale-wood interior could use some "sprucing up."

**Auld Dubliner, The** *Pub Food*                     18 | 20 | 18 | $22

**Long Beach** | Pike at Rainbow Harbor | 71 S. Pine Ave. (Ocean Blvd.) |
562-437-8300 | www.aulddubliner.com

"Beer drinkers" kick back "after a tough day at the office" at this "genuine" Long Beach pub where "personable" bartenders pull pints from 14 brews on tap and the "real-deal" Irish fare like beef stew and fish 'n' chips is "better than it needs to be"; on "weekends" and late nights it draws a rowdier crowd of "tourists" and "college kids" who squeeze in for live music.

**Auntie Em's Kitchen** *American*                    23 | 14 | 16 | $16

**Eagle Rock** | 4616 Eagle Rock Blvd. (Corliss St.) | 323-255-0800 |
www.auntieemskitchen.com

A "homey" setting with "rickety" tables covered with colorful "oilcloth" swatches creates a "charming" backdrop for "wholesome" American breakfast and lunch "staples" like "fluffy" pancakes, "market-fresh salads" and "not-to-be-missed" red-velvet cupcakes at this Eagle Rock cafe; it caters to a "boho" crowd that doesn't mind the "slow" service given the "relaxed" vibe; N.B. there's also an adjacent shop vending an impressive selection of domestic and imported cheeses.

**Aunt Kizzy's Back Porch** *Southern*                19 | 13 | 17 | $22

**Marina del Rey** | 523 Washington Blvd. (Via Marina) | 310-578-1005 |
www.auntkizzys.com

"Down-home" Southern cooking keeps customers contented at this "busy" Marina del Rey "soul fooder" that "warms your heart" with "world-class" fried chicken, "stick-to-your-ribs ribs" and a "surprisingly affordable" Sunday brunch buffet; "relaxed" service suits the casual atmosphere, and as for any qualms about calories, regulars say "forget the diet", "wear loose pants" and just "enjoy"; N.B. the Decor score may not fully reflect a recent move.

| | FOOD | DECOR | SERVICE | COST |
|---|---|---|---|---|

### A Votre Sante  *Vegetarian*
**20 | 13 | 18 | $23**

Brentwood | 13016 San Vicente Blvd. (26th St.) | 310-451-1813 |
www.avotresantela.com

Those in search of "the perfect post-yoga meal" head to this "reasonably priced" Brentwood cafe dishing up "mostly organic" veggie vittles plus a handful of "guilt-free" chicken and salmon dishes that "give health food a good name"; "accommodating" servers add to the overall "low-key" vibe, though on weekend mornings a sprinkling of celebs adds "star" power to the otherwise understated room.

### Axe Ⓜ *Californian*
**22 | 17 | 18 | $39**

Venice | 1009 Abbot Kinney Blvd. (bet. Brooks Ave. & B'way) | 310-664-9787 |
www.axerestaurant.com

"Beloved" by locals, this "health-focused" Venice Californian boasts an "unusual" mostly organic menu served up in "stylishly" "spare" surroundings with a few "communal tables" and vaguely "uncomfortable" bench seating; on weekends, "brunch is the thing" when "beautiful bohos" "spill out onto Abbot Kinney" and "waits" are the norm, though supporters swear the simply "magical" nine-grain pancakes are "worth it."

### Azami Ⓢ Ⓜ *Japanese*
**▽ 25 | 14 | 21 | $41**

Hollywood | 7160 Melrose Ave. (bet. Detroit St. & Formosa Ave.) |
323-939-3816 | www.azamisushi.net

"Incredibly fresh" fish and "creative" omakase menus lure loads of "repeat" visitors to this Hollywood Japanese helmed by "uniquely skilled" Niki Nakayama, one of the few female sushi chefs in the area; though loyalists lament it's "no longer a secret", it retains a "neighborhood-y" feel thanks to an "attentive" staff, "comfortable" strip-mall digs and tabs that are substantial "without feeling overpriced."

### Babalu  *Californian*
**19 | 16 | 17 | $26**

Santa Monica | 1002 Montana Ave. (10th St.) | 310-395-2500

Californian fare with "island flair" describes the "inventive" menu at this "casual" Santa Monica standby dishing out "satisfying" plates of blackened chicken and coconut shrimp plus "fabulous" "homemade" desserts in "kooky" and "colorful" Caribbean-inspired quarters; "erratic" service is a sore spot, as are "cramped" and "noisy" conditions, so "try to sit outside" if you can.

### ⓩ Babita Mexicuisine Ⓜ *Mexican*
**26 | 14 | 22 | $38**

San Gabriel | 1823 S. San Gabriel Blvd. (Norwood Pl.) | 626-288-7265

"Refined Mexican" cooking draws a fanatical following to chef-owner Roberto Berrelleza's "out-of-the-way" "jewel" in San Gabriel offering "inspired" dishes that "bring new life" to "traditional" recipes; with just 10 tables, the brightly hued space is "unpretentious" at best, but that's no matter since customers claim they "always feel pampered" by the staff's "gracious" "hospitality."

### ⓩ Baby Blues BBQ  *BBQ*
**23 | 9 | 18 | $23**

Venice | 444 Lincoln Blvd. (Rose Ave.) | 310-396-7675 |
www.babybluesbarbq.com

"Meaty" babyback ribs arrive "falling-apart tender" at this "down and dirty" Venice joint where BBQ buffs "line up around the block" for Memphis-style grub served with "sauces that will knock your socks

| | FOOD | DECOR | SERVICE | COST |
|---|---|---|---|---|

off" and all the proper "Southern trimmings"; regulars report "it gets very crowded", so go "during off hours" or opt for "takeout"; N.B. they now serve beer and wine.

### Back Home in Lahaina  *Hawaiian*

| | 17 | 13 | 17 | $17 |
|---|---|---|---|---|

**Carson** | 519 E. Carson St. (Grace Ave.) | 310-835-4014
**Manhattan Beach** | 916 N. Sepulveda Blvd. (10th St.) | 310-374-0111
www.backhomeinlahaina.com

These "easygoing" South Bay Hawaiian twins pay homage to the Islands with "Big Kahuna–sized" plates of *lau lau* (slow-cooked pork), fried chicken and other "decent" renditions of traditional dishes served with "hospitality" in tropical-style settings; even if a few are "disappointed" by grub they find "marginal", most say "*mahalo*" for the "great prices."

### Baja Fresh Mexican Grill  *Mexican*

| | 17 | 10 | 14 | $11 |
|---|---|---|---|---|

**Third Street** | 8495 W. Third St. (La Cienega Blvd.) | 310-659-9500
**Beverly Hills** | 475 N. Beverly Dr. (Little Santa Monica Blvd.) | 310-858-6690
**Brentwood** | 11690 San Vicente Blvd. (Barrington Ave.) | 310-826-9166
**Marina del Rey** | Villa Marina Mktpl. | 13424 Maxella Ave. (Del Rey Ave.) | 310-578-2252
**Westwood** | Westwood Vill. | 10916 Lindbrook Ave. (Westwood Blvd.) | 310-208-3317
**Long Beach** | Los Altos Shopping Ctr. | 2090 Bellflower Blvd. (bet. Abbeyfield St. & Britton Dr.) | 562-596-9080
**Pasadena** | 899 E. Del Mar Blvd. (Lake Ave.) | 626-792-0446
**Burbank** | 877 N. San Fernando Blvd. (Burbank Blvd.) | 818-841-4649
**Studio City** | Bistro Ctr. | 12930 Ventura Blvd. (Coldwater Canyon Ave.) | 818-995-4242
**Woodland Hills** | Winnetka Sq. | 19960 Ventura Blvd. (bet. Lubao & Penfield Aves.) | 818-888-3976
www.bajafresh.com
Additional locations throughout Southern California

Surveyors seeking an "emergency taco fix" hit up this SoCal chain that "makes Mexican a little healthier" with "zingy" "made-to-order" eats that "work in a pinch" "as long as you aren't looking for authenticity"; it offers a "comfortably predictable" experience with all branches boasting the same "cheap tabs", "industrial-style settings" and "typical fast-food service" – "the only thing that differs is the parking."

### Baleen Los Angeles  *American*

| | ▽ 20 | 23 | 18 | $51 |
|---|---|---|---|---|

**Redondo Beach** | Portofino Hotel & Yacht Club | 260 Portofino Way (Harbor Dr.) | 310-372-1202 | www.hotelportofino.com

Well-heeled patrons "ogle the boats while dining" at this "lovely" New American "sitting right on the harbor" at Redondo Beach's Portofino Hotel & Yacht Club featuring a candlelit dining room with a fireplace and "beautiful wooden bar"; yet in spite of the "terrific location", detractors dub the "well-presented" seafood dishes "inconsistent" and say the "pricey" tabs might leave you with a sinking feeling.

### Bamboo  *Caribbean*

| | 20 | 13 | 18 | $27 |
|---|---|---|---|---|

**Culver City** | 10835 Venice Blvd. (bet. Overland Ave. & Sepulveda Blvd.) | 310-287-0668 | www.bamboorestaurant.net

"A keeper" gush fans of this "casual" Culver City canteen where the kitchen is "not shy" about spicing up the "nouvelle" Caribbean cuisine and the pitchers of sangria "can make you forget a rough

| | FOOD | DECOR | SERVICE | COST |
|---|---|---|---|---|

week quickly"; despite its location on a "noisy" street, it features a "transporting" shaded patio while inside the color-splashed space, a new bar mixing mojitos and "friendly" service add to the overall festive feel.

### Bamboo Cuisine  Chinese          23 | 17 | 20 | $25

**Sherman Oaks** | 14010 Ventura Blvd. (bet. Hazeltine & Woodman Aves.) | 818-788-0202 | www.bamboocuisine.com

Valley dwellers declare they're always "impressed" by this "top-notch" Sherman Oaks Sino showcasing "fresh", "high-quality" Mandarin dishes (with plenty of "low-calorie" options) on "lazy Susans" planted in the center of "large, round tables"; factor in "personalized" service, and "reasonable" prices, and it's no wonder it's "still going strong" "after all these years."

### Bandera  American/Southwestern          21 | 20 | 20 | $37

**West LA** | 11700 Wilshire Blvd. (Barrington Ave.) | 310-477-3524 | www.hillstone.com

"Good-looking professionals" pack this West LA offshoot of the Houston's chain offering "tasty" Southwestern-American dishes like "fall-off-the-bone ribs" and "delicious grilled artichokes" plus "killer cocktails" in "dark", "moody" environs with a "happening" "bar scene"; "long waits" are the norm, though the "tag-team service approach" turns tables quickly – just don't let the waiters "hurry you out."

### Banzai Sushi  Japanese          22 | 14 | 19 | $36

**Calabasas** | 23508 Calabasas Rd. (Valley Circle Blvd.) | 818-222-5800 | www.banzaisushi.com

Calabasas sushi connoisseurs claim they're "never disappointed" in this "casual" commissary specializing in "customizable" rolls and a variety of tempura and teppanyaki dishes; its traditional bamboo-trimmed setting includes a patio so pleasant you "almost forget you're in a parking lot", while valet attendants raise the bar for service by offering to "hand wash" your car "while you dine."

### Barbara's at the Brewery  🏁 Eclectic       ▽ 14 | 13 | 15 | $19

**Downtown** | Brewery Art Complex | 620 Moulton Ave. (Main St.) | 323-221-9204 | www.bwestcatering.com

Downtown scenesters are drawn to this under-the-radar "hang-out" "hidden" inside The Brewery artists' colony whose "unusual location" in a "warehouse-y" complex of buildings makes it "worth a detour" in itself; unfortunately, the "standard" Eclectic bar eats don't quite match up, but "happy-hour" deals on "snacks and drinks" keep patrons pleased, as does the trio of patios that are "good for smokers."

### Bar Celona  Spanish          16 | 19 | 17 | $32

**Pasadena** | 46 E. Colorado Blvd. (bet. Fair Oaks & Raymond Aves.) | 626-405-1000

A "happening" place in Old Town Pasadena, this "high-energy" Spaniard pulls in a "trendy" "young" crowd that "eyes the scene" and nibbles "a bite of this and a bite of that" in between swigs of "outstanding sangria"; though the "vibrant" crimson-hued room exudes a "sexy" vibe, since it's mainly known as a "real pickup bar", those focusing on the fare alone are likely to find it "disappointing."

| | FOOD | DECOR | SERVICE | COST |
|---|---|---|---|---|

**Barefoot Bar & Grill** *Californian/Eclectic* | 18 | 20 | 18 | $34

**Third Street** | 8722 W. Third St. (bet. George Burns Rd. & Robertson Blvd.) | 310-276-6223 | www.barefootrestaurant.com

Locals appreciate this "casual" "neighborhood spot" on Third Street featuring "a varied menu" of Cal-Eclectic eats (think "solid" salads and seafood dishes) augmented by "friendly service", a "pleasant" plant-filled dining area and a "lovely" outdoor patio; it also sports a private room upstairs that's "perfect" for "wedding and baby showers", while its proximity to Cedars-Sinai makes it a natural lunchtime "favorite" for "doctors and nurses."

**Bar Hayama** ⊠ *Japanese* | 24 | 23 | 21 | $49

**West LA** | 1803 Sawtelle Blvd. (Nebraska Ave.) | 310-235-2000 | www.bar-hayama.com

"Sake-friendly noshes" are the focus of this Westside Japanese "gem" helmed by "longtime maestro" Frank Toshi Sugiura (head of the California Sushi Academy) and his "outgoing" team of chefs turning out "top-of-the-line" fin fare and macrobiotic dishes in a "cozy" setting made warmer by a "lovely" fire pit out on the patio; "pricey" tabs are a deterrent to only a few – even though it's relatively new, a number of converts claim they're "already regulars."

**Barney Greengrass** *Deli* | 20 | 17 | 17 | $32

**Beverly Hills** | Barneys New York | 9570 Wilshire Blvd., 5th fl. (bet. Camden & Peck Drs.) | 310-777-5877 | www.barneygreengrass.com

"Homesick New Yorkers" hail this "fiercely busy" Beverly Hills deli above Barneys department store that's "chicer and more polished than its NYC namesake", but serves up similarly "delish" "hand-cut" smoked fish on H&H bagels and other "delicacies" like blintzes, eggs and overstuffed sandwiches; even if it's "overpriced" and "a bit lacking in service", given the "beautiful views" from the terrace and great "celeb-spotting" and "eavesdropping" inside, "what's not to like?"

**Barney's Gourmet Hamburgers** *Burgers* | 20 | 10 | 16 | $15

**Brentwood** | 11660 San Vicente Blvd. (bet. Darlington & Mayfield Aves.) | 310-447-6000

**Brentwood** | Brentwood Country Mart | 225 26th St. (San Vicente Blvd.) | 310-899-0133

**Sherman Oaks** | Westfield Fashion Sq. | 14006 Riverside Dr. (Woodman Ave.) | 818-808-0680

www.barneyshamburgers.com

"Messy", "mouthwatering" burgers come in "every conceivable variety" at this "super-casual" chain out of San Francisco whose Brentwood and Sherman Oaks outposts also offer "addictive" fries ("skinny, steak-cut or curly") and salads that "ain't bad either"; service "varies in enthusiasm and attention", but considering the eats are this "cheap", even the "zero atmosphere" gets a positive spin, with one surveyor glad to be rid of the "annoying '50s music" that seems to be required-listening at "joints" like these.

**NEW** **Bar Pintxo** ☽ *Spanish* | 19 | 16 | 18 | $32

**Santa Monica** | 109 Santa Monica Blvd. (Ocean Ave.) | 310-458-2012

"Bustling" from day one, this Santa Monica newcomer from Joe Miller (Joe's) "re-creates" a "Barcelona"-style tapas joint with a "diverse" selection of Iberian wines and "authentic" Spanish bites that "pack a

|  | FOOD | DECOR | SERVICE | COST |
|---|---|---|---|---|

punch"; some say the "tiny" space is "best designed for snacking" especially considering the "uncomfortable" barstool seating and tabs so "steep" that "a full meal would break the bank" anyhow.

**Barsac Brasserie** ⓩ *Californian/French*     21 | 19 | 21 | $39

**North Hollywood** | 4212 Lankershim Blvd. (bet. Moorpark St. & Ventura Blvd.) | 818-760-7081 | www.barsac.com

A "go-to spot" for "studio types", this "charming" NoHo bistro "just up the street from Universal" is an "island of quality" in an area "without a lot of choices" where "quite good" Cal-French fare is pumped out of an open kitchen and a martini bar draws "crowds" after work; though it's certainly "not cheap", the "charming" staff treats everyone like a "regular", creating a "lovely" ambiance even for those without a "high credit limit."

**NEW Bashan** Ⓜ *American*     26 | 17 | 25 | $49

**Montrose** | 3459 N. Verdugo Rd. (bet. Oceanview & Sunview Blvds.) | 818-541-1532 | www.bashanrestaurant.com

"LA foodies" laud this Montrose "find" that "adds a new spark" to the area dining scene with "talented" chef Nadav Bashan's "exciting" New American menu showing "astounding attention to detail" with "beautifully presented" dishes (including a burrata appetizer "to fight your dining partner over") brought out in a "small" storefront space with grass wall coverings; even if a few are irked by "tiny" portions, the "genuinely cordial" staff makes that – and "high prices" – easy to overlook.

**Basix Cafe** *Californian/Italian*     19 | 14 | 17 | $23

**West Hollywood** | 8333 Santa Monica Blvd. (N. Flores St.) | 323-848-2460 | www.basixcafe.com

"As the name implies", this WeHo "hang" is a "dependable" pick for "simple", "affordable" Cal-Italian selections like "tasty" thin-crust pizzas and "skinny" brunch options served up by an "eager" (if "flaky") staff; both patio and sidewalk seating offer "the full West Hollywood experience", with "boys, their dogs, their boyfriends and their boyfriend's dogs" all contributing to the overall "lively" scene.

**ⓩ Bastide** ⓈⓂ *French*     27 | 27 | 27 | $145

**West Hollywood** | 8475 Melrose Pl. (La Cienega Blvd.) | 323-651-5950

A "delight for every sense" awaits at this recently "revamped" New French in West Hollywood, where, after several high-profile chef changes, Paul Shoemaker (ex Providence) took the helm post-Survey offering four- and seven-course tasting menus complemented by "outstanding" wines from a 1,500-bottle cellar; the "sensational" service sans "attitude" (voted Tops in this year's Survey) and "whimsical, yet elegant" decor by Andrée Putman lend themselves to a "memorable" "five-hour" evening, so while "it ain't cheap", gastronomes insist that for "serious dining", it leaves others "in the dust."

**Bay Cities Deli** Ⓜ *Italian*     - | - | - | I

**Santa Monica** | 1517 Lincoln Blvd. (B'way) | 310-395-8279 | www.bcdeli.com

With only a handful of concrete tables on the front patio for seating, this Italian deli and bakery fills up fast at lunch with Santa Monicans hungry for stuffed Godmother sandwiches, homemade pasta salads and cannoli; while its recipes give a nod to the old country, its online ordering option helps keep service up to speed.

| | FOOD | DECOR | SERVICE | COST |
|---|---|---|---|---|

**BCD Tofu House** *Korean*  19 | 11 | 13 | $16

**Downtown** | 1201 S. Los Angeles St. (12th St.) | 213-746-2525 🗷
**Koreatown** | 3575 Wilshire Blvd. (Kingsley Ave.) | 213-382-6677 ●
**Koreatown** | 869 S. Western Ave. (9th St.) | 213-380-3807 ●
**Cerritos** | 11818 South St. (Pioneer Blvd.) | 562-809-8098
**Torrance** | 1607 Sepulveda Blvd. (Western Ave.) | 310-534-3480
**Reseda** | 18044 Saticoy St. (Lindley Ave.) | 818-342-3535 ●
**Rowland Heights** | 1731 Fullerton Rd. (Colima Rd.) | 626-964-7073
www.bcdtofu.com

"Simmering" "mini-cauldrons" of "spicy tofu soup" are the stars of this "Korean comfort-food" chain also dishing out bulgogi, bibimbop and a variety of "banchan" ("small plates") that really "hit the spot"; the settings are "plain" and "bright", and some guests gripe that service tends to be "subpar" even with a "call button" at each table; still, when a "craving" hits, "you can't beat the value"; N.B. the Garden Grove and Koreatown locations are open 24/7.

**Beacon** *Pan-Asian*  22 | 17 | 20 | $36

**Culver City** | Helms Bldg. | 3280 Helms Ave. (Washington Blvd.) | 310-838-7500 | www.beacon-la.com
Still "holding its own against flashier arrivals" in "now-hip" Culver City, this "inventive" canteen from chefs/co-owners Kazuto Matsusaka and Vicki Fan showcases "tiny" Pan-Asian bites that offer "big rewards" and larger plates like the "scrumptious" miso-glazed cod and hanger steak with wasabi relish; though some say "poor acoustics" in the high-ceilinged dining room "makes conversation difficult", the two "cute patios" redeem as does "courteous and prompt" service and "surprisingly affordable" tabs.

**Beau Rivage** *Mediterranean*  21 | 21 | 21 | $50

**Malibu** | 26025 PCH (Corral Canyon Rd.) | 310-456-5733 | www.beaurivagerestaurant.com
One of the "prettiest places in Malibu" declare devotees of this "romantic" Mediterranean overlooking the shoreline, where diners linger over "pâté" and rare Bordeaux "while watching the sun set"; though the staff is "charming" some say the "inconsistent" fare doesn't live up to the "potential" of the flower-filled setting (or its "pricey" tabs) – even so, it's "always busy", especially during Sunday's champagne brunch.

**Beckham Grill** *American*  18 | 19 | 20 | $35

**Pasadena** | 77 W. Walnut St. (Fair Oaks Ave.) | 626-796-3399 | www.beckhamgrill.com
There's "not too many places like this left" say Pasadenans who pick this "beef-eater's dream" for Traditional American fare with a taste of "ye olde England" thanks to "hearty portions" of prime rib and Yorkshire pudding plus a fine selection of single-malts served by a "friendly crew"; though modernists maintain the "dark", traditional "hunting lodge ambiance" needs a little "refurbishing", diehards declare it wouldn't feel the same without it.

**Beechwood** *American*  18 | 22 | 16 | $37

**Marina del Rey** | 822 Washington Blvd. (Abbot Kinney Blvd.) | 310-448-8884 | www.beechwoodrestaurant.com
"Scruffy Westside hipsters" convene at this "beautiful hang" in Marina del Rey whose "ultramodern" "indoor/outdoor setup" includes a

"lively" patio with fire pit where you can "warm yourself while sipping a sweet blood-orange martini"; though a "creative" New American menu is offered in the "quieter" dining room, given the "spacey" service and often "crowded" scene, many prefer it for "drinks and apps."

### Bel-Air Bar & Grill  *Californian*    19 | 18 | 21 | $46

**Bel-Air** | 662 N. Sepulveda Blvd. (bet. Moraga Dr. & Ovada Pl.) | 310-440-5544 | www.belairbarandgrill.com

"Convenience" is key at this Bel-Air eatery well-located "in between the valley and the Westside" serving upscale Californian cuisine (but despite the name, "no burgers") in a "lovely" marble-floored dining room that's "cozy" in winter "when the fireplace is lit"; though the entrance "through a gas station" leaves some scratching their heads, "efficient" servers aim to "please" and it's "reasonably priced considering the location."

### Bella Cucina Italiana  *Italian*    ∇ 23 | 19 | 19 | $33

**Hollywood** | 1708 N. Las Palmas Ave. (Hollywood Blvd.) | 323-468-8815 | www.dolcegroup.com

This "glitzy" "Hollywood hang" from the Dolce Group pulls in a "young crowd" for "large" helpings of Southern Italian cuisine set down by "great-looking" waitresses who work the "faux-nostalgic" setting with chandeliers, a marble bar and *The Godfather* playing on the TV); given such a "trendy" "scene", cynics are surprised the food's "a lot better than expected", while the "fair prices" keep it in several surveyors' rotation for a pre-clubbing meal.

### Bella Roma SPQR  Ⓜ *Italian*    ∇ 23 | 14 | 25 | $29

**Pico-Robertson** | 1513 S. Robertson Blvd. (Horner St.) | 310-277-7662 | www.bellaromaspqr.com

Customers "can't rave enough" about this "darling" Pico-Robertson newcomer where "the nicest proprietor" – chef Roberto Amico – offers "a taste of Rome" via "mouthwatering" regional dishes served in a cafe-style setting with soccer on the TV on Sundays; although the BYO policy keeps prices "remarkably low", the "tiny" space means it's often tough "to get a table."

### Bellavino Wine Bar  Ⓢ *Eclectic*    ∇ 19 | 17 | 19 | $48

**Westlake Village** | Paseo Market Pl. | 3709 E. Thousand Oaks Blvd. (Marmon Ave.) | 805-557-0202 | www.bellavinowinebar.com

Boasting an award-winning cellar with 50 wines available by the glass, this Westlake Village "hideaway" is where locals in-the-know go for "unique" sips matched with "creative" bites from a midpriced Eclectic menu; though detractors dis "erratic" service and "expensive" prices, the "romantic" setting compensates, especially on the patio when "the fireplace is going."

### Belmont Brewing Co.  *American*    16 | 17 | 16 | $25

**Long Beach** | 25 39th Pl. (1 block south of Ocean Blvd.) | 562-433-3891 | www.belmontbrewing.com

Enthusiasts attest you "can't beat the location" of this "seaside" Long Beach "hangout" drawing a "boisterous" bunch of "families" and "students" for "simple" American eats and 12 "tasty" microbrews on tap; with only "average" grub and "mediocre" service, most grab "a table outside" and focus on the "ocean views."

### ☑ Belvedere, The  *American*    | 25 | 26 | 27 | $75 |

**Beverly Hills** | Peninsula Hotel of Beverly Hills | 9882 S. Santa Monica Blvd. (Wilshire Blvd.) | 310-788-2306 | www.peninsula.com

This "enchanting" "oasis" inside Beverly Hills' Peninsula Hotel channels "classic five-star dining" – "a fading joy" for some – with an "impeccable" staff that takes "service to an art form" ferrying "excellent" New American feasts favored for "power breakfasts", "special-occasion" dinners and a "sublime Sunday brunch"; though the "elegant" gold-toned setup strikes some as "dated" ("expect to see Krystal Carrington coming out of the ladies room at any moment"), the "serene" patio redeems with a "gardenlike" setting that's perfect for "lingering"; N.B. the Food score does not reflect a post-Survey chef change.

### Benihana  *Japanese*    | 18 | 17 | 19 | $37 |

**Beverly Hills** | 38 N. La Cienega Blvd. (Wilshire Blvd.) | 323-655-7311
**Santa Monica** | 1447 Fourth St. (Santa Monica Blvd.) | 310-260-1423
**Ontario** | 3760 E. Inland Empire Blvd. (N. Haven Ave.) | 909-483-0937
**Encino** | 16226 Ventura Blvd. (bet. Libbet & Woodley Aves.) | 818-788-7121
**City of Industry** | Plaza at Puente Hills | 17877 Gale Ave. (Fullerton Rd.) | 626-912-8784
www.benihana.com

"Dinner and a show" takes on new meaning at this "entertaining" Japanese steakhouse chain, the "original teppanyaki experience" complete with "acrobatic", "knife-flipping" chefs who "slice and dice" your meal tableside; party-poopers protest "bland" grub, "hokey" theatrics and "chop-chop" service, noting that "if you go without kids", it helps to "drink a lot."

### ☑ Benley Vietnamese Kitchen ☒ *Vietnamese*    | 24 | 15 | 21 | $23 |

**Long Beach** | 8191 E. Wardlow Rd. (Los Alamitos Blvd.) | 562-596-8130
Chowhounds cheer this "haven for outstanding Vietnamese cuisine" in Long Beach offering "amazingly spiced pho" and "table-pounding good" curry chicken all crafted from "wonderfully fresh ingredients" and served in "minimalist" quarters with black-and-white framed photographs hung on the bright, white walls; factor in "good prices" and "unrushed" service, and aside from the "sketchy" mini-mall setting, the only downside is that it's not open on Sundays; N.B. it now has a full liquor license.

### Berri's Pizza Cafe  *Pizza*    | 16 | 14 | 14 | $27 |

**Third Street** | 8412 W. Third St. (S. Orlando Ave.) | 323-852-0642 ◑
**Playa del Rey** | 8415 Pershing Dr. (Manchester Ave.) | 310-823-6658
This "decent" Italian duo (with a third Hollywood location in the works) fills the need for New York–style pizzas, pastas and salads deemed "ok", but "nothing to call your mama about"; the Playa del Rey branch is more of a "neighborhood" spot while the Third Street outpost is open till 4 AM, making it a "late-night alternative to drive-thru", albeit one that's "expensive for what is."

### NEW Beso ☒ *Spanish*    | - | - | - | M |

**Hollywood** | 6350 Hollywood Blvd. (Ivar Ave.) | 323-467-7991
Celebrity chef Todd English teams up with Desperate Housewife Eva Longoria Parker for this Hollywood haunt getting plenty of "hype"

| | FOOD | DECOR | SERVICE | COST |
|---|---|---|---|---|

thanks to a boldfaced-name crowd tucking into midpriced Spanish dishes both classic and modern; though early samplers say they're "still working out the kinks" with food and service, the bustling bar scene wins "*besos*", as does the "cozy" space done up in a warm palette of caramel, bronze and gold.

### NEW Best Fish Taco in Ensenada, The 🖼 Ⓜ Mexican
▽ 21 | 8 | 14 | $7

**Los Feliz** | 1650 Hillhurst Ave. (Prospect Ave.)

Los Feliz locals "love the simplicity" of this "bare-bones" stand on Hillhurst offering a "basic" but "brilliant" menu of "two items" – "fish or shrimp tacos" – "made fresh while you wait" and customized with "homemade salsas"; prices are "cheap", and even those who "haven't been to Ensenada" still count on it for a "quick snack."

### Big Mama's Rib Shack Ⓜ BBQ/Soul Food
19 | 11 | 16 | $20

**Pasadena** | 1453 N. Lake Ave. (Rio Grande St.) | 626-797-1792 | www.bigmamas-ribshack.com

"Gut-busting portions" of "crispy fried chicken" and "slow-cooked ribs" taste "just like your grandma could have made them" at this Pasadena Southerner putting "lots of soul" into its "comforting" cuisine; though prices are "cheap", some say service needs an "attitude" adjustment and the "depressing" no-frills interior could use a "makeover" too.

### Billingsley's Steak
15 | 11 | 18 | $23

**West LA** | 11326 W. Pico Blvd. (Sawtelle Blvd.) | 310-477-1426 | www.billingsleysrestaurant.com

"Big vinyl booths", "stiff drinks" and "waitresses who call you 'sweetie'" transport "nostalgic" diners to "another era" at this "dark", atmospheric West LA steakhouse serving up "reliable" "well-priced" square meals with a side of "garlic cheese bread"; opened by actress Barbara Billingsley's husband in 1946, it's still popular with an "old-time crowd", especially during the nightly early-bird dinner ($14.95, 4:30–6:30 PM daily).

### Bistro de la Gare Ⓜ French
19 | 20 | 17 | $39

**South Pasadena** | 921 Meridian Ave. (bet. El Centro & Mission Sts.) | 626-799-8828 | www.bistrodelagare.com

"Simple, satisfying food" is at the soul of this "busy" bistro in South Pasadena earning its "strong following" with "traditional" cooking and "reasonably priced" wines set down in a "noisy" "Parisian"-style space with deep-red walls and an antique mahogany bar; the French "flavor" extends all the way down to the servers' accents, leading the less-impressed to label it "a touch pretentious" and "expensive" to boot.

### Bistro 45 Ⓜ Californian
26 | 22 | 24 | $56

**Pasadena** | 45 S. Mentor Ave. (bet. Colorado Blvd. & Green St.) | 626-795-2478 | www.bistro45.com

A "true delight" declare those dazzled by this area "mainstay" that's "still a high point of Pasadena dining" thanks to "wonderful" French-accented Californian cuisine matched with "a dream" of a wine list; its "intimate" setting in a "vintage art deco building" offers a "lovely" terrace and "warm" service, so even if tabs can feel "awfully pricey", most maintain it's "hard to beat" "for that one special meal."

|  | FOOD | DECOR | SERVICE | COST |
|---|---|---|---|---|

## ☑ Bistro Garden at Coldwater, The  *Continental*

| 21 | 26 | 22 | $51 |

**Studio City** | 12950 Ventura Blvd. (Coldwater Canyon Ave.) | 818-501-0202 | www.bistrogarden.com

A "wealthy" crowd frequents this "elegant" Studio City respite where the "gorgeous" "gardenlike" setting with 30-ft. ceilings, "white twinkle lights" and a baby grand piano make it "wonderful for a special occasion", whether a "business lunch" or an "intimate dinner"; "attentive" waiters and a "lovely" menu of Continental cuisine, including "heavenly soufflés" and signature chicken curry, also win raves, so even though some snipe "it's getting by on reputation", many return to "relax" and "enjoy the ambiance."

## Bistro Provence ☒ *French*

| 23 | 16 | 20 | $37 |

**Burbank** | Lakeside Ctr. | 345 N. Pass Ave. (Rte. 134) | 818-840-9050 | www.bistroprovence.net

"An unexpected pleasure" in an "unlikely" strip-mall setting, this "wonderful" French "find" proffers "creative" takes on bistro classics and features a three-course $27.50 prix fixe dinner that deal-hunters deem a "delicious steal"; the "convivial atmosphere" is heightened by the "welcoming" staff, so while the "quiet" mustard-hued room is "not quite France" it still feels "far from Burbank."

## Bistro 767 ☒Ⓜ *Californian*

| ▽ 22 | 19 | 21 | $40 |

**Rolling Hills Estates** | 767 Deep Valley Dr. (bet. Drybank & Roxcove Drs.) | Rolling Hills | 310-265-0914 | www.bistro767.com

"Consistently good" Californian cuisine is enhanced by a "solid wine list" at this "pricey" Rolling Hills Estates destination that Peninsula dwellers deem "worth a try" for "special occasions"; given the "efficient" service and "appealing" low-lit space whose "cozy" banquettes "allow for privacy", some say they only wish they "could afford to go more often."

## NEW Bistrotek  *American*

| - | - | - | M |

**Westchester** | Custom Hotel | 8639 Lincoln Blvd. (W. Manchester Ave.) | 310-258-5757 | www.customhotel.com

"A welcome addition" to the "anemic Westchester dining scene", this midpriced American on the ground floor of the Custom Hotel presents "pimped up" comfort foods like Maine lobster pot pie and grilled mascarpone sandwiches in a "cool" loftlike space with exposed pipes and concrete floors; though the staff is "well meaning", critics are left "unsatisfied" by "mediocre" eats, even if they concede it's "convenient" for a quick bite "before flying from nearby LAX."

## NEW Bistro 39  *French*

| - | - | - | M |

**Alhambra** | 39 W. Main St. (Garfield Ave.) | 626-282-0600

Amid Alhambra's cache of Asian eateries, this French bistro bucks the trend; white tablecloths and lots of mirrors and flowers serve as backdrop for a midpriced menu of old-school Gallic fare such as soupe à l'oignon and sole amandine.

## Bistro 31 ☒ *Californian*

| ▽ 18 | 17 | 17 | $26 |

**Santa Monica** | Art Institute of Los Angeles | 2900 31st St. (Ocean Park Blvd.) | 310-314-6057

"Young foodies" run the show at this student training ground in the Art Institute in Santa Monica where "the best table" in the house is the one overlooking the glassed-in kitchen pumping out often "incredible" Californian dishes for "amazingly cheap prices"; though the cooking can be "uneven" and service verges on "cringe-worthy", most survey-ors "cut them some slack" since "they're just learning" and try "des-perately to please"; N.B. open Monday–Wednesday only and hours are seasonal, so call ahead.

## BJ's  *Pub Food*                    17 | 16 | 16 | $20

**Cerritos** | 11101 183rd St. (I-605) | 562-467-0850
**Westwood** | 939 Broxton Ave. (bet. Le Conte & Weyburn Aves.) | 310-209-7475 ●
**Long Beach** | 5258 E. Second St. (bet. Covina & La Verne Aves.) | 562-439-8181
**Moreno Valley** | 22920 Centerpoint Dr. (Frederick St.) | 951-571-9370 ●
**Arcadia** | 400 E. Huntington Dr. (Gateway Dr.) | 626-462-1494 ●
**Burbank** | 107 S. First St. (Olive Ave.) | 818-557-0881 ●
**Woodland Hills** | 6424 Canoga Ave. (bet. Erwin St. & Victory Blvd.) | 818-340-1748 ●
**NEW** **Montebello** | 1716 Montebello Town Ctr. (N. San Gabriel Blvd.) | 323-201-5290 ●
**Westlake Village** | 3955 E. Thousand Oaks Blvd. (Westlake Blvd.) | 805-497-9393
**Valencia** | Valencia Town Ctr. | 24320 Town Center Dr. (McBean Pkwy.) | 661-288-1299 ●
www.bjsbrewhouse.com
Additional locations throughout Southern California
There's always "lots of action at the bar" at this "lively" chain of SoCal pubs serving a "fine selection of house-crafted beers" (some branches have on-site breweries) along with a "varied" lineup of "affordable" American noshes like "thick-crust" Chicago-style pizzas and "amaz-ing" 'pizookis' (a warm cookie topped with ice cream); "unconsciona-bly slow" service is a sore spot, as is the "deafening" noise – just make sure you "bring earplugs" along with a "hearty" appetite.

## Blair's  *American*                 24 | 19 | 21 | $42

**Silver Lake** | 2903 Rowena Ave. (bet. Glendale & Hyperion Blvds.) | 323-660-1882 | www.blairsrestaurant.com
Silver Lake "foodies" find "bliss" in this "inviting" Eastside "hideaway" that "pleases on every level" with "gutsy" New American cooking and "carefully chosen" beers and wines served up in a "small" "storefront" space exuding a "New York" vibe; "gracious" servers maintain the "quiet energy" of the "hip, but not too hip" candlelit dining room, so in spite of a few quibbles about "close" quarters and "steep pricing", the majority admits "we need more places like this in LA."

## bld  *American*                     21 | 19 | 19 | $35

**Beverly Boulevard** | 7450 Beverly Blvd. (N. Vista St.) | 323-930-9744 | www.bldrestaurant.com
"Simple" New American cuisine gets some "interesting twists" at this "casual" "little sister" of Neal Fraser's Grace on Beverly Boulevard that's "best" for the "wonderful breakfasts" starring "dreamy" blueberry-ricotta pancakes and a "great cup of joe"; the "sleek, mod-ern" space is blessed with "lots of natural light", but "quirky" service can be "hit-or-miss" and wallet-watchers lament it's "just a bit too ex-pensive" "to go every day."

| | FOOD | DECOR | SERVICE | COST |
|---|---|---|---|---|

**Bloom Cafe**  *American/Californian*　　22 | 15 | 15 | $23

**Mid-City** | 5544 W. Pico Blvd. (S. Sierra Bonita Ave.) | 323-934-6900 |
www.go2bloom.com

Eco-happy eaters say it's "worth seeking out" this "definite stand-out" in a "cute" colorful storefront on an "up-and-coming block of Pico" showcasing "imaginative" Californian–New American creations that put the focus on "fresh" "organic" ingredients, sustainable seafood and grass-fed beef; "lackadaisical service" can feel "downright European" at times, but the mood's kept "pleasant" thanks to such "reasonable prices"; N.B. it's BYO with no corkage fee.

**Blossom** ⊠ *Vietnamese*　　▽ 22 | 12 | 18 | $14

**Downtown** | 426 S. Main St. (Winston St.) | 213-623-1973 |
www.blossomrestaurant.com

"Huge bowls" of "flavorful pho" and a bevy of blended teas draw Downtown office dwellers to this "simply decorated" Vietnamese parked on a "gentrified" strip of Main Street across from "gallery row"; "fast service" and pleasing prices make it a "team favorite" for lunch, and a recent expansion means more elbow room for those dining in.

**NEW BLT Steak**  *Steak*　　▽ 23 | 23 | 18 | $79

**West Hollywood** | Sunset Plaza | 8720 Sunset Blvd. (Sherbourne Dr.) |
310-360-1950 | www.bltsteak.com

West Hollywood habitués call this Sunset Strip outpost of Laurent Tourondel's meaty empire a "worthy addition to the LA chophouse scene" with its "predictably stellar" steaks, "well-executed" sides and "towering" Gruyère popovers set down in a "sleek" yet "inviting" "transformation" of the old Le Dome space; "steep prices" come with the territory, though some surveyors are surprised that the "service does not measure up" to the otherwise "fantastic" experience.

**Blue Hen**  *Vietnamese*　　▽ 14 | 11 | 14 | $16

**Eagle Rock** | 1743 Colorado Blvd. (Argus Dr.) | 323-982-9900 |
www.eatatbluehen.com

"Convenience" is key at this Eagle Rock "neighborhood haunt" where the "limited" menu of "healthy", "homey" Vietnamese cooking relies on local suppliers and organic meats and veggies; though prices are "cheap" and "earnest" service perks up the minimalist interior, "disappointed" diners say that while they "appreciate" the concept, they wish the food could be "better than it actually is."

**blue on blue**  *American*　　19 | 20 | 19 | $48

**Beverly Hills** | Avalon Hotel | 9400 W. Olympic Blvd. (Cañon Dr.) |
310-407-7791 | www.avalonbeverlyhills.com

The "sexy, poolside" setting is the main attraction at this "cool" restaurant on the ground floor of Beverly Hills' Avalon Hotel where a "tragically hip" clientele lounge inside semiprivate cabanas amid sleek midcentury decor evoking "Palm Springs"; though a few find the seasonal New American menu "not worth the prices", "free valet parking" takes the sting off, while "Sunday brunch" and cocktail hour offers the same "chic" experience with a more modest bill.

| | FOOD | DECOR | SERVICE | COST |
|---|---|---|---|---|

### Blue Velvet  *American*

| | 20 | 25 | 19 | $53 |

**Downtown** | The Flat | 750 S. Garland Ave. (bet. 7th & 8th Sts.) | 213-239-0061 | www.bluevelvetrestaurant.com

The "stunning" eco-friendly design alone "makes it worth the trip" to this "über-hip" venue in Downtown LA sporting "beautiful" skyline views, indoor and outdoor fireplaces and a "MOCA-worthy" unisex bathroom; an "innovative" American menu featuring "organic" ingredients follows through on the green-centric theme, and if a few deem it "a little style over substance", for most it's a welcome "oasis" in an "otherwise seedy" part of town.

### Bluewater Grill  *American/Seafood*

| | 19 | 18 | 18 | $36 |

**Redondo Beach** | King Harbor Marina | 665 N. Harbor Dr. (Beryl St.) | 310-318-3474 | www.bluewatergrill.com

"Consistency is a virtue" at this waterside American in Redondo Beach, part of a SoCal chainlet that pleases with "economically priced" portions of "really fresh" seafood; though the fare is "solid", it's the "lovely views" from the terrace (a "great place for dates") that steal the show, upstaging the "casual" interior and "friendly" if sometimes "scattered" service; N.B. the Decor score does not reflect a July 2008 remodel.

### Blvd, The  *Californian*

| | 20 | 24 | 20 | $52 |

**Beverly Hills** | Beverly Wilshire | 9500 Wilshire Blvd. (Rodeo Dr.) | 310-385-3901 | www.fourseasons.com

"Sit outside" for a view "straight down Rodeo Drive" at this "lovely" eatery in the Beverly Wilshire where a "haute couture crowd" "lingers" over "pricey" Californian cuisine and "celeb sightings abound" in the deco-inspired interior; service is "excellent" (especially "if they recognize you"), and though it's quite "the scene" for "power breakfasts" and "afternoon meetings", live jazz on Fridays and Saturdays loosens up the usually "stuffy" feel at night.

### NEW Blvd 16  *American*

| | - | - | - | M |

**Westwood** | Hotel Palomar | 10740 Wilshire Blvd. (Selby Ave.) | 310-474-7765 | www.blvd16.com

Situated along the increasingly stylish Wilshire Corridor, this mid-priced New American in Westwood's Hotel Palomar provides a modernist, earth-toned backdrop for the cooking of chef Simon Dolinky (a veteran of August and Cobalt in New Orleans); with his locally sourced, seasonally changing menu, Dolinky's out to prove that the Corridor isn't just a strip for pedal-to-the-metal cruising, but rather a bona fide dining destination.

### Boa  *Steak*

| | 23 | 23 | 21 | $61 |

**West Hollywood** | Grafton Hotel | 8462 W. Sunset Blvd. (La Cienega Blvd.) | 323-650-8383
**Santa Monica** | 101 Santa Monica Blvd. (Ocean Blvd.) | 310-899-4466
www.innovativedining.com

"Imaginative cocktails" fuel the "sexy" "scene" at these "high-energy" "nouveau steakhouses" in West Hollywood and Santa Monica packing in a "VIP crowd" for "well-marbled" meats matched with "tasty" rubs and sauces and accompanied by sides so "imaginative" they could be "the main attraction"; "seriously friendly service" provides a nice counterpoint to the "ultrahip" (and ultraloud) settings with tufted leather walls and dramatic floor-to-ceiling wine displays, but some warn of "remarkable" tabs – "it gets pricey since everything is à la carte"; N.B. the WeHo branch will relocate in 2009.

**Boccaccio's** *European/Italian* ▽ 22 | 22 | 22 | $41

**Westlake Village** | 32123 Lindero Canyon Rd. (Lakeview Canyon) | 818-889-8300 | www.boccacciosrestaurant.com

An "outstanding location" blessed with "peaceful lake views" distinguishes this Westlake Village "standby" that's "especially lovely" on the "comfortable patio"; though some admirers assert the "beautiful setting" trumps the "high-quality" European-Italian steaks and seafood, "exceptional" servers who "know how to please" pave the way for a "pleasant" evening.

**boé** *American* ▽ 22 | 23 | 21 | $37

**Beverly Hills** | The Crescent | 403 N. Crescent Dr. (Brighton Way) | 310-247-0505 | www.crescentbh.com

Nestled in the stylish Crescent hotel, this "intimate", mostly outdoor venue proffers "inventive" New American cuisine – from "fancy brunches" to "late-night drinks" and snacks – in modern digs with a "flickering fireplace"; given such a "quiet and peaceful" setting, some say it's hard to believe this celebrity hang is still a Beverly Hills "secret."

**Bollywood Cafe** *Indian* ▽ 19 | 13 | 18 | $21

**Studio City** | 11101 Ventura Blvd. (Vineland Ave.) | 818-508-8472 | www.bollywoodcafela.com

**NEW** **Studio City** | 3737 Cahuenga Blvd. (Lankershim Blvd.) | 818-508-5533 | www.bollywoodcafe2.com ⓢ

"Dependable" Indian cooking comes in "generous portions" at these family-run twins in Studio City scoring well for their "solid" lunch buffets and servers who are "always helpful with recommendations"; despite lackluster settings, prices are "great", so hungry fans are "hoping they'll open more."

**Bombay Bite** *Indian* ▽ 20 | 17 | 19 | $23

**Westwood** | 1051 Gayley Ave. (bet. Le Conte & Weyburn Aves.) | 310-824-1046 | www.bombaybite.com

Devotees "dine regularly" at this "underrated" Westwood Indian where a dash of Chinese fusion mixes up a menu of "traditional Bombay favorites"; "kind" service and a "trendy" yet "comfortable" atmosphere contribute to the overall "enjoyable" experience that's conducive to "inexpensive dates" or a "nice lunch."

**Bombay Cafe** *Indian* 23 | 15 | 18 | $31

**West LA** | 12021 W. Pico Blvd. (Bundy Dr.) | 310-473-3388 | www.bombaycafe-la.com

"Simply delicious all the way around" proclaim proponents of this "modern" West LA Indian that "opens your eyes to a whole new world" with "inventive dishes not seen elsewhere" plus "perfectly spiced curries" and an "amazing chutney selection" all brought by a "knowledgeable" staff that's at the ready with "recommendations"; frugal sorts say that tabs can feel "expensive", especially given the "low-key" blue-and-yellow setting, though converts conclude it's "worth it", given such "high quality."

### Bombay Palace *Indian*  | 21 | 20 | 19 | $36 |

**Beverly Hills** | 8690 Wilshire Blvd. (bet. Hamel & Willaman Drs.) | 310-659-9944

Acolytes attest this Beverly Hills subcontinental is "among the best" in the area for "gourmet" cuisine presented in a "nice-looking space" with white walls, "dim" lighting and antiques displayed throughout; though it's "on the pricey side" for the genre, service is "welcoming" and "you can always count on it"

### NEW BonChon Chicken *Korean*  | - | - | - | I |

**Koreatown** | 3407 W. Sixth St. (S. Catalina St.) | 213-487-7878 | www.bonchon.com

This Korean fried chicken chain clucks about its 'specially engineered sauce' that sticks to the bird and not to your hands for neat meat in regular and hot options; the corner spot in a K-town office building is much fancier than your basic cheep-eats place, with low lighting and a clubby feel nice enough to eat in.

### NEW Bond Street Beverly Hills *Japanese*  | 19 | 24 | 17 | $67 |

**Beverly Hills** | Thompson Beverly Hills Hotel | 9360 Wilshire Blvd. (N. Crescent Dr.) | 310-601-2255 | www.thompsonbeverlyhills.com

"Nestled" within the "swanky, new" Thompson Beverly Hills Hotel, this Manhattan import caters to a "Prada-clad" crowd (including "the occasional superstar") with a "chic" "energetic" atmosphere done up in a "black-and-white check" motif and "innovative" Japanese dishes, both raw and cooked; still, in spite of some "unique" offerings, it "doesn't live up to the hype" (or the "expense-account prices") for those "underwhelmed" by the food and "all-over-the-place" service.

### Boneyard Bistro *BBQ/Eclectic*  | 21 | 16 | 20 | $34 |

**Sherman Oaks** | 13539 Ventura Blvd. (Woodman Ave.) | 818-906-7427 | www.boneyardbistro.com

"Gourmet barbecue" featuring three different styles of "succulent" ribs heads up the Eclectic menu at this "quaint" Sherman Oaks eatery also serving a lineup of bistro selections alongside a "killer" list of 125 brews to wash it all down; though some deem the "Q" too "froufrou" and the art-filled dining room "loud", a "personable" staff keeps it "popular" as does Monday's "awesome" "fried-chicken and half-priced beer special."

### Bono's *Californian*  | 20 | 20 | 18 | $43 |

**Long Beach** | 4901 E. Second St. (St. Joseph Ave.) | 562-434-9501 | www.bonoslongbeach.com

This "upscale" Long Beach boîte owned by Christy Bono (Sonny's daughter) traffics in "well-executed" Californian cuisine matched with an "impressive wine and martini list" set down in "chic, contemporary" surroundings that feel like you're dining at a "well-heeled friend's beach house"; a few critics cite "hit-or-miss" fare and service as cause for complaint, but the prime location and breezy patio make it "one of the nicer places to 'lunch' on Belmont Shore."

| | FOOD | DECOR | SERVICE | COST |
|---|---|---|---|---|

**Bora Bora** ⓜ *Californian/Polynesian*  ▽ 22 | 18 | 21 | $35

**Manhattan Beach** | 3505 Highland Ave. (35th St.) | 310-545-6464
"Amazing" spicy ribs and "ultrarich" mac 'n' cheese are the standouts on the "reasonably priced" Cal-Polynesian menu at this Manhattan Beach "sleeper" where the "decadent" dishes arrive via "chatty" waiters who look like they just stepped "out of the pages of *GQ*"; it's "very much a neighborhood spot" favored for "dates", thanks to "large" "cozy" booths and a "dark, intimate" atmosphere illuminated by tropical light fixtures.

**Border Grill** *Mexican*  21 | 17 | 18 | $34

**Santa Monica** | 1445 Fourth St. (bet. B'way & Santa Monica Blvd.) | 310-451-1655 | www.bordergrill.com
It "always feels like a party" at this "rollicking" Santa Monica Mexican mainstay from celeb owners Susan Feniger and Mary Sue Milliken that "still delivers" "tons of flavor" via "nouveau" eats with a "Californian kick" and "magnificent" margaritas made from a selection of 95 tequilas; though the staff is "accommodating" and pricing "affordable for the neighborhood", a few find the "'90s-style" interior "screaming for an update" and add that "nightmare acoustics" make "conversation impossible" (bring "earplugs" or "in-laws").

**Bossa Nova** *Brazilian*  20 | 13 | 17 | $22

**Hollywood** | 7181 W. Sunset Blvd. (Formosa Ave.) | 323-436-7999 ●
**Pico-Robertson** | 10982 W. Pico Blvd. (bet. Greenfield & Veteran Aves.) | 310-441-0404
**West Hollywood** | 685 N. Robertson Blvd. (bet. Melrose Ave. & Santa Monica Blvd.) | 310-657-5070 ●
**Beverly Hills** | 212 S. Beverly Dr. (Charleville Blvd.) | 310-550-7900
www.bossafood.com
A "broad menu" of "zesty" South American standards characterizes this "lively" chainlet "catering to big groups" with "huge" platters of grilled meats, black beans and fried plantains that really "hit the spot", especially "late at night" (the Hollywood branch is "fired up" till 4 AM); "too-bright" atmosphere gets some surveyors down, as does "slow" service that always seems to be "running on Brazilian time."

**Boss Sushi** *Japanese*  ▽ 25 | 14 | 21 | $42

**Beverly Hills** | 270A S. La Cienega Blvd. (Gregory Way) | 310-659-5612 | www.bosssushi.com
Sushi buffs say this Beverly Hills "favorite" is "tops" for a "wide assortment" of both "traditional" Japanese dishes and "innovative" "fresh fish" expertly cut by a "friendly team" of chefs; "dismal" digs are a drawback, but many maintain it's "well worth trying" anyway.

**BottleRock** *European*  16 | 15 | 16 | $30

**Culver City** | 3847 Main St. (bet. Culver & Venice Blvds.) | 310-836-9463 | www.bottlerock.net
A "nice place to lounge and sip", this Culver City wine bar/shop and patio features a seemingly "infinite" cellar and a "fantastic tasting policy" ("they'll open any bottle if you order two glasses"); a "limited" lineup of well-priced European "munchies" like charcuterie plates provides a "light complement" to the drinks, but sticklers say the "skimpy" portions and "uncomfortable" seating are not well-suited to a "full meal."

| | FOOD | DECOR | SERVICE | COST |
|---|---|---|---|---|

### Boulevard Lounge ●Ⓜ *Californian* ▽ 19 | 20 | 18 | $32

**West Hollywood** | 1114 N. Crescent Heights Blvd. (Santa Monica Blvd.) | 323-654-6686 | www.theboulevardlounge.com

Fans of "strong drinks" cheer this "funky", "friendly" stop on the West Hollywood "happy-hour" circuit offering "deals" twice nightly in a "cool" powder-blue bungalow with a covered patio and two oak trees growing up through the floor; though service can be "slow", most are pleasantly "surprised" by the "gussied up" Cal cuisine that's served late (till 1 AM on weekends) and is "affordable" too.

### Bowery ● *American/French* 20 | 20 | 18 | $26

**Hollywood** | 6268 W. Sunset Blvd. (bet. Argyle Ave. & Vine St.) | 323-465-3400 | www.theboweryhollywood.com

Channeling the "look and feel of a New York City watering hole" ("you can almost feel the 6-train rumbling under you"), this well-priced Hollywood French-American turns out "tasty" fare – including "standout" blue-cheese burgers – and a "nice selection" of wines and single-malt scotches in a "cool" space decked out with black-and-white tile and a tin ceiling; despite the "funky" feel, a few find fault with "cramped quarters" and "noisy" acoustics, and given the "tiny" space and "no-reservations" policy, loyalists lament it's often hard to "get a seat."

### Ⓩ Brandywine Ⓢ *Continental* 27 | 20 | 27 | $60

**Woodland Hills** | 22757 Ventura Blvd. (Fallbrook Ave.) | 818-225-9114

A "charming owner" presides over this "sweet", "little" Woodland Hills "gem" that embodies "old-world elegance" with "lovingly prepared" Continental cuisine and "quaint" decor that makes you feel "swept away" to a "French countryside home"; it's certainly "not cheap" but the smitten swear it's "worth dressing up and paying a little bit extra" for such a "memorable", "romantic" meal.

### Brass.-Cap. *French* 19 | 20 | 18 | $56

**Santa Monica** | 100 W. Channel Rd. (PCH) | 310-454-4544 | www.brasseriecapo.com

An "upscale clientele" frequents this Santa Monica "nook", a "little cousin" of Bruce Marder's Capo serving up "straightforward" French bistro fare in an art-filled setting with a heated patio; while many are pleasantly surprised to find such a "sophisticated" place "right by the beach", critics complain the food is "too expensive for what it is", and prefer it for drinks at the "beautiful" zinc bar.

### Bravo Cucina *Italian/Pizza* ▽ 17 | 11 | 14 | $24

**Santa Monica** | 1319 Third St. Promenade (bet. Arizona Ave. & Santa Monica Blvd.) | 310-394-0374

### Bravo Pizzeria *Italian/Pizza*

**Santa Monica** | 2400D Main St. (bet. Hollister Ave. & Ocean Park Blvd.) | 310-392-7466
www.bravosantamonica.com

With a pizzeria on Main Street (open till 3 AM on weekends) and a full "East Coast" Italian-style menu at the Promenade locale, surveyors say this "comfortable" Santa Monica duo from the owners of NYC's Ferrara is hard to beat for a "quick" "bite" "before a movie" or when the "late-night" munchies hit; though tabs are kept pleasantly low, the

| | FOOD | DECOR | SERVICE | COST |
|---|---|---|---|---|

less-enthused attest that "uninspired" service and "so-so" decor mean they're otherwise "unremarkable."

**Breadbar** *American/Bakery*　　　　　| 18 | 14 | 15 | $20 |

**West Hollywood** | 8718 W. Third St. ( Robertson Blvd.) | 310-205-0124
**Century City** | Westfield Century City Shopping Ctr. | 10250 Santa Monica Blvd. (bet. Ave. of the Stars & Century Park W.) | 310-277-3770
www.breadbar.net

You'll want to "check your no-carbs policy at the door" of these "innovative bakeries" in Century City and West Hollywood specializing in a "delectable" selection of "freshly made" artisanal breads and pastries as well as "nice soups", salads and other New American dishes deemed "healthy, if you don't nosh too much"; "communal tables" and patio seating at both locations encourage a "casual" vibe, but "disorganized" service prompts some patrons to recommend it for "takeout" only; P.S. check their website for info on their ongoing "guest chef" series.

**Breeze** *Californian/Seafood*　　　| 17 | 19 | 18 | $45 |

**Century City** | Hyatt Regency Century Plaza Hotel | 2025 Ave. of the Stars (Constellation Ave.) | 310-551-3334 | www.centuryplaza.hyatt.com

A "safe bet for a client lunch", this Californian inside the Hyatt Regency Century Plaza Hotel proffers "typical, but well-executed" seafood-focused fare in a "pleasant" semi-"formal" room furnished in browns and greens with patio seating; antagonists, however, allege it's "nothing special" and are chilly over "expense account" prices and servers who sometimes pull a "Houdini" and "disappear."

**Z Brent's Deli** *Deli*　　　　　　| 26 | 15 | 22 | $20 |

**Northridge** | 19565 Parthenia St. (bet. Corbin & Shirley Aves.) | 818-886-5679
**Westlake Village** | 2799 Townsgate Rd. (Westlake Blvd.) | 805-557-1882
www.brentsdeli.com

Even "ex-New Yorkers don't kvetch about the food" at this "legendary" 40-year-old Northridge deli and its spiffier Westlake Village spin-off famed for their "sky-high sandwiches" fashioned from "fabulous" fixings like "killer chopped liver", "delicious corned beef" and "crusty" rye bread; though there's "often a wait", "old-time waitresses" deliver "prompt service", leading boosters to brand them "hands (and tongue) down" "the best in town."

**Brentwood, The** *American*　　　| 21 | 18 | 19 | $46 |

**Brentwood** | 148 S. Barrington Ave. (Sunset Blvd.) | 310-476-3511 | www.brentwoodrestaurant.com

Likened to a "pricey dive for rich locals", this "dependable" Brentwood "retreat" from Bruce Marder is where Westside "power-players" tuck into "tasty" New American dishes like Kobe-style burgers and "falling-off-the-bone short ribs" and knock back "icy-cold martinis"; the "undeniably masculine" decor is trimmed in dark mahogany, though a few find the "dimly lit" atmosphere ("it's like eating in a mineshaft") "takes dark, moody lighting to a kind of silly extreme."

|  | FOOD | DECOR | SERVICE | COST |
|---|---|---|---|---|

### Briganti  *Italian* | 23 | 18 | 21 | $35

**South Pasadena** | 1423 Mission St. (bet. Fair Oaks & Fremont Aves.) | 626-441-4663 | www.brigantisouthpas.com
Fans of "real-deal" Italian cooking tout this "rising star" in the South Pasadena dining scene where the "rustic" fare – like "exquisite pasta" – is set down by "genuinely happy" servers who "treat you like family"; though some guests gripe the "comfortable" atmosphere with white tablecloths and tile floors is only "so-so", it gets a lift from patio seating, and all appreciate the "fair prices."

### Brighton Coffee Shop  *Diner* | 18 | 8 | 17 | $16

**Beverly Hills** | 9600 Brighton Way (Camden Dr.) | 310-276-7732
A "Beverly Hills institution", this "cheery" "little" 1930s-era coffee shop off Rodeo Drive plates "simple", "hearty" American fare – like "great meatloaf sandwiches" and tuna melts – at "fair prices"; somewhat "harried servers" "keep up with the rapid tempo" of "junior agents", "shoppers" and "office workers" filing in and out, making it a good bet for a "quick" bite.

### NEW Brix @ 1601  *American* | - | - | - | M

**Hermosa Beach** | 1601 PCH (16th St.) | 310-698-0740 | www.brix1601.com
Situated in a shiny new shopping complex just north of Pier Avenue, this sprawling 10,000-sq.-ft. New American/wine bar – boasting brick archways, warm bronze lighting, deep leather booths, stone fireplaces and a vaulted ceiling – feels like it's been there forever; its midpriced, casually creative menu (e.g. duck confit spring rolls) plays off an extensive list of vintages, including esoteric glasses from Slovenia and Greece.

### Broadway Deli  *Deli* | 15 | 13 | 14 | $23

**Santa Monica** | 1457 Third St. Promenade (B'way) | 310-451-0616 | www.broadwaydeli.com
For "brunch at the beach" Santa Monicans say you can't beat the location of this Third Street Promenade deli and wine bar featuring a "massive menu" of Eclectic "comfort food" from "smoked fish platters" to more "health conscious" items like salads; nonbelievers note that while the "big and brash" looks give it the feel of "a New York deli", "it doesn't taste like one", citing "merely adequate" eats and concluding that its "only saving grace is that they're open late" (till 1 AM on weekends).

### NEW Brunello Trattoria  *Italian* | - | - | - | I

**Culver City** | 6001 Washington Blvd. (La Cienega Blvd.) | 310-280-3856
The married team of Cinzia and Bruno Morra (Da Pasquale) expands the family empire to the eastern edge of Culver City with this Italian newcomer where the pasta sauces are made to order and the panini are prepared with freshly baked bread; pictures of Naples lend the space a traditional feel, while the central square bar offers a smart, social dining option.

### Buca di Beppo  *Italian* | 15 | 17 | 17 | $24

**Santa Monica** | 1442 Second St. (bet. B'way & Santa Monica Blvd.) | 310-587-2782
**Redondo Beach** | 1670 S. PCH (Palos Verdes Blvd.) | 310-540-3246
**Pasadena** | 80 W. Green St. (De Lacey Ave.) | 626-792-7272
**Encino** | 17500 Ventura Blvd. (Encino Ave.) | 818-995-3288

*(continued)*

*(continued)*

### Buca di Beppo
**Universal City** | Universal CityWalk | 1000 Universal Studios Blvd.
(off Rte. 101) | 818-509-9463
**Claremont** | 505 W. Foothill Blvd. (Indian Hill Blvd.) | 909-399-3287
**Thousand Oaks** | Janss Mall | 205 N. Moorpark Rd. (Hillcrest Dr.) |
805-449-3688
**Valencia** | 26940 Theater Dr. (Magic Mountain Pkwy.) | 661-253-1900
www.bucadibeppo.com

An "ode to excess", this "campy" chain draws "noisy families" and
"birthday" celebrants with a "1950s Italian" menu served in family-
style portions that could "feed an army"; "memorabilia"-laden settings and "cheap" tabs ratchet up the "boisterous" goings-on, though
"more-is-less" proponents say "food quality is not its strong suit."

### Buddha's Belly  *Pan-Asian*                    | 19 | 17 | 19 | $27 |
**Beverly Boulevard** | 7475 Beverly Blvd. (Gardner St.) | 323-931-8588
**NEW** **Santa Monica** | 205 Broadway (2nd St.) | 310-458-2500
www.bbfood.com

"Healthy" Angelinos attest they "can't get enough" of the "modern"
Pan-Asian plates and "creative" sake and soju cocktails at these "self-
consciously hip" "casual" "favorites" on Beverly Boulevard and in Santa
Monica featuring a black-cod with miso that's especially "enticing" and
"well priced" too; both play host to a "hopping" scene helped along by
some of the "friendliest service in LA" so even if purists pooh-pooh
the "lack of authenticity", they remain "popular" nonetheless.

### Buffalo Club  🗷 *American*                    | 20 | 21 | 18 | $56 |
**Santa Monica** | 1520 Olympic Blvd. (bet. 14th & 16th Sts.) | 310-450-8600 |
www.thebuffaloclub.com

Only the valet sign out front identifies this "secret rendezvous" in
Santa Monica that works the "speakeasy-chic" angle with a "dark",
"clubby" interior that opens out onto a "fabulous patio" playing host
to live entertainment and a "big pickup scene" on weekends; though
the "rich" "all-American" menu earns raves from some, many "don't
get the appeal" considering the "exorbitant prices" and the "almost
French-like" attitude of the "snooty" staff.

### Buggy Whip  *Seafood/Steak*                   | 19 | 16 | 18 | $38 |
**Westchester** | 7420 La Tijera Blvd. (74th St.) | 310-645-7131
Sentimentalists swoon over this Westchester "throwback" from 1952
that "still has some snap" thanks to its "dependable" surf 'n' turf menu
featuring "excellent prime rib" and salad with Green Goddess dressing
served amid "retro" surroundings with a lounge singer in the bar
Wednesdays–Saturdays; modernists label it "tired" and "unexciting",
but prices are "reasonable" (especially the "early-bird specials") and
decor "comfortable", so most find it "fits like a glove."

### Bulan Thai Vegetarian Kitchen  *Thai*         | ▽ 25 | 13 | 18 | $19 |
(fka Busaba Thai)
**Melrose** | 7168 Melrose Ave. (La Brea Ave.) | 323-857-1882
**NEW** **Silver Lake** | 4114 Santa Monica Blvd. (Myra Ave.) | 323-913-1488
www.bulanthai.com

"You won't miss the meat" swear supporters of this "small" Melrose
Thai turning out "delicious" vegetarian fare, including "faux chicken

| | FOOD | DECOR | SERVICE | COST |
|---|---|---|---|---|

satay" that could "please the most avid carnivore"; avocado-colored walls echo the earthy theme, while "fast" service, "cheap" prices and delivery options are icing on the (sugar-free) cake; N.B. the Silver Lake branch opened post-Survey.

### Buona Sera   *Italian*    ▽ 22 | 16 | 19 | $43

**Redondo Beach** | 247 Avenida del Norte (S. Catalina Ave.) | 310-543-2277 | www.buonasera-ristorante.com

With "so many wonderful choices" – especially among the "fresh pastas" – regulars insist "it's hard to decide what to order" at this "charming" "little Italian" in Redondo Beach; since the "understated" interior and "welcoming" service are well suited to both "dates" and a family meal, "pricey" tabs are singled out as the only sticking point.

### Burger Continental   *Mideastern*    17 | 10 | 15 | $18

**Pasadena** | 535 S. Lake Ave. (California Blvd.) | 626-792-6634

"A true Pasadena original", this "offbeat" "destination" "mixes up" a "tremendous variety" of "cheap" Middle Eastern specialties and "huge burgers" in a covered patio setting made "raucous" with "belly dancing" Thursday–Sunday; it's long been a "favorite" for "Cal-Tech students" who insist it's "wacky, but you gotta love it."

### Burger 90210   *Burgers*    16 | 12 | 16 | $13

**Beverly Hills** | 242 S. Beverly Dr. (Olympic Blvd.) | 310-271-7900

"Juicy" burgers are at the forefront of this order-at-the-counter Beverly Hills "joint" where the usual "beef, turkey and veggie patties" are customizable with a multitude of toppings; though the eats are served up "fast", antagonists allege the grub's "nothing special" and are less-than-impressed by paper plates ("for these prices?") and "bare-bones" atmosphere dominated by "big-screen TVs."

### Ca'Brea ⊠ *Italian*    22 | 20 | 21 | $44

**La Brea** | 346 S. La Brea Ave. (bet. 3rd & 4th Sts.) | 323-938-2863 | www.cabrearestaurant.com

"Still a pleasure" sigh guests grateful that this La Brea eatery reopened last year, finding "you can still count on it" for "consistently delicious" Northern Italian "country cooking" served up in a "warm atmosphere" that utterly lacks "pretense"; add in "good value" and many agree that dinner here is a "totally enjoyable" experience.

### Ca' del Sole   *Italian*    22 | 22 | 21 | $41

**North Hollywood** | 4100 Cahuenga Blvd. (Lankershim Blvd.) | 818-985-4669 | www.cadelsole.com

An "unexpected" bit of "bliss" "in the shadow of Universal Studios", this "classy" North Hollywood Italian "fallback" lures "execs" and other loyalists for "classic" Venetian dishes "prepared with care" and matched with wines from a 700-label list; "wonderful service" adds to the "pleasant" atmosphere, while eating "under the trees" in the garden "is a bit of heaven" on "sultry evenings."

### Café Beaujolais ⓜ *French*    23 | 19 | 22 | $34

**Eagle Rock** | 1712 Colorado Blvd. (bet. Argus & Mt. Royal Dr.) | 323-255-5111

Eagle Rock diners declare they "practically live" at this "comfortable" bistro inspiring "ooh-la-las" with "simple" French fare at "great prices"; "darling" "Parisian" decor abets the "authentic" vibe (the "flirtatious"

| | FOOD | DECOR | SERVICE | COST |
|---|---|---|---|---|

"heavily accented" waiters "don't disappoint" either) – just be sure to "make a reservation" or you may find yourself "waiting in line."

### ⓩ Café Bizou  *Californian/French*  | 23 | 19 | 21 | $33 |

**Pasadena** | 91 N. Raymond Ave. (Holly St.) | 626-792-9923
**Sherman Oaks** | 14016 Ventura Blvd. (bet. Costello & Murietta Aves.) |
818-788-3536
www.cafebizou.com

"Longtime" patrons proclaim "you just can't miss" with these "bargain" Cal-French bistros in Pasadena and Sherman Oaks, which win *"bizoux"* thanks to a "tasty" "traditional" menu and a "$2 corkage fee" that "sweetens" the deal for "wine aficionados"; "unflappable" servers and a "bustling" atmosphere are part of the appeal, but given the constant "crowds", "don't expect to linger."

### Café Brasil  *Brazilian*  | 19 | 13 | 14 | $18 |

**Palms** | 10831 Venice Blvd. (Westwood Blvd.) | 310-837-8957
**West LA** | 11736 W. Washington Blvd. (McLaughlin Ave.) | 310-391-1216
www.cafe-brasil.com

These "kitschy" "little" Brazilians in Palms and West LA thrive in "quirky" colorful environs with "cute outdoor" dining areas that fans find "relaxing on a perfect California day"; both "satisfy cravings" with "plentiful" plates of "flavorful" "traditional" fare (think rice, black beans, and various meats and fish) at prices that can feel "a bit high", but still a "great deal."

### Cafe Del Rey  *Californian/Mediterranean*  | 21 | 22 | 20 | $49 |

**Marina del Rey** | 4451 Admiralty Way (bet. Bali Way & Via Marina) |
310-823-6395 | www.cafedelreymarina.com

"Ocean breezes" enhance the already "marvelous setting" with "drop-dead gorgeous" views of the Marina del Rey harbor at this "longtime favorite" for "special occasions" and "impressing" "out-of-town guests" with "nouveau" Cal-Med cuisine and "accommodating" service; a few find "pricey" tabs and the "noise level" a "turnoff", though most still consider it a "standard-bearer" for the area, especially for its "excellent Sunday brunch."

### Cafe des Artistes  *French*  | 20 | 22 | 19 | $43 |

**Hollywood** | 1534 N. McCadden Pl. (Sunset Blvd.) | 323-469-7300 |
www.cafedesartistes.info

This "charming little bungalow" "tucked away on a quiet street" in Hollywood endears itself to locals with "agreeable" French bistro classics and a "delightfully bohemian" setting complete with a "beautiful patio" loaded with plants and furnished with "twinkly lights"; though some say service can be "lacking", the mood is decidedly "romantic", so bring a date for "a special night out."

### Cafe 50's  *Diner*  | 16 | 17 | 17 | $15 |

**Venice** | 838 Lincoln Blvd. (Lake St.) | 310-399-1955 ⊞
**West LA** | 11623 Santa Monica Blvd. (bet. Barry & Federal Aves.) |
310-479-1955 | www.cafe50s.com ☾
**Sherman Oaks** | 4609 Van Nuys Blvd. (Hortense St.) | 818-906-1955 ☾

Fans of "retro kitsch" favor these "'50s-themed" juke joints proffering "passable" American diner eats that are "comforting in their greasiness" plus some of "the best milkshakes west of the 110"; "kid-friendly" service and "easy-on-the-wallet" tabs both earn a thumbs-up, though more than a few cynics say these "throwbacks" have seen happier days.

### Café 14 *Californian/Continental* | 24 | 18 | 21 | $46 |

**Agoura Hills** | Reyes Adobe Plaza | 30315 Canwood St. (Reyes Adobe Rd.) | 818-991-9560 | www.cafe-14.com

Enthusiasts adore this "grown-up restaurant" "hidden away" in an "obscure" Agoura Hills strip mall where "welcoming" chef-owner Neil Kramer does a "brilliant" job crafting "outstanding" dishes from his "oft-changing" Cal-Continental menu; prices offer "exceptional value" too so even if the "intimate" setup divides some diners ("charming" vs. "sterile"), most maintain it's an "absolute jewel" that's "lovely in every way."

### Cafe Med *Italian* | 18 | 16 | 18 | $37 |

**West Hollywood** | 8615 Sunset Blvd. (Sunset Plaza Dr.) | 310-652-0445 | www.cafemedsunsetplaza.com

A "prime Sunset location", complete with "celebrity spotting" on the patio, keeps this "dependable" WeHo Italian "filled with regulars" (notwithstanding the "teeth-rattling vibrations from the Harleys going by on Friday nights"); while some critics call the "basic" food a "tad expensive for what you get", most don't mind on account of the "friendly" crew and "sexy" "scene."

### Café Montana *Californian* | 19 | 15 | 17 | $32 |

**Santa Monica** | 1534 Montana Ave. (16th St.) | 310-829-3990

This "semi-upscale" Santa Monica Californian is "a step up from the usual neighborhood cafe", beckoning Montana Avenue shoppers from its "giant windows" with "big salads", "tempting brunch items" and "unbelievable desserts"; despite somewhat "cramped" seating, both the service and the space strike a "cheerful" tone.

### Café Mundial Ⓜ *Californian/Mediterranean* | ▽ 21 | 20 | 20 | $33 |

**Monrovia** | 514 S. Myrtle Ave. (Colorado Blvd.) | 626-303-2233 | www.cafemundial.net

Set in the "bustle of Downtown Monrovia", this "romantic" Californian-Mediterranean with a "casually elegant" atmosphere presents "varied, good quality" dishes for a "reasonable price"; while the service gets mixed reviews and some say the "menu needs a makeover", supporters praise the patio for a "nice Friday night out in the summer."

### Café Pacific *American* | ▽ 24 | 25 | 23 | $53 |

**Rancho Palos Verdes** | Trump Nat'l Golf Course | 1 Ocean Trails Dr. (Palos Verdes Dr. S.) | 310-303-3260 | www.trumpgolf.com

Tucked amid Trump National Golf Club, this Rancho Palos Verdes cafe attracts patrons with "fabulous views" from an "upscale casual" dining room, as well as "excellent", "well-presented" New American fare; even if you need "the Donald's money to afford it", most argue it's "worth the trip" to savor the "beautiful" grounds and one of the "best wine lists" in the area.

### Café Pierre *French* | 22 | 18 | 20 | $45 |

**Manhattan Beach** | 317 Manhattan Beach Blvd. (bet. Highland Ave. & Morningside Dr.) | 310-545-5252 | www.cafepierre.com

"Both classy and super laid-back", this "trendy" Manhattan Beach "diamond in the South Bay rough" boasts "delightful" French fare (the cheese selection is a "highlight") served to "pretty people" amid recently remodeled "red, red, red" decor; while the staff is "accommodating", some critics note that seating is tight and it gets so "crowded" you may "end up waiting even with reservations."

**Cafe Pinot** *Californian/French*  | 22 | 23 | 21 | $49 |

**Downtown** | 700 W. Fifth St. (Flower St.) | 213-239-6500 | www.patinagroup.com

"Delightful" for "first dates", "pre-theater dinners" and "power lunches", this Cal-French Dowtowner – a "beautiful glass box next to the towering public library" – boasts a "leafy" garden so "magical" "you won't believe you're in LA"; customers commend the "courteous" service and "fresh", "well-executed" fare that "always reflects the seasons", so even if a few fault it for following the "ubiquitous Patina mold", most find the "high prices" justified.

**Café Provencal** *French*  | ∇ 23 | 17 | 23 | $41 |

**Thousand Oaks** | 2310 E. Thousand Oaks Blvd. (Conejo School Rd.) | 805-496-7121 | www.cafeprovencal.biz

Possibly the "best-kept secret of the Conejo Valley", this "intimate" "hideaway" in a Thousand Oaks strip mall is an "unexpected find" that offers "out-of-this-world" Provençal "home cooking" and "gracious" service, not to mention a "fantastic" lunch special and a five-course prix fixe menu Wednesday–Thursday; right by the Civic Arts Plaza, it's a natural for "pre-theater dining."

**Cafe Rodeo** *Californian*  | ∇ 18 | 17 | 15 | $41 |

**Beverly Hills** | Luxe Hotel Rodeo Dr. | 360 N. Rodeo Dr. (bet. Santa Monica & Wilshire Blvds.) | 310-273-0300 | www.luxehotelrodeodrive.com

"After a day of shopping", customers drop their bags for a "bite with a view" from a "front row seat on Rodeo Drive" at this Californian "retreat" in the Luxe Hotel; while most call the food "just ok" and the service "slow", others find it "special" enough to warrant the "expensive" tab.

**Café Santorini** *Mediterranean*  | 20 | 20 | 20 | $34 |

**Pasadena** | 64 W. Union St. (bet. De Lacey & Fair Oaks Aves.) | 626-564-4200 | www.cafesantorini.com

"Perfect for a date under the stars", this "informal" Mediterranean "gem" in Old Town Pasadena beckons with its "lovely" balcony and "delicious", "reasonably priced" food with lots of Greek flavor; though the service can range from "attentive" to "spotty", that hardly dampens the "busy" scene on "sunny afternoons and warm summer evenings."

**Cafe Stella** *French*  | 21 | 22 | 16 | $45 |

**Silver Lake** | 3932 W. Sunset Blvd. (bet. Hyperion & Sanborn Aves.) | 323-666-0265

"Like dining on a Parisian side street" effuse fans of this "cozy escape in Silver Lake" with its "fabulous outdoor cafe scene" and "beautifully prepared" French bistro fare accompanied by "amazing wines"; while some say the servers can be as "surly" as their Continental counterparts and the food is "no longer a bargain", others rave it's the next best thing to "dining along the Seine."

| | FOOD | DECOR | SERVICE | COST |
|---|---|---|---|---|

### Cafe Surfas  *American*  `19` `10` `13` `$14`

**Culver City** | 8777 W. Washington Blvd. (National Blvd.) | 310-558-1458 |
www.cafesurfas.com

"Clever sandwich creations" and other "delicious" "seasonal food
served deli-style" at this daytime Culver City American provide a
"quick fix" for customers after cruising the aisles of the Surfas family's
"chef's paradise" store next door; since the seating is on a patio "overlooking the parking lot" and the service can be "snooty", regulars recommend packing up the grub for a "picnic lunch at a nearby park."

### Cafe Sushi ● *Japanese*  ▽ `20` `14` `18` `$34`

**Beverly Boulevard** | 8459 Beverly Blvd. (N. La Cienega Blvd.) | 323-651-4020
It "still rocks" say followers of this Beverly Boulevard "institution" that
dishes out "generous portions" of "fresh" sushi (including some "unusual" choices) from a "varied" Japanese menu; though the decor is
seriously "underwhelming", customers appreciate the service at the
bar and say you "definitely get your money's worth."

### Café Tu Tu Tango  *Eclectic*  `19` `19` `16` `$27`

**Universal City** | Universal CityWalk | 1000 Universal Studios Blvd.
(off Rte. 101) | 818-769-2222 | www.cafetututango.com

Noshers "nibble on the small plates specialties" while "checking out
the artwork" and the "performers wandering through the restaurant"
at this "funky", "lively" Eclectic tapas spot at Universal CityWalk;
while some call the sustenance only "so-so", satisfied samplers say a
"light meal" is "easy on the wallet", plus all the "sangria, laughs" and
"silly antics" might "make you want to shake your tutu" too.

### Caffé Delfini  *Italian*  `23` `18` `21` `$43`

**Santa Monica** | 147 W. Channel Rd. (PCH) | 310-459-8823 |
www.caffedelfini.com

"Darling" and "delightfully homey", this "real Italian trattoria" delivers
the "classics" "at reasonable prices" near the beach in Santa Monica;
"the lighting is so dim you need a flashlight (provided by the waiters) to
read the menu", but the food remains "excellent after all these years"
and the "owners really care about the diners"; P.S. you might "see a star."

### Caffe Luxxe  *Coffeehouse*  ▽ `24` `20` `20` `$8`

**Santa Monica** | 925 Montana Ave. (bet. 9th & 10th Sts.) | 310-394-2222 |
www.caffeluxxe.com

"Finally, a place in California that knows how to make a true ris-
tretto!" affirm admirers of this "chic" Santa Monica coffeehouse
whose "skillful" baristas fashion "artistic", "quality espresso
drinks" accompanied by "excellent pastries"; with a standing bar,
the "modern" room is a "close approximation of a real Italian
neighborhood place", though it does get "crowded" and seats are
scarce, so it's not ideal for lingering.

### Caffe Pinguini  Ⓜ *Italian*  `21` `18` `21` `$36`

**Playa del Rey** | 6935 Pacific Ave. (Culver Blvd.) | 310-306-0117 |
www.caffepinguini.com

This "casually elegant" Playa del Rey "sleeper" "known to locals for
years" brings together "simply prepared" Italian eats, an "attentive" staff
and a "chill Cali vibe" courtesy of the patio's ocean breezes; for most,
it's "well worth a visit if you're in the neighborhood."

| | FOOD | DECOR | SERVICE | COST |
|---|---|---|---|---|

### Caffe Primo *Italian*

▽ 19 | 20 | 16 | $18

**West Hollywood** | Sunset Millennium Plaza | 8590 Sunset Blvd.
(La Cienega Blvd.) | 310-289-8895 | www.iloveprimo.com

Customers at this "upscale" Italian cafe smack-dab in the middle of
the Sunset Strip scene are "pleasantly surprised" by its "European-
style sandwiches", "savory" salads and "amazing" gelato; while some
say it needs to "fine-tune" its "inconsistent" service, others call it their
"favorite place to hang", plus the "free WiFi is a draw."

### Caffe Roma ● *Italian*

17 | 15 | 17 | $35

**Beverly Hills** | 350 N. Cañon Dr. (bet. Brighton & Dayton Ways) |
310-274-7834 | www.cafferomabeverlyhills.com

Like a "Fernando's Hideaway" for "old-timer celebs" and other "low-key"
types, this "offbeat" Beverly Hills retreat co-owned by Ago Sciandri
(Ago) makes guests "feel at home" from lunch to "late-night"; while the
quality of the well-priced Italian food ranges from "delicious" to
"fair", many seek it out just for the "pleasant", "remarkably improved"
patio, even if smokers complain that there are "no more cigars!"

### Caioti Pizza Cafe *Pizza*

22 | 12 | 16 | $20

**Studio City** | 4346 Tujunga Ave. (Moorpark St.) | 818-761-3588 |
www.caiotipizzacafe.com

"Some of the tastiest pizzas in the Valley" (with "unique toppings and
crusts") and "fine" salads can be found at this Studio City "hole-in-
the-wall", a "relaxing" BYO where wine drinkers "save a bundle" since
there's no corkage fee; despite the passing of longtime chef-owner Ed
LaDou – largely considered the "originator" of the "California-style"
pie – passionate fans say "they are making it work with his blessing."

### California Chicken Cafe 🖾 *American*

21 | 9 | 16 | $12

**Hollywood** | 6805 Melrose Ave. (Mansfield Ave.) | 323-935-5877
**Santa Monica** | 2401 Wilshire Blvd. (24th St.) | 310-453-0477
**Venice** | 424 Lincoln Blvd. (Sunset Ave.) | 310-392-3500
**West LA** | 2005 Westwood Blvd. (bet. Olympic & Santa Monica Blvds.) |
310-446-1933
**Encino** | 15601 Ventura Blvd. (bet. Haskell Ave. & Sepulveda Blvd.) |
818-789-8056
**Northridge** | University Plaza | 18445 Nordhoff St. (Reseda Blvd.) |
818-700-9977
**Woodland Hills** | 22333 Ventura Blvd. (Shoup Ave.) |
818-716-6170
www.californiachickencafe.com

Devotees of this "healthy" "fast-food" chain cluck over the "succulent", "crisp" rotisserie chicken that's "light on the waist" but "fills the
belly" without "depleting the wallet"; its "fresh", "quick" salads and
sides also satisfy vegetarians, but be warned that it can be a "mad
house at lunch"; P.S. lots of "pumped-up", "post-workout Gold's Gym"
hardbodies make the Venice branch extra buff.

### California Pizza Kitchen *Pizza*

18 | 14 | 17 | $21

**Downtown** | Wells Fargo Ctr. | 330 S. Hope St. (bet. 3rd & 4th Sts.) |
213-626-2616
**Hollywood** | Hollywood & Highland Ctr. | 6801 Hollywood Blvd.
(Highland Ave.) | 323-460-2080
**Beverly Hills** | Beverly Ctr. | 121 N. La Cienega Blvd. (bet. Beverly Blvd. &
3rd St.) | 310-854-6555

*(continued)*

## California Pizza Kitchen

**Beverly Hills** | 207 S. Beverly Dr. (bet. Olympic & Wilshire Blvds.) | 310-275-1101

**Santa Monica** | 210 Wilshire Blvd. (bet. 2nd & 3rd Sts.) | 310-393-9335

**Westwood** | Westwood Vill. | 1001 Broxton Ave. (Weyburn Ave.) | 310-209-9197

**Manhattan Beach** | Manhattan Vill. | 3280 N. Sepulveda Blvd. (Rosecrans Ave.) | 310-796-1233

**Pasadena** | Plaza Las Fuentes | 99 N. Los Robles Ave. (Union St.) | 626-585-9020

**Burbank** | 601 N. San Fernando Blvd. (Cypress Ave.) | 818-972-2589

**Studio City** | 12265 Ventura Blvd. (Laurel Grove Ave.) | 818-505-6437
www.cpk.com
Additional locations throughout Southern California

Like a "poor man's Spago", this Beverly Hills–bred pizza chain "mainstay" dishes up "gourmet" pies with "exotic" toppings like shrimp, pineapple and BBQ chicken (though some "work better than others") and "tasty salads"; "iffy service", "hectic" vibes and "bright, clinical" decor can be downers, but "inexpensive" tabs keep most branches "crowded" and parents proclaim them "a godsend if you have kids."

## California Wok  *Chinese*

| 17 | 8 | 14 | $17 |

**Third Street** | Cienega Plaza | 8520 W. Third St. (La Cienega Blvd.) | 310-360-9218

**Brentwood** | 12004 Wilshire Blvd. (Bundy Dr.) | 310-479-0552

**Encino** | Encino Mktpl. | 16656 Ventura Blvd. (Petit Ave.) | 818-386-0561 | www.caliwok.com

"Cheap eats" with a "healthy twist" draw a "well-deserved" following (especially for lunch) to these separately owned branches that boosters consider some of "the better Chinese take-out joints around"; since "lackluster" service and "zilch" ambiance are part of the "bargain", many opt for "fast delivery."

## Calitalia  M  *Californian/Italian*

| – | – | – | E |

**Calabasas** | 23536 Calabasas Rd. (El Canon Ave.) | 818-223-9600 | www.calitaliarestaurant.com

Situated in the heart of historic Old Calabasas, what used to be the ambiguously named Native Cafe has been relaunched to reflect the menu's mix of Californian and Italian cooking with a healthful focus, complemented by high-end specialty cocktails; featuring a separate wine room and lounge, it's popular for birthdays, showers and the like.

## Camilo's  M  *Californian*

| 23 | 21 | 21 | $30 |

**Eagle Rock** | 2128 W. Colorado Blvd. (Caspar Ave.) | 323-478-2644

An "anchor for Eagle Rock dining", this "neighborhood bistro" and "brunch favorite" serves "creative" Californian fare in a setting that's "bright and airy" by day and "intimate" by night; the "warm" staff makes customers feel "at home", and while some "carefully selected" wines are available, the $5 corkage fee makes BYO an attractive option.

## Campanile  *Californian/Mediterranean*

| 26 | 24 | 23 | $57 |

**La Brea** | 624 S. La Brea Ave. (bet. 6th St. & Wilshire Blvd.) | 323-938-1447 | www.campanilerestaurant.com

Chef-owner Mark Peel "continues to shine" at this "LA classic", presenting "splendid" Cal-Mediterranean meals, including an "excep-

FOOD | DECOR | SERVICE | COST

tional" brunch, famed "Thursday gourmet grilled-cheese night" and "terrific Friday night flights", inside a "beautiful", "historic" La Brea space with a touch of "Spanish style"; most agree "the same respect" is shown to the customers as to each "imaginative" dish, and while it "ain't cheap", it's "worth it" for fans who leave "feeling nurtured spiritually as well as gastronomically."

### Canal Club  *Californian/Eclectic*
18 | 18 | 18 | $35

**Venice** | 2025 Pacific Ave. (N. Venice Blvd.) | 310-823-3878 | www.canalclubvenice.com

Diners and drinkers "drop in for happy hour" (when many of the plates are half-price) at this "laid-back" "local joint" in Venice where Cal-Eclectic fare such as "reliable" sushi and mesquite-grilled steaks are served by a "sweet" staff; the "gondola hanging from the back room ceiling" adds extra whimsy to the already "hip" beachside scene.

### C & O Cucina  *Italian*
18 | 16 | 18 | $24

**Marina del Rey** | 3016 Washington Blvd. (Thatcher Ave.) | 310-301-7278 | www.cocucina.com

### C & O Trattoria  *Italian*

**Marina del Rey** | 31 Washington Blvd. (Pacific Ave.) | 310-823-9491 | www.cotrattoria.com

"Hokey, but fun", this Marina del Rey Italian duo wins props from *amici* for its "irresistible" "gratis garlic rolls", "toothsome" pastas and "free-flowing" Chianti that fuels "'That's Amore' sing-a-longs" led by a "friendly" crew; though detractors deem the fare "mediocre", at least the "gigantic" portions offer lots of "bada bing, bada bang" for the buck.

### Canelé  M  *Mediterranean*
23 | 18 | 20 | $36

**Atwater Village** | 3219 Glendale Blvd. (bet. Brunswick & Edenhurst Aves.) | 323-666-7133 | www.canele-la.com

"Up-and-coming" chef/co-owner Corina Weibel turns ingredients "fresh from the farmer's market" into "robust, soulful" Mediterranean dishes with some "highly original specials" at this "bohemian", moderately priced Atwater Village "find"; though visitors call the staff "sometimes friendly, sometimes surly", and much of the seating can be a "tight squeeze", most agree the communal table is "a kick."

### Canter's  ●  *Deli*
18 | 10 | 15 | $20

**Fairfax** | 419 N. Fairfax Ave. (bet. Oakwood & Rosewood Aves.) | 323-651-2030 | www.cantersdeli.com

"They film 'deli scenes' here for a reason" nod noshers about this 24-hour Fairfax "icon" whose kosher-style menu features "healing" chicken soup and "traditional", "expensive" pastrami sandwiches "so impossibly huge they look like something Bluto would eat"; it's all dished up by the "crustiest waitresses in LA" to "twentysomething rockers and 80-year-olds" alike, who soak up the "unintentionally ironic oldster decor" as well as "retro cool jam sessions" at the adjoining Kibitz Room bar.

### Cantina Joannafina y Bar La Luna  *Mexican*
∇ 19 | 14 | 21 | $19

**Westlake Village** | 3637 Thousand Oaks Blvd. (Marmon St.) | 805-374-7744 | www.cantinajoannafina.com

"Homemade tamales" and a "gracious" welcome are highlights of the "delicious" Mexican meals at this Westlake Village cantina; even

| | FOOD | DECOR | SERVICE | COST |
|---|---|---|---|---|

though it's less atmospheric than the beachside Ventura original, guests say *"gracias"* for the "good value" at both; N.B. the kitchen closes between lunch and dinner on weekdays.

### ☑ Capo ☒Ⓜ *Italian* | 26 | 23 | 23 | $78 |

**Santa Monica** | 1810 Ocean Ave. (Pico Blvd.) | 310-394-5550 | www.caporestaurant.com

Enthralled diners declare "everything is amazing" at this "superior" Santa Monica Italian, from the "smell of the wood-burning grill" to the "romantic", "rustic" room to the "seductive" cuisine by chef/co-owner Bruce Marder; while critics note that the bill is equally "stunning" (partly due to the "outstanding" but "ridiculously marked up" wine list) and the service ranges from "skillful" to "snobby", that hardly keeps away the "elite" clientele.

### NEW Captain Crab *Seafood* | - | - | - | M |

**San Gabriel** | 250 W. Valley Blvd. (Del Mar Ave.) | 626-293-8338

Occupying two stories in a mini-mall just west of sprawling San Gabriel Square, this Vietnamese-run seafooder offers Louisianan takes on shellfish, including Dungeness, blue and king crab; rounding out the reasonably priced menu are plenty of sides, beer and gumbo, which, despite its misspelling as 'gumbi', isn't green.

### NEW Carbon Beach Club *Californian/Pacific Rim* | ∇ 13 | 22 | 13 | $56 |

**Malibu** | Malibu Beach Inn | 22878 PCH (Malibu Pier) | 310-456-6444 | www.malibubeachinn.com

The "vast Pacific" beckons from the "spectacular oceanside" patio at this breezy locale in the Malibu Beach Inn, which was recently purchased and renovated by David Geffen; early samplers, however, say the "expensive" Cal-Pacific Rim "food doesn't match the view" and service can be "snobbish", so curious customers might just "go for beachside drinks."

### ☑ Carlitos Gardel *Argentinean/Steak* | 23 | 19 | 23 | $51 |

**Melrose** | 7963 Melrose Ave. (bet. Edinburgh & Hayworth Aves.) | 323-655-0891 | www.carlitosgardel.com

"Heaven" for "beef snobs", this "inviting" family-owned Argentinean steakhouse on Melrose serves up "wonderful" rib-eyes, "to-die-for" garlic fries ("make sure everyone is having some!") and "excellent" wines; with "warm" service and live piano and violin on the weekends, it's a "gem" for an upscale "date or dinner with friends."

### Carney's Express *Hot Dogs* | 19 | 14 | 15 | $10 |

**West Hollywood** | 8351 W. Sunset Blvd. (Sweetzer Ave.) | 323-654-8300 ☏
**Studio City** | 12601 Ventura Blvd. (Whitsett Ave.) | 818-761-8300
www.carneytrain.com

"Snappy dogs" "served in a train car in the middle of the Sunset Strip" in WeHo (and on Ventura in Studio City) draw "throngs of loyal fans" to these "funky, inexpensive" stops where the "greasy" chili burgers, fries and shakes also "hit the spot"; with "friendly, efficient service" too, it's perennial "fun for kids" and anyone who agrees the "food might kill you, but you'll die happy."

| | FOOD | DECOR | SERVICE | COST |
|---|---|---|---|---|

### Carnival  *Lebanese*

22 | 8 | 15 | $21

**Sherman Oaks** | 4356 Woodman Ave. (bet. Moorpark St. & Ventura Blvd.) | 818-784-3469 | www.carnivalrest.com

If it "catered a Middle East summit, we'd have peace at last" assure admirers of this "Lebanese food lover's dream", a "popular" Sherman Oaks eatery plating up "gigantic portions" of "scrumptious" dishes and "delicious" desserts served by "saucy waitresses" to a clientele speaking a "Babel of languages"; though critics note it's "usually crowded" and resembles a cross between a "hospital cafeteria" and a "Denny's", a planned expansion should give it a lift.

### Carousel  Ⓜ *Mideastern*

22 | 14 | 19 | $27

**East Hollywood** | High Plaza | 5112 Hollywood Blvd. (Normandie Ave.) | 323-660-8060

**Glendale** | 304 N. Brand Blvd. (California Ave.) | 818-246-7775 | www.carouselrestaurant.com

"Terrific" Middle Eastern dining with a "communal vibe" appeals to plenty of "party" people at this festive pair where a "helpful" staff sets down "incredible amounts" of "beautifully done" apps, kebabs and other "tasty" fare for a "bargain"; while the East Hollywood strip-mall locale scores low on atmosphere, the larger Glendale branch offers "better decor" as well as live entertainment on the weekends.

### Casa Bianca  ●Ⓢ Ⓜ ⨝ *Pizza*

23 | 11 | 16 | $19

**Eagle Rock** | 1650 Colorado Blvd. (Vincent Ave.) | 323-256-9617 | www.casabiancapizza.com

"Legions of devoted fans" ("cops, college locals, trendy artists") line up for "one of the best pies west of Brooklyn" at this "old-style, family-owned" Italian in Eagle Rock, complete with "iconic red-and-white checkered tablecloths"; both the pizza and the less-esteemed entrees are wallet-friendly (and cash-only), but "call your order ahead" for pickup since the wait can be "interminable."

### Casablanca  *Mexican*

18 | 16 | 19 | $25

**Venice** | 220 Lincoln Blvd. (Rose Ave.) | 310-392-5751 | www.casablancacatering.com

"Fresh handmade tortillas" and "delightful" calamari steaks are the specialties of this "accommodating", "reasonably priced" Venice Mexican where live guitar lends a "special ambiance" to dinner; though some critics call the food "average" and say the memorabilia "reminiscent of the Bogie movie" is "showing its years", more forgiving guests "rarely remember much after sampling the tequilas" from the 300-plus selection.

### ⭐NEW Casablanca

▽ 18 | 16 | 16 | $29

### Mediterranean  *Mediterranean*

**Claremont** | The Packing House | 500 W. First St. (Cornell Ave.) | 909-626-5200 | www.casablancaclaremont.com

Housed in a onetime lemon packing house, this affordable Claremont newcomer produces "generous servings" of "tasty", "aromatic" Mediterranean and Middle Eastern eats; though a few say it's still "working out some kinks in service" and call the wood-heavy interior "uninspired", many agree that hookahs on the patio and weekend belly dancing "add to the fun."

### NEW Casa Don Rolando 🅼 *Cuban*

| | | | |
|---|---|---|---|
| – | – | – | M |

**North Hills** | 8755 Parthenia Pl. (Sepulveda Blvd.) | 818-920-2272 | www.casadonrolando.com

Namesake toque Don Rolando (ex the defunct Madre's) showcases his Cuban chops at this moderately priced North Hills newcomer dishing out authentic fare like *ropa vieja* in a traditional space with terra-cotta-colored walls and a plant-filled patio with wrought-iron detailing; despite the lack of libations (a liquor license is pending), it has a festive feel with live Latin bands spicing things up most Friday nights.

### Casa Vega ◐ *Mexican*

| | | | |
|---|---|---|---|
| 18 | 16 | 17 | $24 |

**Sherman Oaks** | 13301 Ventura Blvd. (bet. Fulton & Nagle Aves.) | 818-788-4868 | www.casavega.com

"Right out of *Pulp Fiction*", this "dark", "kitschy" "Valley landmark" (and "godsend for late diners") in Sherman Oaks delivers "generous" plates of "traditional", "good but not gourmet" Mexican food to an "entertaining crowd mixed between families and those in the adult film industry"; while the booths and the "jumping" bar are often "jam-packed", guests say the "strong margaritas" "make the wait almost bearable."

### Cassell's 🅼 *Burgers*

| | | | |
|---|---|---|---|
| ▽ 19 | 5 | 10 | $13 |

**Koreatown** | 3266 W. Sixth St. (bet. S. Berendo St. & S. New Hampshire Ave.) | 213-480-5000

Known to the devoted as the "gold standard" for "top" hamburgers (cooked "true to old form") and "exceptional" potato salad prepared with housemade mayo (complete with a horseradish "bite"), this Koreatown anchor has become a "legend" since opening in 1948; still, detractors demur that the quality has gone "downhill" of late, the service is middling at best and the "antediluvian tables and chairs" were last tended to "after California gained statehood."

### Castaway *Californian*

| | | | |
|---|---|---|---|
| 13 | 19 | 15 | $38 |

**Burbank** | 1250 E. Harvard Rd. (Sunset Canyon Dr.) | 818-848-6691 | www.castawayrestaurant.com

"It's all about location" say diners of these Burbank and San Bernardino establishments known for "killer" views, brunch buffets and "drinks at sunset" on the ample outdoor patios; otherwise, many cite a "staid" Californian menu that's grown "tired" with the years, not to mention disproportionate prices and "unreliable" service.

### NEW Catalina ◐ *American*

| | | | |
|---|---|---|---|
| ▽ 24 | 22 | 25 | $45 |

**Redondo Beach** | 320 S. Catalina Ave. (Torrance Blvd.) | 310-374-6929 | www.320catalina.com

An "adorable" addition to the South Bay, this go-getter with real "potential" in Redondo Beach impresses early samplers with its "rich, complex" New American dishes by chef Arthur Martinez (ex the shuttered Avenue); with "excellent" service and "intimate charm" too, "it's just the place for a romantic night out."

### Catch *Californian/Seafood*
(fka Oceanfront)

| | | | |
|---|---|---|---|
| 22 | 25 | 21 | $60 |

**Santa Monica** | Hotel Casa Del Mar | 1910 Ocean Way (Pico Blvd.) | 310-581-7714 | www.catchsantamonica.com

"Gorgeous" surroundings with a "mother of pearl bar" and "unbeatable" ocean views through the floor-to-ceiling windows set the scene for "romantic" evenings at this recently revamped Santa Monica retreat in the Casa del Mar, where the largely "excellent", "costly" Californian menu stands out with "creative" sushi and crudo; while the "elegant" service comes with a bit too much "attitude" for some, most find the whole experience a "special treat."

**CBS Seafood** 🅢🅜 *Seafood*                                   - | - | - | M

Chinatown | 700 N. Spring St. (Ord St.) | 213-617-2323 |
www.cbsseafoodrestaurant.com

Though it's not on the network's fall lineup, this Hong Kong–style seafood palace wins over everyone from Chinatown regulars to media giants like Sumner Redstone with its terrific dim sum and fish plucked live from tanks in back; set in sprawling digs, it often draws an overflow crowd – luckily there's a steam table up front offering numerous items to go.

**Celestino** 🅢 *Italian*                                   23 | 18 | 23 | $41

Pasadena | 141 S. Lake Ave. (bet. Cordova & Green Sts.) | 626-795-4006 |
www.calogerodrago.com

Devotees declare this Drago brothers destination in Pasadena "the standard" for "delicious pastas" and other Tuscan fare of "fantastic quality"; though a few grouse that the "menu doesn't change" and the tables are "packed too tightly", its "stupendous" service and "good value" in an atmosphere of "European elegance" help earn it a "loyal" following.

**Central Park** *American/Californian*                      17 | 17 | 16 | $26

Pasadena | 219 S. Fair Oaks Ave. (bet. Orange Pl. & Valley St.) |
626-449-4499 | www.centralparkrestaurant.net

Customers of this "cute" Pasadena cafe with "views of the park" say its midpriced Cal-American meals provide a "satisfying" repast a bit outside of the area "frenzy"; while it can be too "safe" and "slow" for some, its "Old Town charm" gives it a boost for breakfast and "relaxed dinners."

**Cézanne** *Californian/French*                      ▽ 21 | 23 | 22 | $55

Santa Monica | Le Merigot Hotel | 1740 Ocean Ave. (bet. Colorado Ave. & Pico Blvd.) | 310-899-6122 | www.lemerigothotel.com

"Wonderful" Cal-French cuisine, a "serene" atmosphere and "excellent" service make admirers say "ooh-la-la" at this "special place for a leisurely dinner" in Santa Monica's Le Merigot Hotel; while a few feel it "misses the mark", especially considering the "expense", many commend it as a real "sleeper" – "you'd never know" the venue's "a Marriott."

**Chaba** *Thai*                                   20 | 19 | 18 | $28

Redondo Beach | 525 S. PCH (Ruby St.) | 310-540-8441 |
www.chabarestaurant.com

"Fresh, flavorful" Thai food from a "diverse" menu pleases patrons who "go with friends and share plates" at this Redondo Beach hot spot on PCH; even if the cuisine is "too Western" in style and a little "pricey" for some, the "consistent" kitchen, "colorful" decor and "excellent" service make it a South Bay staple.

**Chabuya Tokyo Noodle Bar** *Japanese*                      19 | 17 | 16 | $16

West LA | 2002 Sawtelle Blvd. (La Grange Ave.) | 310-473-1013 ◐
🆕 Torrance | 24231 Crenshaw Blvd. (Lomita Blvd.) | 310-530-2749
"Tasty", "freshly made" bowls of ramen with "unique" broths send fans to "noodle heaven" at these Japanese siblings in West LA and

Torrance; while the staff can sometimes be "inefficient" and the cooking style and cost not for the "traditionalist", the "modern" decor on Sawtelle is "better than the average" joint, and the tab is still "inexpensive."

### ☑ Cha Cha Cha  *Caribbean*
20 | 19 | 18 | $26

**Silver Lake** | 656 N. Virgil Ave. (Melrose Ave.) | 323-664-7723 | www.theoriginalchachacha.com

Silver Lakers "blissfully pig out" on "amazing jerk chicken" and other "inexpensive" Caribbean fare, washed down with "wonderful" sangria, at this longtime local "favorite" that's "wildly popular with a young, noisy crowd"; its "wacky" island atmosphere and "upbeat" staff add to the "kitschy fun", so even if the service is a bit "laid-back" for some, it's still "perfect for parties and for defusing first dates."

### Cha Cha Chicken  *Caribbean*
21 | 13 | 16 | $13

**Santa Monica** | 1906 Ocean Ave. (Pico Blvd.) | 310-581-1684 | www.chachachicken.com

This "colorful" Santa Monica "shack by the beach" with outdoor seating and "plastic tablecloths" on an "enclosed patio" feels like a "quick trip to the Caribbean", serving up "fantastic" "tangy" dishes for "a steal"; a few wayfarers wish "they had a liquor license", but many are happy to BYO and kick back with the "flirty" staff for a "memorable" feast.

### Chadaka  *Thai*
24 | 23 | 22 | $24

**Burbank** | 310 N. San Fernando Blvd. (Palm Ave.) | 818-848-8520 | www.chadaka.com

"Delightful, delicious, delovely" describes this "cool, unexpected" Burbank "oasis" that dishes up "bright", "creative" Thai fare for a song amid "beautiful" surroundings; with a "terrific" staff too, regulars call it a "refreshing switch from storefront" eateries and "one of the few respites from chaindom" in the area.

### Chakra  *Indian*
21 | 22 | 19 | $32

**Beverly Hills** | 151 S. Doheny Dr. (Wilshire Blvd.) | 310-246-3999 | www.chakracuisine.com

Intrepid diners embark on a "novel", "flavorful journey" at this "trendy" Indian destination in Beverly Hills serving "unique", "first-rate" dishes in "lovely" digs that exhibit a tuned-in "attention to detail"; most also give "kudos" to the service and appreciate the cuisine (and the cocktails) as a "nice change from standard fare", even if a few balk at "not so authentic" preparations for "above-average prices."

### Chameau  🗷Ⓜ  *French/Moroccan*
22 | 21 | 21 | $41

**Fairfax** | 339 N. Fairfax Ave. (bet. Beverly Blvd. & Oakwood Ave.) | 323-951-0039 | www.chameaurestaurant.com

"Fabulous" French-Moroccan cuisine served in "plentiful" portions "spoils your palate for anything else" at this Fairfax "find"; though it's on the "small" side and the menu isn't cheap, many gladly shell out for the "welcoming" service and "imaginative", "mod" decor ("like *Austin Powers* in the Middle East"), not to mention the chance to "have a b'steeya without enduring a belly dance."

**Chan Dara** *Thai*      20 | 17 | 18 | $26

**West LA** | 11940 W. Pico Blvd. (Bundy Dr.) | 310-479-4461 |
www.chandararestaurant.com

**Chan Darae** *Thai*

**Hollywood** | 1511 N. Cahuenga Blvd. (Sunset Blvd.) | 323-464-8585

**House of Chan Dara** *Thai*

**Hancock Park** | 310 N. Larchmont Blvd. (Beverly Blvd.) |
323-467-1052 | www.chandararestaurant.com

These "old, reliable and tasty" Thai standbys serve up "delicate"
dishes in "fun", "busy" locales where the "gorgeous", "distractingly"
attired waitresses look like "models waiting for their big break";
though the three locations strike some as "overpriced" "fading lo-
tuses", most maintain they're "always a favorite" where the food is
"actually very good"; N.B. the Hollywood branch is separately owned.

**Chao Krung** *Thai*      ▽ 20 | 14 | 19 | $22

**Fairfax** | 111 N. Fairfax Ave. (bet. Beverly Blvd. & 1st St.) | 323-932-9482 |
www.chaokrungrestaurant.com

Fans head to this Fairfax "secret" for "solid", "reasonable" Thai fare
that's delivered in "healthy portions" by an "efficient", "friendly" staff,
or self-served at the "great lunch buffet"; while the "dark" "ornate" interior is "aging" and a bit "gaudy" to some, others say its "peaceful"
vibe will instantly "transport you to a cafe in Thailand."

**Chapter 8 Steakhouse &**      ▽ 17 | 23 | 18 | $49
**Dance Lounge** 🅂 Ⓜ *Steak*

**Agoura Hills** | 29020 Agoura Rd. (Kanan Rd.) | 818-889-2088 |
www.chapter8lounge.com

"Glitzy" "bordello" decor that's a "throwback to the Rat Pack days"
lures the "beautiful people" to this accommodating Agoura Hills
steakhouse that invites "fishing for singles" and "relaxing" by the fire
pit as much as carnivorous chowing down; while a number of surveyors say the food "needs to be better" to stand up to the atmosphere
and the cost, it's still a "romantic must" for its main clientele – just not
so much "if you're over 45."

**Charcoal** *American*      11 | 17 | 12 | $36

**Hollywood** | 6372 W. Sunset Blvd. (Ivar St.) | 323-465-8500 |
www.charcoalhollywood.com

"More of a scene than a restaurant", this Geisha House sib boasts a
"killer location" next to Hollywood's ArcLight Cinemas; unfortunately,
critics say the kitchen flops with "overpriced" burgers and other "pedestrian" American fare, the staff is "clueless" and even the "overly
designed rustic decor" looks "like a TGI Fridays trying to be cool";
sure, it's "convenient" and sometimes "decent", but most agree
"you'd need a lot more lighter fluid to get this fire started."

**Chart House** *Seafood/Steak*      19 | 22 | 19 | $43

**Malibu** | 18412 PCH (Topanga Canyon Rd.) | 310-454-9321
**Marina del Rey** | 13950 Panay Way (Via Marina) | 310-822-4144
**Redondo Beach** | 231 Yacht Club Way (Harbor Dr.) | 310-372-3464
www.chart-house.com

"Scenic locations" make the "delicious fish" and "good steaks" all the
tastier at this "upscale" surf 'n' turf chain where the "expensive" tariffs

| | FOOD | DECOR | SERVICE | COST |
|---|---|---|---|---|

are blunted by "elegant", "nautical" atmospheres; though the crowd skews "touristy" and the staff gets mixed marks – "exceptional" vs. "too young" – most report "reliable" dining.

### Chateau Marmont  *Californian/French*

| 20 | 25 | 20 | $57 |

**West Hollywood** | Chateau Marmont | 8221 W. Sunset Blvd. (bet. Havenhurst Dr. & Marmont Ln.) | 323-656-1010 | www.chateaumarmont.com

"Sit in the gardens and eat well among the stars" (including some "lovely ghosts") sigh fans of this pricey West Hollywood "landmark" boasting "almost daily celeb sightings" in a "chill", "sophisticated" setting with a "beautiful" patio; most find the "simple" seasonal Cal-French fare a "pleasant surprise", but since the staff caters to an "industry" crowd, some say "if you aren't in 'the biz' fuhgeddaboudit."

### Chaya Brasserie  *Asian/French*

| 24 | 23 | 22 | $51 |

**West Hollywood** | 8741 Alden Dr. (bet. Beverly Blvd. & 3rd St., off Robertson Blvd.) | 310-859-8833 | www.thechaya.com

"Creative", "delectable" Asian-French cuisine, an "excellent" staff and a "stylish", "old-school Hollywood" environment that "buzzes" at happy hour (which runs all night Sunday–Monday) make this "upscale" WeHo brasserie a "long-standing attraction that never fails to deliver"; while a few quibblers complain that it's "loud" and "crammed", most are "loath to give it anything but praise."

### Chaya Venice  *Japanese/Mediterranean*

| 22 | 20 | 20 | $46 |

**Venice** | 110 Navy St. (Main St.) | 310-396-1179 | www.thechaya.com

Locals and visitors alike "love" this Venice "favorite" with "staying power" for its "astounding fusion" of Japanese-Med cuisine that "bursts with flavor" (especially the "high-quality" sushi); boasting "hip" servers and a "lovely, comfortable" space, it's "always lively", though some warn that the scene can be "ear-splitting" during the "bargain" happy hour – so "learn to yell."

### Checkers Downtown  *Californian*

| 20 | 23 | 21 | $49 |

**Downtown** | Hilton Checkers | 535 S. Grand Ave. (bet. 5th & 6th Sts.) | 213-624-0000 | www.checkershotel.com

"Quiet" and a little "corporate", this Downtown eatery "hidden" in the historic Hilton Checkers provides "sumptuous" Californian cuisine and "accommodating" service in a setting suitable for both "important meetings" and "secluded trysts"; though some find it "bland" and balk at the bill, pre-concert diners call the free car to the Music Center the "crowning touch."

### Cheebo  *Italian*

| 19 | 14 | 16 | $26 |

**Hollywood** | 7533 W. Sunset Blvd. (bet. Gardner St. & Sierra Bonita Ave.) | 323-850-7070 | www.cheebo.com

Hollywood "hipsters" gravitate to this "groovy" spot that serves "terrific" slab pizzas, "winning" high-end sandwiches and other "eclectic", largely organic Italian bites in a "bright" (some say "dizzying") atmosphere where you're encouraged to "doodle on the tablecloths"; despite gripes about "crowded" digs and "grumpy" service, it's an "easy" choice for "hanging out with good friends or a special date."

| | FOOD | DECOR | SERVICE | COST |
|---|---|---|---|---|

**☑ Cheesecake Factory** *American* — 19 | 18 | 18 | $27

**Fairfax** | The Grove | 189 The Grove Dr. (Beverly Blvd.) | 323-634-0511
**Beverly Hills** | 364 N. Beverly Dr. (Brighton Way) | 310-278-7270
**Brentwood** | 11647 San Vicente Blvd. (bet. Barrington Ave. & Wilshire Blvd.) | 310-826-7111
**Marina del Rey** | 4142 Via Marina (Admiralty Way) | 310-306-3344
**Redondo Beach** | 605 N. Harbor Dr. (190th St.) | 310-376-0466
**Pasadena** | 2 W. Colorado Blvd. (Fair Oaks Ave.) | 626-584-6000
**Sherman Oaks** | Sherman Oaks Galleria | 15301 Ventura Blvd. (Sepulveda Blvd.) | 818-906-0700
**Woodland Hills** | Warner Ctr. | 6324 Canoga Ave. (Victory Blvd.) | 818-883-9900
**Thousand Oaks** | Thousand Oaks Mall | 442 W. Hillcrest Dr. (Lynn Rd.) | 805-371-9705
www.thecheesecakefactory.com
Additional locations throughout Southern California

The menu's "mammoth" – and "so are the crowds" – at this "family-pleasing" chain where the "endless" American options arrive in equally "colossal" portions (ironically, "they give you so much there's no room" for their "heavenly" namesake desserts); despite "ordinary" settings, "spotty" staffing and "lots of commotion", these "well-oiled machines" are so "busy" that they're best accessed "off-hours" to avoid "waits."

**Chef Melba's Bistro** Ⓜ *Californian* — ▽ 24 | 13 | 21 | $42

**Hermosa Beach** | 1501 Hermosa Ave. (15th St.) | 310-376-2084 | www.chefmelbasbistro.com

A "rising star" in Hermosa Beach, this deceptively "small, quaint" Californian "knocks your socks off" with "exciting" cuisine prepared with the "freshest ingredients" by chef-owner Melba Rodriguez who "welcomes you" from the open kitchen; though diners wish the "packed" space were "a bit more inviting", the meal packs an "impressive" punch for the price.

**Chez Jay** *Steak* — 16 | 15 | 17 | $33

**Santa Monica** | 1657 Ocean Ave. (Colorado Ave.) | 310-395-1741 | www.chezjays.com

There's "sawdust on the floor and Sinatra on the box" at this "classic" Santa Monica "beach dive", a "mainstay with heart" serving up a "simple" surf 'n' turf menu, a "buzzing barfly scene" and decor that's in a "time warp from the 1970s"; it's a "rare night when Jay doesn't pay a visit to your table", so while some say the "underwhelming" eats "shouldn't cost this much", no one disputes that it has "real history" as a "great old Westside joint."

**☑ Chez Mélange** *Eclectic* — 25 | - | 24 | $45

**Redondo Beach** | 1611 Catalina Ave. (Ave. I) | 310-540-1222 | www.chezmelange.com

This "venerable" Redondo Beach Eclectic – which shuttered its doors on PCH and is moving to Catalina Avenue at press time – delivers "spectacular" seasonal cuisine complemented by a "wonderful wine list" featuring a number of "reasonable selections"; the staff is "spot-on" too, and guests who griped about its former digs may be pleased by its new larger space with a cocktail bar and gastropub offerings to match.

| | FOOD | DECOR | SERVICE | COST |
|---|---|---|---|---|

### Chez Mimi ☑ *French*

| | 22 | 24 | 22 | $48 |

**Santa Monica** | 246 26th St. (San Vicente Blvd.) | 310-393-0558 | www.chezmimirestaurant.com

"Intimate and special", this Santa Monica "charmer" woos guests with its "French country" cottage setting and "darling" outdoor patio presided over by "delightful" chef-owner Mimi Hebert; the "honest", "graciously" served Gallic "home cooking" is "delicious" too, so while it's moderately "pricey", most agree it's "worth a visit for any Francophile."

### Chichen Itza *Mexican*

| | 24 | 15 | 20 | $24 |

**Downtown** | 2501 W. Sixth St. (Carondelet St.) | 213-380-0051 ☑
**Downtown** | Mercado La Paloma | 3655 S. Grand Ave. (bet. Jefferson Blvd. & 37th St.) | 213-741-1075
www.chichenitzarestaurant.com

"True Yucatán food" provides a "sensational" alternative to typical Mexican at these Downtowners known for their "superb", "unusual" dishes to please both meat lovers and veggies; though the Mercado La Paloma locale is for takeout only, the newer, pricier West Sixth Street branch is "elegantly decorated" and staffed by "helpful" servers, creating an ambiance that's "upscale but not pretentious."

### Chi Dynasty *Chinese*

| | 21 | 16 | 21 | $24 |

**Los Feliz** | 1813 Hillhurst Ave. (Franklin Ave.) | 323-667-3388 | www.chidynasty.com

Enthusiasts applaud this "enjoyable", recently relocated Los Feliz "family place" for "standout" Chinese food presented by a largely "top-notch" staff; while the new "improved" space has a more "modern" look, a few grumble that they're still "settling in" and "working out the kinks", and it's now a little more "expensive" with valet parking.

### Chili John's ☒ *American*

| | ▽ 17 | 10 | 17 | $12 |

**Burbank** | 2018 W. Burbank Blvd. (Keystone St.) | 818-846-3611

"Chili a Texan would be proud to eat" keeps the faithful flocking to this "Burbank legend", a "throwback" where the U-shaped counter is "crammed shoulder-to-shoulder with men" ("try not to think of the campfire scene in *Blazing Saddles*"); even if the "cheap" grub is "a bit oily" for some, it's ladled out "faster than fast food" by servers who are like "good bartenders" and make newcomers feel "welcome"; N.B. closed July through Labor Day.

### Chili My Soul *Southwestern/Tex-Mex*

| | 21 | 6 | 16 | $13 |

**Encino** | 4928 Balboa Blvd. (Ventura Blvd.) | 818-981-7685 | www.chilimysoul.com

"Come hungry" say fans of this Southwestern Tex-Mex Encino staple, since its "spicy, delicious" chilis – in rotating varieties from "traditional" to "way out" – will "keep you full" for hours; it's your "basic storefront operation" and some cite "hiked-up" prices of late, but most are pleased to find it offers "something a little different" that's particularly "perfect for the rare cold day in LA."

### China Beach Bistro *Vietnamese*

| | ▽ 16 | 9 | 15 | $18 |

**Venice** | 2024 Pacific Ave. (Venice Blvd.) | 310-823-4646 | www.chinabeachbistro.com

"Ok for a quick bite" say reviewers about the inexpensive Vietnamese fare that's "better than you would expect from the hole-in-the-wall

| | FOOD | DECOR | SERVICE | COST |

surroundings" at this Venice "dive"; though there's "not much charm" all around, it's a rarity in the area and its location near the beach is a bonus.

**China Grill** *Californian/Chinese*  19 | 15 | 16 | $28

**Manhattan Beach** | Manhattan Vill. | 3282 N. Sepulveda Blvd. (Rosecrans Ave.) | 310-546-7284 | www.chinagrillbistro.com

Manhattan Beach customers clamor for the "creative" "fresh" food with "excellent sauces" made from "high-quality ingredients" at this slightly "upscale" but "affordable" Cal-Cantonese bistro; even if its strip-mall surroundings are "not exactly inviting", it's "relaxing" on the patio, so many find it "wonderful for sharing and people-watching."

**Chin Chin** *Chinese*  16 | 13 | 16 | $24

**West Hollywood** | Sunset Plaza | 8618 W. Sunset Blvd. (Sunset Plaza Dr.) | 310-652-1818

**Beverly Hills** | 206 S. Beverly Dr. (Charleville Blvd.) | 310-248-5252

**Brentwood** | San Vincente Plaza | 11740 San Vicente Blvd. (bet. Barrington & Montana Aves.) | 310-826-2525

**Studio City** | 12215 Ventura Blvd. (Laurel Canyon Blvd.) | 818-985-9090

www.chinchin.com

A "predictable" chain for Cal-style "nouveau Chinese food", this "lunchtime favorite" is sought out for its "classic" signature Chinese chicken salad ("a must") and roster of dim sum choices (as well as Pan-Asian dishes at the more upscale WeHo branch); still, it's just "ho-hum" to those who feel it's gone "downhill" and call the "skimpy portions" "chin chin chintzy."

**⚡ Chinois on Main** *Asian/French*  26 | 21 | 23 | $61

**Santa Monica** | 2709 Main St. (Hill St.) | 310-392-9025 | www.wolfgangpuck.com

"Spectacular" Asian-French dishes "served family-style" "justify the pull at your pocketbook" at Wolfgang Puck's Santa Monica draw that still "lives up to its name" "after all these years"; fans say the "fine" staff is "knowledgeable" and the open kitchen makes for an entertaining "floor show", though the chinoiserie-clad room strikes doubters as "dated" and "way too loud" considering the "close-together" tables.

**Chipotle** *Mexican*  18 | 11 | 15 | $11

**Fairfax** | 110 S. Fairfax Ave. (1st St.) | 323-857-0608

**Third Street** | 121 N. La Cienega Blvd. (3rd St.) | 310-855-0371

**Beverly Hills** | 244 S. Beverly Dr. (bet. Charles Blvd. & Gregory Way) | 310-273-8265

**Marina del Rey** | 4718 Admiralty Way (Mindanao Way) | 310-821-0059

**Torrance** | 24631 Crenshaw Blvd. (Skypark Dr.) | 310-530-0690

**Pasadena** | Hastings Ranch Shopping Ctr. | 3409 E. Foothill Blvd. (Madre St.) | 626-351-6017

**Burbank** | 135 E. Palm Ave. (1st St.) | 818-842-0622

www.chipotle.com

"Fresh", "build-your-own" burritos assembled from "high-quality ingredients" keep the lines "long" at this *muy* "popular" Mexican chain where portion sizes approximate "one day's worth of food in one sitting"; "great dollar value" compensates for the "cafeteria-style" service, though "stark", "no-frills" settings make them "best for carryout."

|  | FOOD | DECOR | SERVICE | COST |
|---|---|---|---|---|

### NEW Chloe 🗷 American/French — ▽ 18 | 22 | 17 | $33

**Santa Monica** | 1449 Second St. (B'way) | 310-899-6999 | www.barchloe.com
An "intimate" "date place" with burgundy sofas and marble-topped tables, this Santa Monica lounge in the old Voda space offers a "warm", "relaxing" atmosphere with a "perfect bar menu" of "creative" New American–French small plates to "pair with the cocktails"; on the downside, there's "fierce competition for seating" and the wine and mixed drinks are "none too cheap."

### Z Cholada Thai — 24 | 9 | 19 | $22

**Malibu** | 18763 PCH (Topanga Beach Dr.) | 310-317-0025 | www.choladathaicuisine.com
This "funky beach shack" delivers "wonderful", "highly memorable" Thai meals for a "bargain" at two separately owned branches in Malibu and Ventura; though regulars advise "just close your eyes" since the "tight quarters" with "no atmosphere" are hardly an attraction, they overwhelmingly call it a "real find" for "quick", "cheap" eats served by a "friendly" crew.

### Z ChoSun Galbee Korean — 23 | 21 | 19 | $36

**Koreatown** | 3330 W. Olympic Blvd. (bet. Manhattan Pl. & Western Ave.) | 323-734-3330 | www.chosungalbee.com
"Succulent" meats and other "crave-able" Korean dishes you grill at your table make both regulars and "first-timers" swoon over this "sleek", "accessible" K-town BBQ with a "pleasant, efficient" staff and a "beautiful" open-air space that "accommodates large groups"; while the bill is "steeper than some", most are happy to chip in for the "perfect-for-sharing" platters.

### Z Christine Mediterranean/Pacific Rim — 26 | 19 | 24 | $44

**Torrance** | Hillside Vill. | 24530 Hawthorne Blvd. (Via Valmonte) | 310-373-1952 | www.restaurantchristine.com
The "adventurous" Mediterranean–Pacific Rim menu by "genius" chef Christine Brown continues to "surprise" patrons of this Torrance "jewel of the South Bay" who feel "lucky" to have it in the neighborhood; its "intimate" quarters can get a bit "cramped" (there's "more privacy" on the patio), but "personal" service helps make it "tops" for "special occasions" "without extreme prices."

### Christy's Italian — 22 | 22 | 22 | $46

**Long Beach** | 3937 E. Broadway (bet. Mira Mar & Termino Aves.) | 562-433-7133 | www.christysristorante.com
"Superb", "traditional" Tuscan fare and an "extensive" wine list at "fair prices" attract a following to this "venerable", "off-the-beaten-path" "Long Beach haunt"; despite some complaints of "inconsistency" in food and service, most feel it has just the right "dark, romantic" ambiance when you want to "impress a first date."

### Chung King ⊭ Chinese — ▽ 25 | 8 | 17 | $19

**Monterey Park** | 206 S. Garfield Ave. (bet. Garvey & Newmark Aves.) | 626-280-7430
"If you like it spicy and hot, this is the place!" exclaim lovers of this "rock-solid" Monterey Park "miracle" whose "damn good" Sichuan fare induces the "ultimate burn, sweat and swear" reaction; the "reasonable" tabs help keep tempers soothed, but since the dining room is

a "bare-bones strip-mall box" and the staff "speaks minimal English", many recommend opting for takeout.

**Cialuzzi's** Ⓜ *Italian* ▽ 20 | 10 | 16 | $22

**Redondo Beach** | 601 N. PCH (bet. Beryl & 190th Sts.) | 310-374-8511

Loyalists "load up" on "red-sauce" pasta and "authentic New York-style" pizza while "talking Yankee baseball" with the owner at this "unpretentious", unadorned Redondo Beach Italian; the "noise and crowds" are drawbacks for some, but to others that's all part of the "atmosphere."

**Ciao Trattoria** Ⓢ *Italian* 20 | 19 | 20 | $36

**Downtown** | 815 W. Seventh St. (bet. Figueroa & Flower Sts.) | 213-624-2244 | www.ciaotrattoria.com

"Before a game at Staples" or a night at the theater, this Downtown "sleeper" provides "fine" Italian fare that's "reliable if not revelatory" and served in the "upscale" art deco interior of an "old classic" building; moderate prices and service that "gets you in and out quickly" keep it "busy" for lunch and dinner.

**Ⓩ Cicada** Ⓜ *Californian/Italian* 23 | 27 | 23 | $56

**Downtown** | 617 S. Olive St. (bet. 6th & 7th Sts.) | 213-488-9488 | www.cicadarestaurant.com

An "art deco dream", this "dazzling" Downtown "oasis of class, elegance" and "Lalique splendor" is reminiscent of "old Hollywood" with its "jaw-dropping" dining room that's known for appearing in *Pretty Woman*; "amazing" Cal-Italian cuisine presented by a "tip-top" staff completes the picture, so even if it's "expensive", smitten surveyors say it "never disappoints."

**Circa 55** *American/Californian* ▽ 19 | 22 | 21 | $59

**Beverly Hills** | Beverly Hilton | 9876 Wilshire Blvd. (Santa Monica Blvd.) | 310-887-6055 | www.circa55beverlyhills.com

Gadflies groove to "watching the action out by the pool" from a dining room decked out in vintage earth tones at this otherwise "ok" New American-Californian in the Beverly Hilton; some critics call the food "uneven" and "meh for the price you're paying", but Sunday brunch enhances the value with a bounty of "fresh seafood" from the raw bar.

**Citizen Smith** ❶ *American* 17 | 23 | 15 | $41

**Hollywood** | 1600 N. Cahuenga Blvd. (bet. Hollywood & Sunset Blvds.) | 323-461-5001 | www.citizensmith.com

A "young crowd" heads to this "dark", "late-night" Hollywood hang whose "cool" surroundings are clinched by a "lively" bar scene and "lovely patio"; while the New American menu offers what some call "better than expected" "country-style home cooking", detractors deem the chow "uninspired" and "ridiculously" priced, and are irked by "inattentive" service.

**NEW Citrus at Social** Ⓢ Ⓜ *Eclectic/French* 21 | 24 | 21 | $64

**Hollywood** | 6525 Sunset Blvd. (Schrader Blvd.) | 323-337-9797 | www.citrusatsocial.com

Stirring up "quite a scene", this new Hollywood hotbed with a "lemon-lime" twist is "sexy" and "luxurious", boasting "vaulted ceilings", "flattering lighting and plush seating" that delights a deep-pocketed "forever-21 crowd"; most agree that DC-superstar chef Michel

| | FOOD | DECOR | SERVICE | COST |
|---|---|---|---|---|

Richard "makes his LA comeback" in style, preparing "imaginative", "delicious" French-Eclectic fare that's served by a "surprisingly pleasant", "well-mannered" staff.

### City Bakery  *Bakery*

| 19 | 11 | 13 | $17 |

**Brentwood** | Brentwood Country Mart | 225 26th St. (San Vicente Blvd.) | 310-656-3040 | www.thecitybakery.com

Home of "heaven in a chocolate chip cookie" and other "killer" baked goods (including "unique" pretzel croissants), this daytime Brentwood spin-off of the NYC cafe also offers a "fresh", "eclectic" salad bar, mac 'n' cheese and other American fare; among its drawbacks are "limited seating", "cafeteria"-like looks and a "distracted" staff, not to mention goods "so expensive you won't be able to send your kids to college", but the faithful would "sit in traffic all day" for its signature sweet stuff.

### Ciudad  *Nuevo Latino*

| 21 | 19 | 19 | $41 |

**Downtown** | Union Bank Plaza | 445 S. Figueroa St. (5th St.) | 213-486-5171 | www.ciudad-la.com

"Still spicy" pronounce fans of this Downtown Nuevo Latino owned by the Too Hot Tamales, Mary Sue Milliken and Susan Feniger (Border Grill), whose "brilliantly flavored", "intriguing" dishes, "exotic" drinks, "bright", "funky" setting and "hospitable" service all win kudos; while some dissenters deem it "overpriced", "chaotic" and "rock-concert loud" ("not a good biz place"), most are won over by touches like the "Sunday tapas menu on the patio – the way to go."

### Clafoutis  ● *French/Italian*

| 19 | 17 | 17 | $33 |

**West Hollywood** | Sunset Plaza | 8630 W. Sunset Blvd. (Sunset Plaza Dr.) | 310-659-5233

"Similar to its Parisian cousins", this WeHo bistro turns out "good quality" French-Italian "standards" for a "gregarious" "Euro" crowd that gathers on the "cute" Sunset Plaza terrace for "awesome" people-watching; service "leaves a little to be desired", but many forgive it since the place is "open late" and "truly a value on the Strip"; P.S. "free and copious parking" is a bonus.

### Claim Jumper  *American*

| 19 | 18 | 18 | $25 |

**Long Beach** | Marketplace Shopping Ctr. | 6501 E. PCH (2nd St.) | 562-431-1321
**Torrance** | Torrance Crossroads | 24301 Crenshaw Blvd. (Lomita Blvd.) | 310-517-1874
**Monrovia** | 820 W. Huntington Dr. (bet. 5th & Monterey Aves.) | 626-359-0463
**Northridge** | Northridge Fashion Ctr. | 9429 Tampa Ave. (Plummer St.) | 818-718-2882
**City of Industry** | 18061 Gale Ave. (Fullerton Rd.) | 626-964-1157
**Valencia** | 25740 N. The Old Rd. (McBean Pkwy.) | 661-254-2628
www.claimjumper.com

"Holy healthy portions!" crow fans of this "family-focused" chain dishing out "comforting", "super-size" all-American eats that are "humanly impossible to consume in one sitting"; the "excellent value" and "pleasant" service are pluses, even if some sniff at the "old-timey" decor and "long waits", and assess what the "homey" dishes "lack in quality they make up for with butter."

|  | FOOD | DECOR | SERVICE | COST |
|---|---|---|---|---|

### Clay Pit *Indian*
| 21 | 15 | 20 | $32 |

**Brentwood** | 145 S. Barrington Ave. (Sunset Blvd.) | 310-476-4700
"Solid", "refined" Indian fare is presented with "class" at this Brentwood neighborhood eatery, where a "reasonable" lunch buffet makes up for the higher-end dinner menu; most say the "stale" furnishings lend it "no ambiance", but still find the meals "above-average" overall.

### Clementine ⊠ *American/Bakery*
| 23 | 12 | 14 | $19 |

**Century City** | 1751 Ensley Ave. (Santa Monica Blvd.) | 310-552-1080 | www.clementineonline.com
"Fall in love" with chef-owner Annie Miler's "outstanding" "seasonal" American breakfast and lunch dishes and "masterful" desserts at this "upscale" Century City staple where the "lines are long" and "tables difficult to find" but the cost is "worth it"; though parking is "almost impossible", curbside pickup is now available for takeout.

### ☑ Cliff's Edge *Californian/Italian*
| 21 | 26 | 18 | $41 |

**Silver Lake** | 3626 Sunset Blvd. (Edgecliffe Dr.) | 323-666-6116 | www.cliffsedgecafe.com
Like something "out of a fairy tale", the "lush" garden at this unmarked Silver Lake "hideaway" feels like a "tropical oasis" for "romantic" dinners and weekend brunches of "enticing", "creative" Cal-Italian cuisine; some call the bill "too high" for the "random" service they receive, but smitten surveyors say the "ambiance makes up for it."

### Coast *Californian/Seafood*
| 21 | 24 | 22 | $43 |

**Santa Monica** | Shutters on the Bch. | 1 Pico Blvd. (Ocean Ave.) | 310-458-0030 | www.coastsantamonica.com
Set in Santa Monica's Shutters on the Beach, this "light, airy" yearling with a "lovely patio and comfy indoor booths" "feels like Martha's Vineyard", complete with an "awesome" ocean backdrop and a thoroughly "laid-back vibe"; most call the high-end Californian fare "simple, fresh" and a "big improvement from the previous incarnation", though some prefer it just for "sunset drinks" since the view is "still the lure"; N.B. a new Santa Barbara spin-off has opened in the Canary Hotel.

### Cobras & Matadors *Spanish*
| 21 | 17 | 16 | $35 |

**Beverly Boulevard** | 7615 W. Beverly Blvd. (bet. Curson & Stanley Aves.) | West Hollywood | 323-932-6178
**NEW** **La Brea** | 460 S. La Brea Ave. (6th St.) | 323-936-7622 ●⊠
**Los Feliz** | 4655 Hollywood Blvd. (Vermont Ave.) | 323-669-3922
Fans ask why "fly to Spain"? when you can enjoy "killer" tapas with "big flavors" at Steven Arroyo's "provocative", "dark", "screamingly loud" joints that are always "packed"; while critics carp "they try to be a little too hip for their own good" and service can be "iffy", a "reasonable" menu and no-corkage BYO policy at the Beverly Boulevard branch (with a wine shop next door) keeps the bill from getting out of bounds; N.B. La Brea's former Goat location has joined the pack, and the Los Feliz locale has a new wine bar attached called Sgt. Recruiter.

### Coco Noche *Dessert/Eclectic*
| ▽ 17 | 14 | 19 | $28 |

**Manhattan Beach** | 1140 Highland Ave. (Manhattan Beach Blvd.) | 310-545-4925 | www.coconoche.com
A "strange fusion of Korean restaurant, wine bar and chocolatier", this Eclectic Manhattan Beach entry has gained a foothold as an

"after-dinner place to gather with friends" over "decadent" sweets, "nice tapas" and vino; still, it's literally too "cool" and spare inside for some, and the plates from the "limited" menu are "not for the starving."

### Colony Café & Papa's Porch  *American*  ∇ | 18 | 16 | 13 | $14

**West LA** | 10939 W. Pico Blvd. (bet. Veteran Ave. & Westwood Blvd.) | 310-470-8909 | www.thecolonycafe.com

Customers head to this "casual", "family-friendly" West LA eatery for "tasty" breakfast and lunch "comfort food" in a "cute" if "strangely" arranged setting with a nautical "East Coast feel"; however, disappointed diners call the quality "unpredictable" and service "indifferent", making it too much "like going to a fast-food joint."

### NEW Comme Ça  *French*  21 | 20 | 19 | $54

**West Hollywood** | 8479 Melrose Ave. (La Cienega Blvd.) | 323-782-1104 | www.commecarestaurant.com

"*C'est magnifique!*" claim connoisseurs of the "sumptuous" "meal of the moment" at this new West Hollywood brasserie by Sona's David Myers, boasting "classic French preparations" that "hit the mark" – along with a "terrific" cheese course and oysters from the raw bar – complemented by "extraordinary cocktails"; while some gripe that the food "doesn't live up to the hype" and cite "sporadic" service – and many call the "jet-runway" noise level "downright unpleasant" – most eat up its "hip ambiance", "sleek" bistro decor and occasional "star sightings."

### Coral Tree Café  *Californian/Italian*  18 | 14 | 13 | $17

**Brentwood** | 11645 San Vicente Blvd. (Darlington Ave.) | 310-979-8733

**Encino** | 17499 Ventura Blvd. (Encino Ave.) | 818-789-8733

### Coral Tree Express  *Californian/Italian*

**Century City** | Century City Westfield Mall | 10250 Santa Monica Blvd. (bet. Ave. of the Stars & Century Park W.) | 310-553-8733

**Canoga Park** | Topanga Canyon Mall | 6600 Topanga Canyon Blvd (Victory Blvd.) | 818-587-3330

www.coraltreecafe.com

Those craving "healthy" breakfasts and "well-done" salads and sandwiches with "wholesome" ingredients dig these "popular", "down-to-earth" Cal-Italian cafes whose Brentwood and Encino branches offer patio seating and WiFi (ideal for "aspiring writers"); still, some mumble there's "no decor to speak of", lines to place your order "extend to the back door" and you may do a "double-take" when you see the bill.

### Cora's Coffee Shoppe  *Diner*  21 | 14 | 17 | $21

**Santa Monica** | 1802 Ocean Ave. (Pico Blvd.) | 310-451-9562 | www.corascoffee.com

It "takes the grease out of greasy spoon" say Santa Monicans who savor "hearty" "contemporary" breakfasts and lunches among a "hip" crowd at this "high-end diner" adjacent to parent restaurant Capo and a block from the beach; though the menu is "limited", sitting inside can be "claustrophobic" and the "location isn't perfect due to the proximity to the road", "they make it work" with a "pretty" patio where you dine "under a bougainvillea canopy."

| | FOOD | DECOR | SERVICE | COST |
|---|---|---|---|---|

## Corkscrew Cafe ⓜ *Eclectic* ▽ 21 | 17 | 17 | $26

**Manhattan Beach** | 2201 Highland Ave. (Marine Ave.) |
310-546-7160

"Authentic Philly cheese steak meets upscale wine bar" in Manhattan Beach at this "engaging, one-of-a-kind" Eclectic cafe proffering "delicious" sandwiches and small plates, "top-notch" beers and "reasonable" vino; customers are also lulled by "views of the ocean" from the "charming" upstairs patio with a fire pit, but dissenters opine that dining downstairs feels "cramped and awkward" and that the staff, while "knowledgeable", can "take forever."

## Counter, The *Burgers* 21 | 13 | 16 | $17

**NEW Marina del Rey** | 4786 Admiralty Way (Fiji Way) |
310-827-8600
**Santa Monica** | 2901 Ocean Park Blvd. (29th St.) | 310-399-8383
www.thecounterburger.com

"Design your own patty from heaven" by choosing from an "arm-long list" of "eclectic" toppings to enjoy with "life-changing" sweet potato fries and "out-of-this world malts" advise aficionados of this "crowded" "retro-mod" Santa Monica–based burger chain; "healthy items" including a "fabulous" veggie burger are available, but "bring an extra stomach" for the "generous portions" and "call your order in to avoid long waits"; N.B. new branches are set to open soon in El Segundo, Studio City and Westlake Village.

## Coupa Café *Eclectic* 17 | 16 | 17 | $24

**Beverly Hills** | 419 N. Cañon Dr. (bet. Brighton Way & Santa Monica Blvd.) | 310-385-0420 | www.coupacafe.com

A "slightly offbeat" Eclectic menu with Latin arepas, all-day breakfast and "flavorful" Venezuelan java means this modestly priced "sleeper" brings something "different" to Beverly Hills; sure, nonbelievers simper about edibles they find "uninspiring" and inconsistent service, but it's "casual" and "cute", and a "table by the fire on a cold winter's night is just right"; P.S. on Tuesday nights there's "great Venezuelan music too."

## Courtyard, The ☾ *Spanish* ▽ 19 | 20 | 17 | $34

**West Hollywood** | 8543 Santa Monica Blvd. (La Cienega Blvd.) |
310-358-0301

It's the "perfect atmosphere for relaxing and drinking a glass of sangria" say habitués of this West Hollywood "gem" with a "charming" patio amid "N'Awlins-like dwellings"; the kitchen's "varied" Spanish tapas are often "very good", but "can add up in cost before you're full" and might take time to arrive since the "service could use some work."

## Coyote Cantina *Southwestern* 20 | 15 | 18 | $25

**Redondo Beach** | King Harbor Ctr. | 531 N. PCH (Beryl St.) | 310-376-1066 |
www.coyotecantina.net

"Fantastic" Southwestern fare, "killer" margaritas and a staff that "works hard for you" wins over fans of this "not fancy" but "popular" Redondo Beach hangout that offers a change of pace from "typical Mexican"; despite an "impressive wall of tequila", the jaded find the decor "a little tired" and the room "noisy", but defenders exclaim "it's always packed for a reason!"

|  | FOOD | DECOR | SERVICE | COST |
|--|------|-------|---------|------|

**Cozymel's** *Mexican* · 16 · 16 · 16 · $22

**El Segundo** | 2171 Rosecrans Ave. (Continental Way) | 310-606-5464 | www.cozymels.com

The food is "up and down" at this "mid-level" Mexican chain link in El Segundo, but it's still "popular at lunch and happy hour" for "large", "gringo"-friendly plates and "huge, delicious" margaritas enjoyed by groups in a "playful" atmosphere; even if service isn't stellar, the staff is "accommodating" and will let your party "make a lot of noise."

**Craft** *American* · 25 · 25 · 24 · $74

**Century City** | 10100 Constellation Blvd. (bet. Ave. of the Stars & Century Park E.) | 310-279-4180 | www.craftrestaurant.com

"Exceptional on every level" laud fans of *Top Chef* Tom Colicchio's "knock-your-socks-off" NYC transplant and "power meeting spot" in Century City boasting "astounding" New American dishes that "wow" with their "freshness, simplicity and flavor" and "unique" family-style presentation (though "you won't want to share one morsel"); "gorgeous", "serene" surroundings and an "exemplary" staff lead mavens to muse "if I could afford it, I'd be here every night."

**Crazy Fish** *Japanese* · 16 · 7 · 13 · $27

**Beverly Hills** | 9105 W. Olympic Blvd. (Doheny Dr.) | 310-550-8547

Many call it "second-rate", but bargain-hunters beeline to this Beverly Hills joint for "designer sushi" with "novel" styles and "portions double" the size you get elsewhere; "long waits", "noisy, cramped" digs in need of a redo and "inattentive" service come with the "cheap" tab.

**Creole Chef, The** *Creole* · - · - · - · I

**Baldwin Hills** | Baldwin Hills Plaza | 3715 Santa Rosalia Dr. (Stocker St.) | 323-294-2433

Some of the "best Creole food in Los Angeles" (including bread pudding "to die for") and "plenty of Southern hospitality" ensure that this "little place" tucked into Baldwin Hills Plaza is "packed constantly" with crawfish lovers; those who don't care for its "semi-fast food" atmosphere may prefer takeout or "outside tables that work very well in good weather."

**NEW Creperie by Jack n' Jill's** *Creole* · ▽ 21 · 17 · 19 · $20

**Third Street** | 8738 W. Third St. (S. Robertson Blvd.) | 310-858-4900 | www.creperiebyjacknjills.com

"Delicious" crêpes, from "innovative" savory selections to an "amazing" chocolate banana cream variety, as well as "fantastic" Creole cooking attract locals to this Jack n' Jill's spin-off, a "cute addition to Third Street" with a choice "people-watching" location; considering the "accommodating" service and affordable prices, some ask "are we sure we're only a block from Robertson?"

**CrêpeVine, The** Ⓜ *French* · 21 · 19 · 20 · $27

**Pasadena** | 36 W. Colorado Blvd. (bet. De Lacey & Fair Oaks Aves.) | 626-796-7250 | www.thecrepevine.com

"You'll be transported back to Paris" by the "fab" crêpes and other "delicious" French fare at this "tiny", sometimes "hectic" bistro that's

| | FOOD | DECOR | SERVICE | COST |

"hidden" in an alley off Pasadena's Colorado Boulevard; locals appreciate the "large" wine selection, "accommodating" service and "reasonable" prices, though a few lament that the "menu's changed" and "pared-down" due to a kitchen fire last year; N.B. there's live music Wednesday–Saturday nights.

### Crocodile Cafe  *Californian*

| 16 | 15 | 17 | $24 |

**Pasadena** | 140 S. Lake Ave. (bet. Cordova & Green Sts.) | 626-449-9900 | www.crocodilecafe.com

This Pasadena go-to by the Smith brothers (Arroyo Chop House, Parkway Grill) offers "inexpensive" Californian cuisine that admirers call "consistently good" for lunch or a "light dinner" in a "coffee-shop" atmosphere with a "relaxing" patio; meanwhile, a number of surveyors beef that the menu is "average" and "tired" and the space can get "noisy", especially in back "where they stick all the kids and large parties."

### NEW Crudo Bar & Ristorante ⑤ *Italian*

| - | - | - | M |

**West Hollywood** | 8570 W. Sunset Blvd. (La Cienega Blvd.) | 310-289-1131

Far more casual than the space's previous tenant (the short-lived Norman's), this Italian seafood arrival on the Sunset Strip dropped its predecessor's booths with gauzy curtains in favor of functional chairs and orange-backed barstools; the midpriced menu features a selection of crudo, a dish well suited for the outdoor patio where diners can watch West Hollywood's legion of supermodels click by in their stilettos.

### ⚡ Crustacean  *Asian Fusion/Vietnamese*

| 24 | 25 | 21 | $62 |

**Beverly Hills** | 9646 Little Santa Monica Blvd. (Bedford Dr.) | 310-205-8990 | www.houseofan.com

"Beyond mouthwatering" say satisfied suppers of the "divine crab and garlic noodles" at this Beverly Hills "can't-miss" where the fine Vietnamese and Asian fusion cuisine is served in "gorgeous" digs (most memorable for the "koi fish swimming undefoot") with "excellent" service to boot; just "bring your piggy bank", since the tabs are suited to "special occasions."

### Cuban Bistro Ⓜ *Cuban*

| ▽ 18 | 18 | 17 | $26 |

**Alhambra** | 28 W. Main St. (Garfield Ave.) | 626-308-3350 | www.cubanbistro.com

"Love the plantains!" coo buffs of this Alhambra bistro serving up "solid Cuban food" for affordable prices; while the less-enthused call the eats "nothing exciting", many say it's worth "going for the mojitos" and live music on the weekends.

### cube ⑤ *Italian*

| 22 | 16 | 22 | $31 |

**La Brea** | 615 N. La Brea Ave. (Clinton St.) | 323-939-1148 | www.cubemarketplace.com

This "little" La Brea "hideaway" that's both a cafe and a gourmet shop sates with "quality", "unpretentious" food including an "almost overwhelming selection" of "amazing" cheeses from the "prominently displayed" *fromage* case, as well as "fresh-made" pasta and charcuterie served by a "prompt, helpful" staff; the no-corkage BYO policy helps keep tabs "affordable."

| | FOOD | DECOR | SERVICE | COST |
|---|---|---|---|---|

### Cucina Paradiso  *Italian*    ▽ 21 | 18 | 22 | $36

**Palms** | 3387 Motor Ave. (bet. National Blvd. & Woodbine St.) | 310-839-2500 | www.cucinaparadiso.net

Palms patrons admire the "creative", "delicately flavored" pasta and other Northern Italian dishes served by a "friendly", "efficient" staff at this midpriced "old-time neighborhood" place that's "charming" and "comfortable" with Tuscan-style surroundings; live entertainment on the weekends in the adjacent Palmer Room is a bonus.

### ✷ CUT ⊠ *Steak*    26 | 24 | 24 | $97

**Beverly Hills** | Beverly Wilshire | 9500 Wilshire Blvd. (Rodeo Dr.) | 310-276-8500 | www.wolfgangpuck.com

Beef eaters boast that Wolfgang Puck's steakhouse in the Beverly Wilshire is "a cut above", living up to the "hype" with the "most sublime beef known to man" as well as "incredible appetizers and side dishes"; while even those who snag a "hard-to-get" reservation may need to "take out that second mortgage" when the check arrives ("$90 for a steak? please!"), most say it's "worth it" to sit in the "modern", "celeb-filled" dining room designed by Richard Meier and be catered to by the "exceptional", "not stuffy" staff.

### Daily Grill  *American*    18 | 17 | 18 | $31

**Brentwood** | Brentwood Gdns. | 11677 San Vicente Blvd. (Barrington Ave.) | 310-442-0044

**El Segundo** | 2121 Rosecrans Ave. (bet. Apollo & Nash Sts.) | 310-524-0700

**LAX** | LA Int'l Airport | 280 World Way (Tom Bradley Terminal) | 310-215-5180

**Burbank** | Burbank Marriott | 2500 Hollywood Way (bet. Empire & Thornton Aves.) | 818-840-6464

**Studio City** | Laurel Promenade | 12050 Ventura Blvd. (Laurel Canyon Blvd.) | 818-769-6336

**Universal City** | Universal CityWalk | 1000 Universal Studios Blvd. (off Rte. 101) | 818-760-4448

www.dailygrill.com

"Dependable, hearty" and as "comfortable as a pair of slippers" is how regulars describe this chain with a "diverse", "homestyle" American menu offering plenty of "options for fussy eaters"; though critics call the fare "mediocre" and a bit "pricey for nothing special", others are satisfied by "huge" plates delivering enough for "leftovers."

### Dakota  *Steak*    22 | 23 | 20 | $60

**Hollywood** | Roosevelt Hotel | 7000 Hollywood Blvd. (Orange Dr.) | 323-769-8888 | www.dakota-restaurant.com

"Lots of leather" and "dark, intimate lighting" set the stage for steaks you can "cut with a butter knife" at this "swanky" Hollywood "haunt" in the Roosevelt Hotel that does a "respectable" job in the kitchen despite the "scene" up front; most commend the "informed" service too, which helps support the "expensive" tab.

### ✷ Dal Rae  *Continental*    25 | 21 | 25 | $51

**Pico Rivera** | 9023 E. Washington Blvd. (Rosemead Blvd.) | 562-949-2424 | www.dalrae.com

It's a "time warp to the multi-martini lunch days" at this "classic" Pico Rivera "institution" where the kitchen turns out "excellent steaks" and "divine desserts" from a Continental menu that's "straight out of the '50s", and the staff proves that "customer service is still king"; throw in live piano music Tuesday–Sunday nights, and it's "expensive but worth it."

### Damon's Steakhouse  Steak     | 18 | 17 | 19 | $29 |

**Glendale** | 317 N. Brand Blvd. (bet. California Ave. & Lexington Dr.) | 818-507-1510 | www.damonsglendale.com
"Tacky tiki at its best" can be found at this "rich-in-tradition" Glendale "flashback" bringing together "old-fashioned mai tais" and "decent", "bang-for-the-buck" steaks in a room with "hilariously" retro Polynesian stylings; even if it's "past its glory days", the staff generally ensures a "pleasant" meal that's a "quirky" change of pace.

### D'Amore's Pizza Connection  Pizza     | 20 | 5 | 14 | $15 |

**Malibu** | 22601 PCH (Cross Creek Rd.) | 310-317-4500
**Westwood** | 1136 Westwood Blvd. (bet. Kinross Ave. & Lindbrook Dr.) | 310-209-1212
**Canoga Park** | 7137 Winnetka Ave. (Sherman Way) | 818-348-5900
**Encino** | 15928 Ventura Blvd. (bet. Gavlota & Gloria Aves.) | 818-907-9100
**Sherman Oaks** | 12910 Magnolia Blvd. (Coldwater Canyon Ave.) | 818-505-1111
**Sherman Oaks** | 14519 Ventura Blvd. (Van Nuys Blvd.) | 818-905-3377
**Thousand Oaks** | Skyline Shopping Ctr. | 2869 Thousand Oaks Blvd. (Skyline Dr.) | 805-496-0030
"Makes me weep with joy" cry committed customers about this "neighborhood pizza" chain serving "fresh", "Boston-style" "thin-crust" pies made with water actually shipped from Massachusetts; a little more "expensive" than the competition, it pays off with "huge" portions and "healthy" options, though takeout is recommended since most branches have "all the ambiance of an emergency room."

### Danny's Venice  Deli     | ▽ 17 | 16 | 16 | $23 |

**Venice** | 23 Windward Ave. (bet. Pacific Ave. & Spdwy.) | 310-566-5610 | www.dannysvenicedeli.com
The "location can't be beat" for a "bite by the beach" say reviewers of this Venice boardwalk eatery from the team behind James Beach and Canal Club, serving simple but "good" Traditional American plates and sandwiches; it's "a bit pricey for the area" and service can be "inconsistent", but the "terrific happy hour" means it's "fun to bring a date."

### Dan Tana's ● Italian     | 23 | 18 | 22 | $56 |

**West Hollywood** | 9071 Santa Monica Blvd. (Doheny Dr.) | 310-275-9444 | www.dantanasrestaurant.com
"Wonderful" for "people-watching" and "old-school Hollywood" "celebrity sightings", this "pricey", "throwback" WeHo establishment has that "dark" "hush-hush feel" that makes it "the place to go if you're having an extramarital affair", but "you can take your grandmother too" for "fabulous" Italian dishes and "perfect steak"; just "be prepared to wait for your table" ("regulars are definitely given preference") and "laugh" off the waiters' "salty" attitudes ("it's part of the shtick").

### Danube Bulgarian  Bulgarian     | ▽ 19 | 9 | 19 | $21 |

**Westwood** | 1303 Westwood Blvd. (Wellworth Ave.) | 310-473-2414
"I just found out I like Bulgarian food!" exclaim initiates about this Westwood eatery serving "flavorful" "working-class" Eastern

| | FOOD | DECOR | SERVICE | COST |
|---|---|---|---|---|

European dishes that also "reach to Greece and Turkey"; it's a "hole-in-the-wall", but the staff is "very nice" and the BYO-only policy with a $3.50 corkage fee adds to the bargain.

### Da Pasquale ⊠Ⓜ *Italian*    | 20 | 13 | 20 | $35 |

**Beverly Hills** | 9749 Little Santa Monica Blvd. (bet. Linden & Roxbury Drs.) | 310-859-3884 | www.dapasqualecaffe.com

"Terrific daily specials" and "fantastic" homemade pastas by "mamma in the kitchen" keep bellies full at this "quintessential" "neighborhood trattoria" "conveniently located right in front of a metered parking lot in Beverly Hills"; some call the space "a little worn" and often "loud, loud, loud", but most feel "right at home" since the staff is "pleasant" and "welcomes everyone as if they're family."

### Dar Maghreb *Moroccan*    | 20 | 25 | 22 | $48 |

**Hollywood** | 7651 Sunset Blvd. (bet. Fairfax & La Brea Aves.) | 323-876-7651 | www.darmaghrebrestaurant.com

"Atmospheric" and "convivial" with "North African seating" and belly dancers "swirling about the tables", this Hollywood Moroccan is "entertaining" for groups and couples who dine on "sensuous" "finger-eaten delicacies" you can "feed your date" (just "wash your hands – there's no silverware"); still, despite an "accommodating" staff, critics find it a bit too "cheesy" and "shabby", citing a "Disneyland" feel that puts a damper on the "expensive" prix fixe meal.

### NEW Darren's ⊠ *Californian*    | ▽ 26 | 22 | 22 | $52 |

**Manhattan Beach** | 1141 Manhattan Ave. (Manhattan Beach Blvd.) | 310-802-1973 | www.darrensrestaurant.com

"Exquisite, exciting food" makes this "small" Manhattan Beach bistro in the former Avenue space a "new and worthy find" for "top-notch" Cal-New American meals by chef-owner Darren Weiss; enhanced by "warm, inviting" decor, "unobtrusive" service and a "lively scene at the bar" (with its own "impressive menu"), it pleases even customers who call it "a little pricey."

### NEW D'Cache ⊠Ⓜ *Pan-Latin*    | - | - | - | M |

**Toluca Lake** | 10717 Riverside Dr. (Cahuenga Blvd.) | 818-506-9600 | www.dcacherestaurant.com

This lovingly restored 1928 Mission Revival cottage in Toluca Lake lets diners journey back to Hollywood before it was spoiled by talkies; its midpriced Pan-Latin menu delivers tapas, paella and entrees with a contemporary twist (such as salmon blackened with coffee), plus there's nightly live Spanish music.

### NEW Del, The ⊠Ⓜ *American*    | 20 | 17 | 19 | $37 |

**Playa del Rey** | 119 Culver Blvd. (Vista del Mar) | 310-823-6800 | www.thedelrestaurant.com

"A slice of coolness in sleepy Playa del Rey", this new "little out-of-the-way place" shows "culinary flair" in its "well-prepared", "reasonably priced" New American fare that's a "step up" from that of its predecessor, the La Marina Inn; while some early samplers say it's "still trying to find its way", enthusiasts approve of the "ultra-modern" space (infused with "a touch" of the old inhabitant's retro ambiance), sporting three "cozy" fireplaces plus an "ace bar" tended by a "sweet" staff.

| | FOOD | DECOR | SERVICE | COST |
|---|---|---|---|---|

**NEW Delancey Hollywood** ● *Italian* | - | - | - | M

**Hollywood** | 5936 Sunset Blvd. (Tamarind Ave.) | 323-924-2093 |
www.delanceyhollywood.com

The largely ungentrified eastern edge of Hollywood shows signs of
colonization with this casual late-night Italian, a new spin-off of the
Bowery sporting old brick, purplish banquettes and menus written on
the mirrors (à la Paree); its refreshingly affordable fare includes
dishes like pizza topped with Gorgonzola and fennel, and the tap beer
selection is impressive – call it a taste of the new East Hollywood.

**Delmonico's Lobster House** *Seafood* | 22 | 20 | 21 | $46

**Encino** | 16358 Ventura Blvd. (Hayvenhurst Ave.) | 818-986-0777

"One of the few fresh fish houses in the Valley", this "clubby" Encino
seafooder serves a "high-end" menu of "old favorites" in "generous
portions"; its "enclosed booths" are "lovely for a couple or foursome"
and the service is "attentive without being cloying", so even if some
sniff that it "lacks inspiration", others say "they've been around for
eons and there's a reason for it."

**Delphi Greek Cuisine** Ⓢ *Greek* | 17 | 12 | 17 | $23

**Westwood** | 1383 Westwood Blvd. (Wilshire Blvd.) | 310-478-2900 |
www.delphirestaurant.com

"Decent Greek grub" makes for "quick, healthy lunches" at this
"quaint" Westwood locale with a "welcoming" feel; some say it
"lacks the homemade quality you want", and even after a hyper-
Mediterranean renovation, with blue-and-white accents and floors re-
sembling old stone streets, few give the decor a nod, but most agree
the "price is right."

**Depot, The** Ⓢ *Eclectic* | 24 | 21 | 22 | $42

**Torrance** | 1250 Cabrillo Ave. (Torrance Blvd.) | 310-787-7501 |
www.depotrestaurant.com

"We aren't in Torrance anymore, are we, Toto?" ask those transported by this "top-notch" establishment where "mingling" chef-
owner Michael Shafer "impresses" with "artful" Eclectic cuisine
amid a "charming" "historical" setting in a "former railroad station"; a
few find both the cooking and service too "variable", but most salute
it as a "solid" choice, especially for "power lunches" with the
"SoCal automotive scene."

**Derby, The** *Steak* | 23 | 22 | 22 | $43

**Arcadia** | 233 E. Huntington Dr. (bet. Gateway Dr. & 2nd Ave.) |
626-447-2430 | www.thederbyarcadia.com

"Top off a day at the races" at this "old-fashioned" Arcadia steakhouse
near Santa Anita Park that provides "all the red leather you could
yearn for" and so much memorabilia (thanks to its former owner,
Seabiscuit jockey George Woolf) it's practically a "museum for horse-
racing history"; most find the meaty fare "consistently good" and the
service "professional", making it a prime place to "take clients for lunch."

**Ⓩ Derek's** Ⓢ Ⓜ *Californian/French* | 27 | 23 | 26 | $61

**Pasadena** | 181 E. Glenarm St. (bet. Arroyo Pkwy. & Marengo Ave.) |
626-799-5252 | www.dereks.com

"Intimate dining in a strip mall" can be found at this "refined"
Cal-French "special-event place" in Pasadena where the cooking is

"superb" and the "tasting menu with wine pairings never misses"; despite the "off-putting" exterior, its "romantic" setting ("sit by the fireplace on a cold night") and "fine", "considerate" staff round out an experience that justifies the "expensive" tab.

### Devon, Restaurant Ⓜ *Californian/French* ▽ 23 | 18 | 20 | $50

**Monrovia** | 109 E. Lemon Ave. (Myrtle Ave.) | 626-305-0013

An "excellent" Cal-French menu featuring "wonderful" game, unusual signatures ("try the blue cheese ice cream") and "fantastic" wines attracts enthusiasts to this "cozy" Monrovia bistro; still, a few assert that it's "declined" and could use some improvements to match the price.

### Ⓩ Din Tai Fung *Chinese* 25 | 13 | 15 | $21

**Arcadia** | 1088 S. Baldwin Ave. (Arcadia Ave.) | 626-446-8588

**Arcadia** | 1108 S. Baldwin Ave. (bet. Arcadia Ave. & Duarte Rd.) | 626-574-7068

www.dintaifungusa.com

"Transcendent" Shanghai soup dumplings so "delicate" and "juicy" "you may need a bib" are sought out by supplicants at this Arcadia "mecca" by a "world-famous" Taipei-based chain; those in-the-know "line up early on the weekend" to minimize the "long, long" wait, but once inside the "intimate" original dining room or the "more upscale" new space next door, the "phenomenal" "food comes fast and furious" and "lives up to the hype."

### Dish *American* 16 | 14 | 15 | $23

**La Cañada Flintridge** | 734 Foothill Blvd. (Commonwealth Ave.) | 818-790-5355 | www.dishbreakfastlunchanddinner.com

"Good old Americana" is the draw of this "pleasant", "affordable" standby in La Cañada Flintridge serving "decent" "home cooking" in a quirky environment with toasters on the tables during breakfast; still, opinions are split on whether it has "panache" or is just plain "boring", with a number of guests glazing over at the "slow-as-molasses" service.

### Divino *Italian* 22 | 17 | 21 | $42

**Brentwood** | 11714 Barrington Ct. (Sunset Blvd.) | 310-472-0886

A "neighborhood standout", this Brentwood Italian boasts "delicious" Adriatic-influenced creations and "lovely" desserts by "hospitable" chef-owner Goran Milic who "always has some special dishes reflecting his latest travels"; while the "tiny" room tends to get "crowded" and even difficult to "maneuver", most feel the "expense" is rewarded by a meal that's "extremely well prepared and served."

### Dolce Enoteca e Ristorante *Italian* 17 | 21 | 18 | $52

**Melrose** | 8284 Melrose Ave. (Sweetzer Ave.) | 323-852-7174 | www.dolcegroup.com

Even with a "fire blazing behind the bar", this "pricey", "modern" Melrose Italian by the Dolce Group is "not the hot scene" it once was according to critics, but it's still "beautiful", with "better-than-expected" food; DJs spinning "chill music" help override bumps in service.

### NEW Dolce Isola Ⓢ *American* ▽ 24 | 17 | 23 | $19

**Pico-Robertson** | 2869 S. Robertson Blvd. (Cattaraugus Ave.) | 310-776-7070

From "famous parent" The Ivy, this "quaint" newcomer in an "unlikely" Pi-Ro locale proffers "brilliant baking", "huge, wonderful" sandwiches

| | FOOD | DECOR | SERVICE | COST |

and other "delicious" daytime American bites; with scarce seating, it's "not really an eat-in place", but fans "love" the staff and only lament that if it keeps up the "awesome" work, "soon it will be too crowded."

**Dominick's** ● *Italian*                    21 | 22 | 20 | $41

**Beverly Boulevard** | 8715 Beverly Blvd. (San Vicente Blvd.) | West Hollywood | 310-652-2335 | www.dominicksrestaurant.com

A "trendy spot with staying power", this "upscale" "oasis" on Beverley Boulevard is "atmospheric" with "New York" style and two fireplaces (including one on the "fantastic" patio) as well as accommodating "night-owl" service; most guests appreciate the "simple", "homestyle" Italian cooking, giving "major props" to the weekly three-course Sunday supper for $15.

**Doña Rosa** *Bakery/Mexican*                    16 | 13 | 15 | $14

**Arcadia** | Westfield Shoppingtown Santa Anita | 400 S. Baldwin Ave. (Huntington Dr.) | 626-821-3556

**Pasadena** | 577 S. Arroyo Pkwy. (California Blvd.) | 626-449-2999 ●
www.dona-rosa.com

These slightly "dolled-up" spin-offs of El Cholo are most notable for their "homemade tortillas" and "nice" baked goods among a "hit-or-miss" "fast Mex" menu that seems "geared for those with the last-minute munchies"; while the Arcadia location only serves beer and wine, "cheap margaritas" are a pick-me-up at the Pasadena branch with a "happening" patio.

**Drago** *Italian*                    24 | 20 | 23 | $54

**Santa Monica** | 2628 Wilshire Blvd. (26th St.) | 310-828-1585 |
www.celestinodrago.com

Pleased patrons say the "inspired" cuisine is "still satisfying" (and ideal for "special occasions") at this Santa Monica Italian, the oldest in Celestino Drago's "empire", where the service is so "gracious" that "even the busboys are charming"; sure, it's "pricey" and some complain the "handsome" setting has become a little "fusty", but most forgive it in light of the "terrific" meal.

**Dr. Hogly Wogly's BBQ** *BBQ*                    22 | 7 | 18 | $22

**Van Nuys** | 8136 Sepulveda Blvd. (Roscoe Blvd.) | 818-780-6701 |
www.hoglywogly.com

"Bodacious BBQ" leads smoke lovers to "hog heaven" at this longtime Van Nuys staple providing "giant portions" of "delectable" ribs and "melt-in-your-mouth" brisket served by "feisty waitresses" in a real "pit" ("ambiance is not what this place is about"); some snobs sniff, however, it's "not good enough for a Texan – but probably good enough for those who wish they were."

**Duke's** *Pacific Rim*                    17 | 21 | 19 | $34

**Malibu** | 21150 PCH (Las Flores Canyon Rd.) | 310-317-0777 |
www.hulapie.com

"Join the surfer dudes", "order a tropical drink and drift away" at this "Hawaiian-style" "hangout" in Malibu featuring a "barefoot bar" and an "aloha atmosphere"; it's a little "touristy", the "average" Pacific Rim fare "seems like an afterthought" and you'll "pay for" the "dynamite" ocean views, but "time it right" and you could "see whales or dolphins frolicking in the waves."

|  | FOOD | DECOR | SERVICE | COST |
|---|---|---|---|---|

### Duke's Coffee Shop  *Diner*  18 | 10 | 17 | $15

**West Hollywood** | 8909 Sunset Blvd. (San Vicente Blvd.) | 310-652-3100 |
www.dukescoffeeshop.com

"You can come in your PJs" and have "breakfast with the rockers (that
means 2 PM)" along with "hipsters, truckers" and others chowing down
at communal tables inside this WeHo coffee shop that "hasn't changed
in decades on the Strip"; it may not be "the scene it once was", but for
"quick", "inexpensive" "all-American" diner food, it's a "classic."

### Du-par's  *Diner*  16 | 11 | 15 | $17

**Fairfax** | Grove at Farmers Mkt. | 6333 W. Third St. (Fairfax Ave.) |
323-933-8446  ●

**Studio City** | Studio City Plaza | 12036 Ventura Blvd. (Laurel Canyon Blvd.) |
818-766-4437  ●

**Thousand Oaks** | Best Western Thousand Oaks Inn |
75 W. Thousand Oaks Blvd. (bet. Moorpark Rd. & Rte. 101) | 805-373-8785
www.dupars.com

"Genuine retro appeal" is the lure of these "dependable" diners where
"ancient" "beehived waitresses in uniform call you 'hon' while happily
refilling your coffee cup"; though the food itself is "not outstanding",
most say "mmm" to the pancakes "no matter what time of day" and
appreciate the "good prices for early-bird dinners" from 4-5 PM;
N.B. the Farmers Market and Studio City branches are open 24 hours.

### Dusty's  *American/French*  18 | 19 | 19 | $33

**Silver Lake** | 3200 W. Sunset Blvd. (Descanso Dr.) | 323-906-1018 |
www.dustysbistro.com

Silver Lakers "slide into the booths" and dine on "tasty" French-
American dishes with a "Québécois" touch ("they have poutine!") at
this "hip" "little bistro" with a "cozy" interior and "cheerful" service;
the brunch is often "top-notch", but some are less impressed with dinner, finding it "overpriced" despite "generous" servings.

### eat. on sunset  🅢🅜  *American*  18 | 20 | 17 | $42

**Hollywood** | 1448 N. Gower St. (Sunset Blvd.) | 323-461-8800 |
www.patinagroup.com

Staking a claim as "Paramount's commissary", this "slick" American in
the Patina Group draws a "young" Hollywood crowd hungry for "simple",
"high-end comfort food"; it's "lively" with a "fantastic" patio, but many
still see "room for improvement" in both the cuisine and "spotty" service.

### Eat Well Cafe  *American*  16 | 12 | 16 | $16

**West Hollywood** | 8252 Santa Monica Blvd. (N. Harper Ave.) | 323-656-1383
**Glendale** | 1013 S. Brand Blvd. (Chevy Chase Blvd.) | 818-243-5928

"Old-fashioned 1950s breakfasts" and other "typical" diner eats keep
bellies full at these Glendale and West Hollywood "hipster mainstays"
slinging plenty of "greasy" American grub (though the "healthy alternatives" on offer are popular with WeHo "muscle boys"); service can be
"lacking", but they're "affordable" and have a "nice neighborhood feel."

### E. Baldi  🅢  *Italian*  22 | 16 | 16 | $58

**Beverly Hills** | 375 N. Cañon Dr. (bet. Brighton & Dayton Ways) |
310-248-2633 | www.ebaldi.com

"Unbelievable" pastas and other "delicious" Northern Italian
dishes attract fans (including plenty of "celebrities") to this

| | FOOD | DECOR | SERVICE | COST |
|---|---|---|---|---|

"casually elegant" Beverly Hills arrival by Giorgio Baldi's son, Edoardo; unfortunately, while the "showbiz scene" has its charms, the less-impressed report that "crowded" seating and "surly" service (the "attitude meter is off the charts") leave a few feeling "ripped off."

### Ebizo's Skewer  *Japanese*

▽ 22 | 9 | 15 | $23

**Manhattan Beach** | 229 Manhattan Beach Blvd. (Highland Ave.) | 310-802-0765

The "place for a shabu-shabu fix in the South Bay", this Manhattan Beach "joint" also serves up "juicy" Kobe burgers and "flavorful" Japanese skewers that are "easy on the wallet"; while the interior is rather "minimalist", you can angle for a seat outside and "watch the sun go down over the ocean."

### Echigo  🄈 *Japanese*

25 | 8 | 19 | $39

**West LA** | 12217 Santa Monica Blvd. (Amherst Ave.) | 310-820-9787

With "nothing fried, no miso and no edamame", this West LA Japanese from "master" chef-owner Hitoshi Kataoka (ex Sushi Sasabune) wins over "traditional sushi lovers" with "super-fresh" fish and a "stellar" omakase for lunch and dinner; the strip-mall setting is a "drab" "hole-in-the-wall", but fortunately prices are "rock-bottom" too.

### Edendale Grill  *American*

16 | 23 | 18 | $36

**Silver Lake** | 2838 Rowena Ave. (bet. Auburn & Rokeby Sts.) | 323-666-2000 | www.edendalegrill.com

The "inviting patio and gorgeous bar" combined with a "high hipster factor" win over admirers of this Traditional American "restored fire station" in Silver Lake; still, "disappointed" diners recommend "sticking to the drinks", citing "uneven", "overpriced" dishes and "variable" service, and concluding that the experience "could easily be so much better."

### Eight-18  🄈 *Mediterranean*

▽ 20 | 19 | 19 | $33

**Toluca Lake** | 10151 Riverside Dr. (bet. Forman & Talofa Aves.) | 818-761-4243 | www.eight-18.com

Providing "a welcome bit of LA in the Valley", this plush, "grown-up" "little" boîte attracts a "trendy" Toluca Lake crowd for its "huge selection" of bottles and "excellent" Mediterranean small plates; a number of critics complain, however, about the "loud" atmosphere and "too expensive" dishes that are "so small they can't be shared", advising diners to "grab a glass of wine after work, but don't go there hungry."

### NEW 8 oz.  🄈 *Burgers*

- | - | - | I

**Melrose** | 7661 Melrose Ave. (Spaulding Ave.) | 323-852-0008 | www.8ozburgerbar.com

While Govind Armstrong transfers Table 8 to a larger location, he's converted its former Melrose home into a hamburger joint with a more casual, woodsy interior; the hand-formed patties of hormone-free Black Angus and Estancia grass-fed meat are stored in Himalayan salt, grilled on exotic hardwoods and served on toasted Yukon potato bread buns with housemade condiments.

|  | FOOD | DECOR | SERVICE | COST |
|---|---|---|---|---|

### El Cholo Cafe  *Mexican*  | 18 | 18 | 18 | $24 |

**Mid-City** | 1121 S. Western Ave. (bet. 11th & 12th Sts.) | 323-734-2773
**Santa Monica** | 1025 Wilshire Blvd. (bet. 10th & 11th Sts.) | 310-899-1106
**Pasadena** | 958 S. Fair Oaks Ave. (bet. Arlington Dr. & Hurlbut St.) | 626-441-4353

### El Cholo Cantina  *Mexican*

**LAX** | LA Int'l Airport | 209 World Way (Terminal 5) | 310-417-1910
www.elcholo.com

"Olé!" applaud amigos of this Mexican chain serving "relatively inexpensive" "gringo-fied" food that many call "delish", especially the "tableside guac" and "phenomenal" seasonal green corn tamales; though some dismiss it as "ordinary" and "cheesy", the "legendary" margaritas are a hit for "parties", and the "octogenarian original" in Mid-City still has "character."

### El Coyote Cafe  *Mexican*  | 13 | 14 | 17 | $22 |

**Beverly Boulevard** | 7312 Beverly Blvd. (bet. Fuller Ave. & Poinsetta Pl.) | 323-939-2255 | www.elcoyotecafe.com

"It's all about the drinks and the atmosphere" at this "critic-proof" Mexican "guilty pleasure" on Beverly Boulevard that's "been around forever" and still delivers "hallucinogenic" margaritas and a "campy", "colorful" ambiance courtesy of "Christmas lights" and "red leather booths"; waitresses in "traditional dress" sling "lackluster", "low-cost, low-quality" fare, including tostadas made with "canned mixed vegetables", but unfazed fans are sold since it's a "crowd-pleasing" "hoot."

### Electric Lotus  ❂ *Indian*  | 18 | 19 | 16 | $27 |

**Los Feliz** | 4656 Franklin Ave. (Vermont Ave.) | 323-953-0040 | www.electriclotus.com

Fans feel like they're "dining in Jeannie's bottle" at this "dimly lit" Los Feliz "date spot" where decorative saris, throw pillows and "hypnotic" DJ tunes on the weekends create an "intimate" atmosphere; yet opinions are mixed on the "above-average-priced" Indian fare, which some call "flavorful" and others maintain is so "mild" it's "bland", and made less enticing by "hipper-than-thou" service.

### Elf Café  Ⓜ☐ *Mediterranean/Vegetarian*  | ▽ 25 | 18 | 22 | $24 |

**Echo Park** | 2135 W. Sunset Blvd. (N. Alvarado St.) | 213-484-6829

"Elfin in size but not in taste", this "scene-y" Echo Park BYO has fast become a "new LA landmark" for "fresh, inventive" and modestly priced Mediterreanean veggie dishes that "even meat eaters" adore, served in a "super-cute" space with a handful of tables and sidewalk seating out front; "long waits" are a drawback, but the "wonderful" staff keeps the mood welcoming; N.B. open Wednesday–Sunday for dinner only.

### El Pollo Inka  *Peruvian*  | 19 | 12 | 16 | $17 |

**Lawndale** | Lawndale Plaza | 15400 Hawthorne Blvd. (154th St.) | 310-676-6665
**Gardena** | Gateway Plaza | 1425 W. Artesia Blvd. (Normandie Ave.) | 310-516-7378
**Hermosa Beach** | 1100 PCH (Aviation Blvd.) | 310-372-1433
**Torrance** | 23705 Hawthorne Blvd. (bet. Lomita Blvd. & PCH) | 310-373-0062
www.elpolloinka.com

"To-die-for" lomo saltado, "fabulous" rotisserie chicken and other "addictive" Peruvian plates come in portions so big at this "busy"

| | FOOD | DECOR | SERVICE | COST |
|---|---|---|---|---|

chain that customers have to "prepare to share or take some home"; given the "bargain prices", most overlook the spotty service and decor that's "getting a bit worn"; N.B. there's live South American music on the weekends at the Torrance and Hermosa Beach branches.

### ☑ El Tepeyac  *Mexican*

| | 24 | 8 | 18 | $13 |
|---|---|---|---|---|

**East LA** | 812 N. Evergreen Ave. (Winter St.) | 323-267-8668

"Home of the Hollenbeck burrito" – a "classic must" that's a "challenge to finish" – this "small", "revered" East LA joint offers "more for your money" than most with its "flavorful" and generous "homestyle" Mex fare; though service is "fast", vets advise "go early" to avoid "waiting in line" and "don't expect" much in the way of decor beyond "family photos on the wall", since it's the "real" deal.

### El Torito  *Mexican*

| | 15 | 14 | 15 | $21 |
|---|---|---|---|---|

**Hawthorne** | 11855 Hawthorne Blvd. (bet. 118th & 119th Sts.) | 310-679-0233
**Marina del Rey** | 13715 Fiji Way (Lincoln Blvd.) | 310-823-8941
**Long Beach** | 6605 PCH (bet. 2nd St. & Westminster Ave.) | 562-594-6917
**Redondo Beach** | Fisherman's Wharf | 100G Fisherman's Wharf (S. Catalina Ave.) | 310-376-0547
**Pasadena** | 3333 E. Foothill Blvd. (Sierra Villa Madre Ave.) | 626-351-8995
**Burbank** | 4012 W. Riverside Dr. (Pass Ave.) | 818-848-4501
**Northridge** | 8855 Tampa Ave. (bet. Nordhoff & Parthenia Sts.) | 818-349-1607
**Sherman Oaks** | 14433½ Ventura Blvd. (Van Nuys Blvd.) | 818-990-5860
**Woodland Hills** | Warner Ctr. | 6040 Canoga Ave. (Oxnard St.) | 818-348-1767
**Thousand Oaks** | 449 N. Moorpark Rd. (bet. Brazil St. & Wilbur Rd.) | 805-497-3952
www.eltorito.com
Additional locations throughout Southern California

Spread all over Southern California, this "family-friendly" chain with a "faux Mexican setting, matching food and extremely gentle margaritas" serves up meals some call "cheap, filling" and "reliable" and others sum up as "bland as our weather"; it can be a "zoo at the bar", but the "popularity" puzzles critics given "all the choices in LA."

### El Torito Grill  *Mexican*

| | 18 | 17 | 18 | $24 |
|---|---|---|---|---|

**Beverly Hills** | 9595 Wilshire Blvd. (Camden Dr.) | 310-550-1599
**Torrance** | 21321 Hawthorne Blvd. (Torrance Blvd.) | 310-543-1896
**Sherman Oaks** | Sherman Oaks Galleria | 15301 Ventura Blvd. (Sepulveda Blvd.) | 818-907-7172
www.etgrill.com

"Don't fill up on" the "fresh" "handmade tortillas" say amigos of these "upscale" sibs of the El Torito chain that are deemed "better and different" (if "not truly authentic"), plating up Mexican fare with a "Southwest twist"; while "happy hour" is popular with the after-work set, "kids enjoy" chowing down there too, so "bring the family" because "they handle big groups well" and it's "affordable."

### Emles  *Californian/Mediterranean*

| | ▽ 19 | 13 | 20 | $19 |
|---|---|---|---|---|

**Northridge** | 9250 Reseda Blvd. (Prairie St.) | 818-772-2203 | www.emlesrestaurant.com

"You'll feel like part of the family" at this "fairly priced" Northridge "sleeper" where the "earnest" staff "puts a lot of effort" into the "flavorful" Cal-Med fare, and the "killer breakfasts" and "early-bird dinners" earn special praise; as for its "odd" "strip-mall" space in a former fast-food venue, some patrons proclaim it deserves "a better location."

**Empress Harbor Seafood Restaurant** *Chinese* | 19 | 13 | 12 | $24 |

**Monterey Park** | Atlantic Plaza | 111 N. Atlantic Blvd., Ste. 350 (Garvey Ave.) | 626-300-8833
Adventurous eaters "nibble on chicken feet" and other "tasty" "authentic" Chinese dishes at this budget-friendly Monterey Park dim sum specialist also famed for its "no-fuss" Cantonese fin fare; the spacious marble-and-wood-trimmed interior provides plenty of seating, though service "can be nonexistent when they're bogged down."

**Empress Pavilion** *Chinese* | 21 | 13 | 14 | $22 |

**Chinatown** | Bamboo Plaza | 988 N. Hill St. (Bernard St.) | 213-617-9898 | www.empresspavilion.com
The "grande dame" of Chinatown dim-sum "palaces", this low-cost Sino "standby" delivers a "diverse" lineup of "steaming hot dishes" "straight off the rolling carts"; even if diehards declare the staff "surly" and say it "can't compete with the places in the San Gabriel Valley", it remains as "popular" as ever, with "Soviet-era" waits on weekends.

**Encounter** *Eclectic* | ∇ 14 | 23 | 16 | $35 |

**LAX** | LA Int'l Airport | 209 World Way (bet. Terminals 1, 2 & 6) | 310-215-5151 | www.encounterlax.com
A "classic", set in LAX's *Jetsons*-esque Theme Building, this offbeat eatery earns kudos for its "swinging" 1960s feel with lava lamps and retro-futuristic decor courtesy of Walt Disney Imagineering; though it also boasts "spectacular views" of the runway and the city skyline, only "marginal" Eclectic eats mean it may not be a "destination" on its own, but is a "great place to pass the time waiting for a flight."

**Engine Co. No. 28** *American* | 19 | 21 | 20 | $39 |

**Downtown** | 644 S. Figueroa St. (bet. 7th St. & Wilshire Blvd.) | 213-624-6996 | www.engineco.com
Housed in a restored 1912 Los Angeles fire station – "fire pole included" – this Downtown American is a "perennial favorite" for the "pre-theater", "sports" and "business" crowds thanks to its "convenient locale" and "unfussy" "homestyle" cooking presented in a "comfortable" atmosphere with red-brick floors and a tin ceiling; though skeptics say it's "unexceptional" "for the price", the majority concurs that it's "a good bet" if you're in the area; N.B. they also have a free shuttle to the Music and Staples Centers.

**Enoteca Drago** *Italian* | 21 | 19 | 20 | $47 |

**Beverly Hills** | 410 N. Cañon Dr. (Brighton Way) | 310-786-8236 | www.celestinodrago.com
"Remarkably unpretentious for the neighborhood", this "inviting" Beverly Hills wine bar/restaurant from the Drago family conjures up "a slice of Italy" with a "fantastic" selection of vintages (50 available by the glass or in flights) paired with "wonderful" antipasti, thin-crust pizzas and pastas; it flaunts a "sophisticated" setting and a "dedicated" staff, so even if some say "it's not up to" its Santa Monica sib, it's a "local" "favorite" nonetheless.

|  | FOOD | DECOR | SERVICE | COST |
|---|---|---|---|---|

## Enoteca Toscana
**Wine Bistro** Ⓜ *Italian/Spanish*

▽ 19 | 18 | 20 | $31

Camarillo | 2088 E. Ventura Blvd. (Fir St.) | 805-445-1433 |
www.enotecatoscanawinebistro.com

A "pleasant" hideaway in "charming" Old Town Camarillo, this "casual" snackery touts a "simple" menu of Italian and Spanish small plates (think cured meats and cheeses plus empanadas and panini) alongside an extensive "variety of imported wines" set down in Tuscan-style digs; though a few find it "pricey for the area", it's a "comfortable" spot where the "attentive" staff ensures "your glass is never empty."

## Enterprise Fish Co.  *Seafood*

19 | 17 | 18 | $34

Santa Monica | 174 Kinney St. (Main St.) | 310-392-8366 |
www.enterprisefishco.com

"Solid, but unspectacular" sums up this Santa Monica seafooder and its Santa Barbara sib where "locals and tourists" chow down on "huge plates" of "simply prepared" fin fare that makes for a "good value", especially during Monday and Tuesday's "bargain" lobster special; on the downside are "long waits" and a "warehouse"-like atmosphere at both locations, but insiders insist "if you drink a fruity cocktail", none of that will "matter too much."

## Enzo & Angela  *Italian*

22 | 16 | 23 | $35

West LA | 11701 Wilshire Blvd. (Barrington Ave.) | 310-477-3880 |
www.enzoandangela.com

"Please don't list this place" beg boosters who "don't want the word getting out" about this "reasonably priced" West LA "gem" – a "modest" "mom-and-pop" operation "hidden" on the second floor of a "busy" mini-mall; with a "hard-at-work" team sending out "plentiful" portions of "homemade" pastas and "intriguing" Italian specials, supporters say "it's hard not to love it."

## e3rd Steakhouse & Lounge ⊘ *Steak*

19 | 22 | 20 | $35

Downtown | 734 E. Third St. (bet. S. Alameda St. & Santa Fe Ave.) |
213-680-3003 | www.eastthird.com

"Sleek" and "cavernous" with "fabulous" decor, this "clublike" Downtown spin-off of Zip Fusion serves an "affordable" Asian-accented steakhouse menu that ranges in quality from "addictive" to merely "palatable"; still, some guests like "sitting at the bar" and appreciate the "professional" service even if the place "hasn't quite found its niche yet."

## Fabiolus Café, The  *Italian*

20 | 15 | 19 | $27

Hollywood | 6270 W. Sunset Blvd. (bet. Argyle Ave. & Vine St.) |
323-467-2882 | www.fabiolus.com

Cinephiles frequent this "affordable" Hollywood standby near the ArcLight for "reliable" "pre-theater" meals of "basic", "well-executed" Italian standards served "quickly"; the trattoria-style interior strikes some as "blah", but it gets a boost from a back patio that's "beautiful on a spring day"; N.B. the Melrose location has closed.

## Factor's Famous Deli  *Deli*

16 | 10 | 17 | $21

Pico-Robertson | 9420 W. Pico Blvd. (Beverly Dr.) | 310-278-9175 |
www.factorsdeli.com

Noshers craving "Jewish comfort food" seek out this "family-run" "old-time" Pico-Robertson deli, a "neighborhood standby" for

| | FOOD | DECOR | SERVICE | COST |
|---|---|---|---|---|

"smoked fish platters", "huge salads", matzo ball soup and over-stuffed sandwiches; even though the "decor could use an update", it thrives on "character", thanks to waitresses who are a "crack up" and little "showbiz" touches like film posters on the wall and valet parking.

### Falafel King  *Mideastern*
| 18 | 6 | 14 | $11 |
|---|---|---|---|

**Santa Monica** | The Promenade | 1315 Third St. Promenade (bet. Arizona Ave. & Santa Monica Blvd.) | 310-587-2551
**Westwood** | 1059 Broxton Ave. (bet. Kinross & Weyburn Aves.) | 310-208-4444

"Tasty" falafel, "creamy hummus" and "numerous" salad options head up the menu at this "utterly no-frills" Middle-Eastern pair in Santa Monica and Westwood; cynics say they've "gone downhill" since their "heyday", but "students" and folks on-the-go insist they still "hit the spot" for a "quick", "cheap" meal.

### Farfalla Trattoria  *Italian*
| 22 | 16 | 19 | $30 |
|---|---|---|---|

**Los Feliz** | 1978 Hillhurst Ave. (Finley Ave.) | 323-661-7365 | www.farfallatrattoria.com

Champions contend that "LA needs more places like this" "unstuffy" Italian "hang" in "hipster-heavy" Los Feliz where the "solid" thin-crust pizzas and "terrific" pastas "are the stars" of the "straightforward" well-priced menu; its "tiny" mirror-and-brick space with "close-set" tables makes for occasional "waits" and "little elbow room" to spare, but a "friendly" staff keeps the mood "warm" on most nights.

### Farm of Beverly Hills  *American*
| 19 | 16 | 17 | $29 |
|---|---|---|---|

**Fairfax** | Grove at Farmers Mkt. | 189 The Grove Dr. (bet. Fairfax Ave. & 3rd St.) | 323-525-1699
**Beverly Hills** | 439 N. Beverly Dr. (bet. Brighton Way & Santa Monica Blvd.) | 310-273-5578
**Woodland Hills** | Topanga Mall | 6600 Topanga Canyon Blvd. (Randi Ave.) | 818-888-6738
www.thefarmofbeverlyhills.com

"Simple country fare" gets a "designer" "twist" at this New American chainlet, a "haven for shoppers", "moms and tots" and "pretty people in oversized sunglasses" who "munch on salads" and "sophisticated" "diner"-like staples then indulge in "delicious" desserts; yet in spite of its "homey" appeal, some city-folks take a pass, citing "sketchy" service and tabs that seem "expensive for what you get."

### Farm Stand  *Eclectic*
| 21 | 17 | 20 | $27 |
|---|---|---|---|

**El Segundo** | 422 Main St. (Holly Ave.) | 310-640-3276 | www.farmstand.us
"Creative homecooking from around the world" "impresses" the locals at this "sweet", "unassuming" spot on El Segundo's Main Street proffering "fantastic", "fresh-tasting" Eclectic dishes – many with a "Middle-Eastern influence" – and plenty of options for vegetarians; a few find the "casual", "urban country"-style space "cramped", but they're usually won over by the "easygoing service" and "decent" prices.

### Far Niente  *Italian*
| 25 | 19 | 22 | $41 |
|---|---|---|---|

**Glendale** | 204½ N. Brand Blvd. (Wilson Ave.) | 818-242-3835 | www.farnienteristorante.net
"A winner" cheer champions of this "beloved" Glendale Northern Italian where the "outstanding", if "pricey", meals are kicked off with "fragrant", "addictive" flatbread and follow through with "gracious" service in the

| | FOOD | DECOR | SERVICE | COST |

two terra-cotta–appointed dining areas; given that it's often "filled with regulars", occasionally "noisy" environs are to be expected.

**Fat Fish** *Asian Fusion/Japanese*     20 | 20 | 18 | $37

**Koreatown** | 3300 W. Sixth St. (Berendo St.) | 213-384-1304
**West Hollywood** | 616 N. Robertson Blvd. (bet. Melrose Ave. & Santa Monica Blvd.) | 310-659-3882
www.fatfishla.com

It's "often a scene" at this "hip" WeHo sushi specialist where "pretty people" down "lethal" cocktails before digging into "creative" rolls and "tasty" Asian fusion plates made even more "affordable" by the happy-hour prices (5–7 PM daily); the newer Koreatown branch may not have its liquor license yet, but it features an almost identical menu and similarly "stunning", "modern" decor and "cute" waiters.

**☒ Father's Office** *American/Burgers*     24 | 14 | 11 | $22

**NEW Culver City** | Helms Bakery | 3229 Helms Ave. (Washington Blvd.) | 310-736-2224
**Santa Monica** | 1018 Montana Ave. (bet. 10th & 11th Sts.) | 310-393-2337
www.fathersoffice.com

The "line swings out the door" at this "legendary" Santa Monica "gastropub" that's "famous" for both its "sublime" burgers and strict "no customization" policy ("don't even try to order ketchup"); "fantastic" fries served "in adorable shopping carts" and an "unparalleled" selection of "hard-to-find" microbrews are additional perks, so diehards urge you to overlook the "cattle-call" atmosphere and "inhospitable" service, insisting this area "classic" is well "worth the trouble"; N.B. the newer Culver City branch features a larger space with patio, plus an expanded American menu.

**Fatty's & Co.** Ⓜ *Vegetarian*     ∇ 23 | 18 | 17 | $24

**Eagle Rock** | 1627 Colorado Blvd. (Vincent Ave.) | 323-254-8804 | www.fattyscafe.com

Even "non-veggies" say they "can't get enough" of the "imaginative" meat-free eats, "sinful desserts" and "vast array of wines" at this "real find" in Eagle Rock touting a menu made from mostly organic and local ingredients; service is a weak point, but the "lovely" setting redeems with a brick-walled space that's filled with fresh flowers.

**Feast from the East** Ⓢ *Asian*     20 | 7 | 15 | $13

**West LA** | 1949 Westwood Blvd. (bet. Olympic & Santa Monica Blvds.) | 310-475-0400 | www.ffte.com

"The Chinese chicken salad still reigns" at this West LA "one-dish-wonder" where connoisseurs claim "nothing else" on the "affordable" Pan-Asian menu even "comes close" to their signature tossed greens and its "fabulous" sesame dressing (also available in bottles); though service is "efficient" and they spruced up the simple interior in 2007, most "addicts" still opt to "take out."

**Figaro Bistrot** *French*     19 | 22 | 17 | $35

**Los Feliz** | 1802 N. Vermont Ave. (bet. Franklin Ave. & Hollywood Blvd.) | 323-662-1587 | www.figarobistrot.com

Los Feliz Francophiles "*adore*" the "Gallic ambiance" of this "genuine" bistro turning out "authentic", if "inconsistent", eats in a 1920s cafe-style setting with antique mirrors, "tiny tables placed close together"

|  | FOOD | DECOR | SERVICE | COST |
|---|---|---|---|---|

and sidewalk seating providing prime "people-watching"; unfortunately, a few find the "very French attitude" extends to the "aloof" servers, while others call the prices "expensive for what you get."

### Fins  *Continental/Seafood*  | 22 | 20 | 21 | $42 |

**Calabasas** | 23504 Calabasas Rd. (Mulholland Dr.) | 818-223-3467
**Westlake Village** | Westlake Plaza | 982 S. Westlake Blvd. (bet. Agoura & Townsgate Rds.) | 805-494-6494
www.finsinc.com

"Consistently fresh" fin fare and "well-prepared" Continental dishes make this "classy" valley duo a "delight" for fans who also give props to the "lovely" outdoor seating at both branches, especially Calabasas' "romantic", "creekside" patio; foes find them "overrated", though an "attentive" staff is a plus and "live music" keeps them "noisy and crowded" most nights.

### Firefly ●Ⓩ *American*  | 22 | 25 | 18 | $42 |

**Studio City** | 11720 Ventura Blvd. (Colfax Ave.) | 818-762-1833
"Chic" "twentysomethings" slip into this "sexy" Studio City "hideaway" to sip a drink at the handsome library-themed bar or nibble "moderately high-priced" New American dishes in the "elegant" Moroccan-style tent illuminated by candles; it's about "as close to 'Hollywood in the Valley' as you can get", with critics cautioning about "crowds" and a "meat market" atmosphere.

### Firefly Bistro Ⓜ *American*  | 18 | 18 | 19 | $38 |

**South Pasadena** | 1009 El Centro St. (Meridian Ave.) | 626-441-2443 | www.eatatfirefly.com
A "charming" tented patio makes a "lovely" open-air setting for this South Pasadena New American where an "adventurous" chef turns out "well-balanced" "seasonal" dishes and proponents praise the especially "satisfying brunch" with "great blues" playing in the background; a few chafe at tabs they find "pricey", but "smart" service redeems, as does the overall "relaxed" mood.

### Fish Grill  *Seafood*  | 19 | 7 | 13 | $15 |

**Beverly Boulevard** | 7226 Beverly Blvd. (Alta Vista Blvd.) | 323-937-7162
**Pico-Robertson** | 9618 W. Pico Blvd. (Beverwil Dr.) | 310-860-1182
**Brentwood** | 12013 Wilshire Blvd. (Bundy Dr.) | 310-479-1800
www.fishgrill.com
Seafood-seekers "get their Omega-3's on" at this order-at-the-counter kosher mini-chain pumping out "simply prepared" mesquite-grilled fish plus salads and chowders, all priced on the "affordable" side; decor is "purely utilitarian", prompting some patrons to opt for "takeout" – just remember, they're "closed on the Sabbath" (Friday evenings and Saturdays).

### 555 East  *Steak*  | 24 | 22 | 23 | $55 |

**Long Beach** | 555 E. Ocean Blvd. (Linden Ave.) | 562-437-0626 | www.555east.com
Long Beach locals insist "there's no better place for steak" than this "classic" "upper-end" chophouse matching "quality" meats with "well-thought-out" sides and a "fabulous" 1,000-plus label wine list; "veteran" servers add to the "old-school" feel, as does the "elegant" decor with "rich wood" accents, tin ceilings and marble floors.

| | FOOD | DECOR | SERVICE | COST |
|---|---|---|---|---|

### NEW Five Guys
### Famous Burger & Fries *Burgers*

- | - | - | I

**Carson** | South Bay Pavilion | 20700 Avalon Blvd. (E. Del Amo Blvd.) | 310-515-7700 | www.fiveguys.com

A Carson shopping center houses the first West Coast branch of this popular Right Coast hamburger chain, identifiable by its red-and-white checker motif and inexpensive, fast food–style burgers, hot dogs and fries; toppings like sautéed mushrooms and fried onions are gratis, as are unlimited soda refills.

### Five Sixty-One 🅂 *Californian/French*

▽ 22 | 19 | 22 | $43

**Pasadena** | California School of Culinary Arts | 561 E. Green St. (Madison Ave.) | 626-405-1561 | www.561restaurant.com

Aspiring chefs deliver a "unique" experience at this "delightful" Cal-French canteen in the CA School of Culinary Arts in Pasadena turning out often "terrific" food (including a "special" prix fixe tasting menu on Thursday and Friday nights) in a brick-walled space decorated with paintings by local artists; as for service, "they are, after all, students", so expect an "earnest" effort, but allow "some leniency for mess-ups."

### NEW Flake *American*

- | - | - | I

**Venice** | 513 Rose Ave. (5th Ave.) | 310-396-2333 | www.veniceflake.com

In an airy Venice space just a few blocks from the beach, this breakfast-intensive hang lets patrons mix-and-match any of 34 cereals with 32 toppings, allowing unusual combinations like Lucky Charms with wheat germ or Grape Nuts with gummi bears; sandwiches with names like the Nutty Munkee provide further sustenance through the afternoon.

### Flavor of India *Indian*

22 | 16 | 19 | $29

**West Hollywood** | 9045 Santa Monica Blvd. (Doheny Dr.) | 310-274-1715
**NEW Burbank** | 161 E. Orange Grove Ave. (San Fernando Blvd.) | 818-558-1199
www.flavorofindia.com

"Authentic" Indian cooking full of "complex" flavors awaits at this "inexpensive" West Hollywood "neighborhood joint" and its newer Burbank brother that customers count on for "takeout and delivery", buffets lunches or a "casual" dinner on the covered patio; "outdated" decor draws a few detractors, as does occasionally "spotty" service.

### Fleming's Prime Steakhouse & Wine Bar *Steak*

25 | 22 | 24 | $58

**El Segundo** | 2301 Rosecrans Ave. (Douglas St.) | 310-643-6911
**Woodland Hills** | 6373 Topanga Canyon Blvd. (Victory Blvd.) | 818-346-1005
www.flemingssteakhouse.com

"Not as stuffy" as the competition, this "inviting" chophouse chain purveys "classic" steaks and sides in "relaxed", "clubby" digs conducive to both "business and romance"; "low-profile" service and an "excellent wine-by-the-glass program" add to its allure, but since "everything's à la carte", be prepared for "high-end" tabs.

### Fogo de Chão *Brazilian*

24 | 20 | 24 | $52

**Beverly Hills** | 133 N. La Cienega Blvd. (Clifton Way) | 310-289-7755 | www.fogodechao.com

"Paradise for Atkins diet–lovers", this Beverly Hills churrascaria imported from Brazil rolls out all-you-can-eat meats on skewers for folks seeking to "embrace their inner caveperson"; the "meal-in-itself" salad bar is equally "tasty" and the drinks sure "pack a punch", but be careful and "pace yourself" to avoid the inevitable "protein swoon."

### Fonz's  *Seafood/Steak*                    22 | 18 | 22 | $42

**Manhattan Beach** | 1017 Manhattan Ave. (bet. 10th Pl. & 11th St.) | 310-376-1536 | www.fonzs.com
"Regulars" give "a big thumbs-up" to this "feel-good" spot with a "prime" Manhattan Beach address proffering "surprisingly good" (if somewhat "pricey") steaks and seafood in a "warm" atmosphere that's both casual and clubby; the "high-energy" bar area is "not for the claustrophobic", but the "down-to-earth" servers always "take care of you" ensuring most "keep coming back."

### NEW FOOD  *American*                    - | - | - | I

**Rancho Park** | 10571 W. Pico Blvd. (Prosser Ave.) | 310-441-7770 | www.food-la.com
Expect to see both duffers and studio execs from nearby 20th Century Fox fueling up at this breakfast-and-lunch-only American diagonally across from Rancho Park Golf Course; the affordable fare includes the likes of organic eggs and sandwiches named for classic films, all served in a modernist earth-colored setting.

### Ford's Filling Station  *Gastropub*          19 | 17 | 18 | $40

**Culver City** | 9531 Culver Blvd. (Irving Pl.) | 310-202-1470 | www.fordsfillingstation.net
Gourmands "secretly craving a great burger" and other "fancy bar" fare flock to this "trendy" Culver City gastropub where chef-owner Ben Ford (son of Harrison) concocts an "eclectic mix" of daily changing and "definitely filling" "comfort foods" enhanced by a "wonderful variety of beers" in a "boisterous" setting (i.e. "lots of noise"); still, a number of naysayers feel that it's "overhyped, over-priced and overcrowded", concluding the "buzz can get in the way of a good meal."

### Formosa Cafe  ❶ *Asian Fusion*             12 | 18 | 16 | $28

**West Hollywood** | 7156 Santa Monica Blvd. (Formosa Ave.) | 323-850-9050 | www.formosacafe.com
"The golden age of Hollywood" lives on at this circa-1939 "historic hangout" (a former Bugsy Șiegel hangout, it was used as a set in *LA Confidential*) featuring a "limited" menu of "greasy" Asian fusion "hangover food" that most maintain pales next to the drinks and atmosphere; even if old faithfuls worry it's "lost its glow", crowds keep coming for the "train-trolley" decor and "Raymond Chandler" vibe.

### Foundry on Melrose, The  Ⓜ *American*       23 | 21 | 23 | $57

**Melrose** | 7465 Melrose Ave. (N. Gardner St.) | 323-651-0915 | www.thefoundryonmelrose.com
"Ask for the prix fixe of the night" or choose from the "small, well-thought-out menu" at "genial" chef Eric Greenspan's "high-quality" New American, a "cozy, intimate" space bringing "much-needed class to this part of Melrose"; while a few call the fare "hit-or-miss", most agree that the "staff makes you feel special" and the "really cool patio" is "lovely in warm weather"; N.B. a jazz trio plays on weekends.

FOOD DECOR SERVICE COST

### Fountain Coffee Room  *Diner*
▽ 20 | 20 | 22 | $32

**Beverly Hills** | Beverly Hills Hotel | 9641 Sunset Blvd. (bet. Beverly & Crescent Drs.) | 310-276-2251 | www.thebeverlyhillshotel.com

"Pink-clad waitresses" add to the "'50s" feel of this "charming" classic coffee shop tucked beneath the Beverly Hills Hotel lobby where Tinseltown types "sit at the counter" and dig into "wonderful" diner-style breakfasts and lunches; prices are "affordable" and "celebrity" sightings a regular occurrence – no wonder some say it's a "secret favorite."

### 410 Boyd ⓩ  *Californian*
17 | 14 | 17 | $27

**Downtown** | 410 Boyd St. (San Pedro St.) | 213-617-2491

"Feel like an edgy urban pioneer" at this "longtime" "hangout" on a "seedy" stretch of Downtown where the "uncomplicated" California cuisine (think burgers and BLTs) and "quite strong" drinks make it a perennial "inexpensive" "lunch" pick for the "lawyers, journalists and artists" laboring nearby; in the evening, the "modern" industrial space features rotating gallery exhibits and plays host to DJs as well.

### NEW Foxtail ●ⓩ  *French*
- | - | - | E

**West Hollywood** | 9077 Santa Monica Blvd. (Doheny Blvd.) | 310-859-8369 | www.sbe.com\foxtail

Decorated to the nines with art nouveau wallpaper and malachite tables, this opulent 1930s-style supper club from nightlife impresarios SBE ratchets up West Hollywood's glamour quotient; servers sport outfits from Brit clothier Biba, while swells and celebutantes dine on French bistro fare from ex-Spago chef Antonia Lofaso, a contestant on *Top Chef*; after dinner, the high-wattage set shakes their moneymakers in the ultraexclusive nightclub upstairs.

### ⓩ Fraîche  *French/Mediterranean*
24 | 22 | 20 | $49

**Culver City** | 9411 Culver Blvd. (Main St.) | 310-839-6800 | www.fraicherestaurantla.com

"Culver City's gone gourmet" gush the hordes of diehards who declare "it doesn't get much better" than Jason Travi's "inventive" French-Med fare (and "specialty cocktails") that's "worth every penny" at this "comfortable, clubby" "bistro with a neighborhood feel"; so though a few claim "if you're not the biggest name in the room, service can be challenging", the majority labels it a "breath of fraîche air" – making reservations "tough" to nab.

### Frascati  *Italian*
24 | 17 | 21 | $39

**Rolling Hills Estates** | Promenade on the Peninsula | 550 Deep Valley Dr. (Crossfield Dr.) | Rolling Hills | 310-541-8800 | www.frascatirestaurant.com

"Locals meet and eat" at this "delightful" midpriced "surprise" in Rolling Hills Estates where an "especially tasty" lineup of antipasti proves the perfect precursor to "excellent" Northern Italian preparations and "superb" wines brought by an "amiable" staff; its "small", but "comfortable" space is often "packed", so those in-the-know say "reservations are a must", "even during the week."

### Fred 62 ●  *Diner*
17 | 16 | 14 | $18

**Los Feliz** | 1850 N. Vermont Ave. (Russell Ave.) | 323-667-0062 | www.fred62.com

Like a "hipster Denny's", this "kitschy" 24/7 Los Feliz "gathering spot" is a "favorite" for "cool kids" and "a celeb or two" who pile into vinyl booths "that feel like the backseat of your grandpa's Buick" and chow down on "gussied up" American diner standards; "service issues" are legendary ("62 is the number of tries it takes to flag down your waiter"), but when the "late-night munchies" strike, denizens declare it's "everything a hungry clubber could want."

### French Crêpe Co.  *French*    21 | 9 | 15 | $14

**Fairfax** | Grove at Farmers Mkt. | 6333 W. Third St. (Fairfax Ave.) | 323-934-3113
**Hollywood** | Hollywood & Highland Ctr. | 6801 Hollywood Blvd., Ste. 403 (Highland Ave.) | 323-960-0933
www.frenchcrepe.com

"Delicious" "savory and sweet" crêpes come in "every combination you can imagine" at these "modest little French joints" set amid the "hustle and bustle" of the Farmers Market and the Hollywood & Highland Center, also offering other "tasty treats" like waffles, sandwiches and soups; service is "friendly", but be forewarned that the alfresco settings draw "long waits on weekends."

### ☒ Frenchy's Bistro  Ⓜ *French*    26 | 17 | 23 | $48

**Long Beach** | 4137 E. Anaheim St. (bet. Termino & Ximeno Aves.) | 562-494-8787 | www.frenchysbistro.com

"Superlative in every way" sing those smitten with this "top-notch" Long Beach bistro where "genuinely French" chef-owner Andre Angles prepares "outstanding" Provençal dishes – like *magnifique* soufflés – brought by an "informed" staff and deemed a "great value"; it's "definitely a destination", even if a few find the decidedly "un-chic" storefront setting an "incongruous" match with the "stunning" fare.

### Frida  *Mexican*    21 | 18 | 21 | $34

**Beverly Hills** | 236 S. Beverly Dr. (bet. Charleville Blvd. & Gregory Way) | 310-278-7666 | www.fridarestaurant.com

"Distinctive" "gourmet Mexican" fare "surprises" surveyors at this "upscale" Beverly Hills eatery "right off Rodeo" where the "authentic" menu includes "lots of nice touches" like fresh fruit margaritas and a "scrumptious" tres leches cake; its "lively" gallerylike interior sports colorful tile and wrought-iron accents, though comfort-hounds criticize the "uncomfortable" "closely set" tables and say service can be "spotty" as well.

### Fritto Misto  *Italian*    21 | 12 | 19 | $22

**Santa Monica** | 601 Colorado Ave. (6th St.) | 310-458-2829
**Hermosa Beach** | 316 Pier Ave. (Monterey Blvd.) | 310-318-6098

"Picky" pastaphiles praise the "customizable" plates at these "crowd-pleasing" Italians in Hermosa Beach and Santa Monica also boasting bargain wines and a "liberal" $2 corkage policy; "there's not much in the way of ambiance", but the "laid-back" settings and "kid-friendly" vibe keep them "crowded", so occasional "waits" are to be expected.

### Fromin's Deli  *Deli*    14 | 9 | 16 | $18

**Santa Monica** | 1832 Wilshire Blvd. (19th St.) | 310-829-5443
**Encino** | 17615 Ventura Blvd. (bet. Encino & White Oak Aves.) | 818-990-6346

"East Coast" expats in search of "New York flavor" seek out these rather "basic" separately owned delis in Encino and Santa Monica where "seasoned" servers deliver "piles" of pickles, "real brisket" and bowls of matzo ball soup to the "early bird set" in "drab" "1970s"-style digs; several surveyors kvetch these "throwbacks" are "past their glory days" and "too expensive" to boot, but true Angelenos attest they're "ok", if only for the "convenient parking."

### Fu-Shing  *Chinese*                        19 | 11 | 18 | $23

**Pasadena** | 2960 E. Colorado Blvd. (El Nido Ave.) | 626-792-8898 | www.fu-shing.com

"Firecracker"-hot Sichuan specialties augment the well-priced menu of "high-quality" Sino standards at this "better-than-average" Pasadena "standby" that locals label a "favorite for takeout"; even if the "endearingly shabby" bi-level digs "need redecorating" most appreciate the "quiet sound level" and "efficient service."

### Gaby's                                    19 | 7 | 14 | $18
**Mediterranean** ● *Lebanese/Mediterranean*

**Marina del Rey** | 20 Washington Blvd. (Stanford Ave.) | 310-821-9721
**West LA** | 10445 Venice Blvd. (Motor Ave.) | 310-559-1808
**Gaby's Express**  *Mediterranean*
**Marina del Rey** | 3216 Washington Blvd. (Lincoln Blvd.) | 310-823-7299
www.gabysexpress.com

For a "nutritious alternative to fast food", "munch lazily through several meze" at these "casual" cafes specializing in "inexpensive", "full-of-flavor" Lebanese-Mediterranean meals that are "reliably good"; the West LA outpost is "half-a-block from the beach" and recently underwent a major renovation, while the Marina del Rey branches are "great" for "family takeout."

### Gale's  Ⓜ *Italian*                        24 | 18 | 22 | $31
**Pasadena** | 452 S. Fair Oaks Ave. (Bellevue Dr.) | 626-432-6705 | www.galesrestaurant.com

"One of Pasadena's not-so-well-kept secrets", this "bustling" Northern Italian "gem" attracts "locals in-the-know" for "magnificent pastas" and "stellar" regional dishes that taste "like someone's grandmother from Sienna is in the kitchen making them by hand"; the "informal" brick-and-marble-clad space gets a "warm" touch from "welcoming" owner Gale Kohl while prices that are an "incredible value" ensure most customers "keep coming back."

### Galletto Bar and Grill  *Brazilian/Italian*   ▽ 23 | 15 | 17 | $37
**Westlake Village** | Westlake Plaza | 982 S. Westlake Blvd. (bet. Agoura & Townsgate Rds.) | 805-449-4300 | www.gallettobarandgrill.com

A "big-city vibe" prevails at this Westlake Village boîte where "killer caipirinhas" kick off a "moderately priced" meal of "inspired" Brazilian and Italian eats set to the tunes of live jazz, rock and soul; because the "energetic" atmosphere can "slow" the service and make the white-tablecloth space "tough for conversation", some suggest you hit it "before the evening rush."

### Galley, The  *Seafood/Steak*                18 | 17 | 20 | $35
**Santa Monica** | 2442 Main St. (bet. Ocean Park & Pico Blvds.) | 310-452-1934 | www.thegalleyrestaurant.net

It's "Xmas all year round" at this "campy" Santa Monica "dive" that "hasn't changed in decades" with holiday lights, "big booths", nautical details and wood paneling lending it a certain "crusty appeal"; a few longtimers lament that "prices have climbed" in recent years, though the "well-mixed drinks" and "large portions" of solid surf 'n' turf-style eats remain the same.

### Gardens  *Californian/Mediterranean*  | 23 | 25 | 25 | $67 |

**Beverly Hills** | Four Seasons Hotel | 300 S. Doheny Dr. (Burton Way) | 310-273-2222 | www.fourseasons.com

A well-heeled crowd lingers over a "leisurely" meal at this "luxurious" hideaway in the Beverly Hills Four Seasons Hotel where "excellent" servers roll out "fine" Cal-Med cuisine with an "abundant" Sunday brunch "worth every penny and calorie"; though a recent renovation expanded the patio dining area, the indoor space awash in reds and golds remains as "lovely" as ever and a prime source of excellent "people-watching."

### Gardens on Glendon  *Californian*  | 19 | 21 | 19 | $37 |

**Westwood** | 1139 Glendon Ave. (Lindbrook Dr.) | 310-824-1818 | www.gardensonglendon.com

Regulars report "no surprises and no disappointments" at this "pleasant" pick in Westwood that's long been a destination for "well-prepared" Californian "comfort food" (the guacamole made tableside "is still the must-have") in "pleasant" roomy surroundings with "twinkling lights" and trees sprouting up through the floor; despite a few grumbles about "expensive" tabs and "spotty service", most appreciate its "convenient" location near UCLA's Royce Hall and The Geffen Playhouse, and add that "considering the alternatives in the area", it's one of the "best bets."

### Gate of India  *Indian*  ∇ | 21 | 13 | 13 | $26 |

**Santa Monica** | 115 Santa Monica Blvd. (Ocean Ave.) | 310-656-1664

Chowhounds cherish the "outstanding curries" at this Santa Monica subcontinental where the "seriously rich" specialties prove a "reliable" choice for an inexpensive Indian meal; cynics, however, chafe at "cramped" conditions and say the less-than-stellar service "mars" an otherwise appealing meal.

### Gaucho Grill  *Argentinean/Steak*  | 17 | 14 | 17 | $26 |

**Brentwood** | 11754 San Vicente Blvd. (Gorham Ave.) | 310-447-7898
**Santa Monica** | 1251 Third St. Promenade (3rd St.) | 310-394-4966
**Pasadena** | 121 W. Colorado Blvd. (bet. De Lacey & Pasadena Aves.) | 626-683-3580
**Studio City** | 12050 Ventura Blvd. (Laurel Canyon Blvd.) | 818-508-1030
**Woodland Hills** | 6435 Canoga Ave. (Victory Blvd.) | 818-992-6416
www.gauchogrillrestaurant.com

"Addictive" chimichurri dipping sauce spices up the "hearty" plates of grilled steaks and chicken at this "reliable" Argentinean chain "meat mecca" catering to "families" with spacious digs and a "budget-friendly" bill; sticklers say they're "nothing special" and add that "distracted" service detracts, though if you "manage your expectations", many maintain you'll leave "satisfied."

### Geisha House ◐ *Japanese*  | 20 | 25 | 18 | $50 |

**Hollywood** | 6633 Hollywood Blvd. (Cherokee Ave.) | 323-460-6300 | www.geishahousehollywood.com

"Once a celebrity magnet", this "glammed-up" Hollywood Japanese may not attract the "A-listers" it used to, but it still stirs up a "sexy" "scene" thanks to plenty of "potent cocktails", "unusual" sushi rolls and slick red-and-black "Tokyo"-themed decor that screams "sensory overload"; in spite of many who deem it "outrageously" priced and "overrated" to boot, even if it's "not cool anymore", "trendsetters" grudgingly admit it's still "a great deal of fun."

**Genghis Cohen** *Chinese* — 20 | 14 | 18 | $29

**Fairfax** | 740 N. Fairfax Ave. (Melrose Ave.) | 323-653-0640
Your "bubbe would love" this midpriced Fairfax Sino specializing in "New Yorkish" Chinese "staples" like "thick egg rolls", crispy duck and non-kosher Sichuan standards "with a twist"; though it attracts an "interesting mix of young and old", some patrons are put off by "cranky" service and "tired decor" and say the nightly live music in the adjacent performance space can make the dining area too "noisy."

**Gennaro's Ristorante** ⊠ *Italian* — ▽ 20 | 20 | 22 | $47

**Glendale** | 1109 N. Brand Blvd. (Dryden St.) | 818-243-6231 | www.gennarosristorante.com
Insiders insist this "off-the-radar" Glendale Italian is a "real find" for its "well-prepared" pastas, "professional" service and "quiet, elegant" candlelit setting; it's certainly not "edgy" and a few entrees may "occasionally miss the mark", yet it remains a local "standard" for celebrating "special occasions."

**☑ Geoffrey's** *Californian* — 21 | 27 | 21 | $59

**Malibu** | 27400 PCH (¼ mi. west of Latigo Canyon Rd.) | 310-457-1519 | www.geoffreysmalibu.com
"It's all about the amazing views" at this mostly open-air eatery "perched over the Pacific" on the "Malibu Riviera" where those looking for "romance" revel in the "dreamy" setting and nibble on "prettily arranged" Californian cuisine; though the less-smitten single out "inconsistent" service and "outrageously expensive" tabs as cause for complaint, supporters swear all are "easy to overlook" given the "stunning" setting.

**George's Greek Café** *Greek* — 22 | 14 | 20 | $22

**Downtown** | Seventh Street Market Pl. | 735 S. Figueroa St., Ste. 131 (7th St.) | 213-624-6542 ⊠
**Long Beach** | 318 Pine Ave. (bet. 3rd & 4th Sts.) | 562-437-1184
**Long Beach** | 5316 E. Second St. (Pomona Ave.) | 562-433-1755
www.georgesgreekcafe.com
A homegrown Greek chain with "lots of heart", this "casual" trio showcases "satisfying" Hellenic cooking "at its unfussy best" with "hearty" plates of souvlaki and saganaki dished up at "very low prices"; what it lacks in "atmosphere", it makes up for in "exuberance", with a "bustling" crowd, "nice outside patios" and live music featured at both Long Beach locations.

**Getty Center, Restaurant at the** ⓜ *Californian* — 22 | 25 | 22 | $46

**Brentwood** | The Getty Ctr. | 1200 Getty Center Dr. (N. Sepulveda Blvd.) | 310-440-6810 | www.getty.edu
Gallery-goers make a beeline for this "pristine and airy venue" "beautifully sited" in the Getty museum complex offering "glorious" views of the hills and "flavorful" market-driven Californian cuisine "nicely served" by an "attentive" staff; in spite of "quite pricey" tabs, groupies

gush it's the "perfect place" to take "out-of-town guests" for a "leisurely lunch" or "civilized dinner" (on weekends only) – and the best part is you can "walk it all off" afterwards in the "lovely" gardens below.

### NEW Giggles 'n Hugs  *American*

| | | | - | - | - | I |

West LA | 11701 Wilshire Blvd. (Barrington Ave.) | 310-478-4847 | www.gigglesnhugs.com

It's all about kids at this rollicking pre-tween party palace in West LA featuring child-size tables, mini-cars, makeup stations and games galore; dishes have giggle-worthy names such as Madeleine's Milanese and Gaston's Grilled Ham and Cheese, and come at prices that will make parents grin.

### Z Gina Lee's Bistro M  *Asian/Californian*

26 | 15 | 23 | $40

Redondo Beach | Riviera Plaza | 211 Palos Verdes Blvd. (bet. Catalina Ave. & PCH) | 310-375-4462

Owners Scott and Gina Lee "make everyone feel welcome" at their "foodie" "favorite" in a Redondo Beach strip mall featuring a "tantalizing" lineup of "beautifully presented", "affordable" Cal-Asian dishes, including their "outstanding" signature crispy catfish that "loyal" locals deem a "must"; the sole drawback is that the "small", "nicely decorated" interior can be "as loud as a frat party" – if "acoustics" are an issue, "go early."

### Gingergrass  *Vietnamese*

21 | 14 | 17 | $22

Silver Lake | 2396 Glendale Blvd. (Brier Ave.) | 323-644-1600 | www.gingergrass.com

"California-ized" Vietnamese cooking takes center stage at this Silver Lake standby specializing in "light and healthy" renditions of South Asian dishes – like wok-tossed noodles and "refreshing" housemade drinks and elixirs – deemed "darn tasty" by fans who also like the "reasonable" prices; though it cultivates a "happening" vibe, the modern-industrial setting makes for "noisy" dining while its "popularity" makes it "hard to get a seat on weekends."

### Giorgio Baldi M  *Italian*

24 | 17 | 18 | $70

Santa Monica | 114 W. Channel Rd. (PCH) | 310-573-1660 | www.giorgiobaldi.com

"Dark and De Niro-esque", this "romantic" Santa Monica Italian brings in the "glitterati" and "wealthy locals" for its "fabulous" fare like "homemade ravioli" and "sublime" specials tagged with prices that just might "make your eyes pop"; though the "stargazing" shines, considering constant "waits" and "cramped" conditions, noncelebs deem it "not worth the trouble" and say the "attitude" from "haughty" servers can leave you needing "Xanax."

### Girasole Cucina Italiana S M  *Italian*

23 | 16 | 22 | $31

Hancock Park | 225½ N. Larchmont Blvd. (bet. Beverly Blvd. & 3rd St.) | 323-464-6978 | www.girasolecucina.com/Girasole/Main.html

"A tiny place with big flavor", this "informal" Hancock Park Italian delivers "delish" dishes from the Veneto region like "homemade pastas" and "melt-in-your-mouth" osso buco all "served with care" in a "shoe box" of a space with sidewalk seating out front ("reservations are essential"); its BYO policy with no corkage fee "keeps the bill down" as well, making it also "one of the best deals in town."

| | FOOD | DECOR | SERVICE | COST |
|---|---|---|---|---|

### NEW Gjelina  American
**-** | **-** | **-** | **M**

**Venice** | 1429 Abbot Kinney Blvd. (California Ave.) | 310-450-1429
This Venice newcomer's name is a mouthful, and so is its midpriced New American cuisine, built around what's available at local farmer's markets; the 'green' space, made of old brick and reclaimed wood and adorned with recycled chandeliers, boasts a groaning board of charcuterie and a trio of communal tables, plus a fire pit on the back patio.

### Gladstone's Malibu  Seafood
**14** | **18** | **14** | **$39**

**Pacific Palisades** | 17300 PCH (Sunset Blvd.) | 310-573-0212 | www.gladstones.com
"Tourists meet the ocean" at this beachfront seafooder in Pacific Palisades moving "monstrous" portions of "lackluster" fin fare in a "crowded" outdoor setting offering "unparalleled views" of the coast; considering the "lax" service, "pesky seagulls" and "premium" pricing, most locals are content to cede it to "out-of-towners", but if you must, insiders instruct: "buy a drink, look at the sunset, then go home."

### Golden Deli  ⊅ Vietnamese
**23** | **7** | **11** | **$11**

**San Gabriel** | Las Tunas Plaza | 815 W. Las Tunas Dr. (Mission Dr.) | 626-308-0803 | www.goldendelirestaurant.com
Devotees "devour" big bowls of "intensely aromatic" pho, and other "deliriously delicious" dishes at this bare-bones San Gabriel Vietnamese where one has to "make a big effort to spend more than $15"; though "long waits" (even with "rushed service") and "crowded" quarters prove a deterrent to some, converts claim it's "worth every jostle."

### Z Gonpachi  Japanese
**18** | **27** | **19** | **$51**

**Beverly Hills** | 134 N. La Cienega Blvd. (Wilshire Blvd.) | 310-659-8887 | www.globaldiningca.com
Simply "stunning" say surveyors of this sprawling Beverly Hills Japanese, a multileveled "complex" constructed from actual folk dwellings that evokes a shogun's palace with other "authentic" architectural details like a Zen garden and tatami rooms; given the "high expectations" aroused by the "exquisite" decor, some are let down by the rather "ordinary" "high-priced" sushi, "homemade" soba and robata dishes and uneven service, but many proclaim it "promising" and are rooting for it to "iron out the kinks."

### Gordon Biersch  Pub Food
**16** | **16** | **16** | **$23**

**Pasadena** | 41 Hugus Alley (Colorado Blvd.) | 626-449-0052
**Burbank** | 145 S. San Fernando Blvd. (Angeleno Ave.) | 818-569-5240
www.gordonbiersch.com
"Beer is the star" of this "upbeat" brewpub chain where the "pretty standard" American grub plays second fiddle to the suds (though aficionados say the "to-die-for garlic fries" are the thing to order); the "too loud" decibel levels don't seem to faze its "rollicking" "frat-boy" following.

### NEW Gordon Ramsay  Continental
**-** | **-** | **-** | **E**

**West Hollywood** | The London West Hollywood | 1020 N. San Vicente Blvd. (Sunset Blvd.) | 310-358-7788 | www.gordonramsay.com
The first West Coast opening by Gordon Ramsay is a budget-busting modern Continental set in the hyperelegant London West Hollywood hotel; in contrast to Ramsay's Sweeney Todd–like persona on TV's *Hell's Kitchen,* his eponymous eatery is a raw-ther sedate place

adorned with gold filigree and brocade, off-white marble and an impressive view from the picture windows; perhaps for a few extra dollars, Gordo will come to your table and call you a 'bleeping yob.'

### Gorikee ⓂCalifornian    22 | 11 | 20 | $29

**Woodland Hills** | Warner Plaza Shopping Ctr. | 21799 Ventura Blvd. (bet. Canoga Ave. & Topanga Canyon Blvd.) | 818-932-9149

"Palate-pleasing" Californian cuisine is made all the more "intriguing" by "Asian influences" and a garlic-centric focus at this Woodland Hills eatery also earning praise for its "polite service" and "bargain" prices; its "unfortunate" strip-mall setting doesn't win any raves, but even if it's "hard to find", most maintain it's "worth the search."

### Grace Ⓜ American    25 | 24 | 25 | $60

**Beverly Boulevard** | 7360 Beverly Blvd. (Fuller Ave.) | 323-934-4400 | www.gracerestaurant.com

"Classy, classy, classy" describes chef-owner Neal Fraser's "elegantly understated" "gem" on Beverly Boulevard that acts as "a magnet to the stars" thanks to its "cozy, clubby" atmosphere, "striking" New American dishes, "to-die-for" desserts ("save room for the doughnut holes" on Wednesdays) and "interesting" wine list, all overseen by a "professional" staff; although a few exclaim "oh, those prices!", the vast majority designates it a "gourmet's dream."

### Grand Lux Cafe Eclectic    18 | 18 | 18 | $28

**Beverly Hills** | Beverly Ctr. | 121 N. La Cienega Blvd. (bet. Beverly Blvd. & 3rd St.) | 310-855-1122 | www.grandluxcafe.com

"Spun-off from the Cheesecake Factory", this somewhat "fancier" version in the Beverly Center features an "everything-for-everybody" Eclectic menu that spans the globe and arrives in "huge", "tasty" portions; if vaguely Venetian decor and "speedy" "aspiring-actor" service aren't enough, it's "not too expensive" either.

### Great Greek Greek    21 | 16 | 20 | $29

**Sherman Oaks** | 13362 Ventura Blvd. (bet. Dixie Canyon & Nagle Aves.) | 818-905-5250 | www.greatgreek.com

The "ouzo is always flowing" at this "exhilarating" Sherman Oaks Greek that's like "one big noisy party" complete with a live band, "plate breaking" and "dancing waiters" adding to the overall "convivial" feel; the "traditional" Hellenic fare is "tasty" too – some just wish the "music would stop just long enough to order."

### Greenblatt's Deli & Fine Wines ● Deli    18 | 12 | 15 | $21

**Hollywood** | 8017 Sunset Blvd. (Laurel Ave.) | 323-656-0606

"Generous helpings" of "Jewish comfort food" get washed down with "Merlot" instead of Cel-Ray at this Hollywood deli "standby" famed for its "restorative" matzo ball soup, "tasty sandwiches" and "marvelous" in-house wine shop; no one minds the "nothing fancy" interior given that service is swift and they're open till 1 AM – "the only bummer" is the somewhat "pricey" tabs.

### Green Field Churrascaria Brazilian    21 | 16 | 19 | $37

**Long Beach** | 5305 E. PCH (Anaheim St.) | 562-597-0906 | www.greenfieldchurrascaria.com

(continued)

*(continued)*

### Green Field Churrascaria

**West Covina** | 381 N. Azusa Ave. (Workman Ave.) | 626-966-2300 |
www.greenfieldbbq.com

"Meat, meat and more meat" lies in store at these Long Beach and West Covina Brazilian chain links specializing in a huge "variety" of "skewered" cuts proffered by "gallivanting" gaucho-clad waiters who load up your plate with BBQ until you "just can't take it anymore"; "romantic, it's not", but it's a "pleasant" pick for a festive meal and "gluttons" say you get "good value for your money" too.

### Green Street Restaurant  *American*                ▁ | ▁ | ▁ | I

**Pasadena** | 146 Shoppers Ln. (Cordova St.) | 626-577-7170 |
www.greenstreetrestaurant.com

On a Pasadena street chock-full of small-town charm, this warmly decorated cafe remains a local standby thanks to its crowd-pleasing menu of Traditional American favorites like their signature salad Dianne; the casual space boasts a shaded patio, and its location just off the area's main shopping drag makes it a natural draw for the ladies-who-lunch.

### NEW Green Street Tavern  *Californian/European*   23 | 18 | 20 | $29

**Pasadena** | 69 W. Green St. (De Lacey Ave.) | 626-229-9961 |
www.greenstreettavern.net

Pasadenans praise this "divine new arrival" "on the edge of Old Town" sending out "uniformly well-prepared" meals of Californian cuisine with European touches in an "attractive" earth-toned space exuding a "masculine elegance"; some say it's still finding its footing with service, but "reasonable prices" mean it "has the makings" of a "solid" new "neighborhood choice."

### Griddle Cafe, The  *American*                      22 | 11 | 16 | $17

**Hollywood** | 7916 Sunset Blvd. (bet. N. Fairfax & N. Hayworth Aves.) |
323-874-0377 | www.thegriddlecafe.com

The "holy mother" of LA pancake houses, this "sceney" breakfast and lunch-only Hollywood American slings "hangover-killing" standards – like "incredible flapjacks" and "wonderful egg dishes" – in "coma-inducing" portions while the solid service comes via a "cute", "aspiring actor" staff; the "tiny" space makes for a perpetually "jammed" interior, though regulars report it's "worth the wait (but boy will you wait)."

### Grill on Hollywood, The  *American*                22 | 21 | 22 | $43

**Hollywood** | Hollywood & Highland Ctr. | 6801 Hollywood Blvd.
(Highland Ave.) | 323-856-5530 | www.thegrill.com

"Solid in every way" praise proponents of this American "standby", an offshoot of The Grill on the Alley, serving up "expertly cooked" chops and steaks in "classy" deco surroundings that befit the "pricey" tabs; given its Hollywood & Highland address, it caters to a tourist-heavy clientele, and though the original is a tough reservation, you "can almost always walk in" here, making it a "best bet" for the area.

### ☑ Grill on the Alley, The  *American*              24 | 20 | 24 | $58

**Beverly Hills** | 9560 Dayton Way (Wilshire Blvd.) | 310-276-0615 |
www.thegrill.com

"Showbiz insiders" swear the "charm has not faded" from this "expensive" Beverly Hills American "icon" hosting a "heavy-hitting"

| | FOOD | DECOR | SERVICE | COST |
|---|---|---|---|---|

lunchtime crowd ("directors, agents, stars") for "outstanding" steaks and chops set down by "warm", "witty waiters" in a "comfortable" room oozing with "old-style glamour"; though dinner is a quieter affair (with the "coveted" green-leather booths up for grabs), even without the "priceless people-watching", regulars report it's "never a disappointment."

### Grub *American*  19 | 15 | 17 | $19

**Hollywood** | 911 N. Seward St. (bet. Melrose Ave. & Santa Monica Blvd.) | 323-461-3663 | www.grub-la.com

Boosters boast this "quirky" and "sweet" daytime Hollywood eatery "hits the spot" with "wholesome" American comfort fare like "creamy tomato soup" (served with a grilled-cheese sandwich) and say "you'll feel right at home" in its "colorful" converted bungalow setting with "pleasant" patio seating; service is "suitably casual", so the mood remains "relaxed" in spite of "cramped" environs and "noisy" acoustics; N.B. dinner service is reportedly in the works.

### Guelaguetza *Mexican*  22 | 11 | 16 | $19

**Huntington Park** | 2560 E. Gage Ave. (bet. Pacific Blvd. & Rugby Ave.) | 323-277-9899
**Koreatown** | 3014 W. Olympic Blvd. (S. Normandie Ave.) | 213-427-0608
**Koreatown** | 3337½ W. Eighth St. (Irolo St.) | 213-427-0601
**Lynwood** | 11215 Long Beach Blvd., Ste. 1010 (Beechwood Ave.) | 310-884-9234
**Palms** | 11127 Palms Blvd. (Sepulveda Blvd.) | 310-837-1153
www.guelaguetzarestaurante.com

A "fiesta" of "exceptional moles" heads up the menu at these separately owned Mexicans dotted across LA turning out "real-deal" Oaxacan dishes like "flawless" banana leaf–wrapped tamales and other dishes deemed a "revelation" in their "complexity"; in spite of "divey" decor, they maintain a "family-friendly" feel with live mariachi and "great bang for your buck."

### Guido's *Italian*  19 | 19 | 22 | $42

**Malibu** | 3874 Cross Creek Rd. (PCH) | 310-456-1979 | www.guidosmalibu.com
**West LA** | 11980 Santa Monica Blvd. (Bundy Dr.) | 310-820-6649

"Old-school charm" abounds at these "retro" twins on the Westside "still cranking out" "reliable" renditions of Northern Italian classics in a "dimly lit" atmosphere with "comfortable" leather booths adding to the "'70s" feel; the West LA outpost gets a boost from "tuxedoed waiters" and tableside presentations, while Malibu is a more casual affair that loyalists liken to the *Cheers* of the neighborhood.

### Gulfstream *American/Seafood*  21 | 20 | 20 | $39

**Century City** | Westfield Century City Shopping Ctr. | 10250 Santa Monica Blvd. (bet. Ave. of the Stars & Century Park W.) | 310-553-3636 | www.hillstone.com

"Yuppies" munch and "mingle" at this "upscale" Houston's offshoot in Century City that specializes in "solid, if not dynamic" seafood dishes – like a "tremendous tuna burger" – and also plays host to a "lively" "after-work" bar scene; an "efficient" staff provides solid service, though some complain the constant "buzz" ("and the occasional crash") from the open kitchen creates an overall "noisy" atmosphere.

| | FOOD | DECOR | SERVICE | COST |
|---|---|---|---|---|

### Gumbo Pot  Cajun

| | 19 | 7 | 13 | $14 |
|---|---|---|---|---|

**Fairfax** | Grove at Farmers Mkt. | 6333 W. Third St. (Fairfax Ave.) |
323-933-0358 | www.thegumbopotla.com

"Cajun cravings" are well-sated by this "dependable" food stall "in the
heart of the Farmers Market" on Fairfax offering up "down-home"
"'N'Awlins'" grub like gumbo and po' boys plus chicory coffee and beig-
nets; though it's cheap and counter service is "fast" (if a little "gruff"),
a number of "native New Orleanians" claim the food may taste "decent", but "it's not anything close to authentic."

### NEW Gus's BBQ  BBQ

| | - | - | - | I |
|---|---|---|---|---|

**South Pasadena** | 808 Fair Oaks Ave. (Mission St.) | 626-799-3251 |
www.gussbbq.com

The new owners of this venerable (circa 1946) South Pas rib shop take
their 'cue from the past, albeit with some modern updates: the setting's been remodeled with dark-wood floors, pewter ceiling tiles, a
new bar and booths, and the menu includes meats done Memphis-
and St. Louis–style plus non-BBQ entrees such as dry-aged steaks and
sides-of-the-moment (e.g. pecan rice and sugar snap peas); low
prices are a retro touch.

### NEW Gyenari Korean BBQ & Lounge  Korean

| | - | - | - | M |
|---|---|---|---|---|

**Culver City** | 9540 Culver Blvd. (W. Washington Blvd.) | 310-838-3131 |
www.gyenari.com

Downtown Culver City's culinary jigsaw puzzle gets another piece with
this barbecue arrival, an upscale Korean with a modern menu and an impressive cocktail selection; the space boasts a massive mountainscape
mural and 32 tables on which to grill your own beef, pork and chicken.

### Gyu-Kaku  Japanese

| | 20 | 17 | 18 | $31 |
|---|---|---|---|---|

**Beverly Hills** | 163 N. La Cienega Blvd. (Clifton Way) | 310-659-5760
**West LA** | 10925 W. Pico Blvd. (bet. Kelton & Midvale Aves.) | 310-234-8641
**Torrance** | Cross Road Plaza | 24631 Crenshaw Blvd. (Sky Park Dr.) |
310-325-1437
**Pasadena** | 70 W. Green St. (De Lacey Ave.) | 626-405-4842
**Canoga Park** | 6600 Topanga Canyon Blvd. (Victory Blvd.) |
310-415-7555  🅢 🅜
**Sherman Oaks** | 14457 Ventura Blvd. (Van Nuys Blvd.) | 818-501-5400
www.gyu-kaku.com

"Interactive dining" is the draw at this Japanese yakiniku chain where
you can "be your own chef" and "grill up" "tasty morsels" of "tender"
meats (like "genuine Kobe beef") and veggies in "lively" contemporary
settings that prove "great for groups"; the less-enthusiastic find fault
with "skimpy portions" and "top-dollar" prices and say that once the
"novelty" wears off, they're left feeling "hungry and broke."

### NEW Hall, The  French

| | - | - | - | M |
|---|---|---|---|---|

**West Hollywood** | Palihouse | 8465 Holloway Dr. (La Cienega Blvd.) |
323-656-4020 | www.palihouse.com

Few have found this under-the-radar new eatery in West Hollywood's
Palihouse hotel, but those who have laud it as a "nice addition" to the
area with a French brasserie–style menu served up by a "knowledgeable" staff in "modern" surroundings with metallic banquettes and a
"beautiful" shaded courtyard; moderate tabs may help gain it a local
following, though for now it's mostly populated with hotel guests.

| | FOOD | DECOR | SERVICE | COST |
|---|---|---|---|---|

### Hal's Bar & Grill  *American* | 20 | 19 | 18 | $37 |

**Venice** | 1349 Abbot Kinney Blvd. (bet. Main St. & Venice Blvd.) |
310-396-3105 | www.halsbarandgrill.com

"Always bustling", this "classic" Abbot Kinney "hangout" proves a
"home away from home" for Venice locals thanks to its "cool" art-filled
setting, "can't-go-wrong" New American menu and "sweet bartenders" who pour some of "the strongest cocktails on the Westside";
though it "can get a bit noisy", "inexpensive" prices win over the "diverse" crowd, as do "great gimmicks" like live jazz on Sundays and
Mondays and half-price wines available on Tuesdays.

### Hamasaku  ☒ *Japanese* | 26 | 18 | 21 | $61 |

**West LA** | 11043 Santa Monica Blvd. (Sepulveda Blvd.) | 310-479-7636 |
www.hamasakula.com

Those smitten with this "trendy" West LA sushi specialist "salivate
just thinking about" the "phenomenal" menu offering "unique tastes
for the palate" with "designer" rolls, "artistic" cooked creations and
"flashy desserts" that may not please "purists", but are "spectacular"
nonetheless; though the strip-mall digs are on the modest side, given
its reputation as a "hot-shot" "hangout", expect a palpable "buzz"
along with "celebrity pricing"; N.B. a Melrose branch in the former
Kumo space is set to open this fall.

### Hama Sushi  *Japanese* | 21 | 14 | 18 | $38 |

**Venice** | 213 Windward Ave. (Main St.) | 310-396-8783 |
www.hamasushi.com

"Incredibly fresh" sushi and free-flowing sake come together at this
Venice "tradition" – a fixture on the "local party scene" – where a
"friendly" team delivers "perfectly prepared" fish in a "rock 'n' roll" setting so "hip" "you feel like you're invading the practice space for a garage
band"; those preferring a more "beachy setting" commandeer a table
on the spacious patio that's "delightful" on a "warm summer evening."

### Hamburger Mary's  ◑ *Diner* | 15 | 14 | 15 | $20 |

**West Hollywood** | 8288 Santa Monica Blvd. (Sweetzer Ave.) | 323-654-3800 |
www.hamburgermarysweho.com

Like a "gay TGI Fridays", this West Hollywood American pulls in a
"freaky" crowd for "happy-hour drinks" and "basic bar food" in a "tacky-
chic" setting where there's "always a party" going on (Wednesday's
"dragalicious" Bingo Night is a "hoot"); there's "plenty of eye candy to
tantalize" – especially the "servers" – so even if it's "not a place to
bring your parents", "it's a fun night out with the boys" nonetheless.

### Hamlet Restaurant  *American* | 16 | 15 | 17 | $22 |
### (fka Hamburger Hamlet)

**West Hollywood** | 9201 Sunset Blvd. (N. Doheny Dr.) |
310-278-4924
**West LA** | 2927 Sepulveda Blvd. (National Blvd.) | 310-478-1546
**Pasadena** | 214 S. Lake Ave. (bet. E. Colorado & E. Del Mar Blvds.) |
626-449-8520
**Sherman Oaks** | 4419 Van Nuys Blvd. (Ventura Blvd.) | 818-784-1183
www.hamletrestaurants.com

"Despite the name change" and "menu upgrade", longtime loyalists
say this "enduring and endearing" mini-chain remains a "steady fallback" for "affordable" American fare like "big, juicy burgers", frosty

| | FOOD | DECOR | SERVICE | COST |
|---|---|---|---|---|

"schooners" of beer and an "extensive lineup" of lighter salads, soups and sandwiches for "health conscious" diners; although "throwback decor" with "dark-wood paneling" makes it an "enjoyable" "time warp" for some (you can still sit at Dean Martin's table at the Sunset branch) ex-allies label it a "has-been" and say the new identity "can't disguise" that it's "just not what is used to be."

**🄩 Hampton's** 🄼 *Californian*                    | 23 | 27 | 26 | $62 |

**Westlake Village** | Four Seasons Westlake Vill. | 2 Dole Dr. (Lindero Canyon Rd.) | 818-575-3000 | www.fourseasons.com

"East Coast sophistication" comes to Westlake Village via this "elegant" "fine-dining" room inside the Four Seasons hotel featuring a "light", "innovative" Californian menu – think "spa food", only less "froufrou" – crafted from the "freshest ingredients" and served by a "respectful" team that "never rushes" you; though enthusiasts insist the "serene" red-and-gold setting with "wonderful views" of the gardens and waterfalls stands up to the "beautifully presented" cuisine, the less-impressed are irked by "big prices" given such "small servings" and wish it weren't so "focused on being healthful."

**Hard Rock Cafe** *American*                    | 14 | 23 | 16 | $24 |

**Universal City** | Universal CityWalk | 1000 Universal Studios Blvd. (off Rte. 101) | 818-622-7625 | www.hardrock.com

An "iconic part of the tourist landscape", this rock 'n' roll–themed American chain link in Universal CityWalk was "cool" once but many feel it's "past its sell date", citing "mundane" grub, "haphazard" service and "way too loud" acoustics; despite a "surprisingly decent burger", "kid"-friendly vibe and all that "fun music memorabilia", some opt to "buy the T-shirt" instead.

**Harold & Belle's** *Creole*                    ▽ | 24 | 15 | 21 | $30 |

**Mid-City** | 2920 W. Jefferson Blvd. (bet. Arlington Ave. & Crenshaw Blvd.) | 323-735-3376

Cognoscenti claim this "wonderful" Mid-City staple is "as good as it gets" for Creole cuisine with "sinfully good" specialties like "impressive étouffée" and jambalaya brought out in "amazingly huge" helpings that taste even "better as leftovers"; though the budget-conscious note it's "pricey" for the genre, boosters say that's only fair given that "sincere" service and an "elegant" New Orleans–themed dining room mean it's "a notch better" than competitors too.

**🄩 Hatfield's** 🄩 *American*                    | 27 | 20 | 25 | $66 |

**Beverly Boulevard** | 7458 Beverly Blvd. (Gardner St.) | 323-935-2977 | www.hatfieldsrestaurant.com

"Hats off!" cheer champions of "husband-and-wife duo" Quinn and Karen Hatfield's Beverly Boulevard "jewel" presenting an "intelligent" New American menu showcasing "bold and clean flavors" from "farm-fresh" ingredients in "memorable" à la carte selections or in a "luxurious" seven-course tasting menu; the "graceful" staff provides "smooth service", and if some customers quibble about the "spare", "tiny" space, proponents proclaim it's just proof that "great things come in small packages."

| | FOOD | DECOR | SERVICE | COST |
|---|---|---|---|---|

### Hayakawa Ⓜ Japanese | ▽ 28 | 15 | 20 | $41 |

Covina | 750 Terrado Plaza (bet. Citrus & Workman Aves.) | 626-332-8288
Sushi buffs are "blown away" by the "fresh" fin fare at this Covina Japanese boasting an "imaginative" omakase menu by chef Kazuhiko Hayakawa (ex Matsuhisa) who always "makes sure you leave happy"; though some say the atmosphere – with lanterns and Shoji screens – is "lacking", considering prices are a relative "bargain" "compared to other high-end restaurants", most maintain they'd "go back in a heartbeat."

### Heroes and Legends Pub Food | 17 | 17 | 18 | $21 |

Claremont | 131 N. Yale Ave. (bet. 1st & 2nd Sts.) | 909-621-6712
"College" kids cram into this "rowdy" "watering hole" in Claremont, where an "endless" variety of brews on tap pairs well with a "crowd-pleasing" menu of American "pub grub" plated in "huge" portions; though its "always packed" with a "shoulder-to-shoulder" crowd, regulars say it remains "relaxed" thanks to "friendly and fast enough" service and "comfortable" quarters with "peanut shells on the floor" and "sports" playing on the "high-def" TVs.

### NEW Hidden Restaurant Eclectic | 15 | 21 | 18 | $46 |

Santa Monica | 3110 Main St. (Marine St.) | 310-399-4800 | www.hiddenrestaurant.com
Diners can "mix-and-match" from five different cuisines (Italian, Mexican, Vietnamese, Japanese and Spanish) at this "funky" Santa Monica Eclectic literally "hidden" from the street, where "fancy cocktails" and a "DJ on weekends" add to the "nightclub"-esque feel; though loungers laud the "beautiful" setting, skeptics call the concept "overly ambitious" and say the "gigantic" menu results in "a muddle of unmemorable dishes" – why not "pick one style and perfect it"?

### Hide Sushi Ⓜ⇱ Japanese | 24 | 10 | 17 | $28 |

West LA | 2040 Sawtelle Blvd. (bet. La Grange & Mississippi Aves.) | 310-477-7242
"Delectable" sushi comes "without all the LA glitz" at this "been-there-forever" Little Osaka Japanese sending out "expertly cut" fish in a "family-style" setting that "utterly lacks pretension"; given the "unbeatable" prices that seem "blissfully unaware of inflation" champions claim that "curt service", a "cash-only policy" and "way-too-crowded" seating are just a few "small sacrifices" to make.

### Hirosuke Japanese | 19 | 12 | 18 | $32 |

Encino | Plaza de Oro | 17237 Ventura Blvd. (Louise Ave.) | 818-788-7548
An "early" entrant on the Ventura Boulevard sushi scene, this Encino Japanese earns kudos from "neighborhood" denizens for its "freshly prepared" fish, casual quarters and "reasonable prices"; although new ownership took over in 2008 and made few "significant changes to the menu or style", longtimers lament that "quality has dropped" and add that "just average" eats mean it's "no longer a first choice" for fans.

### Hirozen ⊠ Japanese | 25 | 12 | 19 | $40 |

Beverly Boulevard | 8385 Beverly Blvd. (Orlando Ave.) | West Hollywood | 323-653-0470 | www.hirozen.com
Despite its "unassuming" mini-mall locale, acolytes attest this Beverly Boulevard Japanese is "serious about sushi" with "innovative" chefs

offering an "exceptional" experience from the "meticulously crafted fish" and "unusual" cooked selections "right through to the beautifully presented desserts"; given that the "tiny" space only holds "a handful of tables", insiders insist you "call ahead for reservations" or try to snag "a seat at the bar."

**Hokusai** Ⓜ *French/Japanese*                         24 | 20 | 21 | $56

**Beverly Hills** | 8400 Wilshire Blvd. (S. Gale Dr.) | 323-782-9717 | www.hokusairestaurant.com

Situated "in the middle of no-man's land on Wilshire", this relative newcomer in Beverly Hills is gaining a following for its "inventive" French-Japanese creations like roasted salmon with lobster bisque sauce and "wonderfully fresh" sushi; given the well-appointed space and staff that "takes very good care" of you, allies insist it could be a "nice, little neighborhood restaurant" if only it weren't so "pricey."

**Holdren's Steaks & Seafood** *Steak*         ▽ 21 | 19 | 20 | $42

**Thousand Oaks** | 1714 Newbury Rd. (N. Ventu Park Rd.) | 805-498-1314 | www.holdrens.com

Carnivores claim you'll "clean your plate" at this surf 'n' turf duo in Santa Barbara and Thousand Oaks roping up cowboy-cut rib-eyes with all the trimmings at prices deemed "reasonable when you consider they all come with soup or salad"; both locations thrive in "crowded" quarters done up in dark-wood paneling with bustling bar areas, but if "noise" is an issue, "make sure to reserve a booth" ahead of time.

**Holly Street Bar & Grill** *Californian*         19 | 17 | 20 | $34

**Pasadena** | 175 E. Holly St. (bet. Marengo & Raymond Aves.) | 626-440-1421 | www.hollystreetbarandgrill.com

Tucked away in a "charming" "ivy-covered" brick building, this reasonably priced Pasadena mainstay offers a "wide range" of Californian "standards" in "laid-back" digs conducive to "quiet conversation"; things take a "lively" turn on weekends when "live jazz" takes over the front room, though the "lovely patio" provides an ideal respite "on a sunny day."

**Holy Cow Indian Express** *Indian*         ▽ 20 | 7 | 15 | $15

**Third Street** | 8474 W. Third St. (La Cienega Blvd.) | 323-852-8900 | www.holycowindianexpress.com

"Spice" buffs say they're "hooked" on this "little sister to Surya" on Third Street offering "amazing" "light" Indian fare at "modest prices" (the lunch menu especially "is an incredible value"); though servers working the cafeteria-style line are "cordial", digs have a "sparse" "fast-food" feel, so most "take out."

**NEW Honda-Ya** ❶ *Japanese*         22 | 16 | 19 | $25

**Little Tokyo** | Mitsuwa Shopping Ctr. | 333 S. Alameda St. (E. 3rd St.) | 213-625-1184

The "splendid" "little dishes" are made for "sharing" at this "traditional Japanese gastropub" in Little Tokyo where a "staggering variety" of inexpensive izakaya standards – like "perfectly cooked" yakitori – goes so well with "amazing sakes" and "beer" that "it's easy to drink too much"; bamboo detailing adds to the "authentic" feel while the tatami rooms are perfect for "carousing" in private.

|  | FOOD | DECOR | SERVICE | COST |
|---|---|---|---|---|

## NEW Hong Yei *Chinese*  — | — | — | I

**San Gabriel** | 288 S. San Gabriel Blvd. (B'way) | 626-614-8188
Diners get a lot of spice for their buck at this latest entry in the how-hot-can-you-make-it world of San Gabriel Valley Chinese; its understated, brightly lit room gets added glow from inexpensive dishes that begin at fiery and grow considerably more combustible from there.

## Hop Li *Chinese*  20 | 10 | 15 | $21

**Chinatown** | 526 Alpine St. (N. Hill St.) | 213-680-3939
**West LA** | 10974 W. Pico Blvd. (Westwood Blvd.) | 310-441-3708
**West LA** | 11901 Santa Monica Blvd. (Armacost Ave.) | 310-268-2463
**Arcadia** | 855 S. Baldwin Ave. (Huntington Dr.) | 626-445-3188 ●
www.hoplirestaurant.com
Hungry Angelenos "hop on over" to this "family-friendly" Chinese mini-chain favored for "tasty" Cantonese and Hong Kong–style cooking; though service is "abrupt" and "no-frills" decor "leaves much to be desired", spacious settings make them "great for large groups" and prices are such "a bargain", that fans find them "worth repeat trips."

## Hop Woo *Chinese*  18 | 9 | 13 | $19

**Chinatown** | 845 N. Broadway (bet. Alpine & College Sts.) | 213-617-3038 ●♿
**West LA** | 11110 W. Olympic Blvd. (S. Sepulveda Blvd.) | 310-575-3668
**Alhambra** | 1 W. Main St. (Garfield Ave.) | 626-289-7938
www.hopwoo.com
Chowhounds craving "Chinese comfort food" like BBQ duck and Cantonese seafood plates seek out these SoCal sibs serving up a "huge" variety of Sino specialties at "1950s prices"; though the "food comes out fast", foes fault the "too bright" settings and say that because the quality "fluctuates", "you never know what you'll be getting."

## ☑ Hotel Bel-Air Restaurant *Californian/French*  25 | 29 | 27 | $76

**Bel-Air** | Hotel Bel-Air | 701 Stone Canyon Rd. (Sunset Blvd.) | 310-472-1211 | www.hotelbelair.com
A "peaceful oasis" "far from the LA bustle", this "idyllic" Bel-Air "hideaway" is once again voted No. 1 for Decor thanks to its "utterly gorgeous" "lush" garden that "even Eden can't match" and "elegant" English-style interior that "makes any occasion a special one"; a "perfectly gracious" staff treats everyone "like an A-lister", so even if a few find the "elaborate" Cal-French feasts aren't as "transcendent" as the setting, acolytes insist it's an experience of "pure decadence" worthy of a "once-a-year treat" and the appropriately "celestial prices."

## House of Blues *Southern*  16 | 21 | 17 | $34

**West Hollywood** | 8430 Sunset Blvd. (Olive Dr.) | 323-848-5100 | www.hob.com
Reviewers report "surprisingly good fare for a concert venue" at this "down-home, feel-good" chain link in West Hollywood purveying a "standard" selection of "Southern comfort food" in a faux honky-tonk setting goosed up by "A-list" "band performances"; "loud, bustling" and always jammed with "tourists", it may be "nothing to write home about", though disciples sing "hallelujah for the Sunday gospel brunch."

| | FOOD | DECOR | SERVICE | COST |
|---|---|---|---|---|

### 🅩 Houston's  American          21 | 19 | 20 | $35

**Century City** | Westfield Century City Shopping Ctr. |
10250 Santa Monica Blvd. (bet. Ave. of the Stars & Century Park W.) |
310-557-1285
**Santa Monica** | 202 Wilshire Blvd. (2nd St.) | 310-576-7558
**Manhattan Beach** | Bristol Farms | 1550 Rosecrans Ave. (bet. Aviation &
Sepulveda Blvds.) | 310-643-7211
**Pasadena** | 320 S. Arroyo Pkwy. (Del Mar Blvd.) | 626-577-6001
www.hillstone.com

A "chain that doesn't feel like one", this "reliable" national franchise
"clicks" thanks to a "pretty darn good" menu of "all-American comfort" items (including a notoriously "addicting spinach dip") and a
"modern metropolitan" ambiance that brings in "mingling singles" after work; despite debate on the cost – "inexpensive" vs. "overpriced" –
most report "solid quality" here.

### Hugo's  Californian          21 | 14 | 19 | $24

**West Hollywood** | 8401 Santa Monica Blvd. (bet. Kings Rd. & Orlando Ave.) |
323-654-3993
**Studio City** | 12851 Riverside Dr. (Coldwater Canyon Ave.) | 818-761-8985
www.hugosrestaurant.com

"Bravo for a healthy alternative" say believers in this "recently updated" WeHo "favorite" and its "down-home" Studio City sib that deliver "delicious" Californian–New American fare ranging from "super
green" to "indulgent", prepared with sustainably produced meat and
produce; despite a few naysayers ("does anyone go to a restaurant to
eat mung beans?"), most tout their "fairly priced" "fabulous breakfasts", "hearty" dinners and "top-of-the-line" teas, plus a sprinkling of
"star sightings" too.

### Hump, The  Japanese          25 | 21 | 20 | $63

**Santa Monica** | Santa Monica Airport | 3221 Donald Douglas Loop S.
(Airport Ave.) | 310-313-0977 | www.thehump.biz

The "unexpected" setting "next to the runway at the Santa Monica
Airport" is actually a fitting spot to feast on fish "flown in from Japan"
among other "incredibly inventive" Nipponese cuisine at this "inviting" destination; connoisseurs commend the "uniquely presented"
omakase meu ("full of surprises"), but warn that even if eating sushi
"so fresh" it's "served with the head still moving" doesn't "shock" you,
the prices just might – so make sure your "wallet can handle it."

### NEW Hunan Seafood  Chinese          - | - | - | I

**Rosemead** | 8772 E. Valley Blvd. (Rosemead Blvd.) | 626-280-8389

While the decor and the name may be generic at this affordable
Rosemead newcomer, the range of Hunan seafood (such as fish-head
casserole and dried squid) in pungent sauces more than compensates;
those who like it hot will be pleased by the intensity of the peppers.

### Hungry Cat, The ⏺ Seafood          24 | 16 | 20 | $43

**Hollywood** | 1535 N. Vine St. (Sunset Blvd.) | 323-462-2155 |
www.thehungrycat.com

Chef-owner David Lentz (hubby of Lucques' Suzanne Goin) serves up a
"New England seafood fantasy" in an "austere" but recently "expanded"
Hollywood setting (with a Santa Barbara outpost) that draws a "hip"
crowd oozing "foodie energy"; raw bar specialties and other "inspired"

| | FOOD | DECOR | SERVICE | COST |
|---|---|---|---|---|

plates are washed down with "top-notch" cocktails, so it's "a blast" to "eat at the bar and watch the mixologists work their magic", and "perfect" for a "late-night snack" "after catching a flick at the ArcLight."

### Hurry Curry of Tokyo  *Japanese*
18 | 14 | 17 | $15

**West LA** | 2131 Sawtelle Blvd. (bet. Mississippi Ave. & Olympic Blvd.) | 310-473-1640
**Pasadena** | 37 S. Fair Oaks Ave. (Colorado Blvd.) | 626-792-8474
www.hurrycurryoftokyo.com

"If you've never had Japanese curry before, start here" say fans of this "budget" Pasadena and West LA duo serving "tasty" Tokyo "comfort food" in a "cool atmosphere" accentuated by servers "with asymmetrical haircuts who look like they just stepped out of anime"; while a few complain that the plates are just "passable", the "lines for lunch" attest to its "popularity."

### Hu's Szechwan  *Chinese*
21 | 4 | 15 | $17

**Palms** | 10450 National Blvd. (bet. Motor & Overland Aves.) | 310-837-0252 | www.husrestaurant.com

A Palms "institution" for "decades", this "neighborhood dive with upscale Chinese cuisine" "always satisfies" by providing "quality" Sichuan fare for an "excellent value"; some surveyors bemoan the "dumpy" decor and the "tough parking" ("make sure you get it to go") but loyalists overlook the "no-frills service and atmosphere" and keep the place "crowded."

### i Cugini  *Italian/Seafood*
21 | 22 | 20 | $43

**Santa Monica** | 1501 Ocean Ave. (B'way) | 310-451-4595 | www.icugini.com

"Ocean breezes" and "lovely" views from the patio provide the backdrop for "Italian seafood lovers" to feast at this "tasteful" Santa Monica sib of Water Grill; service is "steady" and the "must-try" Sunday jazz brunch and "wonderful happy hour" (till 8 PM daily) are both favorites, though some critics gripe that the "big open room" with marble countertops gets "painfully loud", and the food is a bit "ordinary" for the price.

### Il Boccaccio  *Italian*
∇ 22 | 15 | 20 | $42

**Hermosa Beach** | 39 Pier Ave. (bet. Hermosa Ave. & The Strand) | 310-376-0211 | www.ilboccaccio.com

"You know someone back in the kitchen really loves their job!" at this little Hermosa Beach Italian that earns raves for its "homemade pastas" and other "excellent" dishes; though critics call the service "a bit stiff" and the brick-walled room too "crowded" and "dated", most agree that the upscale eats make for a "pleasant" break from the "loud bars" lining the pier.

### Il Buco  *Italian*
22 | 16 | 24 | $37

**Beverly Hills** | 107 N. Robertson Blvd. (Wilshire Blvd.) | 310-657-1345 | www.giacominodrago.com

Loyalists laud the "warm", "personal" service ("very accommodating to granddad") at this "dependable" "Drago brothers eatery", an "affordable" Beverly Hills trattoria turning out "hearty" pastas and pizzas; the room is "intimate" and "relaxed", so despite its modest decor (Venetian masks, photos of old Sicily), most find it's "just what a neighborhood restaurant should be."

### Il Capriccio on Vermont  *Italian*                20 | 14 | 18 | $25

**Los Feliz** | 1757 N. Vermont Ave. (bet. Kingswell & Melbourne Aves.) | 323-662-5900

### Il Capriccio Wood Fire Pizzeria  *Italian*

**Los Feliz** | 4518 Hollywood Blvd. (Sunset Blvd.) | 323-644-9760
www.ilcapriccioonvermont.com

"Packed" with Los Feliz "locals", this "charming" "family-owned" trattoria wins hearts with "fresh pastas" and other "consistent", "affordable" Italian dishes, while its newer pizzeria branch turns out "good thin-crust" pies from the brick oven; though the original can get "cramped" "when it's hopping", the patios at both locations offer some breathing room; the Wood Fire location is BYO-only.

### NEW Il Carpaccio  *Italian*                23 | 17 | 20 | $50

**Pacific Palisades** | 538 Palisades Dr. (Sunset Blvd.) | 310-573-1411 | www.ilcarpaccioristorante.com

A "small neighborhood Italian with big ambition", this Palisades newcomer by chef-owner Antonio Muré (ex La Botte and Piccolo) provides "top-notch", "inventive" food served by a "knowledgeable" staff; while some surveyors protest that it's "priced way out of the strip mall", many agree the humble setting "is forgotten" after a gander at the "notable wine list", and the six-course tasting menu is simply "transporting."

### Il Chianti  Ⓜ *Italian*                ▽ 20 | 15 | 19 | $33

**Lomita** | 24503 Narbonne Ave. (Lomita Blvd.) | 310-325-5000

"Unique in the South Bay", this "hidden" Japanese-influenced Italian is known for its "refreshing, original spins" on old-country dishes that attract "super long lines" of Lomita fans in the mood for "delicious fusion"; a spare setting and sometimes "tricky" communication with the staff are part of the moderately priced package.

### Il Cielo  Ⓩ *Italian*                21 | 26 | 22 | $52

**Beverly Hills** | 9018 Burton Way (bet. Almont & Wetherly Drs.) | 310-276-9990 | www.ilcielo.com

"Twinkling lights" on the "gorgeous" patio and a "cozy fireplace" inside "cannot fail to impress anyone even mildly in love" say surveyors swept away by this "exquisitely romantic" Northern Italian in Beverly Hills, where the "attentive but not cloying" staff makes you "feel like the most important guest there, even if George Clooney is in the house"; while the "pricey", "tasty" fare is a bit less "memorable" than the setting, most agree you "go for the ambiance" more than the food.

### Il Fornaio  *Italian*                20 | 19 | 19 | $34

**Beverly Hills** | 301 N. Beverly Dr. (Dayton Way) | 310-550-8330
**Santa Monica** | 1551 Ocean Ave. (Colorado Ave.) | 310-451-7800
**Manhattan Beach** | Manhattan Gateway Shopping Ctr. | 1800 Rosecrans Ave. (bet. S. Sepulveda Blvd. & Village Dr.) | 310-725-9555
**Pasadena** | One Colorado | 24 W. Union St. (Fair Oaks Ave.) | 626-683-9797
www.ilfornaio.com

The name translates as 'the baker', so naturally there's the "smell of fresh bread" in the air at this "higher end" Italian chain where the "consistently tasty" offerings arrive in "elegantly casual" environs; "super weekly specials" and a "solid wine selection" add to its "reliable" reputation and help explain the somewhat "upscale" price point.

### Il Forno  *Italian*

20 | 15 | 20 | $32

**Santa Monica** | 2901 Ocean Park Blvd. (bet. 29th & 30th Sts.) | 310-450-1241 | www.ilfornocaffe.com

"Pasta's the thing here" (along with "hot, fresh" bread) say patrons of this strip-mall "neighborhood standby" in Santa Monica that's frequently "slammed" with guests chowing down on "solid", modestly priced Northern Italian fare; even if it's "not as exciting as it once was", the "gracious" "born-in-The-Boot" servers "make you feel welcome", and there's a "nice patio" too.

### Il Forno Caldo  ⌧ *Italian*

22 | 18 | 20 | $30

**Beverly Hills** | 9705 Santa Monica Blvd. (Roxbury Dr.) | 310-777-0040

For a "red-sauce fix", diners head to this "sleeper in Beverly Hills" that dishes up "homey Italian" lunches and "quick" dinners in a "cozy", "casual" atmosphere; considering the "reasonable prices", it stands out as a "real value find."

### Il Grano  ⌧ *Italian*

26 | 21 | 22 | $58

**West LA** | 11359 Santa Monica Blvd. (Purdue Ave.) | 310-477-7886

Chef-owner Salvatore Marino is an "artist" who "has a way with everything he touches" say those who adore his "delectable" Italian cuisine with an emphasis on "seasonal" dishes and seafood ("kudos to the crudo bar") at this West LA "wonder"; a "ready-to-please" staff and "understated" dining room round out the "amazing" experience, perhaps one of the "most underrated in the city", though a few fault it for "drastic pricing"; N.B. a vegetarian tasting menu is offered daily.

### Il Moro  *Italian*

23 | 22 | 22 | $43

**West LA** | 11400 W. Olympic Blvd. (Purdue Ave.) | 310-575-3530 | www.ilmoro.com

"Tucked away" in an "odd" "office building location" in West LA, this "unexpected treasure" nonetheless wins praise for its "beautifully" remodeled "contemporary" space (with a "peaceful" patio) as well as its "creative", "refreshing" Italian fare; the "unpretentious" service is "winning" too, and though some claim the bill "keeps going up", those in-the-know recommend noshing at happy hour for "a steal."

### Il Pastaio  *Italian*

25 | 17 | 20 | $42

**Beverly Hills** | 400 N. Cañon Dr. (Brighton Way) | 310-205-5444 | www.giacominodrago.com

It's an "instant addiction" say Beverly Hills locals who "love" the "authentic", "superb" Italian dishes by chef-owner Giacomino Drago at this "bustling" bistro staffed by a "friendly" team; given its high-end shopping locale, the patio is "fun for people-watching", but "expect to wait" to slip into "tight seating" as "they don't take reservations."

### Il Sole  *Italian*

24 | 19 | 20 | $65

**West Hollywood** | 8741 Sunset Blvd. (Sherbourne Dr.) | 310-657-1182

"Stargazers won't be disappointed" at this West Hollywood "paparazzi magnet" dishing out "wonderful" Italian food and a "high glam quotient" in equal measure; smitten suppers say the "lively" atmosphere "exudes warmth", though some critics cite "fusty" decor and a "pretentious" attitude, also cautioning that "the bill adds up pretty quickly", so watch out for waiters "pushing truffles."

| | FOOD | DECOR | SERVICE | COST |
|---|---|---|---|---|

### Il Tiramisù Ristorante & Bar Ⓜ *Italian*    `23` `19` `23` `$37`

**Sherman Oaks** | 13705 Ventura Blvd. (Woodman Ave.) | 818-986-2640 | www.il-tiramisu.com

"Fantastic service" sets apart this white-tablecloth Sherman Oaks Italian "gem" where the "perfect hosts", father-son owners Ivo and Peter Kastelan, "always make patrons feel like part of the family"; most visitors find the "affordable" food "first-class" too and appreciate the "pleasant" "bistro ambiance", particularly during the "incredible" monthly wine dinners.

### Il Tramezzino *Italian*    `20` `10` `15` `$20`

**Beverly Hills** | 454 N. Cañon Dr. (Santa Monica Blvd.) | 310-273-0501
**Studio City** | 13031 Ventura Blvd. (Coldwater Canyon Ave.) | 818-784-2244
**NEW Tarzana** | 18636 Ventura Blvd. (bet. Reseda Blvd. & Yolanda Ave.) | 818-996-8726
www.iltram.net

"Nice for a quick bite", this trio of "informal" Italian cafes serves up a "classy version of fast food", including "delicious" grilled panini and "tasty" salads, in a "relaxed" atmosphere; even if the interiors feel rather "tired", the outdoor patios are appealing ("bring your dog"), and the Beverly Hills locale is "perfect after a night out" on the weekends.

### India's Oven *Indian*    `19` `11` `17` `$25`

**Beverly Boulevard** | 7233 Beverly Blvd. (bet. Alta Vista Blvd. & Formosa Ave.) | 323-936-1000

The "spicy" fare attracts a following to this "local" Indian on Beverly Boulevard that's "one of the top places" around for "quality" South Asian cooking; while its decor is unremarkable and it costs "a little more" than some competitors, many agree it's a "no-brainer" for takeout.

### India's Tandoori *Indian*    `19` `9` `16` `$21`

**Mid-Wilshire** | 5468 Wilshire Blvd. (Cochran Ave.) | 323-936-2050 | www.indiastandoori.net
**Hawthorne** | 4850 W. Rosecrans Ave. (bet. Inglewood & Shoup Aves.) | 310-675-5533 | www.indiastandoorilax.net
**West LA** | 11819 Wilshire Blvd. (bet. Granville & S. Westgate Aves.) | 310-268-9100
**Tarzana** | Windsor Ctr. | 19006 Ventura Blvd. (Donna Ave.) | 818-342-9100

"Extremely generous", "flavorful" Indian meals ("enough for a second dinner") keep bellies full at this chain of separately owned "reliables"; while they're "not much to look at", the service is "pleasant" and the lunch buffet (at all locations except Tarzana) provides real "bang for the buck."

### Indo Cafe *Indonesian*    `▽ 19` `15` `18` `$18`

**Palms** | 10428½ National Blvd. (Motor Ave.) | 310-815-1290 | www.indocaferestaurant.com

"Fresh", "exotic" Indonesian specialties for a "good value" are the draw at this "veggie"-friendly Palms "standby" where even the avocado shake is "amazing"; with "amiable" service and a "newly decorated" space featuring Javanese wall art, many agree it's now "taken it up a notch."

| | FOOD | DECOR | SERVICE | COST |
|---|---|---|---|---|

### Indochine Vien ⓜ *Vietnamese*

| 16 | 14 | 16 | $16 |

**Atwater Village** | 3110 Glendale Blvd. (Glenhurst Ave.) | 323-667-9591 |
www.indochinevien.com

"Authentic enough for Atwater", this Vietnamese "joint" cooks up
"fragrant pho" and other "snacky" dishes with "crisp flavors" in a
small, "minimalist" space; though some find the "no-frills" menu "limited" and "dumbed-down" (for those "unfamiliar with cow's stomach"), others appreciate that it's "fast", "convenient" and "beats
trekking across town" to Little Saigon.

### ☒ Inn of the Seventh Ray *Californian*

| 20 | 26 | 20 | $44 |

**Topanga** | 128 Old Topanga Canyon Rd. (4 mi. north of PCH) | 310-455-1311 |
www.innoftheseventhray.com

"Eco-conscious" "creekside dining for the posh hippie" wins raves
from surveyors swept away by the "wooded", "magical fairyland" setting in "rustic" Topanga Canyon (bring your "in-laws from Iowa" and
your best "harmonic vibrations" for "a spiritual California experience"); many agree that the organic Cal menu, with options for every-
body from vegans to meat lovers, "could use some sprucing up" along
with the service, as they're no match for the "idyllic" atmosphere.

### ☒ In-N-Out Burger ◐ *Burgers*

| 23 | 10 | 19 | $8 |

**Hollywood** | 7009 Sunset Blvd. (N. Orange Dr.)
**Culver City** | 13425 Washington Blvd. (bet. Glencoe & Walnut Aves.)
**West LA** | 9245 W. Venice Blvd. (Exposition Dr.)
**Westwood** | 922 Gayley Ave. (Levering Ave.)
**Westchester** | 9149 S. Sepulveda Blvd. (bet. Westchester Pkwy &
W. 92nd St.)
**North Hollywood** | 5864 Lankershim Blvd. (bet. Califa & Emelita Sts.)
**Sherman Oaks** | 4444 Van Nuys Blvd. (bet. Milbank &
Moorpark Sts.)
**Studio City** | 3640 Cahuenga Blvd. (bet. Fredonia Dr. & Regal Pl.)
**Van Nuys** | 7930 Van Nuys Blvd. (bet. Blythe & Michaels Sts.)
**Woodland Hills** | 19920 Ventura Blvd. (bet. Lubao & Oakdale Aves.)
800-786-1000 | www.in-n-out.com
Additional locations throughout Southern California

"A quantum leap beyond other fast-food joints", this "SoCal classic" and top Bang for the Buck in LA delivers "amazing" burgers,
fries (get them "crispy") and milkshakes all made from ingredients
"so fresh" that "even the slow-food lover likes to sneak there once
in a while"; the "efficient" staff will "serve you something 'animal
style' with a smile", leaving the "long lines" at the drive-thru
("more of a park-thru" at peak hours) and the calories as the "only
downsides", though "these are burgers even your cardiologist
would say are worth having."

### Iroha ◐ *Japanese*

| 25 | 17 | 20 | $38 |

**Studio City** | 12953 Ventura Blvd. (Coldwater Canyon Ave.) |
818-990-9559

"Forget the fancier places": this long-standing "hole-in-the-wall"
Japanese on the Studio City "side of the hill" lures a "cool neighborhood crowd of music and industry folk" to its "covered outdoor patio"
for "excellent" sushi served by a "competent" staff; while some prefer
the kitchen's more "innovative", "pricier" preparations, traditionalists
say "stick with the fish."

| | FOOD | DECOR | SERVICE | COST |
|---|---|---|---|---|

**NEW Isla** *Mexican* — | — | — | M

**West Hollywood** | 8788 W. Sunset Blvd. (Holloway Dr.) | 310-657-8100
A circular space at the busy West Hollywood intersection of Sunset and Holloway is now home to this moderately priced Mexican newcomer; true to its name, an island theme plays out on the coastal-focused menu that offers ceviche, seafood tacos and calamari in diablo sauce.

**Islands** *American* 16 | 15 | 17 | $17

**Beverly Hills** | 350 S. Beverly Dr. (Olympic Blvd.) | 310-556-1624
**Marina del Rey** | 404 Washington Blvd. (Via Dolce) | 310-822-3939
**West LA** | 10948 W. Pico Blvd. (Veteran Ave.) | 310-474-1144
**Manhattan Beach** | 3200 Sepulveda Blvd. (bet. 30th & 33rd Sts.) | 310-546-4456
**Torrance** | 2647 PCH (Crenshaw Blvd.) | 310-530-5383
**Pasadena** | 3533 E. Foothill Blvd. (Rosemead Blvd.) | 626-351-6543
**Burbank** | 101 E. Orange Grove Ave. (N. 1st St.) | 818-566-7744
**Encino** | 15927 Ventura Blvd. (Gloria Ave.) | 818-385-1200
**Glendale** | 117 W. Broadway (Orange St.) | 818-545-3555
**Woodland Hills** | 23397 Mulholland Dr. (Calabasas Rd.) | 818-225-9839
www.islandsrestaurants.com
Additional locations throughout Southern California
"Surf's up!" at this "tiki-themed" "kid-friendly" chain for "huge" burgers" ("lots of tasty choices"), "irresistible" fries in "Mount Everest" portions and bowls of "endless tortilla soup"; "surf and ski videos" please the young 'uns and provide "ample zoning-out opportunities" while "adults unwind", so they earn a "thumbs-up" for "family fun."

**Ita Cho** 𝕊 *Japanese* 21 | 12 | 20 | $36

**Beverly Boulevard** | 7311 Beverly Blvd. (bet. Fuller Ave. & Poinsettia Pl.) | 323-938-9009 | www.itachorestaurant.com
"Go with a group" because "you're supposed to share" the "tasty tapas", "traditional" cooked fare and platters of sushi at this Japanese on Beverly Boulevard; though the jury's still out on its "new owners" and expanded menu, and most agree the space provides "absolutely no ambiance", "loyal crowds" (including "low-key actors") still like the "smiles" of the staff and feel that it's a "perfect last-minute" "neighborhood go-to."

**Ivy, The** *Californian* 22 | 22 | 20 | $62

**West Hollywood** | 113 N. Robertson Blvd. (bet. Beverly Blvd. & 3rd St.) | 310-274-8303
"No one really goes for the food" quip observers of this West Hollywood "paparazzi-stalked" "celeb hangout" where "gawking" on the "French-country", "shabby-chic" patio is tops on the menu – though the "ample salads and other Californian fare are "surprisingly good" too; while some praise the "professional" service, more than a few bridle at the "snobby" attitude ("only stars get the star treatment") and "exotic" prices, but then again, you're paying to "see and be seen."

**Ivy at the Shore** *Californian* 22 | 22 | 21 | $60

**Santa Monica** | 1535 Ocean Ave. (bet. Broadway & Colorado Ave.) | 310-393-3113
"More laid-back" than the original WeHo locale, this Santa Monica "destination" is nonetheless "energetic" and "always delivers a star

"sighting" as well as "delicious" Californian fare in "Texas-size" portions with prices to match; the location "right across the street from the beach" is "lovely", though some feel the tropical decor may be a "little too Tommy Bahama", and the service can range from "cordial" to "snooty."

## Izaka-Ya by Katsu-Ya *Japanese*     25 | 15 | 18 | $42

**Third Street** | 8420 W. Third St. (Orlando Ave.) | 323-782-9536
"Like sushi crack", the "inventive" Japanese cuisine by Katsuya Uechi (Katsu-ya) inspires feverish devotion ("I would knock people over to get to the spicy tuna on crispy rice"), at this somewhat "nautical-themed" Third Street izakaya that's "expensive" but still more affordable than the original; given its "trendy" rep, it's "hard to catch a table even with reservations", which may be why some find the servers "rushing" them through the meal.

## Izayoi ⓩ *Japanese*     20 | 12 | 17 | $32

**Little Tokyo** | 132 S. Central Ave. (bet. 1st & 2nd Sts.) | 213-613-9554
"You can get some Japanese bar specialties you can't find elsewhere" at this "jumping" Little Tokyo izakaya serving up "lots of well-made" small plates and sushi in a "neo-industrial" setting that "draws upscale diners from the lofts" of Downtown; though critics complain that it's "nondescript" and "the check runs up quickly", others call it "satisfying" and say the bento boxes "will make jury duty" at the nearby courthouse "seem worth it."

## Jack n' Jill's *American*     19 | 13 | 16 | $19

**Beverly Hills** | 342 N. Beverly Dr. (bet. Brighton & Dayton Ways) | 310-247-4500
**Santa Monica** | 510 Santa Monica Blvd. (5th St.) | 310-656-1501
www.eatatjacknjills.com
"Homey" American eating comes in the form of "creative breakfast options" till 5 PM along with "big salads" and sandwiches at these "kid-friendly" but "upscale" daytime bakery/cafes in Beverly Hills and Santa Monica; just "don't come to lunch expecting to get in and out" as "lines for tables can be a nightmare" and service is "lacking", but most feel "it's all worth it once you get your food."

## Jackson's Village Bistro Ⓜ *American*     24 | 15 | 20 | $39

**Hermosa Beach** | 517 Pier Ave. (bet. Bard St. & Cypress Ave.) | 310-376-6714
This "genuine chef-owned and -operated" New American "neighborhood hangout" is beloved by Hermosa Beach "locals" for its "excellent bistro food" at a "great value" ("you think you're eating at a much higher-priced restaurant"); its "warm", "unassuming" vibe and "amazing corkage policy" ("just $5!") help keep it "popular."

## Jack Sprat's Grille *Californian*     19 | 12 | 16 | $23

**West LA** | 10668 W. Pico Blvd. (Overland Ave.) | 310-837-6662 | www.jackspratsgrille.com
"Healthier than usual" fare, including "lots of vegetarian dishes" and "killer" air-baked fries, is the draw at this "reliable" West LA Californian, though it's the pre-meal "hot pretzels" with mustard that keep guests "going back"; while it can get "loud", most find it family-friendly and "comfortable", plus half-price wine bottles Monday–Tuesday add to the "bargain."

| | FOOD | DECOR | SERVICE | COST |
|---|---|---|---|---|

### Jacopo's  *Pizza* | 16 | 10 | 14 | $18

**Beverly Hills** | 326 S. Beverly Dr. (bet. Gregory Way & Olympic Blvd.) | 310-858-6446 ◐
**Pacific Palisades** | 15415 Sunset Blvd. (Via de la Paz) | 310-454-8494
www.jacopos.com

Local families favor these pizzerias in Pacific Palisades and Beverly Hills (at a new "roomier" location) for "good" pies and other "decent" affordable fare; frequenters say a "not fancy", "neighborhood" feel and "kid-friendly" attitude make them a top pick for "team parties" or "takeout in a pinch", even if some feel they've "lost their mojo" over the years.

### James' Beach  *American* | 18 | 18 | 20 | $39

**Venice** | 60 N. Venice Blvd. (Pacific Ave.) | 310-823-5396 | www.jamesbeach.com

"Dinner meets nightclub" "a Frisbee throw from the beach" at this "shabby-chic" Venice American turning out "comfort-food" classics in an airy bungalow while "gaggles of women" and guys with "popped collars" mingle over mojitos at the patio bar; the service can be "wonderful", though critics call the "homecooking" "average for beach prices", so some assess it's "better for drinking than for eating."

### Jan's ◐ *Diner* | ∇ 14 | 6 | 17 | $19

**West Hollywood** | 8424 Beverly Blvd. (Croft Ave.) | 323-651-2866

A "quintessential coffee shop" that recalls "the one in *Seinfeld*", this "old standby" in WeHo draws an "interesting mixture of wheelchairs, walkers and police officers" for "decent" diner food in "portions that could feed a small country"; with "green Naugahyde booths" and a "no-frills approach", it's a "steady" antidote to trendier breakfast spots and, even if the food is a little "greasy", it's "perfect for the morning after."

### Japon Bistro  *Japanese* | ∇ 25 | 18 | 20 | $33

**Pasadena** | 927 E. Colorado Blvd. (bet. Lake & Mentor Aves.) | 626-744-1751 | www.japonbistro-pasadena.com

"This one is special" say surveyors smitten with the "inventive appetizers", "quality sushi" and "top sake list" at this moderate Pasadena Japanese where the "smart" servers "take good care of you"; while it's on the "quiet" side, insiders say it's "resurfacing" and advise "make sure you have a reservation" to nab a seat among the "young clientele."

### Jar  *American/Steak* | 25 | 22 | 23 | $59

**Beverly Boulevard** | 8225 Beverly Blvd. (Harper Ave.) | West Hollywood | 323-655-6566 | www.thejar.com

Chef-owner Suzanne Tracht's "old-school steakhouse with new-school flavor" on Beverly Boulevard wins raves for its "stylish" takes on "traditional" American dishes ("awesome" deviled eggs, "heavenly" pot roast) and "sophisticated" service; even if the "acoustics need work", most find the "mod", wood-paneled room "handsome" enough for the "Rat Pack", though a few newbies are "jarred by the prices"; P.S. "mozzarella Mondays are a real treat."

### Javan  *Persian* | 20 | 15 | 19 | $24

**West LA** | 11500 Santa Monica Blvd. (Butler Ave.) | 310-207-5555 | www.javanrestaurant.com

"The standard for Persian cuisine", this "popular", "inexpensive" West LA eatery provides "bountiful" plates of "succulent meats and mountains of rice" that are ideal for "sharing"; most call the "airy" space "pleasant" and the staff "excellent", even if the "Las Vegas–type pianist" is "trying for a vibe that isn't quite there."

**Jer-ne** *Californian*                  20 | 24 | 21 | $58

**Marina del Rey** | Ritz-Carlton, Marina Del Rey | 4375 Admiralty Way (off Lincoln Blvd.) | 310-574-4333 | www.ritzcarlton.com

A "beautiful" waterside setting is the top selling point of this "civilized" Californian small-plates specialist in the Marina del Rey Ritz-Carlton, making it sought out for "special occasions" and "springtime Sunday brunches"; surveyors are split, however, on both the food ("terrific" to "uninspired") and service, leaving some to surmise it's more "show" than "substance" and you're really "paying for the Ritz name."

**NEW** **Jian Korean BBQ** ⑤ *Korean*            - | - | - | M

**Beverly Boulevard** | 8256 Beverly Blvd. (N. Sweetzer Ave.) | 323-655-6556

At this Korean arrival on Beverly Boulevard, the midpriced, barbecue-focused menu is supplemented by classic dishes and more modern fare, including phyllo-wrapped scallops with a pomegranate vinaigrette; designwise it also offers an interesting mix: the logo is an imposing Korean warrior, there are pachinko machines behind the bar and a robot statue stands guard in the corner.

**Jinky's** *Southwestern*               19 | 11 | 16 | $16

**West Hollywood** | 8539 W. Sunset Blvd. (Alta Loma Rd.) | 310-659-9670
**Santa Monica** | 1447 Second St. (bet. Broadway & Santa Monica Blvd.) | 310-917-3311
**Sherman Oaks** | 14120 Ventura Blvd. (Stansbury Ave.) | 818-981-2250
www.jinkys.com

Giving "comfort food" a Southwestern spin, this daytime chain offers the "perfect cure for the Sunday morning blues" say buffs who love the "huge menu" ("it may take you longer to read it than to eat your breakfast") including 20 different chilis for eating by the bowl or topping the "ultimate" omelet; on the downside, don't expect more than "diner"-level looks and service, and "bring a book 'cos there's a bit of a wait"; N.B. the Sherman Oaks branch is now open for dinner.

**☑ Jin Patisserie** Ⓜ *Bakery/French*          25 | 19 | 18 | $21

**Venice** | 1202 Abbot Kinney Blvd. (Argon Ct.) | 310-399-8801 | www.jinpatisserie.com

'Bakery' is a woefully inadequate term for this "jewel box" patisserie and teahouse in Venice serving chef-owner Kristy Choo's "exquisite" cakes and "handmade chocolates" along with upscale French cafe bites; the "hideaway" "garden setting", right off Abbot Kinney, is a surprisingly "serene" spot for a "real foodie's tea" featuring "delectable" sandwiches and "artful" sweets, so even if the service "could be better", the experience is "lovely" all around.

**☑ JiRaffe** *American/French*           26 | 21 | 24 | $56

**Santa Monica** | 502 Santa Monica Blvd. (5th St.) | 310-917-6671 | www.jirafferestaurant.com

"A gem on just about every level", this Santa Monica bistro rewards guests with "sublime", "imaginative" French–New American fare by wave-riding chef-owner Raphael Lunetta, "superb" service and an "ele-

| | FOOD | DECOR | SERVICE | COST |

gant" ambiance accented with dark wood and chandeliers; though the atmosphere can feel "hectic" and "noisy on the ground floor", most "enjoy the whole experience" at this "surfer's high-end dream restaurant."

### Z Jitlada  *Thai*
26 | 12 | 20 | $26

**East Hollywood** | 5233½ W. Sunset Blvd. (bet. Harvard Blvd. & Kingsley Dr.) | 323-667-9809

"Different and exponentially better than the standard" dishes found elsewhere rave fans about the "hot, hot, hot" (some say "defibrillating") Southern Thai specialties at this "real find" "elbowed into a strip mall" in East Hollywood; the "charming" service trumps the "hole-in-the-wall" setting and sets the stage for "unique" meals that make it a serious contender for the "very best Thai spot in all of LA."

### JJ Steak House  Ⓜ *Steak*
23 | 23 | 22 | $57

**Pasadena** | 88 W. Colorado Blvd. (De Lacey Ave.) | 626-844-8889 | www.jjsteakhouse.net

"It's all about the romantic atmosphere" ("sit by the fireplace" or on the patio) at this "quiet", "old-line" steakhouse "perched above the main drag" in Old Town Pasadena; most find the kitchen has "mastered the classics" and the service is "professional", so even if some deem it only "decent" for the "expensive" tab, it's still sought out for "special celebrations."

### Joan's on Third  *American/Bakery*
23 | 17 | 17 | $23

**Third Street** | 8350 W. Third St. (bet. Fairfax Ave. & La Cienega Blvd.) | West Hollywood | 323-655-2285 | www.joansonthird.com

An "epicurean" "delight", this "airy", "bustling" cafe and marketplace on Third Street, with bountiful deli cases for "unrivaled" sandwiches and platter after platter of "tempting" baked goods, sets the "standard" for "sophisticated" American eat-in or take-out "picnic" fare; still, even after a 2007 expansion it's "not the most relaxing place" to grab lunch, as you'll have to "put up with long lines, a confusing ordering system, a lack of parking and the paparazzi chasing Nicole Richie."

### Jody Maroni's Sausage Kingdom  *Hot Dogs*
19 | 6 | 13 | $10

**Culver City** | Howard Hughes Ctr. | 6081 Center Dr. (Sepulveda Blvd.) | 310-348-0007
**Venice** | 2011 Ocean Front Walk (20th Ave.) | 310-822-5639
**LAX** | LA Int'l Airport | 201 World Way (Terminals 3 & 6) | 310-646-8056
**Torrance** | South Bay Galleria | 1815 Hawthorne Blvd. (Redondo Beach Blvd.) | 310-370-6921
**NEW Arcadia** | 1 W. Duarte Rd. (Santa Anita Ave.) | 626-254-8600
**Universal City** | Universal CityWalk | 1000 Universal Studios Blvd. (off Rte. 101) | 818-622-5639
**Camarillo** | Camarillo Premium Outlet Mall | 740 E. Ventura Blvd. (Camarillo Outlet) | 805-384-9300
www.jodymaroni.com

"Hot diggity" these are "tasty dogs" say connoisseurs who "love all the choices" of "juicy" sausages served up at this chain whose original Venice stand makes a "stroll down the boardwalk complete"; even if critics compare the franchised fare to "mall food", it's "quick", "cheap" and still "quenches a hankering" "after all these years."

| | FOOD | DECOR | SERVICE | COST |
|---|---|---|---|---|

**Z Joe's M** *Californian/French* — 26 | 20 | 23 | $52

**Venice** | 1023 Abbot Kinney Blvd. (B'way) | 310-399-5811 |
www.joesrestaurant.com

"A must-visit for any foodie", this "pioneering" Cal-French in Venice,
serving "exquisite" cuisine at "fair prices", is "not hip, trendy or
groovy", but "rock steady" under the guidance of chef-owner Joe
Miller; patrons praise the "elegant but simple" bungalow setting displaying colorful "contemporary art", and appreciate "welcoming"
servers who "make you feel like you're in their home", which may explain why the restaurant itself is "like an old friend"; P.S. "brunch on
the patio" is one of the "best on the Westside."

**Joe's Crab Shack** *Seafood* — 13 | 15 | 15 | $26

**Long Beach** | 6550 E. Marina Dr. (Studebaker Rd.) | 562-594-6551
**Redondo Beach** | 230 Portofino Way (Harbor Dr.) | 310-406-1999
**City of Industry** | 1420 S. Azusa Ave. (Colima Rd.) | 626-839-4116
www.joescrabshack.com

It's "totally gimmicky but has a draw" for "lively" "children's birthday
parties" and "crazy-loud" "get-togethers with friends" say fans of this
"touristy" chain with an "old-salt" feel and "shack-shaking entertainment" from servers "forced to sing and dance"; though it gets knocked
for "assembly-line" seafood, it's "ok to have a drink" and the coastal
locations offer "super water views."

**NEW Joe's Pizza ●⇆** *Pizza* — 20 | 6 | 13 | $11

**Santa Monica** | 111 Broadway (Ocean Ave.) | 310-395-9222 |
www.joespizza.com

The "New York slice" "finally comes to LA" at this Santa Monica newcomer, a Manhattan import serving "pizza the way it's supposed to
be" that "tastes just like it did on Bleecker Street"; seating is minimal
and service can be "chaotic", but all in all it's the "real deal" and
"cheaper than the roundtrip back to the Village."

**Joey's Smokin' BBQ** *BBQ* — 18 | 9 | 14 | $17

**Manhattan Beach** | Manhattan Vill. | 3564 N. Sepulveda Blvd.
(Rosecrans Ave.) | 310-563-9072 | www.joeyssmokinbbq.com

"Fall-off-the-bone" BBQ scores points with surveyors who "love" the
ribs, pulled pork and other meaty fare at this Manhattan Beach chain
link co-owned by the Lakers' Luke Walton; it's "tiny" ("definitely for
takeout") and the staff has "gotta work on that order-desk charm", but
otherwise it fills a "clear need" in SoCal for "Memphis-style" 'cue.

**Johnnie's New York Pizzeria** *Pizza* — 18 | 9 | 14 | $17

**NEW Downtown** | City Nat'l Plaza | 505 S. Flower St. (bet. 5th & 6th Sts.) |
213-488-0299 **S**
**Mid-Wilshire** | Museum Park Sq. | 5757 Wilshire Blvd. (Courtyard Pl.) |
323-904-4880
**West Hollywood** | 8166 Sunset Blvd. (Havenhurst Dr.) | 323-650-8172
**Century City** | Fox Apts. | 10251 Santa Monica Blvd. (bet. Ave. of the Stars &
Beverly Glen Blvd.) | 310-553-1188
**Malibu** | 22333 PCH (bet. Carbon Canyon Rd. & Malibu Pier) | 310-456-1717
**Santa Monica** | 1444 Third St. Promenade (Colorado Ave.) | 310-395-9062
**Venice** | Hoyt Plaza | 2805 Abbot Kinney Blvd. (Washington Blvd.) |
310-821-1224

*(continued)*

(continued)

### Johnnie's New York Pizzeria

**West LA** | 11676 Olympic Blvd. (Barrington St.) | 310-477-2111
www.johnniesnypizza.com

It "does the trick" for lunch or dinner say surveyors about this "reliable" chain, though controversy rages over whether it delivers the "closest thing to New York pizza out here" or is simply "not" worthy of the name; either way, most call the offerings "consistently good", and given the humble digs, agree takeout is the "best bet."

### Johnnie's Pastrami ●🎔 *Deli*

| 20 | 9 | 16 | $14 |

**Culver City** | 4017 Sepulveda Blvd. (bet. Washington Blvd. & Washington Pl.) | 310-397-6654

"Long live carnivores!" exclaim fans of this Culver City deli, a "step back in time" where the "juicy" hot pastrami sandwiches "rule" (and can feed "two people") and the "retro-diner" decor "hasn't changed in 50 years"; sure, the waitresses are "cranky", but "they know how to sling meat", so "bring your antacids", join the "police officers and blue-collar workers" at tables by the fire pit and pile on the pickles.

### Johnny Rebs' *BBQ*

| 22 | 17 | 21 | $21 |

**Bellflower** | 16639 Bellflower Blvd. (bet. Alondra Blvd. & Flower St.) | 562-866-6455
**Long Beach** | 4663 Long Beach Blvd. (bet. 46th & 47th Sts.) | 562-423-7327
www.johnnyrebs.com

"Come for the catfish, stay for the cobbler!" crow customers about this morning-to-night Southern chain plating up "gut-busting" "home cooking" and "super" BBQ in a "joint" that feels so "authentic you could almost be in Carolina"; while "peanut shells on the floor" might not be for everyone, most call it "friendly", "fun" and "hard on the arteries, but worth it."

### Johnny Rockets *Burgers*

| 15 | 15 | 16 | $14 |

**Fairfax** | Grove at Farmers Mkt. | 6333 W. Third St. (Fairfax Ave.) | 323-937-2093
**Hollywood** | Hollywood & Highland Ctr. | 6801 Hollywood Blvd. (Highland Ave.) | 323-465-4456
**Melrose** | 7507 Melrose Ave. (Gardner St.) | 323-651-3361
**Culver City** | Howard Hughes Ctr. | 6081 Center Dr. (Sepulveda Blvd.) | 310-670-7555
**Long Beach** | Pine Ct. | 245 Pine Ave. (bet. Broadway & 3rd St.) | 562-983-1332
**Manhattan Beach** | Manhattan Mktpl. | 1550 Rosecrans Ave. (Sepulveda Blvd.) | 310-536-9464
**Arcadia** | Westfield Shoppingtown Santa Anita | 400 S. Baldwin Ave. (Huntington Dr.) | 626-462-1800
**Burbank** | Media City Ctr. | 201 E. Magnolia Blvd. (3rd St.) | 818-845-7055
**Encino** | 16901 Ventura Blvd. (Balboa Blvd.) | 818-981-5900
**Alhambra** | 19 E. Main St. (Garfield Ave.) | 626-281-8831
www.johnnyrockets.com
Additional locations throughout Southern California

Travel back in time to the days of "cherry Cokes" and "tabletop jukeboxes" at these faux "'50s malt shops" featuring "decent all-American" eats, most notably "above-average burgers" and "thick shakes"; while the "singing, dancing" staff is particularly "good for kids", grown-ups gripe about "slow service" and a "formulaic" approach.

|  | FOOD | DECOR | SERVICE | COST |
|---|---|---|---|---|

### John O'Groats *American* | 21 | 12 | 18 | $18 |

**Rancho Park** | 10516 W. Pico Blvd. (½ block west of Beverly Glen Blvd.) | 310-204-0692 | www.ogroatsrestaurant.com

"Sit at the counter and feel like it's the '50s again" at this family-run daytime eatery in Rancho Park known for "terrific" American breakfasts (complete with "killer biscuits") served in a "hodgepodge" multiroom setting; though some just "don't get" the "long lines on the weekends", advocates commend the "hospitable" host and say "complimentary coffee while you wait" for a table doesn't hurt, either.

### Jones Hollywood ● *American/Italian* | 18 | 18 | 16 | $32 |

**West Hollywood** | 7205 Santa Monica Blvd. (Formosa Ave.) | 323-850-1726

"Still knocks out some tender roast chicken", "addictive" "late-night pizza" and an "honest pour of Jack Daniels" say faithful fans of this "laid-back" WeHo Italian-American with a "rock 'n' roll" vibe and a staff that pays "just enough attention to guests"; sure, it can be "louder than a street gun battle" and "too dark" to see and be seen, but that's just fine by the "cool" crowd that "comes for dinner and stays for drinks."

### Joseph's Cafe ⌧ *Greek* | ▽ 18 | 17 | 16 | $29 |

**Hollywood** | 1775 N. Ivar Ave. (Yucca St.) | 323-462-8697 | www.josephscafe.com

"Classic Greek" food fuels up party people in the "clubby environment" decked out with columns and colorful draperies at this Hollywood longtimer; while some of the focus has left the "reliable" cooking, many find it satisfying for sharing a bite "after work" and "hanging out" to the tune of DJ sets on weekends and Monday nights.

### Josie *American* | 26 | 22 | 24 | $61 |

**Santa Monica** | 2424 Pico Blvd. (25th St.) | 310-581-9888 | www.josierestaurant.com

"Not one for over-the-top trends", "gifted" chef Josie Le Balch nonetheless produces "stellar", "adventurous" New American cuisine matched by "wonderful", "reasonably priced" wines at this "hidden gem on Pico" in Santa Monica; attracting a somewhat "older crowd", the hearth-warmed room has a "mellow", "comfortable" feel that, combined with "phenomenal" service, adds up to a "rewarding experience" all around.

### J Restaurant & Lounge ⌧ *Mediterranean* | 16 | 22 | 16 | $38 |

**Downtown** | 1119 S. Olive St. (bet. 11th & 12th Sts.) | 213-746-7746 | www.jloungela.com

A "snazzy" detour on the "Downtown scene", this "huge" tri-level restaurant and lounge appeals more for its "sexy" atmosphere than for Mediterranean fare that many call "uninspiring" and "slow" to arrive; still, the location is convenient for "pre-theater" dining, the patio with a fire pit is "welcoming" and "what the food lacks" may well be "made up for with ambiance – wow!"

### JR's BBQ ⌧ *BBQ* | 21 | 8 | 20 | $17 |

**Culver City** | 3055 S. La Cienega Blvd. (Blackwelder St.) | 310-837-6838 | www.jrs-bbq.com

"When they say spicy, they mean it" at this "down-home" BBQ joint in Culver City, where the "tender" ribs, pulled pork and brisket are cooked "low and slow" and plated in "ample" portions for a "decent" price; mother-son owners Jeanie Jackson and Bobby Johnson lead an "incredibly friendly" staff, lending the '50s-style place a "family feel."

**NEW JuJu Cereal Bar** *American*  `-` `-` `-` `I`

**Westwood** | 1248 Westwood Blvd. (Ashton Ave.) | 310-474-8571 | www.jujucerealbar.com

"A nice addition to the morning routine", this "novel" Westwood cereal bar offers a large menu of boxed breakfast favorites from Lucky Charms to muesli with a variety of toppers (hint: "banana milk makes everything taste good"); while some wonder "how exciting can cereal really be, even if you're mixing eight together?", the "cool" daytime counter spot is bringing comfort-craving UCLA students "back for seconds."

**Juliano's Raw** *Vegan*  ▽ `19` `16` `17` `$33`

**Santa Monica** | 609 Broadway (6th St.) | 310-587-1552 | www.planetraw.com

"Weird but tasty" say samplers of this Santa Monica vegan where chef-owner Juliano Brotman crafts "hard-core" raw dishes like mock salmon sushi, 'cheezeburgers' and faux pasta made of zucchini strips; on the downside, it's "pricier than expected", service is "inconsistent" and the space is lackluster aside from its "recommended" patios, but it may just do the trick when you're ready to "test your palate."

**Julienne** 🅂 *French*  `25` `21` `20` `$26`

**San Marino** | 2651 Mission St. (bet. El Molino & Los Robles Aves.) | 626-441-2299 | www.juliennetogo.com

"San Marino's version of The Ivy" is the "local place to see and be seen" for the "ladies-who-lunch" crowd ("my wife would live there if they set her up a bed") that dishes over "delightful" French bistro fare; admirers say sitting on the "beautiful" front patio will "remind you why you live in SoCal", but if the "inevitable wait" for a table is too "long", there are "fabulous" prepared foods available to take out from the marketplace; N.B. closes at 3:30 PM.

**Junior's** *Deli*  `16` `9` `16` `$21`

**West LA** | 2379 Westwood Blvd. (Pico Blvd.) | 310-475-5771

After nearly 50 years, this West LA Jewish deli is "still holding on", serving "reliable" kosher-style fare morning to night, including "giant" sandwiches and matzo ball soup that's "a meal in itself"; even if many find it "past its prime", "overpriced" and merely "decent" ("it's no East Coast pastrami"), it remains a "family favorite" that "caters to the 70-plus crowd" – especially with the "good-value" early-bird special.

**Kanpai Japanese Sushi Bar & Grill** *Japanese*  ▽ `22` `15` `18` `$42`

**Westchester** | 8325 Lincoln Blvd. (bet. 83rd & 84th Sts.) | 310-338-7223

The "creative" sushi and grilled dishes plus a "good sake list" offer plenty to cheer about at this "small", "unassuming" Westchester Japanese that's a bit publike with its assorted TV screens; even if it's "slightly expensive" for a local place, guests who return "again and again" are "grateful" to have it nearby.

**Kansas City BBQ Company** *BBQ*  ▽ `21` `4` `16` `$18`

**Studio City** | 4141 Lankershim Blvd. (Aqua Vista St.) | 818-754-0030

Even Kansas City "natives" give the nod to this Studio City BBQ joint that serves up "melt-in-your-mouth" hickory-smoked ribs slathered with "real K.C. sauce" and "winning" sandwiches like the Big Cheese, boast-

FOOD  DECOR  SERVICE  COST

ing three pounds of brisket and a spot for your photo on the wall if you finish it; the basic furnishings mean it's no feast for the eyes, but 'cue connoisseurs "adore" the easy-on-the-wallet grub too much to mind.

**Katana** ◐ *Japanese*                23 | 25 | 20 | $57

**West Hollywood** | 8439 W. Sunset Blvd. (bet. La Cienega Blvd. & Sweetzer Ave.) | 323-650-8585 | www.katanarobata.com

"As places to see and be seen go, it's got better chow than most" say those who join the "gorgeous" "models-and-Ferraris" crowd ("catch Hugh Hefner and the girls") for "high-quality" sushi and "delicious robata goodies" at this Japanese "party-starter" in WeHo (soon to open a Vegas branch); the space itself is "well designed" with a "fantastic" patio overlooking the Sunset Strip, and the sushi chefs add "personality" too, though it's "way too expensive" and "pretentious" for some.

**Kate Mantilini** *American*            18 | 18 | 18 | $35

**Beverly Hills** | 9101 Wilshire Blvd. (Doheny Dr.) | 310-278-3699 ◐
**Woodland Hills** | 5921 Owensmouth Ave. (bet. Califa & Oxnard Sts.) | 818-348-1095

"Essentially a fancy diner", this "bustling" Beverly Hills "standby" (with a Woodland Hills sib) serves "satisfying", "reliable" interpretations of American comfort food like meatloaf and chicken pot pie; its "late hours and celebrity clients are a huge plus", especially "after an Academy or WGA screening", though some guests feel "nickel and dimed" for somewhat "dull" cuisine, dissing it as "Denny's on wallet steroids."

**NEW Katsu Sushi** Ⓢ *Japanese*          - | - | - | M

**Beverly Hills** | 260 N. Beverly Dr. (Dayton Way) | 310-858-0535 | www.katsusushibar.com

One of LA's most respected longtime sushi chefs, Katsu Michite (of the defunct Katsu in Los Feliz and the very-much-alive Tama Sushi in Studio City), has taken over a former sushi bar in the heart of Beverly Hills and transformed it into this traditional Japanese; the moderately priced menu offers old-school dishes that utilize handpicked organic ingredients and daily selected seafood.

**Ⓩ Katsu-ya** *Japanese*                27 | 15 | 19 | $42

**Encino** | 16542 Ventura Blvd. (Hayvenhurst Ave.) | 818-788-2396
**Studio City** | 11680 Ventura Blvd. (Colfax Ave.) | 818-985-6976
www.sushikatsu-ya.com

Boasting "brilliant", "inventive" sushi and cooked dishes, these Encino and Studio City Japanese "gems" provide "exceptional" culinary quality while offering a "better deal" "without the attitude" of their "flashier" unhyphenated cousins; their "small" "nothing-to-look-at" digs are "always crowded" with a "cult" following and then some, so vets advise "make reservations" and "order from the board for a gastronomic treat."

**Ⓩ Katsuya** *Japanese*                24 | 25 | 19 | $58

**NEW Hollywood** | 6300 Hollywood Blvd. (Vine St.) | 323-871-8777 ◐
**Brentwood** | 11777 San Vicente Blvd. (Montana Ave.) | 310-207-8744
**NEW Glendale** | Americana at Brand | 702 Americana Way (Brand Blvd.) | 818-244-5900 ◐
www.sbeent.com/katsuya

"TMZ is permanently staked outside", but these Japanese destinations actually "have the food to back up" the "glitzy" "scene", as "wizard" chef Katsuya Uechi crafts a "superb" menu of "memorable" sushi and other "sensational" dishes; the "stunning", white-accented Philippe Starck design wins applause too, and if some warn about "self-important" service and the "accompanying price tag", most feel that all is "redeemed" by the quality of the cuisine.

### Kay 'n Dave's  Mexican

| 18 | 14 | 17 | $20 |

**Pacific Palisades** | 15246 W. Sunset Blvd. (bet. Monument St. & Swarthmore Ave.) | 310-459-8118
**Rancho Park** | 10543 W. Pico Blvd. (bet. Patricia & Prosser Aves.) | 310-446-8808
**Santa Monica** | 262 26th St. (San Vicente Blvd.) | 310-260-1355
www.kayndaves.com

Offering a "tasty, healthy take on traditional Mexican" plates, this trio of "inexpensive" Westside "family favorites" turns out "lard-free" staples, including south-of-the-border breakfast items served all day; it's "not as wildly flavorful" as some would like, and the simple digs are so "kid-friendly" they verge on "adult-unfriendly at times", but perks like a "charming" patio on Pico make for a "pleasant" stop.

### NEW Ken & Kent's NY Style Deli  Deli

| - | - | - | I |

**Hermosa Beach** | 844 Hermosa Ave. (8th St.) | 310-376-3354
This inexpensive arrival fills the South Bay's deli void with a wide range of New York–style sandwiches and grub; located in a warehouselike space (formerly Hana Sushi) just a short stroll from the ocean, it may be one of the few spots where you can experience borscht and board shorts at the same time.

### Kendall's Brasserie  French

| 17 | 19 | 17 | $46 |

**Downtown** | Dorothy Chandler Pavilion | 135 N. Grand Ave. (bet. Temple St. & Tom Bradley Blvd.) | 213-972-7322 | www.patinagroup.com
A "captive audience" hits this "old-world"-style Downtown French eatery (in the Patina Group) for a "traditional bistro" bite before or after catching a performance nearby; while some critcs say both the food and service can be "spotty" ("stick with the simple stuff") and lament "what used to be an affordable brasserie has turned into quite an expensive evening", many agree the "convenience" of the location "trumps any shortcomings."

### Ketchup ● American

| 15 | 19 | 18 | $43 |

**West Hollywood** | Millennium Ctr. | 8590 W. Sunset Blvd. (Alta Loma Rd.) | 310-289-8590 | www.dolcegroup.com
"Like a diner from the *Jetsons*", this "hip", red-accented Dolce Group hot spot in WeHo is packed with "beautiful" "twentysomethings" digging into a retro American menu full of "fun" "twists on comfort food" (with its own homemade 'sup) alongside playful cocktails; some guests regret "paying too much for hot dogs and fries" among other eats that slide from "decent" to "disappointing", but for many the "young", "upbeat" vibe and "clever" concept warrants a night out.

### Kincaid's  Seafood/Steak

| 20 | 23 | 19 | $43 |

**Redondo Beach** | Redondo Beach Pier | 500 Fisherman's Wharf (Torrance Blvd.) | 310-318-6080 | www.kincaids.com
Admirers "love sitting outside on the pier" and also appreciate the "tasteful" interior of this Redondo Beach surf 'n' turf chain link that's

"better than your average waterside dining option", serving "old-school", upscale" fare that's "reliable" if "not subtle"; despite somewhat "inconsistent" service, it stays "packed" with "business types", "tourists" and those out for a "romantic" evening complete with "sunset views."

### King's Fish House  *Seafood*  | 21 | 18 | 19 | $34 |

**Long Beach** | 100 W. Broadway Ave. (Pine Ave.) | 562-432-7463
**Calabasas** | The Commons | 4798 Commons Way (Calabasas Rd.) |
818-225-1979
www.kingsfishhouse.com

"Incredibly fresh seafood" "any way you like it" is the hook at these "unpretentious" chain bistros deemed a "good value" for "safe, not spectacular" "basics" and "ice-cold" "oysters served right" "year-round"; "great cocktails" and "happy-hour deals" reel in a "loud", "lively" cantina crowd, but "pleasant" dining rooms with "attractive" patios are "relaxing" for "businesspeople, parents or your date."

### Kings Road Cafe  *American*  | 18 | 12 | 15 | $20 |

**Beverly Boulevard** | 8361 Beverly Blvd. (Kings Rd.) | West Hollywood |
323-655-9044 | www.kingsroadcafe.com

"Extra-strong", "individually brewed" cups of coffee and "homestyle" American food make it "worth getting dressed in the morning to have breakfast" at this Beverly Boulevard cafe populated with "actors" and "bored hipsters" vying for "coveted sidewalk tables"; though it's not as memorable for dinner, the "hearty" brunches there are "ideal for those rough morning-afters", offering "something to love for vegetarians and carnivores alike."

### Kitchen, The ● *American*  | 19 | 12 | 18 | $23 |

**Silver Lake** | 4348 Fountain Ave. (Sunset Blvd.) | 323-664-3663 |
www.thekitchen-silverlake.com

"Where else are you going to get your late-night meatloaf fix?" ask fans of this "unpretentious", "low-cost" Silver Lake eatery serving a "simple", "honest" menu of American comfort food in a "small", "unfinished"-looking setting; it plays host to a "colorful" crowd tended to by "familiar", quirky servers (don't be surprised if they offer to "read your palms"), but it's a little "too funky for some" and too "unimaginative" for others.

### NEW Kitchen 24 ● *American*  | - | - | - | I |

**Hollywood** | 1608 N. Cahuenga Blvd. (Hollywood Blvd.) | 323-465-2424 |
www.kitchen24.info

The food may be Traditional American, but the decor at this Hollywood arrival is futuristic-modern, with whitewashed brick walls and lamps worthy of *Star Trek*; open 24/7, it offers inexpensive options all day, including omelets, sandwiches and even a chicken-fried pork chop, while the bar pours exotic libations with names like the Thumb Sucker and the Willie Nelson.

### Koi  *Japanese*  | 24 | 25 | 20 | $68 |

**West Hollywood** | 730 N. La Cienega Blvd. (bet. Melrose &
Willoughby Aves.) | 310-659-9449 | www.koirestaurant.com

Amid the "star-seekers" and "paparazzi", this West Hollywood "celeb"-magnet that amped up the trend of tuna on crispy rice continues to "deliver the goods" with "exquisite" sushi and other "creative"

|  | FOOD | DECOR | SERVICE | COST |
|---|---|---|---|---|

Japanese dishes that make even the staff's "attitude" worth "tolerating"; with a "plush", "stunning" ambiance", fans say it's one of the few "hot" restaurants whose "hype is warranted" – just remember, you "pay for the glamour."

### Kokomo Cafe  *Southern*

| | ▽ 19 | – | 17 | $19 |
|---|---|---|---|---|

**Beverly Boulevard** | 7385 Beverly Blvd. (Martell Ave.) | West Hollywood | 323-933-0773 | www.kokomocafe.com

"That's where we want to go" croon customers who commend the "very good" breakfasts (including "great waffles" and "boffo bacon") at this casual Southern nook, which recently moved from the Farmers Market to larger digs on Beverly Boulevard; some of the offerings are fairly "average", and the service could use work, but many "like it" for the "occasional brunch or light meal."

### Koo Koo Roo  *American*

| | 15 | 9 | 13 | $13 |
|---|---|---|---|---|

**Downtown** | 255 S. Grand Ave. (3rd St.) | 213-620-1800 🆂
**Downtown** | 445 S. Figueroa St. (5th St.) | 213-629-1246 🆂
**Hancock Park** | 301 N. Larchmont Blvd. (Beverly Blvd.) | 323-962-1500
**Mid-City** | 5779 Wilshire Blvd. (bet. Courtyard Pl. & Curson Ave.) | 323-954-7200
**West Hollywood** | 8520 Santa Monica Blvd. (La Cienega Blvd.) | 310-657-3300
**Beverly Hills** | 262 S. Beverly Dr. (bet. Charleville Blvd. & Gregory Way) | 310-274-3121
**Marina del Rey** | Villa Marina Mktpl. | 4325 Glencoe Ave. (bet. Maxella Ave. & Mindanao Way) | 310-305-8100
**West LA** | 11066 Santa Monica Blvd. (Sepulveda Blvd.) | 310-473-5858
**Manhattan Beach** | Manhattan Vill. | 3294 N. Sepulveda Blvd. (Rosecrans Ave.) | 310-546-4500
**Pasadena** | 238 S. Lake Ave. (bet. Cordova St. & Del Mar Blvd.) | 626-683-9600
www.kookooroo.com
Additional locations throughout Southern California

"Serviceable and pretty healthy for fast food", this LA chain turns out "juicy" skinless rotisserie chicken and sides for "on-the-go" meals; the "tacky" "cafeteria surroundings" can be a turnoff, and some call the eats "only so-so", but otherwise it's a "no-brainer" for a "quick", "inexpensive" bite.

### Koutoubia  Ⓜ *Moroccan*

| | ▽ 20 | 20 | 19 | $45 |
|---|---|---|---|---|

**Westwood** | 2116 Westwood Blvd. (bet. Mississippi Ave. & Olympic Blvd.) | 310-475-0729 | www.koutoubiarestaurant.com

At this Moroccan "oasis" in Westwood, elaborate furnishings of North African tents and pillows set the scene for a "different" dining experience, complete with largely "excellent" b'steeya, kebabs and fresh mint tea; it's a touch "expensive", but weekend belly dancing makes it a "fun" change from the usual.

### NEW Kress, The  Ⓢ Ⓜ *Pan-Asian*

| | – | – | – | M |
|---|---|---|---|---|

**Hollywood** | 6608 Hollywood Blvd. (Whitley Ave.) | 323-785-5000

Only in Hollywood: a four-story Spanish Colonial Revival structure that last housed Frederick's is now home to this flashy restaurant and nightclub (with a lounge on the roof for good measure); those who show up for the moderately priced menu can taste the cuisine of Troy Thompson (ex Jer-ne), which includes Pan-Asian bites as well as sushi.

|  | FOOD | DECOR | SERVICE | COST |
|---|---|---|---|---|

## NEW Kula Ⓢ *Japanese* ▽ 15 | 20 | 15 | $35

**Century City** | 10351 Santa Monica Blvd. (S. Beverly Glen Blvd.) |
310-282-8870 | www.kulasushi.com

Part of a chain from Japan, this new midpriced Japanese in Century
City aims to distinguish itself by using organic products and wasabi
"made freshly" in-house, but the jury is still out on its success; set in
the space previously home to Aphrodisiac, it boasts a "very roomy"
setting sporting "beautiful" midcentury decor.

## Kung Pao Bistro *Chinese* 19 | 11 | 18 | $20

**West Hollywood** | San Fair | 7853 Santa Monica Blvd. (Fairfax Ave.) |
323-848-9888 | www.kpbistro.com
**Sherman Oaks** | 15025 Ventura Blvd. (bet. Kester & Noble Aves.) |
818-788-1689 | www.kpchinabistro.com
**Studio City** | 11838 Ventura Blvd. (bet. Colfax Ave. & Laurel Canyon Blvd.) |
818-766-8686 | www.kpbistro.com

This "popular", "fairly priced" trio (the Sherman Oaks location is separately owned) provides "healthy", "tasty", "American-style" Chinese
fare including all-white meat chicken entrees, vegetarian substitutions and "half-orders for many of the dishes"; though reviewers call
the rooms "run-down" with tables that "seem to be on top of each
other", at least the servers are "friendly as can be."

## K-Zo Ⓢ *Japanese* 23 | 20 | 22 | $41

**Culver City** | 9240 Culver Blvd. (Ince Blvd.) | 310-202-8890 | www.k-zo.com

"In a town where there are almost as many sushi bars as Starbucks",
this Culver City "jewel" stands out for "fabulous" (if "somewhat
pricey") fish and "artful" small plates by chef-owner Keizo Ishiba; despite its "random location next to Trader Joe's", the space is "beautiful" and staffed by servers who "treat you well."

## Ⓩ La Boheme *Californian* 22 | 26 | 22 | $55

**West Hollywood** | 8400 Santa Monica Blvd. (Orlando Ave.) | 323-848-2360 |
boheme.globaldiningca.com

"Opulent" and "otherworldly", this recently renovated and reopened
West Hollywood "date" place "looks like Anne Rice's dining room"
with its "dramatic" ("sort of Transylvania modern") design; the
"movie"-ready setting is supported by "skillfully prepared" Cal cuisine
and "wonderful" service, so even if a few find it "passé", others appreciate the "enchantment" it brings to "special occasions."

## La Botte *Italian* 25 | 20 | 23 | $61

**Santa Monica** | 620 Santa Monica Blvd. (7th St.) | 310-576-3072 |
www.labottesantamonica.com

"Spectacular" Italian food that's among the "finest" on the Westside can
be found at this "hidden", "high-end" Santa Monican whose "housemade pastas" are the stuff of "dreams"; wooden barrel planks covering
the walls and floor lend a "warm feel" to the "dark" dining room, and the
staff is largely "simpatico" too, though some diners cite "too many
rules" concerning how the meal is served, including "no outside wine."

## La Bottega Marino *Italian* 21 | 13 | 18 | $20

**Hancock Park** | Larchmont Vill. | 203 N. Larchmont Blvd. (bet. Beverly Blvd. &
1st St.) | 323-962-1325

*(continued)*

*(continued)*

**La Bottega Marino**

**West LA** | 11363 Santa Monica Blvd. (Purdue Ave.) | 310-477-7777
www.labottegausa.com

Granted these "little delis" in Hancock Park and West LA by chef-owner Salvatore Marino (Il Grano) are "not much to look at", but "boy" do they deliver with "fresh", "rustic" "trattoria comfort food" from "pizzas to salads to ravioli"; service is "sincere", but "could be a little sharper", so "plan on a leisurely lunch" or dinner; N.B. the Hancock Park location is BYO (with no corkage fee) and serves breakfast too.

**La Bruschetta Ristorante** *Italian*    23 | 18 | 24 | $42

**Westwood** | 1621 Westwood Blvd. (bet. Massachusetts & Ohio Aves.) | 310-477-1052

"It's like coming home to dinner" at this Westwood "standby" whose "charming" chef-owner Angelo Peloni and his "impeccable" staff "never disappoint", serving "thoughtful" Italian fare matched by a "good, not expensive" wine list; even if the room is a little "old-fashioned", guests are grateful that it's "quiet enough to talk and hear your companions."

**La Cabanita** *Mexican*    24 | 14 | 18 | $20

**Montrose** | 3447 N. Verdugo Rd. (Ocean View Blvd.) | 818-957-2711

For "real-deal Mexican cooking" "beyond the usual fare", this "homey", affordable Montrose stalwart hits the spot with "one-of-a-kind mole" dishes, chicken soup that "can cure all ills" and other "terrific" specialties; given the "fantastic" margaritas and "cheerful" service, no wonder it's "always crowded."

**Z La Cachette** Z *French*    27 | 25 | 25 | $71

**Century City** | 10506 Little Santa Monica Blvd. (Thayer Ave.) | 310-470-4992 | www.lacachetterestaurant.com

"What fine dining should be", this "jewel box" in Century City treats fans to a "first-rate" "taste of France" by chef-owner Jean Francois Meteigner, who reinvents "classic" dishes with "imagination", "elegance" and a "light" touch; service is "seamless" too, and though the "spacious" Provençal-inspired dining room feels a bit "sedate" and "elite" to some, most find it "marvelous" enough to warrant the "hefty price tag."

**La Creperie Cafe** *French*    23 | 22 | 19 | $25

**Long Beach** | 4911 E. Second St. (bet. Argonne & St. Joseph Aves.) | 562-434-8499

**NEW Manhattan Beach** | 1209 Highland Ave. (Beach Blvd.) | 310-545-3509
www.lacreperiecafe.net

Sweet and savory crêpes provide a "rich, attractive" repast at this "cool" Long Beach bistro (with a Manhattan Beach sib) whose "extravagant" surroundings cheekily look "as if France threw itself against the walls"; it plays host to a "hip", "noisy" scene, but when it's "crowded", expect "service delays" to "provide the authentic Paris experience."

**NEW La Défence** Z *Eurasian*    – | – | – | M

**Koreatown** | 3701 Wilshire Blvd. (S. Serrano Ave.) | 213-384-9500
www.ladefencerestaurant.com

When restaurants in K-town decide to go upscale, they give themselves a fancy French name, open a karaoke lounge and amp up the cuisine; in this case there's exotic sushi (all-you-can-eat most week-nights till 10 PM), as well as Eurasian fusion fare blending Japanese and Italian flavors.

### La Dijonaise Café et Boulangerie  *French*   18 | 14 | 15 | $22

**Culver City** | Helms Bldg. | 8703 Washington Blvd. (Helms Ave.) | 310-287-2770 | www.ladijonaise.com

One of the "cheapest places for good French food in LA", this "quaint" Culver City bistro and bakery offers a "consistent" menu featuring "fresh" pastries and baguettes and "fantastic" breakfasts among other "traditional", "reliable" fare; though the "aloof" service ("not rude, just French") can ruffle feathers, it's still a popular "place to sit and have a bite before hitting the stores" in the Helms Building.

### La Dolce Vita 🗷 *Italian*   22 | 20 | 23 | $59

**Beverly Hills** | 9785 Santa Monica Blvd. (Wilshire Blvd.) | 310-278-1845 | www.ladolcevitabeverlyhills.com

The "drinks are strong, the lights low" at this "time warp" in Beverly Hills where mature, well-heeled customers settle into "comfortable booths" for "tried-and-true" "East Coast-style" Italian dishes served by a "smooth" staff; though the food strikes some as "heavy", others call the "old-school" preparations part of the "charm."

### L.A. Farm 🗷 *Californian*   20 | 21 | 20 | $40

**Santa Monica** | 3000 W. Olympic Blvd. (Stewart St.) | 310-449-4000

Following a number of chef changes, this "solid" Californian in Santa Monica is still evolving while the "lovely" space continues to be reno-vated and operate with limited hours; known to attract "showbiz" types for "straightforward", "fresh" fare, it's a "comfortable" "escape" even in the midst of transition; N.B. only open Monday–Friday for lunch, with plans for dinner service to return in November 2008.

### LA Food Show  *American*   18 | 16 | 17 | $26

**Manhattan Beach** | Manhattan Vill. | 3212 N. Sepulveda Blvd. (Rosecrans Ave.) | 310-546-5575 | www.cpk.com

As a fallback for "hearty", "decent" American fare, this "California Pizza Kitchen offshoot" in the Manhattan Village Mall is a "kid-friendly" staple, with a "wide-ranging" menu suitable for "picky" eaters; though detractors deem it "middle of the road", it satisfies those seeking a "casual" atmosphere complete with "pleasant" ser-vice and a "fair" bill; N.B. a new location is set to open in Beverly Hills in fall 2008.

### La Frite  *French*   18 | 15 | 18 | $29

**Sherman Oaks** | 15013 Ventura Blvd. (Lemona Ave.) | 818-990-1791

**Woodland Hills** | 22616 Ventura Blvd. (Sale Ave.) | 818-225-1331

"Longtime local favorites", these "quirky" French bistros balance "de-pendable", no-"fuss" dishes (including the namesake "skinny" fries), "friendly" service and prices that won't "break the bank" against "tight seating" in "noisy" surroundings that are a bit "frayed around the edges" (but "more atmospheric" in Sherman Oaks than in Woodland Hills); critics contend they "used to be better", but ardent supporters say "after 1,000 meals here, I still look forward to the next one."

| | FOOD | DECOR | SERVICE | COST |
|---|---|---|---|---|

### NEW La Grande Orange  *American*

| - | - | - | M |

**Pasadena** | 260 S. Raymond Ave. (Del Mar Blvd.) | 626-356-4444
Pasadena pop-ins find this Old Town newcomer (part of a Phoenix-based chainlet) "endearing" thanks to the historic setting in the "beautifully restored" Del Mar depot, spiffed up with dark wood, lush colors and leather booths, and enhanced by "pleasant" outdoor seating with "trains running by"; its "clever", "reasonable" menu of American comfort fare tends to satisfy, though some are longing for "a little more excitement" in the cuisine and say the service "needs work."

### La Huasteca  *Mexican*

| ▽ 26 | 19 | 24 | $30 |

**Lynwood** | Plaza Mexico | 3150 E. Imperial Hwy., Ste. 100 (bet. Peach & State Sts.) | 310-537-8800 | www.lahuasteca.com
"Wonderfully authentic", "lovingly prepared" plates rooted in Southern Mexico, including "well-done" moles and "excellent" but "unusual" Sunday brunch dishes, served by an "attentive" staff "delight" diners at this "lively", slightly "upscale" Lynwood locale; handcrafted furniture and folk art lend the airy space extra soul (indeed the "funky bare-breasted women in the murals offer wholesome fun for the entire family"), and a "talented" mariachi band plays on the weekends.

### Lal Mirch  *Indian*

| ▽ 20 | 12 | 20 | $22 |

**Studio City** | 11138 Ventura Blvd. (Vineland Ave.) | 818-980-2273 | www.lmdining.com
The "spice" is right at this new Studio City "standout" where "flavorful", "aromatic" Indian dishes, including a wide veggie selection, place it on "a level above the rest"; though the "low-key" dining room doesn't turn heads, patrons say the "professional" service makes it a "strong addition" to the Valley scene.

### La Loggia  *Italian*

| 22 | 20 | 22 | $41 |

**Studio City** | 11814 Ventura Blvd. (bet. Colfax Ave. & Laurel Canyon Blvd.) | 818-985-9222
Occasional "celebrity" sightings lend a spark to this "intimate", "slightly upscale" Studio City "staple" with a covered patio, where "charming" servers present a "simple", "consistent" Italian menu that "hasn't changed in years"; even if there are "no surprises" for veteran visitors, the same owner's tapas lounge next door offers a bit more of a "scene" at night.

### La Maschera Ristorante  🗷 *Italian*

| ▽ 22 | 17 | 19 | $35 |

**Pasadena** | 82 N. Fair Oaks Ave. (Holly St.) | 626-304-0004 | www.lamascheraristorante.com
In restaurant-saturated Old Town, this "off-the-beaten-path" Pasadena Italian "impresses" with "wonderful" cooking complemented by a large cheese and salumi selection and a "great wine list", all for a relative "bargain"; though a few find the "interesting" environs with a "Middle Eastern" look a bit too "dark", the ambiance gets a lift from projections of "old movies" on the wall.

### NEW LAMILL Coffee Boutique  *Californian*

| 23 | 23 | 19 | $23 |

**Silver Lake** | 1636 Silver Lake Blvd. (Effie St.) | 323-663-4441 | www.lamillcoffee.com
There's "nothing in LA like it" say early adopters of this "beautiful" Silver Lake coffeehouse where "every minute detail" has been thoroughly

| | FOOD | DECOR | SERVICE | COST |
|---|---|---|---|---|

"thought out", from the "exquisite" if "minimal" Californian menu by chef/co-owner Michael Cimarusti (Providence) to the "sensational" cups of java; the "bright, modern" space is staffed by "intelligent" servers in "high-waisted jeans" who are "happy to explain" the choices, but some say a "pretentious" feel and "top-dollar" prices leave a bitter taste.

### Lamonica's NY Pizza ●⊅ *Pizza*    21 | 11 | 14 | $11

**Westwood** | 1066 Gayley Ave. (Kinross Ave.) | 310-208-8671
More than an "affordable" pit stop "before Bruin games", this "classic" Westwood pizzeria serves "one of the best New York slices" around, keeping it "real" with dough shipped from the Big Apple; it's not big on looks, but fans call it "perfect" for what it is, especially when the "late-night munchies" hit.

### ☒ Langer's Deli ☒ *Deli*    25 | 9 | 18 | $19

**Downtown** | 704 S. Alvarado St. (7th St.) | 213-483-8050 | www.langersdeli.com
Mavens "make a pilgrimage" to this 1947-vintage daytime deli that's "world-renowned" for its hand-sliced "pastrami perfection" ("order the No. 19" sandwich), homemade pickles and "kugel to kvell for"; though some are deterred by the "dodgy" Downtown location, the "always hospitable, no-nonsense" staff and a panoply of patrons (from "LAPD" to "yuppies" to "blue-collar types") make it a "true LA treasure"; P.S. "call ahead" for curbside service.

### ☒ Langham Huntington Dining Room ☒Ⓜ *Californian*    26 | 27 | 26 | $67
### (fka Ritz-Carlton Huntington Dining Room)

**Pasadena** | Langham Huntington Hotel & Spa | 1401 S. Oak Knoll Ave. (Huntington Dr.) | 626-568-3900 | www.langhamhotels.com
"Dining here makes you feel like old money" say surveyors spoiled by this Pasadena "grande dame" where "each bite is a jewel" thanks to "ingenious" chef Craig Strong, whose "inventive and well-conceived" Californian dinners are bolstered by "fabulous" service; a "quiet" "respite from all the ultratrendy places", it's "where you go to impress someone"; N.B. jacket suggested.

### La Paella ☒ *Spanish*    23 | 18 | 20 | $37

**Beverly Hills** | 476 S. San Vicente Blvd. (bet. La Cienega & Wilshire Blvds.) | 323-951-0745 | www.usalapaella.com
"Textbook" tapas, "paella from heaven" and a "fabulous" wine list have those in-the-know calling this moderately priced Beverly Hills Spaniard a "treat for the senses", blowing away all the "pretenders passing off small plates" of non-Iberian fare; a "welcoming" staff adds to the "convivial" atmosphere of the "homey", ceramic-accented dining room, which feels "like a little village spot in Spain."

### La Pergola *Italian*    22 | 20 | 23 | $41

**Sherman Oaks** | 15005 Ventura Blvd. (Lemona Ave.) | 818-905-8402
"Freshly picked" produce from the restaurant's own garden supports "inventive" Italian meals at this "high-end" yet "reasonable" Sherman Oaks "find" where "everyone looks happy" to be there; tended to by a "charming" staff and "friendly" chef-owner who likes to talk "vegetables" with the patrons, the flower-filled space is "adorable" with Florentine "pottery on display."

|  | FOOD | DECOR | SERVICE | COST |
|---|---|---|---|---|

### Larchmont Grill  *American*

| 22 | 22 | 25 | $37 |

**Hollywood** | 5750 Melrose Ave. (Lucerne Ave.) | 323-464-4277 | www.larchmontgrill.com

"You can't get friendlier service" gush guests of this "cozy" Hollywood New American housed in a converted Craftsman that's "well-lit with a fireplace", boasts a second-floor balcony and "wonderfully doesn't feel like LA"; the "simple", "delicious" cooking is "comforting" too, and there are "plenty of selections at good prices" on the wine list, which is half-off on Tuesdays.

### Lares ● *Mexican*

| 19 | 16 | 19 | $23 |

**Santa Monica** | 2909 Pico Blvd. (29th St.) | 310-829-4559 | www.laresrestaurant.com

"Holy mole" exclaim amigos of this affordable, "dependable" family-owned Mexican in Santa Monica dishing up "lovely home-cooked" meals and "strong" margaritas; there's still a "noisy" scene going on "after all these years", especially in the airy upstairs room, and "live music adds to the ambiance."

### La Rive Gauche  *French*

| ▽ 19 | 15 | 20 | $44 |

**Palos Verdes Estates** | 320 Tejon Pl. (Palos Verdes Dr.) | 310-378-0267

This "aging classic" in Palos Verdes has an air of "elegance", offering "traditional" if "not consistent" French cuisine in a subdued fashion; the "tired" atmosphere is a sticking point, however, with a number of guests deeming it "pretentious" and "living in the past", concluding that it "needs an update" *tout de suite.*

### Larkin's Ⓜ *Southern*

| 20 | 23 | 21 | $26 |

**Eagle Rock** | 1496 Colorado Blvd. (Loleta Ave.) | 323-254-0934 | www.larkinsjoint.com

Offering a "clever" "spin on soul food", this "super-charming" BYO in Eagle Rock by chef-owner Larkin Mackey serves up "flavorful", "inexpensive" contemporary Southern fare in a "beautifully restored Craftsman home" filled with local artwork; "gracious" service completes the picture, making it a new "personal favorite" of many.

### NEW Larsen's Steakhouse  *Steak*

| - | - | - | E |

**Encino** | 16101 Ventura Blvd. (Woodley Ave.) | 818-386-9500 | www.larsensteakhouse.com

Situated on the second floor of a glitzy shopping center, this Encino steakhouse offers caveman portions of a full range of classic dishes to locals lusting for a beef fix; the setting is dark and plush with polished wood and rich colors, and prices are correspondingly upscale.

### La Scala Ⓢ *Italian*

| 21 | 17 | 21 | $35 |

**Beverly Hills** | 434 N. Cañon Dr. (bet. Brighton Way & Santa Monica Blvd.) | 310-275-0579

### La Scala Presto Ⓢ *Italian*

**Brentwood** | 11740 San Vicente Blvd. (bet. Barrington & Montana Aves.) | 310-826-6100

The "legendary" chopped salad still "rules" at this "old-line" Beverly Hills Italian that attracts "lunching ladies" and others who sink into the "comfy red booths" and remember "how restaurants used to be"; the Brentwood location is a bit lower-key, but offers the same "dependable", moderate menu and "consistent" service.

| | FOOD | DECOR | SERVICE | COST |
|---|---|---|---|---|

## La Serenata de Garibaldi  *Mexican/Seafood*  22 | 14 | 18 | $29

**Boyle Heights** | 1842 E. First St. (bet. Boyle Ave. & State St.) | 323-265-2887
**Santa Monica** | 1416 Fourth St. (Santa Monica Blvd.) | 310-656-7017

## La Serenata Gourmet  *Mexican/Seafood*

**West LA** | 10924 W. Pico Blvd. (Westwood Blvd.) | 310-441-9667
www.laserenataonline.com

"Don't expect a burrito" at this "high-quality" Mexican trio preparing "spectacular" seafood with "tantalizing" sauces, among other "delectable", "affordable" specialties; while both the "colonial" decor and the service "vary" depending on the location, many recommend taking "out-of-town foodies" on a "trek" to the Boyle Heights original.

## Lasher's Ⓜ *American*  23 | 22 | 23 | $43

**Long Beach** | 3441 E. Broadway (bet. Newport & Redondo Aves.) | 562-433-0153 | www.lashersrestaurant.com

"Solid", "high-end American comfort food" surprises with a "touch" of Southern "spice" at this "adorable" "little Craftsman" where couples nestle into "romantic nooks", whether "by the fireplace" or on the "sun-dappled patio"; though it's "a little out of the way" in Long Beach, the "helpful but not intrusive" owners, Ray and Lynn Lasher, and a "lively, capable staff" make it extra "inviting."

## La Sosta Enoteca Ⓜ *Italian*  ∇ 26 | 21 | 23 | $51

**Hermosa Beach** | 2700 Manhattan Ave. (27th St.) | 310-318-1556

"Terrific" Northern Italian fare, featuring "top-notch" gnocchi and a "cutting board of cheeses and meats" sliced to order, is complemented by a "fantastic" wine list at this "quaint", "romantic" Hermosa Beach bistro; most agree "engaging" owner Luca Manderino and his staff provide a "warm" welcome, though some critics feel cool about the "costly" specials and "small portions for big prices."

## La Terza  *Italian*  22 | 19 | 20 | $51

**Third Street** | Orlando Hotel | 8384 W. Third St. (Orlando Ave.) | West Hollywood | 323-782-8384

"Beautifully prepared" "regional Italian delicacies" and a "wicked" wine list delight "foodie" followers of this Third Street sib to Angelini Osteria with a "minimalist" look ("think Milan"); some feel it "lacks ambiance", however, and would like finer service considering the "expense."

## La Vecchia Cucina  *Italian*  21 | 17 | 20 | $35

**Santa Monica** | 2654 Main St. (bet. Hill St. & Ocean Park Blvd.) | 310-399-7979 | www.lavecchiacucina.com

Santa Monica "swoons" over this "sleeper" offering "delicious" Italian fare and "one of the best happy hours in town" for a bar bite ("get there early" or "you won't get a seat"); though the "cozy" dining room means tables are a bit "close together", "accommodating" service helps make up for the squeeze.

## 🆕 Lawry's Carvery  *American*  19 | 11 | 15 | $20

**Century City** | Westfield Century City Shopping Ctr. | 10250 Santa Monica Blvd. (bet. Ave. of the Stars & Century Park W.) | 310-432-0101 | www.lawrysonline.com

"Lawry's famed prime rib on-the-go" is the draw at this "deli-style walk-up" in Century City, where mall shoppers and business lunchers make "quick" meals of "hearty", "hand-carved" sandwiches; fussy

FOOD | DECOR | SERVICE | COST

voters sniff it's "not as good" as the original, but fans say it's an "excellent low-cost alternative" for a "red-meat fix."

## ☑ Lawry's The Prime Rib  *Steak*  24 | 21 | 24 | $53
**Beverly Hills** | 100 N. La Cienega Blvd. (Wilshire Blvd.) | 310-652-2827 | www.lawrysonline.com

Like the name says, it's all about the "first-class prime rib" at this Beverly Hills "legend" and flagship of the "high-quality" steakhouse chain where "beautiful slabs" are "carved tableside" by an "attentive" crew; harking back to a "bygone era", it's often "crowded with tourists" hungry for a taste of "old LA", so its "quaint style" now feels a bit too "commercial" to some.

## Lazy Dog Cafe, The  *Eclectic*  19 | 20 | 19 | $23
**Torrance** | Del Amo Fashion Ctr. | 3525 W. Carson St. (Torrance Blvd.) | 310-921-6080 | www.thelazydogcafe.com

A "cute theme" with appealing decor for "dog lovers" sets an "upbeat" tone at this "casual", "family-friendly" Torrance link in a SoCal chain offering a "creative yet comfortable" Eclectic menu with a number of international "twists and turns"; service is "efficient", but given the "busy" atmosphere, there are often "long waits, especially on the weekends."

## Leaf Cuisine  *Vegan*  17 | 12 | 14 | $16
**Culver City** | 11938 W. Washington Blvd. (Inglewood Blvd.) | 310-390-6005
**Sherman Oaks** | 14318 Ventura Blvd. (Beverly Glen Blvd.) | 818-907-8779
www.leafcuisine.com

"Health" is the watchword at these "affordable" Culver City and Sherman Oaks vegans specializing in "creative", "filling" raw cuisine that some call "delicious" and others deem too "bland and green" ("I went back to meat!"); considering the "lackluster" digs and "subpar" service, critics contend "you need to be a die-hard" veggie fan to enjoy it.

## Le Chêne  *French*  ▽ 23 | 17 | 20 | $42
**Saugus** | 12625 Sierra Hwy. (Sierra Vallejo Rd.) | 661-251-4315 | www.lechene.com

An "original" in a "land of lacquered menus and boxy chains", this "fine" "slice of France" in Saugus wins over wayfarers with its "unbelievable" wine list and "inventive" upscale menu featuring "lots of game"; enhanced by a rustic river rock exterior and an "inviting" atmosphere, it's a "true destination" for many, though some feel it should be "better for the price."

## ☑ Leila's ⑤Ⓜ *Californian*  27 | 19 | 24 | $46
**Oak Park** | RE/MAX Plaza | 706 Lindero Canyon Rd. (Golden Eagle Dr.) | 818-707-6939 | www.leilasrestaurant.com

"Quite a surprise" considering its "strip-mall exterior", this "always fabulous" Californian in Oak Park provides "awesome", "frequently changing" seasonal fare by "superb" chef Richie DeMane, who "obviously loves food"; "reasonable" choices on the "outstanding" wine list and "personable" service add to the "positive" experience, though some feel the colorful, "eclectic" setting "could use some work."

|  | FOOD | DECOR | SERVICE | COST |
|---|---|---|---|---|

### Le Marmiton  *French*

| 18 | 16 | 14 | $28 |

**Santa Monica** | 1327 Montana Ave. (bet. Euclid & 14th Sts.) | 310-393-7716

### Le Marmiton Marina  *French*

**Marina del Rey** | 4724 Admiralty Way (Mindanao Way) | 310-773-3560

"Good" French breakfast dishes, pastries and "lots of carry-out choices" attract Westsiders to this scaled-down Santa Monica French (open till 8 PM), while the "breezy" patio and slightly more "formal" interior at Marina del Rey play host to "pleasant" meals from morning to night; they can be "terrific" at times, but a number of diners leave "disappointed", citing "inconsistent" cooking and "poor" service.

### NEW Lemonade Cafe  ⊠ *Californian*

| - | - | - | I |

**Downtown** | 505 S. Flower St. (5th St.) | 213-488-0299
**Beverly Hills** | 9001 Beverly Blvd. (Almont Dr.) | 310-247-2500
www.lemonadela.com

Having opened two branches just weeks apart – in Beverly Hills (for shoppers) and Downtown (for workers) – this casual Californian cafeteria appears confident in its ability to provide good cheap dining in bad economic times; its serve-yourself breakfast and lunch fare, including made-in-house breads and pastries, can be consumed under umbrellas on an outdoor patio or at a handful of tables inside.

### Lemon Moon  ⊠ *Californian/Mediterranean*

| 20 | 14 | 15 | $17 |

**West LA** | Westside Media Ctr. | 12200 W. Olympic Blvd. (S. Bundy Dr.) | 310-442-9191 | www.lemonmoon.com

West LA workers "can't get enough of those prepared salads", "inventive" sandwiches or "excellent" breakfast items at this high-end cafeteria-style Cal-Med by the team of Josiah Citrin (Mélisse) and Raphael Lunetta (JiRaffe); located in an office building and open weekday mornings and afternoons only, it's industrial yet "light and airy" with a patio, but be prepared to "fight the crowds" at the counter at lunch.

### Le Pain Quotidien  *Bakery/Belgian*

| 19 | 16 | 15 | $20 |

**West Hollywood** | 8607 Melrose Ave. (bet. Huntley & Westbourne Drs.) | 310-854-3700
**Beverly Hills** | 320 S. Robertson Blvd. (bet. Burton Way & 3rd St.) | 310-858-7270
**Beverly Hills** | 9630 Little Santa Monica Blvd. (bet. Bedford & Camden Drs.) | 310-859-1100
**Brentwood** | Barrington Ct. | 11702 Barrington Ct. (Barrington Ave.) | 310-476-0969
**NEW Brentwood** | 13050 San Vicente Blvd. (26th St.) | 310-393-8909
**Santa Monica** | 316 Santa Monica Blvd. (4th St.) | 310-393-6800
**Westwood** | 1055 Broxton Ave. (bet. Kinross & Weyburn Aves.) | 310-824-7900
**Manhattan Beach** | Metlox Ctr. | 451 Manhattan Beach Blvd. (bet. Morningside & Valley Drs.) | 310-546-6411
**Pasadena** | 88 W. Colorado Blvd. (De Lacey Ave.) | 626-396-0956
**Studio City** | 13045 Ventura Blvd. (Valley Vista Blvd.) | 818-986-1929
www.lepainquotidien.com

This "civilized", slightly "pricey" Belgian bakery/cafe chain "pleases" patrons with "amazing" pastries, "excellent" organic breads and "refreshing" salads and tartine sandwiches; its rustic communal tables are conducive to a "convivial atmosphere", making it a "sure bet" for a "quick bite" as long as "you can get the attention of the staff."

### Le Petit Bistro  *French*

22 | 17 | 19 | $37

**West Hollywood** | 631 N. La Cienega Blvd. (Melrose Ave.) | 310-289-9797 | www.lepetitbistro.us

"Just like a Paris bistro", this WeHo French is "brimming with joie de vivre", with tables so close "you can share a baguette with a stranger", not to mention "hearty" plates of other "delicious" "delicacies"; "expats" and somewhat "snooty service" are also part of the package, making it feel all the more "genuine."

### Le Petit Cafe  ⓩ *French*

21 | 15 | 20 | $34

**Santa Monica** | 2842 Colorado Ave. (bet. Stewart & Yale Sts.) | 310-829-6792 | www.lepetitcafebonjour.com

"Charming" and "cozy" as its name suggests, this family-run French "farmhouse amid studios" in Santa Monica provides an "escape to Provence" with its "wholesome", "traditional" bistro fare for an "excellent value", "delightful" service and classic blue-and-yellow decor; since it tends to feel "cramped", insiders insist it's "best with no more than four people."

### Le Petit Four  *French*

19 | 18 | 17 | $35

**West Hollywood** | Sunset Plaza | 8654 W. Sunset Blvd. (Sunset Plaza Dr.) | 310-652-3863 | www.lepetitfour.net

"Show up in your Ferrari" at this Sunset Plaza bistro, a magnet for the "fashion crowd", "modelizers" and "European expats" that provides plenty of West Hollywood "people-watching" from the sidewalk tables; though the French fare is "secondary to the scene", admirers admit it's "consistently tasty" and not too extravagant "after shopping on the Strip"; P.S. there's lots of free "parking in the back."

### Le Petit Greek  *Greek*

19 | 15 | 19 | $30

**Hancock Park** | 127 N. Larchmont Blvd. (1st St.) | 323-464-5160 | www.lepetitgreek.com

"Always predictably good", this "casual", family-owned Greek in Hancock Park can be counted on for "tender" lamb, "fresh" salads and other "steady" dishes; "welcoming" service and the "added bonus" of a "chill" patio make it a "favorite neighborhood" stop, even if some call it "a little pricey for what it is."

### Le Petit Restaurant  *French*

21 | 18 | 20 | $37

**Sherman Oaks** | 13360 Ventura Blvd. (Dixie Canyon Ave.) | 818-501-7999 | www.lepetitrestaurant.net

"Smartly prepared" French staples satisfy "appreciative guests" at this "reasonably priced" Sherman Oaks bistro tended to by a "cordial" staff; as it's "noisy, crowded" and "charming", "you could be in Paris", but the "popular" lobster special Monday–Tuesday nights "reminds you it's good to be in the U.S."

### Le Saigon  Ⓜ⊅ *Vietnamese*

21 | 11 | 19 | $16

**West LA** | 11611 Santa Monica Blvd. (bet. Barry & Federal Aves.) | 310-312-2929

This "solid" Vietnamese "fullfills a pho craving" for West LA customers who commend its "excellent savory meals" served on the "cheap" by a "warm, helpful" staff; it's strictly "no-frills" and "cash-only", but "worth a trip to the ATM."

| | FOOD | DECOR | SERVICE | COST |
|---|---|---|---|---|

### Le Sanglier French Restaurant 🅼 *French* ▽ 24 | 21 | 23 | $54

**Tarzana** | 5522 Crebs Ave. (Ventura Blvd.) | 818-345-0470 |
www.lesanglierrestaurant.com

Big game hunters are in for a "treat" at this "upscale" Tarzana "tradition" whose "extensive" menu of "imaginative" French fare highlights delicacies like roast duck and wild boar; its "lodge"-like interior is "lowkey" and often filled with longtime "regulars", and though a few critics find it "overpriced", most agree it's "lovely" for "special occasions."

### 🆉 Les Sisters Southern Kitchen 🅼 *Southern* 23 | 10 | 20 | $22

**Chatsworth** | 21818 Devonshire St. (Jordan Ave.) | 818-998-0755

"Killer fried chicken", "slabs of ribs" and "gumbo from heaven" are the thing at this Chatsworth joint where the "authentic" Southern soul cooking is just as "down-home" as the service; sure, it's a "tiny" "hole-in-the-wall", but the "large portions mean you never leave hungry."

### Liberty Grill *American* 18 | 17 | 19 | $29

**Downtown** | 1037 S. Flower St. (11th St. & Olympic Blvd.) | 213-746-3400 |
www.liberty-grill.com

"Convenient to Staples", this "casual" Downtown American with a "wonderful" patio serves up "simple", "decent" plates of "comfort food" (the fried mac 'n' cheese bites "hurt so good") to a "sports" crowd; the staff makes it "easy to get in and out", though you may need a reservation "before the game."

### Library Alehouse *Eclectic* 18 | 16 | 17 | $23

**Santa Monica** | 2911 Main St. (bet. Ashland Ave. & Marine St.) |
310-314-4855 | www.libraryalehouse.com

"Artists, musicians and interesting professionals" gather "after stressful days" and on "lazy weekends" at this "hopping" Santa Monica "hang" for "upscale", "well-executed" Eclectic "pub grub" and an "amazing" selection of microbrews (the "main event"); it's "cozy" and often "jammed" inside, but savvy guests "get there early" to stake out a table on the "charming" patio – "the place to be."

### Lido di Manhattan *Italian/Mediterranean* ▽ 19 | 16 | 20 | $33

**Manhattan Beach** | 1550 Rosecrans Ave. (bet. Market Pl. & Parkway Dr.) |
310-536-0730 | www.lidodimanhattan.com

"A big menu" of pizza, pasta and other "consistently good" Italian-Med eats "satisfies everyone" at this "comfortable" Manhattan Beach strip-maller that's strong on "value"; with servers who "remember" you and occasional live music, it suits an "impromptu evening out."

### 🆕 Lido Grill *Mediterranean* - | - | - | M

**Venice** | 417 Washington Blvd. (Clune Ave.) | 310-577-3030

In the Restaurant Row at the western end of Venice's Washington Boulevard, this affordable Mediterranean offers an extensive roster of tapas, paella and cioppino; grab a seat by the front windows, where you can watch a parade of humanity that's hard to match.

### Lilly's French Cafe & Wine Bar *French* 19 | 20 | 16 | $37

**Venice** | 1031 Abbot Kinney Blvd. (Westminster Ave.) | 310-314-0004 |
www.lillysfrenchcafe.com

At this "sweet", "affordable Abbot Kinney mainstay", the Gallic fare is "reliable" and the service is "reliably nonexistent", but some say,

| | FOOD | DECOR | SERVICE | COST |
|---|---|---|---|---|

"they're French" so "get over it"; just have some wine (120 are available by the glass) and "relax" on the "lovely" patio, which is particularly "delightful on summer evenings" and the "way to go" for brunch.

**Limon Latin Grill** *Pan-Latin* ▽ 18 | 19 | 15 | $31

**Simi Valley** | 1555 Simi Town Center Way (1st St.) | 805-955-9277 | www.limongrill.com

"Bringing a little Latin love" to Simi Valley, this eatery decked out with "excellent" decor (ironwork on the walls, champagne-toned booths) whips up inexpensive Cuban sandwiches, Brazilian *churrasco* and Argentinean steak all under one roof; live music on the weekends adds extra flavor, though lackluster service and "inconsistent" food make the fiesta fizzle for some.

**Literati Café** *Californian/Eclectic* 19 | 17 | 17 | $32

**West LA** | 12081 Wilshire Blvd. (S. Bundy Dr.) | 310-231-7484 | www.literaticafe.com

**Literati II** *Californian/Eclectic*

**West LA** | 12081 Wilshire Blvd. (S. Bundy Dr.) | 310-479-3400 | www.literati2.com

This "casual" cafe in West LA and its next-door "upscale" offshoot offer two distinct dining experiences: one has a "cerebral coffee-shop vibe", plying "laptop"-laden "students and writers" with "simple, fresh" salads, sandwiches and pastries, while the "sequel" serves up "winning" Cal-Eclectic dishes in "sleek but homey" white-tablecloth digs; the service "could stand a little perking up" at both, however, which some tag "a tad pricey."

**NEW Little Dom's** *Italian* 17 | 22 | 20 | $38

**Los Feliz** | 2128 Hillhurst Ave. (Avocado St.) | 323-661-0055 | www.littledoms.com

Boasting "beautiful" "deco decor" like marble-topped tables "right out of the '30s", this Dominick's spin-off is "abuzz" with a "hip" Los Feliz crowd sampling "simple", "rich" pastas, pizzas and other Italian eats served by a "thoughtful" staff; some lament that it's "overpriced" and "average" with "lots of kinks to be worked out", but hopeful types urge "improve the food and you have a hit!"

**Z Little Door, The** *Mediterranean* 23 | 26 | 21 | $58

**Third Street** | 8164 W. Third St. (bet. Kilkea Dr. & La Jolla Ave.) | 323-951-1210 | www.thelittledoor.com

A "scintillating" place that will "wow your date and ensure a second", this high-end Third Street Mediterranean "defines romantic" thanks to its "gorgeous" garden, "phenomenal" decor and "superb", "memorable" dishes with a hint of "French North Africa", matched by a "stellar" wine list; "charming" service that's "attentive yet never intrusive" "seals the deal."

**Little Tokyo Shabu Shabu** *Japanese* ▽ 20 | 14 | 18 | $23

**Rowland Heights** | Diamond Plaza | 1330 S. Fullerton Rd. (Hwy. 60, ext. 19) | 626-810-6037 | www.littletokyoshabushabu.com

Handy "if you want to cook your own food", this affordable Rowland Heights Japanese offers neophytes a "unique experience" of swishing Angus beef, seafood and veggies shabu-shabu style; its "trendy" environs get a mixed response, but "fast", "friendly" servers compensate.

|  | FOOD | DECOR | SERVICE | COST |
|---|---|---|---|---|

### Lobster, The  *Seafood*
22 | 23 | 21 | $54

**Santa Monica** | 1602 Ocean Ave. (Colorado Ave.) | 310-458-9294 | www.thelobster.com

Guests navigate "crowded" waters for "awe-inspiring" ocean views at this "happy, noisy" and sustainably focused seafooder at the Santa Monica pier serving "shellfish galore" and other "fresh, well-presented" dishes along with "spectacular" Bloody Marys concocted by "top-notch" bartenders; though some cry "tourist trap", most say "go anyway" and splurge for a "pleasant surprise"; N.B. it's certified 'green' with solar panels on the roof.

### Local Place, The  *American/Hawaiian*
18 | 13 | 16 | $11

**Torrance** | 18605 S. Western Ave. (W. 186th St.) | 310-523-3233

"Quick" "'local-kine' food" is the draw at this Hawaiian "fast-food eatery and bakery" in Torrance where the dishes are "decent" but the "sweet" bread and "light" cakes are "a slice of paradise"; while it's "no-frills" all around, everything comes at a "good price."

### Locanda del Lago  *Italian*
21 | 18 | 20 | $37

**Santa Monica** | 231 Arizona Ave. (2nd St.) | 310-451-3525 | www.lagosantamonica.com

"We need to keep this one quiet" say fans of this "intimate" Santa Monican by the Promenade serving "flavorful" Northern Italian fare that's "reasonably priced for the quality", complemented by wines from the 400-bottle cellar; "courteous" service and sidewalk tables perfect for "people-watching" complete the picture.

### Locanda Veneta  *Italian*
24 | 17 | 21 | $52

**Third Street** | 8638 W. Third St. (Willaman Dr.) | 310-274-1893

"After all these years" this "tiny", "expensive" Third Street Italian is "still the king" of Venetian cuisine in the eyes of admirers, with "pleasant" servers delivering "delicious" homemade pastas and other "savory" dishes matched by "wonderful wines"; though the "classic" space is a bit "too cramped" (especially with all the "big Hollywood attitudes" in the room), that can be overlooked when the "real star is what's on the plate."

### Lodge Steakhouse, The  *Steak*
19 | 20 | 18 | $63

**Beverly Hills** | 14 N. La Cienega Blvd. (Wilshire Blvd.) | 310-854-0024 | www.thelodgesteakhouse.com

"Am I in Banff or Beverly Hills?" ask guests of this "swanky", "wood-paneled ski lodge" that plays host to "posh" dinners and "late-night" bites (till midnight on the weekends) of "scrumptious" steaks, "magnificent" martinis and even "bacon strips at the bar"; some are "disappointed" by the service, however, and cite "hit-or-miss" meals, sighing "if only the food lived up to the setting."

### Loft, The  *Hawaiian*
19 | 13 | 18 | $15

**Cerritos** | 20157 Pioneer Blvd. (Del Amo Blvd.) | 562-402-3538 Ⓜ
**Torrance** | 23305 Hawthorne Blvd. (Lomita Blvd.) | 310-375-4051
www.thelofthawaii.com

Fans say *"mahalo"* to "tasty" Hawaiian "comfort food" served in "portions so big" that "take-home boxes are almost mandatory" at this "accommodating", "kid-friendly" and "funky" mini-chain; the "reasonable" tabs impress mainlanders and ex-islanders alike, though many deem it a place to "eat and get out as soon as you've filled your belly."

|  | FOOD | DECOR | SERVICE | COST |
|---|---|---|---|---|

**L'Opera** *Italian* | 23 | 23 | 22 | $51

**Long Beach** | 101 Pine Ave. (bet. B'way & Ocean Blvd.) | 562-491-0066 | www.lopera.com

Romantics rate this "expensive" Northern Italian in Long Beach a winner for "that special night out", a "true gourmet experience" with "sophisticated" cuisine, an "unbelievable" wine list and a staff that makes "helpful" recommendations; while it's "noisy" at times, the atmosphere inside a vintage converted bank has a "plush, old-world" feel, embellished by live opera singers on the weekends.

**Los Balcones del Peru** Ⓜ *Peruvian* | ▽ 18 | 7 | 16 | $22

**Hollywood** | 1360 N. Vine St. (De Longpre Ave.) | 323-871-9600

Ceviche and other "wonderfully flavorful" dishes attract diners to this inexpensive Hollywood Peruvian that's a "good choice before the ArcLight"; while the colonial-accented decor doesn't fly with most ("please fix"), it makes the grade for a "laid-back", "casual" meal, and has the "potential" to be even better.

**Lotería! Grill** *Mexican* | 24 | 8 | 13 | $15

**Fairfax** | Grove at Farmers Mkt. | 6333 W. Third St. (Fairfax Ave.) | 323-930-2211 | www.loteriagrill.com

🆕 **Hollywood** | 6627 Hollywood Blvd. (N. Cherokee Ave.) | 323-465-2500

"Wade through the tourists" at the Farmers Market and pull up a stool at this Mexican stall where "addictive" mole and other "authentic", "unusual" dishes promise a "fiesta of flavor" and win massive support ("long lines" are a given) even if service "can be a bit dicey"; its new Hollywood branch is a folk art–adorned sit-down venue with an expanded menu and an encyclopedic selection of tequilas.

🆕 **Lot 1** Ⓜ *American* | - | - | - | M

**Echo Park** | 1533 Sunset Blvd. (Echo Park Ave.) | 213-481-8400

With nine tables inside and three on the sidewalk, this New American in increasingly gentrified Echo Park has an intimate feel, with a black-and-tan color scheme and a jazz soundtrack; the moderately priced fare exhibits a quirky modern sensibility, as in gazpacho made with beets and chicharrones.

**Lou** ●🅱 *Eclectic/Mediterranean* | 23 | 19 | 21 | $38

**Hollywood** | 724 Vine St. (Melrose Ave.) | 323-962-6369 | www.louonvine.com

Guests go ga-ga for the "outrageous" pig candy ("makes me want to dance naked") and other "unusual", "beautiful" bites "perfect for sharing" at this Med-Eclectic Hollywood "boîte" whose "inspired" cellar offers plenty of "big wines to go with the small plates"; despite its "unlikely" strip-mall setting, the "intimate" interior with a "New York feel" is "just lovely" and tended to by a "knowledgable" staff, though some warn that the bill "adds up quickly"; P.S. the prix fixe "Monday suppers are a fun adventure."

**Louise's Trattoria** *Californian/Italian* | 17 | 14 | 17 | $24

**Hancock Park** | 232 N. Larchmont Blvd. (Beverly Blvd.) | 323-962-9510
**Los Feliz** | 4500 Los Feliz Blvd. (Hillhurst Ave.) | 323-667-0777
**Melrose** | 7505 Melrose Ave. (Gardner St.) | 323-651-3880
**Brentwood** | 264 26th St. (San Vicente Blvd.) | 310-451-5001

|  | FOOD | DECOR | SERVICE | COST |
|--|------|-------|---------|------|

*(continued)*

**Louise's Trattoria**

**Santa Monica** | 1008 Montana Ave. (10th St.) | 310-394-8888
**West LA** | 10645 W. Pico Blvd. (bet. Manning & Pelham Aves.) |
310-475-6084
**Pasadena** | 2-8 E. Colorado Blvd. (Fair Oaks Ave.) | 626-568-3030
**Studio City** | 12050 Ventura Blvd. (Laurel Canyon Blvd.) | 818-762-2662
www.louises.com

"Huge portions" and a "large selection" of "predictable" Cal-Italian dishes have earned this chain a "loyal following" that relies on it for "relaxed" "everyday dining"; though the service is "mediocre" and the decor is "ordinary", it "serves a purpose", especially for "budget"-minded "families."

**Lucille's Smokehouse Bar-B-Que** *BBQ* | 22 | 18 | 19 | $27 |

**NEW Cerritos** | 11338 E. South St. (Gridley Rd.) | 562-916-7427
**Long Beach** | 4828 E. Second St. (bet. Park & St. Joseph Aves.) | 562-434-7427
**Long Beach** | Long Beach Towne Ctr. | 7411 Carson St. (Nectar Ave.) |
562-938-7427
**Torrance** | Del Amo Fashion Ctr. | 21420 Hawthorne Blvd.
(Del Amo Circle Blvd.) | 310-370-7427
www.lucillesbbq.com

Hefty plates of "savory" BBQ with "all the soul food fixin's" ensure "you'll never leave hungry (unless you're a vegan)" from these "crowded", "noisy" joints where "two can easily eat for the price of one" if you share; "friendly" "college-kid" servers and "well-executed" theme decor with mismatched furniture encourage a "Southern roadhouse" vibe, but "long waits" are part of the package, especially on weekends.

**Lucky Devils** *American* | 20 | 15 | 16 | $22 |

**Hollywood** | 6613 Hollywood Blvd. (Whitley Ave.) | 323-465-8259 |
www.luckydevils-la.com

"Right in the thick" of "Hollyweird", this "tiny", "happy-go-lucky" joint (open till midnight on the weekends) offers a "cool twist on American diner food", turning out "jazzed-up", "pricey" burgers, "deadly" milkshakes and an "amazing" beer selection; though some dis the decor as "anonymously sterile", it's always a kick to catch a "glance" of hunky owner-actor Lucky Vanous "behind the grill."

**NEW Luckyfish** *Japanese* | ∇ 18 | 22 | 22 | $36 |

**Beverly Hills** | 338 N. Cañon Dr. (Dayton Way) | 310-274-9800 |
www.luckyfishsushi.com

Fans are "totally hooked" on the "instant gratification" of conveyor-belt sushi at this "energetic" Beverly Hills newcomer (from the Sushi Roku team) sporting a "hip" interior with a photographic cherry tree mural and relatively "inexpensive" "color-coded plates" of "quality" fish; there's "knowledgeable" service too, and the system lets you "get in and out at your own pace", though some feel the offerings are ultimately "commonplace", making it a "novelty restaurant for sushi novices."

**Z Lucques** *Californian/Mediterranean* | 27 | 24 | 25 | $61 |

**West Hollywood** | 8474 Melrose Ave. (La Cienega Blvd.) | 323-655-6277 |
www.lucques.com

Dining is a "dream" at this "casually elegant" Cal-Med in West Hollywood where "brilliant" chef/co-owner Suzanne Goin (A.O.C.)

| | FOOD | DECOR | SERVICE | COST |
|---|---|---|---|---|

continues to "surprise and delight" with "inventive" dishes highlighting the "farms' freshest" ingredients, served by a "spot-on" staff; "warm" with a "cozy fireplace" and "charming" patio, the converted carriage house has an "inviting", "grown-up" atmosphere to suit the "unpretentious" crowd; P.S. most nights it's a "splurge", but the prix fixe Sunday Supper still has it "goin' on" as one of the "best deals in town."

### Lula *Mexican* | 18 | 16 | 18 | $24 |

**Santa Monica** | 2720 Main St. (bet. Ashland Ave. & Hill St.) | 310-392-5711 | www.lulacocinamexicana.com

Offering a "distinctive" taste of Mexico in the "middle of trendy Main Street", this "inexpensive", "enjoyable" Santa Monica cantina satisfies with "interesting, tasty" dishes and "lethal margaritas" delivered by a "cheerful" staff; "splashes of bright color everywhere", both inside and on the bougainvillea-laced patio, make it extra festive.

### Luna Park *American* | 17 | 19 | 18 | $31 |

**La Brea** | 672 S. La Brea Ave. (Wilshire Blvd.) | 323-934-2110 | www.lunaparkla.com

"Delicious drinks" and "solid", "homestyle" American fare served in a "cool, not too sceney" space draw an "eclectic" "after-work" crowd to this La Brea locale that "doesn't break the bank"; "pleasant" service and "booths at the back with curtains" are pluses, but since most of the room has the "acoustics of a gym", "be prepared to yell to be heard."

### Macau Street ● *Chinese* | ∇ 19 | 12 | 14 | $19 |

**Monterey Park** | 429 W. Garvey Ave. (bet. Atlantic & Garfield Blvds.) | 626-288-3568

Excelling at "unbelievable" seafood (especially the "garlic crab") and other Cantonese specialties, this Monterey Park "treat" is a "budget dream"; some customers caution "choose wisely", while adventurous eaters advise "go with a group, so you can try a variety of dishes."

### Madame Matisse *American* | 19 | 11 | 17 | $19 |

**Silver Lake** | 3536 W. Sunset Blvd. (bet. Golden Gate & Maltman Aves.) | 323-662-4862

Silver Lakers roll out of bed for a "lazy brunch" at this "tiny" daytime "sidewalk hangout" that serves a "reasonable" menu of "simple, tasty" American fare, including the "fluffiest pancakes"; though some call it "pretentious", all in all it's a "neighborly" place for "people-watching."

### Madeleine Bistro ◨ *French/Vegan* | ∇ 24 | 20 | 22 | $32 |

**Tarzana** | 18621 Ventura Blvd. (Amigo Ave.) | 818-758-6971 | www.madeleinebistro.com

Chef-owner David Anderson performs a "miracle" with "sparkling fresh produce and exotic spices" at this uniquely "upscale" Tarzana vegan, employing "traditional French culinary techniques" to craft "superb", "innovative" dishes that are "comforting" too; commending the "pretty" "candlelit" atmosphere and quality service, even "serious carnivores" "love it"; N.B. closed Monday–Tuesday.

### Madeleine's ◨ *Californian* | 24 | 23 | 21 | $46 |

**Pasadena** | 1030 E. Green St. (Catalina Ave.) | 626-440-7087 | www.madeleinesrestaurant.com

The "place for a romantic rendezvous" in Pasadena, this "elegant" Californian delights with "lovely fireplaces", a historic New Orleans-style building and several "secluded dining areas" setting the stage for "creatively prepared", "well-presented" seasonal fare by chef Claud Beltran; it's "expensive" and the meals are "long", but the "earnest", "accommodating" staff adds to its "fine" reputation.

### Madeo  *Italian*

24 | 18 | 22 | $63

**West Hollywood** | 8897 Beverly Blvd. (Swall Dr.) | 310-859-4903

"High-end locals" and "movie-industry" honchos hit this "top-notch" WeHo Northern Italian for "seductive" veal and other "simple, satisfying" fare served by an "experienced, professional" staff; while the "below-ground" setting with "heavy" decor makes you "feel like someone from *The Sopranos* is going to make a hit", somehow it's "fitting" in an "old-school" way.

### ⊠ Madison, The ● ⊠  *Seafood/Steak*

20 | 27 | 21 | $55

**Long Beach** | 102 Pine Ave. (1st St.) | 562-628-8866 | www.themadisonrestaurant.com

Housed in a "beautiful" restored bank decked out with crystal chandeliers and "deep, dark" mahogany walls, this "gorgeous" Long Beach "special-occasion" place exudes "old-fashioned elegance" and follows through with "well-prepared" (if less memorable) steaks and seafood served by a "fine" staff; many reserve it for "expense-account" meals, but find it "fabulous" for "romance or business."

### Maggiano's Little Italy  *Italian*

18 | 19 | 18 | $30

**Fairfax** | Grove at Farmers Mkt. | 189 The Grove Dr. (bet. Fairfax Ave. & 3rd St.) | 323-965-9665

**Woodland Hills** | Westfield Promenade | 6100 Topanga Canyon Blvd. (bet. Erwin & Oxnard Sts.) | 818-887-3777

www.maggianos.com

You almost "expect to see Sinatra walk in behind you" at this checkered-tablecloth chain where "monster portions" of "red-sauce" Italiana are dished out in "enjoyably hectic" surroundings; some dub it a "mixed bag", citing a "mass-production", "quantity-trumps-quality" approach, but fans tout this "crowd-pleaser" as a "big night out" for "not a lot of money."

### Magnolia ●  *American*

19 | 19 | 17 | $33

**Hollywood** | 6266½ Sunset Blvd. (bet. Argyle Ave. & Vine St.) | 323-467-0660 | www.magnoliahollywood.com

"A hit if you're eating late", this "trendy neighborhood" joint in Hollywood delivers "solid" New American eats in a "hip" 1940s-inspired atmosphere with "laid-back" couch seating; though the servers tend to "meet their obligations, nothing more", patrons give props to the "quick, attentive" bartenders.

### Magnolia Lounge  *Contemp. Louisiana*

19 | 23 | 16 | $26

**Pasadena** | 492 S. Lake Ave. (California Blvd.) | 626-584-1126 | www.magnoliaonlake.com

Bar food gets the Southern treatment at this "classy" Pasadena "hideaway" where "delicious" Contemporary Louisiana bites help "soak up the great cocktails" as customers unwind in the "charming" "indoor/outdoor" space; fans call it "tops for nightlife" in the area ("Old Town crowds, please stay on Colorado Boulevard"), though some find it "better for the twentysomethings who like the scene" than for serious diners.

| | FOOD | DECOR | SERVICE | COST |
|---|---|---|---|---|

### Maison Akira ⓜ *French/Japanese* — 25 | 22 | 25 | $54

**Pasadena** | 713 E. Green St. (bet. El Molino & Oak Knoll Aves.) | 626-796-9501 | www.maisonakira.com

Fans fawn over the "first-class" dining at this Pasadena "gem" where chef Akira Hirose's "fabulous, unusual" French-Japanese cuisine is "poetry on a plate", complemented by a "romantic" setting and "top-notch" service; though it feels "slightly stuffy", "old-world" and "expensive" to some, the lunchtime bento boxes are a "bargain."

### ☒ Mako ☒ *Asian Fusion* — 26 | 20 | 24 | $55

**Beverly Hills** | 225 S. Beverly Dr. (Charleville Blvd.) | 310-288-8338 | www.makorestaurant.com

"Delectable" "flavor sensations" abound at this "surprising" Beverly Hills Japanese where the "delicately prepared" dishes by chef-owner Makoto Tanaka are ideal "when you have a yen" for Asian fusion ("and lots of yen" in your pocket); while the minimalist backdrop is less "memorable" than the food, "gracious" service enhances the meal.

### NEW Malibu Pier Club *Californian* — - | - | - | E

**Malibu** | 23000 PCH (Malibu Pier) | 310-456-9800 | www.thebeachcombercafe.com

After being closed to the public for years, the Malibu Pier is undergoing a major overhaul that includes re-creating it as a dining destination overlooking Surfrider Beach; enter this casual, polished wood-and-glass Californian with signature cocktails like Gidget's Gimlet and modern beach bites like Kobe burgers – all served with a side of cool ocean breeze.

### Malibu Seafood *Seafood* — 22 | 12 | 14 | $20

**Malibu** | 25653 PCH (Corral Canyon Rd.) | 310-456-6298 | www.malibufishandseafood.com

"No pretentiousness" here, just a patio full of "picnic tables and an amazing view" of the Pacific at this roadside "shack" and seafood market in Malibu serving "incredibly fresh" deep-fried fish for "refueling" after a "day at the beach"; with "reasonable" prices to boot, wave-riders ask "who could ask for anything more, except faster service?"; N.B. closes between 7 and 8:30 PM depending on the season.

### Malo *Mexican* — 17 | 16 | 14 | $27

**Silver Lake** | 4326 W. Sunset Blvd. (Fountain Ave.) | 323-664-1011 | www.malorestaurant.com

"Cooked-to-order chips", salsa "flights" and "small, tasty" tacos star on the "simple" yet "interesting" menu at this "dark, clubby" Silver Lake Mexican (a sib of Cobras & Matadors) boasting an "excellent" tequila list; some cite "spotty" service and "California portions" that are just "ok", but the "hip" surroundings with a lounge and patio tend to please with a "good vibe for groups."

### Mama D's *Italian* — 21 | 12 | 22 | $22

**NEW Hermosa Beach** | 1031 Hermosa Ave. (bet. 10th St. & Pier Ave.) | 310-379-6262

**Manhattan Beach** | 1125 Manhattan Ave. (Manhattan Beach Blvd.) | 310-546-1492

"A Manhattan Beach favorite", this "generous" mama serves up "affordable" "homestyle Italian" dishes that "consistently satisfy" cus-

|  | FOOD | DECOR | SERVICE | COST |
|--|------|-------|---------|------|

tomers who sit "elbow to elbow" in "tight quarters" (just like "grandma's kitchen"); regulars recommend "arrive early to avoid lines" and "don't eat too much bread while you wait", or try the new, less-crowded outpost in Hermosa (open for dinner only).

## Mandarette  *Chinese*
**18 | 14 | 16 | $29**

**West Hollywood** | 8386 Beverly Blvd. (bet. N. Kings Rd. & Orlando Ave.) | 323-655-6115 | www.mandarettecafe.com

"For those who won't drive" to Chinatown or Monterey Park, this "underappreciated" WeHo Sichuan fills the area "void" with "fresh", "traditional" dishes that are slightly more "spendy" than the usual Chinese; due to "dull" decor and a fairly "indifferent" staff, though, critics assess it's "not the place you'd spend the night dining, more like an hour."

## Mandarin Deli  *Chinese*
**20 | 7 | 14 | $14**

**Northridge** | 9305 Reseda Blvd. (Prairie St.) | 818-993-0122
**Monterey Park** | 701 W. Garvey Ave. (Chandler Ave.) | 626-570-9795 ⊅

"Juicy", "incredible steamed dumplings" and "huge bowls of noodle soups" come out of the kitchen at this "authentic", "dirt-cheap" "haunt for lunch" in Monterey Park and Northridge; insiders insist the low-caliber service and dated decor are a "small price to pay" for some of the "best" Chinese eats around.

## Mandevilla  *Continental*
**22 | 18 | 22 | $40**

**Westlake Village** | 951 S. Westlake Blvd. (bet. Hampshire & Townsgate Rds.) | 805-497-8482 | www.mandevillarestaurant.com

It "rarely disappoints" say faithful diners of this upscale Westlake Village Continental where "leisurely" meals of "tasty" seasonal cuisine are served by "respectful" servers in a "warm" setting enhanced by a "nice patio"; still, critics call it "nothing exciting", citing "predictable" food and "tired" decor that could use a "face-lift."

## Mäni's Bakery Café  *Bakery/Vegan*
**18 | 10 | 15 | $16**

**Santa Monica** | 2507 Main St. (Ocean Park Blvd.) | 310-396-7700
## Mäni's on Fairfax  *Bakery/Vegan*
**Fairfax** | 519 S. Fairfax Ave. (bet. 5th St. & Maryland Dr.) | 323-938-8800 | www.manisbakery.com

"Fantastic vegan baked goods" and "no-sugar" desserts that "make you forget what's missing" are the "healthful" stars at these "easy-breezy" Fairfax and Santa Monica cafes that also offer the "usual salad and sandwich suspects" (for both "vegetarians and carnivores"); service is on the "slow" side and it can be "hard to get a table", but otherwise they appeal to a "hip crowd."

## Manna  *Korean*
**16 | 8 | 9 | $24**

**Koreatown** | 3377 W. Olympic Blvd. (bet. Gramercy Dr. & St. Andrews Pl.) | 323-733-8516 | www.mannakoreanrestaurant.com

A "gluttonous feast" of "all-you-can-eat" grill-your-own meat is the draw at this "cheap", "super-crowded" K-town BBQ joint that pulls in "true carnivores" and "college kids" on a "budget" who don't care that it's "not the finest dining" in the world; indeed, the service "leaves much to be desired" and the "smoke gets in your eyes" (and your "clothes"), but the "outdoor seating minimizes" the fumes.

| | FOOD | DECOR | SERVICE | COST |
|---|---|---|---|---|

### Maria's Italian Kitchen  *Italian*                 17 | 13 | 17 | $22

**Brentwood** | 11723 Barrington Ct. (Barrington Ave.) | 310-476-6112
**West LA** | 10761 Pico Blvd. (Malcolm Ave.) | 310-441-3663
**Pasadena** | Hastings Ranch Shopping Ctr. | 3537 E. Foothill Blvd.
(N. Rosemead Blvd.) | 626-351-2080
**Encino** | 16608 Ventura Blvd. (Rubio Ave.) | 818-783-2920
**Northridge** | 9161 Reseda Blvd. (bet. Dearborn & Nordhoff Sts.) |
818-341-5114
**Sherman Oaks** | 13353 Ventura Blvd. (bet. Dixie Canyon & Fulton Aves.) |
818-906-0783
**Woodland Hills** | El Camino Shopping Ctr. | 23331 Mulholland Dr.
(Calabasas Rd.) | 818-225-0586
**Agoura Hills** | Ralph's Shopping Ctr. | 29035 Thousand Oaks Blvd.
(Kanan Rd.) | 818-865-8999
www.mariasitaliankitchen.com
"Consistency is key" at this "inexpensive", "kid-friendly" Italian chain
serving up "average" pizza and other plates that "work in a pinch"
thanks to "quick turnarounds"; as the setting and service have a "formulaic" feel, regulars have two words of advice: "take out."

### Marino  ☒ *Italian*                 ▽ 21 | 14 | 22 | $45

**Hollywood** | 6001 Melrose Ave. (Wilcox Ave.) | 323-466-8812
A quarter-century old, this Hollywood "classic" is still welcoming "one
and all like family" (including "power-lunching Paramount execs") to
feast on "wonderful" Italian fare amid surroundings that feel like "Little
Italy in 1965"; it's "expensive", but you're "made to feel special", as the
"old-fashioned" staff "cares about details and always remembers you."

### ☑ Mario's Peruvian & Seafood  *Peruvian*        25 | 7 | 15 | $18

**Hollywood** | 5786 Melrose Ave. (Wilcox Ave.) | 323-466-4181
"Not fancy by any means, but the food is delectable" at this Hollywood
"gem" serving "ridiculously good", "cheap" *lomo saltado,* ceviche and
other "hard-to-find" Peruvian specialties; while "parking is a hassle"
and it "takes forever to get seating", that doesn't deter the devoted.

### Marix Tex Mex Café  *Tex-Mex*               16 | 14 | 17 | $26

**West Hollywood** | 1108 N. Flores St. (Santa Monica Blvd.) | 323-656-8800
### Marix Tex Mex Playa  *Tex-Mex*

**Santa Monica** | 118 Entrada Dr. (PCH) | 310-459-8596
www.marixtexmex.com
This "lively" Tex-Mex duo with "popular" patios offers two distinct
vibes – a "rolicking" "mostly gay" scene (where you "go to see the
fauna") "in the heart of Boystown" in WeHo and a "family-friendly
beach-bum hangout" (complete with koi pond) in Santa Monica – but
both can be counted on for "powerful" potables, notably the "mouthwatering" margs; a "young, eager" staff keeps it "jumping", so even
though many call the food "so-so", it's still a "safe bet."

### Market City Caffe  *Californian/Italian*          17 | 16 | 17 | $24

**Burbank** | 164 E. Palm Ave. (bet. N. 1st St. & San Fernando Blvd.) |
818-840-7036
"Bring on the breadsticks" and "simple pizza and pastas" at this "predictable" but affordable Cal-Italian in Burbank that keeps bellies full with its
"wonderful salad bar" – an "antipasto oasis"; though the decor "could be
spruced up", a "courteous" staff keeps it a "standby" for "easy eating."

### Mark's Restaurant  *Californian*
**17** | **17** | **17** | **$36**

**West Hollywood** | 861 N. La Cienega Blvd. (bet. Waring & Willoughby Aves.) | 310-652-5252 | www.marksrestaurant.com

"Gorgeous" waiters who "play up to the gay crowd" are a "large part of the appeal" of this "relaxing", "upscale" and recently remodeled WeHo fixture, in business for more than 20 years; while the seasonal Californian fare strikes many as "reliable" but "standard", regulars call the bargain Monday night menu "the bomb."

### Marmalade Café  *American/Californian*
**17** | **17** | **18** | **$26**

**Fairfax** | Grove at Farmers Mkt. | 6333 W. Third St. (Fairfax Ave.) | 323-954-0088

**Rolling Hills Estates** | Avenue of the Peninsula Mall | 550 Deep Valley Dr. (Crossfield Dr.) | Rolling Hills - 310-544-6700

**Malibu** | 3894 Cross Creek Rd. (PCH) | 310-317-4242

**Santa Monica** | 710 Montana Ave. (7th St.) | 310-395-9196

**El Segundo** | Plaza El Segundo | 2014 E. Park Pl. (bet. Apollo & Nash Sts.) | 310-648-7200

**Calabasas** | The Commons | 4783 Commons Way (Calabasas Rd.) | 818-225-9092

**Sherman Oaks** | 14910 Ventura Blvd. (Kester Ave.) | 818-905-8872

**Westlake Village** | Promenade at Westlake | 140 Promenade Way (Thousand Oaks Blvd.) | 805-370-1331

www.marmaladecafe.com

Though it's "nothing fancy", this "steady" Cal-American chain is "always a favorite for brunch" with "hearty" plates that "fill you up for the day", though dinner quality tends to be "coffee-shop" caliber; while the "folksy ambiance" rankles some ("like grandma's house from hell"), others say it makes for a "warm family atmosphere", especially considering the "child-friendly" service and "moderate" tabs.

### Marouch  Ⓜ *Lebanese*
▽ **23** | **15** | **19** | **$25**

**East Hollywood** | 4905 Santa Monica Blvd. (N. Edgemont St.) | 323-662-9325 | www.marouchrestaurant.com

"Oh, the spices!" exclaim enthusiasts of the "sumptuous, unique" Lebanese eats (including "just-right" falafel) at this East Hollywood "classic" "on the cheap" that's a prime place for "sharing with a group"; though the strip-mall space is a little "tacky", it's "better looking inside than out" and tended to by a "helpful" staff.

### Marrakesh  *Moroccan*
▽ **19** | **20** | **19** | **$38**

**Studio City** | 13003 Ventura Blvd. (Coldwater Canyon Ave.) | 818-788-6354 | www.marrakeshrestaurant.com

Tasters are "transported to where Ali Baba roams" at this midpriced Studio City Moroccan where the "heavily-spiced" "multicourse meals" are ideal for "eating with your fingers"; despite complaints that the traditionally styled room is "a bit run-down", live belly dancing "keeps the atmosphere light" and "great for a party."

### Marston's  Ⓜ *American*
**23** | **15** | **20** | **$22**

**Pasadena** | 151 E. Walnut St. (bet. N. Marengo & Raymond Aves.) | 626-796-2459 | www.marstonsrestaurant.com

"Pasadena's iconic breakfast spot", this "cute, little" American plates up "delicious" omelets, "crunchy" French toast and "special" pancakes among other "satisfying" fare served by a "personable" staff in a "cozy" Craftsman bungalow; though the tables are "crowded together" and there's a "long wait on weekends", fans are willing to "stand in line" for a seat ("hold out for the porch"), and the lower-key lunches and dinners are "nicely done" too.

**Martha's 22nd St. Grill**  *American*            21 | 13 | 18 | $16

**Hermosa Beach** | 25 22nd St. (bet. Beach Dr. & Hermosa Ave.) | 310-376-7786

It's "worth the wait" for some of the "best breakfasts" in the South Bay, including "one-of-a-kind" scrambles and milkshakes, at this "kid-friendly" "bare-bones" American "steps from the beach" in Hermosa; with an "ocean breeze" and "unbeatable views" from the patio, it's "the place to be on a sunny weekend day."

**Marty's**  *Californian*            ∇ 18 | 15 | 18 | $24

**Highland Park** | 5137 York Blvd. (bet. Aves. 51 & 52) | 323-256-2400

Adding an "infusion of hipness to Highland Park", this dark, "loungey" sib of Mia Sushi draws an "interesting mix of young college kids and locals" with "strong drinks" and a Californian menu that's "limited" but offers upscale burgers, fries and other "gastropub" grub "done well"; an "attractive" staff amps up the "sexy" vibe, though many seek it out more for the bar than for the food.

**Massimo**  *Italian*            22 | 19 | 22 | $51

**Beverly Hills** | 9513 Little Santa Monica Blvd. (bet. Camden & Rodeo Drs.) | 310-273-7588 | www.massimobh.com

A "well-edited" menu of "terrific" "homemade" Tuscan cuisine served in a "romantic" setting appeals to guests in a "grown-up" mood at this high-end Beverly Hills "jewel" where the "fantastic", "European"-style service features "visits by Massimo himself", and "star sightings" are a plus.

**☑ Mastro's Steakhouse**  *Steak*            26 | 23 | 24 | $73

**Beverly Hills** | 246 N. Cañon Dr. (bet. Clifton & Dayton Ways) | 310-888-8782
**Thousand Oaks** | 2087 E. Thousand Oaks Blvd. (bet. Conejo School Rd. & Los Feliz Dr.) | 805-418-1811
www.mastrosoceanclub.com

"The bone-in filet is like butta" rave fans of these "showy", "top-notch steak- and chophouses" where "huge" is the watchword, from the cocktails to the bill to the "power scene" – a "who's who of LA" at the Beverly Hills original; "professional" service and live piano "complete the dining experience", though critics contend the bar can be a "middle-aged meat market."

**☑ Matsuhisa**  *Japanese*            27 | 16 | 23 | $78

**Beverly Hills** | 129 N. La Cienega Blvd. (bet. Clifton Way & Wilshire Blvd.) | 310-659-9639 | www.nobumatsuhisa.com

"Raw fish guru" Nobu Matsuhisa "hasn't lost a step" at his first "home" in Beverly Hills, "turning out unbelievably fresh sushi" and "imaginative" Japanese dishes with Peruvian twists that "entice you to return" "even if you have to wait until your next paycheck" to afford it; the "helpful" staff "makes you feel welcome and at ease", and though some say the decor is "in need of a serious face-lift", most agree it still "sets the standard" for LA cuisine.

|  | FOOD | DECOR | SERVICE | COST |
|--|------|-------|---------|------|

### Matteo's ⓜ *Italian*
19 | 19 | 20 | $43

**West LA** | 2321 Westwood Blvd. (bet. Pico Blvd. & Tennessee Ave.) | 310-475-4521 | www.matteosla.com

"Sinatra and Dino thought this was great Italian – who are we to argue" reason supporters of this upscale former "Rat Pack hang" in West LA, the "real deal" with "leapord-print" barstools, "lipstick-red" booths, "classic cocktails" and pastas and seafood that are fairly "basic" but "carefully prepared"; with "competent" service, it easily suits a "special night out", especially if you get table number eight – Ol' Blue Eyes' favorite corner booth.

### Max *Asian Fusion*
24 | 19 | 23 | $47

**Sherman Oaks** | 13355 Ventura Blvd. (bet. Dixie Canyon & Fulton Aves.) | 818-784-2915 | www.maxrestaurant.com

Adventurous eaters beat a path to Sherman Oaks for "unique" Asian fusion by "master in the kitchen", chef-owner André Guerrero (The Oinkster), who "takes it to the max" by "blending several food cultures seamlessly and deliciously"; though it's "loud", the "space is tight" and it's "rather expensive for the Valley, a "bubbly" staff and "NYC"-style art deco design make the atmosphere "delightful" for most.

### Maxwell's Cafe *American*
19 | 11 | 17 | $15

**Venice** | 13329 W. Washington Blvd. (Walgrove Ave.) | 310-306-7829

A "favorite" for "homemade" "hangover" breakfasts, this American "greasy spoon" opened over 36 years ago in Venice and still looks like a "'70s kitchen" – "funky" and "not pretentious in any way"; with a "friendly" staff keeping it real, it's no wonder "people line up to get in" on weekends.

### M Café de Chaya *Vegetarian*
21 | 13 | 16 | $20

**Melrose** | 7119 Melrose Ave. (La Brea Ave.) | 323-525-0588
**NEW** **Culver City** | 9343 Culver Blvd. (Ince Blvd.) | 310-838-4300
www.mcafedechaya.com

"Rocking" vegan dishes (with the option of fish) and "unbelievable" desserts define this Melrose "macrobiotic heaven" and its new Culver City spin-off where even carnivores "don't miss the meat or dairy"; the mood is "hip" with "starlets and models" waiting in line, but despite the presence of a "patient" staff, "crowds can be overwhelming" and lunchtime "insane."

### McCormick & Schmick's *Seafood*
19 | 19 | 19 | $41

**Downtown** | US Bank Tower | 633 W. Fifth St. (Grand Ave.) | 213-629-1929
**Beverly Hills** | Two Rodeo | 206 N. Rodeo Dr. (Wilshire Blvd.) | 310-859-0434
**El Segundo** | 2101 Rosecrans Ave. (Parkway Dr.) | 310-416-1123
**Pasadena** | 111 N. Los Robles Ave. (Union St.) | 626-405-0064
**Burbank** | The Pinnacle | 3500 W. Olive Ave. (W. Riverside Dr.) | 818-260-0505
www.mccormickandschmicks.com

An "endless menu" that "changes daily depending on what's freshly caught" reels in the "business crowd" at this "elevated seafood" chain with "comfortable" "steakhouse decor"; while some call the preparations "predictable" and the prices a little "lofty", many are impressed by the "happy-hour noshes" for "a steal."

| | FOOD | DECOR | SERVICE | COST |
|---|---|---|---|---|

### McKenna's on the Bay  *Seafood/Steak*   `19` `23` `20` `$46`

**Long Beach** | 190 Marina Dr. (PCH) | 562-342-9411 |
www.mckennasonthebay.com

With "stunning" waterfront views of Alamitos Bay, "you think you're on vacation" at this "pricey" Long Beacher that's more favored for it's "fresh" seafood than its often "average" steaks; the staff is "attentive", and lots of windows brighten up the "cozy" nautical atmosphere, which turns "lively" as the sun sets with piano entertainment Wednesday–Sunday.

### Mediterraneo  *Mediterranean*   `20` `19` `19` `$31`

**Hermosa Beach** | 73 Pier Ave. (Hermosa Ave.) | 310-318-2666 |
www.mediterraneohb.com

"Sit on the patio" on a "nice summer evening" with a "pitcher of sangria" to best experience this Hermosa Beach Mediterranean that matches a "variety" of "tasteful", "tiny" tapas with "wines by the glass at reasonable prices"; even if some credit its success to being "one of the few non-greasy options on the pier", it attracts a following during the "fantastic" happy hour and on Tuesday nights when bites are "two for one."

### Mediterraneo  *Mediterranean*   ▽ `17` `21` `17` `$39`

**Westlake Village** | 32037 Agoura Rd. (Lakeview Canyon Rd.) | 818-889-9105 |
www.med-rest.com

"Pleasantly surprised" patrons praise the "serene" view of the lake and "relaxing" atmosphere at this two-year-old Mediterranean bistro serving a "decent", "reasonable" menu on the grounds of the Westlake Village Inn; though some deem the food "disappointing" and call the vaulted interior with black crystal chandeliers "a bit overdone", most find its "romantic" setting a "positive change" from the past.

### 🆕 Medusa Lounge  🅂🅼 *Eclectic*   `-` `-` `-` `M`

**Beverly Boulevard** | 3211 Beverly Blvd. (S. Hoover St.) | 213-382-5723 |
www.medusaloungela.com

In the Beverly Boulevard space that used to house Lowenbrau Keller, this high-concept newcomer has covered every surface with some manner of curlicue and kitsch – imagine an Ernst Lubitsch fever dream to get the picture; the midpriced menu has an Eclectic bent too, meandering from the U.S. to France.

### 🆉 Mélisse  🅂🅼 *American/French*   `28` `25` `27` `$97`

**Santa Monica** | 1104 Wilshire Blvd. (11th St.) | 310-395-0881 |
www.melisse.com

"Marvelous evenings" are made at Josiah Citrin's "sublime" French-New American in Santa Monica, renowned for "meticulously prepared" seasonal dishes and "exceptional" tasting menus that "open new vistas" of experience, earning it the No. 1 Food score in LA; rounded out by an "elegant", "quiet" atmosphere and "impeccable" (if "serious") service, it wins accolades as a "national treasure" – just "be prepared to pay for this pursuit of perfection."

### 🆕 Melograno  🅼 *Italian*   ▽ `23` `20` `20` `$51`

**Hollywood** | 6541 Hollywood Blvd. (Schrader Blvd.) | 323-465-6650 |
www.melogranohollywood.com

"Amid the hubbub of Hollywood Boulevard", this "soulful" Piedmontese newcomer by chef/co-owner Alberto Lazzarino (ex Piccolo) provides

|  | FOOD | DECOR | SERVICE | COST |
|---|---|---|---|---|

a "welcome change from slick-over-substance spots" with its "off-the-hook" seasonal menu starring homemade gnocchi and other "outstanding" "rustic" dishes (many incorporating the eponymous pomegranate); service is largely "professional", and while the "simple" "bistro atmosphere" receives mixed responses, guests appreciate that opening the patio "doubles its size."

### NEW Melrose Bar & Grill ☒ *American* | 18 | 18 | 19 | $40

**West Hollywood** | 8826 Melrose Ave. (N. Robertson Blvd.) | 310-278-3684 | www.melrosebarandgrill.com

Blending "casual and classy" in the former Doug Arango's space (by the same owners), this WeHo newcomer feels "very Cape Cod" with its taupe tones and stone fireplace, and generally "satisfies" with its "creative", "upscale" American "comfort food" (including a few "exotic" choices) served in "unrushed" style; though it strikes some as "bland", many find it promising as a "not-too-sceney" "hangout."

### Mel's Drive-In ● *American* | 15 | 16 | 16 | $18

**Hollywood** | 1650 N. Highland Ave. (Hollywood Blvd.) | 323-465-2111
**West Hollywood** | 8585 Sunset Blvd. (Sunset Plaza Dr.) | 310-854-7200
**Sherman Oaks** | 14846 Ventura Blvd. (Kester Ave.) | 818-990-6357
www.melsdrive-in.com

"Retro nostalgia" rules at this trio decked in "quintessential diner" decor, where the "classic" American fare like "greasy" burgers and "late-night milkshakes" require "loosening your belt a notch"; the servers "will either love you or hate you, but they'll get you your food on time", and when you're up in the wee hours with the "post-party" crowd, the 24/7 WeHo locale just might "save your life."

### Meltdown Etc. ☒ *American* | 18 | 8 | 16 | $13

**Culver City** | 9739 Culver Blvd. (bet. Duquesne & Lincoln Aves.) | 310-838-6358 | www.meltdownetc.com

"Fancy grilled cheese" is the focus of this "tiny storefront eatery" in Culver City where a "wide variety of melted, gooey sandwiches" and "tasty soup" fulfill a "clever concept" for lunch; it's "casual", "quick" and "popular among the younger set", but price is a sticking point, as is the limited seating, especially "on cold days."

### Melting Pot *Fondue* | 18 | 18 | 19 | $46

**Pasadena** | 88 W. Colorado Blvd. (De Lacey Ave.) | 626-792-1941
**Westlake Village** | 3685 E. Thousand Oaks Blvd. (bet. Auburn & Marmon Aves.) | 805-370-8802
www.meltingpot.com

"Change-of-pace" mavens and "do-it-yourself" types are fond of this "novel" fondue franchise for its "interactive" approach, i.e. the chance to "cook your own dinner"; the "long, slow meals" make it appropriate for "first dates" or "large crowds", and though the morsels are "tasty", you'll "end up spending a lot of money" for them.

### NEW Mes Amis *French* | ∇ 16 | 17 | 17 | $39

**Los Feliz** | 1739 N. Vermont Ave. (Prospect Ave.) | 323-665-7810 | www.mes-amis-cuisine.com

Opinions vary, but the French bistro dishes are generally "decent" at this Los Feliz newcomer where servers are "thankfully unchatty" and

| | FOOD | DECOR | SERVICE | COST |
|---|---|---|---|---|

the "pleasant" Provençal-style space features a large sidewalk patio; some call it "overpriced", while others shrug it's "trying hard, but not quite there yet."

### Mexicali ◐ *Californian/Mexican*

| 15 | 16 | 16 | $24 |

**Studio City** | 12161 Ventura Blvd. (bet. Laurel Canyon Blvd. & Vantage Ave.) | 818-985-1744

An "Americanized" menu of "huge burritos, lots of grilled dishes" and "margatinis" keeps this inexpensive Studio City Cal-Mexican "rocking through lunch and dinner", but "it might rock a little too much" given that it's the "noisiest restaurant around"; factor in late hours and "crowds" of "aging frat boys" and "industry" types, and regulars have two words of advice: "*más tequila!*"

### Mexico City  *Mexican*

| 18 | 13 | 16 | $24 |

**Los Feliz** | 2121 Hillhurst Ave. (bet. Ambrose Ave. & Avocado St.) | 323-661-7227

The kitchen does a "solid" job with Mexican grub at this "raucous", "hipped-up" Los Feliz "cantina" with "colorful" (if "divey") "diner"-like looks; though peso-pinchers posit "it's a little pricey for what you get", especially considering the "spotty" service and general "noise", "it's nothing a margarita can't help."

### Mia Sushi  *Japanese*

| ∇ 18 | 22 | 19 | $35 |

**Eagle Rock** | 4741 Eagle Rock Blvd. (bet. Las Colinas & Ridgeview Aves.) | 323-256-2562 | www.mia-sushi.com

"A stylish oasis" on a "drab" stretch of Eagle Rock Boulevard, this "small", "high-end" Japanese offers an "adorable" patio for chowing down on "elaborate" "specialty rolls" and tempura; yet while some guests are glad to finally have a worthy "date spot" in the area, critics sniff it's "overpriced" and "out of place."

### Miceli's  *Italian*

| 17 | 18 | 19 | $27 |

**Hollywood** | 1646 N. Las Palmas Ave. (bet. Hollywood Blvd. & Selma Ave.) | 323-466-3438
**Universal City** | 3655 Cahuenga Blvd. W. (Regal Pl.) | 323-851-3344
www.micelis1949.com

"Singing waiters" are the "star attraction" at these old-time "charmers" in Hollywood and Universal City, where Chianti bottles hang from the ceiling and the "well-priced", "basic-red-sauce" Southern Italian fare is "not as easy on the hips as it is on the lips"; even if they're "not wowed" by the cooking, many call it a "real kick", especially for "anyone entertaining out-of-town guests."

### Michael's ⧄ *Californian*

| 24 | 25 | 24 | $67 |

**Santa Monica** | 1147 Third St. (bet. California Ave. & Wilshire Blvd.) | 310-451-0843 | www.michaelssantamonica.com

This "historic" Santa Monican where owner Michael McCarty ushered in "Cal cuisine" still has the "subtle, hideaway mystique" of what many consider "the most romantic patio in the city" and "superb" seasonal dishes delivered by a "wonderful" staff; some longtimers lament, however, that it's "resting on its laurels", with an "outdated" interior and "overpriced" fare, making them yearn for the "Michael's of yore."

| | FOOD | DECOR | SERVICE | COST |
|---|---|---|---|---|

### NEW Michael's on Naples Ristorante 🏵️Ⓜ️ *Italian*    | - | - | - | M |

**Long Beach** | 5620 E. Second St. (Campo Walk) | 562-439-7080 | www.michaelsonnaples.com

Long Beach restaurants tend toward the casual, so this white-tablecloth Italian stands out for its sense of style and elegance, with boldly colored art adorning the brightly lit dining room; it's nice enough that you won't feel lost wearing a tie, yet prices are down to earth; N.B. the Naples in the name refers to the section of Long Beach rather than the Italian town.

### Michel Richard *Bakery/French*    | 23 | 14 | 20 | $36 |

**Beverly Hills** | 310 S. Robertson Blvd. (bet. Burton Way & 3rd St.) | 310-275-5707 | www.maisonrichard.com

This "charming" Beverly Hills bakery and bistro that helped "put LA on the foodie map" remains a standout for "delicious desserts" that are "still Richard-esque" even though the legendary namesake chef "has not been involved for a long time"; some supporters suggest that the "wholesome", "leisurely" French meals for a "low cost" appeal to customers "more concerned with what they eat than where they eat on Robertson."

### Mijares *Mexican*    | 17 | 16 | 18 | $23 |

**Pasadena** | 145 Palmetto Dr. (Pasadena Ave.) | 626-792-2763
**Pasadena** | 1806 E. Washington Blvd. (N. Allen Ave.) | 626-794-6674
www.mijaresrestaurant.com

"Always filled with people in-the-know", this "Pasadena institution" on Palmetto, run by the same family since 1910, appeals with its "sense of history" lending heft to the "consistent" Mexican combo plates and "gotta-have" margaritas; its "big, noisy setting, mariachis included", feels a bit "old-fashioned", but the patio is "the place to while away a summer night"; P.S. the "long wait" is eased somewhat by its spin-off on Washington Boulevard.

### Mike & Anne's Ⓜ️ *American*    | 21 | 19 | 19 | $33 |

**South Pasadena** | 1040 Mission St. (Fairview Ave.) | 626-799-7199 | www.mikeandannes.com

The seasonal New American menu "ranges from safe to adventurous" at this "pleasant", airy South Pasadenan offering moderately priced "fine dining on Mission" to a "mixed clientele" of both "jeans and suits"; "competent" service, a "wonderful" garden and proximity to the Gold Line and "antique stores" win local approval.

### Milky Way *Californian*    | ▽ 19 | 14 | 23 | $25 |

**Pico-Robertson** | 9108 W. Pico Blvd. (Doheny Dr.) | 310-859-0004

Leah Adler, the "sweetheart of Pico Boulevard", "greets the patrons personally" at this kosher kitchen dishing up "delicious" meals of "blintzes and other homestyle Jewish dairy cooking" as well as specials with a Californian twist; sure, the flower-filled room is "not too hip", but "how could you not love eating with Steven Spielberg's mommy – she's a riot!"

### Mimi's Cafe *Diner*    | 17 | 17 | 18 | $19 |

**Atwater Village** | 2925 Los Feliz Blvd. (bet. Revere & Seneca Aves.) | 323-668-1715

*(continued)*

(continued)

## Mimi's Cafe

**Cerritos** | Cerritos Towne Ctr. | 12727 Towne Center Dr. (Bloomfield Ave.) |
562-809-0510

**Downey** | 8455 Firestone Blvd. (bet. Brookshire & Dolan Aves.) |
562-862-2828

**Long Beach** | 6670 E. PCH (N. Studebaker Rd.) | 562-596-0831

**Torrance** | 25343 S. Crenshaw Blvd. (PCH) | 310-326-4477

**Monrovia** | 500 W. Huntington Dr. (S. Mayflower Ave.) | 626-359-9191

**Chatsworth** | 19710 Nordhoff Pl. (Corbin Ave.) | 818-717-8334

**City of Industry** | 17919 Gale Ave. (S. Azusa Ave.) | 626-912-3350

**Whittier** | Whittwood Town Ctr. | 15436 E. Whittier Blvd.
(Santa Gertrudes Ave.) | 562-947-0339

**Santa Clarita** | 24201 W. Magic Mountain Pkwy. (Auto Center Dr.) |
661-255-5520

www.mimiscafe.com

Additional locations throughout Southern California

Providing "generous portions" of "American comfort food" and "fresh" baked goods at a pace that "keeps the queues moving", this cross between "New Orleans Square in Disneyland" and a "chain restaurant off the freeway in Kentucky," dishes up a heaping plate of coffee-shop "kitsch" to the "post-church" family crowd; though the food is fairly "standard" and there's often a "wait", it's "cheap", "cute and easy", making it a "nice place to bring grandparents or break up with someone."

## Mimosa ⚟Ⓜ French — 20 | 18 | 19 | $47

**Beverly Boulevard** | 8009 Beverly Blvd. (bet. N. Edinburgh & Laurel Aves.) |
323-655-8895 | www.mimosarestaurant.com

"In the new world of Beverly Boulevard über restaurants" this cousin of Café des Artistes is still "kicking" "after all these years" say customers keen on its "quintessential" bistro fare prepared in an "understated manner" and "bargain" prix fixe menus "served with Gallic flair"; it's "comfortable" and "homey", so even if foes find it "unimaginative", many recommend it for the "genuine" French touch that's an "LA rarity."

## Minotaure ● Spanish — 20 | 18 | 22 | $36

**Playa del Rey** | 333 Culver Blvd. (Vista Del Mar) | 310-306-6050

"Terrific" tapas that "break the mold" with their "gigantic" size matched by "great wines" really "wow" at this "tiny" Spaniard in Playa del Rey, set in a "romantic" room (embellished with "red ostrich feathers" above the bar) featuring flamenco guitarists Thursday–Sunday; the service "makes you feel welcome", but critics contend that with so much going on, it can sometimes get "claustrophobic" and "expensive" to boot.

## Minx Eclectic — ∇ 18 | 22 | 16 | $40

**Glendale** | 300 Harvey Dr. (bet. Hwys. 2 & 134) | 818-242-9191 |
www.minx-la.com

Glendale guests are enticed by the "innovative" seasonal Eclectic fare with presentations that would be "equally at home in Las Vegas or Hollywood" at this "loungey" upscale "destination", though many come away more impressed with the "chic", "sleek" stone and glass setting with views of the Verdugos; still, "deafening" decibels and "unjustified attitude" can detract from the atmosphere, and some diners warn "don't go too late on weekends unless you want a really crazy party scene"; N.B. the Food score may not reflect a recent chef change.

|  | FOOD | DECOR | SERVICE | COST |
|---|---|---|---|---|

### Mio Babbo's  *Italian*    ▽ 22 | 17 | 23 | $25

**Westwood** | 1076 Gayley Ave. (bet. Kinross Ave. & Weyburn Dr.) |
310-208-5117 | www.miobabbos.com

"One of the few bargains left", this "unpretentious" Italian in Westwood
plates up "addictive" pastas and other "homestyle comfort food" in
"small", "charming" digs that are "quiet enough to carry on a conversation"; with a staff that "treats you like family" and a "mixed crowd of
seniors and college students", it has a hearty "community feel."

### Mi Piace  *Californian/Italian*    20 | 19 | 17 | $33

**Pasadena** | 25 E. Colorado Blvd. (bet. Fair Oaks & Raymond Aves.) |
626-795-3131 ●
**Calabasas** | Commons, The | 4799 Commons Way (Calabasas Rd.) |
818-591-8822
www.mipiace.com

Serving "enjoyable" Italian cuisine with "character", including "fabulous"
desserts, this "reasonable" Cal-Italian duo in Calabasas and Pasadena is
"popular" among groups and families who groove to the "vibrant" (if
"noisy") atmosphere in a "clean, modern" setting; it's "not adventurous"
and the service can be "slow", but luckily it's an "easy place to linger."

### Mirabelle ● *Californian/Eclectic*    19 | 19 | 19 | $41

**West Hollywood** | 8768 W. Sunset Blvd. (bet. Horn Ave. &
N. Sherbourne Dr.) | 310-659-6022

"Stepping in brings you back to the old LA" at this "long-lived", late-
night Cal-Eclectic bistro offering a "low-key" respite from the Sunset
Strip hubbub with its "amber-lit", dark-wood dining room and a "hip"
outdoor patio for drinks and smokes; most find the dishes "well made"
and served by an "efficient" staff, so even if it's "not spectacular", it
"will be here after the big earthquake."

### Mi Ranchito Family Mexican  *Mexican*    18 | 15 | 18 | $17

**Culver City** | 12223 W. Washington Blvd. (bet. Centinela Ave &
Grand View Blvd.) | 310-398-8611

It has "more kitsch on the walls than a drag bar", but the "tacky decor
adds to the ambiance" at this "tiny", "family-run" and child-friendly
Culver City joint turning out "Vera Cruz–style" eats that are "better than
the average" Mexican; some cite "shortcuts" in the cooking, but many
find it "appealing", "affordable" and "a bit of a dive, just as it should be."

### Mirü8691  *Pan-Asian*    ▽ 25 | 20 | 21 | $30

**Beverly Hills** | Beverly Palm Plaza | 9162 W. Olympic Blvd. (S. Palm Dr.) |
310-777-8378 | www.miru8691.com

A small but ardent following applauds the "overwhelming array of sushi
rolls" (named after Chanel, Prada and the like) and "unique" menu of "innovative" Pan-Asian cuisine "served with flair" at this midpriced Beverly
Hills Japanese where "each dish is a happy surprise" and lunchtime offers "great specials"; evening brings even more scintillation, when the
modern white interior is washed over with changing neon-colored lights.

### Mishima  *Japanese*    20 | 12 | 18 | $18

**Third Street** | 8474 W. Third St. (La Cienega Blvd.) | 323-782-0181 |
www.mishima.com

Oodles of noodles are the thing at this cheap, "fast" and "delicious"
Japanese "staple" on Third Street that "never fails" for bowls of "sat-

| | FOOD | DECOR | SERVICE | COST |
|---|---|---|---|---|

isfying" soba and udon along with other "dependable" "bento box-style food"; a "family favorite", it's not big on looks, but the "friendly" staff keeps it "comfortable" enough.

**Mission 261** *Chinese*                              20 | 18 | 15 | $25

**San Gabriel** | 261 S. Mission Dr. (W. B'way) | 626-588-1666 | www.mission261.com

This San Gabriel Chinese offers "wonderful dim sum and then some", upping the ante with "fancier takes on traditional Cantonese seafood" and an "unexpectedly nice setting" free of "roving carts"; service is "iffy" and the tabs "higher than average", but most patrons are appeased by the atmosphere and a walk through the "beautiful" old surrounding neighborhood.

**Misto Caffé & Bakery** *Californian/Eclectic*      20 | 13 | 20 | $24

**Torrance** | Hillside Vill. | 24558 Hawthorne Blvd. (bet. Newton St. & Via Valmonte) | 310-375-3608 | www.mistocaffe.com

It's a "keep-in-the-back-pocket" kind of place enthuse eaters at this "family-friendly", "crowded" Cal-Eclectic in Torrance, whose afford-able menu "pleases everyone" with salads, sandwiches and pizzas as well as some "fantastic" desserts; despite lackluster looks, it comes through as a "comfortable" option for "comfort food."

**Mistral** ⊠ *French*                                25 | 22 | 25 | $55

**Sherman Oaks** | 13422 Ventura Blvd. (bet. Dixie Canyon & Greenbush Aves.) | 818-981-6650

"Still terrific after all these years", this "sophisticated", "high-end" Sherman Oaks bistro impresses with "impeccably prepared" French fare and "art deco decor" that "transports you to an earlier era"; as the "superb" staff ensures a "festive evening", diners say the "decibel level" is the only "downer."

**Modo Mio Cucina Rustica** *Italian*                22 | 19 | 21 | $41

**Pacific Palisades** | 15200 W. Sunset Blvd. (La Cruz Dr.) | 310-459-0979 | www.modomiocucinarustica.com

"Consistency" is key at this Pacific Palisades "locals' favorite" for "homemade pasta dishes" and other "reliable" Italian eats served by a "pleasant" staff in a "homey" muraled room; though it's "a bit more upscale" than others in the area, reviewers feel rewarded by the "high quality/price ratio."

**Moishe's** ⊄ *Mideastern*                          ∇ 21 | 6 | 13 | $13

**Fairfax** | Grove at Farmers Mkt. | 6333 W. Third St. (Fairfax Ave.) | 323-936-4998

"Sensational" hummus, "terrific" kebabs and other "flavorful" plates of "fresh" Middle Eastern fare are the stock and trade of this small stand in the Farmers Market where there's "always a line and for good reason"; given the "reasonable" prices for "fabulous" eats, "unsmil-ing" service is the only "sour" note.

**NEW Mojitos Restaurant & Rum Bar** *Cuban*        ∇ 24 | 21 | 21 | $36

**Pasadena** | 69 N. Raymond Ave. (Holly St.) | 626-796-2520 | www.mojitosrestaurant.com

The name says it all at this "updated" Cuban (housed in the former Xiomara) in Old Town Pasadena, where patrons "love" the namesake drink ("hand-muddled and made with cane juice") as well as the

|  | FOOD | DECOR | SERVICE | COST |
|--|------|-------|---------|------|

"nicely prepared" dishes served by a staff that "remembers you"; details like fresh orchids and live Latin jazz on weekends add some extra spice.

### Momoyama *Japanese* ▽ 19 | 21 | 18 | $38

**Redondo Beach** | 1810 S. PCH (Vista Del Parque) | 310-540-8211
Diners differ over whether this Redondo Beach "secret" is geared toward the more "adventurous eater" or is overly "familiar", but most agree the midpriced sushi menu (augmented by steak and other seafood options) offers "quality" fish; above all, the "beautiful", "quiet" setting, embellished by a starlit ceiling and indoor waterfall, is what makes it stand out in the South Bay.

### Monsieur Marcel *French* 21 | 16 | 16 | $26

**Fairfax** | Grove at Farmers Mkt. | 6333 W. Third St. (Fairfax Ave.) | 323-939-7792
**NEW Santa Monica** | 1260 Third St. Promenade (Arizona Ave.) | 310-587-1166
www.breadwineandcheese.com
"Smack in the middle of the Farmers Market", this "bustling" bistro (with a smaller Santa Monica spin-off) offers "amazing" cheeses and fondue along with other "classic" Gallic dishes matched by "extraordinary" wines by the glass, all for a "decent" price; most appreciate its "cool" outdoor vibe and attached gourmet market, but find the staff "way too authentically French."

### Monsoon Cafe *Pan-Asian* 18 | 21 | 16 | $31

**Santa Monica** | 1212 Third St. Promenade (bet. Arizona Ave. & Wilshire Blvd.) | 310-576-9996
"Tasty" "sizzling" dishes, sushi and "stiff drinks" fuel the scene at this Pan-Asian on Santa Monica's Promenade where customers go to "collapse after a movie or shopping" or celebrate with a "large party"; though some cite "forgettable" food and "spotty" service, many are taken by the "fabulous" "Polynesian-style" room and frequent live bands (often with a cover) that play to a "packed" house.

### Monte Alban ● *Mexican* 21 | 11 | 17 | $19

**West LA** | 11927 Santa Monica Blvd. (bet. Armacost & Brockton Aves.) | 310-444-7736
"Fresh", "well-seasoned" Oaxacan dishes delight diners who "dive into the mole sauces" at this West LA strip-maller that you "can't beat for the price"; "comfortable and casual", it's "not fancy" but "nicer" than it looks from the outside (murals of "Aztec trompe l'oeil notwithstanding").

### Monty's Steakhouse *Steak* 20 | 16 | 20 | $52

**Woodland Hills** | 5371 Topanga Canyon Blvd. (Ventura Blvd.) | 818-716-9736
"Old-school" all around, this Woodland Hills chophouse delivers "good" steaks and sides in "huge portions"; it's "expensive" and the clientele is none too "young", but the "comfortable" atmosphere, "friendly" staff and "happy-hour scene" keep it a local "institution."

### Moonshadows *American* 17 | 21 | 17 | $43

**Malibu** | 20356 PCH (Big Rock Dr.) | 310-456-3010 |
www.moonshadowsmalibu.com
"Grab a table overlooking the water" and "watch the waves roll in" at this Malibu "singles" "hangout" (a "tourist attraction" since "Mel Gibson got drunk here") sporting an outdoor deck and tiki bar perfect

for "pre-dinner drinks and frivolity"; though service "could be better" and the "pricey" New American menu is on the "tired" side, game guests are energized by the "spectacular" setting.

**Morels First Floor Bistro** *French*  17 | 17 | 15 | $32

**Fairfax** | Grove at Farmers Mkt. | 189 The Grove Dr. (bet. Fairfax Ave. & 3rd St.) | 323-965-9595

At this "perfect people-watching locale" in The Grove, patrons "pass pleasant afternoons" on the patio sipping wine (50 are available by the glass) and dunking into "proper" fondue made with cheeses from the on-site 'cave'; though critics call much of the French bistro fare "pretentious, overpriced" and served by a staff with "attitude", it satisfies those who "stick to appetizers" for a bite "while shopping."

**Morels French Steakhouse** Ⓜ *French/Steak*  18 | 19 | 17 | $46

**Fairfax** | Grove at Farmers Mkt. | 189 The Grove Dr. (bet. Fairfax Ave. & 3rd St.) | 323-965-9595

This "convenient" French steakhouse at The Grove is *magnifique* for "watching the show" from the balcony overlooking the fountain, but while some customers call the cuisine "well prepared", many are "disappointed" by the food, the "lacking" service and a somewhat "corporate" feel, finding it "pricey" "for what you get."

**Ⓩ Mori Sushi** Ⓢ *Japanese*  27 | 17 | 21 | $68

**West LA** | 11500 W. Pico Blvd. (Gateway Blvd.) | 310-479-3939 | www.morisushi.org

"Scintillating combinations of ingredients" showcasing "sparkling fresh" fish presented on "beautiful" "handcrafted" plates dazzle diners who say "splurge on the omakase" by "Mori-san" (chef-owner Morihiro Onodera) at this West LA Japanese; while the digs "feel a bit spartan", that hardly matters when you're savoring "sushi from the gods."

**Mo's** *American*  17 | 13 | 16 | $20

**Burbank** | 4301 W. Riverside Dr. (bet. N. Rose & N. Valley Sts.) | 818-845-3009 | www.eatatmos.com

"Don't expect fancy" at this Burbanker, just a "reliable" American menu starring "big" burgers with "lots of toppings" from the salad bar, along with a Sunday brunch boasting bottomless champagne; the casual setting provides a "real *Cheers* feel" for the "studio crowd" (it's "the Warner Bros. commissary"), but in place of Sam Malone are "actor-wannabe" waiters, which means "if you're a talent scout, you'll get good service."

**Moun of Tunis** *Moroccan/Tunisian*  ▽ 21 | 19 | 21 | $38

**Hollywood** | 7445½ W. Sunset Blvd. (Gardner St.) | 323-874-3333 | www.mounoftunisrestaurant.com

Gung-ho guests say "they get everything right" at this pillow-strewn Hollywood fixture serving "huge" plates of "great Moroccan" and Tunisian food in set menus that are "good for groups" and "less expensive" than comparable feasts elsewhere; "first-rate" belly dancing adds to the experience, even if a few find it "cheesy."

**MOZ Buddha Lounge** *Asian Fusion*  20 | 21 | 18 | $41

**Agoura Hills** | 30105 W. Agoura Rd. (Reyes Adobe Rd.) | 818-735-0091 | www.mozbar.com

A "happening" place in Agoura Hills, this "dark", "crowded" destination for drinks, music and Asian fusion often succeeds with "innovative" dishes that can be shared amid "interesting" digs adorned with red-and-gold details and the requisite Buddha; the staff is "friendly" enough, but some surveyors sniff that it's "pretty expensive" and "trying too hard."

### Mr. Cecil's California Ribs  *BBQ*   | 18 | 11 | 15 | $25 |

**West LA** | 12244 W. Pico Blvd. (Bundy Blvd.) | 310-442-1550
**Sherman Oaks** | 13625 Ventura Blvd. (Woodman Ave.) |
818-905-8400
www.mrcecilscaribs.com

"Shticky but still smokin'", this West LA joint (inside a "rotund" former '40s-era Chili Bowl) and its Sherman Oaks spin-off plate up "damn good ribs" that have "so much flavor" adding sauce is a "disservice"; though detractors say it's "second-rate", service is "not so good" and "you don't get much for the money", supporters let their "taste buds speak, and they overwhelmingly approve."

### Mr. Chow ● *Chinese*   | 21 | 20 | 20 | $71 |

**Beverly Hills** | 344 N. Camden Dr. (bet. Brighton Way & Wilshire Blvd.) |
310-278-9911 | www.mrchow.com

"Daily celeb sightings" are a "blast" at this "over-the-top" "Beverly Hills favorite for being seen and making scenes", where the collision of "A-listers" and "paparazzi jumping out of nowhere" provides nightly "dinner theater", while the tightly "packed" black-and-white interior graced by original Warhols still looks "chic"; the "exorbitantly priced" Chinese food ranges from "run-of-the-mill" to "fabulous", and though the servers "sparkle", cautious customers warn "if you listen to their specials, you're sure to get ripped off."

### **NEW** Mucho Ultima Mexicana  *Mexican*   | 19 | 22 | 16 | $41 |

**Manhattan Beach** | 903 Manhattan Ave. (9th St.) | 310-374-4422 |
www.muchomb.com

A "spicy addition to Manhattan Beach", this "swanky" arrival by restaurateur/hotelier Mike Zislis (Rock'n Fish, Shade Hotel) delivers "wicked" margaritas and "trendy nouveau" Mexican fare that's a "notch above the usual combo plates" inside a "sleek" but "warm" space; though service is still "working out the kinks" and the bill can add up, it gets plenty of "style points" for both the setting and the "people-watching scene."

### Mulberry Street Pizzeria  *Pizza*   | 23 | 9 | 16 | $14 |

**Beverly Hills** | 240 S. Beverly Dr. (bet. Charleville Blvd. & Gregory Way) |
310-247-8100
**Beverly Hills** | 347 N. Cañon Dr. (bet. Brighton & Dayton Ways) |
310-247-8998
**Encino** | 17040 Ventura Blvd. (Oak Park Ave.) | 818-906-8881
www.mulberrypizza.com

"Now this is New York pizza (right down to the *Post* on the counter)" exclaim even "hard-core" East Coasters about these Beverly Hills and Encino parlors specializing in "just-about-perfect" "thin-crust" pies with "wonderful toppings"; the other Italian eats receive less acclaim, but with "minuscule" tabs, "you can't beat it."

### ☑ Murano Ⓜ *Italian*   | 20 | 27 | 20 | $61 |

**West Hollywood** | 9010 Melrose Ave. (N. Almont Dr.) | 310-246-9118 |
www.murano9010.com

Serving up a "splashy dining experience", this "sexy" WeHo "knockout" flaunts "stunning" all-white decor (red "Murano chandeliers impart a warm glow") and "hot waiters" who "know it"; though "imaginative", the French-accented Italian food "can't quite keep up" with all the eye candy, and the service generally "doesn't warrant the prices", but it's still "fun on the weekends" for a "Boystown" crowd.

**Musha** *Japanese*  | 24 | 16 | 19 | $32 |

**Santa Monica** | 424 Wilshire Blvd. (bet. 4th & 5th Sts.) | 310-576-6330 ●
**Torrance** | 1725 W. Carson St. (S. Western Ave.) | 310-787-7344
"Spectacular" small plates of "savory" Japanese "pub food" "give your taste buds a wild ride" ("don't be afraid of the octopus omelet") at these "affordable" izakayas in Santa Monica and Torrance; with flowing beer and sake, "polite" service and a "hopping", "noisy" scene, they have an "authentic Tokyo" feel.

**Musso & Frank Grill** Ⓢ Ⓜ *American*  | 18 | 19 | 19 | $42 |

**Hollywood** | 6667 Hollywood Blvd. (bet. Cherokee & Las Palmas Aves.) | 323-467-7788
"A chilled martini, curt service and retro fare make for an authentic evening circa 1939" at this third-generation "landmark" that played host to Charlie Chaplin, Douglas Fairbanks, "Faulkner and Fitzgerald" and still exudes "old Hollywood" appeal, from the "unchanged" booths and wood-paneled walls to the "classically styled" American menu starring "good" "grilled meats"; though it "disappoints" some, many find it "musty but still mighty" – "long may she live."

**NEW Nakkara** *Thai*  | – | – | – | M |

**Fairfax** | 7669 Beverly Blvd. (N. Spaulding Ave.) | 323-937-3100 | www.nakkaraonbeverly.com
"Why fight the crowds at The Grove?" when "across the street" is this "wonderful" Fairfax newcomer where "inventive" spins on Thai standards are the order of the day; the "tiny" dining room is decorated in "clean blue" hues, and though service gets a mixed response, most find the overall quality "above-average" for the tab.

**Nak Won Korean** ● *Korean*  | ▽ 16 | 7 | 10 | $18 |

**Koreatown** | 3879 Wilshire Blvd. (Western Ave.) | 213-388-8889
"No-fuss" Korean BBQ and "home cooking" satisfies "people looking for a quick fix with variety" at this "bargain" 24-hour K-town eatery; it's "friendly" despite the language barrier, but just be warned "if you want ambiance, it's not the place for you."

**Nanbankan** *Japanese*  | ▽ 24 | 15 | 19 | $29 |

**West LA** | 11330 Santa Monica Blvd. (Corinth Ave.) | 310-478-1591
"Tough to find" but "worth the effort", this "hidden" Japanese "gem" in West LA offers "amazing", "authentic" "char-grilled yakitori" prepared right in the middle of the otherwise "bland", "dark" room; regulars are "welcomed like family" and advise "sitting at the counter to watch the action" – "just don't wear your best" since it gets pretty "smoky."

**Napa Valley Grille** *Californian*  | 20 | 21 | 20 | $43 |

**Westwood** | 1100 Glendon Ave. (Lindbrook Dr.) | 310-824-3322 | www.napavalleygrille.com
"You feel like you're dining in a major winery" at this "serene" Westwood branch of an "upscale" chain, thanks to the "extensive"

| | FOOD | DECOR | SERVICE | COST |
|---|---|---|---|---|

vino selection and "generous pours" by a "knowledgable" staff, not to mention the "tremendously yuppie" vibe; the rustic decor with fireplaces and grapevines on the patio drives home the theme, as does the "light, reliable" Cal-New American cuisine, adding up to what some diners deem a "blandly enjoyable" meal.

### Natalee Thai  *Thai*
18 | 16 | 16 | $22

**Beverly Hills** | 998 S. Robertson Blvd. (Olympic Blvd.) | 310-855-9380
**Palms** | 10101 Venice Blvd. (Clarington Ave.) | 310-202-7003
www.nataleethai.com

"A cut above average", this "trendy" Thai pair delivers an "eclectic" menu in a "futuristic", "idiosyncratic" setting in Beverly Hills and Palms (which also features a sushi bar); it's "loud, crowded" and the service is variable, but at least the cocktails "add a little spice to the typical Thai experience."

### Nate 'n Al  *Deli*
20 | 10 | 16 | $24

**Beverly Hills** | 414 N. Beverly Dr. (bet. Brighton Way & Santa Monica Blvd.) | 310-274-0101 | www.natenal.com

The "mile-high" sandwiches of "heavy-duty corned beef", matzo ball soup with "healing properties" and other "Jewish soul food" served at this Beverly Hills "tradition" are "perfect" "when you're on the Left Coast and your tummy is on the East"; "true to deli form", it gives "old-timers" and "celebrities" ("Cindy Crawford", "Larry King", "an Olsen twin") the same "sassy" treatment, and though some nudges knock the "lousy" environs, maybe they've never seen the "real deal" before.

### ❷ Native Foods  *Californian/Eclectic*
22 | 11 | 16 | $17

**Westwood** | 1110½ Gayley Ave. (Wilshire Blvd.) | 310-209-1055 | www.nativefoods.com

If you didn't think "vegan comfort food" existed, this "inexpensive" "cafeteria-style" Cal-Eclectic in Westwood will make you think again with its "fresh", "satisfying" plates of "creative" eats including home-made tempeh and "addictive" pizza that leave surveyors "stuffed but feeling insanely healthy"; there's "no atmosphere", but it works as a "quick, nutritious" option that "kids love" too.

### Nawab of India  *Indian*
21 | 15 | 19 | $28

**Santa Monica** | 1621 Wilshire Blvd. (bet. 16th & 17th Sts.) | 310-829-1106 | www.nawabindia.com

"Wonderful curries", "spicy appetizers" and other "delectable" dishes make this Santa Monica Indian a favorite for "bargain" buffets during lunch and weekend brunch (though it's "pricier" for dinner); the antiques-adorned setting gets mixed reviews, but most find it "pleasant" and appreciate the "steady" service.

### NBC Seafood  *Chinese/Seafood*
19 | 10 | 11 | $22

**Monterey Park** | 404 S. Atlantic Blvd. (bet. Harding & Newmark Aves.) | 626-282-2323

This "popular" Monterey Park "palace" purveys "fabulous dim sum" as well as Cantonese dinnertime "delights from the sea" that are "brought to your table for approval before cooking"; though service is "curt" and the atmosphere "tacky", it's all "appropriately authentic" and the space is so "humongous" at least you "won't get smacked by a passing cart."

| | FOOD | DECOR | SERVICE | COST |
|---|---|---|---|---|

### Neomeze  *Eclectic*
▽ 23 | 23 | 23 | $37

**Pasadena** | 20 E. Colorado Blvd. (Fair Oaks Ave.) | 626-793-3010 | www.neomeze.com

"Cool" customers "love the design" and the "loft vibe" of this "ultramodern" newcomer whose "hopping" lounge has a "retractable roof", creating a "sexy" prelude for "refreshing", "unusual and attractive" Eclectic small plates, complemented by the "best martinis"; the staff is "awesome" too, so many deem it a Pasadena "must" for the "late", spendy crowd; N.B. the Food score may not reflect a recent chef change.

### Neptune's Net  *Seafood*
18 | 10 | 10 | $21

**Malibu** | 42505 PCH (Yerba Buena Rd.) | 310-457-3095 | www.neptunesnet.com

It's "Harley heaven" at this "biker dive/seafood hut" on the Malibu coastline, where a "spectacular" view of the Pacific along with a "beer and a basket of shrimp", among a "varied artery-stopping" lineup of fried fish, keep the "locals and surfers" coming too; with its beachy setting and "major people-watching", "it doesn't get any more Southern Californian than this little shack."

### New Moon  *Chinese*
21 | 19 | 18 | $25

**Downtown** | 102 W. Ninth St. (S. Main St.) | 213-624-0186 🛃
**Montrose** | 2138 Verdugo Blvd. (Clifton Pl.) | 818-249-4868
**NEW** **Valencia** | Gateway Vill. | 28281 Newhall Ranch Rd. (Rye Canyon Rd.) | 661-257-4321
www.newmoonrestaurants.com

"Upscale Asian food" is "made with fresh ingredients" at these well-priced Sino sibs where the "tasty", if "not particularly authentic" eats include their "famous" Chinese chicken salad as well as a variety of "old favorites"; service can be "erratic", but given the "comfortable" contemporary settings, families contend they're "lucky to have" them around.

### Newsroom Café  *Vegetarian*
18 | 14 | 15 | $25

**West Hollywood** | 120 N. Robertson Blvd. (bet. 3rd St. & W. Beverly Blvd.) | 310-652-4444

West Hollywood's "hip and healthy" head to this "venerable" cafe for "wonderfully fresh" food featuring "tons of vegan and vegetarian options" plus "tasty baked goods" and "booze" on offer for less-virtuous types; its Robertson Boulevard location affords plenty of "stargazing" from the front patio, so even if service is "inconsistent" it's still "dependable" for a "cheap" bite.

### Nick & Stef's Steakhouse  *Steak*
23 | 20 | 21 | $56

**Downtown** | Wells Fargo Ctr. | 330 S. Hope St. (bet. 3rd & 4th Sts.) | 213-680-0330 | www.patinagroup.com

"Simple pleasures" like "incredible" dry-aged steaks and "impressive wines" are the hallmarks of this chophouse "splurge" from the Patina Group whose "convenient" Downtown location makes it "popular" for "power lunches" and "pre-theater" dinners; service is usually "attentive", and though some find the "sophisticated" wood-lined setting a little "worn around the edges", at least the eye-catching "glassed-in meat locker" adds a "unique" touch.

| | FOOD | DECOR | SERVICE | COST |
|---|---|---|---|---|

### Nicola's Kitchen  *Californian/Italian*   | 20 | 13 | 19 | $22 |

**Woodland Hills** | French Quarter | 20969 Ventura Blvd. (De Soto Ave.) | 818-883-9477 | www.nicolaskitchen.com

Woodland Hills residents rely on this "neighborhood joint" for "simple" "well-prepared" Cal-Italian dishes like penne pomodoro, chicken parmigiana and "terrific chopped salads" served in "generous portions"; digs are "nothing fancy", but "personal" service adds a "homey" touch and prices are a "good value" too.

### Nic's ●🗷 *American*   | 19 | 20 | 20 | $45 |

**Beverly Hills** | 453 N. Cañon Dr. (Little Santa Monica Blvd.) | 310-550-5707 | www.nicsbeverlyhills.com

"Moody lighting" and "Bossa nova" on the speakers set the scene at this "Rat-Pack-inspired" Beverly Hills watering hole famed for its "delicious martinis" offered up in 21 varieties, from "classic gin" to "jalapeño"; service is "pleasant" and "solid" New American cuisine "never takes a backseat to the booze", though some say it's the "walk-in vodka freezer" (where you can sample various spirits) that proves to be the real "centerpiece" of the evening.

### Nine Thirty  *American*   | ▽ 21 | 25 | 20 | $56 |

**Westwood** | W Los Angeles Westwood | 930 Hilgard Ave. (bet. La Conte & Weyburn Aves.) | 310-443-8211 | www.ninethirtyw.com

"Über-hip" describes both the atmosphere and the "too-cool" clientele at this "slick" venue inside the W hotel in Westwood turning out "perfectly presented" New American dishes with an "organic" focus in a modern space with bamboo-and-coconut detailing; service is "attentive", and given such a "stylish" scene, "pricey" tabs should come as no surprise – "you'll spend your down payment on the valet" alone.

### Nishimura 🗷 *Japanese*   | ▽ 26 | 23 | 20 | $105 |

**West Hollywood** | 8684 Melrose Ave. (N. San Vicente Blvd.) | 310-659-4770

Purists proclaim this "secret" West Hollywood Japanese sets "the gold standard" for sushi with "fabulously fresh" fish set atop "exquisitely beautiful" "handmade ceramic" platters and set down in a "well-designed" "Zen-minimalist" space with a bamboo garden; yet while supporters say it's "not to be missed", the less-smitten say that service is "arrogant" and most "memorable" are the "truly expensive" prices.

### Nizam  *Indian*   | 18 | 13 | 18 | $23 |

**West LA** | 10871 W. Pico Blvd. (Westwood Blvd.) | 310-470-1441

"Traditional Indian dishes" and a notable lunch buffet attract a "neighborhood" following to this West LA "old-timer" that's convenient for "takeout" or "before or after a movie at Westside Pavilion"; though prices are pleasing, ex-allies attest the decor is "tired", and add that the food's not "up to par" with its former standards.

### Noah's New York Bagels  *Sandwiches*   | 17 | 11 | 14 | $9 |

**Hancock Park** | 250 N. Larchmont Blvd. (Beverly Blvd.) | 323-466-2924
**Palos Verdes Estates** | 895 Silver Spur Rd. (Crenshaw Blvd.) | 310-541-7824
**Brentwood** | 11911 San Vicente Blvd. (Montana Ave.) | 310-472-5651
**Marina del Rey** | Marina del Rey Shopping Ctr. | 546-548 Washington Blvd. (Via Marina) | 310-574-1155

*(continued)*

*(continued)*

**Noah's New York Bagels**

**Westwood** | 10910 Lindbrook Dr. (Westwood Blvd.) | 310-209-8177
**Manhattan Beach** | 330 Manhattan Beach Blvd. (Highland Ave.) |
310-937-2206
**Pasadena** | Hastings Ranch Shopping Ctr. | 3711 E. Foothill Blvd.
(Rosemead Blvd.) | 626-351-0352
**Pasadena** | 605 S. Lake Ave. (E. California Blvd.) | 626-449-6415
**Sherman Oaks** | 14622 Ventura Blvd. (Cedros Ave.) | 818-907-9570
www.noahs.com

For a "quick nosh on the run" surveyors say this national sandwich
chain is "as good as it gets outside of the Big Apple" for "endless varieties" of "fresh, fat" bagels "with all the trimmings"; though the
counter staff usually keeps the "intimidating lines on weekends"
"moving fast", "ex-New Yorkers" avow these "puffed-up" "dough
balls" are certainly "not authentic", but they'll do "in a pinch."

**NEW Nobu Los Angeles** ◑ *Japanese*          26 | 22 | 24 | $81

**West Hollywood** | 903 N. La Cienega Blvd. (Willoughby Ave.) |
310-657-5711 | www.noburestaurants.com

"Master of miso" Nobu Matsuhisa "hasn't lost his touch" say longtime
supporters savoring the "perfect marriage" of Peruvian and Japanese
flavors at this "trendy" new West Hollywood outpost of the sushi
chef's international empire; allies attest the "total package is a knockout", from the "accommodating" service to the "amazing" David
Rockwell–designed space, however, critics knock "exorbitant prices"
and claim it's not "up to par" with the "original" – Matsuhisa – right
"down the street."

**Z Nobu Malibu** *Japanese*          27 | 20 | 22 | $73

**Malibu** | 3835 Cross Creek Rd. (PCH) | 310-317-9140 |
www.nobumatsuhisa.com

"Near perfection" is how devotees describe Nobu Matsuhisa's
Malibu Japanese "hot spot" where "A-listers abound" in the "casually luxe" setting, but the "food is the star" with "spectacular"
sushi and "phenomenal carpaccio dishes" all delivered by a "warm
crew"; though it thrives on a "laid-back" feel, don't let the "tacky strip-
mall locale" fool you – this "spectacular culinary experience" is "not
for the faint of wallet."

**Noé** *American*          24 | 23 | 23 | $59

**Downtown** | Omni Los Angeles Hotel | 251 S. Olive St. (2nd St.) |
213-356-4100 | www.noerestaurant.com

Theatergoers thrill to this "elegant" entry in the Omni Hotel
Downtown that's "ideal" for a "pre-show" meal thanks to its "delicious" New American cuisine with "lovely" "Asian influences" and a
"terrific location" "near MOCA and Disney Hall"; "intelligent" service enhances the "wonderful ambiance", as do the "floor-to-
ceiling windows" flaunting "breathtaking views" of the city and live
piano Tuesday–Saturday.

**NEW Nonna** *Italian*          ▽ 18 | 19 | 22 | $56

**West Hollywood** | 9255 Sunset Blvd. (Doheny Dr.) | 310-270-4455

A "warm, professional" team is behind this WeHo entry on a busy
stretch of Sunset where a "pleasant" setting with "well-spaced" tables

and a "nice sheltered patio" make it a natural fit for the "over-65 Beverly Hills set"; though the rustic Italian dishes (like pizzas from a wood-burning oven) are deemed "solid" by supporters, a number of naysayers feel it's not impressive enough "to justify" the relatively high prices.

### ☑ Nook Bistro ⑤ *American/Eclectic*

24 | 17 | 21 | $32

**West LA** | Plaza West | 11628 Santa Monica Blvd. (Barry Ave.) | 310-207-5160 | www.nookbistro.com

"Aptly named", this "cute" little "hole-in-the-wall" in a West LA strip mall doles out "impressive" "grown-up versions" of American-Eclectic "childhood favorites" like grilled Albacore sandwiches and three-cheese macaroni backed by a "snappy" wine list; it thrives on an "easygoing" vibe thanks to the "amiable staff", "reasonable prices" and a "modest" white-walled interior with a communal table; in fact, the only downside, attest enthusiasts, is that it's so "popular", reservations can be "tough to get."

### Nyala Ethiopian *Ethiopian*

21 | 17 | 19 | $21

**Fairfax** | 1076 S. Fairfax Ave. (bet. Whitworth Dr. & W. Olympic Blvd.) | 323-936-5918 | www.nyala-la.com

Fairfax diners "dig in, hands and all" at this family-run "Little Ethiopia" "favorite" where "richly spiced stews" (in meat and vegetarian varieties) are "scooped up" with "spongy" injera bread offering the ultimate in "finger-licking good" experiences; "kind service", "moderate prices" and a "quiet" colorful setting seal the deal for "adventuresome" eaters who recommend it for both "group" dining and a low-key "date."

### NEW O!Burger *Burgers*

- | - | - | I

**West Hollywood** | 8593 Santa Monica Blvd. (La Cienega Blvd.) | 310-854-0234

Everything's organic at this fast-fooder in the midst of West Hollywood's Boystown, including the burgers – made from grass-fed beef, free-range turkey or spinach-and-corn – and drinks like oat milk vegan shakes and kombucha tea; the polished metal-and-glass setting, on the other hand, is strictly high-tech.

### NEW Oak Room, The *Californian*

- | - | - | E

**Pacific Palisades** | 1035 Swarthmore Ave. (Sunset Blvd.) | 310-454-3337 | www.oakroompantry.com

Former Mayor Richard Riordan – owner of Gladstone's, the Original Pantry and Riordan's Tavern – lobbies to make the Pacific Palisades a dining destination by opening this high-end Californian right next to his Village Pantry; chef Douglas Silberg (ex Water Grill, Michael's) creates dishes with a focus on seasonal ingredients, served in an oak-accented room decorated with local art.

### O-Bar *American*

21 | 25 | 22 | $41

**West Hollywood** | 8279 Santa Monica Blvd. (N. Sweetzer Ave.) | 323-822-3300 | www.obarrestaurant.com

A "gorgeous" room done up in frosty blues gets a boost from "eye candy galore" at this "very hip", "very gay" New American in West Hollywood serving "creative" "comfort food" like fried chicken and waffles with rosemary-infused syrup; cuisine can be "inconsistent",

| | FOOD | DECOR | SERVICE | COST |

but the "wonderful" cocktails always hit their mark, so most reviewers report they're "never disappointed", in spite of occasional "attitude" from the "hot" staff.

### NEW Oba Sushi Izakaya *Japanese*

| - | - | - | M |

**Pasadena** | 181 E. Glenarm St. (Arroyo Pkwy.) | 626-799-8543 | www.obasushi.com

Far from the madding crowds of Old Town Pasadena, this understated izakaya in an off-the-beaten-path mini-mall showcases an unusual lineup of Japanese small plates alongside a selection of sushi, maki and tempura; prices are modest, so for those who don't want to venture into Little Tokyo or Gardena for their sake and snacks, this peaceful venue is a fine alternative.

### Ocean & Vine *American*

| ▽ 21 | 24 | 23 | $51 |

**Santa Monica** | Loews Santa Monica Beach Hotel | 1700 Ocean Ave. (Pico Blvd.) | 310-576-3180 | www.oceanandvine.com

Affording "beautiful ocean views", this "upscale" "surprise" "tucked into" the Loews Santa Monica offers a "romantic ambiance" both out on the "lovely patio" complete with a fire pit and in the "chic" pillow-strewn interior; as for the New American cuisine, pleased patrons say it's "better than you'd expect for a hotel", with "tasty" signatures like fondue backed by an "excellent wine list."

### Ocean Ave. Seafood *Seafood*

| 23 | 20 | 21 | $49 |

**Santa Monica** | 1401 Ocean Ave. (Santa Monica Blvd.) | 310-394-5669 | www.oceanave.com

Enthusiasts applaud this "lively" Santa Monica seafooder that "continues to impress" with "as-fresh-as-it-gets" fin fare – including an "extensive oyster selection" – that some say is "second only to cousin Water Grill", and a "heck of a lot cheaper" too; "plenty of attention from servers" is a definite plus, yet those who find the "nautically themed" dining room a little "tired" are advised to gaze outward for prime "sunset views."

### Ocean Seafood *Chinese/Seafood*

| 20 | 15 | 16 | $24 |

**Chinatown** | 750 N. Hill St. (bet. Alpine & Ord Sts.) | 213-687-3088 | www.oceansf.com

An "oldie but goodie" on the dim sum circuit, this Chinatown "banquet hall" specializes in dumplings, turnip cakes and "loads" of other "little morsels" in addition to "fresh seafood" plates that "come close" to those in "NYC"; a few find the "cattle calls" of "cart pushers" leave something to be desired, but the "low prices" and "beautifully tacky" chandeliered decor redeem, prompting some to recommend it as a less "crowded" "alternative" to other nearby spots.

### Ocean Star *Chinese*

| 21 | 14 | 15 | $23 |

**Monterey Park** | 145 N. Atlantic Blvd. (bet. Emerson & Garvey Aves.) | 626-308-2128

An "endless" array of carts deliver "delicious" dim sum at this "top" tier Monterey Park Sino specialist that fans favor for its "amazing" "variety" ("the usual favorites" plus more "adventuresome" offerings) and "traditional" "Hong Kong" feel; despite ample seating in the "cavernous" interior, "long waits" and "crowded" conditions are a regular occurrence, especially on "weekends."

**Odyssey** *Continental/Seafood* | 14 | 18 | 16 | $36 |

Granada Hills | 15600 Odyssey Dr. (Buchner Ave.) | 818-366-6444 |
www.theodysseyrestaurant.com

The "fabulous views" of the Valley are the stars at this "mountaintop"
Granada Hills venue favored for "banquets and weddings", "romantic
dinners" and other "special occasions"; though foes find the seafood-
focused Continental menu merely "mediocre" (and "expensive" to
boot), a smattering of surveyors suggest it's worth it to "go at least
once" – if only for the "sunsets" and a "drink on the patio."

**Oinkster, The** *BBQ* | 20 | 9 | 15 | $13 |

Eagle Rock | 2005 Colorado Blvd. (Shearin Ave.) | 323-255-6465 |
www.oinkster.com

A "throwback to old LA", this "retro" Eagle Rock American from fine-
dining chef André Guerrero (Max) offers up a "fresh" "interpretation
of fast food" with "old-fashioned" burgers with "homemade" condiments, "rockin' pastrami" and a "BBQ pulled-pork sandwich" to make
you "weak in the knees" all rustled up by an "accommodating" counter
staff; though regulars report "long waits, even if you call ahead", it's
relatively "cheap" and "outdoor seating with umbrellas" and "pitchers
of beer" prove "nice on a summer night."

**Olé! Tapas Bar** *Spanish* | 16 | 18 | 15 | $32 |

Studio City | 13251 Ventura Blvd. (Longridge Ave.) | 818-986-3190 |
www.oletapasbar.com

Tipplers tout this Studio City Spaniard where "creative small plates"
get a boost from sangria, specialty martinis and a well-considered
wine list; "flamenco dancing" on Tuesday adds to the "lively" feel, but
some find it focuses "too much on atmosphere", citing "overpriced"
"inauthentic" fare and service that can border on "nonexistent."

**Oliva** *Italian* | 21 | 18 | 21 | $31 |

Sherman Oaks | 4449 Van Nuys Blvd. (Moorpark St.) | 818-789-4490 |
www.olivarestaurant.com

"Lots of regulars" say they return "again and again" to this "sweet"
Sherman Oaks trattoria offering "ample portions" of Italian cooking at
"fair prices"; though it's "recently expanded", it's "so popular" that the
"warm" staff is sometimes strained and some suggest "it's best to
come early to get a table."

**Omelette Parlor** *American* | 19 | 14 | 18 | $18 |

Santa Monica | 2732 Main St. (Ocean Park Blvd.) | 310-399-7892

It's "all about the breakfast" at this "chummy" American eatery on
Santa Monica's Main Street, a "local staple" for 30 years for its
"nice selection" of "enormous" "specialty" egg dishes and waffles and
pancakes with "tasty" toppings; longtimers say "the back patio is the
only way to go", but "weekends are a zoo", so arrive "early" or "be
prepared to wait."

**Omino Sushi** *Japanese* | ▽ 25 | 9 | 20 | $35 |

Chatsworth | 20957 Devonshire St. (De Soto Ave.) | 818-709-8822 |
www.ominosushi.com

"Artistic chefs" slice up an "extensive selection" of "phenomenal
sushi" at this Chatsworth Japanese set in a "middle-of-nowhere strip
mall" but deemed "worth the schlep"; though it doesn't score high for

| | FOOD | DECOR | SERVICE | COST |
|---|---|---|---|---|

looks, regulars report the "congenial" staff "treats you like royalty", so just sit at the bar and "ask what they recommend."

**O-Nami** *Japanese* | 17 | 11 | 15 | $27 |

**Torrance** | 1925 W. Carson St. (Cabrillo Ave.) | 310-787-1632
Groupies "go hungry" to take advantage of the "spectacular spreads" at this Torrance Japanese seafood buffet offering "freshly made" sushi and maki as well as a "multitude" of hot entrees, salads and desserts; though cynics say it offers all the "quality implied by all-you-can-eat", defenders declare "it's a good deal if you aren't too picky."

**ｚ One Pico** *Californian/Mediterranean* | 22 | 26 | 23 | $58 |

**Santa Monica** | Shutters on the Bch. | 1 Pico Blvd. (Ocean Ave.) | 310-587-1717 | www.shuttersonthebeach.com
"Fabulous ocean views" add to the "aura of tranquility" at this "understated" respite in Santa Monica's Shutters on the Beach; most find the Cal-Med cuisine "creative without being too edgy", while "white-glove service" makes it "perfect for a special evening"; N.B. a post-Survey renovation may not be reflected in the Decor score.

**One Sunset** ●ｚ *American* | 20 | 25 | 17 | $56 |

**West Hollywood** | 8730 W. Sunset Blvd. (N. Sherbourne Dr.) | 310-657-0111 | www.theonerestaurants.com
"Beautiful people" "soak in the scene" at this velvet-roped West Hollywood lounge/restaurant – an offshoot of a "trendy" NYC original – where the "stunning" luxe leather-and-wood interior with "low tables" and banquettes set the scene for "flavorful" New American small plates that "lend themselves to sharing"; some say the "noisy" room with a nightly DJ isn't conducive to conversation, and a few fret that it's "overpriced" and best for "apps and drinks."

**On Sunset** *Californian* | ▽ 22 | 27 | 20 | $43 |

**Brentwood** | Luxe Hotel | 11461 Sunset Blvd. (Church Ln.) | 310-476-6571 | www.luxehotelsunsetblvd.com
"Amazing night views" from the "top floor" of the "secluded" Luxe Hotel in Brentwood create a "lovely" ambiance at this Californian yearling well-suited for both "business meetings" or a "girls' night out"; the "imaginative" menu earns kudos too, so the only thing that gives diners pause is the somewhat posh pricing.

**Onyx** *Japanese* | ▽ 25 | 27 | 24 | $50 |

**Westlake Village** | Four Seasons Westlake Vill. | 2 Dole Dr. (Via Rocas) | 818-575-3043 | www.fourseasons.com
Gastronomes sing the praises of this "little-known" Japanese "gem" in the Four Seasons hotel in Westlake Village that goes "beyond" your standard raw fish dishes with "buttery" sashimi and "impressive chef's specials" like Chilean sea bass and Kobe beef; it gets its "cool" looks thanks to wall panels of semiprecious stones and a saltwater aquarium, and there's also a patio "overlooking the beautiful grounds."

**Original Pancake House** *Diner* | 23 | 10 | 18 | $15 |

**Redondo Beach** | 1756 S. PCH (bet. Palos Verdes Blvd. & Paseo De Las Delicias) | 310-543-9875 | www.originalpancakehouse.com
A "seemingly endless variety of pancakes" (especially the "don't-miss" apple and "unusual" Dutch Baby versions) makes fans flip for

this "real-deal" breakfast chain that supplies "Sunday morning comfort" for many; service is "swift" and the price is right, so the "only drawback is long lines on the weekends."

### Original Pantry Cafe ●✓ Diner | 15 | 9 | 16 | $17 |

**Downtown** | 877 S. Figueroa St. (9th St.) | 213-972-9279 | www.pantrycafe.com

"A greasy spoon with character", this Downtown "relic" that opened in 1924 feels "right out of a Chandler story" with "spunky waitresses" setting down "no-nonsense" American diner food like "bargain breakfasts" and "cooked-to-order steaks" 24 hours a day; even if many maintain the food's "not the best", "nostalgics" note "you can't beat it for authentic charm" (or the "cheap prices").

### Original Texas BBQ King, The ✓ BBQ | 21 | - | 13 | $15 |
### (aka BBQ King)

**Mid-City** | 5309 S. Vermont Ave. (W. 53rd St.) | 213-437-0881 | www.texasbbqking.com

Recently relocated from Downtown digs, this "real-deal" BBQ emporium is now smoking up "tender ribs" and "tasty tri-tip" in a similarly "no-frills" Mid-City locale with table seating and full service; a few 'cue connoisseurs find the sauce "cloying", but for "an occasional fix", it does the trick; N.B. they also deliver.

### Orris Ⓜ French/Japanese | 26 | 15 | 22 | $40 |

**West LA** | 2006 Sawtelle Blvd. (La Grange Ave.) | 310-268-2212 | www.orrisrestaurant.com

The "delectable" French-Japanese small plates make for "superb grazing" at chef-owner Hideo Yamashiro's West LA destination rolling out "refined" cuisine and "intriguing wines and sakes" at prices that won't "break the bank"; though the setting is "minimalist", the staff is "upbeat" and an open kitchen offers "lots to watch" while you dine, leading the satisfied to sigh "now, if only they would take reservations . . ."

### Orso Italian | 21 | 21 | 20 | $46 |

**Third Street** | 8706 W. Third St. (S. Hamel Rd.) | 310-274-7144 | www.orsorestaurant.com

Loyalists "love" to "linger" on the "serene" garden patio at this Third Street Italian whose "industry"-heavy scene promises "almost guaranteed celebrity sightings" daily; like its sibling outposts in NYC and London, it maintains its "high standards" with "consistently good" cuisine and a "top-notch" staff adding to the overall "warm" ambiance.

### NEW Ortega 120 Mexican | - | - | - | I |

**Redondo Beach** | 1814 S. PCH (Palos Verdes Blvd.) | 310-792-4120 | www.ortega120.com

Day of the Dead artifacts line the walls at this South Bay cantina set in a space that's been a revolving door for many concepts; the low-priced menu is notable for large portions of Mexican chow, plus 120 tequilas.

### Ortolan ⓈⓂ French | 25 | 24 | 24 | $85 |

**Third Street** | 8338 W. Third St. (bet. Orlando & Sweetzer Aves.) | West Hollywood | 323-653-3300 | www.ortolanrestaurant.com

"Playful" New French creations are executed with "obsessive attention to detail" at "world-class" chef Christophe Émé's "memorable" Third

Street boîte set in a "sexy", "stylish" room with cream leather booths and crystal chandeliers; though the less-impressed label the presentations almost "comically pretentious" ("test-tube appetizers" "chilled forks?"), the "surprisingly unstuffy" staff offers such "gracious" service that many find it "delightful" "down to the last petit four."

**Osteria La Buca** *Italian* | 25 | 18 | 19 | $38 |

**Melrose** | 5210 Melrose Ave. (Wilton Pl.) | 323-462-1900 | www.osterialabuca.com

"Sublime pastas" "made from scratch" lead the popularity parade at this Melrose "secret", a "fabulous go-to" for "wonderful" Northern Italian cuisine at "reasonable prices"; though regulars report the "handsome" interior is "much more comfortable" since a recent expansion, several surveyors say it's "lost" some of its "quaint charm", though it still feels "cozy when the fireplace is going" and a "friendly" crew adds another nice touch.

**Osteria Latini** *Italian* | 24 | 16 | 20 | $46 |

**Brentwood** | 11712 San Vicente Blvd. (Barrington Ave.) | 310-826-9222 | www.osterialatini.com

"Delighted" diners cheer this "hidden find" on a "street full of Italian restaurants" in Brentwood where a "talented chef" turns out "honest" "authentic" dishes in a "low-key" space with white tablecloths and racks of regional wines on display; add in a "welcoming" staff and a "good price-to-food value", and the only downside, say some, is the somewhat "claustrophobic" seating.

**Z Osteria Mozza ●** *Italian* | 26 | 22 | 23 | $62 |

**Hollywood** | 6602 Melrose Ave. (Highland Ave.) | 323-297-0100 | www.mozza-la.com

"You'll need the patience of a saint" to snag a reservation at this "high-end" Hollywood "foodie magnet" from celeb chefs Mario Batali and Nancy Silverton – a "delicious counterpart" to their Pizzeria Mozza – that "lives up to its much-hyped reputation" with "sensational" cooking, "fabulous breads" and "dreamworthy" "fresh" cheeses from the in-house mozzarella bar; "wonderful" servers "encourage you to linger over every morsel" in the "elegant" space, but some guests gripe that the "mind-numbingly loud" "'80s music" "seems misplaced" in what otherwise feels like a "a truly authentic Italian experience."

**Outback Steakhouse** *Steak* | 17 | 15 | 17 | $28 |

**Lakewood** | 5305 Clark Ave. (Candlewood St.) | 562-634-0353
**Torrance** | Del Amo Fashion Ctr. | 21880 Hawthorne Blvd. (bet. Carson St. & Sepulveda Blvd.) | 310-793-5555
**Arcadia** | 166 E. Huntington Dr. (bet. 1st & 2nd Aves.) | 626-447-6435
**Burbank** | Empire Ctr. | 1761 N. Victory Pl. (W. Empire Ave.) | 818-567-2717
**Northridge** | 18711 Devonshire St. (Reseda Blvd.) | 818-366-2341
**City of Industry** | Puente Hills Mall | 1418 S. Azusa Ave. (Colima Rd.) | 626-810-6765
**Covina** | 1476 N. Azusa Ave. (Arrow Hwy.) | 626-812-0488
**Thousand Oaks** | 137 E. Thousand Oaks Blvd. (Moorpark Rd.) | 805-381-1590
**Valencia** | 25261 N. The Old Rd. (Chiquella Ln.) | 661-287-9630
www.outback.com
Additional locations throughout Southern California

"Meat lovers on a budget" report that this "midtier", Aussie-themed chain chophouse provides terrific "bang for the buck", not to mention

| | FOOD | DECOR | SERVICE | COST |
|---|---|---|---|---|

"basic" steaks and "hefty sides" (the famed bloomin' onion supplies "a week's worth of calories" in a single serving); it's "not known for subtlety" – starting with the "overly friendly, chat 'n' squat" service – but when you "don't want to splurge", it's a "decent" enough option.

### Outlaws Bar & Grill  *American*

| 18 | 12 | 18 | $22 |
|---|---|---|---|

**Playa del Rey** | 230 Culver Blvd. (Vista del Mar) | 310-822-4040

"Funky as ever", this "homey" "hangout" in Playa del Rey is a "reliable" pick for well-priced American pub grub (they're "known for their burgers") and a "fantastic" suds selection in a "friendly" setting that feels "like hanging out in your pal's rec room"; given its address just a block from the beach, some say the "perfect patio" with "seagulls overhead" is the best option.

### Pace  *Italian*

| 21 | 21 | 19 | $41 |
|---|---|---|---|

**Laurel Canyon** | 2100 Laurel Canyon Blvd. (Kirkwood Dr.) | 323-654-8583 | www.peaceinthecanyon.com

"Romantic, but in a bohemian way", this "dark", "intimate" Laurel Canyon "hideaway" dishes up "rustic" Italian specialties made from "fresher than fresh" organic ingredients in a "gorgeous subterranean setting" featuring "frequent celeb sightings"; despite some quibbles about "steep prices", most maintain it's a "wonderful experience" that's well "worth the windy drive" to get there.

### Pacific Dining Car ● *Steak*

| 22 | 21 | 23 | $57 |
|---|---|---|---|

**Downtown** | 1310 W. Sixth St. (bet. Valencia & Witmer Sts.) | 213-483-6000

**Santa Monica** | 2700 Wilshire Blvd. (Princeton St.) | 310-453-4000
www.pacificdiningcar.com

"Open around the clock", this "old-line" Downtown "martini and steak emporium" (with a Santa Monica offshoot) is "still a standout after all these years" thanks to "impeccable service" from "veteran waiters" and a "terrifically dated" "rail-car" setting with "big booths" and "white-linen tablecloths"; the "wonderful breakfasts" are the "most reasonable meal of the day here", but beware the "à la carte" dinners, which some say require a "second mortgage."

### Paco's Tacos  *Mexican*

| 20 | 15 | 18 | $18 |
|---|---|---|---|

**Mar Vista** | 4141 S. Centinela Ave. (bet. Culver & Washington Blvds.) | 310-391-9616

**Westchester** | 6212 W. Manchester Blvd. (bet. La Tijera & Sepulveda Blvds.) | 310-645-8692
www.pacoscantina.com

"Better-than-average" Mexican cooking gets a lift from "freshly made corn and flour tortillas" at these colorful "family-friendly" Mar Vista and Westchester cantinas also famed for their "excellent" "pitchers of margaritas"; though lines are "out the door" "at prime times", "complimentary chips and salsa" "make the waits bearable."

### Padri  *Italian*

| 21 | 22 | 20 | $40 |
|---|---|---|---|

**Agoura Hills** | 29008 Agoura Rd. (bet. Cornell & Kanan Rds.) | 818-865-3700 | www.padrirestaurant.net

A "big-city restaurant in little Agoura Hills", this "casual" Italian is always "a pleasure" thanks to "killer cocktails" and "solid" cooking; "couples" claim the "romantic" Tuscan-farmhouse-style dining room "feels like a fairy tale cottage", though "singles" say the "real scene" is

| | FOOD | DECOR | SERVICE | COST |
|---|---|---|---|---|

at the "crowded bar" or out on the "wonderful" patio; N.B. there's live music Wednesday–Friday.

### NEW Palate Food + Wine  *American*

| - | - | - | M |
|---|---|---|---|

**Glendale** | 933 S. Brand Blvd. (bet. Acacia & Garfield Aves.) | 818-662-9463 | www.palatefoodwine.com

After helping to redefine French bistro fare at Pinot Bistro, chef Octavio Becerra turns his playful sensibility to New American at this arrival parked in Glendale's former Cinnabar space; pork plays prominently on the menu, from the 'porkfolio' (an assortment of piggy charcuterie) to potted shoulder in Mason jars, while a checkerboard floor and purple-and-green design touches comprise the fanciful decor.

### Palermo  *Italian*

| 19 | 16 | 21 | $21 |
|---|---|---|---|

**Los Feliz** | 1858 N. Vermont Ave. (bet. Franklin & Prospect Aves.) | 323-663-1178 | www.palermorestaurant.net

"The party never stops" at this "old-school" Los Feliz Italian where "gracious" owner Tony Fanara presides over the "awesomely tacky" muraled dining room and an accordion player who "plays for tips" adds to the "fun" on Sunday nights; the "filling" fare – like "classic pizzas" – is "nothing "fancy", but red-sauce regulars say there's "plenty of it" and prices are "affordable" too.

### Palm, The  *Seafood/Steak*

| 23 | 19 | 22 | $62 |
|---|---|---|---|

**Downtown** | 1100 S. Flower St. (11th St.) | 213-763-4600
**West Hollywood** | 9001 Santa Monica Blvd. (bet. Doheny Dr. & Robertson Blvd.) | 310-550-8811
www.thepalm.com

"Old-school dining" is alive and well at the Downtown and WeHo branches of this "distinguished" chain carnivorium, born in NYC in 1926 and drawing "movers and shakers" ever since with its "enormous" steaks and lobsters plated in "distinguished" settings adorned with celebrity "caricatures"; sure, the tabs are reminiscent of "mortgage payments" and service can career from "top-notch" to "surly", but ultimately the quality is "consistently good."

### Palmeri  *Italian*

| 22 | 21 | 22 | $43 |
|---|---|---|---|

**Brentwood** | 11650 San Vicente Blvd. (bet. Darlington & Mayfield Aves.) | 310-442-8446

*Amici* avow this "gem" is a "standout" among "many fine Italians" in Brentwood thanks to chef Ottavio Palmeri's "lovingly prepared" Sicilian dishes enhanced by a "solid, midrange wine list"; add in "exceptionally good" servers "full of recommendations" and a "comfy" modern setting where "you can hear yourself speak", and fans insist that if it weren't on the "expensive" side, they could "eat here every night."

### Palms Thai ◐ *Thai*

| 20 | 13 | 17 | $20 |
|---|---|---|---|

**East Hollywood** | 5900 Hollywood Blvd. (Bronson Ave.) | 323-462-5073 | www.palmsthai.com

"Out-of-towners on a budget" will "thank you very much" for taking them to this East Hollywood joint featuring a "crooning Thai Elvis impersonator" (Wednesday–Sunday) and "lots of fantastic" South Asian dishes, both "Americanized" and "wildly authentic"; the somewhat "sterile "cafeterialike" setting is nothing to write home about, but that's no matter since servers tend to "rush you out."

| | FOOD | DECOR | SERVICE | COST |
|---|---|---|---|---|

### Palomino  *American/European*   `19` `20` `19` `$37`

**Westwood** | 10877 Wilshire Blvd. (Glendon Ave.) | 310-208-1960 |
www.palomino.com

A "steal at happy hour" "with the crowds to prove it", this Westwood "watering hole" attracts a varied clientele, from the "UCLA graduate students' drinking symposium" to "bargain-hunting senior citizens"; sure, it's part of a "chain", but servers are "personable", the decor "light and airy" and the European–New American grub "if not spectacular, is consistent"; N.B. the three-course early-bird special is $25 before 6 PM.

### Panda Inn  *Chinese*   `21` `18` `20` `$26`

**Ontario** | Centrelake Plaza | 3223 Centre Lake Dr. (Guasti Rd.) |
909-390-2888
**Pasadena** | 3488 E. Foothill Blvd. (Rosemead Blvd.) | 626-793-7300
**Glendale** | 111 E. Wilson Ave. (bet. Brand Blvd. & Maryland Ave.) |
818-502-1234
www.pandainn.com

These "upscale cousins" of the Panda Express fast-food chain are "perennial favorites" for fans who dig the "American-style" Chinese cooking – "especially the honey-walnut shrimp" – delivered in "large portions" at "affordable" prices; the "tasteful" settings done up in reds and orange creates a "comfortable atmosphere" while "white chocolate–dipped fortune cookies" cap a "satisfying" if not exactly "authentic" meal.

### Pane e Vino  *Italian*   `21` `21` `21` `$39`

**Beverly Boulevard** | 8265 Beverly Blvd. (Sweetzer Ave.) | 323-651-4600 |
www.panevinola.com

"Always reliable", these independently owned trattorias on Beverly Boulevard and in Santa Barbara live up to "what a neighborhood restaurant should be" with "simple" "rustic" Italian "standards" "served with a smile"; each features an "inviting" patio ("perfect for a date"), a "laid-back" yet "convivial" ambiance and "value" pricing.

### Panini Cafe  *Italian/Mediterranean*   `17` `15` `17` `$20`

**NEW** **Downtown** | 600 W. 9th St. (Hope St.) | 213-489-4200
**Beverly Hills** | 9601 Santa Monica Blvd. (Camden Dr.) |
310-247-8300
www.mypaninicafe.com

"Packed at lunch", this "friendly" Beverly Hills cafe supplies "bargain"-priced Italian pressed sandwiches, Mediterranean salads and platters in ample patio-blessed digs; antis allege it's "nothing to write home about" and say that while it's "good" for a "quick" bite, they "wouldn't do dinner there"; N.B. the Downtown branch is new and unrated.

### Panzanella  *Italian*   `22` `21` `22` `$47`

**Sherman Oaks** | 14928 Ventura Blvd. (bet. Sepulveda & Van Nuys Blvds.) |
818-784-4400 | www.giacominodrago.com

For a "leisurely dinner", Valley dwellers who don't want to "drive over the hill" select this "upscale" Sherman Oaks Sicilian from the Drago group for "dependable" Italian cooking, including a "superb" signature bread salad that "lives up to their name"; though it strikes some as "overpriced", defenders declare it pays off with "unobtrusive" service and a "soothing" Tuscan-inspired setting.

| | FOOD | DECOR | SERVICE | COST |
|---|---|---|---|---|

**Z Papa Cristo's** Ⓜ *Greek*    22 | 9 | 16 | $17

**Mid-City** | 2771 W. Pico Blvd. (Normandie Ave.) | 323-737-2970 | www.papacristos.com

"An old-country oasis of charm" on a gritty stretch of Pico, this "lively" Mid-City Greek restaurant/market dishes up "delicious" Hellenic specialties in a "humble" atmosphere that feels like a cross between an "Athens cafe" and a "high-school gymnasium"; though prices are always "cheap", there's a "bargain" "buffet" on Thursdays (with belly dancing as an added attraction) that may have you "unbuttoning your pants and going back for seconds."

**Z Papadakis Taverna** *Greek*    21 | 18 | 26 | $43

**San Pedro** | 301 W. Sixth St. (Centre St.) | 310-548-1186 | www.papadakistaverna.com

"Hospitable" brothers John and Tom Papadakis run this longtime San Pedro Greek "staple" that owes its "effervescent" "party feel" to "belly dancing" and "plate-tossing" nightly; the eats are "pretty darn good" too, so as long as you aren't expecting "a quiet dinner", it's "worth" a spin.

**NEW Paperfish** Ⓩ *Seafood*    23 | 24 | 22 | $62

**Beverly Hills** | 345 N. Maple Dr. (Alden Ave.) | 310-858-6030 | www.patinagroup.com/paperfish

It's a "foodie must" insist admirers of Joachim Splichal's new Beverly Hills entry delivering "beautifully presented" seafood selections – like the signature Thai snapper *en papillote* served tableside – in a "fabulous" ultramodern space done up in vibrant red and orange; though a chorus of critics says they "still have some kinks" to work out with "uneven" food and service, even if it "may not live up to the hype" just yet, the "potential for greatness" is certainly there.

**Paradise Cove** *American/Seafood*    15 | 19 | 16 | $32

**Malibu** | 28128 PCH (Paradise Cove Rd.) | 310-457-2503 | www.paradisecovemalibu.com

"There's nothing quite like" dining with "sun on your shoulders" at this beachside Malibu seafooder where "regular folks" sink into "Adirondack chairs", "kick off their shoes and crack open a cold one right on the sand"; even if service is "inconsistent" and American eats merely "adequate", it earns a legion of supporters who insist "the views are outstanding" – "what more do you want?"

**Parc** ●ⓏⓂ *Asian/French*    ∇ 21 | 21 | 19 | $51

**Hollywood** | 6683 Hollywood Blvd. (N. Las Palmas Ave.) | 323-465-6200 | www.parchollywood.com

A 14-ft. tree surrounded by Swarovski crystal light fixtures is the centerpiece of this Hollywood "scene" offering "interesting" Asian-French-inspired small plates designed for "sharing"; though "tabs can add up quickly", it's still drawing a "trendy" young crowd thanks to the "fantastic" design with white leather banquettes and "clublike" feel with a "live DJ playing a good mix" on Thursday–Saturday nights.

**NEW Park, The** Ⓜ *American*    - | - | - | M

**Echo Park** | 1400 W. Sunset Blvd. (Douglas St.) | 213-482-9209 | www.thepark1400sunset.com

Further proof of the gentrification of the neighborhoods just north of Downtown, this new Echo Park BYO is the very essence of the small chef-owner eatery, gaining a word-of-mouth following from fans of the New American dishes (such as sirloin burgers and corn cakes with shrimp and chipotle butter) by Joshua Siegel; decorated with flea-market decor with mismatched chairs, it supports the belief that good food at a good price trumps million-dollar design every time; N.B. closed Monday–Tuesday.

### Parker's Lighthouse  *Seafood*

| FOOD | DECOR | SERVICE | COST |
|------|-------|---------|------|
| 18 | 21 | 17 | $36 |

**Long Beach** | 435 Shoreline Village Dr. (E. Shoreline Dr.) | 562-432-6500 | www.parkerslighthouse.com

For "one hell of a view" of the Queen Mary insiders insist you "dine outdoors" at this Long Beach seafooder where the "fresh fish", if "ordinary", is "well prepared", but the "real allure" is the "harborfront locale"; add in "pleasant" service, live jazz Wednesdays and Thursdays and a somewhat "touristy" crowd, and some say that eating here "feels like being on vacation."

### ☑ Parkway Grill  *Californian*

| FOOD | DECOR | SERVICE | COST |
|------|-------|---------|------|
| 26 | 25 | 25 | $53 |

**Pasadena** | 510 S. Arroyo Pkwy. (bet. California & Del Mar Blvds.) | 626-795-1001 | www.theparkwaygrill.com

Pasadena patrons praise this "sophisticated" "local treasure" from the Smith brothers (Arroyo Chop House, Smitty's Grill) that "continues to pack 'em in" "after all these years" thanks to a "fabulous" Californian menu with choices to "fit every taste"; service is "stellar" while the "polished" setting "has the right mix of intimacy and class" – no wonder so many say they "always count on it" as "a sure thing" "for any occasion."

### Pastina  ☒ *Italian*

| FOOD | DECOR | SERVICE | COST |
|------|-------|---------|------|
| 20 | 16 | 20 | $34 |

**West LA** | 2260 Westwood Blvd. (bet. Olympic & Pico Blvds.) | 310-441-4655

Westsiders feel "lucky to have" this "warm" "family-run" trattoria in their midst because the "classic" Southern Italian dishes are not only "reliable", but "fairly priced" too; the ambiance, while "not hip by any stretch", is "pleasant" enough, and the "friendly" staff "aims to please."

### Pastis  *French*

| FOOD | DECOR | SERVICE | COST |
|------|-------|---------|------|
| 21 | 17 | 20 | $47 |

**Beverly Boulevard** | 8114 Beverly Blvd. (Crescent Heights Blvd.) | 323-655-8822 | www.lapastis.com

For a "taste of Provence" "without the attitude", diners head to this "delightful" Beverly Boulevard bistro where "well-prepared" French "classics" are conveyed by a "knowledgeable" staff; though "tables are set a bit close to each other", for most that only adds to the "intimate" atmosphere; P.S. there's an "amazing" "two-for-one" special on vino every Wednesday.

### Patina  Ⓜ *American/Californian*

| FOOD | DECOR | SERVICE | COST |
|------|-------|---------|------|
| 25 | 24 | 24 | $77 |

**Downtown** | Walt Disney Concert Hall | 141 S. Grand Ave. (2nd St.) | 213-972-3331 | www.patinagroup.com

"Perfect" for a "pre-symphony" meal, Joachim Splichal's Downtown flagship may be set adjacent to the Walt Disney Concert Hall, but this is "no Mickey Mouse" operation insist those savoring "world-class" Cal-New American cuisine (available à la carte or in a "rapturous" prix fixe tasting menu) enhanced by "wonderful wines" and a "fabulous" cheese course that's "an art unto itself"; a "top-notch" team provides "deft" service in the "luxe" "high-concept" dining room, so even if prices can feel "very expensive", the majority agrees "this one's worth saving for."

| | FOOD | DECOR | SERVICE | COST |
|---|---|---|---|---|

### Patrick's Roadhouse  *Diner*
▽ 17 | 16 | 16 | $22

**Santa Monica** | 106 Entrada Dr. (PCH) | 310-459-4544 |
www.patricksroadhouse.info

Locals insist you've "got to love" this "funky" Santa Monica "mainstay" right by the beach slinging "more-than-ample" portions of eclectic diner fare in a "divey" space adorned with "junkyard trinkets"; though it's often "jammed on weekends", it retains a "friendly" feel thanks to "minimal attitude" from the "laid-back" staff.

### Pat's  *Californian/Italian*
22 | 17 | 20 | $37

**Pico-Robertson** | 9233 W. Pico Blvd. (Glenville Dr.) | 310-205-8705

"Who knew kosher could be so fashionable?" ask admirers of this "sophisticated" Pico-Robertson venue serving "wonderful" glatt Cal-Italian dishes in a "stylish" setting with a view of the open kitchen; everyone appreciates the "excellent" service, though a few demur on prices they find "on the high side."

### Paul's Cafe  *Californian/French*
17 | 16 | 18 | $32

**Tarzana** | 18588 Ventura Blvd. (Mecca Ave.) | 818-343-8588

This "unpretentious local bistro" in Tarzana is well suited for those seeking "simple" Cal-French food with "no bother or fuss"; disappointed diners, however, say that while the menu "offers good variety", "nothing seems particularly new or creative", although at least the bill won't "break the bank."

### Pearl Dragon  *Pan-Asian*
17 | 16 | 14 | $37

**Pacific Palisades** | 15229 Sunset Blvd. (bet. Antioch St. & La Cruz Dr.) | 310-459-9790 | www.thepearldragon.com

"The only game in town" for "hard liquor" and sushi in Pacific Palisades, this midrange Pan-Asian is "never empty" say locals who "keep returning" in spite of "underwhelming" sushi, "disinterested service" and "high prices"; expect a "Chuck E. Cheese atmosphere" "before 7:30 PM" (when it's "taken over by families") that makes way for a "lively" bar scene later on – either way, it's "unbelievably noisy."

### Pecorino  *Italian*
22 | 19 | 22 | $52

**Brentwood** | 11604 San Vicente Blvd. (Mayfield Ave.) | 310-571-3800 | www.pecorinorestaurant.com

"Loyal" customers insist they "can't say enough good things" about this "delightful" Brentwood *cucina* where "charming" chef Raffaele Sabatini turns out "delicious" Italian dishes and his brother, "amiable host" Mario, oversees the front-of-the-house; servers are also "eager-to-please" while the "relaxed" "country" atmosphere with exposed brick and a beamed ceiling belies the otherwise unassuming "strip-mall" location.

### Pei Wei Asian Diner  *Pan-Asian*
16 | 13 | 14 | $16

**Torrance** | 2777 PCH (Crenshaw Blvd.) | 310-517-9366
**Pasadena** | 3455 E. Foothill Blvd. (bet. N. Rosemead Blvd. & Sierra Madre Villa Ave.) | 626-325-9020
**Santa Clarita** | Valencia Crossroads | 24250 Valencia Blvd. (McBean Pkwy.) | 661-600-0132
www.peiwei.com

"Lazy pickup dinners" are an easy option at this Pan-Asian chain (a "downscale" "little cousin" of P.F. Chang's) where the chow is "tasty" enough, the menus "limited" and the service primarily "cafeteria-style"; a few sigh "boring", but "kids like it", the food "seems healthy" and, not incidentally, the "prices are really good."

**Z Penthouse, The** *American* | 18 | 26 | 19 | $58 |

**Santa Monica** | Huntley Santa Monica Beach Hotel | 1111 Second St. (Wilshire Blvd.) | 310-394-5454 | www.thehuntleyhotel.com
"Dress flashy and carry a big wallet" instruct the "young and beautiful" inhabitants of this Santa Monica "scene" set on the top floor of the Huntley Hotel where the "spectacular" all-white decor with "private cabanas" and indoor fire pit is bested only by the "360 degree views" of "ocean and city"; the New American cuisine is judged "surprisingly good", though many agree it "doesn't stand out" amid such "raucous" surroundings.

**Peppone** *Italian* | 23 | 18 | 23 | $60 |

**Brentwood** | 11628 Barrington Ct. (Barrington Ave.) | 310-476-7379 | www.peppone.com
"Old-fashioned in the best sense", this "real-deal" Italian "hang" is "still a destination" for "rich" Brentwood locals thanks to its "home-style" dishes fit for "Don Corleone"; an "inviting" atmosphere with "red leather booths" and "Tiffany lamps" and "excellent" service provide additional appeal for those who insist "it's been here for 1,000 years and for good reason!"

**Pete's Cafe & Bar** ◗ *American* | 19 | 19 | 16 | $28 |

**Downtown** | 400 S. Main St. (W. 4th St.) | 213-617-1000 | www.petescafe.com
"On the gentrifying edge" of Downtown, this "white-tablecloth" "diner" draws "loft and gallery" dwellers for "dependable" New American eats like "good burgers" and "addictive blue cheese fries" in a "vintage-feeling space" well-suited to the "historic" San Fernando building that houses it; service can be "unpredictable", but at least prices are "fair" and they're open late too (every night till 1:45 AM).

**Petrelli's Steakhouse** *Italian/Steak* | 16 | 13 | 19 | $30 |

**Culver City** | 5615 Sepulveda Blvd. (Jefferson Blvd.) | 310-397-1438 | www.georgepetrellisteaks.com
A "neighborhood" crowd appreciates this circa-1931 Culver City Italian steakhouse famed for its "value" filets and "big, cold martinis" served by "sassy" waitresses; cushy "leather booths" add to the "comfortable" feel, though the less-charmed dub it "drab" and claim this "once great" "institution" crosses the line from "retro" into "just plain old."

**Z Petros** *Greek* | 24 | 21 | 20 | $45 |

**Manhattan Beach** | 451 Manhattan Beach Blvd. (Valley Dr.) | 310-545-4100 | www.petrosrestaurant.com
"Mykonos comes to Manhattan Beach" via this "stylish" venue proffering "marvelous" "nouveau" Hellenic cuisine that's "a refreshing change from the usual"; the "modern decor" with "clean lines", "whitewashed walls" and outdoor seating create a "pleasant" atmosphere, though some find "the service is lacking" given the "near fine-dining price tags."

| | FOOD | DECOR | SERVICE | COST |
|---|---|---|---|---|

**Petrossian Paris** *French*  ▽ 23 | 16 | 18 | $70

**West Hollywood** | 321 N. Robertson Blvd. (W. Beverly Blvd.) | 310-271-0576 | www.petrossian.com

"Fabulous caviar" and other French "delicacy dishes" are on offer at this petite West Hollywood offshoot of New York's restaurant and gourmet shop also famed for its "one-of-a-kind" Sunday champagne brunch; "exorbitant" pricing is to be expected, but some also knock "attitude" from servers; N.B. they close at 8 PM Fridays and Saturdays.

**P.F. Chang's China Bistro** *Chinese*  19 | 19 | 18 | $29

**Beverly Hills** | Beverly Ctr. | 121 N. La Cienega Blvd. (bet. Beverly Blvd. & 3rd St.) | 310-854-6467
**Santa Monica** | 326 Wilshire Blvd. (4th St.) | 310-395-1912
**El Segundo** | 2041 E. Rosecrans Ave. (Nash St.) | 310-607-9062
**Pasadena** | Paseo Colorado | 260 E. Colorado Blvd. (Garfield Ave.) | 626-356-9760
**Sherman Oaks** | Sherman Oaks Galleria | 15301 Ventura Blvd. (Sepulveda Blvd.) | 818-784-1694
**Woodland Hills** | The Promenade at Woodland Hills | 21821 Oxnard St. (Topanga Canyon Blvd.) | 818-340-0491
www.pfchangs.com

Expect "major hustle-bustle" at this "noisy" Chinese chain where the "sanitized", "mass-produced" menus "aren't really authentic" yet do "appeal to most palates" (when in doubt, the "lettuce wraps rule"); no one minds the "spotty" service and "ersatz" Sino decor since they "have the formula down" – starting with "nothing-fancy" prices and an overall "fun" vibe.

**Philippe the Original** ⇝ *Sandwiches*  21 | 13 | 16 | $12

**Chinatown** | 1001 N. Alameda St. (Ord St.) | 213-628-3781 | www.philippes.com

A visit to this 100-year-old Chinatown "landmark" and self-proclaimed "originator of the French Dip" is like a "trip down nostalgia lane" where "longtime waitresses" plate up "heavenly sandwiches" like they have for "decades" and "coffee is still only nine cents a cup"; it owes its "tremendous character" in part to its "egalitarian" setup with "order-at-the-counter" service and "communal tables" where folks of all stripes – from "bankers to bus drivers" – chow down "side-by-side."

**Ⓩ Phillips Bar-B-Que** *BBQ*  25 | 7 | 13 | $16

**Leimert Park** | 4307 Leimert Blvd. (43rd St.) | 323-292-7613 ⑤
**Mid-City** | 2619 Crenshaw Blvd. (W. Adams Blvd.) | 323-731-4772 Ⓜ
**Inglewood** | 1517 Centinela Ave. (Beach Ave.) | 310-412-7135 ⑤

"Now *this* is some BBQ" exclaim fans of this "lip-smacking good" trio where "excellent ribs, brisket, hot links and chicken" are slathered with "off-the-chain" sauce and served up with "lots of napkins" and bread; they're basically for "takeout" only (though the Mid-City branch has limited outdoor seating), and regulars recommend you "call in your order" first for "fast service."

**Pho Café** ●⇝ *Vietnamese*  21 | 13 | 17 | $14

**Silver Lake** | 2841 W. Sunset Blvd. (Silver Lake Blvd.) | 213-413-0888

Eastside "hipsters" jam into this "unmarked" Silver Lake Vietnamese proffering "delicious" pho and other "healthy-tasting" dishes that "hit the spot"; a few find the minimalist design overly "sparse", but "incredibly quick" (if "impersonal") service redeems and "affordable" tabs mean you can "eat like a king for next to nothing."

### Pho 79  *Vietnamese*

| 20 | 9 | 11 | $12 |

**Alhambra** | 29 S. Garfield Ave. (Main St.) | 626-289-0239

"Pho-nominal" Vietnamese cooking pleases the masses at this no-frills Alhambra joint rolling out an "incredible selection" of "authentic" specialties, including "flavorful" noodle soups that are "wonderful" in their "simplicity"; despite "dingy" decor and "curt" service, it's "always crowded", thanks in part to its "cheap" prices.

### Piatti  *Italian*

| 19 | 19 | 19 | $36 |

**Thousand Oaks** | 101 S. Westlake Blvd. (Thousand Oaks Blvd.) | 805-371-5600 | www.piatti.com

These "reasonably priced" chain outposts in Montecito and Thousand Oaks serve up "solid" Italian cooking "with some surprises" (the latter uses "locally sourced ingredients for better-than-average salads"); though doubters deride the overall "generic" feel, all boast patios and fireplaces, and defenders declare they're "enjoyable" for a "quick meal."

### Picanha Churrascaria  *Brazilian*

| 21 | 16 | 21 | $40 |

**Burbank** | 269 E. Palm Ave. (bet. San Fernando Blvd. & 3rd St.) | 818-972-2100 | www.picanharestaurant.com

A veritable "orgy" of beef is on offer at this "belt-busting" Burbank churrascaria (and its new Cathedral City offshoot) where "efficient gauchos" supply "tasty skewers" of Brazilian barbecue; though a few find the "noisy" "strip mall-like ambiance" detracts, ample seating makes it good for groups.

### Piccolo  *Italian*

| 27 | 17 | 24 | $53 |

**Venice** | 5 Dudley Ave. (Spdwy.) | 310-314-3222 | www.piccolovenice.com

"A secret hideaway" just "steps from the beach", this "charming" Venice Italian showcases "big-flavored" cooking that's "always delicious, even with the changes in chefs", and "splendid vino" in a "postage-stamp"-sized setting; a no-reservations policy means you can "expect to wait", but once you snag a seat, regulars report you're in for a "treat", albeit a somewhat "expensive" one.

### Piccolo Paradiso  *Italian*

| 23 | 16 | 21 | $45 |

**Beverly Hills** | 150 S. Beverly Dr. (Wilshire Blvd.) | 310-271-0030 | www.giacominodrago.com

"Wonderfully authentic" *cibo* pleases patrons of this "upscale" Beverly Hills "delight" from Giacomino Drago that hosts "a definite power scene at lunch" ("Sumner Redstone asked to borrow my cell phone!") and a "more relaxed" gathering at dinner; despite a few quibbles about "noisy" acoustics at peak hours, the "intimate" *Cinema Paradiso*-themed dining room "has a real homey feel to it" thanks to a "genuinely warm team" providing "most gracious" service.

### Pie 'N Burger  ⌨ *Diner*

| 19 | 8 | 16 | $14 |

**Pasadena** | 913 E. California Blvd. (bet. S. Lake & S. Mentor Aves.) | 626-795-1123 | www.pienburger.com

Harking back to "a simpler time" this circa-1963 Pasadena coffee shop channels "classic Americana" with "notoriously messy" burgers, hand-mixed sodas and "mountain-high" fruit pies topped with "real whipped cream"; sure, service at the wraparound counter can be "surly", but in spite of that, and decidedly un-"retro" pricing, most patrons proclaim they "hope it stays around forever."

**Pig 'n Whistle**  *Continental*          13 | 18 | 14 | $27

**Hollywood** | 6714 Hollywood Blvd. (bet. Highland & Las Palmas Aves.) | 323-463-0000 | www.pignwhistle.com

One of the last of the "classic Hollywood hangouts", this "reclaimed" 1927 "landmark" with an "ornate wood ceiling" features an "acceptable" Continental menu that takes a backseat to the "historic" atmosphere; still, "it's a lively place to eat on the Boulevard", filled with "T-shirt-clad tourists" by day and "young grungy types" who "congregate at the bar" at night.

**Pink's Famous Chili Dogs**  ●⊭ *Hot Dogs*     19 | 7 | 13 | $10

**La Brea** | 709 N. La Brea Ave. (Melrose Ave.) | 323-931-4223 | www.pinkshollywood.com

As "quintessentially" LA as the "seashore and the freeways", this almost-70-year-old La Brea hot dog stand "tickles" patrons "pink" with "snappy" franks "piled high" with "chili and onions" and a slew of other "outrageous" condiments; "tourists" and "slumming celebs" all endure the "fabled lines" (with waits sometimes approaching "an hour"), and since it's open till 3 AM on weekends, the "late-night drunk food cravings" of "clubgoers" are well-served too.

**Pink Taco**  *Mexican*          15 | 18 | 16 | $27

**Century City** | Westfield Century City Shopping Ctr. | 10250 Santa Monica Blvd. (bet. Ave. of the Stars & Century Park W.) | 310-789-1000 | www.pinktaco.com

It "always feels like there's a fiesta going on" at this Vegas import, a "Century City margarita meat market", where *Entourage* wannabes" "party after work" amid "racy" rock 'n' roll-style decor with "loud music blasting"; yet, a number of naysayers "can't get past the name", and insist that "strong drinks" and "sexy" waitresses in "scantily clad ensembles" don't make up for "spotty service" and "underwhelming", "gringo-Mex" eats; N.B. a Hollywood branch is in the works.

**Pinot Bistro**  *French*          23 | 22 | 22 | $48

**Studio City** | 12969 Ventura Blvd. (Coldwater Canyon Ave.) | 818-990-0500 | www.patinagroup.com

"Classy and relaxed all at once", this "welcoming" Patina Group bistro in Studio City "still delivers" "wonderful" French fare in a "beautiful" wood-paneled setting that's as "comfortable as your favorite pair of jeans"; the "dependable" menu strikes some as a little "tired", but at least prices are "decent" thanks to "no corkage charges", free meals for children 10 and under and a "bargain" prix fixe dinner offered every Sunday.

**Pistachio Grill**  *Persian*        ▽ 21 | 10 | 19 | $23

**Beverly Hills** | 8560 Wilshire Blvd. (bet. Le Doux & Stanley Rds.) | 310-854-1020

"Flavorful Persian dishes" including "great grilled offerings" and "nice vegan alternatives" comprise the menu at this "wonderful" Beverly Hills BYO; though the "hole-in-the-wall" decor "leaves a lot to be desired", regulars report that service is congenial and say it's "never crowded" either.

| | FOOD | DECOR | SERVICE | COST |
|---|---|---|---|---|

**Pizza Rustica** *Pizza*     ▽ 22 | 15 | 20 | $17

**West Hollywood** | 8410 W. Sunset Blvd. (Kings Rd.) | 323-656-6800 ◐
**Beverly Hills** | 9497 S. Santa Monica Blvd. (N. Rodeo Dr.) |
310-550-7499
www.pizza-rustica.com

"Gourmet pizza by the slice" is on offer at these "South Beach transplants" topping their traditional and whole-wheat-crusted pies with an "amazing variety" of ingredients; though most diners rely on them for takeout, the Beverly Hills branch features "fast delivery" and an eat-in space tricked out with recycled aluminum detailing and free WiFi; N.B. the Downtown and Sherman Oaks locations have closed.

**Z Pizzeria Mozza** ◐ *Pizza*     26 | 19 | 21 | $36

**Hollywood** | 641 N. Highland Ave. (Melrose Ave.) | 323-297-0101 |
www.mozza-la.com

The "hottest ticket in town", this "instant classic" in Hollywood from "rock-star chefs" Mario Batali and Nancy Silverton might just "change your worldview about pizza" with "ethereal" pies sporting perfectly "charred" crusts and "esoteric toppings" like squash blossoms and burrata; given the frequently "packed house", servers are "overwhelmed" and the noise level "much too loud", yet acolytes insist they "could eat here every night" if only they "could get in" (psst - "reserve well ahead" or "try the bar" for impromptu dining).

**Pizzicotto** *Italian*     23 | 16 | 21 | $32

**Brentwood** | 11758 San Vicente Blvd. (bet. Gorham & Montana Aves.) |
310-442-7188

"You can feel the love" they put into each "delectable" dish at this "quaint" Brentwood ristorante plating "simple", "authentic" Italian fare at "decent prices"; though the "warm" staff maintains a "relaxed vibe", it's "usually packed to the gills", so to avoid "getting jostled by the take-out crowd", "ask to be seated upstairs."

**NEW Point, The** Ⓩ *Eclectic*     ▽ 18 | 12 | 16 | $14

**Culver City** | Conjunctive Points | 8522 National Blvd. (Fay Ave.) |
310-836-8400 | www.thepoint-la.com

"From the creators of Beacon" comes this stainless-steel "lunch stand" stationed in a Culver City "office park" proffering "reasonably priced" Eclectic eats like "tasty" custom-made salads and panini all "with an accent on freshness"; counter service is "quick", but given the scarcity of seating, most opt to get their order "to-go"; N.B. open Monday–Friday only.

**Polo Lounge** ◐ *Californian/Continental*     22 | 25 | 24 | $62

**Beverly Hills** | Beverly Hills Hotel | 9641 Sunset Blvd. (bet. Beverly &
Crescent Drs.) | 310-887-2777 | www.beverlyhillshotel.com

"Drinks on the patio can make anyone feel like a movie star" at this "legendary" eatery inside the Beverly Hills Hotel whose "genteel" art deco setting evokes "the elegance of times past" with "beautiful china and silver" and piano playing nightly; given the "celeb-studded room" and "effortlessly" "formal" service, some suggest the "outrageously expensive" Cal-Continental cuisine is "probably beside the point", although acolytes insist it's "quite well-done" too.

| | FOOD | DECOR | SERVICE | COST |
|---|---|---|---|---|

### Pomodoro Cucina Italiana  *Italian*    | 18 | 14 | 18 | $22

**West Hollywood** | West Hollywood Gateway Ctr. | 7100 Santa Monica Blvd. (La Brea Ave.) | 323-969-8000
**Manhattan Beach** | 401 Manhattan Beach Blvd. (Morningside Dr.) | 310-545-5401
**Burbank** | Burbank Town Ctr. | 201 E. Magnolia Blvd. (San Fernando Blvd.) | 818-559-1300
**Sherman Oaks** | La Reina Pl. | 14622 Ventura Blvd. (Vesper Ave.) | 818-501-7400
**Woodland Hills** | 21600 Victory Blvd. (bet. Canoga & Owensmouth Aves.) | 818-340-2400
www.pastapomodoro.com
Surveyors seeking "an Italian quickie" "pop into" one of the many links of this "reliable" chain dishing out "respectable" renditions of "simple" trattoria favorites; everything comes via "pleasant" waiters at "inexpensive" prices, though critics knock the "too-bright, too-loud" settings.

### Poquito Más  *Mexican*    | 21 | 10 | 16 | $12

**West Hollywood** | 8555 Sunset Blvd. (Londonderry Pl.) | 310-652-7008
**West LA** | 2215 Westwood Blvd. (Olympic Blvd.) | 310-474-1998
**Torrance** | Rolling Hills Plaza | 2625 PCH (Crenshaw Blvd.) | 310-325-1001
**Burbank** | 2635 W. Olive Ave. (Buena Vista St.) | 818-563-2252
**Chatsworth** | 9229 Winnetka Ave. (Prairie St.) | 818-775-1555
**North Hollywood** | 10651 Magnolia Blvd. (Cartwright Ave.) | 818-994-8226
**Studio City** | 3701 Cahuenga Blvd. (bet. Barham & Lankershim Blvds.) | 818-760-8226 ◗
**Woodland Hills** | 21049 Ventura Blvd. (Alhama Dr.) | 818-887-2007
**Valencia** | Valencia Town Ctr. | 24405 Town Center Dr. (McBean Pkwy.) | 661-255-7555
www.poquitomas.com
"Freshly made tortillas make all the difference" at this "no-nonsense" chain of cantinas where the "flavorful", relatively "healthy" eats "spoil you for all other fast-food Mexican"; they don't offer much in the way of decor, but service is "quick-ish", the prices "dirt-cheap" and the "free soup on rainy days is a nice touch" too.

### Porta Via  *Californian*    | 24 | 19 | 22 | $38

**Beverly Hills** | 424 N. Cañon Dr. (Santa Monica Blvd.) | 310-274-6534
Although "often overlooked", this "casual" Beverly Hills bistro features "fabulous" Californian cuisine ferried by "personable" servers who "make you feel at home"; in spite of a newly expanded dining room, most allies angle for "an outdoor table", especially during Sunday's "special" brunch – "it's the perfect place to wind down after a long week."

### 🆕 Porta Via Italian Foods  *Italian*    ▽ | 23 | 18 | 21 | $17

**Pasadena** | 1 W. California Blvd. (S. Fair Oaks Ave.) | 626-793-9000 | www.portaviafoods.com
*Paesani* praise this "wonderful" Italian marketplace and restaurant in Pasadena supplying "every delicacy a kid from the Bronx could imagine" from "homemade meatballs" to baked ziti, panini and cannoli; cafeteria-style service is all "smiles", and though most opt to "carry out", there's also a "lovely" shaded patio out back and a handful of tables inside as well; N.B. they close at 7 PM.

| | FOOD | DECOR | SERVICE | COST |
|---|---|---|---|---|

### Porterhouse Bistro  *Steak*
20 | 18 | 19 | $45

**Beverly Hills** | 8635 Wilshire Blvd. (Carson Rd.) | 310-659-1099 | www.porterhousebistro.com

"The prix fixe is the way to go" at this Beverly Hills chophouse offering "excellent bang for the buck" with a $43.20 meal that includes four courses and two cocktails; yet in spite of a "pleasant" pastel-hued setting and staff that "tries hard to please", unimpressed eaters cite "ordinary" fare and say that even with "value" pricing, "there are better steaks in town."

### 🆕 Portillo's Hot Dogs  *Hot Dogs*
18 | 15 | 15 | $11

**Moreno Valley** | 12840 Day St. (Gateway Dr.) | 951-653-1000 | www.portillos.com

"Chi-town" transplants "feel right at home" at this Moreno Valley link in a Midwestern chain famed for "authentic" Italian beef sandwiches and "delish" dogs "with all the fixin's"; faithful fans know that prices are cheap and the "lines are fast" and put it in their "regular" rotation for their "Windy City" fix.

### Porto Alegre  *Brazilian/Steak*
▽ 20 | 23 | 18 | $49

**Pasadena** | Paseo Colorado | 260 E. Colorado Blvd. (Garfield Ave.) | 626-744-0555

Instead of "filling up on the salad bar", insiders insist you "save room" for the "wonderful meats" that get top billing at this "good-quality" all-you-can-eat Brazilian steakhouse in Pasadena; though service can be "inconsistent", decor is "pleasing" and live jazz gives it a lift on Friday and Saturday nights.

### ⓩ Porto's Bakery  *Bakery/Cuban*
24 | 14 | 16 | $12

**Burbank** | 3614 W. Magnolia Blvd. (Cordova St.) | 818-846-9100
**Glendale** | 315 N. Brand Blvd. (California Ave.) | 818-956-5996
www.portosbakery.com

"Sweet-toothed" surveyors seek out this Cuban bakery/cafe duo in Burbank and Glendale specializing in "sinfully good" pastries and "terrific" savory lunch items like "heavenly potato ball sandwiches" ("take that Dr. Atkins!"); "seemingly endless" lines are a deterrent to some, but prices are such a "bargain" that most are "willing to wait."

### ⓩ Prado  *Caribbean*
22 | 17 | 20 | $31

**Hancock Park** | 244 N. Larchmont Blvd. (bet. Beverly Blvd. & 1st St.) | 323-467-3871 | www.pradola.com

Hancock Park residents hail this "sentimental favorite" for its "satisfying" Caribbean cooking, "reasonable prices" and "accommodating service"; the "colorful, comfortable" decor exudes a "small-town feel", but given the quirky vibe, just "don't expect any of the chairs at your table to match."

### Prana Cafe  *Pan-Asian*
▽ 18 | 12 | 10 | $24

**West Hollywood** | 650 N. La Cienega Blvd. (Melrose Pl.) | 310-360-0551 | www.pranacafela.com

"Pleasant" for "brunch", this "casual" venue peddles "good, healthy" Pan-Asian cuisine that's best appreciated from the "outdoor" seating area; service is "friendly, but disorganized", so cons caution that "waits for a table" and then "for your order" can be especially "frustrating"; N.B. the Studio City branch has closed.

| | FOOD | DECOR | SERVICE | COST |
|---|---|---|---|---|

**NEW Press Panini** 🍴 *Sandwiches* — | — | — | | I
**Studio City** | 4389 Tujunga Ave. (Moorpark Ave.) | 818-487-2564 | www.presspanini.com

This spare, Italian-style panini bar in Studio City comes from the son of the owner of the wildly popular Gelato Bar nearby; patrons can order their sandwiches (27 to choose from) à la carte or as part of the $14 Meal Deal, which also includes a side and a beverage.

**Primitivo Wine Bistro** *Mediterranean* 20 | 19 | 18 | $39
**Venice** | 1025 Abbot Kinney Blvd. (bet. Brooks Ave. & Westminster Ave.) | 310-396-5353 | www.primitivowinebistro.com

"Attractive" Venice beachers "make the scene" at this "happening" Mediterranean tapas bar boasting a "long" list of vino and "tasty" small bites that prove a "perfect pre-night out" meal "since you leave satisfied, but not in the 'let me unbutton my pants' kind of way"; lots of "chatter and clinking glasses" make for a "noisy" atmosphere, but luckily there's an "intimate" patio providing a "quieter" respite.

**Prizzi's Piazza** *Italian* ▽ 21 | 17 | 15 | $30
**Hollywood** | 5923 Franklin Ave. (bet. Bronson Ave. & Gower St.) | 323-467-0168 | www.prizzispiazza.com

For "deep-dish pizza even a Chicagoan would approve of", "neighborhood" denizens descend on this Hollywood Italian also delivering "homemade pastas", "garlic breadsticks" ("mmm") and "reasonably priced wines" in an "offbeat" setting decorated with local art for sale; yet in spite of a recent spruce up and "cordial" service, longtimers lament "it lost some of its magic" when ownership changed hands last year.

**Prosecco** 🚫 *Italian* 19 | 17 | 21 | $37
**Toluca Lake** | 10144 Riverside Dr. (Forman Ave.) | 818-505-0930

Toluca Lakers insist this "sweet little eatery" lives up to "what a neighborhood restaurant should be" with "reliable" Northern Italian cooking set down by "friendly help" in a "cozy" white-tablecloth setting; the less-charmed label it "pedestrian", but since it offers such "good value", most locals insist "we need more places like this."

**Z Providence** *American/Seafood* 26 | 25 | 26 | $90
**Hollywood** | 5955 Melrose Ave. (Cole Ave.) | 323-460-4170 | www.providencela.com

"Every bite is a delight" at this "unmatched" Hollywood "jewel" showcasing "talented" chef-owner Michael Cimarusti's "beyond exquisite" New American seafood creations best appreciated via the "heavenly tasting menu" ("a must for any serious foodie"); given the "elegant, but not flashy" beige-toned dining room and "impeccable" service from "consummate pros", the majority contends it has "not a single complaint" about this true "epicurean experience", except for the "pocketbook shocker" of a bill.

**P6 Restaurant & Lounge** *American* ▽ 22 | 25 | 20 | $44
**Westlake Village** | 2809 Agoura Rd. (Westlake Blvd.) | 805-778-0123 | www.p6lounge.com

One of the "hippest places in the Conejo Valley", this Westlake Village "lounge" boasts a "beautiful" "Vegas-style" atmosphere with bamboo detailing and an outdoor fire pit; though the "creative" New American menu showcases some "great flavors", cons claim it's more about the

|  | FOOD | DECOR | SERVICE | COST |
|--|------|-------|---------|------|

"scenery" than the food, especially at "happy hour" when it plays host to a "noisy meet market" for "dressed-up" young "singles."

## Quincy's BBQ *BBQ* | 16 | 11 | 15 | $22 |

**Encino** | Plaza de Oro | 17201 Ventura Blvd. (Louise Ave.) | 818-784-6292 | www.quincysbbq.com

"No bones about it", this rib and chicken joint named after the owner's pooch brings "homestyle" chow to "barbecue-starved" Encino; though the "simple backyard"-style atmosphere with a "dog-friendly" patio elicits barks of approval, petless patrons call it "average", but concede it's "ok for a quick bite."

## Qusqo ☒ *Peruvian* | ▽ 19 | 16 | 19 | $24 |

**West LA** | 11633 Santa Monica Blvd. (Barry Ave.) | 310-312-3800 | www.qusqo.com

Diners declare they're "glad to have" this relatively new storefront Peruvian bringing "simple, but good" "traditional" specialties (like ceviche and lomo saltado) to West LA; pricing is inexpensive, and the "tiny" digs owe their "funky" feel to a rotating lineup of local art for sale.

## NEW R+D Kitchen *American* | - | - | - | I |

**Santa Monica** | 1323 Montana Ave. (14th St.) | 310-395-3314

In a Santa Monica space that has seen many restaurants come and go, the power players behind Houston's have opened this New American, whose initials stand for 'research and development'; a Frank Lloyd Wright look defines the dining room, wherein patrons graze on inexpensive fare like burgers and salads while gazing through floor-to-ceiling windows at Montana Avenue's parade of well-heeled shoppers.

## Rack, The ● *Californian* | ▽ 16 | 17 | 17 | $25 |

**Woodland Hills** | Westfield Promenade | 6100 Topanga Canyon Blvd. (bet. Erwin & Oxnard Sts.) | 818-716-0123 | www.therack.us

Fifteen billiards tables, a patio and "plenty of beer on tap" make this pool hall and dining room in Woodland Hills' Westfield Promenade a "great place to hang out with friends"; though the "overpriced" Californian "comfort food" doesn't always "hit the mark", since the "extensive" menu offers "everything under the rainbow", it's usually "packed" anyway; N.B. open till 2 AM Thursdays–Saturdays.

## Radhika's *Indian* | ▽ 22 | 17 | 20 | $24 |

**Pasadena** | The Commons | 140 Shoppers Ln. (Cordova St.) | 626-744-0994 | www.radhikas.com

"More sophisticated than your average Indian restaurant", this Pasadenan attracts heat-seeking chowhounds thanks to its "creative" subcontinental cuisine, including a "terrific lunch buffet"; given that it's "more ambitious than most", expect more "formal" service, contemporary decor and higher prices too.

## Rae's ⇆ *Diner* | 18 | 12 | 20 | $13 |

**Santa Monica** | 2901 Pico Blvd. (29th St.) | 310-828-7937

"Greasy spoon" aficionados adore this "real-deal" Santa Monica diner that's been "dishing out carbs" for over 50 years; its "old-school" touches include "insanely cheap tabs", "tough waitresses" and "time-warp" decor that's "not even trying to be kitschy"; N.B. cash only.

| | FOOD | DECOR | SERVICE | COST |
|---|---|---|---|---|

**Ragin' Cajun Cafe** Ⓜ *Cajun*     20 | 17 | 19 | $20

**Hermosa Beach** | 422 Pier Ave. (PCH) | 310-376-7878 | www.ragincajun.com

"Authentic, right down to the owner's accent", this Hermosa Beach Cajun "is where locals go" for crawfish étouffée, gumbo and other "down-home" standards sure to "put a little spice in your life"; maybe the "funky" setting isn't winning any design awards, but the "festive" feel means it's "always a hoot."

**Rainforest Cafe** *American*     12 | 23 | 14 | $25

**Ontario** | Ontario Mills | 4810 Mills Circle (4th St.) | 909-941-7979 | www.rainforestcafe.com

"Appease the kids" at this "jungle"-themed chain, a "gimmicky" franchise where the "mediocre" American grub is overshadowed by its "Disney-like animatronics" and faux thunderstorms; "jet-plane noise levels", "so-so service" and rather "expensive" tabs come with the territory, though after a "couple of drinks, it seems more parent-friendly."

**Rambutan Thai** *Thai*     21 | 19 | 18 | $26

**Silver Lake** | 2835 W. Sunset Blvd. (Silver Lake Blvd.) | 213-273-8424 | www.rambutanthai.com

"Refined" Thai dishes pair up with "exotic" soju cocktails at this "stylish" Silver Laker whose "moody", "modern" decor makes it "great for dates"; though "rough parking" and "so-so" service are among the downsides, it's "bustling" most nights because the food really "shines"; N.B. they also deliver.

**RA Sushi** *Japanese*     ▽ 16 | 20 | 16 | $30

**Torrance** | Del Amo Fashion Ctr. | 3525 W. Carson St. (Torrance Blvd.) | 310-370-6700 | www.rasushi.com

"Loud music" and "sake bombs" animate the scene at this Torrance Asian fusion and sushi chain by Benihana that's become a magnet for "twentysomethings" at "happy hour"; doubters dismiss the food and service as "disappointing", and add that while they'd "go back for drinks", "there are much better Japanese restaurants in the South Bay."

**Raymond, The** Ⓜ *Californian*     24 | 24 | 23 | $50

**Pasadena** | 1250 S. Fair Oaks Ave. (Columbia St.) | 626-441-3136 | www.theraymond.com

"Romance is in the air" at this "charming cottage" in Pasadena that owes its "wonderfully quaint" feel to its "historic" Craftman-style setting divided into a "collection of small, intimate rooms" with several patios; it attracts a "well-heeled" clientele that savors the "fantastic" seasonal Californian dishes and "unobtrusive" service while otherwise overlooking the "high prices."

**Ⓩ Real Food Daily** *Vegan*     21 | 14 | 18 | $23

**West Hollywood** | 414 N. La Cienega Blvd. (bet. Beverly Blvd. & Melrose Ave.) | 310-289-9910

**Santa Monica** | 514 Santa Monica Blvd. (bet. 5th & 6th Sts.) | 310-451-7544 www.realfood.com

Supporters swear "you won't miss the meat" at these "informal" Santa Monica and West Hollywood health-fooders where the "fantastically fresh" organic fare includes "crave-worthy" "vegan re-creations" of "Americana" like cashew cheddar nachos and "to-die-for fake meatloaf"; some complain that service can be "preachy", but that's no matter to most who "rely" on it for a "quick" meal.

### NEW RED Steak
| — | — | — | E |

**City of Industry** | Pacific Palms Conference Resort | 1 Industry Hills Pkwy. (Azusa Ave.) | 626-854-2496

Adjacent to a golf course in San Gabriel Valley East, this hilltop steakhouse (with steep prices to match) is the latest addition to the Pacific Palms Resort; while beef is the menu's focus, there's also plenty of seafood plus a nightly changing selection of Asian dishes, all served in a modern but cozy space complete with blazing fireplaces.

### Red Corner Asia ● Thai
| ▽ 25 | 15 | 20 | $18 |

**East Hollywood** | Hollywood Plaza | 5267 Hollywood Blvd. (Normandie Ave.) | 323-466-6722 | www.redcornerasia.com

"Mouthwatering curries" and more "adventurous" specialties await at this "modern" Thai joint set in an East Hollywood shopping center; though a few fret about "difficult parking", all is forgiven thanks to such "quick" service and "ridiculously reasonable" prices.

### Reddi Chick BBQ ⊠⇄ BBQ
| 21 | 7 | 16 | $12 |

**Brentwood** | Brentwood Country Mart | 225 26th St. (San Vicente Blvd.) | 310-393-5238

"It ain't organic or free range, but, lord, this is good chicken" crow fans of the "succulent" BBQ and rotisserie birds at this "funky" stall inside the Brentwood Country Mart, a neighborhood "institution" since 1948; its bare-bones setup with outdoor seating and order-at-the-counter service offers little in the way of perks, but for a "casual" meal or "takeout", it sure "beats KFC."

### NEW Red Fish Seafood
| ▽ 21 | 23 | 23 | $44 |

**Simi Valley** | Simi Valley Town Ctr. | 1555 Simi Town Center Way (1st St.) | 805-823-4756 | www.sparkredfish.com

Bringing "LA cool" to Simi Valley, this new "high-end" seafooder spun off from the Spark Woodfire chain boasts a "dramatic" interior crafted from reclaimed woods with a striking open kitchen; early samplers rate the fare "excellent" and staff "attentive", hailing this "destination restaurant" as a "wonderful addition" to the area, even if prices can sometimes feel "too high for what you get."

### Red Pearl Kitchen Pan-Asian
| 17 | 21 | 16 | $38 |

**Hollywood** | 6703 Melrose Ave. (Citrus Ave.) | 323-525-1415 | www.redpearlkitchen.com

"Dim red lighting" lends a "sexy" feel to this "stylish" Hollywood Pan-Asian whose high quotient of "beautiful people" leads patrons to ponder if they're "dining in the middle of a model casting"; some who are ruffled by the "loud" environs and "snooty" service suggest it for "fruity drinks" and "apps" over a full meal of the "less-than-authentic" cuisine.

### Red Seven ⊠ Pan-Asian
| ▽ 24 | 23 | 24 | $31 |

**West Hollywood** | Pacific Design Ctr. | 700 N. San Vicente Blvd. (Melrose Ave.) | 310-289-1587 | www.wolfgangpuck.com

Wolfgang Puck "gets it right" at this "chic" lunch-only "bistroette" in WeHo's Pacific Design Center providing "flavorful" Pan-Asian fare like sashimi salad and Kobe burgers; prices are moderate and service is "attentive beyond expectations", so the only complaint, claim converts, is that they "wish it were open for dinner and on weekends" too.

**redwhite+bluezz** *American*                    22 | 19 | 20 | $36

**Pasadena** | 70 S. Raymond Ave. (Green St.) | 626-792-4441 |
www.redwhitebluezz.com

"Great jazz acts" steal the spotlight every night at this "crowded" Pasadena stop for "enjoyable" New American bites like "well-matched wine and cheese flights"; "friendly" servers "cater to your every need", and aficionados give a "a big thumbs-up" to the heated patio outfitted with speakers "so you don't miss what's being played inside."

**Reel Inn** *Seafood*                             20 | 12 | 11 | $24

**Malibu** | 18661 PCH (Topanga Canyon Rd.) | 310-456-8221

"Shorts" and flip-flops define the dress code at this "funky" seafood shack "right on PCH" in Malibu where "fresh" fin fare is cooked up "any way you like it"; "cheap beer" and "picnic tables" affording "nice views of the water" create a "carefree atmosphere", so perhaps it's no wonder so many locals "love this place after a day at the beach."

**NEW Restaurant 15** ☒ *American*        ▽ 20 | 20 | 20 | $27

**Echo Park** | 1320 Echo Park Ave. (Sunset Blvd.) | 213-481-0454 |
www.restaurant15.com

"Fancy" for Echo Park, this "fine-looking" New American lures locals who insist it's a "welcome addition" thanks to its "reasonably priced" menu with a $19 "early-bird special" offered till 6:30 PM daily; service is generally "attentive" and the earth-toned interior combines a "modern" look with a "comfortable" feel, spurring most reviewers to "recommend it."

**Ribs USA** *BBQ*                                 19 | 7 | 15 | $21

**Burbank** | 2711 W. Olive Ave. (bet. Buena Vista & Florence Sts.) |
818-841-8872 | www.ribsusa.com

"Sawdust and peanut shells on the floor" add to the "no-frills" feel of this Burbank BBQer trading in "big, messy" plates of ribs, wings and links; cons call the 'cue "underwhelming", yet it's popular for "takeout" and for "casual" "family" meals.

**NEW Richie Palmer's Pizzeria** *Pizza*     ▽ 15 | 12 | 12 | $15

**Santa Monica** | 1355 Ocean Ave. (Santa Monica Blvd.) | 310-255-1111
**Glendale** | Americana at Brand | 658 Americana Way (Central Ave.) |
818-240-4440

"East Coasters" exclaim that Santa Monica has become "a little slice of heaven" thanks to an abundance of new 'za entries, including this "New York–style" parlor from one of the founders of Mulberry Street Pizzeria; even if detractors declare it doesn't quite measure up to competitors, most are grateful to have "another great" "thin-crust" option in the neighborhood; N.B. the Glendale branch is new and unrated.

**Riordan's Tavern** *Steak*                      ▽ 15 | 18 | 19 | $39

**Downtown** | 875 S. Figueroa St. (9th St.) | 213-627-6879 |
www.riordanstavern.com

Former Mayor Richard Riordan is behind this relatively new Downtown steakhouse adjacent to his Original Pantry Cafe; though most find the fare "nothing special" (and "overpriced" to boot), "nice" barkeeps and a "clubby" tavern atmosphere mean it's a "good place for lunch" or "drinks" "on the way to a Kings game."

| | FOOD | DECOR | SERVICE | COST |
|---|---|---|---|---|

### Rive Gauche Cafe ⓜ *French* | 19 | 21 | 19 | $38 |

**Sherman Oaks** | 14106 Ventura Blvd. (Hazeltine Ave.) |
818-990-3573

This "understated" bistro in Sherman Oaks is a standby for "quiet, romantic" dining thanks to its "pretty" country-style setting and "beautiful" courtyard; "traditional French" feasts are "reliable", if "not exceptional", and a smattering of surveyors suggests the menu and service could use an upgrade.

### Riviera Restaurant & Lounge *Italian* | 24 | 22 | 22 | $47 |

**Calabasas** | 23683 Calabasas Rd. (Park Granada) | 818-224-2163

Calabasas' "upper-crust locals" come to this "hip" sib of Westlake Village's Rustico for a "consistently delicious" lineup of seasonal Italian cooking; a "gracious" team provides "professional" service, though the "nice atmosphere" can turn "noisy at times", especially on weekends, when "reservations are a must."

### NEW Robata Bar ◑ *Japanese* | 21 | 21 | 20 | $43 |

**Santa Monica** | 1401 Ocean Ave. (Santa Monica Blvd.) | 310-458-4771 |
www.robatabar.com

"Delicious" grilled "tidbits" are the focus of this Japanese sib of next-door Sushi Roku in Santa Monica also showcasing raw offerings like sashimi and ceviche with soju cocktails and beer to wash it all down; though the "attractive" lantern-lit atmosphere earns praise, a few suspect they prize "hipness above service", and add that "tiny" portions and "pricey" tabs can leave both "stomachs and wallets" feeling "empty."

### Robin's Woodfire BBQ & Grill ⓜ *BBQ* | 17 | 14 | 16 | $22 |

**Pasadena** | 395 N. Rosemead Blvd. (Foothill Blvd.) | 626-351-8885

A BBQ "oasis" in an area overrun by "fast-food" outlets, this "dependable" Pasadenan plies patrons with "huge portions" of ribs and such from a "virtually all-meat menu"; the mood is "family-friendly", although some say the "gaudy" decor done up with "vintage" beer signs and license plates is more like a "dive bar" than a "TGI Fridays."

### NEW Röckenwagner | - | - | - | I |

**Bakery Cafe** *Bakery/Californian*

**Santa Monica** | 311 Arizona Ave. (3rd St.) | 310-394-4267

Now that he's closed the last of his formal restaurants, chef Hans Röckenwagner has found a niche in the world of gourmet-casual at this inexpensive Santa Monica arrival; he's serving sandwiches on pretzel bread (baked in-house) plus other Californian fare in a modern space with green-and-white walls and a patio boasting a fine view of Third Street Promenade.

### Rock'n Fish *Seafood/Steak* | 21 | 17 | 18 | $36 |

**Manhattan Beach** | 120 Manhattan Beach Blvd.
(bet. Manhattan Ave. & Manhattan Bch.) | 310-379-9900 |
www.rocknfishmb.com

"Always bustling", this "fairly priced" Manhattan Beach "hangout" just "30 seconds from the sand" brings together "solid steaks" and "wonderful seafood" with a "huge selection" of wines and specialty cocktails; on weekends, the already "energetic" atmosphere gets a boost from a "pickup" scene at the bar, so those seeking a respite from the "loud", "tight quarters" say "upstairs" offers a "more romantic" experience.

| | FOOD | DECOR | SERVICE | COST |
|---|---|---|---|---|

## NEW RockSugar
### Pan Asian Kitchen *Pan-Asian*

| - | - | - | M |
|---|---|---|---|

**Century City** | Westfield Century City Shopping Ctr. | 10250 Santa Monica Blvd. (Century Park W.) | 310-552-9988 | www.rocksugarpanasiankitchen.com

In the space that used to be the Century City Food Court, this moderately priced Cheesecake Factory spin-off serves food from Southeast Asia – including dishes from Thailand, Vietnam, Indonesia, Malaysia and India – in a high-ceilinged, temple-inspired room decorated with dozens of Buddhas; N.B. true to the restaurant's roots, the menu offers cheesecake, albeit one made with tofu.

### Rocky Cola Café *Diner*

| 13 | 14 | 15 | $15 |
|---|---|---|---|

**Hermosa Beach** | 1025 PCH (Aviation Blvd.) | 310-798-3111 ☻
**Montrose** | 2201 Honolulu Ave. (Verdugo Rd.) | 818-249-2233
**Whittier** | 6757 Greenleaf Ave. (Philadelphia St.) | 562-907-3377

"Popular with families", this "1950s"-style trio offers an "ample menu" of "typical" diner favorites alongside "healthy alternatives" that "cater to the slim-obsessed of South Bay"; "listless" service is a sore spot, but at least tabs are cheap, and they're "open late" on weekends too.

### Roll 'n Rye Deli *Deli*

| 17 | 12 | 19 | $19 |
|---|---|---|---|

**Culver City** | Studio Village Shopping Ctr. | 10990 W. Jefferson Blvd. (Machado Rd.) | 310-390-3497

A "loyal following" applauds this "friendly, neighborhood" deli in Culver City offering an "extensive" lineup of "nice, large sandwiches", soups and other "traditional" favorites; sepia-toned photos on the walls lend it a "homey" feel, though most agree it's on the "pricey" side.

### Romano's Macaroni Grill *Italian*

| 17 | 17 | 17 | $24 |
|---|---|---|---|

**Cerritos** | 12875 Towne Center Dr. (bet. Bloomfield Ave. & 183rd St.) | 562-916-7722
**El Segundo** | 2321 Rosecrans Ave. (Aviation Blvd.) | 310-643-0812
**Torrance** | Rolling Hills Plaza | 25352 S. Crenshaw Blvd. (Airport Dr.) | 310-534-1001
**Monrovia** | 945 W. Huntington Dr. (5th Ave.) | 626-256-7969
**Northridge** | Northridge Fashion Ctr. | 19400 Plummer St. (Tampa Ave.) | 818-725-2620
**Thousand Oaks** | Promenade Shopping Ctr. | 4000 E. Thousand Oaks Blvd. (Westlake Blvd.) | 805-370-1133
**Santa Clarita** | 25720 N. The Old Rd. (McBean Pkwy.) | 661-284-1850 www.macaronigrill.com

"Solid Italian mainstays" fill out the menu of this "busy" chain tricked up with "open kitchens", "singing waiters" and "crayon"-ready paper tablecloths; though the food quality is debatable – "delicious" vs. "as bland as a jar of Ragu" – there's consensus on its "reasonable prices", helped along by that "wine-on-the-honor-system" program.

### Roscoe's House of
### Chicken 'n Waffles *Soul Food*

| 20 | 8 | 15 | $17 |
|---|---|---|---|

**Hollywood** | 1514 N. Gower St. (bet. Hollywood & Sunset Blvds.) | 323-466-7453 ☻
**Mid-City** | 106 W. Manchester Ave. (S. Main St.) | 323-752-6211
**Mid-City** | 5006 W. Pico Blvd. (La Brea Ave.) | 323-934-4405 ☻
**Long Beach** | 730 E. Broadway (bet. Alamitos & Atlantic Aves.) | 562-437-8355

*(continued)*

## Roscoe's House of Chicken 'n Waffles

**Pasadena** | 830 N. Lake Ave. (bet. Mountain St. & Orange Grove Blvd.) | 626-791-4890

www.roscoeschickenandwaffles.com

"Folks of all ages and races" "worship the bird and batter" at this LA soul food chain "classic" proffering the "unbeatable combination" of "crisp" fried chicken and "syrup-drenched" waffles ("it all makes sense after you take your first bite"); lines can be "long" and the "fluorescent-lit" interiors don't offer much in the way of ambiance, but loyalists insist you sample the "feel-good" fare "at least once", even if you'll have to "fast for two days afterwards."

## Rose Cafe  *Californian*

19 | 18 | 17 | $21

**Venice** | 220 Rose Ave. (Main St.) | 310-399-0711 | www.rosecafe.com

A "favorite haunt" for Venice locals, this "casual" cafe touts a "delightfully fresh" Californian menu and a "sun-dappled patio" that's the site of "relaxed" breakfasts and lunches; service is "swift", so afterwards, you can "browse" the attached gift shop for "unique tchotchkes."

## Rosti  *Italian*

16 | 12 | 15 | $23

**Beverly Hills** | 233 S. Beverly Dr. (bet. Olympic & Wilshire Blvds.) | 310-275-3285

**Santa Monica** | 931 Montana Ave. (10th St.) | 310-393-3236

**Encino** | Encino Mktpl. | 16403 Ventura Blvd. (Hayvenhurst Ave.) | 818-995-7179

www.rostituscankitchen.com

"Almost like Italian fast food", this "reasonably priced" Tuscan chain can be counted on for "tasty" rosemary roast chicken, plus sandwiches, salads, pizzas and other dishes that "get the job done" for an "easy" meal; though all branches boast patio seating, most find the "casual" setup and "ok service" a better fit for "takeout."

## Roy's  *Asian Fusion/Hawaiian*

23 | 22 | 22 | $49

**Downtown** | 800 S. Figueroa St. (8th St.) | 213-488-4994

**NEW** **Pasadena** | 641 E. Colorado Blvd. (El Molino Ave.) | 626-356-4066

**Woodland Hills** | 6363 Topanga Canyon Blvd. (Victory Blvd.) | 818-888-4801

www.roysrestaurant.com

"Bringing back memories of the Big Island", this "haute Hawaiian" chain via celeb chef Roy Yamaguchi stays "exciting" thanks to a "top-shelf" Asian-inspired fusion menu that's as "eye-pleasing as it is palate-pleasing"; "first-class" service and "upscale casual" atmospheres add to its luster, though given the "upmarket pricing", it does "taste better when someone else is paying."

## R23  ⓩ  *Japanese*

26 | 22 | 22 | $52

**Downtown** | 923 E. Second St. (bet. Alameda St. & Santa Fe Ave.) | 213-687-7178 | www.r23.com

Inside one of Downtown's converted warehouses dwells this "stylish" Japanese whose "cutting-edge" design decked out with "museum-quality" ceramics, paintings and corrugated cardboard chairs "makes you feel like you're eating in a gallery" (indeed you are, since much of the art is for sale); fans find the food – "unbelievable sushi" and "creative" cooked dishes – similarly "fabulous", even if critics tut it's too "expensive."

| | FOOD | DECOR | SERVICE | COST |
|---|---|---|---|---|

**Ruby's** *Diner*     17 | 17 | 18 | $16

**Rolling Hills Estates** | Avenue of the Peninsula Mall | 550 Deep Valley Dr.
(Crossfield Dr.) | Rolling Hills | 310-544-7829
**LAX** | L.A. Int'l Airport | 209 World Way (Terminal 6) |
310-646-2480
**Long Beach** | 6405 E. PCH (2nd St.) | 562-596-1914
**Redondo Beach** | 245 N. Harbor Dr. (Beryl St.) | 310-376-7829
**Woodland Hills** | Westfield Promenade | 6100 Topanga Canyon Blvd.
(bet. Erwin & Oxnard Sts.) | 818-340-7829
**Whittier** | Whittwood Mall | 10109 Whittwood Ln. (Cullen St.) |
562-947-7829
www.rubys.com

"Kids beg to go" for the burgers, shakes and other "classic diner
food" at this "upbeat" "retro malt shoppe" chain that's the "place to go
after a Little League game"; less gaga grown-ups call it only "ok if you
gotta", but acknowledge that the "fast", "cheery" staff adds
to the "convenience."

**Ruen Pair** ●♿ *Thai*     ▽ 24 | 9 | 17 | $18

**East Hollywood** | 5257 Hollywood Blvd. (Western Ave.) |
323-466-0153

"Only the valet" signals that you're "not in Thailand" at this "authentic" joint in East Hollywood famed for its "unusual", "spicy" fare that
goes beyond basic curries; tabs are "cheap" and "bohemians" hankering for a little "late-night" "stir-fried morning glory" will be glad to
know it stays open till 4 AM.

**NEW** **Rush Street** *American*     - | - | - | M

**Culver City** | 9546 Washington Blvd. (Culver Blvd.) | 310-837-9546
An homage to Chicago set in a former signage company, this New
American is the latest example of Culver City's revival, boasting polished concrete floors and perfectly restored bow truss ceilings, along
with a mezzanine for parties and a roof garden; the midpriced menu is
both eclectic and familiar, with Chi-Town specialties served nightly
(Chicago dogs on Mondays; deep-dish pizza Fridays).

**Russell's Burgers** *Diner*     ▽ 19 | 11 | 16 | $18

**Pasadena** | 30 N. Fair Oaks Ave. (bet. Colorado Blvd. & Union St.) |
626-578-1404
Supporters "sit at the counter and soak in the 1950s vibe" at this "unfussy" Pasadena coffee shop that delivers "good old-fashioned diner
food" headlined by "great burgers" and "meatloaf just like mom could
never make"; it's especially busy at breakfast, so prepare for "waits",
though service is "prompt" once you're seated.

**Rustic Canyon** *Californian/Mediterranean*     21 | 18 | 20 | $45

**Santa Monica** | 1119 Wilshire Blvd. (bet. 11th & 12th Sts.) | 310-393-7050 |
www.rusticcanyonwinebar.com
"Excellent" small-production wines and an "innovative" Cal-Med
menu that "changes frequently" come together at this Santa
Monica small-plater showcasing "fresh, local" ingredients in its
"deliciously uncomplicated" selections; since the "elegant", "austere" setting is often packed with a "good-looking" crowd, expect
"noisy" acoustics, unless you're lucky enough to snag one of the
few "cozy booths."

| | FOOD | DECOR | SERVICE | COST |
|---|---|---|---|---|

### Rustico  *Italian*
▽ 23 | 17 | 21 | $40

**Westlake Village** | 1125 Lindero Canyon Rd. (off Kanan Rd.) | 818-889-0191 | www.rustico-restaurant.com

Admirers announce they've "never had a bad meal" at this strip-mall Italian in Westlake Village whose "solid" cooking and "friendly" service help rank it as "one of the neighborhood's best"; wallet-watchers call it "a little pricey", but concede it's "lovely" for "weekend" dining.

### ⊠ Ruth's Chris Steak House  *Steak*
26 | 22 | 24 | $63

**Beverly Hills** | 224 S. Beverly Dr. (bet. Olympic & Wilshire Blvds.) | 310-859-8744

**Pasadena** | 369 E. Colorado Blvd. (bet. Euclid & Los Robles Aves.) | 626-583-8122

**Woodland Hills** | Westfield Promenade | 6100 Topanga Canyon Blvd. (bet. Erwin & Oxnard Sts.) | 818-227-9505
www.ruthschris.com

"Nothing beats a steak sizzling in butter" at this "special-occasion", New Orleans–based chain where the "melt-in-your-mouth" chops are "cooked to perfection" and presented on "hot plates"; opinions of the clubby, "old-fashioned" decor range from "beautiful" to "bland", but service is "attentive" and the "off-the-charts" pricing manageable "so long as your boss doesn't care how much you spend."

### ⊠ Saddle Peak Lodge  Ⓜ *American*
26 | 27 | 26 | $65

**Calabasas** | 419 Cold Canyon Rd. (Piuma Rd.) | 818-222-3888 | www.saddlepeaklodge.com

"If it walks on all fours", you just might find it on the New American menu at this "elegant" Calabasas "retreat" rolling out "perfectly prepared" game dishes ("try the elk") in an "ineffably romantic" "woodsy" lodge setting with fireplace; add in "impeccable" service, and it's easy to see why this "destination" is deemed "a fixture" for so many "holiday" gatherings.

### Saddle Ranch Chop House  ● *Steak*
14 | 18 | 16 | $30

**West Hollywood** | 8371 Sunset Blvd. (bet. Crescent Heights & La Cienega Blvds.) | 323-656-2007

**Universal City** | 666 Universal Hollywood Dr. (off Rte. 101) | 818-760-9680
www.srrestaurants.com

You've "gotta get on the mechanical bull for the full effect" of this "cheesy" pair of steakhouses on the Sunset Strip and Universal City's CityWalk catering to "frat boys" and "drunken cowgirls" with "Texas-sized" portions of "cheap" grub; despite the "adorable" "young actor" staff ("you really feel for them"), the food's barely "average" – fortunately the cocktails are "strong enough to make you forget the mediocre meal you just ate."

### Safire  *American*
▽ 21 | 22 | 18 | $42

**Camarillo** | 4850 Santa Rosa Rd. (Verdugo Way) | 805-389-1227 | www.safirebistro.com

Residents of "sleepy" Camarillo laud this "nice addition" to the dining scene delivering "daring" New American dishes courtesy of chef Mike Muirhead who once worked the stoves at Spago; though service is "spotty", many "love the look" of the space whose open kitchen and "sexy bar area" give it a "modern" air that certainly feels "hip" for the 'burbs.

|  | FOOD | DECOR | SERVICE | COST |
|---|---|---|---|---|

**Sagebrush Cantina** *Southwestern*  | 13 | 16 | 15 | $25 |

**Calabasas** | 23527 Calabasas Rd. (El Canon Ave.) | 818-222-6062 |
www.sagebrushcantina.com

More "hangout than a restaurant", this Calabasas canteen attracts a
"colorful" "crowd" – "yuppies", "porn stars", "Hells Angels" – who "sit
outside" on "sunny weekends" and sip drinks on the "patio"; though
the Southwestern food and service are both "substandard", given such
"scenery", "who can complain?"

**Sai Sai** ⑤ *Japanese/Pan-Asian*  | ∇ 18 | 19 | 19 | $45 |

**Downtown** | Millennium Biltmore Hotel | 501 S. Olive St. (5th St.) |
213-624-1100 | www.milleniumhotels.com

"Unusual" Pan-Asian dishes augment the selection of sushi at this
"high-end" eatery in the Millenium Biltmore Downtown; though insiders
insist it's "better than your typical hotel restaurant", critics dub the fare
"surprisingly mundane" considering the tony locale and upmarket tabs.

**Saito's Sushi** ⑤ *Japanese*  | ∇ 24 | 6 | 23 | $41 |

**Silver Lake** | 4339 W. Sunset Blvd. (Fountain Ave.) | 323-663-8890

Champions cheer this "one man show" in Silver Lake where "genius"
chef-owner Saito Taka turns out "unbelievable" sushi and sashimi aimed
at "purists"; its "bare-bones" strip-mall space is often jammed with "lots
of regulars", so those-in-the-know arrive "early" for a "seat at the bar."

**Saketini** *Asian Fusion*  | ∇ 20 | 14 | 20 | $29 |

**Brentwood** | 150 S. Barrington Ave. (Sunset Blvd.) | 310-440-5553 |
www.saketini.com

Fusion fans insist this "teeny-tiny" Brentwood Asian is a "treat" for
"delightfully creative" dishes like Korean black cod and yellowtail carpaccio and 12 different varieties of their namesake cocktail; style-
mavens say the sparse decor "could be better", though its "low-key"
feel appeals to a "neighborhood" crowd; P.S. the "bento box lunch" is
priced "under $10 – a bargain in these parts."

**Saladang** *Thai*  | 23 | 19 | 19 | $25 |

**Pasadena** | 363 S. Fair Oaks Ave. (bet. California & Del Mar Blvds.) |
626-793-8123

**Saladang Song** *Thai*

**Pasadena** | 383 S. Fair Oaks Ave. (bet. California & Del Mar Blvds.) |
626-793-5200

"Fantastic" Thai food (and "not just the same old, same old" either)
has patrons "hooked" on these adjacent Siamese "twins" in Pasadena
sending out "spot on" fare ranked among "the best" in town; though
both feature similarly "rapid" service by "eye-candy waitresses", Song
is "a bit more upscale" and sports a "lovely courtyard", making it a
"great budget date spot."

**Salades de Provence** *French*  | ∇ 20 | 16 | 22 | $20 |

**West Hollywood** | 1040 N. La Cienega Blvd. (Holloway Dr.) | 310-657-9696 |
www.saladesdeprovence.com

"Delicious quiches" and "enormous salads" are made from "good-
quality" organic ingredients at this "authentically French" West
Hollywood cafe that also satisfies with gelato and frozen yogurt from
the in-house bar; despite some grumbles that it's "too pricey for lettuce", it earns praise for its "welcoming" staff and "quiet" "sunny" set-

ting whose "unhurried" vibe is conducive to "hanging out" with "coffee" and a "newspaper"; N.B. a Beverly Hills branch will open in fall 2008.

### Salt Creek Grille  *Steak*                     | 18 | 21 | 18 | $38 |

**El Segundo** | Plaza El Segundo | 2015 E. Park Pl. (Sepulveda Blvd.) | 310-335-9288
**Valencia** | Valencia Town Ctr. | 24415 Town Center Dr. (McBean Pkwy.) | 661-222-9999
www.saltcreekgrille.com

"Happy-hour" tipplers sip selections from a "nice list of martinis" at this "lively" steakhouse chain whose "rustic" ambiance gets a lift from "live music" most nights; although portions are "enormous", cons contend the "predictably decent" chops and seafood "aren't as good as the prices suggest they should be."

### Saluzzi  Ⓜ *Italian*                    ▽ 22 | 18 | 16 | $51 |

**Rancho Palos Verdes** | Golden Cove Shopping Ctr. | 31206 Palos Verdes Dr. W. (Hawthorne Blvd.) | 310-377-7200 | www.saluzziristorante.com

"Passionate" chef Michael Saluzzi offers "elegant" "twists" on "traditional" "family recipes" at this "tiny" Rancho Palos Verdes Italian featuring Sistine Chapel–style frescos on the ceiling and views of the Pacific "right out the window"; though the "excellent" food wins raves, some guests gripe that "noisy" environs detract, and say that service needs to "work out the kinks" to measure up with the "expensive" prices.

### 🆕 Sampa Grill  *Brazilian*            | - | - | - | M |

**Encino** | 16240 Ventura Blvd. (Libbit Ave.) | 818-981-8818 | www.sampagrill.net

The churrascaria craze marches on at this lively all-you-can-eater in the heart of Encino decked out in bright, Brazilian carnival–like colors and featuring an enormous salad and hot dish buffet to complement the constant parade of charcoal-grilled meats served by culinary gauchos; moderate prices seal the deal.

### 🔏 Sam's                                  | 26 | 22 | 26 | $49 |
### by the Beach  Ⓜ *Californian/Mediterranean*

**Santa Monica** | 108 W. Channel Rd. (PCH) | 310-230-9100

"Quintessential host" and owner Samer Elias presides over this "adorable hideaway" in Santa Monica whose "cozy" bistro setting and "wonderfully caring" service create a "romantic" atmosphere; diners deem the "eclectic" Cal-Med cooking "delightful" as well, so even if prices fall on the high side, for most this is "one of the great finds in town."

### Sam Woo  *Chinese*                        | 20 | 8 | 12 | $18 |

**Chinatown** | 727 N. Broadway (bet. Alpine & Ord Sts.) | 213-680-7836
**Chinatown** | 803 N. Broadway (Alpine St.) | 213-687-7238 ●🖘
**Cerritos** | 19008 Pioneer Blvd. (South St.) | 562-865-7278 ●
**Van Nuys** | Signature Plaza | 6450 Sepulveda Blvd. (Victory Blvd.) | 818-988-6813 🖘
**Alhambra** | 514 W. Valley Blvd. (bet. 5th & 6th Sts.) | 626-281-0038 ●🖘
**Monterey Park** | 634 W. Garvey Ave. (bet. N. Chandler & N. Moore Aves.) | 626-289-4858 ●🖘
**San Gabriel** | 140 W. Valley Blvd. (Manley Dr.) | 626-572-8418 ●🖘
**San Gabriel** | 425 S. California St. (Agostino Rd.) | 626-287-6528 ●🖾Ⓜ🖘
For "cheap" and "filling" Chinese eats, supporters say "you can't beat" this "no-nonsense" chain churning out "satisfying" specialties like

| | FOOD | DECOR | SERVICE | COST |

BBQ pork, "tasty Peking duck" and a "diverse selection of fresh sea-food"; though decor varies by location, most don't feature much more beyond meats "hanging" in window displays, while servers often "have a brisk style" that some find "rude."

### Sandbag's

**Gourmet Sandwiches** *Sandwiches*

| 16 | 7 | 15 | $11 |

**Downtown** | 818 Wilshire Blvd. (bet. Figueroa & Flower Sts.) | 213-228-1920 🗷
**Mid-Wilshire** | 9404 Wilshire Blvd. (La Jolla Ave.) | 323-655-4250 🗷
**West Hollywood** | 9255 Sunset Blvd. (W. Sunset Blvd.) | 310-888-0112 🗷
**Brentwood** | 11640 San Vicente Blvd. (Bringham Ave.) | 310-207-4888
**Westwood** | 1134 Westwood Blvd. (Wilshire Blvd.) | 310-208-1133 🗷
**Glendale** | 138 S. Brand Blvd. (bet. B'way & Colorado St.) | 818-241-0740
www.sandbagss.com

Nine-to-fivers "love the free cookies" that come with the "creative" sandwiches at this beyond-casual mini-chain that's a lunchtime staple for "takeout" and delivery; skeptics say they're "not sure it's gourmet", but it's a "decent" stop for a "quick" bite nonetheless.

### San Gennaro Cafe *Italian*

| 16 | 13 | 19 | $29 |

**Brentwood** | 140 S. Barrington Pl. (Sunset Blvd.) | 310-476-9696 | www.sangennarocafe.com

The menu's "mammoth" and so are the portions at this Brentwood Italian luring local "families" with "basic" "red-sauce" fare and an "affordable" wine list; most agree the food's "nothing special", but many hold a soft spot for its "longtime" waiters and "cozy" setting that feels "straight out of New York."

### Sapori *Italian*

| ▽ 20 | 16 | 17 | $32 |

**Marina del Rey** | Fishermans Vill. | 13723 Fiji Way (Lincoln Blvd.) | 310-821-1740 | www.sapori-mdr.com

"Sophisticated" Italian fare "surprises" first-timers at this well-priced "little" "sleeper" "tucked away in Marina del Rey's Fisherman Village"; "gracious" service adds to the "charming" atmosphere, as does the patio seating "overlooking the harbor" and affording "great sunset views."

### Sassi Mediterranean *Mediterranean*

| ▽ 21 | 11 | 15 | $24 |

**Encino** | 15622 Ventura Blvd. (Haskell Ave.) | 818-986-5345 | www.sassirestaurant.com

"Terrific" kosher food awaits at this "low-key" Encino Mediterranean cooking up couscous, kebabs and the like in a "basic storefront" setting; service is "fast" and "pleasant", and given its moderate tabs and kid-friendly menu items, it's a natural fit for families; N.B. closed Friday nights and Saturdays.

### Sea Empress *Chinese*

| 19 | 12 | 14 | $21 |

**Gardena** | Pacific Sq. | 1636 W. Redondo Beach Blvd. (bet. Normandie & Western Aves.) | 310-538-6868

South Bay residents salute this Gardena Chinese where "familiar dim sum" favorites plus a "few surprises" arrive "piping hot" off rolling carts; though many find the banquet-style setting has seen better days, the atmosphere provides plenty of "hustle and bustle" and budget-conscious types say it offers "good value" too.

**Sea Harbour**  *Chinese/Seafood*  | 24 | 15 | 14 | $30 |

**Rosemead** | 3939 N. Rosemead Blvd. (Valley Blvd.) | 626-288-3939

The "exquisite" dim sum creations win raves for their "sheer variety and uniqueness" alone at this cart-free Rosemead Cantonese proffering "excellent" made-to-order fare at lunch and "pricey" seafood feasts at dinner; its "typically gaudy" space commands "impossible" lines on weekends, so regulars say "go early" or "be prepared to wait (and wait)."

**Second City Bistro** ⓢ *American*  | 23 | 22 | 23 | $38 |

**El Segundo** | 223 Richmond St. (Grand Ave.) | 310-322-6085 | www.secondcitybistro.com

Admirers adore this "real find" in "sleepy" El Segundo joining up an "inventive" New American menu with an "impressive" lineup of wines; it owes its "warm" vibe to "talented" servers and "Cali-cool" decor featuring exposed beams and an open kitchen plus a patio for "date" night.

**NEW Second Story**  *American*  | - | - | - | M |

**Manhattan Beach** | Belamar Hotel | 3501 Sepulveda Blvd. (Rosecrans Ave.) | 310-750-0300 | www.secondstoryrestaurant.com

Recently opened in Manhattan Beach's boutique Belamar Hotel, this affordable New American is awash in flickering candles and TV screens (mostly there for visual interest, though they're tuned to sports in the bar); the all-day kitchen starts with breakfast fare at 6:30 AM and moves along to sliders, salads and heftier entrees, making it convenient whether you're catching a wave or a flight.

**Señor Fred** ◑ *Mexican*  | 18 | 19 | 17 | $29 |

**Sherman Oaks** | 13730 Ventura Blvd. (Woodman Ave.) | 818-789-3200 | www.senorfred.com

"*Sí, señor!*" say amigos of this "sceney" Sherman Oaks hang where the "wicked margaritas" and semi-"upscale", largely "respectable" grub that's "not the same old American-style Mexican food" attract "local singles" in the mood for happy hour or a "late-night" bite (till midnight on the weekends); with "funky" "bordello" trappings, the "noisy" digs are "almost cavelike", but at least that means "everyone is beautiful because the lights are nearly off."

**NEW Seoul Bros. Korean Grill** ⓢ *Korean*  | - | - | - | I |

**Pasadena** | 851 Cordova St. (Lake Ave.) | 626-795-1777 | www.seoulbros.com

Designed by Sat Garg (Vertical Wine Bistro, Tanzore), this modern Korean fast-fooder in Pasadena is bringing a taste of bulgogi to a part of town that has little in the way of kimchi; patrons order at the counter from a simple, affordable menu that includes BBQ chicken, beef short ribs and organic tofu, then enjoy their eats in an industrial-chic setting accented by a wall that seems to glow with an otherwordly light.

| | FOOD | DECOR | SERVICE | COST |
|---|---|---|---|---|

### Seoul Jung  *Korean*

▽ 20 | 22 | 21 | $42

**Downtown** | Wilshire Grand | 930 Wilshire Blvd. (Figueroa St.) |
213-688-7880 | www.wilshiregrand.com

"Don't let the hotel location fool you" say advocates of this
Downtowner in the Wilshire Grand that delivers "tasty" "traditional"
Korean dishes and grill-it-yourself BBQ; though penny-pinchers pout
that it's "overpriced" compared to "divier" K-town locales nearby, the
"comfortable" contemporary setting and "friendly" service make it fit
for "impressing business clients."

### 750 ml  *French*

19 | 17 | 16 | $44

**South Pasadena** | 966 Mission St. (Prospect Ave.) | 626-799-0711
The latest entry in the Steve Arroyo (Cobras & Matadors) "king-
dom", this South Pas bistro wins praise from patrons who call it a
"great addition to the neighborhood" with an "ambitious" French
menu and a "spot-on wine list" with many bottles under $50; yet
while the "cute" brick-walled space illuminated with Edison bulbs
is often "crowded", some surveyors feel "let down" by the experience, singling out "apathetic" service and an "overpriced" menu
that "hits and misses."

### 17th Street Cafe  *Californian*

19 | 15 | 19 | $28

**Santa Monica** | 1610 Montana Ave. (bet. 16th & 17th Sts.) |
310-453-2771

This "locals' hangout" on Santa Monica's main shopping drag serves
up "dependable" Californian cuisine (think "great breakfasts" and
"fabulous salads") that keeps it "crowded" with "a mixed group" of
"ladies who lunch", "health fanatics" and the "occasional indie film
producer"; service is solid, though some say the "homey decor" with
rotating art exhibits doesn't "do it justice."

### Shabu Shabu House  Ⓜ *Japanese*

23 | 9 | 15 | $22

**Little Tokyo** | 127 Japanese Village Plaza Mall (bet. E. 1st & 2nd Sts.) |
213-680-3890

"What a delight!" declare DIYers of this Little Toyko Japanese
whose "authentic, handmade sauces" and "high-quality beef" hot
pot meals "set it apart" from the competition while providing tremendous "bang for the buck"; "Disneyland-length lines", "so-so
service" and a "scarcely decorated" interior are part of the deal,
but most find the "shabu-shabu makes up for" any shortcomings;
P.S. "get there early and put your name on the list" to help reduce
the "crazy" wait.

### Shack, The  *American*

17 | 10 | 12 | $15

**Playa del Rey** | 185 Culver Blvd. (Vista del Mar) | 310-823-6222
**Santa Monica** | 2518 Wilshire Blvd. (26th St.) | 310-449-1171
www.the-shacks.com

"You can't attack the Shack" swear supporters of these Playa del
Rey and Santa Monica "neighborhood joints" frequented by
"rowdy" locals (and "Eagles fans" at the SM branch) digging into
the "juicy", "legendary" eponymous burger and other "affordable"
American eats; while the "run-down" rooms "live up to the name",
at least that means the staff "doesn't mind sand" tracked in
from the beach.

| | FOOD | DECOR | SERVICE | COST |
|---|---|---|---|---|

### Shaherzad  *Persian*                      21 | 13 | 17 | $26

**Westwood** | 1422 Westwood Blvd. (bet. Santa Monica & Wilshire Blvds.) |
310-470-9131

"Warm flat bread right from the oven" accompanies the "huge portions" of "wonderful", "authentic" grilled meats, veggies and rice
at this casual Westwood Persian that provides an "excellent value"
for the money; despite what some deem a "drab" interior and uneven service, it's "totally satisfying" for "lots of people" making
"lots of noise."

### Sharky's Mexican Grill  *Mexican*        18 | 11 | 15 | $12

**Hollywood** | 1716 N. Cahuenga Blvd. (Hollywood Blvd.) |
323-461-7881
**Beverly Hills** | 435 N. Beverly Dr. (bet. Brighton Way & Santa Monica Blvd.) |
310-858-0202
**Long Beach** | Pike at Rainbow Harbor | 51 The Paseo (Pine Ave.) |
562-435-2700
**Pasadena** | 841 Cordova St. (Lake Ave.) | 626-568-3500
**Burbank** | Burbank Empire Ctr. | 1791 N. Victory Pl. (Empire Ave.) |
818-840-9080
**Calabasas** | Creekside Village Shopping Ctr. | 26527 Agoura Rd.
(Las Virgenes Rd.) | 818-880-0885
**Sherman Oaks** | 13238 Burbank Blvd. (Fulton Ave.) | 818-785-2533
**Tarzana** | 5511 Reseda Blvd. (1 block north of Ventura Blvd.) |
818-881-8760
**Simi Valley** | 2410 Sycamore Dr. (Cochran St.) | 805-522-2270
**Westlake Village** | 111 S. Westlake Blvd. (Thousand Oaks Blvd.) |
805-370-3701
www.sharkys.com
Additional locations throughout Southern California

"You can actually eat Mexican food and not stop your heart" at this
"reliable" counter-service chain serving "surprisingly fresh", "mostly
organic" fare with "low-fat possibilities" at tabs that "won't break the
bank"; even fans think the "bare" digs "could use some design", but
most don't mind when they're out for a "quick, healthy fix."

### Shima  �  *Japanese*                ∇ 27 | 21 | 24 | $52

**Venice** | 1432 Abbot Kinney Blvd. (bet. California Ave. & Palm St.) |
310-314-0882

The sleek "secret townhouse setting" lends a "James Bond" feel to this
"exciting" Venice Japanese where chef Yoshi Shigenobu, keen on both
health and "pleasure", crafts "delectable" brown-rice sushi among
other "exquisite" dishes suited to "special evenings"; sated visitors
advise "don't let the impassive demeanor" of the servers throw you –
"they totally know what they're doing."

### ⚡ Shiro  Ⓜ *French/Japanese*            27 | 18 | 26 | $48

**South Pasadena** | 1505 Mission St. (bet. Fair Oaks & Fremont Aves.) |
626-799-4774 | www.restaurantshiro.com

"Gotta love the deep-fried catfish" crow customers who find the seafood "addictive" at this "sensational", high-end South Pasadena destination where the "quality never fades" thanks to chef-owner Hideo
Yamashiro's intrepid market-going and "memorable" French-
Japanese cooking (no sushi); the staff is "helpful", so even given the
"spartan" surroundings, many agree it's a winning "date place."

|  | FOOD | DECOR | SERVICE | COST |
|---|---|---|---|---|

### NEW Shojin Ⓜ Japanese/Vegan
**- | - | - | M**

**Little Tokyo** | Little Tokyo Sq. | 333 S. Alameda St. (3rd St.) | 213-617-0305 | www.theshojin.com

In a tasteful Little Tokyo setting, this alternative Japanese offers modestly priced Buddhist vegan cuisine that speaks to both Zen principles and 21st-century dietary concerns; among its organically sourced dishes are options such as soybean (rather than crab) cakes and tomato (rather than tuna) tartar, as well as dairy-free, naturally sweetened desserts.

### SHU Italian/Japanese
**21 | 18 | 19 | $50**

**Bel-Air** | The Glen | 2932½ Beverly Glen Circle (Mulholland Dr.) | 310-474-2740 | www.shusushi.com

"Sicilian meets sushi – who woulda thunk it?" ask admirers of this Bel-Air "hideaway" conceived by backer Giacomino Drago (Il Pastaio) that serves "delightful", "healthy" Italian-accented Japanese edibles in a "hip but relaxing" setting that's often "celebrity central" (i.e. "Britney's second home"); a "courteous" staff makes it extra inviting, but be warned that "ordering several of the small plates can ratchet up your bill quickly."

### NEW Siena Italian
**- | - | - | M**

**Pasadena** | 43 E. Union St. (bet. Fair Oaks & Raymond Aves.) | 626-584-6050 | www.sienapasadena.com

There are a few culinary surprises to be found at this budget-friendly Little Italy–style cafe in Pasadena where the menu ranges from greatest Italian hits like fritto misto to more unexpected dishes like black linguine with crab and morels; it's all served in a wood-and-tile room decorated with photos of somebody else's family.

### NEW Sila Bistro American
**- | - | - | M**

**Silver Lake** | 2630 Hyperion Ave. (Griffith Park Blvd.) | 323-664-7979 | www.sila-bistro.com

This dinner-only New American in the heart of Silver Lake isn't just named for the 'hood, but also features walls lined with old photos showing how rural it used to be (and how seminal – don't miss the picture of the original Disney Studio); with the popular Say Cheese fromagerie across the street, it's no surprise that this locavore is planning to offer a series of wine-and-cheese pairings along with its market-based cooking.

### Simon LA American
**21 | 24 | 20 | $55**

**West Hollywood** | Sofitel Los Angeles | 8555 Beverly Blvd. (La Cienega Blvd.) | 310-278-5444 | www.sofitel.com

"Iron Chef" champ Kerry Simon crafts "clever" renditions of American "comfort food" – including "lots of childhood desserts" that "bring back fond memories" – at this "stylish" locale in WeHo's Sofitel LA; though some critics call the cuisine "overhyped" and "inconsistent for the prices", most agree that even if it's a bit "pretentious", the "straight-out-of-a-movie" atmosphere "exudes sexiness", especially on the "romantic" patio with a fire pit.

### Simpang Asia Indonesian
**▽ 18 | 4 | 11 | $11**

**West LA** | 10433 National Blvd. (Motor Ave.) | 310-815-9075 | www.simpangasia.com

"Surprisingly satisfying", this "cafe-style eatery attached to a grocery store" in West LA serves "cheap", "authentic" Indonesian "almost-

|  | FOOD | DECOR | SERVICE | COST |
|---|---|---|---|---|

street food", along with a "don't-miss" avocado smoothie; on the downside, it's a real "hole-in-the-wall" and the "scattered" service tends to "slip when it's busy."

### Sir Winston's  *Continental*    | 21 | 25 | 23 | $59 |

**Long Beach** | Queen Mary | 1126 Queen's Hwy. (south of I-710) | 562-499-1657 | www.queenmary.com

Swept-away suppers "sail back in time" to "what cruise ship dining used to be" at this "top-drawer", "old-school" Cal-Continental inside the Queen Mary docked in Long Beach; the "limited" but largely "excellent" menu is "exquisitely" served amid "gorgeous art deco decor" rife with "fab" oceanfront views, so even if it's a little "stuffy", most don't mind the "pricey" tab; P.S. dress is semiformal, so "men, bring a sportcoat."

### Sisley Italian Kitchen  *Italian*    | 17 | 16 | 17 | $27 |

**West LA** | Westside Pavilion | 10800 W. Pico Blvd. (bet. Overland Ave. & Westwood Blvd.) | 310-446-3030
**Sherman Oaks** | 15300 Ventura Blvd. (Sepulveda Blvd.) | 818-905-8444
**Thousand Oaks** | Oaks Mall | 446 W. Hillcrest Dr. (bet. Lynn Rd. & McCloud Ave.) | 805-777-7511
**Valencia** | Valencia Town Ctr. | 24201 Valencia Blvd. (McBean Pkwy.) | 661-287-4444
www.sisleykitchen.com

"Upscale mall food" is the consensus on this "family-friendly" Italian chain turning out "huge quantities" of "affordable", "reliably edible" eats in Romanesque surroundings; critics call it "mediocre" all around, but fans feel it suffices "when your children are tired of shopping" or you "get a hunger attack on the way to the movies."

### NEW Skaf's Lebanese Cuisine ⑤ *Lebanese*    | ▽ 26 | 11 | 16 | $16 |

**Glendale** | 367 N. Chevy Chase Dr. (N. Verdugo Rd.) | 818-551-5540
"Freshness is the rule" at this new "family-run joint" in Glendale that provides "authentic", "well-made" Lebanese fare for a "bargain"; while it has a "low-end" diner look, that's no obstacle for its growing following of "attorneys, judges" and others who keep it "busy."

### Sky Room ⑤ *American*    | 21 | 25 | 24 | $68 |

**Long Beach** | Historic Breakers Bldg. | 40 S. Locust Ave. (Ocean Blvd.) | 562-983-2703 | www.theskyroom.com

"Spectacular views of the city and the ocean" are the highlights of this Long Beach "special-occasion" place crowning the Historic Breakers Building, where "old-fashioned" live music and dancing invites "dressy" diners "back in time to a bygone era"; though critics call it "over-priced", the New American fare is "well prepared" and the service "makes you feel like a star", adding up to a "memorable" evening out.

### Smitty's Grill  *American*    | 21 | 20 | 21 | $38 |

**Pasadena** | 110 S. Lake Ave. (bet. Cordova & Green Sts.) | 626-792-9999 | www.smittysgrill.com

"Comfort food and martinis" make a fetching pair at this Pasadena "hot spot" by the Smith brothers (Arroyo Chop House, Parkway Grill) where a "30-ish crowd" "unwinds" over "unbelievable" mac 'n' cheese and other elevated "home and hearth" fare; with "warm", wood-accented surroundings and "attentive" service, the only distraction for some is the "loud", "crowded" scene.

| | FOOD | DECOR | SERVICE | COST |
|---|---|---|---|---|

**Smoke House** *Steak*  —  19 | 17 | 19 | $37

**Burbank** | 4420 Lakeside Dr. (Barham Blvd.) | 818-845-3731 |
www.smokehouse1946.com

"Old-fashioned charm" is the main draw at this Burbank "institution"
frequented by "entertainment-industry types" during the "popular
happy hour" for "delicious" martinis, "killer" garlic bread and "predictable" but "perfectly acceptable" steakhouse fare served by a "veteran
staff"; with two "roaring fireplaces" and live music Thursday-
Saturday, it "oozes Hollywood glamour", even if naysayers scoff it's
"lost in time."

**Sofi** *Greek*  —  20 | 20 | 18 | $35

**Third Street** | 8030¾ W. Third St. (bet. Crescent Heights Blvd. & Fairfax Ave.) |
323-651-0346

"Leisurely dinners" are infused with a Mediterranean "island" feel at
this Third Street "hideaway" boasting a "charming" patio that's "perfect for a date night"; most find the Greek cooking "consistent" if a bit
"pricey", and while service could stand to improve, romantics appreciate the "unrushed" pace.

**Soleil Westwood** Ⓜ *Canadian/French*  —  20 | 15 | 22 | $32

**Westwood** | 1386 Westwood Blvd. (Rochester Ave.) | 310-441-5384 |
www.soleilwestwood.com

It's "what every neighborhood should have" assert advocates of this
"pleasant" Westwood "sleeper" where chef-owner Luc Alarie prepares "homey" French-Canadian dishes (including "fabulous" frites)
and might "breeze by your table to see how everything's treating you";
though some say the "service outshines the food" and the "cute" bistro decor, the "not-too-expensive" prices are a plus.

**Ⓩ Sona** ⓈⓂ *French*  —  27 | 24 | 27 | $93

**West Hollywood** | 401 N. La Cienega Blvd. (bet. Beverly Blvd. &
Melrose Ave.) | 310-659-7708 | www.sonarestaurant.com

A "temple for food", this "minimalist" WeHo "favorite" from "wizard"
David Myers showcases a "well-orchestrated" New French menu of
"beautiful, delicate dishes with artfully combined flavors" matched by
an "incredible" wine list; insiders recommend the "sublime" tasting
menu, as it's "worth taking out a loan" just to "sit back and be pampered in every sense of the word" by the "unbeatable" team.

**Sonora Cafe** *Southwestern*  —  22 | 21 | 21 | $42

**La Brea** | 180 S. La Brea Ave. (bet. Beverly Blvd. & 3rd St.) | 323-857-1800 |
www.sonoracafe.com

"Bright, bold flavors with the right amount of spice" (and "no skimping
on portions") plus "decent" margaritas draw La Brea locals to this
"pricey" Southwestern sib of El Cholo that's "stood the test of time";
despite some "cheeseball" touches, the room is "low-key" with a "welcoming" fireplace, and the staff "aims to please."

**Ⓩ Soot Bull Jeep** *Korean*  —  23 | 7 | 12 | $28

**Koreatown** | 3136 Eighth St. (Catalina St.) | 213-387-3865

"Delicious doesn't even begin to describe" the "authentic charcoal
BBQ" at this K-town "institution" where customers table-grill "fresh,
succulent and plentiful" meats accompanied by other "scrumptious"
Korean dishes; never mind the "surly"-seeming staff or the "divey",

| | FOOD | DECOR | SERVICE | COST |
|---|---|---|---|---|

"smoky" digs ("leave your cashmere at home"), diehards declare that the "food is so good you won't care."

## Sor Tino ● *Italian*      19 | 17 | 20 | $38

**Brentwood** | 908 S. Barrington Ave. (San Vicente Blvd.) | 310-442-8466
This "simple", "family-oriented" Brentwood Italian by chef-owner Agostino Sciandri (Ago) offers a "daily menu" of "tasty" (if "not earth-shattering") "rustic" fare for an "acceptable" price that's served by a "witty" staff; some say the "noisy" interior is "part of the charm", but most prefer dining on its "sweet little terrace with greenery and lights."

## Souplantation *American*      16 | 10 | 12 | $12

**Third Street** | Beverly Connection | 100 N. La Cienega Blvd. (W. 3rd St.) | 323-655-0381
**Lakewood** | 4720 Candlewood St. (bet. Clark Ave. & Lakewood Blvd.) | 562-531-6778
**Brentwood** | 11911 San Vicente Blvd. (Montana Ave.) | 310-476-7080
**Marina del Rey** | Villa Marina Mktpl. | 13455 Maxella Ave. (Lincoln Blvd.) | 310-305-7669
**Arcadia** | 301 E. Huntington Dr. (Gateway Dr.) | 626-446-4248
**Pasadena** | 201 S. Lake Ave. (Cordova St.) | 626-577-4798
**Northridge** | 19801 Rinaldi St. (Corbin Ave.) | 818-363-3027
**Alhambra** | 2131 W. Commonwealth Ave. (bet. Date & Palm Aves.) | 626-458-1173
**City of Industry** | Puente Hills Mall | 17411 Colima Rd. (Asuza Ave.) | 626-810-5756
**Camarillo** | 375 W. Ventura Blvd. (S. Las Posas Rd.) | 805-389-3500
www.souplantation.com
Additional locations throughout Southern California
"Families", "vegetarians" and "big eaters" alike come to this "cattle-call" American buffet chain for "all-you-can-graze" salads, soups, pastas and sweets; though some say it "serves its purpose", critics call the goods "cheap" and "low-quality" with a "blahness" to it all.

## South Street *Cheese Steaks*      ∇ 18 | 11 | 12 | $11

**Westwood** | 1010 Broxton Ave. (Weyburn Ave.) | 310-443-9895
**Burbank** | 117 N. Victory Blvd. (Olive St.) | 818-563-2211
www.southstreetcheesesteak.com
Packing "artery-clogging goodness", the "genuine" Philly cheese steaks are "as close to the real thing as you're gonna get" say fans of these Burbank and Westwood joints, who also "love the Tastykakes", water ices and other hometown treats; though some cite "uninviting" digs, all the sports memorabilia makes a few guests misty; N.B. there's also pizza and beer at the Burbank branch.

## ⊿ Spago *Californian*      27 | 25 | 25 | $78

**Beverly Hills** | 176 N. Cañon Dr. (Wilshire Blvd.) | 310-385-0880 | www.wolfgangpuck.com
"A permanent fixture in the LA culinary firmament", this Wolfgang Puck "flagship", voted the city's Most Popular restaurant, has "still got it in spades" thanks to chef Lee Hefter's Californian fare that's "artistically appointed and cooked to perfection", Sherry Yard's "extraordinary" desserts and a staff that "makes a nobody feel like a star"; add in prime Beverly Hills "people-watching" in the "fanciful" room and on the "beautiful" patio, and patrons would pony up the "crown jewels" for the "fabulous" feast.

|  | FOOD | DECOR | SERVICE | COST |
|---|---|---|---|---|

### Spanish Kitchen, The  *Mexican*

| 15 | 19 | 17 | $36 |

**West Hollywood** | 826 N. La Cienega Blvd. (bet. Melrose Pl. & Santa Monica Blvd.) | 310-659-4794 | www.thespanishkitchen.com

"Rocking on the weekends" with a "lively" crowd, this WeHo haunt boasts an "impressive tequila selection" to fuel "amazing" margaritas that tend to outshine the "lackluster" Mexican fare; though the space has "beautiful" touches such as handmade tiles and wrought iron, its "overloaded" servers and "overpriced" menu make the experience "not worth it" for many.

### Spark Woodfire Grill  *American*

| 19 | 17 | 18 | $33 |

**Pico-Robertson** | 9575 W. Pico Blvd. (Beverly Dr.) | 310-277-0133
**Studio City** | 11801 Ventura Blvd. (bet. Carpenter & Colfax Aves.) | 818-623-8883
www.sparkwoodfiregrill.com

Pizzas with a "dime-thin crust" and "delicious" steaks "never disappoint" fans of this "dependable", "comfortable" mini-chain serving up "simple" wood-fired American fare for a "good value"; on the downside, the offerings are too "safe" (and "expensive") for some and the rooms could use "a little updating."

### Spazio  *Californian/Mediterranean*

| 18 | 20 | 19 | $46 |

**Sherman Oaks** | 14755 Ventura Blvd. (bet. Cedros & Willis Aves.) | 818-728-8400 | www.spazio.la

Live jazz "steals the show" at this Sherman Oaks supper club where "world-class" musicians lend both dinner and Sunday brunch an "air of sophistication"; even if the Cal-Med cuisine is just "above average" for "Westside prices", the kitchen is "consistent", the staff "tries hard to please" and the "warm, attractive" space with a "nice patio" completes the picture.

### Spitz  *Turkish*

| 23 | 11 | 20 | $11 |

**Eagle Rock** | 2506 Colorado Blvd. (College View St.) | 323-257-5600 | www.eatatspitz.com

The "finest in 'slow fast food'" can be found at this "Cal-style" Turkish-Med "keeper" where a "devoted" staff serves up a "delish" doner kebab (the "real attraction") along with "tasty" sweet potato fries and "rich, creamy" gelato; it's "off the beaten path", but given the "generous", "inspired" specialties, surveyors surmise "it's worth the drive to Eagle Rock"; N.B. a Little Tokyo branch is set to open in fall 2008.

### Spumoni  *Italian*

| 17 | 12 | 18 | $24 |

**Santa Monica** | 713 Montana Ave. (7th St.) | 310-393-2944
**Calabasas** | 26500 Agoura Rd. (Las Virgenes Rd.) | 818-871-9848
**Sherman Oaks** | 14533 Ventura Blvd. (bet. Van Nuys Blvd. & Vesper Ave.) | 818-981-7218
**Stevenson Ranch** | 24917 Pico Canyon Rd. (The Old Rd.) | 661-799-0360
www.spumonirestaurants.com

This SoCal mini-chain fills a "neighborhood Italian" niche, providing "homemade" "standard" dishes for a "reasonable" cost; though cons call it "mediocre" and criticize the "dearth of ambiance", at least the staff is "accommodating" and the owner "comes by and remembers you, or at least acts like it."

|  | FOOD | DECOR | SERVICE | COST |
|---|---|---|---|---|

### Square One Dining Ⓜ *American*  | 22 | 12 | 17 | $20 |

**East Hollywood** | 4854 Fountain Ave. (bet. N. Berendo & N. Catalina Sts.) | 323-661-1109 | www.squareonedining.com

"A square deal" exclaim enthusiasts of this "popular" East Hollywood "must-try" that "gets every detail right" in its "terrific", "inventive" American breakfast and lunch dishes that are "full of fresh ingredients" from local farms; with an "interesting" location "in the shadow" of a Scientology center, "it's always packed and deservedly so", making for "long" waits and "parking issues."

### Stand, The  *Hot Dogs*  | 18 | 13 | 16 | $13 |

**Century City** | 2000 Ave. of the Stars (Constellation Ave.) | 310-785-0400 Ⓢ

**NEW** **Westwood** | 1116 Westwood Blvd. (Kinross Ave.) | 310-443-0400

**Encino** | 17000 Ventura Blvd. (Genesta Ave.) | 818-788-2700

**NEW** **Woodland Hills** | Warner Center | 5780 Canoga Ave. (Burbank Blvd.) | 818-710-0400

www.thestandlink.com

"Quick, greasy and pretty darn good" declare "die-hard" fans of the "loaded" franks and burgers at these American joints whose "respectable backyard cuisine" make it a "ritual" for the "Little League crowd"; outdoor tables help beef up the digs, while "dollar dogs on Monday nights" bring extra bang for the buck in Encino and Westwood.

### Standard, The ❶ *Eclectic*  | 15 | 21 | 15 | $35 |

**Downtown** | The Standard | 550 S. Flower St. (6th St.) | 213-892-8080

**West Hollywood** | The Standard | 8300 Sunset Blvd. (Sweetzer Ave.) | 323-650-9090

www.standardhotel.com

The "late hours" are key to these "modern but retro" 24/7 locales in the Standard hotel, turning out French–Traditional American fare Downtown and Eclectic eats in WeHo; since the food strikes most as "uninspired" and service can be "dismissive", intrepid "people-gazers" often get their fix with "after-dinner drinks" at the poolside decks; N.B. a chef change Downtown is not reflected by the Food score.

### Stanley's  *Californian*  | 19 | 15 | 18 | $25 |

**Sherman Oaks** | 13817 Ventura Blvd. (bet. Mammoth & Matillja Aves.) | 818-986-4623 | www.stanleys83.com

"Still a local hangout", this Sherman Oaks Californian dating back to 1983 draws former "Valley girls and guys who have become moms and dads" for "tasty", "reasonably priced" fare, including "fantastic" Chinese chicken salad; it can get a little "noisy" inside, so "if you want to talk, the lovely back patio is the place to go."

### Stevie's Creole Cafe  *Cajun*  | ▽ 19 | 16 | 13 | $34 |

**Encino** | 16911 Ventura Blvd. (Balboa Blvd.) | 818-528-3500

"This Cajun joint is jumpin' once the NOLA-style soul singing starts" say reviewers who relish the entertainment (Thursday–Monday) at this Encino honky-tonk; the "big portions" (at "big prices") of gumbo, jambalaya and "Southern-fried" specialties can be "hit-or-miss", however, and the service often "disappoints", so some seek it out just for "music and drinks."

### Stinking Rose, The  *Italian*     18 | 19 | 19 | $37

**Beverly Hills** | 55 N. La Cienega Blvd. (Wilshire Blvd.) | 310-652-7673 | www.thestinkingrose.com

"Garlic, garlic and more garlic" greets guests (including "busloads of tourists") at this SF-export in Beverly Hills that delivers its "flavorful" Italian dishes in a "vibrant" interior with rooms "all themed around the mighty clove"; it's "wacky" and "unique", but disillusioned diners say the "too-expensive" "concept falls flat in execution" ("you realize garlic only has so much to offer") and really "belongs in an amusement park."

### NEW STK ● *Steak*     21 | 23 | 19 | $83

**West Hollywood** | 755 N. La Cienega Blvd. (Waring Ave.) | 310-659-3535 | www.stkhouse.com

"Wow, what a scene!" say samplers of this "hot" NYC import in WeHo that "surprises" with its "haute" steakhouse fare that's "delicious" if sometimes "unnecessarily complicated"; its "chic" double-decker space, which also houses the Coco de Ville lounge, has a "hip" feel, though some find it "overpriced" and "over-trendified", with too much "attitude at the door."

### Stonefire Grill  *BBQ*     18 | 13 | 15 | $17

**West Hills** | Fallbrook Ctr. | 6405 Fallbrook Ave. (Victory Blvd.) | 818-887-4145
**Valencia** | Cinema Park Plaza | 23300 Cinema Dr. (Boquet Canyon Rd.) | 661-799-8282
www.stonefiregrill.com

"Big portions and low prices" are the key to this "informal", "family-friendly" SoCal chain turning out "wonderful" salads, pizzas and "tasty" BBQ items that are "better than fast food" in "quick", order-at-the-counter fashion; since it can get "chaotic", it's often "best for takeout."

### NEW Stork, The  ⊠Ⓜ *American*     - | - | - | E

**Hollywood** | 1738 N. Orange Ave. (Hollywood Blvd.) | 323-462-3663
Situated behind the Kodak Theater, this attempt to re-create the elegance of old Hollywood supper clubs is set in two buildings joined on the second floor and outfitted with windows from Andy Warhol's Factory in New York; the dining room, adorned with sculpted topiary and just enough candles to keep it properly dim, serves pricey New American cuisine Tuesday–Sunday from 8 PM on so revelers can finish at a fashionably late hour and then lounge upstairs in . . . The Lounge.

### NEW sugarFISH  *Japanese*     - | - | - | M

**Marina del Rey** | Waterside, The | 4722¼ Admiralty Way (Mindanao Way) | 310-306-6300
Master sushi chef Kazunori Nozawa has situated this more moderately priced spin-off of his highly rated Sushi Nozawa in a sprawling Marina del Rey shopping center; the modernistic space boasts glowing walls and a long counter at which you can devour any of three preset menus; as ever, don't ask for California rolls – the decor may be contemporary, but the food is resolutely traditional.

### Suki 7  ⊠ *Japanese*     ▽ 19 | 24 | 18 | $49

**Westlake Village** | 925 Westlake Blvd. (Agoura Rd.) | 805-777-7579 | www.suki7lounge.com

"LA comes to the Conejo" at this "gorgeous" Westlake Village arrival (and sib to P6 and Chapter 8) proffering an "eclectic", "interesting"

| | FOOD | DECOR | SERVICE | COST |

Japanese menu of sushi and shabu-shabu along with "potent" libations; despite its "cool" trappings (a flowing water wall, fire pits, golden Buddhas), some disappointed diners cite "pricey", "so-so" dishes, "inattentive" service and a "cheesy" bar scene, saying the "novelty wears off" quickly.

### ☑ Sunnin  *Lebanese* — 24 | 6 | 16 | $15
**Westwood** | 1779 Westwood Blvd. (Santa Monica Blvd.) | 310-477-2358
**Long Beach** | 5110 E. Second St. (bet. Granada & Nieto Aves.) | 562-433-9000
www.sunnin.com
"Delicious" b'steeya, "scrumptious" kebabs and other "authentic" Lebanese food that's "good for the soul as well as the stomach" draws chowhounds to this "cheap", "family-run" duo in Long Beach and Westwood; while "divey" surroundings and "plastic" utensils are part of the package, loyalists assure that "looks are deceiving", so "squeeze in."

### Sur  *Californian/Mediterranean* — 21 | 24 | 21 | $48
**West Hollywood** | 606 N. Robertson Blvd. (Melrose Ave.) | 310-289-2824 | www.sur-restaurant.com
"Very Miami", this "exotic" WeHo Cal-Med features "striking architectural elements" in a virtually all-white candlelit space that's filled with "beautiful people" too; "surprised" by the "winning", "healthy"-leaning dishes and "friendly" service, many find the "reasonably priced" meals "stand up to the imaginative decor."

### ☑ Surya India  *Indian* — 24 | 17 | 22 | $33
**Third Street** | 8048 W. Third St. (bet. S. Crescent Heights Blvd. & S. Laurel Ave.) | 323-653-5151
"One of LA's hidden culinary treasures", this Third Street Indian is a "top pick" for its "innovative", "refined" cooking served in a "pleasant" space with a spicy color palette; the "warm" staff "cheerfully answers" any questions, so most don't mind that it's "a little pricier" than the norm.

### Sushi Duke  *Japanese* — ∇ 23 | 16 | 21 | $32
**Hermosa Beach** | 201 Hermosa Ave. (2nd St.) | 310-406-8986
"A real local hangout", this Hermosa Beach "gem" offers "basic" but mostly "top"-quality sushi in a "relaxed" setting with a wraparound patio; regulars say "happy hour is the time to go" (5:30–6:30 PM nightly) thanks to the half-price drinks and a special menu that makes it "incredibly affordable."

### Sushi Gen  ☒ *Japanese* — 24 | 14 | 18 | $39
**Little Tokyo** | 422 E. Second St. (Central St.) | 213-617-0552
"Fins down", this "moderately priced" Little Toyko Japanese is a "heavenly treat" for "loyal" fans who line up for its "skillfully prepared" and "unadorned" sushi; sure, the "traditionally decorated" room "isn't much" and table service is "lackluster", but if you get a seat at the "crowded" bar, the "animated" chefs make you "feel like an insider."

### Sushi Mac  ⊘ *Japanese* — 16 | 8 | 15 | $15
**Third Street** | 8474 W. Third St. (La Cienega Blvd.) | West Hollywood | 323-653-3959
**West LA** | 2222 Sawtelle Blvd. (Olympic Blvd.) | 310-481-9954
**Sherman Oaks** | 15030 Ventura Blvd. (Lemona Ave.) | 818-986-6450
The "fast-food sushi" at this "popular" Japanese mini-chain draws "poor college students" for "decent budget" rolls that are "nothing wonder-

ful" but "satisfy a craving" on the "cheap"; with its "zero-frills" atmosphere, "ridiculously loud" music and basic counter service, it's "not a place to take someone you want to impress"; N.B. no alcohol or BYO.

**Sushi Masu** Ⓜ *Japanese*     26 | 12 | 21 | $38

**West LA** | 1911 Westwood Blvd. (bet. La Grange & Missouri Aves.) | 310-446-4368

"Masu-san, the master" "expertly prepares" the "freshest fish" with "Zen-like selflessness and a twinkle in his eye" at this West LA "sushi haven" known for its "delectable", "pure and unadulterated" Japanese fare; guests agree the "unassuming" interior "may not be the most elegant on the block", but it "quietly" provides one of the "best values" around.

**Sushi Mon** *Japanese*     19 | 14 | 15 | $31

**Third Street** | 8562 W. Third St. (Holt Ave.) | West Hollywood | 310-246-9230
**Santa Monica** | 401 Santa Monica Blvd. (4th St.) | 310-576-7011

"Generous cuts of fish" and "inexpensive" tabs lure locals to this "unpretentious" Santa Monica and Third Street pair offering an "excellent selection of rolls" among other "creative" Japanese dishes; critics cite "nondescript" digs and "shaky" service, but others commend it as a "solid" sushi choice.

**Sushi Nozawa** Ⓩ *Japanese*     26 | 6 | 12 | $56

**Studio City** | 11288 Ventura Blvd. (bet. Arch & Tropical Drs.) | 818-508-7017

He "makes the Soup Nazi look polite", but "follow his rules and you're in for a culinary treat" advise acolytes of "artisan chef" Kazunori Nozawa who provides a "sublime balance of superb fish and heavenly rice" at this "expensive" "old-school sushi bar" in a Studio City strip mall; true, "it's not cozy and you won't be pampered like royalty" (in fact you could get "kicked out" for using your cell phone), but it's a "must" for the "serious" omakase connoisseur.

**Sushi Ozekii** *Japanese*     ▽ 17 | 16 | 20 | $30

**Beverly Hills** | 480 S. San Vicente Blvd. (La Cienega Blvd.) | 323-852-1799
**Agoura Hills** | 5653 Kanan Rd. (Agoura Rd.) | 818-991-4345 Ⓩ
**Camarillo** | 4421 E. Las Posas Rd., Ste. E (Lewis Rd.) | 805-389-1164 Ⓩ

"Quick", "friendly" service is a highlight at this Japanese mini-chain rolling out sushi of "exceptional size" that a number of reviewers rate "ok but uninspired"; still, the bright, "lively" atmosphere and middle-market prices go a long way in keeping regulars "happy."

**Sushi Roku** *Japanese*     22 | 22 | 19 | $49

**Third Street** | 8445 W. Third St. (bet. Croft Ave. & La Cienega Blvd.) | 323-655-6767 ☽
**Santa Monica** | 1401 Ocean Ave. (Santa Monica Blvd.) | 310-458-4771 ☽
**Pasadena** | One Colorado | 33 Miller Alley (bet. Colorado & Fair Oaks Blvds.) | 626-683-3000
www.sushiroku.com

Setting "the standard for trendy sushi", this "very LA" Japanese trio is "still a scene after all these years" and comes through with "high-quality" fish, "wonderful" cooked dishes and "delicious cocktails" served in a "chic" space; while the staff can be a bit "unpredictable", and some assert it's an "overpriced" "social" spot more than a dining destination, others relish its "nightclub" vibe, recommending you "have an attitude and dress with sex appeal" when you roll in.

| | FOOD | DECOR | SERVICE | COST |
|---|---|---|---|---|

### Sushi Sasabune 🌮 *Japanese*     26 | 13 | 19 | $62

**West LA** | 12400 Wilshire Blvd. (Centinela Ave.) | 310-268-8380

"In-the-know" guests "give it up to the chef and enjoy" at this omakase-only Japanese in West LA where the "delicate" combinations of the "freshest fish and warm rice" are "simply amazing", earning them a place as a "line item" in more than a few personal budgets; the "spacious" location feels too "cafeteria"-like to some, but many agree "the quality makes up for the sterility of the setting"; N.B. closed Saturday–Sunday.

### Sushi Sushi 🌮 *Japanese*     ▽ 24 | 12 | 19 | $62

**Beverly Hills** | 326½ S. Beverly Dr. (bet. Gregory Way & Olympic Blvd.) | 310-277-1165

"Do not show up expecting to get a California roll" at this "top-notch", "authentic" Japanese featuring "elegant" sushi by chef-owner Hiroshige Yamada whose "expensive" omakase is a "real treat"; though the casual space is "tiny", it remains a "favorite" of fans who don't mind "waiting" to "eat at the bar."

### Sushi Zo 🌮 *Japanese*     ▽ 29 | 16 | 19 | $65

**West LA** | 9824 National Blvd. (bet. Castle Heights & Manning Aves.) | 310-842-3977

"Purist heaven", this omakase-only "hidden gem" in West LA provides "unique" sushi that's "superbly prepared and presented" from "stern" "master" chef Keizo Seki and his "authoritative" crew of "soy sauce valkyries" in a "quiet", modern space; though customers say "yikes on the cost" (and "the rules"), they get that they're "paying for the quality of the fish."

### Susina Bakery & Cafe *Bakery*     22 | 19 | 17 | $16

**La Brea** | 7122 Beverly Blvd. (La Brea Ave.) | 323-934-7900 | www.susinabakery.com

An "oasis of sugary bliss", this "little" La Brea bakery packs "big-time calories" with its "exceptional" cakes, "to-die-for" cookies and other "delectable" desserts, not to mention its "fabulous" salads and sandwiches; it can get a little "busy", but there's "service with a smile" at the counter, and the "cute Parisian decor" adds extra "charm."

### Sweet Lady Jane ●🌮 *Bakery*     23 | 13 | 15 | $17

**Melrose** | 8360 Melrose Ave. (bet. N. Kings Rd. & N. Orlando Ave.) | 323-653-7145 | www.sweetladyjane.com

Worthy of a "pilgrimage" for passionate patrons, this "itty-bitty" Melrose bakery is a "shrine" to "marvelous", "memorable" desserts boasting "fancy" "handiwork", as well as "fresh" sandwiches and other savory goods; warier types warn of "counter madness and tiny tables" along with "pricey" tabs, and say "they need a sweeter staff" to match the "fantastic" treats.

### Swingers ● *Diner*     17 | 15 | 15 | $17

**Beverly Boulevard** | Beverly Laurel Motor Hotel | 8020 Beverly Blvd. (Laurel Ave.) | 323-653-5858

**Santa Monica** | 802 Broadway (Lincoln Blvd.) | 310-393-9793

They may be "glorified coffee shops" but they're "all you need" in the wee hours say nightbirds of these "retro" Beverly Boulevard and Santa Monica joints turning out "solid upscale diner" eats (including the "best 2 AM breakfasts") for a "hip" crowd; despite the "attitude" of the staff, they're "chill hangout spots", complete with "cozy booths" and a "wide-ranging" jukebox.

**Swinging Door** ⬛ *BBQ*    ▽ 22 | 7 | 18 | $16

**North Hollywood** | 11018 Vanowen St. (Vineland St.) | 818-763-8996 | www.swingingdoorbbq.com

It's all about the "swingin' ribs" at this "oddly located" North Hollywood joint plating up "huge portions" of "excellent" Texas-style BBQ; though "hole-in-the-wall doesn't even begin to describe it", the "reasonable prices" and perks like live country music keep it jumping.

**Taiko** *Japanese*    20 | 14 | 18 | $25

**Brentwood** | Brentwood Gdns. | 11677 San Vicente Blvd. (Barrington Ave.) | 310-207-7782

**El Segundo** | 2041 Rosecrans Ave. (Sepulveda Blvd.) | 310-647-3100

"Unbeatable udon", "simple" sushi and other "satisfying" Japanese dishes draw diners to these "reasonable", "not-too-fancy" eateries in Brentwood and El Segundo; "innovation is not their strong point" and the surroundings feel "sterile" to some, but their lack of "attitude and snobbery" keeps them "well-populated" with a "diverse local clientele."

**Taix** *French*    16 | 15 | 21 | $29

**Echo Park** | 1911 Sunset Blvd. (Glendale Blvd.) | 213-484-1265 | www.taixfrench.com

"Your grandma will love it" assure surveyors of this Echo Park "institution" where the "fine" "old-school" staff has been dishing out "decent" (if "extremely predictable") "French comfort food", enhanced by an "incredible" wine list, for decades; sure, it's "a bit long in the tooth" and both the menu and "stale" decor "need some fresh air", but, regardless, it's a "wonderful value" and still "fills a niche."

**⎇ Takami Sushi & Robata** *Japanese*    20 | 28 | 19 | $51

**Downtown** | 811 Wilshire Blvd., 21st fl. (bet. Figueroa & Flower Sts.) | 213-236-9600 | www.takamisushi.com

"LA finally has a hip high-rise restaurant" with this "seductive" 21st-floor Downtowner where a "fabulous" clientele savors "stunning" views and an "ethereal" atmosphere; the "innovative" Japanese menu is generally "good", if less dazzling than the design, but it's "expensive" for "minuscule" portions, so reviewers recommend "go for the taste, not to satisfy your hunger."

**Takao** *Japanese*    24 | 12 | 21 | $49

**Brentwood** | 11656 San Vicente Blvd. (bet. Barrington & Darlington Aves.) | 310-207-8636

"Excellent" sushi and "run-down" digs make an "unexpected combination" at this Brentwood Japanese by chef-owner Takao Izumida who prepares an "imaginative variety" of raw and cooked dishes served by a solid staff; while it's a touch "expensive" given the "unimpressive" interior, it remains a "neighborhood favorite" among "Gen-X parents with their children", and "you do run into a few celebrities now and then."

**Talésai** *Thai*    22 | 17 | 20 | $35

**West Hollywood** | 9043 Sunset Blvd. (Doheny Dr.) | 310-275-9724 | www.talesai.com

**Beverly Hills** | 9198 Olympic Blvd. (Oakhurst Dr.) | 310-271-9345 | www.talesai.com

*(continued)*

### Talésai

**Studio City** | 11744 Ventura Blvd. (bet. Colfax Ave. & Laurel Canyon Blvd.) | 818-753-1001 🗗

"Entertaining the taste buds", these "high-end" "gourmet Thai" siblings earn kudos for their "generous" plates of "well-prepared", "addictive" dishes served by an "attentive" staff; "stylish" settings are another plus, though the Beverly Hills location is "tinier" than the others; N.B. the Studio City branch is separately owned.

### Talia's  *Italian*

24 | 21 | 22 | $45

**Manhattan Beach** | 1148 Manhattan Ave. (12th St.) | 310-545-6884 | www.taliasrestaurant.com

A "gem" in Manhattan Beach, this "upscale" Italian "nook" has surveyors smitten with its "terrific" Italian fare served in a "cozy" setting; the service is generally "personable", adding to its rep as a "special" place.

### Tama Sushi  *Japanese*

25 | 16 | 21 | $41

**Studio City** | 11920 Ventura Blvd. (bet. Carpenter Ave. & Laurel Canyon Blvd.) | 818-760-4585 | www.tamasushi.net

Chef-owner Katsu Michite (Katsu Sushi) crafts "superlative" sushi that's "always fresh and creative" as well as "adventurous", "beautiful" cooked dishes at this "outstanding-value" Studio City Japanese whose staff "makes you feel welcome the moment you walk in the door"; since its otherwise "not very special" setting is "less crowded" than some of the competition, loyalists label it "the most underrated on Ventura row."

### Tamayo  🗗  *Mexican*

∇ 18 | 26 | 18 | $25

**East LA** | 5300 E. Olympic Blvd. (bet. Amalia & S. Hillview Aves.) | 323-260-4700

"A bit of grand old Mexico in East LA", this "salon" will "take your breath away" with its original paintings and tapestries by Rufino Tamayo in a restored 1928 "Spanish hacienda"; solid service, occasional entertainment and a "reasonable" bill are other assets, and while the "authentic" food (including "excellent" 'fish of the day' specials) "isn't as inspiring as the surroundings", most say it "doesn't disappoint."

### Tam O'Shanter Inn  *Scottish*

21 | 22 | 23 | $39

**Atwater Village** | 2980 Los Feliz Blvd. (Boyce Ave.) | 323-664-0228 | www.lawrysonline.com

"Wear a kilt and get into the scene" at this "kitschy" Atwater Village "throwback" (in the Lawry's family) that's been turning out "hearty" Scottish "comfort food and strong drinks" since 1922 in a "dark interior" with "old-fashioned booths"; it's a bit "crusty", but with "A-plus service" and "reasonable prices", it's a "family favorite at the holidays."

### Tanino  *Italian*

23 | 21 | 21 | $45

**Westwood** | 1043 Westwood Blvd. (bet. Kinross & Weyburn Aves.) | 310-208-0444 | www.tanino.com

Sated surveyors say it "rocks" to "blow your carb-avoiding diet with amazing pasta" among other "skillfully prepared" Southern Italian fare "served with grace" at this Westwood "oasis" by chef-owner Tanino Drago; while it's "expensive" and the two-story space with antique chandeliers is on the "rococo" side, it's a "favorite" for "special occasions" and convenient "before the Geffen Playhouse"; P.S. "if you're in a rush, ask for the bar area."

**Tantra** ☑ *Indian*  |  20 | 24 | 17 | $33

**Silver Lake** | 3705 W. Sunset Blvd. (Edgecliffe Dr.) | 323-663-8268 | www.tantrasunset.com

"Bringing sexy back", this "trendy" Silver Lake "date spot" attracts "scenesters" to its "sensuous", "palace"-like space for "clever" cocktails and "creative" "New Age" Indian cuisine that's "decent, if not earth-shattering"; foes, however, find it "pretentious", faulting the servers' "attitudes", "small portions" and "pricey" tabs.

**☑ Tanzore** ☑ *Indian*  |  23 | 26 | 23 | $46

**Beverly Hills** | 50 N. La Cienega Blvd. (Wilshire Blvd.) | 310-652-3838 | www.tanzore.com

A "stunning", "sleekly modern" space with a "colorful" lounge displaying "Bollywood videos" sets the stage for "fresh", "updated" and "deftly prepared" subcontinental cuisine presented by a "knowledgeable" staff at this Beverly Hills yearling in the former space of Gaylord; while it's costlier than others, connoisseurs call the quality "right up there with London Indians."

**NEW Tapa Meze** *Mideastern/Spanish*  |  - | - | - | M

**Manhattan Beach** | 1019 Manhattan Beach Blvd. (Sepulveda Blvd.) | 310-545-8500 | www.tapameze.com

In a Manhattan Beach space that's played host to a musical chairs of restaurants, this Middle Eastern–leaning Mediterranean small-dish specialist offers a midpriced menu that, despite the eatery's name, is more about meze (dolmas, baba ghanoush) than tapas – with bigger plates such as paella and steak au poivre also available; there's a small tent over a table in the back for private events.

**Tart** *American*  |  ▽ 16 | 16 | 17 | $33

**Fairfax** | Farmer's Daughter Hotel | 115 S. Fairfax Ave. (bet. Beverly Blvd. & 3rd St.) | 323-937-3930 | www.tartrestaurant.com

"Stick with the burgers" and "killer breakfasts" say guests of this rustic Fairfax New American in the Farmer's Daughter Hotel that's "hanging in there" after some "early misfires" but needs to be more "consistent"; despite its flaws, it's "casual", "affordable" and "nice to sit outside."

**Tasca Winebar** *Spanish*  |  23 | 20 | 21 | $43

**Third Street** | 8108 W. Third St. (Crescent Heights Blvd.) | 323-951-9890 | www.tascawinebar.com

"Such a cool neighborhood spot" say supporters of this Third Street tapas joint where "delectable" French and Spanish plates (including "imaginative" specials) are paired with "fantastic" wines in a "dark", "cozy and romantic" atmosphere; add in owners who "actually care about the customers", plus a "reasonable" tab, and no wonder the scene's "in full swing."

**Taste** *American*  |  23 | 19 | 20 | $36

**West Hollywood** | 8454 Melrose Ave. (La Cienega Blvd.) | 323-852-6888 | www.ilovetaste.com

"Rather tasty", this "petite" WeHo bistro provides "flavorful" New American fare at "moderate" prices in a "lovely" bungalow with an outdoor patio (a "true pleasure" for brunch); "charmed" customers

FOOD | DECOR | SERVICE | COST

say the setting, staff and crowd all make you "feel like a local", striking a "perfect balance of sophisticated yet informal."

### Taste Chicago  *Italian*
▽ 16 | 6 | 13 | $14

**Burbank** | 603 N. Hollywood Way (W. Verdugo Ave.) | 818-563-2800 | www.tastechicago.biz

"Authentic Chicago dogs, pizzas" and Italian beef sandwiches are "the bomb" at this Burbank eatery owned by actor Joe Mantegna that's a "nice reminder" of the Windy City for some, even if critics call it a "far cry" from their favorites back home; given the "nonexistent" decor of the "small" counter joint with just "a few tables inside and outside", those with a craving often opt for "quick" takeout."

### Taverna Tony  *Greek*
20 | 19 | 20 | $38

**Malibu** | Malibu Country Mart | 23410 Civic Center Way (Cross Creek Rd.) | 310-317-9667 | www.tavernatony.com

"A slice of Greece in Malibu", this "lively" "hangout" attracts "celebs" among other locals for "shareable" plates of "terrific" classics delivered by a "well-mannered" team; the "warm" Mediterranean-style space does get "noisy", particularly when there's "kitschy" belly dancing and live music, leading some to opt for the "beautiful" patio ("if you can stand the smokers").

### Taylor's Steak House  *Steak*
21 | 17 | 21 | $37

**Koreatown** | 3361 W. Eighth St. (Ardmore Ave.) | 213-382-8449
**La Cañada Flintridge** | 901 Foothill Blvd. (Beulah Dr.) | 818-790-7668
www.taylorssteakhouse.com

"Can you say old-school?" quip customers of this steakhouse pair with "no airs" whose "solid" "aged beef" and "killer martinis" for a real "value" draw "businessmen, hipsters and those in-the-know"; "dark" and decked with red Naugahyde booths, the Koreatown branch looks "straight out of a film noir set", while the more contemporary, but still "retro", La Cañada Flintridge outpost is currently undergoing an expansion.

### Tender Greens  *American*
23 | 15 | 16 | $17

**Culver City** | 9523 Culver Blvd. (Cardiff Ave.) | 310-842-8300

"I've never gotten so excited over salad before" attest surveyors of this Culver City "alternative to fast food" where the "fresh", "appealing" New American fare prepared with "top-notch", "locally grown" ingredients appeals to "carnivores and vegetarians alike"; while the space is "small" and "utilitarian", and "lines can be long during peak hours" for "cafeteria-style ordering", most call the wait "worth it" and appreciate the "fair" bill ("talk about a cheap date!"); N.B. a new branch is opening in WeHo.

### Tengu  *Japanese*
22 | 21 | 19 | $46

**Westwood** | 10853 Lindbrook Dr. (Tiverton Ave.) | 310-209-0071 | www.tengu.com

### Tengu Santa Monica ● *Japanese*

**Santa Monica** | 1541 Ocean Ave. (bet. B'way & Colorado Ave.) | 310-587-2222

"Inventive" sushi and Asian fusion dishes impress guests at these separately owned "go-tos" – "posh" in Westwood and "hip" in Santa Monica – with an "attractive", "upscale" feel; DJs keep the music flowing at both, while the Ocean Avenue locale gets a boost from happy-hour deals and specialties like blowfish.

| | FOOD | DECOR | SERVICE | COST |
|---|---|---|---|---|

**NEW Terra** M *Californian* ▽ 22 | 20 | 21 | $55

Malibu | 21337 PCH (Las Flores Canyon Rd.) | 310-456-1221 | www.terrarestaurantla.com

Owned by "charming" couple Chris and Christine Bocchino, this new Malibu "jewel" "shines" with a "well-thought-out" menu of "inventive", "fresh" Californian fare served in a "warm", "intimate" cottage setting with a "beautiful" fireplace; as it's one of the area's more "exciting" arrivals of late, surveyors suggest "stay open-minded about the check."

**NEW Terroni** *Italian* 20 | 21 | 17 | $36

Beverly Boulevard | 7605 Beverly Blvd. (N. Curson Ave.) | 323-954-0300 | www.terroni.ca

"Full of pep" affirm samplers of this new Beverly Boulevard Italian, a "cozy" offshoot of a Toronto-based mini-chain, for its "tasty" red-sauce fare, including "homemade pastas" and thin-crust pizzas, at "wallet-friendly" prices; sure, the "wait in line is brutal" and "don't even ask" for substitutions, but the "cool vibe" makes it a "welcome arrival" to the neighborhood.

**Teru Sushi** *Japanese* 19 | 17 | 17 | $38

Studio City | 11940 Ventura Blvd. (bet. Carpenter & Radford Aves.) | 818-763-6201 | www.terusushi.com

"The place that started it all on sushi row", this moderately priced Studio City Japanese keeps rolling with "solid", "tasteful" sushi and a "lovely" outdoor patio; though detractors dub it "a shadow of itself", the dated but "welcoming" space remains "crowded" with "Valleyites" who consider it a "sure bet."

**Tesoro Trattoria** *Italian* 16 | 15 | 16 | $35

Downtown | California Plaza | 300 S. Grand Ave. (3rd St.) | 213-680-0000 | www.tesorotrattoria.com

A "short walk to the Music Center", this Downtown Italian is most sought out for its convenience and "value", though the food is generally "middle-of-the-road" and the interior likened to a "chain restaurant" (despite a "nice waterfall outside"); all in all it's "not a winner", but a "mildly ok" option "if you're seeing a show."

**Thai Dishes** *Thai* 18 | 11 | 16 | $18

Culver City | 9901 W. Washington Blvd. (Hughes Ave.) | 310-559-0987

Malibu | 22333 PCH (Carbon Canyon Rd.) | 310-456-6592

Santa Monica | 111 Santa Monica Blvd. (Ocean Ave.) | 310-394-6189

Santa Monica | 1910 Wilshire Blvd. (19th St.) | 310-828-5634

Inglewood | 11934 Aviation Blvd. (W. 119th Pl.) | 310-643-6199 ⊠

LAX | 6234 W. Manchester Ave. (Sepulveda Blvd.) | 310-342-0046

Manhattan Beach | 1015 N. Sepulveda Blvd. (11th St.) | 310-546-4147

Pasadena | 239 E. Colorado Blvd. (bet. Garfield & Marengo Sts.) | 626-304-9975 | www.mythaidishes.com

Valencia | 23328 Valencia Blvd. (bet. Bouquet Canyon Rd. & Cinema Dr.) | 661-253-3663 | www.thaidishesscv.com

"When you have a craving for Thai" this "dependable" LA chain "satisfies", so though most agree it's "nothing outstanding" and the "nondescript" decor is "wanting", it's "oh-so-affordable" and delivery is "prompt."

| | FOOD | DECOR | SERVICE | COST |
|---|---|---|---|---|

### NEW Third & Olive 🗺 *Californian/French* | - | - | - | E |

**Burbank** | 250 E. Olive Ave. (3rd St.) | 818-846-3900

Chef-owner Miki Zivkovic, of nearby Bistro Provence, goes upscale-casual with this far-more-opulent dining room in Burbank's Media District, featuring a Californian-French menu focusing on the freshest ingredients; N.B. the space was briefly home to Lasher's (from Long Beach), which explains the 'L' engraved on the door.

### 3rd Stop ● *Italian* | 17 | 16 | 17 | $23 |

**West Hollywood** | 8636 W. Third St. (S. Williams Dr.) | 310-273-3605

A seemingly "endless" selection of "specialty brews" on tap is the highlight of this WeHo "pub" that habitués dub a "perfectly pleasant place" to "catch up with friends" over Italian-inflected small plates like pizzas and sausage burgers deemed "good for snacking"; despite the occasional "persnickety" server, it cultivates a "friendly" vibe with happy-hour specials and a plasma TV keeping the concrete-and-marble bar particularly "crowded."

### Thousand Cranes, A *Japanese* | 21 | 25 | 22 | $49 |

**Little Tokyo** | Kyoto Grand Hotel | 120 S. Los Angeles St. (bet. 1st & 2nd Sts.) | 213-253-9255 | www.kyotograndhotel.com

"Waitresses in kimonos" and chefs at the sushi and tempura bar provide "carefully prepared Japanese haute cuisine" at this "lovely", "traditional" Little Tokyo restaurant in the Kyoto Grand Hotel whose "soothing atmosphere" features "tranquil" gardens and a waterfall; a number of customers feel like they're "dining in Tokyo . . . but paying Tokyo prices too."

### NEW Three Forks Chop House *Steak* | ▽ 23 | 24 | 18 | $66 |

**Claremont** | The Packing House | 580 W. First St. (Cornell Ave.) | 888-933-6757 | www.threeforkschops.com

"Forcing foodies to come to the Inland Empire", this new steakhouse in the restored Claremont Packing House provides "excellent", "beautifully presented" beef, game and seafood by "versatile" chef Eric Osley, married with an "extensive wine list"; while the "Montana"-inspired digs are "lovely", many cite "uneven" service, saying it's "not as customer-friendly as a high-end restaurant should be."

### Three on Fourth 🗺 *American/Japanese* | 21 | 17 | 22 | $47 |

**Santa Monica** | 1432 Fourth St. (Santa Monica Blvd.) | 310-395-6765 | www.3onfourth.com

"One block off the hubbub", this Santa Monica "date place" provides "innovative", "fun-to-share" small and large plates (including a "memorable" cheese selection) reflecting American, French and Japanese influences in a "comfortable" setting that's "not too loud to enjoy conversation"; it's "a bit pricey", but considering the "charming, competent" service, fans consider it a "rare find."

### 3 Square Cafe + Bakery *Bakery/Sandwiches* | 20 | 15 | 17 | $24 |

**Venice** | 1121 Abbot Kinney Blvd. (bet. San Juan & Westminster Aves.) | 310-399-6504 | www.rockenwagner.com

"Another hit from Hans Röckenwagner", this "casual" Venice cafe is "always packed" with a "yuppified" crowd thanks to a midpriced menu with "German touches" featuring "wonderful apple pancakes" at breakfast and "swell sandwiches" on pretzel buns at lunch all "whimsically" presented on square plates ("get it?"); dinner draws lower marks and decor is deemed "too minimalist" by some, but the "sunny patio" wins fans, as does the "tempting bakery" next door stocked with "amazing" cakes, scones and breads.

**Tiara Cafe**  *American*  ▽ 23 | 20 | 19 | $23

**Downtown** | 127 E. Ninth St. (Main St.) | 213-623-3663 | www.tiara-cafe.com
"A diamond in the rough", this largely organic New American from "quirky" chef-owner Fred Eric (Fred 62) plates up "fresh, healthy dishes with flair" served by a "funky" staff in "cool" high-ceilinged digs painted with sunset colors; offering plenty of "arty" "people-watching" too, it brings a refreshing dose of "character" Downtown.

**Tibet Nepal House** Ⓜ *Nepalese/Tibetan*  ▽ 19 | 15 | 17 | $23

**Pasadena** | 36 E. Holly St. (N. Fair Oaks Ave.) | 626-585-0955 | www.tibetnepalhouse.com
Pasadenans hungry for Himalayan cooking head to this casual eatery with a "large menu" of "unique" Nepalese-Tibetan fare, including "superb" dumplings and "great yak"; though some find the quality "spotty", many praise the "unbelievably cheap" weekend champagne brunch and say the owner brings a "caring" touch to the "tranquil" setting.

**🆕 Tinto** Ⓢ *Spanish*  ▽ 20 | 18 | 19 | $43

**West Hollywood** | 7511 Santa Monica Blvd. (N. Gardner St.) | 323-512-3095 | www.tintotapas.com
"Bienvenido!" exclaim amigos of this "trendy" new WeHo tapas bar dishing out "tasty", "garlicky" Spanish dishes (that "add up quickly") complemented by "fairly priced" wines; the "super-friendly", "knowledgeable" staff "has a real desire to please", which helps soften the feel of the brick-walled, "hard-surfaced" interior.

**Tlapazola Grill**  *Mexican*  23 | 15 | 22 | $30

**Marina del Rey** | 4059 Lincoln Blvd. (Washington Blvd.) | 310-822-7561 | www.tlapazolagrill.com Ⓜ
**West LA** | 11676 Gateway Blvd. (Barrington Ave.) | 310-477-1577
"Outstanding" Oaxacan food with "savory" sauces "like *abuelita* used to make" win over guests at these "gourmet" Mexican "finds" staffed by a "warm", "knowledgeable" team; though both are "hidden in a mini-mall", the newer Marina del Rey branch (serving "beer and wine only") has a more "intimate" setting that's "better for a date", while the West LA original offers plentiful "tequila options" for "premium margaritas."

**Toast**  *American*  19 | 14 | 16 | $22

**Third Street** | 8221 W. Third St. (bet. S. Harper & S. La Jolla Aves.) | 323-655-5018 | www.toastbakerycafe.net
"People-watch to your heart's content" at this Third Street American that's "jammed" with "celebs, scenesters and gawkers" nibbling on the "brunch with style" as well as other "comfort food", "healthy salads" and "freshly baked" desserts; detractors find it "overrated" and "so 2005", however, dismissing the "hour-plus waits" along with "get 'em in, get 'em out" service.

**🆕 Tofu Villa** ☾ *Korean*  - | - | - | I

**West LA** | 2130 Sawtelle Blvd. (Olympic Blvd.) | 310-477-8987
This low-cost, ultramodern Korean cafe in West LA boasts a white-on-white color scheme, plus an outdoor dining option (with a view of the

| | FOOD | DECOR | SERVICE | COST |
|---|---|---|---|---|

parking lot); it specializes in casseroles – e.g. *soon tofu* and bibimbop – though other dishes like classic barbecue fare are also prepared in the open kitchen; N.B. reasonably priced lunch specials include a soft drink.

**Tofu-Ya** *Korean*                    | 20 | 9 | 14 | $15 |

**West LA** | 2021 Sawtelle Blvd. (La Grange Ave.) | 310-473-2627 | www.tofuyabbq.com

"The lines tell the entire story" at this West LA joint where the "spicy soups" and BBQ draw "students" and others in search of affordable, "flavorful" Korean eats and a "real experience" to boot; though some call it "pricey" compared to the K-town competition, most think it's still a "great deal" and a "refreshing alternative" in the area, even if you "always have to wait."

**Tokyo Table** *Japanese*            ▽ | 19 | 20 | 20 | $34 |

**Beverly Hills** | 50 N. La Cienega Blvd. (bet. Clifton Way & Wilshire Blvd.) | 310-657-9500 Ⓜ

**NEW** **Arcadia** | Westfield Mall | 400 S. Baldwin Ave. (W. Huntington Dr.) | 626-445-4000

www.tokyotable.com

Providing a "huge, affordable" menu of Japanese fare, this "family"-friendly chain in Beverly Hills and Arcadia delivers "silky" homemade tofu among other "interesting" "contemporary" specialties, as well as "fantastic" cocktails; still, some diners are "disappointed", calling it a "Japanese Denny's" that's "struggling to find its identity."

**Tommy's** ◐⇗ *Burgers/Hot Dogs*     | 22 | 5 | 15 | $9 |

**Downtown** | 2575 W. Beverly Blvd. (bet. Coronado St. & Rampart Blvd.) | 213-389-9060 | www.originaltommys.com

"Bring lots of Tums" to this "landmark" 24-hour Downtown "chili-cheeseburger paradise" where the "messy, greasy" patties and dogs make for a "guilty pleasure", particularly after a night of "partying"; as for the "standing-only" space that's in a slightly "sketchy" locale, just remember "you're not here for decor" but for the "legendary experience", and at least the line moves "fast."

**Tony P's Dockside Grill** *American*   | 18 | 18 | 20 | $26 |

**Marina del Rey** | 4445 Admiralty Way (Bali Way) | 310-823-4534 | www.tonyps.com

"Sea breezes" and "beautiful" views are the main attraction at this waterside Marina del Rey "standby" serving "generous" plates of American eats that "stick to your fingers and your ribs"; it's "relaxing" with a partly enclosed patio and a sports bar, so even if there's "nothing spectacular" on the menu, most surveyors are satisfied with the "decent food at a decent price."

**Tony's Bella Vista** *Italian*       ▽ | 21 | 11 | 19 | $24 |

**Burbank** | 3116 W. Magnolia Blvd. (Fairview St.) | 818-843-0164 | www.tonysbellavista.com

"Forget about the trendy pizza cafes" declare Burbank customers of this "real" "old-fashioned" Italian serving "sublime" thin-crust pies among other "East Coast-style" "comfort food" from The Boot; furnished with old red leather booths, the room maintains a "down-home", "1970s" feel, while the "warm" staff "makes you feel like you've come home for dinner."

| | FOOD | DECOR | SERVICE | COST |
|---|---|---|---|---|

**Torafuku** *Japanese* | 24 | 20 | 22 | $45

**West LA** | 10914 W. Pico Blvd. (Westwood Blvd.) | 310-470-0014 |
www.torafuku-usa.com

Featuring "food for traditional Japanese tastes" (including some "real
exotica"), this West LA branch of a Tokyo mini-chain "graciously"
serves "sophisticated" sushi and cooked dishes with "excellent rice" in
a relaxed, earth-toned space; though it's on the "pricey" side, savvy
customers call lunch a "hidden bargain."

**Toscana** *Italian* | 23 | 18 | 20 | $50

**Brentwood** | 11633 San Vicente Blvd. (Darlington Ave.) | 310-820-2448
"Always thunderously noisy", this "popular" Brentwood trattoria attracts an "influential industry clientele" among other deep-pocketed
"locals" for its "primo pasta" and other "superb" Northern Italian specialties served in Tuscan-style surroundings; while the "personable"
staff definitely attends to the "stars", admirers assure "even if you
aren't one you're treated very well."

**Tower Bar** *Californian* | ▽ 21 | 27 | 22 | $66

**West Hollywood** | Sunset Tower Hotel | 8358 Sunset Blvd.
(bet. La Cienega Blvd. & Sweetzer Ave.) | 323-848-6677 |
www.sunsettowerhotel.com

A "sumptuous supper club atmosphere" prevails at this "sexy"
Californian with "stargazing galore" at the top of WeHo's Sunset
Tower Hotel, where "divine" maitre d' Dimitri Dimitrov is a "throwback
to another time in Hollywood", as is the "stunning" art deco design;
most find the food "excellently prepared", even if a few feel that it
"doesn't live up" to the setting.

**Towne** *Californian* | ▽ 18 | 21 | 19 | $40

**Manhattan Beach** | 1142 Manhattan Ave. (Manhattan Beach Blvd.) |
310-545-5405 | www.townebythesea.com

"Gen-Y gals dressed to the nines" are part of the "people-watching" at
this slightly "pricey" Manhattan Beach boîte in a Frank Lloyd Wright–
styled building where the crowd "looks good" and is treated with "care";
while opinions of the Californian fare range from "well-executed" to "just
average" for the price, many go for the drinks and the "action" at the bar.

**Tracht's** *American* | 23 | 23 | 21 | $52

**Long Beach** | Renissance Long Beach Hotel | 111 E. Ocean Blvd. (Pine Ave.) |
562-499-2533 | www.renaissancehotels.com

This "satisfying" New American arrival by chef Suzanne Tracht (Jar)
earns kudos for its "inventive" menu – "mostly a twist on upscale comfort food" – that's "worth the dough", particularly for the "best pot roast
on the planet"; despite its location in a hotel lobby, surveyors say the "elegant" space with 30-ft. windows and a "large patio" provides a "welcome respite", enhanced by "polite" if not always "polished" service.

**Tra Di Noi** *Italian* | 22 | 18 | 19 | $44

**Malibu** | Malibu Country Mart | 3835 Cross Creek Rd. (PCH) | 310-456-0169
"Tucked into" the Malibu Country Mart, this "reliable" Italian provides
a "perfect venue on a warm summer evening" thanks to an "inviting"
patio that's frequented by both "families" and "celebrities"; most call
the red-sauce fare "delicious" if "nothing earth-shaking", though the
slightly "expensive" tab is a deterrent for some.

|  | FOOD | DECOR | SERVICE | COST |
|---|---|---|---|---|

### Trails, The Ⓜ⇗ *American/Vegan* ▽ 16 | 18 | 12 | $13

**Los Feliz** | Griffith Park | 2333 Fern Dell Dr. (Los Feliz Blvd.) | 323-871-2102 |
www.thetrailscafe.com

"How can you go wrong?" ask Los Feliz fans of this "cool little snack shack" that's "tucked away" in Griffith Park, soothing hungry hikers with its "simple" American vegan eats, including "homemade baked goods"; outdoor seating at the picnic tables is "pleasant", offering a WiFi connection for techies.

### NEW Tranquility Base ● *Californian/Eclectic* _ | _ | _ | M

**Downtown** | 801 S. Grand Ave. (8th St.) | 213-404-0588 |
www.tranquilitybaselosangeles.com

Further proof that Downtown is on the rise: the arrival of this dramatic, high-ceilinged Cal-Eclectic on the ground floor of Grand Avenue's new Sky Lofts, an upscale aerie for pioneers colonizing this in-transition neighborhood; the name references Apollo 11's moon landing site, while the decor and globally inspired small plates also take their cues from the celestial, changing quarterly with each equinox and solstice.

### Trastevere *Italian* 17 | 17 | 17 | $33

**Hollywood** | Hollywood & Highland Ctr. | 6801 Hollywood Blvd. (Highland Ave.) | 323-962-3261
**Santa Monica** | 1360 Third St. Promenade (Santa Monica Blvd.) | 310-319-1985
www.trastevereristorante.com

Reviewers "refuel with carbs after hours of shopping" at these twin Italians at Hollywood & Highland and the Santa Monica Promenade turning out "standard" "trattoria basics"; some dismiss the grub as "overpriced" "mall food", but their "busy central locations" make for "top-notch people-watching", especially at the outdoor tables.

### Traxx Ⓧ *American* 20 | 22 | 19 | $42

**Downtown** | Union Station | 800 N. Alameda St. (bet. Cesar Chavez Ave. & Rte. 101) | 213-625-1999 | www.traxxrestaurant.com

"Reminiscent of the days of train travel", this "unique" Union Station destination "feeds all the senses" with its "imaginative" upscale New American fare that's "almost up to the surroundings" of its "retro" art deco room; service can be "variable", but it's offset by prime "people-watching" both inside and on the "beautiful" patio.

### Tre Venezie Ⓜ *Italian* 25 | 21 | 22 | $57

**Pasadena** | 119 W. Green St. (De Lacey St.) | 626-795-4455

"Quirkily authentic", this Pasadena "jewel" offers "genuine", "stunning" Northern Italian fare (some hailing from the "Friuli-Venezia Giulia" region) and "superb" wines in a "tiny" but "cozy" space staffed by "sophisticated" servers who "make you feel like a special guest"; despite "steep" prices, respondents reason that the "cost reflects the effort" and it's worth "booking well in advance."

### Trio Mediterranean Grill *Mediterranean* 20 | 15 | 22 | $26

**Rolling Hills Estates** | Peninsula Ctr. | 46B Peninsula Ctr. (Hawthorne Blvd.) | Rolling Hills | 310-265-5577 | www.triogrille.com

"Reliably tasty" Mediterranean dishes meet the need for a "casual" meal at this "local spot" in a Rolling Hills Estates shopping center that comes in "handy" for "families" thanks to its "reasonable prices" and "comfortable" digs; since the friendly staff is "willing" to pitch in with recommendations too, most find it well "worth" repeated visits.

**Triumphal Palace** *Chinese* | 21 | 17 | 14 | $27 |

**Alhambra** | 500 W. Main St. (5th St.) | 626-308-3222

Devotees "dream about" the "creative" made-to-order dim sum at this "truly special" "gourmet" Chinese in Alhambra that's "a bit more expensive" than competitors, but "worth it" given the "opulent" white-tablecloth surroundings; though a language barrier can impede service, most are willing to overlook that and occasional "waits" given such "sublime" fare.

**Tropicalia Brazilian Grill** ● *Brazilian* | 20 | 13 | 19 | $21 |

**Los Feliz** | 1966 Hillhurst Ave. (Franklin Ave.) | 323-644-1798 | www.tropicaliabraziliangrill.com

"A wonderful variety" of "homestyle" Brazilian specialties (think slow-braised pork and "fresh" salads) "delights the tummies" of Los Feliz locals at this "casual" cafe, also prized for its "unbeatable prices"; the staff is "attentive", and though the vividly hued setting proves "pleasant enough", most prefer to "sit out on the patio" with a "pitcher of sangria" and "watch the people go by"; P.S. afterwards, "hop on over" to the adjacent wine bar.

**Truxton's** *American* | - | - | - | M |

**Westchester** | 8611 Truxton Ave. (Manchester Ave.) | 310-417-8789 | www.truxtonsamericanbistro.com

Just north of LAX, housed in a warmed up industrial space hidden from the street, this casual, environmentally conscious New American eatery incorporates plenty of global and ethnic influences into its menu, producing dishes running the gamut from turkey burritos to grilled pizzas to miso salmon; a menu of martinis and margaritas lends it after-work appeal, while fresh-squeezed juices and a few nonalcoholic cocktails keep teetotalers satisfied too.

**Tsuji No Hana** *Japanese* | 20 | 12 | 18 | $30 |

**Marina del Rey** | 4714 Lincoln Blvd. (Mindanao Way) | 310-827-1433

Customers count this Marina del Rey sushi specialist for "solid" "straightforward" nigiri and maki fit for a "reliable" meal; "small" strip-mall digs are on the basic side too, but "service with a smile" gives it a "neighborly" vibe, and prices are "reasonable" as well.

**Tuk Tuk Thai** *Thai* | 21 | 17 | 18 | $24 |

**Pico-Robertson** | 8875 W. Pico Blvd. (bet. Doheny Dr. & Robertson Blvd.) | 310-860-1872 | www.tuktukla.com

"Perfect for a date", this "cute, little" Thai distinguishes itself from Pico-Robertson competitors with "fresh", "fusion" flavors, fruity soju cocktails and an "attractive" atmosphere with rose-hued walls and "intimate" lighting; "reasonable prices" and an "attentive staff" also make it a "favorite" for locals who rely on it for a "pad Thai fix" and say the "takeout" always arrives "good and hot."

**Tulipano** Ⓜ *Italian* | ▽ 24 | 13 | 25 | $32 |

**Azusa** | 530 S. Citrus Ave. (Gladstone St.) | 626-967-6670

Though it "looks like nothing" from the outside, this well-priced strip-mall Italian in Azusa charms customers with "personal" attention

| | FOOD | DECOR | SERVICE | COST |
|---|---|---|---|---|

from owners-hosts Eduardo and Vincenzo Carrano; after the warm welcome, admirers attest it "only gets better" with "top-notch" "homestyle" cooking proffered by a staff so "accommodating" that "special orders are never a problem."

### Tuscany II Ristorante  *Italian*

**24 | 21 | 24 | $50**

**Westlake Village** | Westlake Plaza | 968 S. Westlake Blvd. (Townsgate Rd.) | 805-495-2768 | www.tuscany-restaurant.com

Westlake customers cherish this "bit of Italy" in the Conejo Valley sending out "well-crafted" regional dishes that consistently "exceed expectations"; "warm" service boosts the "charm" of the "lovely" room done up in muted tones, and though "upscale" pricing may mean some save it for "special occasions", most say it's "always a treat", no matter when you go.

### NEW Twelve + Highland ❶ *American*

**▽ 21 | 20 | 14 | $46**

**Manhattan Beach** | 304 12th St. (Highland Ave.) | 310-545-1881 | www.12andhighland.com

"Unique" for the area, this posh Manhattan Beach newcomer flaunts a sleek "cutting-edge" space done up in shades of gray and lavender with a poured concrete bar; it earns measured praise for its "varied" menu of "well-presented" (if "pricey") New American dishes, but critics say "service suffers" slamming "enormous attitude" and long waits for food; N.B. on Fridays–Saturdays they have a DJ and dancing after 10 PM.

### 25 Degrees ❶ *Burgers*

**21 | 18 | 15 | $25**

**Hollywood** | Roosevelt Hotel | 7000 Hollywood Blvd. (Orange Dr.) | 323-785-7244 | www.25degreesrestaurant.com

Now open 24/7, this "über-cool" "high-end" "burger palace" in the historic Roosevelt Hotel puts the emphasis on "cooked-to-perfection" patties topped with "artisanal cheeses" and a variety of sauces served up in a "dark" "bohemian bordello"-style setting; regulars note that "service can be erratic", luckily "Hollywood Boulevard's loony locals" provide "continuous entertainment" while you wait.

### 2117 Ⓜ *Asian/European*

**23 | 13 | 20 | $37**

**West LA** | 2117 Sawtelle Blvd. (bet. Mississippi Ave. & Olympic Blvd.) | 310-477-1617 | www.restaurant2117.com

"Innovative" chef-owner Hideyo Mitsuno puts on a "wonderful one-man show" whipping up "simple", "elegant" Asian-European dishes at this "still not-too-well-known" "gem" tucked away in a West LA strip mall; though its "austere" setting could use "sprucing up", service is "friendly" and prices a relative "bargain", leading loyalists to insist it "deserves to be more crowded."

### 22nd St. Landing Ⓜ *Seafood*

**18 | 18 | 18 | $35**

**San Pedro** | 141A W. 22nd St. (Harbor Blvd.) | 310-548-4400 | www.22ndstlandingrestaurant.com

"Get a table overlooking the harbor" and dig into some "fresh fish" at this family-friendly seafooder on the San Pedro waterfront offering "plentiful" menu options "for seafarers and landlubbers alike"; surveyors split on the nautically themed decor ("tired" vs. full of "character") and service is sometimes "slow", but supporters swear the "wonderful views" and moderate prices make up for any shortcomings.

|  | FOOD | DECOR | SERVICE | COST |
|--|------|-------|---------|------|

### 26 Beach *Californian*
|  | 20 | 18 | 18 | $26 |

**Marina del Rey** | 3100 Washington Blvd. (Lincoln Blvd.) | 310-823-7526
A "quaint" courtyard and "funky" "shabby-chic" interior make a "charming backdrop" for "eclectic" Californian cuisine at this "popular" Marina del Rey "standby" – a "top-notch pick for a second date" that's also "safe enough" for "the in-laws"; an "extensive" lineup of "terrific" burgers and salads plus an "amazing" brunch mean regulars "never get sick of it", and "enormous portions" signal good "value" too.

### Twin Palms *American*
|  | 18 | 20 | 17 | $35 |

**Pasadena** | 101 W. Green St. (De Lacey Ave.) | 626-577-2567 | www.twin-palms.com
The "stylish" tented setting gives a "quintessentially SoCal" feel to this Pasadena mainstay that plays host to a "lively" bar scene most nights and "live jazz" on Thursdays; the New American menu veers toward "fresh food with a healthy bent" (think "mile-high salads" and herb-crusted filet mignon) though doubters declare "the quality varies" and suggest you "stick to lunch" or "simple items to avoid disappointment."

### Typhoon *Pan-Asian*
|  | 22 | 20 | 19 | $37 |

**Santa Monica** | Santa Monica Airport | 3221 Donald Douglas Loop S. (Airport Ave.) | 310-390-6565 | www.typhoon.biz
Set "at the edge of the Santa Monica airport", this "unique" Pan-Asian "inspires" with both its "unforgettable" location overlooking the runway and "inventive" menu showcasing "exotic" insect dishes – like Singapore-style scorpions and sautéed crickets – alongside a "vast array" of more familiar offerings like fried catfish and curries; factor in "timely" service and an "upbeat vibe", and even if cynics charge it's "gimmicky", most maintain it's a "must" when you're seeking something "a little different."

### Ugo an Italian Bar *Italian*
|  | 17 | 15 | 17 | $24 |

**NEW** **Culver City** | 9501 Culver Blvd. (Cardiff Ave.)
### Ugo an Italian Cafe *Italian*
**Culver City** | 3865 Cardiff Ave. (Culver Blvd.) | 310-204-1222 www.cafeugo.com
This "pleasant" Culver City duo offers up "a lot of bang for your buck" with "better-than-average" Italian eats like "thin-crust pizzas", "simple salads", a "big selection" of regional wines and "indulgent" homemade gelato in 36 flavors (at the cafe only); though the sidewalk seating is well-suited to "lounging", it runs afoul for critics who say the overall package "lacks character."

### Ulysses Voyage *Greek*
|  | 21 | 16 | 18 | $30 |

**Fairfax** | Grove at Farmers Mkt. | 6333 W. Third St. (Fairfax Ave.) | 323-939-9728 | www.ulyssesvoyage.com
"Homestyle" Greek dishes like "delicious salads and dips" and "excellent lamb" prove "surprisingly authentic" at this midpriced Fairfax Hellenic tucked inside The Grove; the interior is "tight, but cute" and features "live bouzouki players" nightly, though converts claim that outside the "relaxing" patio and "passing parade" of shoppers "makes the food taste even better."

|  | FOOD | DECOR | SERVICE | COST |
|---|---|---|---|---|

### Ummba Grill *Brazilian* | 16 | 11 | 13 | $21 |

**Century City** | Westfield Century City Shopping Ctr. |
10250 Santa Monica Blvd. (bet. Ave. of the Stars & Century Park W.) |
310-552-2014

"It's all about the beef" at this Brazilian BBQ in Century City's
Westfield Shopping Center offering a "nice change from the standard
food-court fare" with grilled meats, salads and sides priced by the
pound (beware: "the plates are heavy!"); though some shoppers say
it's "ok for a quick fix", the "lunchroom-type lines" inspire compari-
sons to a "cafeteria", while detractors dis "not that tasty" grub and
claim to save it "for drinks only."

### Uncle Bill's Pancake House *Diner* | 21 | 12 | 19 | $14 |

**Manhattan Beach** | 1305 Highland Ave. (13th St.) | 310-545-5177

A "local legend" in Manhattan Beach, this "do-no-wrong" breakfast
"standby" dishes out "incredibly tasty" inexpensive diner staples like
"fluffy" flapjacks and "amazing omelets" best enjoyed "sitting on the
porch overlooking the ocean"; though the "small" space is "perpetually crowded" (especially "on weekends"), the "personable" staff
"knows how to turn a table" and keeps the "long lines moving" quickly.

### Uncle Darrow's *Cajun/Creole* | 19 | 8 | 19 | $14 |

**Venice** | 2560 S. Lincoln Blvd. (Washington Blvd.) | 310-306-4862 |
www.uncledarrows.com

Venice diners dig this "quick-bite" Cajun-Creole that conjures up a
"South Louisiana roadhouse" with "spicy" jambalaya and po' boys
heading up the beef-and-pork-free menu; despite "basic" "fast-food"-
style digs, "personal attention" adds a "homey" touch, so even if some
say they "wouldn't go out of [their] way for it", "if you're in the neighborhood", it's "worth a shot."

### Upstairs 2 🅂🅜 *Mediterranean* | 24 | 18 | 21 | $44 |

**West LA** | Wine House | 2311 Cotner Ave. (Olympic Blvd.) | 310-231-0316 |
www.upstairs2.com

Stylish sippers "sit at the bar" and "sample" "flavorful" Mediterranean
small plates and "tastes of wine" from a "sensational" list at this West LA
boîte "hidden" above the Wine House retail shop ("you have to know it's
there"); a "knowledgeable" staff that "helps with pairings" keeps the atmosphere "pleasant" in spite of "cramped" digs, though noshers should
note that all this "delicious" "experimentation" can really add up.

### Urasawa 🅂🅜 *Japanese* | ∇ 28 | 22 | 25 | $390 |

**Beverly Hills** | 218 N. Rodeo Dr. (Wilshire Blvd.) | 310-247-8939

"It's more than dinner, it's an experience" insist acolytes of chef and
"artisan" Hiro Urasawa whose "sublime" omakase-only Beverly Hills
Japanese showcases his "masterful techniques" and "exquisite presentations" of "exotic" fish flown in from Japan in 20–30 "luxurious"
courses that "excite all the senses"; add "impeccable service", and it's
an "enlightening" experience sure to "sweep you off your feet", as will
the "breathtakingly expensive" prices.

### Urth Caffé *American* | 20 | 15 | 15 | $19 |

**West Hollywood** | 8565 Melrose Ave. (bet. La Cienega & Robertson Blvds.) |
310-659-0628

*(continued)*

*(continued)*

### Urth Caffé

**Beverly Hills** | 267 S. Beverly Dr. (Gregory Way) | 310-205-9311 | www.urthcaffe.com ◑
**Santa Monica** | 2327 Main St. (bet. Ocean Park & Pico Blvds.) | 310-314-7040 | www.urthcaffe.com

"Fantastic organic coffee drinks" fuel the patio "mob scenes" at this "hyperpopular" trio where a "star-studded" crowd ("especially on Melrose") munches on "healthy" American fare like "expensive granola" and "huge salads" capped with "scrumptious desserts"; "ridiculous lines" and "fights for a table" are regular occurrences, but once the food gets "plonked down", it's really quite "continental" as "übercool" customers "hang casually" for hours.

### uWink *Californian*                     13 | 17 | 13 | $22

**NEW** Hollywood | Hollywood & Highland Ctr. | 6801 Hollywood Blvd. (Highland Ave.) | 323-466-1800
**Woodland Hills** | Westfield Promenade | 6100 Topanga Canyon Blvd. (bet. Erwin & Oxnard Sts.) | 818-992-1100 ◑
www.uwink.com

The "food is second to the 'concept'" at this "novel" Woodland Hills eatery from the founder of Chuck E. Cheese and Atari appealing to "six-year-olds" and "techies" with an "automated" tabletop ordering system and "interactive" video games available during meals; though the "goofy" "*Jetsons*"-style setup is a kick for the little ones ("I couldn't get my kids to leave"), parents have less to praise considering only "average" Californian eats and "deafening" acoustics; N.B. a second location at Hollywood & Highland is now open.

### U-Zen *Japanese*                        22 | 12 | 21 | $32

**West LA** | 11951 Santa Monica Blvd. (Brockton St.) | 310-477-1390
Sushi lovers seek out this West LA "locals' favorite" where "friendly chefs" slice up "excellent quality" fish in a bare-bones setting with a communal table and bar seating; it's "nothing fancy", but regulars report that "reasonable prices" and a "welcoming" vibe are "enough" to keep them coming back.

### ☑ Valentino ⓈItalian                    26 | 24 | 25 | $72

**Santa Monica** | 3115 Pico Blvd. (bet. 31st & 32nd Sts.) | 310-829-4313 | www.welovewine.com

"Still sublime" sigh "well-heeled" customers who cherish this "grande dame" of Santa Monica Italians that "remains superb" after more than 35 years thanks to "flawless" service (overseen by "gracious" host Piero Selvaggio), "masterful" cooking and an "incomparable" 3,000-label wine list that makes oenophiles "cry with joy"; a "beautiful renovation" in 2007 freshened up the "elegant" gold-toned dining areas, though the rooms with semiprivate "alcoves" remain as "romantic" as ever, while a "new wine bar" offers "smaller bites, informal surroundings and lower prices."

### Vault, The *American*                    ▽ 14 | 18 | 14 | $26

**Pasadena** | 2675 E. Colorado Blvd. (N. San Gabriel Blvd.) | 626-683-3344 | www.thevaultpasadena.com

A "stylish" setting in a converted bank proves a draw for the "happy-hour" crowd at this "upscale" watering hole in Pasadena boasting mul-

|  | FOOD | DECOR | SERVICE | COST |
|--|------|-------|---------|------|

tiple plasma TVs and "comfortable" patio seating; yet in spite of some "tasty appetizers", most maintain the "fairly priced" American eats are only "average", and add that even with posh furnishings, it just can't shake the "sports bar feel."

### Vegan Glory  *Vegan*
| 20 | 9 | 20 | $16 |

**Beverly Boulevard** | 8393 Beverly Blvd. (Orlando Ave.) | 323-653-4900 | www.veganglory.com

Surveyors seeking "fresh-tasting" vegan vittles turn to this inexpensive eatery on Beverly Boulevard for "vibrant" Thai-influenced cooking that some say they could "eat every day"; though service is "efficient", given the "standard mini-mall" decor, many opt for "takeout."

### NEW Veggie Grill, The  *Vegan*
| 19 | 15 | 18 | $15 |

**El Segundo** | Plaza El Segundo | 720 Allied Way (Rosecrans Ave.) | 310-535-0025 | www.veggiegrill.com

"Fresh and healthy" fare is the focus of this glossy vegan chainlet whipping up "flavorful" meat-free alternatives that might even "fool hard-core carnivores"; though some say the menu lacks "kick", "good-value" pricing is a plus, as is the "well-meaning" staff that really seems to "care about repeat business."

### Velvet Margarita Cantina ● *Mexican*
| 17 | 23 | 16 | $30 |

**Hollywood** | 1612 N. Cahuenga Blvd. (bet. Hollywood Blvd. & Selma Ave.) | 323-469-2000 | www.velvetmargarita.com

"Loud, crowded and dark", this cavernous Hollywood "hot spot" is beloved by hipsters for its "psychedelic" "Mexi-Goth" decor with black-lit paintings and blue-velvet walls; tipplers tout the "outstanding margaritas" and mariachi nightly and say that even if "there's nothing special" about the south-of-the-border fare, the setting alone (not to mention the "pretty people" that populate it) makes it "worth a look."

### vermont  *American*
| 21 | 21 | 20 | $43 |

**Los Feliz** | 1714 N. Vermont Ave. (Prospect Ave.) | 323-661-6163 | www.vermontrestaurantonline.com

"Still a class act" attest aficionados of this Los Feliz boîte where the "sophisticated" New American cuisine, "welcoming" atmosphere and "romantic" setting with exposed brick and high ceilings make it the "place to impress a first date"; though some suggest it's "overpriced", most insist they're willing to "pay a pretty penny" given that it's such a "pleasure to dine here"; N.B. the Decor score does not reflect a summer 2008 remodel.

### Versailles  *Cuban*
| 21 | 9 | 17 | $19 |

**Mid-City** | 1415 S. La Cienega Blvd. (Pico Blvd.) | 310-289-0392
**Palms** | 10319 Venice Blvd. (Motor Ave.) | 310-558-3168
**Manhattan Beach** | 1000 N. Sepulveda Blvd. (10th St.) | 310-937-6829
**Encino** | 17410 Ventura Blvd. (bet. Louise & White Oak Aves.) | 818-906-0756
**Universal City** | Universal CityWalk | 1000 Universal Studios Blvd. (off Rte. 101) | 818-505-0093
www.versaillescuban.com

"Superlative" chicken "smothered in a savory garlic sauce" is the "main attraction" at this Cuban chainlet, long an "LA institution" channeling "Miami's best" with an "inexpensive" menu featuring

FOOD | DECOR | SERVICE | COST

"gems" like "blissful" roast pork and "divine" fried plantains dished out in "strictly utilitarian" surroundings; "don't be discouraged" by the "mobs" outside – regulars report "almost disconcertingly fast" servers "move you in and out" "quickly."

### Vertical Wine Bistro Ⓜ Eclectic/Mediterranean | 23 | 25 | 21 | $41

**Pasadena** | 70 N. Raymond Ave. (Union St.) | 626-795-3999 | www.verticalwinebistro.com

"A colorful crowd of locals" rubs elbows at this "elegant" Pasadena wine bar offering an "inspired" lineup of Eclectic-Med small plates that "pair well" with the 100 vintages by the glass, and a "knowledge-able" staff smoothes the way for "novice sippers"; "stunning" earth-toned decor earns raves, though a few diners demur on "pricey" tabs they say "can really add up."

### Via Veneto Italian | 26 | 19 | 22 | $54

**Santa Monica** | 3009 Main St. (bet. Marine St. & Pier Ave.) | 310-399-1843 | www.viaveneto.us

It's a "real treasure" assert enthusiasts of this "charming" family-run trattoria in Santa Monica that owes its "authentic" feel to "superb" pastas "made with love" (the ravioli in particular are "not-to-be-missed") and "personal" service from the Italian-speaking staff; though the "candlelit" Tuscan-style room seems made for "romance", foes find the "cramped" setup and "noisy" acoustics make for "uncomfortable" dining.

### Vibrato Grill & Jazz Ⓜ American/Steak | 21 | 25 | 22 | $66

**Bel-Air** | 2930 N. Beverly Glen Circle (Mulholland Dr.) | 310-474-9400 | www.vibratogrilljazz.com

"Perfectly prepared steaks" and "first-rate jazz" prove "the perfect combination" at this "sophisticated" Bel-Air "supper club" co-owned by bandleader Herb Alpert where the added advantage of "wonderful" service makes for a "fabulous evening" all around; though the performances are free, frugal sorts say the menu can feel "pricey", so if budget is an issue, "skip dinner and have a drink at the bar."

### Viet Noodle Bar Ⓜ⊟ Vietnamese | ▽ 22 | 19 | 21 | $14

**Atwater Village** | 3133½ Glendale Blvd. (Glenhurst Ave.) | 323-906-1575

"Minimalist" in menu and decor, this Vietnamese newcomer in Atwater Village presents a "limited" lineup of "cheap and delicious" noodle dishes, soups and spring rolls all enjoyed at communal tables stretching the length of the white-walled space; though they don't serve alcohol, freshly pressed juices are a draw, as is a lending library stocked with books and magazines for solo diners.

### Village Idiot, The ◑ American | 19 | 21 | 20 | $28

**Melrose** | 7383 Melrose Ave. (Martel Ave.) | 323-655-3331 | www.villageidiotla.com

"Friendly bartenders" "pour a good drink" at this "hip" Melrose "haunt" offering a "decently priced" menu of "rustic" American pub fare alongside a "varied" beer selection; open from lunch until late with large windows opening onto a lively street scene, it's equally suited to a "lazy afternoon of people-watching" or a "night out on the town" – the only drawback is that it's always "crowded."

| | FOOD | DECOR | SERVICE | COST |
|---|---|---|---|---|

## NEW Village Pantry *Deli*  | 14 | 12 | 12 | $22 |

**Pacific Palisades** | 1035 Swarthmore Ave. (Sunset Blvd.) | 310-454-3337
Former mayor Richard Riordan expands his restaurant mini-empire (The Original Pantry, Gladstone's Malibu) with this "redo of the Mort's Deli space" in Pacific Palisades, given a "bright" new look and a "jazzed up" American menu; though some say it "shows promise", locals lament this new incarnation has "lost its small-town friendly feel" and complain the "bland" fare, "hi-brow" pricing and "head-in-the-clouds" service all "need work."

## Z Village Pizzeria *Pizza*  | 23 | 12 | 16 | $14 |

**Hancock Park** | 131 N. Larchmont Blvd. (bet. Beverly Blvd. & 1st St.) | 323-465-5566
**NEW Hollywood** | 6363 Yucca St. (bet. Cahuenga Blvd. & Ivar St.) | 323-790-0763
www.villagepizzeria.net

"Outstanding" "thin-crust pizzas" taste like they came "straight from New York" at this Hancock Park Italian on "cute" Larchmont Boulevard deemed a "standout" for "families" who say its worth the parking hassles and "waits" for an "amazing" slice; a few wish they hadn't "imported" East Coast "attitude" from servers, though the majority says "fuhgeddaboudit" – "it's great for a cheap bite"; N.B. the Hollywood branch opened post-Survey.

## Villa Piacere *Eclectic*  | 19 | 22 | 19 | $39 |

**Woodland Hills** | 22160 Ventura Blvd. (bet. Shoup Ave. & Topanga Canyon Blvd.) | 818-704-1185 | www.villapiacere.com

"The perfect place for a romantic meal", this Woodland Hills "old-timer" boasts a "beautiful" courtyard ("prettiest in the valley") that's a popular pick for wedding receptions or outdoor dining on a "summer night"; "solid" Eclectic offerings may not live up to the "unparalleled" setting, but since prices are "affordable" and there's something for everyone" on the menu, most patrons plan on "going back."

## Villa Sorriso *Italian*  | 16 | 21 | 16 | $34 |

**Pasadena** | 168 W. Colorado Blvd. (Pasadena Ave.) | 626-793-8008 | www.sorrisopasadena.com

Regulars recommend "sitting outside" on the "charming" courtyard with "twinkly lights wound around the trees" at this midpriced Pasadena Italian that's "relaxing" for a drink when it's not "crowded"; yet in spite of the "romantic" setting, the "conventional" cooking doesn't win any raves, nor does occasionally "uncooperative" service that harsher critics claim "needs to improve."

## Vincenti Z *Italian*  | 26 | 24 | 23 | $65 |

**Brentwood** | 11930 San Vicente Blvd. (Montana Ave.) | 310-207-0127 | www.vincentiristorante.com

"Absolutely marvelous" purr pleased patrons of "soulful" chef Nicola Mastronardi's "elegant" Brentwood Italian serving "impeccably prepared" "homespun" dishes like "fine roasts of meat and fish" and a lasagna that makes one surveyor "weak in the knees"; "effusive" host/co-owner Maureen Vincenti "greets you like a long-lost friend" and oversees the "lovely" purple-hued dining room, leaving the bill ("ouch!") as the only major downside.

## NEW Vinotéque *Mediterranean*

`-` `-` `-` `I`

**Culver City** | 4437 Sepulveda Blvd. (Braddock Dr.) | 310-482-3490 |
www.vinotequela.com

In a madcap space featuring lights made of wine bottles, this stylish BottleRock spin-off in Culver City offers an encyclopedic selection of more than 250 vintages you've probably never heard of (and will be happy to meet), buttressing them with cheeses, charcuterie and inexpensive, vino-friendly Mediterranean plates such as stuffed dates and lamb burgers; nightly blues and jazz combos add extra body to the chic scene.

## Violet ⓂAmerican

`22` `16` `20` `$39`

**Santa Monica** | 3221 Pico Blvd. (bet. 32nd & 33rd Sts.) | 310-453-9113 |
www.violetrestaurant.com

"Adventurous" chef Jared Simons shows "real flair" with both his "emo-rocker eye makeup" and "imaginative" New American small plates at this Santa Monica spot that also "works the hip factor" with its sleek stainless-steel accented decor; though a handful huff that "service needs work", most maintain they'll "keep coming back", especially since "creative pricing schemes" (like Sunday's $25 prix fixe dinner) keep the costs down.

## V.I.P. Harbor Seafood *Chinese/Seafood*

`18` `12` `14` `$23`

**West LA** | 11701 Wilshire Blvd. (Barrington Ave.) | 310-979-3377 |
www.vipharborseafood.com

Angelenos who "don't want to drive to Monterey Park" sail into this "fairly priced" West LA Sino "standby" that's "sure to please" for "really good" dim sum (at lunch only) that's best appreciated "with a group" so you can "sample everything"; a somewhat "harried" staff means it "takes a while" to get your order, while the "tatty" grandeur of the banquet-style room divides diners – some "love it" and others think it could use some "sprucing up."

## Vitello's *Italian*

`14` `14` `16` `$30`

**Studio City** | 4349 Tujunga Ave. (Moorpark St.) | 818-769-0905 |
www.vitellosrestaurant.com

Made "infamous" by the Robert Blake murder trial, this "old-fashioned" Italian in Studio City soldiers on in somewhat "depressing" digs serving "run-of-the-mill" "red-sauce" fare (including a pasta special named after Blake himself) that "transports" diners to "Long Island" or "New Jersey"; more than a few find the whole experience "creepy" (and the "waiters' stories only make it worse"), though it remains "popular", with live jazz and opera singers most nights.

## Vito *Italian*

`20` `18` `23` `$40`

**Santa Monica** | 2807 Ocean Park Blvd. (28th St.) | 310-450-4999 |
www.vitorestaurant.com

"Hearty" Italian fare is "served the way it should be" – by *Goodfellas* waiters who "take care of you" – at this "family-run" ristorante that's "about as close as you can get" to "New York" in Santa Monica; the "old-world" setting features linen tablecloths and leather booths that are both adequately "romantic" for a "tryst", but "relaxed" enough for "the folks" too.

|  | FOOD | DECOR | SERVICE | COST |
|---|---|---|---|---|

## Vittorio's ☒ *Italian* | 19 | 11 | 18 | $27

**Pacific Palisades** | 16646 Marquez Ave. (Sunset Blvd.) | 310-459-9316 | www.vittoriosla.com

Pacific Palisades "families" frequent this "fine neighborhood joint" for "satisfying" Southern Italian cooking like chicken parmigiana, pizzas and some of "the best" little garlic rolls "this side of heaven"; though it's a "comfortable" spot tended by a "warm" staff, those on-the-go find the take-out and delivery options most appealing.

## Viva Madrid ☒ *Spanish* | ▽ 20 | 22 | 17 | $30

**Claremont** | 225 Yale Ave. (Bonita Ave.) | 909-624-5500 | www.vivamadrid.com

Claremont noshers "nibble a variety" of "interesting" tapas and tuck into "perfectly crafted" paella at this "popular" Spaniard where free-flowing sangria and a "great selection of ports and sherries" fuel the "lively" (read: "loud") scene; the "shoebox" of a space is decked out with bullfighting memorabilia and antiques, with live flamenco guitar on Wednesdays and Thursdays "keeping it hopping" till late; P.S. "expect a wait", especially on weekends.

## Vivoli Café & Trattoria *Italian* | 25 | 16 | 24 | $34

**West Hollywood** | 7994 Sunset Blvd. (Laurel Ave.) | 323-656-5050
**NEW** **Westlake Village** | 3825 E. Thousand Oaks Blvd. (Westlake Blvd.) | 805-373-6060
www.vivolicafe.com

The "utterly charming" staff is always ready with a "*buona sera* and a smile" at this "quaint" Italian slotted into a "nondescript" West Hollywood strip mall that "rewards" regulars with "fabulous" trattoria "classics" – like "heavenly" pastas and "perfect cannoli" – at "reasonable" prices; considering it's already a "tight squeeze" in the dining room, now that "the word has hit the streets" about this "well-kept secret", "better make a reservation"; N.B. the Westlake Village branch opened post-Survey.

## Wa ☒ *Japanese* | ▽ 25 | 10 | 20 | $56

**West Hollywood** | La Cienega Plaza | 1106 N. La Cienega Blvd. (Holloway Dr.) | 310-854-7285

Perched atop the second floor of a West Hollywood shopping center, this "low-key" Japanese may be "nothing special to look at", but afishionados give high marks to sushi so "outstanding" it's "hard to choose" among all the "incredible" creations (hint: "get the omakase"); "friendly" chefs guide the way for initiates so even if "prices add up quickly", most find it "so worth" the "splurge."

## Wabi-Sabi *Asian Fusion* | 22 | 17 | 19 | $41

**Venice** | 1635 Abbot Kinney Blvd. (Venice Blvd.) | 310-314-2229 | www.wabisabisushi.com

"Beautifully prepared" sushi, "creative" Asian fusion plates and "fantastic" lychee martinis draw a dedicated following at this "hip" Venice "standby" "anchoring Abbot Kinney's south side" in a "loft-like" space with "exposed-brick walls"; though it thrives on a "laid-back" "California vibe", it's often "busy", especially during their "excellent" happy hour offering "deals" on fish every evening before 6:30 PM.

| | FOOD | DECOR | SERVICE | COST |
|---|---|---|---|---|

**NEW Waffle, The** ● *American*          ▽ 16 | 13 | 15 | $18

Hollywood | 6255 W. Sunset Blvd. (Vine St.) | 323-465-6901 |
www.thewaffle.us

Sunset's "new kid on the block", this Hollywood arrival proffers "glorified" American "diner fare" based on local ingredients – from "manly
plates" of eggs and hash browns, to chicken pot pie and meatloaf – in
a retro remodel of the ground floor of an office tower; though its late
hours are a boon to nearby nightclubbers, early word on the food is
mixed ("not-too-shabby" vs. "needs help"), while the "inexplicably
slow" service leaves some guests wondering if they've been "punk'd."

**Wahib's Middle East** *Mideastern*          21 | 11 | 17 | $19

Alhambra | 910 E. Main St. (Granada Ave.) | 626-576-1048 |
www.wahibsmiddleeast.com

"Unbelievable falafel" and a "wonderful selection" of inexpensive
"Middle Eastern staples" like kebab and hummus make this "friendly"
mainstay – family-owned and -operated since 1981 – "one of the better" choices in Alhambra; the spacious seating area is a boon for
groups, while belly dancing adds appeal for "adventurous" types on
Friday and Saturday nights.

**Walter's** *Eclectic*          19 | 17 | 18 | $26

Claremont | 308 Yale Ave. (Bonita Ave.) | 909-624-4914 |
www.waltersrestaurant.biz

"A Claremont icon", this Eclectic "staple" since 1957 dishes up "big
plates" of Californian and Afghani cuisine with a "good range of vegetarian choices"; "energetic" "college-age" servers oversee the sprawling interior and "relaxing" patio area, while its "reasonable prices" and
"popularity with locals" add to the overall "small-town feel."

**Warszawa** Ⓜ *Polish*          22 | 18 | 20 | $35

Santa Monica | 1414 Lincoln Blvd. (Santa Monica Blvd.) | 310-393-8831 |
www.warszawarestaurant.com

"Pierogi and pilsner" partisans cheer this Santa Monica stalwart
housed in a "quaint" converted bungalow dishing up "homey" Polish
fare with a "haute" twist (think roast duckling and plums wrapped in
bacon); "accented" "modellike" waitresses provide "charming" service, and given the "surprisingly affordable" prices and "pleasant"
backyard seating, supporters say it's "hard not to love it."

**Warung Cafe** Ⓔ *Pan-Asian*          - | - | - | I

Downtown | 118 W. Fourth St. (Main St.) | 213-626-0718 |
www.warungcafela.com

The Pan-Asian small-plates menu runs the gamut from tuna tartare to
marinated pork ribs at this dimly lit Downtown retreat also boasting a
wide-ranging beer, sake and soju list; prices are affordable, and
though the bamboo-and-brick decor is pleasant enough, speedy delivery sweetens the deal for nearby condo-dwellers.

**Watercress** *Californian*          ▽ 21 | 17 | 19 | $18

Sherman Oaks | 13565 Ventura Blvd. (Woodman Ave.) | 818-385-1448

"Healthy" Californian salads and sandwiches and "good" strong java
from next-door sibling The Coffee Roaster make this "pretty" little
cafe in Sherman Oaks an "excellent" "find" for breakfast and lunch;
though a few fret it's "overpriced" given the "order-at-the-counter"

service, loyalists are won over by the "charming" feel, saying you can tell "they really care about their customers."

## ⚡ Water Grill  *Seafood*      | 27 | 24 | 25 | $66 |

**Downtown** | 544 S. Grand Ave. (bet. 5th & 6th Sts.) | 213-891-0900 | www.watergrill.com

A "perennial favorite" for "fabulous" feasts of "swimmingly delicious" fin fare, this Downtown seafooder proves "all around wonderful" for fans savoring some of "the finest fish in LA" backed by a "broad, creative" wine list and "gracious" service from the "attentive" staff; though the "elegant" yachtlike interior feels "a bit staid" to some, most maintain it's "always a pleasure" for "business lunches", "romantic" dinners and other "splurge"-worthy special occasions.

## West  *Californian/Italian*      | 18 | 22 | 16 | $54 |

**Brentwood** | Hotel Angeleno | 170 N. Church Ln., 17th fl. (I-405) | 310-481-7878 | www.westatangeleno.com

"Breathtaking views" of the 405 freeway are the main selling point of this penthouse venue atop the Hotel Angeleno in Brentwood where the Cal-Italian cuisine and dry-aged steaks are judged "good, but inconsistent"; given that service can be slow, and the posh wood space "loud" on weekends when a DJ takes over, some suggest it's best to "grab a drink" in the inviting lounge area "before heading off to dinner elsewhere."

## Whale & Ale, The  *Pub Food*      ∇ | 16 | 16 | 18 | $26 |

**San Pedro** | 327 W. Seventh St. (bet. Centre & Mesa Sts.) | 310-832-0363 | www.whaleandale.com

"Any Englishman would feel at home" at this San Pedro pub serving ales on tap alongside "fairly authentic" fare in an "old-fashioned" Victorian-style setting with oak-paneled walls and a working fireplace; sticklers say it's a bit "overpriced" given the "average" fare, but Anglophiles attest the atmosphere alone is "well worth the money."

## Wharo Korean BBQ  *Korean*      | 16 | 16 | 17 | $32 |

**Marina del Rey** | 4029 Lincoln Blvd. (Washington Blvd.) | 310-578-7114 | www.wharo.com

Given that "Korean BBQ is hard to find" on the Westside, Marina del Rey patrons welcome this strip-mall option where diners fire up "fresh" meats and veggies on tabletop grills; critics carp it's "overpriced" and insist it's "only good when you need a quick fix."

## NEW  Whisper Cafe  *Eclectic*      | - | - | - | I |

**Encino** | 17312A Ventura Blvd. (Louise Ave.) | 818-386-0061

This Eclectic newcomer set in the former L'Artiste Patisserie space aims for Encino locals with housemade pastries for breakfast, simple salads and sandwiches for lunch and dinner items like eggplant Parmesan and filet mignon served Wednesday–Saturday to the tunes of live jazz; prices are reasonable, while colorful paintings and bric-a-brac lend the modest mini-mall location a lived-in feel.

## Whist  *Californian*      | 20 | 23 | 19 | $61 |

**Santa Monica** | Viceroy Santa Monica | 1819 Ocean Ave. (Pico Blvd.) | 310-260-7500 | www.viceroysantamonica.com

"Pretty girls in huge black sunglasses" "dine in cabanas by the pool" at this Santa Monica "see-and-be-seen spot" in the Viceroy hotel "beauti-

| | FOOD | DECOR | SERVICE | COST |
|---|---|---|---|---|

fully" done up in a "fantasy" white-and-green tea parlor style by designer Kelly Wearstler; as for the "elegantly presented" Californian fare, many find it "overpriced", though Sunday's champagne brunch earns praise.

### Wildflour Pizza  *Pizza*

| 15 | 8 | 13 | $17 |
|---|---|---|---|

**Santa Monica** | 2807 Main St. (bet. Ashland Ave. & Hill St.) | 310-392-3300
"The quintessential beach bum pizza joint", this Santa Monica "hole-in-the-wall" is a "local tradition" for thin-crust pies, pastas and salads best appreciated from the picnic tables on the back patio; doubters dismiss it as "completely mediocre", though it's "convenient" and some swear it's "great for takeout" too.

### Wilshire ●⊠  *American*

| 22 | 25 | 20 | $54 |
|---|---|---|---|

**Santa Monica** | 2454 Wilshire Blvd. (bet. Chelsea Ave. & 25th St.) | 310-586-1707 | www.wilshirerestaurant.com
"Unbeatable on a nice night" thanks to its "stunning" two-tier patio, this "sexy" Santa Monican stirs up "a bit of a scene" with "sophisticated" "black-clad" patrons sipping signature cocktails and swaying to a DJ on weekends; after a chef change in 2008, diners declare the "reworked" market-driven New American menu "much improved" ("delicious!") so even if it's "a bit overpriced", most deem it "appealing" nonetheless.

### Wilson ⊠  *Mediterranean*

| 22 | 16 | 21 | $48 |
|---|---|---|---|

**Culver City** | 8631 Washington Blvd. (Sherbourne Dr.) | 310-287-2093 | www.wilsonfoodandwine.com
"Gutsy" flavor combinations distinguish this "chic" Culver City boîte that owes its "good vibrations" to "delectable" Mediterranean creations by chef-owner Michael Wilson (Beach Boy Dennis Wilson's son); "minimalist" decor with "too-hard chairs" gets a boost from a "comfortable patio" out back, though some loyalists lament that prices are ultimately "too expensive" for what "should be a great neighborhood place."

### Wine Bistro 🅼  *French*

| 21 | 18 | 20 | $42 |
|---|---|---|---|

**Studio City** | 11915 Ventura Blvd. (Laurel Canyon Blvd.) | 818-766-6233 | www.winebistro.net
"A real sleeper" say fans of this "civilized" Studio City standby sending out "authentic" French bistro dishes (bouillabaisse, steak frites) and "superb wines" in a brass-accented room presided over by "gracious host" and co-owner J.B. Tourchon; cushy banquettes contribute to the "relaxing" ambiance and prices are "reasonable" too, no wonder some surveyors say it's a "pleasure to recommend it."

### Wokcano Cafe ●  *Chinese/Japanese*

| 19 | 17 | 18 | $26 |
|---|---|---|---|

**NEW Downtown** | 800 W. Seventh St. (Flower St.) | 213-623-2288
**West Hollywood** | 8408 W. Third St. (Orlando Ave.) | 323-951-1122
**NEW Santa Monica** | 1413 5th St. (Santa Monica Blvd.) | 310-458-3080
**Pasadena** | 33 S. Fair Oaks Ave. (bet. W. Colorado Blvd. & W. Green St.) | 626-578-1818
**Burbank** | 150 S. San Fernando Blvd. (Angeleno Ave.) | 818-524-2288
www.wokcanocafe.com
The Asian menu spans from lo mein to sushi at this Chinese-Japanese chainlet that stays "open very late" catering to a "young crowd" with "inexpensive cocktails" in "clubby" bamboo-and-stone trimmed environs; though more than a few foodies find the cuisine "hit-and-miss", at least prices are a "good value"; N.B. a Long Beach branch is in the works.

### Wolfgang Puck Cafe  *Californian*    | 17 | 13 | 15 | $25 |

**Santa Monica** | Criterion Plaza | 1315 Third St. Promenade (Arizona Ave.) | 310-576-4770

**LAX** | LA Int'l Airport, Terminals 2 & 7 | 310-215-5169

**Universal City** | Universal CityWalk | 1000 Universal Studios Blvd. (off Rte. 101) | 818-985-9653

### Wolfgang Puck LA Bistro 🅂 *Californian*

**Downtown** | Library Court Bldg. | 630 W. Sixth St. (bet. Hope & 6th Sts.) | 213-614-1900

www.wolfgangpuck.com

"Only a hint of the great Wolfgang" is to be found in this "higher-lever" "fast-food" chain offering "decent" renditions from Puck's "standard" Californian repertoire like wood-fired pizzas and Chinois chicken salad; service and decor ratings speak for themselves, but prices are "low", so even if it's not quite "Spago for poor people", it'll do for a "quick bite."

### NEW Wolfgang's Steakhouse  *Steak*    | – | – | – | E |

**Beverly Hills** | 445 N. Cañon Dr. (Little Santa Monica Blvd.) | 310-385-0640 | www.wolfgangssteakhouse.com

Beverly Hills gets a little more steer-crazy with the addition of this up-scale steakhouse from Wolfgang Zwiener (ex–Peter Luger head waiter, now owner of two New York Wolfgang's locations); the room is decked out in classic, über-masculine style and the menu features oversized portions of everything from porterhouse to cottage fries – with schlag (fresh whipped cream) on dessert; N.B. not to be con-fused with Wolfgang Puck's beefed-up CUT just around the corner.

### Wood Ranch BBQ & Grill  *BBQ*    | 20 | 16 | 18 | $28 |

**Fairfax** | Grove at Farmers Mkt. | 189 The Grove Dr. (bet. Fairfax Ave. & 3rd St.) | 323-937-6800

**Cerritos** | Cerritos Towne Ctr. | 12801 Towne Center Dr. (bet. Bloomfield Ave. & 183rd St.) | 562-865-0202

**Arcadia** | Westfield Shoppingtown Santa Anita | 400 S. Baldwin Ave. (Huntington Dr.) | 626-447-4745

**Northridge** | Northridge Fashion Ctr. | 9301 Tampa Ave. (bet. Nordhoff & Plummer Sts.) | 818-886-6464

**Agoura Hills** | Whizins Plaza | 5050 Cornell Rd. (Roadside Dr.) | 818-597-8900

**Camarillo** | 1101 Daily Dr. (Lantana St.) | 805-482-1202

**Moorpark** | 540 New Los Angeles Ave. (Spring Rd.) | 805-523-7253

**Valencia** | Valencia Mktpl. | 25580 N. The Old Rd. (Constitution Ave.) | 661-222-9494

www.woodranch.com

"Meat you can smell for miles" is the draw at this "hectic" American chain crowded with "kids", where "efficient" servers ferry BBQ fare full of "smoky goodness" like "tender tri-tip" and "fall-off-your-fork ribs"; apologists attest "it may not be the most authentic" 'cue in town, but "fair prices" and "generous" portions mean at least "you won't be hun-gry when you leave here (maybe not for days)."

### Woody's Bar-B-Que  *BBQ*    | ▽ 23 | 8 | 16 | $16 |

**Mid-City** | 3446 W. Slauson Ave. (Crenshaw Blvd.) | 323-294-9443

**Inglewood** | 475 S. Market St. (bet. Hillcrest Blvd & La Brea Ave.) | 310-672-4200 🅂

www.woodysla.com

"Awesome" ribs, links and chicken come slathered in an "earthy" sauce at this inexpensive BBQ duo that 'cue connoisseurs rank among the "best in the city"; the Mid-City location is "strictly for takeout", while the Inglewood outpost features a handful of tables as well as homemade red velvet cake on Fridays and Saturdays.

### Woo Lae Oak  *Korean*  | 22 | 22 | 17 | $44 |

**Beverly Hills** | 170 N. La Cienega Blvd. (Clifton Way) | 310-652-4187 | www.woolaeoakbh.com

A "sophisticated" alternative to "traditional" K-town joints, this "fancy" Beverly Hills Korean features similarly "satisfying" "cook-your-own" feasts, albeit at "higher prices"; though the "elegant" contemporary surroundings certainly earn praise, sticklers say the "aspiring actor" staff detracts from an otherwise "authentic" experience.

### W's China Bistro  *Chinese*  | 21 | 20 | 19 | $32 |

**Redondo Beach** | 1410 S. PCH (Ave. F) | 310-792-1600 | www.wschinabistro.com

"Familiar" Chinese favorites get some "edgy" "fusion-ized" twists at this South Bay "staple" specializing in "tasty" creations like wok-seared ahi and velvety shrimp; though the "cute, Asian-inflected" stone-accented decor lends it a "hip" feel that's "upscale for Redondo Beach", regulars report that "affordable" pricing means it's often "filled with families."

### Xi'an  *Chinese*  | 22 | 16 | 18 | $33 |

**Beverly Hills** | 362 N. Cañon Dr. (bet. Brighton Way) | 310-275-3345

"Inspired" Chinese cooking with an emphasis on "healthy" preparations pleases the masses at this Sino "favorite" situated off Rodeo Drive in a "casual, but still date-worthy" blond-wood setting; since tabs are "surprisingly affordable for Beverly Hills", it's "popular" with "neighborhood" types despite "hit-or-miss service" and a "noisy" dining room.

### Xiomara  ⧄ *Nuevo Latino*  | 23 | 22 | 21 | $40 |

**Hollywood** | 6101 Melrose Ave. (Seward St.) | 323-461-0601 | www.xiomararestaurant.com

Admirers of chef-owner Xiomara Ardolina's Hollywood "gem" insist it "keeps getting better and better" with "inventive" Nuevo Latino food bested only by the "justly famous" mojitos "made with real sugarcane juice"; its "gorgeous" Havana-style setting exudes a "sexy" feel, inspiring locals to linger, while being tended to by an "accommodating" staff.

### Yabu  *Japanese*  | 23 | 14 | 20 | $31 |

**West Hollywood** | 521 N. La Cienega Blvd. (Melrose Ave.) | 310-854-0400
**West LA** | 11820 W. Pico Blvd. (bet. Barrington Ave. & Bundy Dr.) | 310-473-9757
www.yaburestaurant.com

Seekers of "authentic Japanese food" cherish this "underrated" Nipponese duo; the "low-key" West LA location puts the focus on "slurpy" "handmade" soba noodles and "tempting" izakaya dishes, while the fancier WeHo branch, with a fireplace and a bamboo-lined back patio, spotlights "sophisticated" sushi and sashimi that "compare favorably" to "much higher-priced places."

### Yai  *Thai*  | ▽ 21 | 6 | 15 | $17 |

**East Hollywood** | 5757 Hollywood Blvd. (Taft Ave.) | 323-462-0292 ⏻
**Los Feliz** | 1627 N. Vermont Ave. (Hollywood Blvd.) | 323-644-1076 Ⓜ

Intrepid eaters hail this East Hollywood strip-mall "jewel" and its Los Feliz spin-off dishing up "well-seasoned", "country"-style Thai cook-

| | FOOD | DECOR | SERVICE | COST |
|---|---|---|---|---|

ing best ordered "really spicy"; given such "authentic" fare and inexpensive prices, most don't mind the "sterile" decor.

### ⏣ Yamashiro  *Asian/Californian*  | 18 | 27 | 21 | $50 |

**Hollywood** | 1999 N. Sycamore Ave. (Franklin Ave.) | 323-466-5125 | www.yamashirorestaurant.com

It's all about the "incredible" views of LA "in all its hazy glory" at this "classic" "hilltop" locale in Hollywood whose "transporting" pagoda setting boasts "lovely grounds" with a koi pond in the center courtyard; critics call the Cal-Asian cuisine "sadly unmemorable" and "too expensive" to boot, and suggest that "tourists" intent on a peek at the scenery try it for "cocktails" – "you'll leave happy."

### NEW Yamato Westwood  *Japanese*  | 19 | 24 | 20 | $37 |

**Westwood** | 1099 Westwood Blvd. (Kinross Ave.) | 310-208-0100 | www.yamatorestaurants.com

At this "welcome addition" to Westwood Village, diners find "creative spins" on Japanese cuisine and a "great sake" selection served up in a "swanky" space in the former bank building that used to house EuroChow; service can be "slow" at times, but prices are "so reasonable" that most find this "new oasis" "deserves every encouragement."

### Yang Chow  *Chinese*  | 22 | 11 | 17 | $23 |

**Chinatown** | 819 N. Broadway (bet. Alpine & College Sts.) | 213-625-0811
**Pasadena** | 3777 E. Colorado Blvd. (Rosemead Blvd.) | 626-432-6868
**Canoga Park** | 6443 Topanga Canyon Blvd. (Victory Blvd.) | 818-347-2610
www.yangchow.com

The signature "slippery shrimp dish is on almost every table" (and "for good reason!") at this "venerable" trio in Canoga Park, Chinatown and Pasadena famed for its "classic" Sino feasts aimed at the "Western palate"; all three thrive in "hectic" and "crowded" environs – "make a reservation" to avoid "long waits" or "stick to takeout if you're easily annoyed."

### Yard House  *American*  | 20 | 18 | 18 | $26 |

**Long Beach** | Shoreline Vill. | 401 Shoreline Village Dr. (Shoreline Dr.) | 562-628-0455
**Pasadena** | Paseo Colorado | 330 E. Colorado Blvd. (bet. Fair Oaks & N. Los Robles Aves.) | 626-577-9273
www.yardhouse.com

"Lively, friendly" and "now ubiquitous", these cavernous chain taverns are "beer snob heaven" for fans drawn to the "outrageous" selection of over 100 brews on tap and "diverse" lineup of "upscale" American bar eats; they're "often crowded", so expect a "noisy, noisy, noisy" atmosphere along with "hit-or-miss" service.

### Yatai Asian Tapas Bar ⏣ *Pan-Asian*  | - | - | - | M |

**West Hollywood** | 8535 W. Sunset Blvd. (N. La Cienega Blvd.) | 310-289-0030 | www.yatai-bar.com

The "tasty" Pan-Asian "treats" are made for "sharing" at this WeHo small-plates specialist set in red-hued digs with a small courtyard patio; happy hour brings "terrific specials" on beer, sake and snacks, so though it flies "under-the-radar", those who've found it claim this "little spot" is nothing less than a "gem."

| | FOOD | DECOR | SERVICE | COST |
|---|---|---|---|---|

## Yen Sushi & Sake Bar  *Japanese*

| 21 | 20 | 19 | $34 |
|---|---|---|---|

**NEW** Little Tokyo | 110 E. 9th St. (bet. Los Angeles & Main Sts.) | 213-627-9709 ⓢ

**Pico-Robertson** | 9618 W. Pico Blvd. (Beverly Dr.) | 310-278-0691

**West LA** | 11819 Wilshire Blvd., Ste. 101 (Granville Ave.) | 310-996-1313

**Long Beach** | 4905 E. Second St. (bet. Argonne & St. Joseph Aves.) | 562-434-5757

**Studio City** | 12930 Ventura Blvd. (Coldwater Canyon Ave.) | 818-907-6400

www.yensushiusa.com

With a handful of locations dotted around LA, this Japanese mini-chain is a "convenient" choice for "fresh and flavorful" (if not especially "adventurous") sushi, noodles and other "nicely presented" specialties; they lure a "kid-friendly" crowd early on, but considering their "hip" feel, smooth service and long list of sakes and cocktails, they're also handy for "dates."

## Ye Olde King's Head  *Pub Food*

| 17 | 17 | 16 | $23 |
|---|---|---|---|

**Santa Monica** | 116 Santa Monica Blvd. (Ocean Ave.) | 310-451-1402 | www.yeoldekingshead.com

"Homesick Brits" "toss darts" and knock back creamy "pints poured to perfection" at this "inviting" Santa Monica pub where "knickknacks" on the walls and soccer on the telly add to the overall "genuine" feel; allies insist the "traditional" grub – like fish 'n' chips and shepherd's pie – "is better than its counterparts in the U.K.", though perhaps, note cynics, "that's not saying much."

## York, The ● *Eclectic*

| 18 | 21 | 17 | $24 |
|---|---|---|---|

**Highland Park** | 5018 York Blvd. (N. Ave. 50) | 323-255-9675 | www.theyorkonyork.com

"An instant favorite" "from the second they opened", this "much-needed" addition to "up-and-coming" Highland Park is a find for unusual draft ales and an Eclectic gastropub-inspired menu judged "satisfying", if "a tad uneven"; although some are irked by the order-at-the-bar service, its "cool" looks redeem, as does the "friendly" vibe that encourages folks to "order another round and chat up some neighbors."

## ☑ Yujean Kang's  *Chinese*

| 25 | 16 | 21 | $38 |
|---|---|---|---|

**Pasadena** | 67 N. Raymond Ave. (bet. Holly & Union Sts.) | 626-585-0855 | www.yujeankangs.com

"Still wonderful" say those sweet on this longtime Pasadena "favorite" catering to "cultivated palates" with "delicately prepared" Chinese dishes whose "flavors linger in memory from visit to visit"; premium pricing and "attentive" service give it a distinctly "fine dining" feel, even if style-mavens insist the "tired" decor could "use some love."

## NEW Yuta Ⓜ *French/Japanese*

| - | - | - | E |
|---|---|---|---|

**Studio City** | 11266 Ventura Blvd. (Tujunga Ave.) | 818-985-9882 | www.yutarestaurant.com

Even against stiff competition in Studio City, connoisseurs claim this French-Japanese newcomer stands out with "inventive" small plates and "artfully" presented sushi; service "aims to please" and the simply decorated room is "quiet enough for conversation", so even if tabs can tally on the "expensive" side, most insist it's a "pleasant experience" nonetheless.

| | FOOD | DECOR | SERVICE | COST |
|---|---|---|---|---|

### Yuzu ⚅ *Japanese*
▽ 23 | 18 | 18 | $43

**Torrance** | 1231 Cabrillo Ave. (Torrance Blvd.) | 310-533-9898
"Japanese expats" seek out this "authentic" Torrance izakaya whose menu offers "a little bit of everything" – from "traditional" "comfort-style" dishes to more "imaginative" small-plate items and sushi; its "modern" decor features bar seating arranged around an open kitchen, but the upscale ambiance also comes with "expensive" prices.

### NEW Zane's *Italian/Steak*
- | - | - | M

**Hermosa Beach** | 1150 Hermosa Ave. (Pier Ave.) | 310-374-7488
In way-casual Hermosa Beach, this Italian steakhouse with high ceilings plates moderately priced cuts of beef plus pastas and more; large windows offer a fine view of the nightly bacchanal on Pier Avenue.

### Zankou Chicken *Mediterranean*
22 | 6 | 12 | $12

**East Hollywood** | 5065 W. Sunset Blvd. (Normandie Ave.) | 323-665-7845 ⑂
**West LA** | 1716 S. Sepulveda Blvd., Ste. 101 (Santa Monica Blvd.) | 310-444-0550
**Pasadena** | 1296 E. Colorado Blvd. (Hill Ave.) | 626-405-1502
**Burbank** | 1001 N. San Fernando Blvd., Ste. 100 (E. Walnut Ave.) | 818-238-0414
**Glendale** | 1415 E. Colorado Blvd., Ste. D (Verdugo Rd.) | 818-244-1937
**Van Nuys** | 5658 Sepulveda Blvd., Ste. 103 (Burbank Blvd.) | 818-781-0615
www.zankouchicken.com
A "cult following" cheers when they see the "big Z in the sky" signaling this "cheap" Med chain and its "juicy, tender" rotisserie chicken served with a "delectable" sauce "garlicky" enough to "ensure a make-out-free evening"; a "less-than-friendly" counter staff "gets you in and out fast" – a good thing since the "fast-food-style" digs with "fluorescent lighting" are "beyond depressing."

### Zazou *Mediterranean*
23 | 20 | 21 | $45

**Redondo Beach** | 1810 S. Catalina Ave. (Vista Del Mar) | 310-540-4884 | www.zazourestaurant.com
The "terrific" Med cooking shows real "love from the kitchen" at this "locals' favorite" in Redondo Beach pairing "exceptional" fare like lamb osso buco with glasses and flights from a 300-label wine list; though it hosts a "busy bar scene", its "upscale" dining area offers a bit of "European elegance" with dim lighting, white linens and "smooth service."

### Zeidler's Café Ⓜ *Californian*
17 | 15 | 16 | $26

**Brentwood** | Skirball Cultural Ctr. | 2701 N. Sepulveda Blvd. (Mulholland Dr.) | 310-440-4515 | www.skirball.org
Museumgoers praise the "nice selection of salads, sandwiches" and meat-free entrees at this kosher Cal cafe in the Skirball Cultural Center; despite "slow" service, most agree the "pleasant" space with courtyard views makes for "convenient" noshing; N.B. lunch only.

### Zeke's Smokehouse *BBQ*
20 | 13 | 16 | $22

**West Hollywood** | West Hollywood Gateway Ctr. | 7100 Santa Monica Blvd. (Formosa Ave.) | 323-850-9353
**Montrose** | 2209 Honolulu Ave. (Verdugo Blvd.) | 818-957-7045
www.zekessmokehouse.com
Converts call the 'cue "finger-lickin' good" at these "no-frills" twins in Montrose and West Hollywood matching their grub with "many differ-

ent sauces" and sides like homemade potato chips and mac 'n' cheese that's "better than your grandmother's"; service is "fast", and though they're "not cheap", defenders declare the "high-quality" meats ("one of the owners runs a top-end supplier") are "worth" a little extra dough.

### Zen Grill  *Pan-Asian*                    ▽ 21 | 12 | 18 | $31

**Beverly Hills** | 9111 W. Olympic Blvd. (Doheny Dr.) | 310-278-7773 | www.zengrillbh.com

Fusion fans praise the "solid" Pan-Asian fare – from Malaysian laksa soup to spicy tuna won tons – at this Beverly Hills eatery; though the "small-ish" space can feel "cramped and crowded", the red-brick decor ramps up the charm, making it an appealing spot for a "cheap" night out; N.B. the Third Street location has closed.

### Zin Bistro Americana  *American*          22 | 24 | 20 | $41

**Westlake Village** | 32131 Lindero Canyon Rd. (bet. Lakeview Canyon Rd. & Ridgeford Dr.) | 818-865-0095 | www.zinbistroamericana.com

The "lovely patio" affords "beautiful views" of "some of the prettiest scenery in SoCal" at this Westlake Villager whose waterside locale makes it well-suited to a "romantic" evening; though service can be "erratic", the "adventurous" New American dishes score well, as do the signature martinis sampled in either in the "smartly decorated" dining room or at the "lively" bar.

### Zip Fusion  *Japanese*                    18 | 15 | 16 | $27

**Downtown** | 744 E. Third St. (Rose St.) | 213-680-3770 ⊠
**West LA** | 11301 W. Olympic Blvd. (Sawtelle Blvd.) | 310-575-3636
www.zipfusion.com

"Pretty decent sushi", "big rolls" and "accessible" fusion dishes keep the various locations of this ever-expanding Japanese chain "packed", even if some guests grumble that the food "lacks zip"; still, "reasonable" tabs prove a pull, as is patio seating that's a magnet for "young people" on "warm nights"; N.B. the West LA branch features private karaoke rooms.

### Zucca Ristorante  *Italian*               21 | 22 | 22 | $48

**Downtown** | 801 Tower | 801 S. Figueroa St. (8th St.) | 213-614-7800 | www.patinagroup.com

"Rustic" Italian cuisine is "always prepared with attention to detail" at Joachim Splichal's "dependable" Downtown dining room catering to a "mixed bag" of "business" types, "concert fans" and "Staples Center" attendees seeking a "pre-event" meal; though some rate the fare "uninspiring", "warm" service redeems, as does the "gorgeous" Tuscan-style setting that feels "transporting" despite the "generic" office tower location.

### Zu Robata  *Japanese*                     ▽ 20 | 23 | 20 | $41

**West LA** | 12217 Wilshire Blvd. (Bundy Dr.) | 310-571-1920 | www.zurobata.com

Jars of fruit-infused sojus "of every possible kind" line the walls of this West LA Japanese drinking den and grill pairing robata-yaki, sushi and "artfully presented" small plates with a lengthy list of beers and housemade cocktails; though the staff is "inviting", antagonists are irked by portions that seem "minuscule" "even for a restaurant of this kind."

# LOS ANGELES INDEXES

## LOCATION MAPS

# Cuisines

Includes restaurant names, locations and Food ratings. ☒ indicates places with the highest ratings, popularity and importance.

## AMERICAN (NEW)

| | |
|---|---|
| Abbey | **W Hollywood** | 14 |
| NEW Akasha | **Culver City** | 22 |
| NEW Animal | **Fairfax** | - |
| Baleen | **Redondo Bch** | 20 |
| NEW Bashan | **Montrose** | 26 |
| Beechwood | **Marina del Rey** | 18 |
| ☒ Belvedere | **Beverly Hills** | 25 |
| Blair's | **Silver Lake** | 24 |
| bld | **Beverly Blvd.** | 21 |
| Bloom Cafe | **Mid-City** | 22 |
| blue on blue | **Beverly Hills** | 19 |
| Blue Velvet | **Downtown** | 20 |
| NEW Blvd 16 | **Westwood** | - |
| boé | **Beverly Hills** | 22 |
| Breadbar | **multi.** | 18 |
| Brentwood, The | **Brentwood** | 21 |
| NEW Brix 1601 | **Hermosa Bch** | - |
| Café Pacific | **Rancho Palos Verdes** | 24 |
| NEW Catalina | **Redondo Bch** | 24 |
| Charcoal | **Hollywood** | 11 |
| NEW Chloe | **Santa Monica** | 18 |
| Circa 55 | **Beverly Hills** | 19 |
| Citizen Smith | **Hollywood** | 17 |
| Craft | **Century City** | 25 |
| NEW Darren's | **Manhattan Bch** | 26 |
| NEW Del, The | **Playa del Rey** | 20 |
| eat. on sunset | **Hollywood** | 18 |
| Farm/Bev. Hills | **multi.** | 19 |
| Firefly | **Studio City** | 22 |
| Firefly Bistro | **S Pasadena** | 18 |
| Ford's | **Culver City** | 19 |
| Foundry, The | **Melrose** | 23 |
| Fountain Coffee | **Beverly Hills** | 20 |
| NEW Gjelina | **Venice** | - |
| Grace | **Beverly Blvd.** | 25 |
| Hal's B&G | **Venice** | 20 |
| ☒ Hatfield's | **Beverly Blvd.** | 27 |
| Hugo's | **W Hollywood** | 21 |
| Ivy at Shore | **Santa Monica** | 22 |
| Jackson's Vill. | **Hermosa Bch** | 24 |
| Jar | **Beverly Blvd.** | 25 |
| ☒ JiRaffe | **Santa Monica** | 26 |
| John O'Groats | **Rancho Pk** | 21 |
| Josie | **Santa Monica** | 26 |
| Larchmont Grill | **Hollywood** | 22 |
| NEW Lot 1 | **Echo Pk** | - |
| Magnolia | **Hollywood** | 19 |
| ☒ Mélisse | **Santa Monica** | 28 |
| NEW Melrose B&G | **W Hollywood** | 18 |

| | |
|---|---|
| Mike & Anne's | **S Pasadena** | 21 |
| Moonshadows | **Malibu** | 17 |
| Napa Valley | **Westwood** | 20 |
| Nic's | **Beverly Hills** | 19 |
| Nine Thirty | **Westwood** | 21 |
| Noé | **Downtown** | 24 |
| ☒ Nook Bistro | **West LA** | 24 |
| O-Bar | **W Hollywood** | 21 |
| Ocean & Vine | **Santa Monica** | 21 |
| One Sunset | **W Hollywood** | 20 |
| NEW Palate | **Glendale** | - |
| Palomino | **Westwood** | 19 |
| NEW Park, The | **Echo Pk** | - |
| Patina | **Downtown** | 25 |
| ☒ Penthouse | **Santa Monica** | 18 |
| Pete's Cafe | **Downtown** | 19 |
| ☒ Providence | **Hollywood** | 26 |
| P6 Rest. | **Westlake Vill** | 22 |
| redwhite+bluezz | **Pasadena** | 22 |
| NEW Rest. 15 | **Echo Pk** | 20 |
| NEW Rush Street | **Culver City** | - |
| ☒ Saddle Peak | **Calabasas** | 26 |
| Safire | **Camarillo** | 21 |
| Second City | **El Segundo** | 23 |
| NEW Second Story | **Manhattan Bch** | - |
| NEW Sila Bistro | **Silver Lake** | - |
| Sky Room | **Long Bch** | 21 |
| NEW Stork, The | **Hollywood** | - |
| Tart | **Fairfax** | 16 |
| Taste | **W Hollywood** | 23 |
| Tender Greens | **Culver City** | 23 |
| Tiara Cafe | **Downtown** | 23 |
| Tracht's | **Long Bch** | 23 |
| Traxx | **Downtown** | 20 |
| Truxton's | **Westchester** | - |
| NEW Twelve + Highland | **Manhattan Bch** | 21 |
| Twin Palms | **Pasadena** | 18 |
| vermont | **Los Feliz** | 21 |
| Violet | **Santa Monica** | 22 |
| Wilshire | **Santa Monica** | 22 |
| Zin Bistro | **Westlake Vill** | 22 |

## AMERICAN (TRADITIONAL)

| | |
|---|---|
| Alcove | **Los Feliz** | 21 |
| American Girl Pl. | **Fairfax** | 11 |
| Apple Pan | **West LA** | 22 |
| Auntie Em's | **Eagle Rock** | 23 |
| Bandera | **West LA** | 21 |

| | |
|---|---|
| Beckham Grill \| **Pasadena** | 18 |
| Belmont Brew. \| **Long Bch** | 16 |
| **NEW** Bistrotek \| **Westchester** | - |
| BJ's \| **multi.** | 17 |
| Bluewater Grill \| **Redondo Bch** | 19 |
| Bowery \| **Hollywood** | 20 |
| Brighton Coffee \| **Beverly Hills** | 18 |
| Buffalo Club \| **Santa Monica** | 20 |
| Burger 90210 \| **Beverly Hills** | 16 |
| Cafe 50's \| **multi.** | 16 |
| Cafe Surfas \| **Culver City** | 19 |
| Cali. Chicken \| **multi.** | 21 |
| Carney's \| **multi.** | 19 |
| Central Park \| **Pasadena** | 17 |
| ☑ Cheesecake Factory \| **multi.** | 19 |
| Chili John's \| **Burbank** | 17 |
| City Bakery \| **Brentwood** | 19 |
| Claim Jumper \| **multi.** | 19 |
| Clementine \| **Century City** | 23 |
| Colony Café \| **West LA** | 18 |
| Coral Tree \| **Canoga Pk** | 18 |
| Daily Grill \| **multi.** | 18 |
| Danny's \| **Venice** | 17 |
| Dish \| **La Cañada Flintridge** | 16 |
| **NEW** Dolce Isola \| **Pico-Robertson** | 24 |
| Du-par's \| **multi.** | 16 |
| Dusty's \| **Silver Lake** | 18 |
| Eat Well Cafe \| **multi.** | 16 |
| Edendale Grill \| **Silver Lake** | 16 |
| **NEW** 8 oz. \| **Melrose** | - |
| Engine Co. 28 \| **Downtown** | 19 |
| ☑ Father's Office \| **multi.** | 24 |
| **NEW** Flake \| **Venice** | - |
| **NEW** Giggles 'n Hugs \| **West LA** | - |
| Gordon Biersch \| **multi.** | 16 |
| Green St. Rest. \| **Pasadena** | - |
| Griddle Cafe \| **Hollywood** | 22 |
| ☑ Grill on Alley \| **Beverly Hills** | 24 |
| Grill on Hollywood \| **Hollywood** | 22 |
| Grub \| **Hollywood** | 19 |
| Gulfstream \| **Century City** | 21 |
| Hamburger Mary's \| **W Hollywood** | 15 |
| Hamlet \| **multi.** | 16 |
| Hard Rock \| **Universal City** | 14 |
| Heroes \| **Claremont** | 17 |
| ☑ Houston's \| **multi.** | 21 |
| Islands \| **multi.** | 16 |
| Jack n' Jill's \| **multi.** | 19 |
| James' Bch. \| **Venice** | 18 |
| Jinky's \| **multi.** | 19 |
| Joan's on 3rd \| **Third St.** | 23 |
| Johnny Rockets \| **multi.** | 15 |
| Jones \| **W Hollywood** | 18 |
| **NEW** JuJu \| **Westwood** | - |
| Kate Mantilini \| **multi.** | 18 |

| | |
|---|---|
| Ketchup \| **W Hollywood** | 15 |
| Kings Road \| **Beverly Blvd.** | 18 |
| Kitchen, The \| **Silver Lake** | 19 |
| **NEW** Kitchen 24 \| **Hollywood** | - |
| Koo Koo Roo \| **multi.** | 15 |
| LA Food Show \| **Manhattan Bch** | 18 |
| Lasher's \| **Long Bch** | 23 |
| **NEW** Lawry's Carvery \| **Century City** | 19 |
| Liberty Grill \| **Downtown** | 18 |
| Local Pl. \| **Torrance** | 18 |
| Lucky Devils \| **Hollywood** | 20 |
| Luna Park \| **La Brea** | 17 |
| Madame Matisse \| **Silver Lake** | 19 |
| Marmalade Café \| **multi.** | 17 |
| Marston's \| **Pasadena** | 23 |
| Martha 22nd St. \| **Hermosa Bch** | 21 |
| Maxwell's Cafe \| **Venice** | 19 |
| Mel's Drive-In \| **multi.** | 15 |
| Meltdown Etc. \| **Culver City** | 18 |
| Mimi's Cafe \| **multi.** | 17 |
| Monty's Steak \| **Woodland Hills** | 20 |
| Mo's \| **Burbank** | 17 |
| Musso & Frank \| **Hollywood** | 18 |
| Neptune's Net \| **Malibu** | 18 |
| **NEW** O!Burger \| **W Hollywood** | - |
| Oinkster, The \| **Eagle Rock** | 20 |
| Omelette Parlor \| **Santa Monica** | 19 |
| Original Pancake \| **Redondo Bch** | 23 |
| Original Pantry \| **Downtown** | 15 |
| Outlaws B&G \| **Playa del Rey** | 18 |
| Paradise Cove \| **Malibu** | 15 |
| **NEW** R+D Kitchen \| **Santa Monica** | - |
| Rainforest Cafe \| **Ontario** | 12 |
| Ruby's \| **multi.** | 17 |
| Russell's Burgers \| **Pasadena** | 19 |
| Shack, The \| **multi.** | 17 |
| Simon LA \| **W Hollywood** | 21 |
| Smitty's Grill \| **Pasadena** | 21 |
| Souplantation \| **multi.** | 16 |
| Spark Woodfire \| **multi.** | 19 |
| Square One Dining \| **E Hollywood** | 22 |
| Stand, The \| **multi.** | 18 |
| Standard, The \| **Downtown** | 15 |
| Swingers \| **multi.** | 17 |
| Three on Fourth \| **Santa Monica** | 21 |
| Toast \| **Third St.** | 19 |
| Tony P's Dock \| **Marina del Rey** | 18 |
| Trails, The \| **Los Feliz** | 16 |
| Urth Caffé \| **multi.** | 20 |
| Vault, The \| **Pasadena** | 14 |
| Vibrato \| **Bel-Air** | 21 |
| Village Idiot \| **Melrose** | 19 |
| **NEW** Waffle, The \| **Hollywood** | 16 |

Wood Ranch BBQ | multi. 20
Yard Hse. | multi. 20

## ARGENTINEAN

☑ Carlitos Gardel | Melrose 23
Gaucho Grill | multi. 17

## ASIAN

Chaya | W Hollywood 24
☑ Chinois | Santa Monica 26
☑ Gina Lee's | Redondo Bch 26
Gordon Biersch | multi. 16
☑ Mako | Beverly Hills 26
Max | Sherman Oaks 24
Parc | Hollywood 21
2117 | West LA 23
Vegan Glory | Beverly Blvd. 20
☑ Yamashiro | Hollywood 18

## ASIAN FUSION

Ahi Sushi | Studio City 20
Asia de Cuba | W Hollywood 23
☑ Crustacean | Beverly Hills 24
Fat Fish | multi. 20
Formosa Cafe | W Hollywood 12
☑ Mako | Beverly Hills 26
Max | Sherman Oaks 24
MOZ Buddha | Agoura Hills 20
RA Sushi | Torrance 16
Roy's | multi. 23
Saketini | Brentwood 20
Tengu | multi. 22
Wabi-Sabi | Venice 22
Zen Grill | Beverly Hills 21

## BAKERIES

Breadbar | W Hollywood 18
City Bakery | Brentwood 19
Clementine | Century City 23
Doña Rosa | multi. 16
Jack n' Jill's | Santa Monica 19
☑ Jin Patisserie | Venice 25
Joan's on 3rd | Third St. 23
Le Pain Quotidien | multi. 19
Mäni's | multi. 18
Michel Richard | Beverly Hills 23
Misto Caffé | Torrance 20
☑ Porto's | multi. 24
NEW Röckenwagner | -
  Santa Monica
Susina | La Brea 22
Sweet Lady Jane | Melrose 23
3 Square | Venice 20

## BARBECUE

Adobe Cantina | Agoura Hills 15
☑ Baby Blues | Venice 23

Big Mama's | Pasadena 19
Boneyard | Sherman Oaks 21
Dr. Hogly Wogly's | Van Nuys 22
NEW Gus's BBQ | S Pasadena -
Joey's BBQ | Manhattan Bch 18
Johnny Rebs' | multi. 22
JR's BBQ | Culver City 21
Kansas City BBQ | Studio City 21
Lucille's BBQ | multi. 22
Mr. Cecil's Ribs | multi. 18
Nanbankan | West LA 24
Oinkster, The | Eagle Rock 20
Original TX BBQ | Mid-City 21
☑ Phillips BBQ | multi. 25
Quincy's BBQ | Encino 16
Reddi Chick BBQ | Brentwood 21
Ribs USA | Burbank 19
Robin's BBQ | Pasadena 17
Stonefire Grill | multi. 18
Swinging Door | N Hollywood 22
Wood Ranch BBQ | multi. 20
Woody's BBQ | multi. 23
Zeke's Smokehse. | multi. 20

## BELGIAN

Le Pain Quotidien | multi. 19

## BRAZILIAN

Bossa Nova | multi. 20
Café Brasil | multi. 19
Fogo de Chão | Beverly Hills 24
Galletto | Westlake Vill 23
Green Field | multi. 21
Picanha Churr. | Burbank 21
Porto Alegre | Pasadena 20
NEW Sampa Grill | Encino -
Tropicalia Brazil | Los Feliz 20
Ummba Grill | Century City 16

## BRITISH

Whale & Ale | San Pedro 16
Ye Olde King's | Santa Monica 17

## BURGERS

Apple Pan | West LA 22
Astro Burger | multi. 19
Barney's Burgers | multi. 20
Burger Continental | Pasadena 17
Burger 90210 | Beverly Hills 16
Cassell's | Koreatown 19
Counter, The | Santa Monica 21
NEW 8 oz. | Melrose -
☑ Father's Office | multi. 24
NEW Five Guys | Carson -
Hamburger Mary's | W Hollywood 15
☑ In-N-Out | multi. 23

| | |
|---|---|
| Islands \| **multi.** | 16 |
| Johnny Rockets \| **multi.** | 15 |
| Mo's \| **Burbank** | 17 |
| **NEW** O!Burger \| **W Hollywood** | - |
| Outlaws B&G \| **Playa del Rey** | 18 |
| Pie 'N Burger \| **Pasadena** | 19 |
| Ruby's \| **multi.** | 17 |
| Russell's Burgers \| **Pasadena** | 19 |
| Shack, The \| **multi.** | 17 |
| Tommy's \| **Downtown** | 22 |
| 25 Degrees \| **Hollywood** | 21 |
| 26 Beach \| **Marina del Rey** | 20 |

## CAJUN

| | |
|---|---|
| Gumbo Pot \| **Fairfax** | 19 |
| Ragin' Cajun \| **Hermosa Bch** | 20 |
| Stevie's Creole \| **Encino** | 19 |
| Uncle Darrow's \| **Venice** | 19 |

## CALIFORNIAN

| | |
|---|---|
| Ammo \| **Hollywood** | 22 |
| **Z** A.O.C. \| **Third St.** | 26 |
| Axe \| **Venice** | 22 |
| Babalu \| **Santa Monica** | 19 |
| Barefoot B&G \| **Third St.** | 18 |
| Barsac Brass. \| **N Hollywood** | 21 |
| Basix Cafe \| **W Hollywood** | 19 |
| Bel-Air B&G \| **Bel-Air** | 19 |
| Bistro 45 \| **Pasadena** | 26 |
| Bistro 767 \| **Rolling Hills Estates** | 22 |
| Bistro 31 \| **Santa Monica** | 18 |
| Bloom Cafe \| **Mid-City** | 22 |
| Blvd \| **Beverly Hills** | 20 |
| Bono's \| **Long Bch** | 20 |
| Bora Bora \| **Manhattan Bch** | 22 |
| Boulevard Lounge \| **W Hollywood** | 19 |
| Breeze \| **Century City** | 17 |
| **Z** Café Bizou \| **multi.** | 23 |
| Cafe Del Rey \| **Marina del Rey** | 21 |
| Café 14 \| **Agoura Hills** | 24 |
| Cafe Montana \| **Santa Monica** | 19 |
| Café Mundial \| **Monrovia** | 21 |
| Cafe Pinot \| **Downtown** | 22 |
| Cafe Rodeo \| **Beverly Hills** | 18 |
| Caioti Pizza \| **Studio City** | 22 |
| Calitalia \| **Calabasas** | - |
| Camilo's \| **Eagle Rock** | 23 |
| Campanile \| **La Brea** | 26 |
| Canal Club \| **Venice** | 18 |
| **NEW** Carbon Beach \| **Malibu** | 13 |
| Castaway \| **Burbank** | 13 |
| Catch \| **Santa Monica** | 22 |
| Central Park \| **Pasadena** | 17 |
| Cézanne \| **Santa Monica** | 21 |
| Chateau Marmont \| **W Hollywood** | 20 |
| Checkers \| **Downtown** | 20 |

| | |
|---|---|
| Chef Melba's \| **Hermosa Bch** | 24 |
| China Grill \| **Manhattan Bch** | 19 |
| **Z** Cicada \| **Downtown** | 23 |
| Circa 55 \| **Beverly Hills** | 19 |
| **Z** Cliff's Edge \| **Silver Lake** | 21 |
| Coast \| **Santa Monica** | 21 |
| Coral Tree \| **multi.** | 18 |
| Crocodile Cafe \| **Pasadena** | 16 |
| **NEW** Darren's \| **Manhattan Bch** | 26 |
| **Z** Derek's \| **Pasadena** | 27 |
| Devon \| **Monrovia** | 23 |
| Emles \| **Northridge** | 19 |
| Farm/Bev. Hills \| **Woodland Hills** | 19 |
| Five 61 \| **Pasadena** | 22 |
| 410 Boyd \| **Downtown** | 17 |
| Fritto Misto \| **multi.** | 21 |
| Gardens \| **Beverly Hills** | 23 |
| Gardens/Glendon \| **Westwood** | 19 |
| **Z** Geoffrey's \| **Malibu** | 21 |
| Getty Ctr. \| **Brentwood** | 22 |
| **Z** Gina Lee's \| **Redondo Bch** | 26 |
| Gorikee \| **Woodland Hills** | 22 |
| **NEW** Green St. Tav. \| **Pasadena** | 23 |
| Hal's B&G \| **Venice** | 20 |
| **Z** Hampton's \| **Westlake Vill** | 23 |
| Holly St. \| **Pasadena** | 19 |
| **Z** Hotel Bel-Air \| **Bel-Air** | 25 |
| Hugo's \| **multi.** | 21 |
| **Z** Inn/Seventh Ray \| **Topanga** | 20 |
| Ivy, The \| **W Hollywood** | 22 |
| Ivy at Shore \| **Santa Monica** | 22 |
| Jack Sprat's \| **West LA** | 19 |
| Jer-ne \| **Marina del Rey** | 20 |
| **Z** Joe's \| **Venice** | 26 |
| **Z** La Boheme \| **W Hollywood** | 22 |
| L.A. Farm \| **Santa Monica** | 20 |
| **NEW** La Grande Orange \| **Pasadena** | - |
| **NEW** LAMILL \| **Silver Lake** | 23 |
| **Z** Langham Huntington \| **Pasadena** | 26 |
| **Z** Leila's \| **Oak Pk** | 27 |
| **NEW** Lemonade Cafe \| **multi.** | - |
| Lemon Moon \| **West LA** | 20 |
| Literati \| **West LA** | 19 |
| Louise's Tratt. \| **multi.** | 17 |
| **Z** Lucques \| **W Hollywood** | 27 |
| Madeleine's \| **Pasadena** | 24 |
| **NEW** Malibu Pier Club \| **Malibu** | - |
| Market City \| **Burbank** | 17 |
| Mark's \| **W Hollywood** | 17 |
| Marmalade Café \| **multi.** | 17 |
| Marty's \| **Highland Pk** | 18 |
| Michael's \| **Santa Monica** | 24 |
| Milky Way \| **Pico-Robertson** | 19 |

| | |
|---|---|
| Mi Piace | multi. | 20 |
| Mirabelle | W Hollywood | 19 |
| Misto Caffé | Torrance | 20 |
| Mr. Cecil's Ribs | West LA | 18 |
| Napa Valley | Westwood | 20 |
| 🖪 Native Foods | Westwood | 22 |
| Nicola's | Woodland Hills | 20 |
| NEW Oak Room | Pacific Palisades | - |
| 🖪 One Pico | Santa Monica | 22 |
| On Sunset | Brentwood | 22 |
| 🖪 Parkway Grill | Pasadena | 26 |
| Patina | Downtown | 25 |
| Pat's | Pico-Robertson | 22 |
| Paul's Cafe | Tarzana | 17 |
| Polo Lounge | Beverly Hills | 22 |
| Porta Via | Beverly Hills | 24 |
| Rack | Woodland Hills | 16 |
| Raymond, The | Pasadena | 24 |
| NEW Röckenwagner | Santa Monica | - |
| Rose Cafe | Venice | 19 |
| Rustic Canyon | Santa Monica | 21 |
| 🖪 Sam's/Beach | Santa Monica | 26 |
| 17th St. Cafe | Santa Monica | 19 |
| Sir Winston's | Long Bch | 21 |
| 🖪 Spago | Beverly Hills | 27 |
| Spazio | Sherman Oaks | 18 |
| Stanley's | Sherman Oaks | 19 |
| Sur | W Hollywood | 21 |
| NEW Terra | Malibu | 22 |
| NEW Third & Olive | Burbank | - |
| Tower Bar | W Hollywood | 21 |
| Towne | Manhattan Bch | 18 |
| NEW Tranquility Base | Downtown | - |
| 26 Beach | Marina del Rey | 20 |
| uWink | multi. | 13 |
| Watercress | Sherman Oaks | 21 |
| West | Brentwood | 18 |
| Whist | Santa Monica | 20 |
| Wolfgang Puck | multi. | 17 |
| 🖪 Yamashiro | Hollywood | 18 |
| NEW Zane's | Hermosa Bch | - |
| Zeidler's | Brentwood | 17 |

## CANADIAN

| | |
|---|---|
| Soleil Westwood | Westwood | 20 |

## CARIBBEAN

| | |
|---|---|
| Bamboo | Culver City | 20 |
| 🖪 Cha Cha Cha | Silver Lake | 20 |
| Cha Cha Chicken | Santa Monica | 21 |
| 🖪 Prado | Hancock Pk | 22 |

## CHEESE STEAKS

| | |
|---|---|
| South St. | multi. | 18 |

## CHINESE

(* dim sum specialist)

| | |
|---|---|
| ABC Seafood* | Chinatown | 19 |
| Bamboo Cuisine | Sherman Oaks | 23 |
| Cali. Wok | multi. | 17 |
| CBS Seafood | Chinatown | - |
| Chi Dynasty | Los Feliz | 21 |
| China Grill | Manhattan Bch | 19 |
| Chin Chin* | multi. | 16 |
| Chung King | Monterey Pk | 25 |
| 🖪 Din Tai Fung | Arcadia | 25 |
| Empress Harbor* | Monterey Pk | 19 |
| Empress Pavilion | Chinatown | 21 |
| Fu-Shing | Pasadena | 19 |
| Genghis Cohen | Fairfax | 20 |
| NEW Hong Yei | San Gabriel | - |
| Hop Li* | multi. | 20 |
| Hop Woo | multi. | 18 |
| NEW Hunan Seafood | Rosemead | - |
| Hu's Szechwan | Palms | 21 |
| Kung Pao | multi. | 19 |
| Macau St. | Monterey Pk | 19 |
| Mandarette | W Hollywood | 18 |
| Mandarin Deli | multi. | 20 |
| Mission 261* | San Gabriel | 20 |
| Mr. Chow | Beverly Hills | 21 |
| NBC Seafood* | Monterey Pk | 19 |
| New Moon | multi. | 21 |
| Ocean Seafood* | Chinatown | 20 |
| Ocean Star* | Monterey Pk | 21 |
| Panda Inn | multi. | 21 |
| P.F. Chang's | multi. | 19 |
| Sam Woo | multi. | 20 |
| Sea Empress* | Gardena | 19 |
| Sea Harbour* | Rosemead | 24 |
| Triumphal Palace* | Alhambra | 21 |
| V.I.P. Harbor* | West LA | 18 |
| Wokcano Cafe | multi. | 19 |
| W's China | Redondo Bch | 21 |
| Xi'an | Beverly Hills | 22 |
| Yang Chow | multi. | 22 |
| 🖪 Yujean Kang's | Pasadena | 25 |

## COFFEEHOUSES

| | |
|---|---|
| Caffe Luxxe | Santa Monica | 24 |
| Coupa Café | Beverly Hills | 17 |
| NEW LAMILL | Silver Lake | 23 |
| Literati | West LA | 19 |
| Urth Caffé | multi. | 20 |
| Watercress | Sherman Oaks | 21 |
| NEW Whisper Cafe | Encino | - |

## COFFEE SHOPS/DINERS

| | |
|---|---|
| Brighton Coffee | Beverly Hills | 18 |
| Cafe 50's | multi. | 16 |

| | |
|---|---|
| Cora's Coffee \| **Santa Monica** | 21 |
| Duke's Coffee \| **W Hollywood** | 18 |
| Du-par's \| **multi.** | 16 |
| Eat Well Cafe \| **W Hollywood** | 16 |
| Fountain Coffee \| **Beverly Hills** | 20 |
| Fred 62 \| **Los Feliz** | 17 |
| Hamburger Mary's \| **W Hollywood** | 15 |
| Jan's \| **W Hollywood** | 14 |
| Kate Mantilini \| **multi.** | 18 |
| Mimi's Cafe \| **multi.** | 17 |
| Original Pancake \| **Redondo Bch** | 23 |
| Original Pantry \| **Downtown** | 15 |
| Patrick's \| **Santa Monica** | 17 |
| Pie 'N Burger \| **Pasadena** | 19 |
| Rae's \| **Santa Monica** | 18 |
| Rocky Cola \| **multi.** | 13 |
| Ruby's \| **multi.** | 17 |
| Russell's Burgers \| **Pasadena** | 19 |
| Swingers \| **multi.** | 17 |
| Uncle Bill's \| **Manhattan Bch** | 21 |

## CONTEMPORARY LOUISIANA

| | |
|---|---|
| Magnolia Lounge \| **Pasadena** | 19 |

## CONTINENTAL

| | |
|---|---|
| ⨂ Bistro Gdn. \| **Studio City** | 21 |
| ⨂ Brandywine \| **Woodland Hills** | 27 |
| Café 14 \| **Agoura Hills** | 24 |
| ⨂ Dal Rae \| **Pico Rivera** | 25 |
| Fins \| **multi.** | 22 |
| NEW Gordon Ramsay \| **W Hollywood** | - |
| Mandevilla \| **Westlake Vill** | 22 |
| Odyssey \| **Granada Hills** | 14 |
| Pig 'n Whistle \| **Hollywood** | 13 |
| Polo Lounge \| **Beverly Hills** | 22 |
| Sir Winston's \| **Long Bch** | 21 |

## CREOLE

| | |
|---|---|
| Creole Chef \| **Baldwin Hills** | - |
| NEW Creperie/Jack n' Jill's \| **Third St.** | 21 |
| Harold & Belle's \| **Mid-City** | 24 |
| Uncle Darrow's \| **Venice** | 19 |

## CUBAN

| | |
|---|---|
| Asia de Cuba \| **W Hollywood** | 23 |
| NEW Casa Don Rolando \| **N Hills** | - |
| Cuban Bistro \| **Alhambra** | 18 |
| NEW Mojitos \| **Pasadena** | 24 |
| ⨂ Porto's \| **multi.** | 24 |
| Versailles \| **multi.** | 21 |

## DELIS

| | |
|---|---|
| Art's Deli \| **Studio City** | 20 |
| Barney Greengrass \| **Beverly Hills** | 20 |

| | |
|---|---|
| ⨂ Brent's Deli \| **multi.** | 26 |
| Broadway Deli \| **Santa Monica** | 15 |
| Canter's \| **Fairfax** | 18 |
| Factor's Deli \| **Pico-Robertson** | 16 |
| Fromin's Deli \| **multi.** | 14 |
| Greenblatt's Deli \| **Hollywood** | 18 |
| Johnnie's Pastrami \| **Culver City** | 20 |
| Junior's \| **West LA** | 16 |
| NEW Ken/Kent's NY Deli \| **Hermosa Bch** | - |
| La Bottega Marino \| **multi.** | 21 |
| ⨂ Langer's Deli \| **Downtown** | 25 |
| Nate 'n Al \| **Beverly Hills** | 20 |
| Roll 'n Rye \| **Culver City** | 17 |
| NEW Village Pantry \| **Pacific Palisades** | 14 |

## DESSERT

| | |
|---|---|
| Alcove \| **Los Feliz** | 21 |
| Auntie Em's \| **Eagle Rock** | 23 |
| Babalu \| **Santa Monica** | 19 |
| Café 14 \| **Agoura Hills** | 24 |
| Cafe Montana \| **Santa Monica** | 19 |
| Campanile \| **La Brea** | 26 |
| Clementine \| **Century City** | 23 |
| Coco Noche \| **Manhattan Bch** | 17 |
| Farm/Bev. Hills \| **multi.** | 19 |
| Grace \| **Beverly Blvd.** | 25 |
| Joan's on 3rd \| **Third St.** | 23 |
| Mäni's \| **multi.** | 18 |
| Max \| **Sherman Oaks** | 24 |
| Melting Pot \| **multi.** | 18 |
| Michel Richard \| **Beverly Hills** | 23 |
| ⨂ Porto's \| **multi.** | 24 |
| Simon LA \| **W Hollywood** | 21 |
| ⨂ Spago \| **Beverly Hills** | 27 |
| Susina \| **La Brea** | 22 |
| Sweet Lady Jane \| **Melrose** | 23 |

## EASTERN EUROPEAN

| | |
|---|---|
| Danube Bulgarian \| **Westwood** | 19 |

## ECLECTIC

| | |
|---|---|
| Barbara's \| **Downtown** | 14 |
| Barefoot B&G \| **Third St.** | 18 |
| Bellavino \| **Westlake Vill** | 19 |
| Boneyard \| **Sherman Oaks** | 21 |
| Broadway Deli \| **Santa Monica** | 15 |
| Buddha's Belly \| **Beverly Blvd.** | 19 |
| Café/Tango \| **Universal City** | 19 |
| Canal Club \| **Venice** | 18 |
| ⨂ Chez Mélange \| **Redondo Bch** | 25 |
| NEW Citrus at Social \| **Hollywood** | 21 |
| Coco Noche \| **Manhattan Bch** | 17 |
| Corkscrew \| **Manhattan Bch** | 21 |
| Coupa Café \| **Beverly Hills** | 17 |

| | |
|---|---|
| Depot | **Torrance** | 24 |
| Encounter | **LAX** | 14 |
| Farm Stand | **El Segundo** | 21 |
| Grand Lux | **Beverly Hills** | 18 |
| **NEW** Hidden | **Santa Monica** | 15 |
| Lazy Dog | **Torrance** | 19 |
| Library Alehse. | **Santa Monica** | 18 |
| Literati | **West LA** | 19 |
| Lou | **Hollywood** | 23 |
| **NEW** Medusa | **Beverly Blvd.** | – |
| Minx | **Glendale** | 18 |
| Mirabelle | **W Hollywood** | 19 |
| Misto Caffé | **Torrance** | 20 |
| **Z** Native Foods | **Westwood** | 22 |
| Neomeze | **Pasadena** | 23 |
| **Z** Nook Bistro | **West LA** | 24 |
| Patrick's | **Santa Monica** | 17 |
| **Z** Penthouse | **Santa Monica** | 18 |
| **NEW** Point, The | **Culver City** | 18 |
| Standard, The | **W Hollywood** | 15 |
| **NEW** Tranquility Base | **Downtown** | – |
| Vertical Wine | **Pasadena** | 23 |
| Villa Piacere | **Woodland Hills** | 19 |
| Walter's | **Claremont** | 19 |
| **NEW** Whisper Cafe | **Encino** | – |
| York, The | **Highland Pk** | 18 |

## ETHIOPIAN

| | |
|---|---|
| Nyala Ethiopian | **Fairfax** | 21 |

## EURASIAN

| | |
|---|---|
| **NEW** La Défence | **Koreatown** | – |

## EUROPEAN

| | |
|---|---|
| BottleRock | **Culver City** | 16 |
| **NEW** Green St. Tav. | **Pasadena** | 23 |
| Palomino | **Westwood** | 19 |
| Three on Fourth | **Santa Monica** | 21 |
| 2117 | **West LA** | 23 |

## FONDUE

| | |
|---|---|
| Melting Pot | **multi.** | 18 |

## FRENCH

| | |
|---|---|
| A Cow Jumped | **Beverly Hills** | 20 |
| **Z** A.O.C. | **Third St.** | 26 |
| **Z** Bastide | **W Hollywood** | 27 |
| Bowery | **Hollywood** | 20 |
| Café Beaujolais | **Eagle Rock** | 23 |
| Café Pierre | **Manhattan Bch** | 22 |
| Cafe Pinot | **Downtown** | 22 |
| Café Provencal | **Thousand Oaks** | 23 |
| Cézanne | **Santa Monica** | 21 |
| Chameau | **Fairfax** | 22 |
| Chateau Marmont | **W Hollywood** | 20 |
| Chaya | **W Hollywood** | 24 |
| Chez Mimi | **Santa Monica** | 22 |

| | |
|---|---|
| **Z** Chinois | **Santa Monica** | 26 |
| **NEW** Chloe | **Santa Monica** | 18 |
| **NEW** Citrus at Social | **Hollywood** | 21 |
| Clafoutis | **W Hollywood** | 19 |
| **NEW** Comme Ça | **W Hollywood** | 21 |
| **Z** Derek's | **Pasadena** | 27 |
| Devon | **Monrovia** | 23 |
| Dusty's | **Silver Lake** | 18 |
| Five 61 | **Pasadena** | 22 |
| **Z** Fraîche | **Culver City** | 24 |
| French Crêpe Co. | **multi.** | 21 |
| Hokusai | **Beverly Hills** | 24 |
| **Z** Hotel Bel-Air | **Bel-Air** | 25 |
| **Z** Jin Patisserie | **Venice** | 25 |
| **Z** JiRaffe | **Santa Monica** | 26 |
| Joe's | **Venice** | 26 |
| **Z** La Cachette | **Century City** | 27 |
| La Creperie Cafe | **Manhattan Bch** | 23 |
| La Frite | **multi.** | 18 |
| La Rive Gauche | **Palos Verdes** | 19 |
| Le Chêne | **Saugus** | 23 |
| Le Sanglier | **Tarzana** | 24 |
| Madeleine Bistro | **Tarzana** | 24 |
| Maison Akira | **Pasadena** | 25 |
| **Z** Mélisse | **Santa Monica** | 28 |
| **NEW** Mes Amis | **Los Feliz** | 16 |
| Morels French Steak | **Fairfax** | 18 |
| Orris | **West LA** | 26 |
| Ortolan | **Third St.** | 25 |
| Parc | **Hollywood** | 21 |
| Paul's Cafe | **Tarzana** | 17 |
| Petrossian | **W Hollywood** | 23 |
| Salades/Provence | **W Hollywood** | 20 |
| **Z** Shiro | **S Pasadena** | 27 |
| Soleil Westwood | **Westwood** | 20 |
| **Z** Sona | **W Hollywood** | 27 |
| Standard, The | **Downtown** | 15 |
| Taix | **Echo Pk** | 16 |
| Tasca Winebar | **Third St.** | 23 |
| **NEW** Third & Olive | **Burbank** | – |
| **NEW** Yuta | **Studio City** | – |

## FRENCH (BISTRO)

| | |
|---|---|
| Angelique Café | **Downtown** | 19 |
| Bistro de la Gare | **S Pasadena** | 19 |
| Bistro Provence | **Burbank** | 23 |
| **NEW** Bistro 39 | **Alhambra** | – |
| Brass.-Cap. | **Santa Monica** | 19 |
| **Z** Café Bizou | **multi.** | 23 |
| Cafe des Artistes | **Hollywood** | 20 |
| Cafe Stella | **Silver Lake** | 21 |
| CrêpeVine | **Pasadena** | 21 |
| Figaro Bistrot | **Los Feliz** | 19 |
| **NEW** Foxtail | **W Hollywood** | – |
| **Z** Frenchy's Bistro | **Long Bch** | 26 |

| | |
|---|---|
| Julienne \| **San Marino** | 25 |
| La Creperie Cafe \| **Long Bch** | 23 |
| La Dijonaise \| **Culver City** | 18 |
| Le Marmiton \| **multi.** | 18 |
| Le Petit Bistro \| **W Hollywood** | 22 |
| Le Petit Cafe \| **Santa Monica** | 21 |
| Le Petit Four \| **W Hollywood** | 19 |
| Le Petit Rest. \| **Sherman Oaks** | 21 |
| Lilly's French Cafe \| **Venice** | 19 |
| Michel Richard \| **Beverly Hills** | 23 |
| Mimosa \| **Beverly Blvd.** | 20 |
| ☑ Mistral \| **Sherman Oaks** | 25 |
| Monsieur Marcel \| **multi.** | 21 |
| Morels First Floor \| **Fairfax** | 17 |
| Pastis \| **Beverly Blvd.** | 21 |
| Pinot Bistro \| **Studio City** | 23 |
| Rive Gauche \| **Sherman Oaks** | 19 |
| 750 ml \| **S Pasadena** | 19 |
| Wine Bistro \| **Studio City** | 21 |

## FRENCH (BRASSERIE)

| | |
|---|---|
| **NEW** Anisette \| **Santa Monica** | - |
| Barsac Brass. \| **N Hollywood** | 21 |
| **NEW** Hall, The \| **W Hollywood** | - |
| Kendall's Brass. \| **Downtown** | 17 |

## GASTROPUB

| | |
|---|---|
| Ford's \| Amer. \| **Culver City** | 19 |
| Whale & Ale \| English \| **San Pedro** | 16 |
| York, The \| Eclectic \| **Highland Pk** | 18 |

## GREEK

| | |
|---|---|
| Delphi \| **Westwood** | 17 |
| George's Greek \| **multi.** | 22 |
| Great Greek \| **Sherman Oaks** | 21 |
| Joseph's Cafe \| **Hollywood** | 18 |
| Le Petit Greek \| **Hancock Pk** | 19 |
| ☑ Papa Cristo's \| **Mid-City** | 22 |
| ☑ Papadakis Tav. \| **San Pedro** | 21 |
| ☑ Petros \| **Manhattan Bch** | 24 |
| Sofi \| **Third St.** | 20 |
| Taverna Tony \| **Malibu** | 20 |
| Ulysses Voyage \| **Fairfax** | 21 |

## HAWAIIAN

| | |
|---|---|
| Back Home \| **multi.** | 17 |
| Local Pl. \| **Torrance** | 18 |
| Loft, The \| **multi.** | 19 |
| Roy's \| **multi.** | 23 |

## HOT DOGS

| | |
|---|---|
| Carney's \| **multi.** | 19 |
| Jody Maroni's \| **multi.** | 19 |
| Pink's Chili Dogs \| **La Brea** | 19 |
| **NEW** Portillo's \| **Moreno Valley** | 18 |
| Stand, The \| **Encino** | 18 |
| Tommy's \| **Downtown** | 22 |

## INDIAN

| | |
|---|---|
| ☑ Addi's Tandoor \| **Redondo Bch** | 26 |
| Agra Cafe \| **Silver Lake** | 21 |
| Akbar \| **multi.** | 22 |
| All India \| **multi.** | 22 |
| Bollywood Cafe \| **Studio City** | 19 |
| Bombay Bite \| **Westwood** | 20 |
| Bombay Cafe \| **West LA** | 23 |
| Bombay Palace \| **Beverly Hills** | 21 |
| Chakra \| **Beverly Hills** | 21 |
| Clay Pit \| **Brentwood** | 21 |
| Electric Lotus \| **Los Feliz** | 18 |
| Flavor of India \| **multi.** | 22 |
| Gate of India \| **Santa Monica** | 21 |
| Holy Cow Indian \| **Third St.** | 20 |
| India's Oven \| **Beverly Blvd.** | 19 |
| India's Tandoori \| **multi.** | 19 |
| Lal Mirch \| **Studio City** | 20 |
| Nawab of India \| **Santa Monica** | 21 |
| Nizam \| **West LA** | 18 |
| Radhika's \| **Pasadena** | 22 |
| ☑ Surya India \| **Third St.** | 24 |
| Tantra \| **Silver Lake** | 20 |
| ☑ Tanzore \| **Beverly Hills** | 23 |

## INDONESIAN

| | |
|---|---|
| Indo Cafe \| **Palms** | 19 |
| Simpang Asia \| **West LA** | 18 |

## IRISH

| | |
|---|---|
| Auld Dubliner \| **Long Bch** | 18 |

## ITALIAN

| | |
|---|---|
| (N=Northern; S=Southern) | |
| Adagio \| N \| **Woodland Hills** | 23 |
| Ago \| N \| **W Hollywood** | 22 |
| Alejo's \| **multi.** | 19 |
| Alessio \| **multi.** | 21 |
| All' Angelo \| **Melrose** | 25 |
| Allegria \| **Malibu** | 20 |
| Amalfi \| **La Brea** | 21 |
| **NEW** Amarone \| **W Hollywood** | 27 |
| Amici \| **multi.** | 21 |
| **NEW** Andiamo \| **Silver Lake** | - |
| Angeli Caffe \| **Melrose** | 23 |
| ☑ Angelini Osteria \| **Beverly Blvd.** | 27 |
| Anna's \| S \| **West LA** | 15 |
| Antica Pizzeria \| **Marina del Rey** | 20 |
| Aroma \| **Silver Lake** | 25 |
| Basix Cafe \| **W Hollywood** | 19 |
| Bay Cities Deli \| **Santa Monica** | - |
| Bella Cucina \| S \| **Hollywood** | 23 |
| Bella Roma \| S \| **Pico-Robertson** | 23 |
| Berri's Pizza \| **multi.** | 16 |
| Boccaccio's \| **Westlake Vill** | 22 |
| Bravo \| **Santa Monica** | 17 |
| Briganti \| **S Pasadena** | 23 |

| | |
|---|---|
| NEW Brunello Trattoria \| Culver City | - |
| Buca di Beppo \| S \| multi. | 15 |
| Buona Sera \| Redondo Bch | 22 |
| Ca'Brea \| N \| La Brea | 22 |
| Ca' del Sole \| N \| N Hollywood | 22 |
| Cafe Med \| W Hollywood | 18 |
| Caffé Delfini \| Santa Monica | 23 |
| Caffe Pinguini \| Playa del Rey | 21 |
| Caffe Primo \| W Hollywood | 19 |
| Caffe Roma \| Beverly Hills | 17 |
| Calitalia \| Calabasas | - |
| C & O \| Marina del Rey | 18 |
| Z Capo \| Santa Monica | 26 |
| Casa Bianca \| Eagle Rock | 23 |
| Celestino \| N \| Pasadena | 23 |
| Cheebo \| Hollywood | 19 |
| Christy's \| N \| Long Bch | 22 |
| Cialuzzi's \| Redondo Bch | 20 |
| Ciao Tratt. \| Downtown | 20 |
| Z Cicada \| Downtown | 23 |
| Clafoutis \| W Hollywood | 19 |
| Z Cliff's Edge \| Silver Lake | 21 |
| Coral Tree \| multi. | 18 |
| NEW Crudo \| W Hollywood | - |
| cube \| La Brea | 22 |
| Cucina Paradiso \| N \| Palms | 21 |
| Dan Tana's \| W Hollywood | 23 |
| Da Pasquale \| S \| Beverly Hills | 20 |
| NEW Delancey \| Hollywood | - |
| Divino \| Brentwood | 22 |
| Dolce Enoteca \| Melrose | 17 |
| Dominick's \| Beverly Blvd. | 21 |
| Drago \| Santa Monica | 24 |
| E. Baldi \| N \| Beverly Hills | 22 |
| Enoteca Drago \| Beverly Hills | 21 |
| Enoteca Toscana \| N \| Camarillo | 19 |
| Enzo & Angela \| West LA | 22 |
| Fabiolus Café \| N \| Hollywood | 20 |
| Farfalla Trattoria \| Los Feliz | 22 |
| Far Niente \| N \| Glendale | 25 |
| Frascati \| N \| Rolling Hills Estates | 24 |
| Fritto Misto \| multi. | 21 |
| Gale's \| N \| Pasadena | 24 |
| Galletto \| Westlake Vill | 23 |
| Gennaro's \| Glendale | 20 |
| Giorgio Baldi \| Santa Monica | 24 |
| Girasole Cucina \| Hancock Pk | 23 |
| Guido's \| N \| multi. | 19 |
| i Cugini \| Santa Monica | 21 |
| Il Boccaccio \| N \| Hermosa Bch | 22 |
| Il Buco \| Beverly Hills | 22 |
| Il Capriccio \| Los Feliz | 20 |
| NEW Il Carpaccio \| Pacific Palisades | 23 |
| Il Chianti \| Lomita | 20 |
| Il Cielo \| N \| Beverly Hills | 21 |
| Il Fornaio \| multi. | 20 |
| Il Forno \| N \| Santa Monica | 20 |
| Il Forno Caldo \| Beverly Hills | 22 |
| Il Grano \| West LA | 26 |
| Il Moro \| West LA | 23 |
| Il Pastaio \| Beverly Hills | 25 |
| Il Sole \| W Hollywood | 24 |
| Il Tiramisù \| N \| Sherman Oaks | 23 |
| Il Tramezzino \| multi. | 20 |
| Jacopo's \| multi. | 16 |
| Johnnie's NY \| Santa Monica | 18 |
| Jones \| W Hollywood | 18 |
| La Botte \| Santa Monica | 25 |
| La Bottega Marino \| multi. | 21 |
| La Bruschetta \| Westwood | 23 |
| La Dolce Vita \| Beverly Hills | 22 |
| La Loggia \| Studio City | 22 |
| La Maschera \| N \| Pasadena | 22 |
| La Pergola \| Sherman Oaks | 22 |
| La Scala \| multi. | 21 |
| La Sosta \| N \| Hermosa Bch | 26 |
| La Terza \| Third St. | 22 |
| La Vecchia \| Santa Monica | 21 |
| Lido/Manhattan \| Manhattan Bch | 19 |
| NEW Little Dom's \| Los Feliz | 17 |
| Locanda/Lago \| N \| Santa Monica | 21 |
| Locanda Veneta \| N \| Third St. | 24 |
| L'Opera \| N \| Long Bch | 23 |
| Louise's Tratt. \| multi. | 17 |
| Madeo \| N \| W Hollywood | 24 |
| Maggiano's \| multi. | 18 |
| Mama D's \| multi. | 21 |
| Maria's Italian \| multi. | 17 |
| Marino \| Hollywood | 21 |
| Market City \| S \| Burbank | 17 |
| Massimo \| N \| Beverly Hills | 22 |
| Matteo's \| West LA | 19 |
| NEW Melograno \| N \| Hollywood | 23 |
| Miceli's \| S \| multi. | 17 |
| NEW Michael's/Naples \| Long Bch | - |
| Mio Babbo's \| Westwood | 22 |
| Mi Piace \| multi. | 20 |
| Modo Mio \| Pacific Palisades | 22 |
| Mulberry St. Pizzeria \| multi. | 23 |
| Z Murano \| W Hollywood | 20 |
| Nicola's \| Woodland Hills | 20 |
| NEW Nonna \| W Hollywood | 18 |
| Oliva \| N \| Sherman Oaks | 21 |
| Orso \| Third St. | 21 |
| Osteria La Buca \| N \| Melrose | 25 |
| Osteria Latini \| Brentwood | 24 |
| Z Osteria Mozza \| Hollywood | 26 |

| | |
|---|---|
| Pace | **Laurel Canyon** | 21 |
| Padri | **Agoura Hills** | 21 |
| Palermo | **Los Feliz** | 19 |
| Palmeri | S | **Brentwood** | 22 |
| Pane e Vino | **Beverly Blvd.** | 21 |
| Panini Cafe | **Beverly Hills** | 17 |
| Panzanella | S | **Sherman Oaks** | 22 |
| Pastina | S | **West LA** | 20 |
| Pat's | **Pico-Robertson** | 22 |
| Pecorino | **Brentwood** | 22 |
| Peppone | **Brentwood** | 23 |
| Petrelli's Steak | **Culver City** | 16 |
| Piatti | **Thousand Oaks** | 19 |
| Piccolo | N | **Venice** | 27 |
| Piccolo Paradiso | **Beverly Hills** | 23 |
| **Ɀ** Pizzeria Mozza | **Hollywood** | 26 |
| Pizzicotto | **Brentwood** | 23 |
| Pomodoro | **multi.** | 18 |
| **NEW** Porta Via Italian | **Pasadena** | 23 |
| **NEW** Press Panini | **Studio City** | - |
| Prizzi's Piazza | **Hollywood** | 21 |
| Prosecco | N | **Toluca Lake** | 19 |
| Riviera Rest. | **Calabasas** | 24 |
| Romano's Macaroni | **multi.** | 17 |
| Rosti | N | **multi.** | 16 |
| Rustico | **Westlake Vill** | 23 |
| Saluzzi | **Rancho Palos Verdes** | 22 |
| San Gennaro | **Brentwood** | 16 |
| Sapori | **Marina del Rey** | 20 |
| SHU | **Bel-Air** | 21 |
| **NEW** Siena | **Pasadena** | - |
| Sisley Italian | **multi.** | 17 |
| Sor Tino | **Brentwood** | 19 |
| Spumoni | **multi.** | 17 |
| Stinking Rose | **Beverly Hills** | 18 |
| Talia's | **Manhattan Bch** | 24 |
| Tanino | S | **Westwood** | 23 |
| Taste Chicago | **Burbank** | 16 |
| **NEW** Terroni | S | **Beverly Blvd.** | 20 |
| Tesoro Tratt. | **Downtown** | 16 |
| 3rd Stop | **W Hollywood** | 17 |
| Tony's Bella Vista | **Burbank** | 21 |
| Toscana | N | **Brentwood** | 23 |
| Tra Di Noi | **Malibu** | 22 |
| Trastevere | **multi.** | 17 |
| Tre Venezie | N | **Pasadena** | 25 |
| Tulipano | **Azusa** | 24 |
| Tuscany | **Westlake Vill** | 24 |
| Ugo/Italian | **Culver City** | 17 |
| **Ɀ** Valentino | **Santa Monica** | 26 |
| Via Veneto | **Santa Monica** | 26 |
| Villa Sorriso | **Pasadena** | 16 |
| Vincenti | **Brentwood** | 26 |
| Vitello's | **Studio City** | 14 |
| Vito | **Santa Monica** | 20 |

| | |
|---|---|
| Vittorio's | S | **Pacific Palisades** | 19 |
| Vivoli Café | **multi.** | 25 |
| West | **Brentwood** | 18 |
| **NEW** Zane's | **Hermosa Bch** | - |
| Zucca | **Downtown** | 21 |

## JAPANESE

(* sushi specialist)

| | |
|---|---|
| Ahi Sushi* | **Studio City** | 20 |
| Asahi Ramen | **West LA** | 20 |
| Asaka* | **Rancho Palos Verdes** | 18 |
| Asakuma* | **multi.** | 20 |
| **Ɀ** Asanebo* | **Studio City** | 28 |
| Asuka* | **Westwood** | 19 |
| Azami* | **Hollywood** | 25 |
| Banzai Sushi* | **Calabasas** | 22 |
| Bar Hayama | **West LA** | 24 |
| Benihana | **multi.** | 18 |
| **NEW** Bond St. | **Beverly Hills** | 19 |
| Boss Sushi* | **Beverly Hills** | 25 |
| Cafe Sushi* | **Beverly Blvd.** | 20 |
| Catch* | **Santa Monica** | 22 |
| Chabuya | **multi.** | 19 |
| Chaya | **Venice** | 22 |
| Crazy Fish* | **Beverly Hills** | 16 |
| Ebizo's | **Manhattan Bch** | 22 |
| Echigo* | **West LA** | 25 |
| Fat Fish* | **multi.** | 20 |
| Geisha Hse.* | **Hollywood** | 20 |
| **Ɀ** Gonpachi | **Beverly Hills** | 18 |
| Gyu-Kaku | **multi.** | 20 |
| Hamasaku* | **West LA** | 26 |
| Hama Sushi* | **Venice** | 21 |
| Hayakawa* | **Covina** | 28 |
| Hide Sushi* | **West LA** | 24 |
| Hirosuke* | **Encino** | 19 |
| Hirozen* | **Beverly Blvd.** | 25 |
| Hokusai* | **Beverly Hills** | 24 |
| **NEW** Honda-Ya | **Little Tokyo** | 22 |
| Hump, The* | **Santa Monica** | 25 |
| Hurry Curry | **multi.** | 18 |
| Iroha* | **Studio City** | 25 |
| Ita Cho | **Beverly Blvd.** | 21 |
| Izaka-Ya | **Third St.** | 25 |
| Izayoi* | **Little Tokyo** | 20 |
| Japon Bistro* | **Pasadena** | 25 |
| Kanpai* | **Westchester** | 22 |
| Katana* | **W Hollywood** | 23 |
| **NEW** Katsu Sushi* | **Beverly Hills** | - |
| **Ɀ** Katsu-ya* | **multi.** | 27 |
| **Ɀ** Katsuya* | **multi.** | 24 |
| Koi* | **W Hollywood** | 24 |
| **NEW** Kula | **Century City** | 15 |
| K-Zo* | **Culver City** | 23 |
| Little Tokyo | **Rowland Hts** | 20 |

| | |
|---|---|
| NEW Luckyfish \| **Beverly Hills** | 18 |
| Maison Akira \| **Pasadena** | 25 |
| Z Matsuhisa* \| **Beverly Hills** | 27 |
| Mia Sushi* \| **Eagle Rock** | 18 |
| Mishima \| **Third St.** | 20 |
| Momoyama* \| **Redondo Bch** | 19 |
| Z Mori Sushi* \| **West LA** | 27 |
| Musha \| **multi.** | 24 |
| Nanbankan \| **West LA** | 24 |
| Natalee* \| **Palms** | 18 |
| Nishimura* \| **W Hollywood** | 26 |
| NEW Nobu \| **W Hollywood** | 26 |
| Z Nobu* \| **Malibu** | 27 |
| NEW Oba Sushi Izakaya* \| **Pasadena** | - |
| Omino Sushi* \| **Chatsworth** | 25 |
| O-Nami* \| **Torrance** | 17 |
| Onyx \| **Westlake Vill** | 25 |
| Orris \| **West LA** | 26 |
| Pearl Dragon* \| **Pacific Palisades** | 17 |
| RA Sushi* \| **Torrance** | 16 |
| NEW Robata Bar \| **Santa Monica** | 21 |
| R23* \| **Downtown** | 26 |
| Sai Sai* \| **Downtown** | 18 |
| Saito's Sushi* \| **Silver Lake** | 24 |
| Shabu Shabu Hse. \| **Little Tokyo** | 23 |
| Shima \| **Venice** | 27 |
| Z Shiro \| **S Pasadena** | 27 |
| NEW Shojin \| **Little Tokyo** | - |
| SHU* \| **Bel-Air** | 21 |
| NEW sugarFISH \| **Marina del Rey** | - |
| Suki 7 \| **Westlake Vill** | 19 |
| Sushi Duke* \| **Hermosa Bch** | 23 |
| Sushi Gen* \| **Little Tokyo** | 24 |
| Sushi Mac* \| **multi.** | 16 |
| Sushi Masu* \| **West LA** | 26 |
| Sushi Mon* \| **multi.** | 19 |
| Sushi Nozawa* \| **Studio City** | 26 |
| Sushi Ozekii* \| **multi.** | 17 |
| Sushi Roku* \| **multi.** | 22 |
| Sushi Sasabune* \| **West LA** | 26 |
| Sushi Sushi* \| **Beverly Hills** | 24 |
| Sushi Zo* \| **West LA** | 29 |
| Taiko* \| **multi.** | 20 |
| Z Takami \| **Downtown** | 20 |
| Takao* \| **Brentwood** | 24 |
| Tama Sushi* \| **Studio City** | 25 |
| Tengu* \| **multi.** | 22 |
| Teru Sushi* \| **Studio City** | 19 |
| Thousand Cranes* \| **Little Tokyo** | 21 |
| Three on Fourth \| **Santa Monica** | 21 |
| Tokyo Table \| **multi.** | 19 |
| Torafuku* \| **West LA** | 24 |
| Tsuji No Hana* \| **Marina del Rey** | 20 |
| Urasawa* \| **Beverly Hills** | 28 |

| | |
|---|---|
| U-Zen* \| **West LA** | 22 |
| Wa* \| **W Hollywood** | 25 |
| Wabi-Sabi* \| **Venice** | 22 |
| Wokcano Cafe* \| **multi.** | 19 |
| Yabu* \| **multi.** | 23 |
| NEW Yamato \| **Westwood** | 19 |
| Yen Sushi* \| **multi.** | 21 |
| NEW Yuta* \| **Studio City** | - |
| Yuzu* \| **Torrance** | 23 |
| Zip Fusion* \| **multi.** | 18 |
| Zu Robata \| **West LA** | 20 |

## KOREAN

(* barbecue specialist)

| | |
|---|---|
| BCD Tofu \| **multi.** | 19 |
| NEW BonChon \| **Koreatown** | - |
| Z ChoSun Galbee* \| **Koreatown** | 23 |
| NEW Gyenari* \| **Culver City** | - |
| NEW Jian* \| **Beverly Blvd.** | - |
| Manna* \| **Koreatown** | 16 |
| Nak Won* \| **Koreatown** | 16 |
| NEW Seoul Bros. \| **Pasadena** | - |
| Seoul Jung* \| **Downtown** | 20 |
| Z Soot Bull Jeep* \| **Koreatown** | 23 |
| NEW Tofu Villa* \| **West LA** | - |
| Tofu-Ya* \| **West LA** | 20 |
| Wharo* \| **Marina del Rey** | 16 |
| Woo Lae Oak \| **Beverly Hills** | 22 |

## KOSHER

| | |
|---|---|
| A Cow Jumped \| **Beverly Hills** | 20 |
| Fish Grill \| **multi.** | 19 |
| Milky Way \| **Pico-Robertson** | 19 |
| Pat's \| **Pico-Robertson** | 22 |
| Sassi Med. \| **Encino** | 21 |
| Zeidler's \| **Brentwood** | 17 |

## LEBANESE

| | |
|---|---|
| Carnival \| **Sherman Oaks** | 22 |
| Gaby's \| **multi.** | 19 |
| Marouch \| **E Hollywood** | 23 |
| NEW Skaf's \| **Glendale** | 26 |
| Z Sunnin \| **multi.** | 24 |

## MEDITERRANEAN

| | |
|---|---|
| Aioli \| **Torrance** | 18 |
| Beau Rivage \| **Malibu** | 21 |
| Cafe Del Rey \| **Marina del Rey** | 21 |
| Café Mundial \| **Monrovia** | 21 |
| Café Santorini \| **Pasadena** | 20 |
| Campanile \| **La Brea** | 26 |
| Canelé \| **Atwater Vill** | 23 |
| NEW Casablanca Med. \| **Claremont** | 18 |
| Chaya \| **Venice** | 22 |
| Z Christine \| **Torrance** | 26 |
| Eight-18 \| **Toluca Lake** | 20 |

| | |
|---|---|
| Elf Café \| **Echo Pk** | 25 |
| Emles \| **Northridge** | 19 |
| 🅔 Fraîche \| **Culver City** | 24 |
| Gaby's \| **multi.** | 19 |
| Gardens \| **Beverly Hills** | 23 |
| J Rest. \| **Downtown** | 16 |
| Lemon Moon \| **West LA** | 20 |
| Lido/Manhattan \| **Manhattan Bch** | 19 |
| **NEW** Lido Grill \| **Venice** | - |
| 🅔 Little Door \| **Third St.** | 23 |
| Lou \| **Hollywood** | 23 |
| 🅔 Lucques \| **W Hollywood** | 27 |
| Mediterraneo \| **Hermosa Bch** | 20 |
| Mediterraneo \| **Westlake Vill** | 17 |
| 🅔 One Pico \| **Santa Monica** | 22 |
| Panini Cafe \| **Beverly Hills** | 17 |
| Primitivo \| **Venice** | 20 |
| Rustic Canyon \| **Santa Monica** | 21 |
| 🅔 Sam's/Beach \| **Santa Monica** | 26 |
| Sassi Med. \| **Encino** | 21 |
| Spazio \| **Sherman Oaks** | 18 |
| Spitz \| **Eagle Rock** | 23 |
| Sur \| **W Hollywood** | 21 |
| **NEW** Tapa Meze \| **Manhattan Bch** | - |
| Trio Med. \| **Rolling Hills Estates** | 20 |
| Upstairs 2 \| **West LA** | 24 |
| Vertical Wine \| **Pasadena** | 23 |
| **NEW** Vinotéque \| **Culver City** | - |
| Wilson \| **Culver City** | 22 |
| Zankou \| **multi.** | 22 |
| Zazou \| **Redondo Bch** | 23 |

## MEXICAN

| | |
|---|---|
| Adobe Cantina \| **Agoura Hills** | 15 |
| Alegria/Sunset \| **Silver Lake** | 21 |
| **NEW** Amaranta \| **Canoga Pk** | 20 |
| Antonio's \| **Melrose** | 19 |
| 🅔 Babita \| **San Gabriel** | 26 |
| Baja Fresh \| **multi.** | 17 |
| **NEW** Best Fish Taco \| **Los Feliz** | 21 |
| Border Grill \| **Santa Monica** | 21 |
| Cantina Joannafina \| **Westlake Vill** | 19 |
| Casablanca \| **Venice** | 18 |
| Casa Vega \| **Sherman Oaks** | 18 |
| Chichen Itza \| **Downtown** | 24 |
| Chipotle \| **multi.** | 18 |
| Cozymel's \| **El Segundo** | 16 |
| Doña Rosa \| **multi.** | 16 |
| El Cholo \| **multi.** | 18 |
| El Coyote \| **Beverly Blvd.** | 13 |
| 🅔 El Tepeyac \| **East LA** | 24 |
| El Torito \| **multi.** | 15 |
| El Torito Grill \| **multi.** | 18 |
| Frida \| **Beverly Hills** | 21 |
| Guelaguetza \| **multi.** | 22 |

| | |
|---|---|
| **NEW** Isla \| **W Hollywood** | - |
| Kay 'n Dave's \| **multi.** | 18 |
| La Cabanita \| **Montrose** | 24 |
| La Huasteca \| **Lynwood** | 26 |
| Lares \| **Santa Monica** | 19 |
| La Serenata \| **multi.** | 22 |
| Lotería! \| **multi.** | 24 |
| Lula \| **Santa Monica** | 18 |
| Malo \| **Silver Lake** | 17 |
| Mexicali \| **Studio City** | 15 |
| Mexico City \| **Los Feliz** | 18 |
| Mijares \| **Pasadena** | 17 |
| Mi Ranchito \| **Culver City** | 18 |
| Monte Alban \| **West LA** | 21 |
| **NEW** Mucho Ultima \| **Manhattan Bch** | 19 |
| **NEW** Ortega 120 \| **Redondo Bch** | - |
| Paco's Tacos \| **multi.** | 20 |
| Pink Taco \| **Century City** | 15 |
| Poquito Más \| **multi.** | 21 |
| Señor Fred \| **Sherman Oaks** | 18 |
| Sharky's Mex. \| **multi.** | 18 |
| Spanish Kitchen \| **W Hollywood** | 15 |
| Tamayo \| **East LA** | 18 |
| Tlapazola Grill \| **multi.** | 23 |
| Velvet Margarita \| **Hollywood** | 17 |

## MIDDLE EASTERN

| | |
|---|---|
| Burger Continental \| **Pasadena** | 17 |
| Carousel \| **multi.** | 22 |
| **NEW** Casablanca Med. \| **Claremont** | 18 |
| Falafel King \| **multi.** | 18 |
| Moishe's \| **Fairfax** | 21 |
| **NEW** Tapa Meze \| **Manhattan Bch** | - |
| Wahib's Mid-East \| **Alhambra** | 21 |

## MOROCCAN

| | |
|---|---|
| Chameau \| **Fairfax** | 22 |
| Dar Maghreb \| **Hollywood** | 20 |
| Koutoubia \| **Westwood** | 20 |
| Marrakesh \| **Studio City** | 19 |

## NEPALESE

| | |
|---|---|
| Tibet Nepal \| **Pasadena** | 19 |

## NOODLE SHOPS

| | |
|---|---|
| Asahi Ramen \| **West LA** | 20 |
| Chabuya \| **West LA** | 19 |
| Mishima \| **Third St.** | 20 |
| Pho Café \| **Silver Lake** | 21 |

## NUEVO LATINO

| | |
|---|---|
| Alegria \| **Long Bch** | 19 |
| Ciudad \| **Downtown** | 21 |
| Xiomara \| **Hollywood** | 23 |

## PACIFIC RIM

NEW Carbon Beach | **Malibu** — 13
Z Christine | **Torrance** — 26
Duke's | **Malibu** — 17

## PAN-ASIAN

Beacon | **Culver City** — 22
Buddha's Belly | **multi.** — 19
Chin Chin | **W Hollywood** — 16
Feast from East | **West LA** — 20
NEW Kress, The | **Hollywood** — –
Mirü8691 | **Beverly Hills** — 25
Monsoon Cafe | **Santa Monica** — 18
Pearl Dragon | **Pacific Palisades** — 17
Pei Wei | **multi.** — 16
Prana Cafe | **W Hollywood** — 18
Red Pearl | **Hollywood** — 17
Red 7 | **W Hollywood** — 24
NEW RockSugar | **Century City** — –
Sai Sai | **Downtown** — 18
Typhoon | **Santa Monica** — 22
Warung Cafe | **Downtown** — –
Yatai Tapas | **W Hollywood** — –
Zen Grill | **Beverly Hills** — 21

## PAN-LATIN

NEW D'Cache | **Toluca Lake** — –
Limon Grill | **Simi Valley** — 18

## PERSIAN

Javan | **West LA** — 20
Pistachio Grill | **Beverly Hills** — 21
Shaherzad | **Westwood** — 21

## PERUVIAN

El Pollo Inka | **multi.** — 19
Los Balcones/Peru | **Hollywood** — 18
Z Mario Peruvian | **Hollywood** — 25
Qusqo | **West LA** — 19

## PIZZA

Abbot's Pizza | **multi.** — 22
Antica Pizzeria | **Marina del Rey** — 20
Berri's Pizza | **multi.** — 16
BJ's | **multi.** — 17
Bravo | **Santa Monica** — 17
Caioti Pizza | **Studio City** — 22
Cali. Pizza Kitchen | **multi.** — 18
Casa Bianca | **Eagle Rock** — 23
Cheebo | **Hollywood** — 19
D'Amore's | **multi.** — 20
Farfalla Trattoria | **Los Feliz** — 22
Il Capriccio | **Los Feliz** — 20
Jacopo's | **multi.** — 16
NEW Joe's Pizza | **Santa Monica** — 20
Johnnie's NY | **multi.** — 18

La Bottega Marino | **multi.** — 21
Lamonica's NY Pizza | **Westwood** — 21
Mulberry St. Pizzeria | **multi.** — 23
Pace | **Laurel Canyon** — 21
Pizza Rustica | **multi.** — 22
Z Pizzeria Mozza | **Hollywood** — 26
Prizzi's Piazza | **Hollywood** — 21
NEW Richie Palmer's | **multi.** — 15
Z Village Pizzeria | **multi.** — 23
Wildflour Pizza | **Santa Monica** — 15
Wolfgang Puck | **Universal City** — 17

## POLISH

Warszawa | **Santa Monica** — 22

## POLYNESIAN

Bora Bora | **Manhattan Bch** — 22

## PUB FOOD

Auld Dubliner | **Long Bch** — 18
BJ's | **multi.** — 17
Gordon Biersch | **Pasadena** — 16
Heroes | **Claremont** — 17
Ye Olde King's | **Santa Monica** — 17

## SANDWICHES

Artisan | **Studio City** — 26
Art's Deli | **Studio City** — 20
Barney Greengrass | **Beverly Hills** — 20
Breadbar | **W Hollywood** — 18
Canter's | **Fairfax** — 18
Danny's | **Venice** — 17
NEW FOOD | **Rancho Pk** — –
Joan's on 3rd | **Third St.** — 23
Johnnie's Pastrami | **Culver City** — 20
Junior's | **West LA** — 16
Z Langer's Deli | **Downtown** — 25
NEW Lawry's Carvery | **Century City** — 19
Meltdown Etc. | **Culver City** — 18
Nate 'n Al | **Beverly Hills** — 20
Nicola's | **Woodland Hills** — 20
Noah's NY Bagels | **multi.** — 17
Philippe/Orig. | **Chinatown** — 21
Z Porto's | **multi.** — 24
NEW Press Panini | **Studio City** — –
Roll 'n Rye | **Culver City** — 17
Sandbag's | **multi.** — 16
3 Square | **Venice** — 20

## SCOTTISH

Tam O'Shanter | **Atwater Vill** — 21

## SEAFOOD

ABC Seafood | **Chinatown** — 19
Admiral Risty | **Rancho Palos Verdes** — 20

| | |
|---|---|
| Baleen | **Redondo Bch** | 20 |
| Bluewater Grill | **Redondo Bch** | 19 |
| Breeze | **Century City** | 17 |
| Buggy Whip | **Westchester** | 19 |
| **NEW** Captain Crab | **San Gabriel** | - |
| Catch | **Santa Monica** | 22 |
| CBS Seafood | **Chinatown** | - |
| Chart House | **multi.** | 19 |
| Delmonico's | **Encino** | 22 |
| Duke's | **Malibu** | 17 |
| Enterprise Fish | **Santa Monica** | 19 |
| Fins | **multi.** | 22 |
| Fish Grill | **multi.** | 19 |
| Fonz's | **Manhattan Bch** | 22 |
| Galley, The | **Santa Monica** | 18 |
| Gladstone's | **Pacific Palisades** | 14 |
| Gulfstream | **Century City** | 21 |
| Hop Woo | **Alhambra** | 18 |
| Hungry Cat | **Hollywood** | 24 |
| i Cugini | **Santa Monica** | 21 |
| Joe's Crab | **multi.** | 13 |
| Kincaid's | **Redondo Bch** | 20 |
| King's Fish | **multi.** | 21 |
| La Serenata | **multi.** | 22 |
| Lobster, The | **Santa Monica** | 22 |
| **Z** Madison, The | **Long Bch** | 20 |
| Malibu Seafood | **Malibu** | 22 |
| McCormick/Schmick | **multi.** | 19 |
| McKenna's | **Long Bch** | 19 |
| NBC Seafood | **Monterey Pk** | 19 |
| Neptune's Net | **Malibu** | 18 |
| Ocean Ave. | **Santa Monica** | 23 |
| Ocean Seafood | **Chinatown** | 20 |
| Odyssey | **Granada Hills** | 14 |
| O-Nami | **Torrance** | 17 |
| Palm, The | **multi.** | 23 |
| **NEW** Paperfish | **Beverly Hills** | 23 |
| Paradise Cove | **Malibu** | 15 |
| Parker's Lighthse. | **Long Bch** | 18 |
| **Z** Providence | **Hollywood** | 26 |
| **NEW** Red Fish | **Simi Valley** | 21 |
| Reel Inn | **Malibu** | 20 |
| Rock'n Fish | **Manhattan Bch** | 21 |
| Sea Harbour | **Rosemead** | 24 |
| 22nd St. Landing | **San Pedro** | 18 |
| V.I.P. Harbor | **West LA** | 18 |
| **Z** Water Grill | **Downtown** | 27 |

## SMALL PLATES

(See also Spanish tapas specialist)

| | |
|---|---|
| All' Angelo | Venetian | **Melrose** | 25 |
| **Z** A.O.C. | Cal./French | **Third St.** | 26 |
| Bar Hayama | Japanese | **West LA** | 24 |
| Beacon | Pan-Asian | **Culver City** | 22 |
| BottleRock | Euro. | **Culver City** | 16 |

| | |
|---|---|
| Broadway Deli | Eclectic | **Santa Monica** | 15 |
| Buddha's Belly | Eclectic | **Beverly Blvd.** | 19 |
| Café/Tango | Eclectic | **Universal City** | 19 |
| **NEW** Carbon Beach | Cal. | **Malibu** | 13 |
| **NEW** Chloe | Amer./French | **Santa Monica** | 18 |
| Coco Noche | Eclectic | **Manhattan Bch** | 17 |
| Corkscrew | Eclectic | **Manhattan Bch** | 21 |
| Eight-18 | Med. | **Toluca Lake** | 20 |
| Enoteca Drago | Italian | **Beverly Hills** | 21 |
| Ita Cho | Japanese | **Beverly Blvd.** | 21 |
| Izaka-Ya | Japanese | **Third St.** | 25 |
| Jer-ne | Cal. | **Marina del Rey** | 20 |
| K-Zo | Japanese | **Culver City** | 23 |
| La Sosta | Italian | **Hermosa Bch** | 26 |
| Lou | Med. | **Hollywood** | 23 |
| **Z** Mako | Asian Fusion | **Beverly Hills** | 26 |
| Musha | Japanese | **multi.** | 24 |
| Orris | French/Japanese | **West LA** | 26 |
| Parc | Asian/French | **Hollywood** | 21 |
| Primitivo | Med. | **Venice** | 20 |
| Red Pearl | Pan-Asian | **Hollywood** | 17 |
| Rustic Canyon | Med. | **Santa Monica** | 21 |
| 3rd Stop | Italian | **W Hollywood** | 17 |
| **NEW** Tinto | Spanish | **W Hollywood** | 20 |
| **NEW** Tranquility Base | Cal./Eclectic | **Downtown** | - |
| Ugo/Italian | Italian | **Culver City** | 17 |
| Upstairs 2 | Med. | **West LA** | 24 |
| Vertical Wine | Eclectic/Med. | **Pasadena** | 23 |
| **NEW** Vinotéque | Eclectic | **Culver City** | - |
| Violet | Amer. | **Santa Monica** | 22 |
| Warung Cafe | Pan-Asian | **Downtown** | - |
| Yatai Tapas | Pan-Asian | **W Hollywood** | - |
| Yuzu | Japanese | **Torrance** | 23 |

## SOUL FOOD

| | |
|---|---|
| Big Mama's | **Pasadena** | 19 |
| Larkin's | **Eagle Rock** | 20 |
| Lucille's BBQ | **multi.** | 22 |
| Roscoe's | **multi.** | 20 |

## SOUTHERN

| | |
|---|---|
| Aunt Kizzy's | **Marina del Rey** | 19 |
| **Z** Baby Blues | **Venice** | 23 |
| House of Blues | **W Hollywood** | 16 |

| | |
|---|---|
| Johnny Rebs' \| **multi.** | 22 |
| Kokomo Cafe \| **Beverly Blvd.** | 19 |
| Larkin's \| **Eagle Rock** | 20 |
| Ⓩ Les Sisters \| **Chatsworth** | 23 |
| Lucille's BBQ \| **multi.** | 22 |

## SOUTHWESTERN

| | |
|---|---|
| Bandera \| **West LA** | 21 |
| Chili My Soul \| **Encino** | 21 |
| Coyote Cantina \| **Redondo Bch** | 20 |
| Jinky's \| **multi.** | 19 |
| Sagebrush Cantina \| **Calabasas** | 13 |
| Sonora Cafe \| **La Brea** | 22 |

## SPANISH

(* tapas specialist)

| | |
|---|---|
| Aioli* \| **Torrance** | 18 |
| Bar Celona* \| **Pasadena** | 16 |
| NEW Bar Pintxo \| **Santa Monica** | 19 |
| NEW Beso \| **Hollywood** | - |
| Cobras/Matadors* \| **multi.** | 21 |
| Courtyard* \| **W Hollywood** | 19 |
| Enoteca Toscana \| **Camarillo** | 19 |
| La Paella* \| **Beverly Hills** | 23 |
| Minotaure* \| **Playa del Rey** | 20 |
| Olé! Tapas Bar* \| **Studio City** | 16 |
| NEW Tapa Meze* \| **Manhattan Bch** | - |
| Tasca Winebar* \| **Third St.** | 23 |
| NEW Tinto \| **W Hollywood** | 20 |
| Viva Madrid* \| **Claremont** | 20 |

## STEAKHOUSES

| | |
|---|---|
| Ⓩ Arnie Morton's \| **multi.** | 25 |
| Arroyo Chop \| **Pasadena** | 25 |
| Beckham Grill \| **Pasadena** | 18 |
| Benihana \| **multi.** | 18 |
| Billingsley's \| **West LA** | 15 |
| NEW BLT Steak \| **W Hollywood** | 23 |
| Boa \| **multi.** | 23 |
| Buggy Whip \| **Westchester** | 19 |
| Ⓩ Carlitos Gardel \| **Melrose** | 23 |
| Chapter 8 \| **Agoura Hills** | 17 |
| Chart House \| **multi.** | 19 |
| Chez Jay \| **Santa Monica** | 16 |
| Ⓩ CUT \| **Beverly Hills** | 26 |
| Dakota \| **Hollywood** | 22 |
| Damon's \| **Glendale** | 18 |
| Derby \| **Arcadia** | 23 |
| e3rd Steak \| **Downtown** | 19 |
| 555 East \| **Long Bch** | 24 |
| Fleming's \| **multi.** | 25 |
| Fogo de Chão \| **Beverly Hills** | 24 |
| Fonz's \| **Manhattan Bch** | 22 |
| Galley, The \| **Santa Monica** | 18 |
| Gaucho Grill \| **multi.** | 17 |

| | |
|---|---|
| Ⓩ Grill on Alley \| **Beverly Hills** | 24 |
| Holdren's Steak \| **Thousand Oaks** | 21 |
| Jar \| **Beverly Blvd.** | 25 |
| JJ Steak \| **Pasadena** | 23 |
| Kincaid's \| **Redondo Bch** | 20 |
| NEW Larsen's Steak \| **Encino** | - |
| Ⓩ Lawry's Prime \| **Beverly Hills** | 24 |
| Lodge Steak \| **Beverly Hills** | 19 |
| Ⓩ Madison, The \| **Long Bch** | 20 |
| Ⓩ Mastro's Steak \| **multi.** | 26 |
| McKenna's \| **Long Bch** | 19 |
| Monty's Steak \| **Woodland Hills** | 20 |
| Morels French Steak \| **Fairfax** | 18 |
| Nick & Stef's Steak \| **Downtown** | 23 |
| Outback \| **multi.** | 17 |
| Pacific Dining Car \| **multi.** | 22 |
| Palm, The \| **multi.** | 23 |
| Petrelli's Steak \| **Culver City** | 16 |
| Porterhouse \| **Beverly Hills** | 20 |
| Porto Alegre \| **Pasadena** | 20 |
| NEW RED \| **City of Industry** | - |
| Riordan's Tav. \| **Downtown** | 15 |
| Rock'n Fish \| **Manhattan Bch** | 21 |
| Ⓩ Ruth's Chris \| **multi.** | 26 |
| Saddle Ranch \| **multi.** | 14 |
| Salt Creek \| **multi.** | 18 |
| Smoke House \| **Burbank** | 19 |
| NEW STK \| **W Hollywood** | 21 |
| Taylor's Steak \| **multi.** | 21 |
| NEW Three Forks \| **Claremont** | 23 |
| Vibrato \| **Bel-Air** | 21 |
| West \| **Brentwood** | 18 |
| NEW Wolfgang's Steak \| **Beverly Hills** | - |
| NEW Zane's \| **Hermosa Bch** | - |

## TEX-MEX

| | |
|---|---|
| Chili My Soul \| **Encino** | 21 |
| Marix Tex Mex \| **multi.** | 16 |

## THAI

| | |
|---|---|
| Bulan Thai \| **multi.** | 25 |
| Chaba \| **Redondo Bch** | 20 |
| Chadaka \| **Burbank** | 24 |
| Chan/Hse. of Chan \| **multi.** | 20 |
| Chao Krung \| **Fairfax** | 20 |
| Ⓩ Cholada \| **Malibu** | 24 |
| Ⓩ Jitlada \| **E Hollywood** | 26 |
| NEW Nakkara \| **Fairfax** | - |
| Natalee \| **multi.** | 18 |
| Palms Thai \| **E Hollywood** | 20 |
| Rambutan Thai \| **Silver Lake** | 21 |
| Red Corner Asia \| **E Hollywood** | 25 |
| Ruen Pair \| **E Hollywood** | 24 |
| Saladang \| **Pasadena** | 23 |
| Talésai \| **multi.** | 22 |

Thai Dishes | **multi.** 18

Tuk Tuk Thai | **Pico-Robertson** 21

Yai | **multi.** 21

**TIBETAN**

Tibet Nepal | **Pasadena** 19

**TUNISIAN**

Moun of Tunis | **Hollywood** 21

**TURKISH**

Spitz | **Eagle Rock** 23

**VEGETARIAN**

(* vegan)

A Votre Sante* | **Brentwood** 20

Bulan Thai | **Melrose** 25

Elf Café | **Echo Pk** 25

Fatty's & Co. | **Eagle Rock** 23

Z Inn/Seventh Ray* | **Topanga** 20

Jack Sprat's | **West LA** 19

Juliano's Raw* | **Santa Monica** 19

Leaf Cuisine* | **multi.** 17

Madeleine Bistro* | **Tarzana** 24

Mäni's* | **multi.** 18

M Café* | **multi.** 21

Z Native Foods* | **Westwood** 22

Newsroom Café | **W Hollywood** 18

Z Real Food Daily* | **multi.** 21

NEW Shojin* | **Little Tokyo** -

Trails, The* | **Los Feliz** 16

Urth Caffé* | **multi.** 20

Vegan Glory* | **Beverly Blvd.** 20

NEW Veggie Grill* | **El Segundo** 19

**VENEZUELAN**

Coupa Café | **Beverly Hills** 17

**VIETNAMESE**

Absolutely Pho | **multi.** 17

Z Benley | **Long Bch** 24

Blossom | **Downtown** 22

Blue Hen | **Eagle Rock** 14

China Beach | **Venice** 16

Z Crustacean | **Beverly Hills** 24

Gingergrass | **Silver Lake** 21

Golden Deli | **San Gabriel** 23

Indochine Vien | **Atwater Vill** 16

Le Saigon | **West LA** 21

Pho Café | **Silver Lake** 21

Pho 79 | **Alhambra** 20

Viet Noodle Bar | **Atwater Vill** 22

**LOS ANGELES**

**CUISINES**

# Locations

Includes restaurant names, cuisines, Food ratings and, for locations that are mapped, top list and map coordinates. ⊠ indicates places with the highest ratings, popularity and importance.

## LA Central

### ATWATER VILLAGE

| | |
|---|---|
| Canelé | *Med.* | 23 |
| Indochine Vien | *Viet.* | 16 |
| Mimi's Cafe | *Diner* | 17 |
| Tam O'Shanter | *Scottish* | 21 |
| Viet Noodle Bar | *Viet.* | 22 |

### BEVERLY BLVD.

(bet. La Brea & La Cienega; see map on back of gatefold)

### TOP FOOD

| | |
|---|---|
| Angelini Osteria | *Italian* | **E8** | 27 |
| Hatfield's | *Amer.* | **E7** | 27 |
| Jar | *Amer./Steak* | **E6** | 25 |
| Hirozen | *Japanese* | **E5** | 25 |
| Grace | *Amer.* | **E8** | 25 |

### LISTING

| | |
|---|---|
| ⊠ Angelini Osteria | *Italian* | 27 |
| bld | *Amer.* | 21 |
| Buddha's Belly | *Pan-Asian* | 19 |
| Cafe Sushi | *Japanese* | 20 |
| Cobras/Matadors | *Spanish* | 21 |
| Dominick's | *Italian* | 21 |
| El Coyote | *Mex.* | 13 |
| Fish Grill | *Seafood* | 19 |
| Grace | *Amer.* | 25 |
| ⊠ Hatfield's | *Amer.* | 27 |
| Hirozen | *Japanese* | 25 |
| India's Oven | *Indian* | 19 |
| Ita Cho | *Japanese* | 21 |
| Jar | *Amer./Steak* | 25 |
| NEW Jian | *Korean* | – |
| Kings Road | *Amer.* | 18 |
| Kokomo Cafe | *Southern* | 19 |
| NEW Medusa | *Eclectic* | – |
| Mimosa | *French* | 20 |
| Pane e Vino | *Italian* | 21 |
| Pastis | *French* | 21 |
| Swingers | *Diner* | 17 |
| NEW Terroni | *Italian* | 20 |
| Vegan Glory | *Vegan* | 20 |

### CHINATOWN

| | |
|---|---|
| ABC Seafood | *Chinese/Seafood* | 19 |
| CBS Seafood | *Seafood* | – |
| Empress Pavilion | *Chinese* | 21 |
| Hop Li | *Chinese* | 20 |
| Hop Woo | *Chinese* | 18 |
| Ocean Seafood | *Chinese/Seafood* | 20 |
| Philippe/Orig. | *Sandwiches* | 21 |
| Sam Woo | *Chinese* | 20 |
| Yang Chow | *Chinese* | 22 |

### DOWNTOWN

(See map on page 278)

### TOP FOOD

| | |
|---|---|
| Water Grill | *Seafood* | **F2** | 27 |
| R23 | *Japanese* | **G5** | 26 |
| Patina | *Amer./Cal.* | **E3** | 25 |
| Arnie Morton's | *Steak* | **F1** | 25 |
| Langer's Deli | *Deli* | **F1** | 25 |
| Noé | *Amer.* | **F3** | 24 |
| Chichen Itza | *Mex.* | **E1** \| **H1** | 24 |
| Roy's | *Asian Fusion/Hawaiian* | **G1** | 23 |
| Cicada | *Cal./Italian* | **G2** | 23 |
| Nick & Stef's Steak | *Steak* | **E3** | 23 |
| Palm, The | *Seafood/Steak* | **H1** | 23 |
| Cafe Pinot | *Cal./French* | **F2** | 22 |
| Pacific Dining Car | *Steak* | **E1** | 22 |
| Tommy's | *Burgers/Hot Dogs* | **C1** | 22 |
| George's Greek | *Greek* | **F1** | 22 |

### LISTING

| | |
|---|---|
| Angelique Café | *French* | 19 |
| ⊠ Arnie Morton's | *Steak* | 25 |
| Barbara's | *Eclectic* | 14 |
| BCD Tofu | *Korean* | 19 |
| Blossom | *Viet.* | 22 |
| Blue Velvet | *Amer.* | 20 |
| Cafe Pinot | *Cal./French* | 22 |
| Cali. Pizza Kitchen | *Pizza* | 18 |
| Checkers | *Cal.* | 20 |
| Chichen Itza | *Mex.* | 24 |
| Ciao Tratt. | *Italian* | 20 |
| ⊠ Cicada | *Cal./Italian* | 23 |
| Ciudad | *Nuevo Latino* | 21 |
| Engine Co. 28 | *Amer.* | 19 |
| e3rd Steak | *Steak* | 19 |
| 410 Boyd | *Cal.* | 17 |
| George's Greek | *Greek* | 22 |
| Johnnie's NY | *Pizza* | 18 |
| J Rest. | *Med.* | 16 |
| Kendall's Brass. | *French* | 17 |
| Koo Koo Roo | *Amer.* | 15 |
| ⊠ Langer's Deli | *Deli* | 25 |
| NEW Lemonade Cafe | *Cal.* | – |
| Liberty Grill | *Amer.* | 18 |

| | |
|---|---|
| McCormick/Schmick | *Seafood* | 19 |
| New Moon | *Chinese* | 21 |
| Nick & Stef's Steak | *Steak* | 23 |
| Noé | *Amer.* | 24 |
| Original Pantry | *Diner* | 15 |
| Pacific Dining Car | *Steak* | 22 |
| Palm, The | *Seafood/Steak* | 23 |
| Panini Cafe | *Italian/Med.* | 17 |
| Patina | *Amer./Cal.* | 25 |
| Pete's Cafe | *Amer.* | 19 |
| Riordan's Tav. | *Steak* | 15 |
| Roy's | *Asian Fusion/Hawaiian* | 23 |
| R23 | *Japanese* | 26 |
| Sai Sai | *Japanese/Pan-Asian* | 18 |
| Sandbag's | *Sandwiches* | 16 |
| Seoul Jung | *Korean* | 20 |
| Standard, The | *Eclectic* | 15 |
| ☑ Takami | *Japanese* | 20 |
| Tesoro Tratt. | *Italian* | 16 |
| Tiara Cafe | *Amer.* | 23 |
| Tommy's | *Burgers/Hot Dogs* | 22 |
| NEW Tranquility Base | *Cal./Eclectic* | - |
| Traxx | *Amer.* | 20 |
| Warung Cafe | *Pan-Asian* | - |
| ☑ Water Grill | *Seafood* | 27 |
| Wokcano Cafe | *Chinese/Japanese* | 19 |
| Wolfgang Puck | *Cal.* | 17 |
| Zip Fusion | *Japanese* | 18 |
| Zucca | *Italian* | 21 |

## EAST HOLLYWOOD

| | |
|---|---|
| Carousel | *Mideast.* | 22 |
| ☑ Jitlada | *Thai* | 26 |
| Marouch | *Lebanese* | 23 |
| Palms Thai | *Thai* | 20 |
| Red Corner Asia | *Thai* | 25 |
| Ruen Pair | *Thai* | 24 |
| Square One Dining | *Amer.* | 22 |
| Yai | *Thai* | 21 |
| Zankou | *Med.* | 22 |

## ECHO PARK

| | |
|---|---|
| Elf Café | *Med./Veg.* | 25 |
| NEW Lot 1 | *Amer.* | - |
| NEW Park, The | *Amer.* | - |
| NEW Rest. 15 | *Amer.* | 20 |
| Taix | *French* | 16 |

## FAIRFAX

| | |
|---|---|
| American Girl Pl. | *Amer.* | 11 |
| NEW Animal | *Amer.* | - |
| Canter's | *Deli* | 18 |
| Chameau | *French/Moroccan* | 22 |
| Chao Krung | *Thai* | 20 |
| ☑ Cheesecake Factory | *Amer.* | 19 |

| | |
|---|---|
| Chipotle | *Mex.* | 18 |
| Du-par's | *Diner* | 16 |
| Farm/Bev. Hills | *Amer.* | 19 |
| French Crêpe Co. | *French* | 21 |
| Genghis Cohen | *Chinese* | 20 |
| Gumbo Pot | *Cajun* | 19 |
| Johnny Rockets | *Burgers* | 15 |
| Lotería! | *Mex.* | 24 |
| Maggiano's | *Italian* | 18 |
| Mäni's | *Bakery/Vegan* | 18 |
| Marmalade Café | *Amer./Cal.* | 17 |
| Moishe's | *Mideast.* | 21 |
| Monsieur Marcel | *French* | 21 |
| Morels First Floor | *French* | 17 |
| Morels French Steak | *French/Steak* | 18 |
| NEW Nakkara | *Thai* | - |
| Nyala Ethiopian | *Ethiopian* | 21 |
| Tart | *Amer.* | 16 |
| Ulysses Voyage | *Greek* | 21 |
| Wood Ranch BBQ | *BBQ* | 20 |

## HANCOCK PARK/
## LARCHMONT VILLAGE

| | |
|---|---|
| Chan/Hse. of Chan | *Thai* | 20 |
| Girasole Cucina | *Italian* | 23 |
| Koo Koo Roo | *Amer.* | 15 |
| La Bottega Marino | *Italian* | 21 |
| Le Petit Greek | *Greek* | 19 |
| Louise's Tratt. | *Cal./Italian* | 17 |
| Noah's NY Bagels | *Sandwiches* | 17 |
| ☑ Prado | *Carib.* | 22 |
| ☑ Village Pizzeria | *Pizza* | 23 |

## HIGHLAND PARK

| | |
|---|---|
| Marty's | *Cal.* | 18 |
| York, The | *Eclectic* | 18 |

## HOLLYWOOD

(See map on page 277)

## TOP FOOD

| | |
|---|---|
| Pizzeria Mozza | *Pizza* | **E7** | 26 |
| Providence | *Amer./Seafood* | **E8** | 26 |
| Osteria Mozza | *Italian* | **E7** | 26 |
| Mario Peruvian | *Peruvian* | **E8** | 25 |
| Katsuya | *Japanese* | **B8** | 24 |
| Hungry Cat | *Seafood* | **B8** | 24 |
| Lotería! | *Mex.* | **B7** | 24 |
| Village Pizzeria | *Pizza* | **A8** | 23 |
| In-N-Out | *Burgers* | **B6** | 23 |
| Lou | *Eclectic/Med.* | **E8** | 23 |
| Xiomara | *Nuevo Latino* | **E7** | 23 |
| Dakota | *Steak* | **B6** | 22 |
| Ammo | *Cal.* | **C7** | 22 |
| Larchmont Grill | *Amer.* | **E8** | 22 |
| Griddle Cafe | *Amer.* | **B4** | 22 |

## LISTING

| | | |
|---|---|---|
| Ammo | *Cal.* | 22 |
| Astro Burger | *Burgers* | 19 |
| Azami | *Japanese* | 25 |
| Bella Cucina | *Italian* | 23 |
| **NEW** Beso | *Spanish* | - |
| Bossa Nova | *Brazilian* | 20 |
| Bowery | *Amer./French* | 20 |
| Cafe des Artistes | *French* | 20 |
| Cali. Chicken | *Amer.* | 21 |
| Cali. Pizza Kitchen | *Pizza* | 18 |
| Chan/Hse. of Chan | *Thai* | 20 |
| Charcoal | *Amer.* | 11 |
| Cheebo | *Italian* | 19 |
| Citizen Smith | *Amer.* | 17 |
| **NEW** Citrus at Social | *Eclectic/French* | 21 |
| Dakota | *Steak* | 22 |
| Dar Maghreb | *Moroccan* | 20 |
| **NEW** Delancey | *Italian* | - |
| eat. on sunset | *Amer.* | 18 |
| Fabiolus Café | *Italian* | 20 |
| French Crêpe Co. | *French* | 21 |
| Geisha Hse. | *Japanese* | 20 |
| Greenblatt's Deli | *Deli* | 18 |
| Griddle Cafe | *Amer.* | 22 |
| Grill on Hollywood | *Amer.* | 22 |
| Grub | *Amer.* | 19 |
| Hungry Cat | *Seafood* | 24 |
| **Z** In-N-Out | *Burgers* | 23 |
| Johnny Rockets | *Burgers* | 15 |
| Joseph's Cafe | *Greek* | 18 |
| **Z** Katsuya | *Japanese* | 24 |
| **NEW** Kitchen 24 | *Amer.* | - |
| **NEW** Kress, The | *Pan-Asian* | - |
| Larchmont Grill | *Amer.* | 22 |
| Los Balcones/Peru | *Peruvian* | 18 |
| Lotería! | *Mex.* | 24 |
| Lou | *Eclectic/Med.* | 23 |
| Lucky Devils | *Amer.* | 20 |
| Magnolia | *Amer.* | 19 |
| Marino | *Italian* | 21 |
| **Z** Mario Peruvian | *Peruvian* | 25 |
| **NEW** Melograno | *Italian* | 23 |
| Mel's Drive-In | *Amer.* | 15 |
| Miceli's | *Italian* | 17 |
| Moun of Tunis | *Moroccan/Tunisian* | 21 |
| Musso & Frank | *Amer.* | 18 |
| **Z** Osteria Mozza | *Italian* | 26 |
| Parc | *Asian/French* | 21 |
| Pig 'n Whistle | *Continental* | 13 |
| **Z** Pizzeria Mozza | *Pizza* | 26 |
| Prizzi's Piazza | *Italian* | 21 |
| **Z** Providence | *Amer./Seafood* | 26 |
| Red Pearl | *Pan-Asian* | 17 |
| Roscoe's | *Soul Food* | 20 |
| Sharky's Mex. | *Mex.* | 18 |
| **NEW** Stork, The | *Amer.* | - |
| Trastevere | *Italian* | 17 |
| 25 Degrees | *Burgers* | 21 |
| uWink | *Cal.* | 13 |
| Velvet Margarita | *Mex.* | 17 |
| **Z** Village Pizzeria | *Pizza* | 23 |
| **NEW** Waffle, The | *Amer.* | 16 |
| Xiomara | *Nuevo Latino* | 23 |
| **Z** Yamashiro | *Asian/Cal.* | 18 |

### HUNTINGTON PARK

| | | |
|---|---|---|
| Guelaguetza | *Mex.* | 22 |

### KOREATOWN

| | | |
|---|---|---|
| BCD Tofu | *Korean* | 19 |
| **NEW** BonChon | *Korean* | - |
| Cassell's | *Burgers* | 19 |
| **Z** ChoSun Galbee | *Korean* | 23 |
| Fat Fish | *Asian Fusion/Japanese* | 20 |
| Guelaguetza | *Mex.* | 22 |
| **NEW** La Défence | *Eurasian* | - |
| Manna | *Korean* | 16 |
| Nak Won | *Korean* | 16 |
| **Z** Soot Bull Jeep | *Korean* | 23 |
| Taylor's Steak | *Steak* | 21 |

### LA BREA

| | | |
|---|---|---|
| Amalfi | *Italian* | 21 |
| Ca'Brea | *Italian* | 22 |
| Campanile | *Cal./Med.* | 26 |
| Cobras/Matadors | *Spanish* | 21 |
| cube | *Italian* | 22 |
| Luna Park | *Amer.* | 17 |
| Pink's Chili Dogs | *Hot Dogs* | 19 |
| Sonora Cafe | *SW* | 22 |
| Susina | *Bakery* | 22 |

### LAUREL CANYON

| | | |
|---|---|---|
| Pace | *Italian* | 21 |

### LEIMERT PARK

| | | |
|---|---|---|
| **Z** Phillips BBQ | *BBQ* | 25 |

### LITTLE TOKYO

| | | |
|---|---|---|
| **NEW** Honda-Ya | *Japanese* | 22 |
| Izayoi | *Japanese* | 20 |
| Shabu Shabu Hse. | *Japanese* | 23 |
| **NEW** Shojin | *Japanese/Vegan* | - |
| Sushi Gen | *Japanese* | 24 |
| Thousand Cranes | *Japanese* | 21 |
| Yen Sushi | *Japanese* | 21 |

### LOS FELIZ

| | | |
|---|---|---|
| Alcove | *Amer.* | 21 |
| **NEW** Best Fish Taco | *Mex.* | 21 |

Chi Dynasty | *Chinese* — 21
Cobras/Matadors | *Spanish* — 21
Electric Lotus | *Indian* — 18
Farfalla Trattoria | *Italian* — 22
Figaro Bistrot | *French* — 19
Fred 62 | *Diner* — 17
Il Capriccio | *Italian* — 20
**NEW** Little Dom's | *Italian* — 17
Louise's Tratt. | *Cal./Italian* — 17
**NEW** Mes Amis | *French* — 16
Mexico City | *Mex.* — 18
Palermo | *Italian* — 19
Trails, The | *Amer./Vegan* — 16
Tropicalia Brazil | *Brazilian* — 20
vermont | *Amer.* — 21
Yai | *Thai* — 21

## MELROSE

(See map on page 277)

### TOP FOOD

All' Angelo | *Italian* | **E6** — 25
Osteria La Buca | *Italian* | **E10** — 25
Sweet Lady Jane | *Bakery* | **E2** — 23

### LISTING

All' Angelo | *Italian* — 25
Angeli Caffe | *Italian* — 23
Antonio's | *Mex.* — 19
Bulan Thai | *Thai* — 25
**Z** Carlitos Gardel | *Argent./Steak* — 23
Dolce Enoteca | *Italian* — 17
**NEW** 8 oz. | *Burgers* — -
Foundry, The | *Amer.* — 23
Johnny Rockets | *Burgers* — 15
Louise's Tratt. | *Cal./Italian* — 17
M Café | *Veg.* — 21
Osteria La Buca | *Italian* — 25
Sweet Lady Jane | *Bakery* — 23
Village Idiot | *Amer.* — 19

## MID-CITY

Bloom Cafe | *Amer./Cal.* — 22
El Cholo | *Mex.* — 18
Harold & Belle's | *Creole* — 24
Koo Koo Roo | *Amer.* — 15
Original TX BBQ | *BBQ* — 21
**Z** Papa Cristo's | *Greek* — 22
**Z** Phillips BBQ | *BBQ* — 25
Roscoe's | *Soul Food* — 20
Versailles | *Cuban* — 21
Woody's BBQ | *BBQ* — 23

## MID-WILSHIRE

India's Tandoori | *Indian* — 19
Johnnie's NY | *Pizza* — 18
Sandbag's | *Sandwiches* — 16

## PICO-ROBERTSON

Bella Roma | *Italian* — 23
Bossa Nova | *Brazilian* — 20
**NEW** Dolce Isola | *Amer.* — 24
Factor's Deli | *Deli* — 16
Fish Grill | *Seafood* — 19
Milky Way | *Cal.* — 19
Pat's | *Cal./Italian* — 22
Spark Woodfire | *Amer.* — 19
Tuk Tuk Thai | *Thai* — 21
Yen Sushi | *Japanese* — 21

## SILVER LAKE

Agra Cafe | *Indian* — 21
Alegria/Sunset | *Mex.* — 21
**NEW** Andiamo | *Italian* — -
Aroma | *Italian* — 25
Blair's | *Amer.* — 24
Bulan Thai | *Thai* — 25
Cafe Stella | *French* — 21
**Z** Cha Cha Cha | *Carib.* — 20
**Z** Cliff's Edge | *Cal./Italian* — 21
Dusty's | *Amer./French* — 18
Edendale Grill | *Amer.* — 16
Gingergrass | *Viet.* — 21
Kitchen, The | *Amer.* — 19
**NEW** LAMILL | *Cal.* — 23
Madame Matisse | *Amer.* — 19
Malo | *Mex.* — 17
Pho Café | *Viet.* — 21
Rambutan Thai | *Thai* — 21
Saito's Sushi | *Japanese* — 24
**NEW** Sila Bistro | *Amer.* — -
Tantra | *Indian* — 20

## THIRD STREET

(bet. La Brea & La Cienega; see map on back of gatefold)

### TOP FOOD

A.O.C. | *Cal./French* | **E6** — 26
Izaka-Ya | *Japanese* | **E5** — 25
Ortolan | *French* | **E5** — 25
Locanda Veneta | *Italian* | **E4** — 24
Surya India | *Indian* | **E6** — 24

### LISTING

**Z** A.O.C. | *Cal./French* — 26
Baja Fresh | *Mex.* — 17
Barefoot B&G | *Cal./Eclectic* — 18
Berri's Pizza | *Pizza* — 16
Cali. Wok | *Chinese* — 17
Chipotle | *Mex.* — 18
**NEW** Creperie/Jack n' Jill's | *Creole* — 21
Holy Cow Indian | *Indian* — 20
Izaka-Ya | *Japanese* — 25

| | |
|---|---|
| Joan's on 3rd \| *Amer./Bakery* | 23 |
| La Terza \| *Italian* | 22 |
| **Z** Little Door \| *Med.* | 23 |
| Locanda Veneta \| *Italian* | 24 |
| Mishima \| *Japanese* | 20 |
| Orso \| *Italian* | 21 |
| Ortolan \| *French* | 25 |
| Sofi \| *Greek* | 20 |
| Souplantation \| *Amer.* | 16 |
| **Z** Surya India \| *Indian* | 24 |
| Sushi Mac \| *Japanese* | 16 |
| Sushi Mon \| *Japanese* | 19 |
| Sushi Roku \| *Japanese* | 23 |
| Tasca Winebar \| *Spanish* | 23 |
| Toast \| *Amer.* | 19 |

## WEST HOLLYWOOD

(See map on back of gatefold)

### TOP FOOD

| | |
|---|---|
| Lucques \| *Cal./Med.* \| **D5** | 27 |
| Bastide \| *French* \| **C5** | 27 |
| Sona \| *French* \| **D5** | 27 |
| Nobu \| *Japanese* \| **C5** | 26 |
| Vivoli Café \| *Italian* \| **A6** | 25 |
| Il Sole \| *Italian* \| **B4** | 24 |
| Koi \| *Japanese* \| **C5** | 24 |
| Madeo \| *Italian* \| **D4** | 24 |
| Chaya \| *Asian/French* \| **E4** | 24 |
| Asia de Cuba \|<br>    *Asian Fusion/Cuban* \| **B5** | 23 |
| Katana \| *Japanese* \| **B5** | 23 |
| Palm, The \| *Seafood/Steak* \| **D4** | 23 |
| Taste \| *Amer.* \| **D5** | 23 |
| Boa \| *Steak* \| **B5** | 23 |
| Yabu \| *Japanese* \| **D5** | 23 |

### LISTING

| | |
|---|---|
| Abbey \| *Amer.* | 14 |
| Absolutely Pho \| *Viet.* | 17 |
| Ago \| *Italian* | 22 |
| **NEW** Amarone \| *Italian* | 27 |
| Asia de Cuba \| *Asian Fusion/Cuban* | 23 |
| Astro Burger \| *Burgers* | 19 |
| Basix Cafe \| *Cal./Italian* | 19 |
| **Z** Bastide \| *French* | 27 |
| **NEW** BLT Steak \| *Steak* | 23 |
| Boa \| *Steak* | 23 |
| Bossa Nova \| *Brazilian* | 20 |
| Boulevard Lounge \| *Cal.* | 19 |
| Breadbar \| *Amer./Bakery* | 18 |
| Cafe Med \| *Italian* | 18 |
| Caffe Primo \| *Italian* | 19 |
| Carney's \| *Hot Dogs* | 19 |
| Chateau Marmont \| *Cal./French* | 20 |
| Chaya \| *Asian/French* | 24 |
| Chin Chin \| *Chinese* | 16 |

| | |
|---|---|
| Clafoutis \| *French/Italian* | 19 |
| **NEW** Comme Ça \| *French* | 21 |
| Courtyard \| *Spanish* | 19 |
| **NEW** Crudo \| *Italian* | - |
| Dan Tana's \| *Italian* | 23 |
| Duke's Coffee \| *Diner* | 18 |
| Eat Well Cafe \| *Amer.* | 16 |
| Fat Fish \| *Asian Fusion/Japanese* | 20 |
| Flavor of India \| *Indian* | 22 |
| Formosa Cafe \| *Asian Fusion* | 12 |
| **NEW** Foxtail \| *French* | - |
| **NEW** Gordon Ramsay \| *Continental* | - |
| **NEW** Hall, The \| *French* | - |
| Hamburger Mary's \| *Diner* | 15 |
| Hamlet \| *Amer.* | 16 |
| House of Blues \| *Southern* | 16 |
| Hugo's \| *Cal.* | 21 |
| Il Sole \| *Italian* | 24 |
| **NEW** Isla \| *Mexican* | - |
| Ivy, The \| *Cal.* | 22 |
| Jan's \| *Diner* | 14 |
| Jinky's \| *SW* | 19 |
| Johnnie's NY \| *Pizza* | 18 |
| Jones \| *Amer./Italian* | 18 |
| Katana \| *Japanese* | 23 |
| Ketchup \| *Amer.* | 15 |
| Koi \| *Japanese* | 24 |
| Koo Koo Roo \| *Amer.* | 15 |
| Kung Pao \| *Chinese* | 19 |
| **Z** La Boheme \| *Cal.* | 22 |
| Le Pain Quotidien \| *Bakery/Belgian* | 19 |
| Le Petit Bistro \| *French* | 22 |
| Le Petit Four \| *French* | 19 |
| **Z** Lucques \| *Cal./Med.* | 27 |
| Madeo \| *Italian* | 24 |
| Mandarette \| *Chinese* | 18 |
| Marix Tex Mex \| *Tex-Mex* | 16 |
| Mark's \| *Cal.* | 17 |
| **NEW** Melrose B&G \| *Amer.* | 18 |
| Mel's Drive-In \| *Amer.* | 15 |
| Mirabelle \| *Cal./Eclectic* | 19 |
| **Z** Murano \| *Italian* | 20 |
| Newsroom Café \| *Veg.* | 18 |
| Nishimura \| *Japanese* | 26 |
| **NEW** Nobu \| *Japanese* | 26 |
| **NEW** Nonna \| *Italian* | 18 |
| **NEW** O!Burger \| *Burgers* | - |
| O-Bar \| *Amer.* | 21 |
| One Sunset \| *Amer.* | 20 |
| Palm, The \| *Seafood/Steak* | 23 |
| Petrossian \| *French* | 23 |
| Pizza Rustica \| *Pizza* | 22 |
| Pomodoro \| *Italian* | 18 |
| Poquito Más \| *Mex.* | 21 |
| Prana Cafe \| *Pan-Asian* | 18 |

| | |
|---|---|
| ☑ Real Food Daily | *Vegan* | 21 |
| Red 7 | *Pan-Asian* | 24 |
| Saddle Ranch | *Steak* | 14 |
| Salades/Provence | *French* | 20 |
| Sandbag's | *Sandwiches* | 16 |
| Simon LA | *Amer.* | 21 |
| ☑ Sona | *French* | 27 |
| Spanish Kitchen | *Mex.* | 15 |
| Standard, The | *Eclectic* | 15 |
| NEW STK | *Steak* | 21 |
| Sur | *Cal./Med.* | 21 |
| Talésai | *Thai* | 22 |
| Taste | *Amer.* | 23 |
| 3rd Stop | *Italian* | 17 |
| NEW Tinto | *Spanish* | 20 |
| Tower Bar | *Cal.* | 21 |
| Urth Caffé | *Amer.* | 20 |
| Vivoli Café | *Italian* | 25 |
| Wa | *Japanese* | 25 |
| Wokcano Cafe | *Chinese/Japanese* | 19 |
| Yabu | *Japanese* | 23 |
| Yatai Tapas | *Pan-Asian* | - |
| Zeke's Smokehse. | *BBQ* | 20 |

## LA East

### BOYLE HEIGHTS

| | |
|---|---|
| La Serenata | *Mex./Seafood* | 22 |

### EAST LA

| | |
|---|---|
| ☑ El Tepeyac | *Mex.* | 24 |
| Tamayo | *Mex.* | 18 |

## LA South

### BELLFLOWER

| | |
|---|---|
| Johnny Rebs' | *BBQ* | 22 |

### CARSON

| | |
|---|---|
| Back Home | *Hawaiian* | 17 |
| NEW Five Guys | *Burgers* | - |

### CERRITOS

| | |
|---|---|
| BCD Tofu | *Korean* | 19 |
| BJ's | *Pub* | 17 |
| Loft, The | *Hawaiian* | 19 |
| Lucille's BBQ | *BBQ* | 22 |
| Mimi's Cafe | *Diner* | 17 |
| Romano's Macaroni | *Italian* | 17 |
| Sam Woo | *Chinese* | 20 |
| Wood Ranch BBQ | *BBQ* | 20 |

### HAWTHORNE

| | |
|---|---|
| El Torito | *Mex.* | 15 |
| India's Tandoori | *Indian* | 19 |

### LAKEWOOD

| | |
|---|---|
| Outback | *Steak* | 17 |
| Souplantation | *Amer.* | 16 |

### LAWNDALE

| | |
|---|---|
| El Pollo Inka | *Peruvian* | 19 |

### LOMITA

| | |
|---|---|
| Il Chianti | *Italian* | 20 |

### LYNWOOD

| | |
|---|---|
| Guelaguetza | *Mex.* | 22 |
| La Huasteca | *Mex.* | 26 |

### PALOS VERDES PENINSULA/ ROLLING HILLS

| | |
|---|---|
| Admiral Risty | *Seafood* | 20 |
| Asaka | *Japanese* | 18 |
| Bistro 767 | *Cal.* | 22 |
| Café Pacific | *Amer.* | 24 |
| Frascati | *Italian* | 24 |
| La Rive Gauche | *French* | 19 |
| Marmalade Café | *Amer./Cal.* | 17 |
| Noah's NY Bagels | *Sandwiches* | 17 |
| Ruby's | *Diner* | 17 |
| Saluzzi | *Italian* | 22 |
| Trio Med. | *Med.* | 20 |

## LA West

### BEL-AIR

| | |
|---|---|
| Bel-Air B&G | *Cal.* | 19 |
| ☑ Hotel Bel-Air | *Cal./French* | 25 |
| SHU | *Italian/Japanese* | 21 |
| Vibrato | *Amer./Steak* | 21 |

### BEVERLY HILLS

(See map on back of gatefold)

#### TOP FOOD

| | |
|---|---|
| Matsuhisa | *Japanese* | **F5** | 27 |
| Spago | *Cal.* | **F2** | 27 |
| Mako | *Asian Fusion* | **F2** | 26 |
| Mastro's Steak | *Steak* | **F2** | 26 |
| CUT | *Steak* | **F2** | 26 |
| Ruth's Chris | *Steak* | **F2** | 26 |
| Il Pastaio | *Italian* | **E2** | 25 |
| Belvedere | *Amer.* | **F1** | 25 |
| Arnie Morton's | *Steak* | **E5** | 25 |
| Fogo de Chão | *Brazilian* | **F5** | 24 |
| Lawry's Prime | *Steak* | **F5** | 24 |
| Grill on Alley | *Amer.* | **F2** | 24 |
| Crustacean | *Asian Fusion/Viet.* | **F2** | 24 |
| Porta Via | *Cal.* | **E2** | 24 |
| Hokusai | *French/Japanese* | **F5** | 24 |

#### LISTING

| | |
|---|---|
| A Cow Jumped | *French* | 20 |
| Amici | *Italian* | 21 |
| ☑ Arnie Morton's | *Steak* | 25 |
| Asakuma | *Japanese* | 20 |

| | | | | |
|---|---|---|---|---|
| Baja Fresh \| *Mex.* | 17 | NEW Lemonade Cafe \| *Cal.* | – |
| Barney Greengrass \| *Deli* | 20 | Le Pain Quotidien \| *Bakery/Belgian* | 19 |
| Z Belvedere \| *Amer.* | 25 | Lodge Steak \| *Steak* | 19 |
| Benihana \| *Japanese* | 18 | NEW Luckyfish \| *Japanese* | 18 |
| blue on blue \| *Amer.* | 19 | Z Mako \| *Asian Fusion* | 26 |
| Blvd \| *Cal.* | 20 | Massimo \| *Italian* | 22 |
| boé \| *Amer.* | 22 | Z Mastro's Steak \| *Steak* | 26 |
| Bombay Palace \| *Indian* | 21 | Z Matsuhisa \| *Japanese* | 27 |
| NEW Bond St. \| *Japanese* | 19 | McCormick/Schmick \| *Seafood* | 19 |
| Bossa Nova \| *Brazilian* | 20 | Michel Richard \| *Bakery/French* | 23 |
| Boss Sushi \| *Japanese* | 25 | Mirü8691 \| *Pan-Asian* | 25 |
| Brighton Coffee \| *Diner* | 18 | Mr. Chow \| *Chinese* | 21 |
| Burger 90210 \| *Burgers* | 16 | Mulberry St. Pizzeria \| *Pizza* | 23 |
| Cafe Rodeo \| *Cal.* | 18 | Natalee \| *Thai* | 18 |
| Caffe Roma \| *Italian* | 17 | Nate 'n Al \| *Deli* | 20 |
| Cali. Pizza Kitchen \| *Pizza* | 18 | Nic's \| *Amer.* | 19 |
| Chakra \| *Indian* | 21 | Panini Cafe \| *Italian/Med.* | 17 |
| Z Cheesecake Factory \| *Amer.* | 19 | NEW Paperfish \| *Seafood* | 23 |
| Chin Chin \| *Chinese* | 16 | P.F. Chang's \| *Chinese* | 19 |
| Chipotle \| *Mex.* | 18 | Piccolo Paradiso \| *Italian* | 23 |
| Circa 55 \| *Amer./Cal.* | 19 | Pistachio Grill \| *Persian* | 21 |
| Coupa Café \| *Eclectic* | 17 | Pizza Rustica \| *Pizza* | 22 |
| Crazy Fish \| *Japanese* | 16 | Polo Lounge \| *Cal./Continental* | 22 |
| Z Crustacean \| *Asian Fusion/Viet.* | 24 | Porta Via \| *Cal.* | 24 |
| Z CUT \| *Steak* | 26 | Porterhouse \| *Steak* | 20 |
| Da Pasquale \| *Italian* | 20 | Rosti \| *Italian* | 16 |
| E. Baldi \| *Italian* | 22 | Z Ruth's Chris \| *Steak* | 26 |
| El Torito Grill \| *Mex.* | 18 | Sharky's Mex. \| *Mex.* | 18 |
| Enoteca Drago \| *Italian* | 21 | Z Spago \| *Cal.* | 27 |
| Farm/Bev. Hills \| *Amer.* | 19 | Stinking Rose \| *Italian* | 18 |
| Fogo de Chão \| *Brazilian* | 24 | Sushi Ozekii \| *Japanese* | 17 |
| Fountain Coffee \| *Diner* | 20 | Sushi Sushi \| *Japanese* | 24 |
| Frida \| *Mex.* | 21 | Talésai \| *Thai* | 22 |
| Gardens \| *Cal./Med.* | 23 | Z Tanzore \| *Indian* | 23 |
| Z Gonpachi \| *Japanese* | 18 | Tokyo Table \| *Japanese* | 19 |
| Grand Lux \| *Eclectic* | 18 | Urasawa \| *Japanese* | 28 |
| Z Grill on Alley \| *Amer.* | 24 | Urth Caffé \| *Amer.* | 20 |
| Gyu-Kaku \| *Japanese* | 20 | NEW Wolfgang's Steak \| *Steak* | – |
| Hokusai \| *French/Japanese* | 24 | Woo Lae Oak \| *Korean* | 22 |
| Il Buco \| *Italian* | 22 | Xi'an \| *Chinese* | 22 |
| Il Cielo \| *Italian* | 21 | Zen Grill \| *Pan-Asian* | 21 |
| Il Fornaio \| *Italian* | 20 | | |
| Il Forno Caldo \| *Italian* | 22 | **BRENTWOOD** | |
| Il Pastaio \| *Italian* | 25 | Amici \| *Italian* | 21 |
| Il Tramezzino \| *Italian* | 20 | A Votre Sante \| *Veg.* | 20 |
| Islands \| *Amer.* | 16 | Baja Fresh \| *Mex.* | 17 |
| Jack n' Jill's \| *Amer.* | 19 | Barney's Burgers \| *Burgers* | 20 |
| Jacopo's \| *Pizza* | 16 | Brentwood, The \| *Amer.* | 21 |
| Kate Mantilini \| *Amer.* | 18 | Cali. Wok \| *Chinese* | 17 |
| NEW Katsu Sushi \| *Japanese* | – | Z Cheesecake Factory \| *Amer.* | 19 |
| Koo Koo Roo \| *Amer.* | 15 | Chin Chin \| *Chinese* | 16 |
| La Dolce Vita \| *Italian* | 22 | City Bakery \| *Bakery* | 19 |
| La Paella \| *Spanish* | 23 | Clay Pit \| *Indian* | 21 |
| La Scala \| *Italian* | 21 | Coral Tree \| *Cal./Italian* | 18 |
| Z Lawry's Prime \| *Steak* | 24 | Daily Grill \| *Amer.* | 18 |

| | |
|---|---|
| Divino | Italian | 22 |
| Fish Grill | Seafood | 19 |
| Gaucho Grill | Argent./Steak | 17 |
| Getty Ctr. | Cal. | 22 |
| ☑ Katsuya | Japanese | 24 |
| La Scala | Italian | 21 |
| Le Pain Quotidien | Bakery/Belgian | 19 |
| Louise's Tratt. | Cal./Italian | 17 |
| Maria's Italian | Italian | 17 |
| Noah's NY Bagels | Sandwiches | 17 |
| On Sunset | Cal. | 22 |
| Osteria Latini | Italian | 24 |
| Palmeri | Italian | 22 |
| Pecorino | Italian | 22 |
| Peppone | Italian | 23 |
| Pizzicotto | Italian | 23 |
| Reddi Chick BBQ | BBQ | 21 |
| Saketini | Asian Fusion | 20 |
| Sandbag's | Sandwiches | 16 |
| San Gennaro | Italian | 16 |
| Sor Tino | Italian | 19 |
| Souplantation | Amer. | 16 |
| Taiko | Japanese | 20 |
| Takao | Japanese | 24 |
| Toscana | Italian | 23 |
| Vincenti | Italian | 26 |
| West | Cal./Italian | 18 |
| Zeidler's | Cal. | 17 |

## CENTURY CITY

| | |
|---|---|
| Breadbar | Amer./Bakery | 18 |
| Breeze | Cal./Seafood | 17 |
| Clementine | Amer./Bakery | 23 |
| Coral Tree | Cal./Italian | 18 |
| Craft | Amer. | 25 |
| Gulfstream | Amer./Seafood | 21 |
| ☑ Houston's | Amer. | 21 |
| Johnnie's NY | Pizza | 18 |
| NEW Kula | Japanese | 15 |
| ☑ La Cachette | French | 27 |
| NEW Lawry's Carvery | Amer. | 19 |
| Pink Taco | Mex. | 15 |
| NEW RockSugar | Pan-Asian | - |
| Stand, The | Hot Dogs | 18 |
| Ummba Grill | Brazilian | 16 |

## CULVER CITY

| | |
|---|---|
| NEW Akasha | Amer. | 22 |
| Bamboo | Carib. | 20 |
| Beacon | Pan-Asian | 22 |
| BottleRock | Euro. | 16 |
| NEW Brunello Trattoria | Italian | - |
| Cafe Surfas | Amer. | 19 |
| ☑ Father's Office | Amer./Burgers | 24 |
| Ford's | Gastropub | 19 |
| ☑ Fraîche | French/Med. | 24 |

| | |
|---|---|
| NEW Gyenari | Korean | - |
| ☑ In-N-Out | Burgers | 23 |
| Jody Maroni's | Hot Dogs | 19 |
| Johnnie's Pastrami | Deli | 20 |
| Johnny Rockets | Burgers | 15 |
| JR's BBQ | BBQ | 21 |
| K-Zo | Japanese | 23 |
| La Dijonaise | French | 18 |
| Leaf Cuisine | Vegan | 17 |
| M Café | Veg. | 21 |
| Meltdown Etc. | Amer. | 18 |
| Mi Ranchito | Mex. | 18 |
| Petrelli's Steak | Italian/Steak | 16 |
| NEW Point, The | Eclectic | 18 |
| Roll 'n Rye | Deli | 17 |
| NEW Rush Street | Amer. | - |
| Tender Greens | Amer. | 23 |
| Thai Dishes | Thai | 18 |
| Ugo/Italian | Italian | 17 |
| NEW Vinotéque | Med. | - |
| Wilson | Med. | 22 |

## MALIBU

| | |
|---|---|
| Allegria | Italian | 20 |
| Beau Rivage | Med. | 21 |
| NEW Carbon Beach | Cal./Pac. Rim | 13 |
| Chart House | Seafood/Steak | 19 |
| ☑ Cholada | Thai | 24 |
| D'Amore's | Pizza | 20 |
| Duke's | Pac. Rim | 17 |
| ☑ Geoffrey's | Cal. | 21 |
| Guido's | Italian | 19 |
| Johnnie's NY | Pizza | 18 |
| NEW Malibu Pier Club | Cal. | - |
| Malibu Seafood | Seafood | 22 |
| Marmalade Café | Amer./Cal. | 17 |
| Moonshadows | Amer. | 17 |
| Neptune's Net | Seafood | 18 |
| ☑ Nobu | Japanese | 27 |
| Paradise Cove | Amer./Seafood | 15 |
| Reel Inn | Seafood | 20 |
| Taverna Tony | Greek | 20 |
| NEW Terra | Cal. | 22 |
| Thai Dishes | Thai | 18 |
| Tra Di Noi | Italian | 22 |

## MARINA DEL REY

(See map on page 279)

### TOP FOOD

| | |
|---|---|
| Tlapazola Grill | Mex. | 23 |
| Akbar | Indian | 22 |
| Cafe Del Rey | Cal./Med. | 21 |
| Jer-ne | Cal. | 20 |
| 26 Beach | Cal. | 20 |

## LISTING

| | |
|---|---|
| Akbar | *Indian* | 22 |
| Alejo's | *Italian* | 19 |
| Antica Pizzeria | *Pizza* | 20 |
| Aunt Kizzy's | *Southern* | 19 |
| Baja Fresh | *Mex.* | 17 |
| Beechwood | *Amer.* | 18 |
| Cafe Del Rey | *Cal./Med.* | 21 |
| C & O | *Italian* | 18 |
| Chart House | *Seafood/Steak* | 19 |
| **Z** Cheesecake Factory | *Amer.* | 19 |
| Chipotle | *Mex.* | 18 |
| Counter, The | *Burgers* | 21 |
| El Torito | *Mex.* | 15 |
| Gaby's | *Lebanese/Med.* | 19 |
| Islands | *Amer.* | 16 |
| Jer-ne | *Cal.* | 20 |
| Koo Koo Roo | *Amer.* | 15 |
| Le Marmiton | *French* | 18 |
| Noah's NY Bagels | *Sandwiches* | 17 |
| Sapori | *Italian* | 20 |
| Souplantation | *Amer.* | 16 |
| **NEW** sugarFISH | *Japanese* | - |
| Tlapazola Grill | *Mex.* | 23 |
| Tony P's Dock | *Amer.* | 18 |
| Tsuji No Hana | *Japanese* | 20 |
| 26 Beach | *Cal.* | 20 |
| Wharo | *Korean* | 16 |

## MAR VISTA

| | |
|---|---|
| Paco's Tacos | *Mex.* | 20 |

## PACIFIC PALISADES

| | |
|---|---|
| Gladstone's | *Seafood* | 14 |
| **NEW** Il Carpaccio | *Italian* | 23 |
| Jacopo's | *Pizza* | 16 |
| Kay 'n Dave's | *Mex.* | 18 |
| Modo Mio | *Italian* | 22 |
| **NEW** Oak Room | *Cal.* | - |
| Pearl Dragon | *Pan-Asian* | 17 |
| **NEW** Village Pantry | *Deli* | 14 |
| Vittorio's | *Italian* | 19 |

## PALMS

| | |
|---|---|
| Café Brasil | *Brazilian* | 19 |
| Cucina Paradiso | *Italian* | 21 |
| Guelaguetza | *Mex.* | 22 |
| Hu's Szechwan | *Chinese* | 21 |
| Indo Cafe | *Indonesian* | 19 |
| Natalee | *Thai* | 18 |
| Versailles | *Cuban* | 21 |

## PLAYA DEL REY

| | |
|---|---|
| Berri's Pizza | *Pizza* | 16 |
| Caffe Pinguini | *Italian* | 21 |
| **NEW** Del, The | *Amer.* | 20 |
| Minotaure | *Spanish* | 20 |

| | |
|---|---|
| Outlaws B&G | *Amer.* | 18 |
| Shack, The | *Amer.* | 17 |

## RANCHO PARK

| | |
|---|---|
| **NEW** FOOD | *Amer.* | - |
| John O'Groats | *Amer.* | 21 |
| Kay 'n Dave's | *Mex.* | 18 |

## SANTA MONICA

(See map on page 279)

### TOP FOOD

| | |
|---|---|
| Mélisse | *Amer./French* | **D2** | 28 |
| Chinois | *Asian/French* | **G1** | 26 |
| Josie | *Amer.* | **F4** | 26 |
| Capo | *Italian* | **E1** | 26 |
| Sam's/Beach | *Cal./Med.* | **B1** | 26 |
| Via Veneto | *Italian* | **G1** | 26 |
| JiRaffe | *Amer./French* | **D2** | 26 |
| Valentino | *Italian* | **F5** | 26 |
| Hump, The | *Japanese* | **G5** | 25 |
| La Botte | *Italian* | **D2** | 25 |
| Musha | *Japanese* | **D2** | 24 |
| Drago | *Italian* | **D4** | 24 |
| Michael's | *Cal.* | **D1** | 24 |
| Giorgio Baldi | *Italian* | **B1** | 24 |
| Father's Office | *Amer./Burgers* | **C2** | 24 |

### LISTING

| | |
|---|---|
| Abbot's Pizza | *Pizza* | 22 |
| Akbar | *Indian* | 22 |
| **NEW** Anisette | *French* | - |
| Babalu | *Cal.* | 19 |
| **NEW** Bar Pintxo | *Spanish* | 19 |
| Bay Cities Deli | *Italian* | - |
| Benihana | *Japanese* | 18 |
| Bistro 31 | *Cal.* | 18 |
| Boa | *Steak* | 23 |
| Border Grill | *Mex.* | 21 |
| Brass.-Cap. | *French* | 19 |
| Bravo | *Italian/Pizza* | 17 |
| Broadway Deli | *Deli* | 15 |
| Buca di Beppo | *Italian* | 15 |
| Buddha's Belly | *Pan-Asian* | 19 |
| Buffalo Club | *Amer.* | 20 |
| Cafe Montana | *Cal.* | 19 |
| Caffé Delfini | *Italian* | 23 |
| Caffe Luxxe | *Coffee* | 24 |
| Cali. Chicken | *Amer.* | 21 |
| Cali. Pizza Kitchen | *Pizza* | 18 |
| **Z** Capo | *Italian* | 26 |
| Catch | *Cal./Seafood* | 22 |
| Cézanne | *Cal./French* | 21 |
| Cha Cha Chicken | *Carib.* | 21 |
| Chez Jay | *Steak* | 16 |
| Chez Mimi | *French* | 22 |
| **Z** Chinois | *Asian/French* | 26 |

| Restaurant | Cuisine | Rating |
|---|---|---|
| Cali. Chicken | Amer. | 21 |
| Canal Club | Cal./Eclectic | 18 |
| Casablanca | Mex. | 18 |
| Chaya | Japanese/Med. | 22 |
| China Beach | Viet. | 16 |
| Danny's | Deli | 17 |
| NEW Flake | Amer. | - |
| NEW Gjelina | Amer. | - |
| Hal's B&G | Amer. | 20 |
| Hama Sushi | Japanese | 21 |
| James' Bch. | Amer. | 18 |
| Z Jin Patisserie | Bakery/French | 25 |
| Jody Maroni's | Hot Dogs | 19 |
| Z Joe's | Cal./French | 26 |
| Johnnie's NY | Pizza | 18 |
| NEW Lido Grill | Med. | - |
| Lilly's French Cafe | French | 19 |
| Maxwell's Cafe | Amer. | 19 |
| Piccolo | Italian | 27 |
| Primitivo | Med. | 20 |
| Rose Cafe | Cal. | 19 |
| Shima | Japanese | 27 |
| 3 Square | Bakery/Sandwiches | 20 |
| Uncle Darrow's | Cajun/Creole | 19 |
| Wabi-Sabi | Asian Fusion | 22 |

## WEST LA

| Restaurant | Cuisine | Rating |
|---|---|---|
| All India | Indian | 22 |
| Anna's | Italian | 15 |
| Apple Pan | Amer./Burgers | 22 |
| Asahi Ramen | Japanese | 20 |
| Asakuma | Japanese | 20 |
| Bandera | Amer./SW | 21 |
| Bar Hayama | Japanese | 24 |
| Billingsley's | Steak | 15 |
| Bombay Cafe | Indian | 23 |
| Café Brasil | Brazilian | 19 |
| Cafe 50's | Diner | 16 |
| Cali. Chicken | Amer. | 21 |
| Chabuya | Japanese | 19 |
| Chan/Hse. of Chan | Thai | 20 |
| Colony Café | Amer. | 18 |
| Echigo | Japanese | 25 |
| Enzo & Angela | Italian | 22 |
| Feast from East | Asian | 20 |
| Gaby's | Lebanese/Med. | 19 |
| NEW Giggles 'n Hugs | Amer. | - |
| Guido's | Italian | 19 |
| Gyu-Kaku | Japanese | 20 |
| Hamasaku | Japanese | 26 |
| Hamlet | Amer. | 16 |
| Hide Sushi | Japanese | 24 |
| Hop Li | Chinese | 20 |
| Hop Woo | Chinese | 18 |
| Hurry Curry | Japanese | 18 |
| Il Grano | Italian | 26 |

| Restaurant | Cuisine | Rating |
|---|---|---|
| Il Moro | Italian | 23 |
| India's Tandoori | Indian | 19 |
| Z In-N-Out | Burgers | 23 |
| Islands | Amer. | 16 |
| Jack Sprat's | Cal. | 19 |
| Javan | Persian | 20 |
| Johnnie's NY | Pizza | 18 |
| Junior's | Deli | 16 |
| Koo Koo Roo | Amer. | 15 |
| La Bottega Marino | Italian | 21 |
| La Serenata | Mex./Seafood | 22 |
| Lemon Moon | Cal./Med. | 20 |
| Le Saigon | Viet. | 21 |
| Literati | Cal./Eclectic | 19 |
| Louise's Tratt. | Cal./Italian | 17 |
| Maria's Italian | Italian | 17 |
| Matteo's | Italian | 19 |
| Monte Alban | Mex. | 21 |
| Z Mori Sushi | Japanese | 27 |
| Mr. Cecil's Ribs | BBQ | 18 |
| Nanbankan | Japanese | 24 |
| Nizam | Indian | 18 |
| Z Nook Bistro | Amer./Eclectic | 24 |
| Orris | French/Japanese | 26 |
| Pastina | Italian | 20 |
| Poquito Más | Mex. | 21 |
| Qusqo | Peruvian | 19 |
| Simpang Asia | Indonesian | 18 |
| Sisley Italian | Italian | 17 |
| Sushi Mac | Japanese | 16 |
| Sushi Masu | Japanese | 26 |
| Sushi Sasabune | Japanese | 26 |
| Sushi Zo | Japanese | 29 |
| Tlapazola Grill | Mex. | 23 |
| NEW Tofu Villa | Korean | - |
| Tofu-Ya | Korean | 20 |
| Torafuku | Japanese | 24 |
| 2117 | Asian/Euro. | 23 |
| Upstairs 2 | Med. | 24 |
| U-Zen | Japanese | 22 |
| V.I.P. Harbor | Chinese/Seafood | 18 |
| Yabu | Japanese | 23 |
| Yen Sushi | Japanese | 21 |
| Zankou | Med. | 22 |
| Zip Fusion | Japanese | 18 |
| Zu Robata | Japanese | 20 |

## WESTWOOD

| Restaurant | Cuisine | Rating |
|---|---|---|
| Asuka | Japanese | 19 |
| Baja Fresh | Mex. | 17 |
| BJ's | Pub | 17 |
| NEW Blvd 16 | Amer. | - |
| Bombay Bite | Indian | 20 |
| Cali. Pizza Kitchen | Pizza | 18 |
| D'Amore's | Pizza | 20 |
| Danube Bulgarian | Bulgarian | 19 |

| | |
|---|---|
| Delphi | *Greek* | 17 |
| Falafel King | *Mideast.* | 18 |
| Gardens/Glendon | *Cal.* | 19 |
| ☑ In-N-Out | *Burgers* | 23 |
| NEW JuJu | *Amer.* | - |
| Koutoubia | *Moroccan* | 20 |
| La Bruschetta | *Italian* | 23 |
| Lamonica's NY Pizza | *Pizza* | 21 |
| Le Pain Quotidien | *Bakery/Belgian* | 19 |
| Mio Babbo's | *Italian* | 22 |
| Napa Valley | *Cal.* | 20 |
| ☑ Native Foods | *Cal./Eclectic* | 22 |
| Nine Thirty | *Amer.* | 21 |
| Noah's NY Bagels | *Sandwiches* | 17 |
| Palomino | *Amer./Euro.* | 19 |
| Sandbag's | *Sandwiches* | 16 |
| Shaherzad | *Persian* | 21 |
| Soleil Westwood | *Canadian/French* | 20 |
| South St. | *Cheese Stks.* | 18 |
| Stand, The | *Hot Dogs* | 18 |
| ☑ Sunnin | *Lebanese* | 24 |
| Tanino | *Italian* | 23 |
| Tengu | *Japanese* | 22 |
| NEW Yamato | *Japanese* | 19 |

## South Bay

### BALDWIN HILLS

| | |
|---|---|
| Creole Chef | *Creole* | - |

### DOWNEY

| | |
|---|---|
| Mimi's Cafe | *Diner* | 17 |

### EL SEGUNDO

| | |
|---|---|
| Cozymel's | *Mex.* | 16 |
| Daily Grill | *Amer.* | 18 |
| Farm Stand | *Eclectic* | 21 |
| Fleming's | *Steak* | 25 |
| Marmalade Café | *Amer./Cal.* | 17 |
| McCormick/Schmick | *Seafood* | 19 |
| P.F. Chang's | *Chinese* | 19 |
| Romano's Macaroni | *Italian* | 17 |
| Salt Creek | *Steak* | 18 |
| Second City | *Amer.* | 23 |
| Taiko | *Japanese* | 20 |
| NEW Veggie Grill | *Vegan* | 19 |

### GARDENA

| | |
|---|---|
| El Pollo Inka | *Peruvian* | 19 |
| Sea Empress | *Chinese* | 19 |

### HERMOSA BEACH

| | |
|---|---|
| Akbar | *Indian* | 22 |
| NEW Brix 1601 | *Amer.* | - |
| Chef Melba's | *Cal.* | 24 |
| El Pollo Inka | *Peruvian* | 19 |

| | |
|---|---|
| Fritto Misto | *Italian* | 21 |
| Il Boccaccio | *Italian* | 22 |
| Jackson's Vill. | *Amer.* | 24 |
| NEW Ken/Kent's NY Deli | *Deli* | - |
| La Sosta | *Italian* | 26 |
| Mama D's | *Italian* | 21 |
| Martha 22nd St. | *Amer.* | 21 |
| Mediterraneo | *Med.* | 20 |
| Ragin' Cajun | *Cajun* | 20 |
| Rocky Cola | *Diner* | 13 |
| Sushi Duke | *Japanese* | 23 |
| NEW Zane's | *Italian/Steak* | - |

### INGLEWOOD

| | |
|---|---|
| ☑ Phillips BBQ | *BBQ* | 25 |
| Thai Dishes | *Thai* | 18 |
| Woody's BBQ | *BBQ* | 23 |

### LAX

| | |
|---|---|
| Daily Grill | *Amer.* | 18 |
| El Cholo | *Mex.* | 18 |
| Encounter | *Eclectic* | 14 |
| Jody Maroni's | *Hot Dogs* | 19 |
| Ruby's | *Diner* | 17 |
| Thai Dishes | *Thai* | 18 |
| Wolfgang Puck | *Cal.* | 17 |

### LONG BEACH

| | |
|---|---|
| Alegria | *Nuevo Latino* | 19 |
| Auld Dubliner | *Pub* | 18 |
| Baja Fresh | *Mex.* | 17 |
| Belmont Brew. | *Amer.* | 16 |
| ☑ Benley | *Viet.* | 24 |
| BJ's | *Pub* | 17 |
| Bono's | *Cal.* | 20 |
| Christy's | *Italian* | 22 |
| Claim Jumper | *Amer.* | 19 |
| El Torito | *Mex.* | 15 |
| 555 East | *Steak* | 24 |
| ☑ Frenchy's Bistro | *French* | 26 |
| George's Greek | *Greek* | 22 |
| Green Field | *Brazilian* | 21 |
| Joe's Crab | *Seafood* | 13 |
| Johnny Rebs' | *BBQ* | 22 |
| Johnny Rockets | *Burgers* | 15 |
| King's Fish | *Seafood* | 21 |
| La Creperie Cafe | *French* | 23 |
| Lasher's | *Amer.* | 23 |
| L'Opera | *Italian* | 23 |
| Lucille's BBQ | *BBQ* | 22 |
| ☑ Madison, The | *Seafood/Steak* | 20 |
| McKenna's | *Seafood/Steak* | 19 |
| NEW Michael's/Naples | *Italian* | - |
| Mimi's Cafe | *Diner* | 17 |
| Parker's Lighthse. | *Seafood* | 18 |

| | |
|---|---|
| Roscoe's | *Soul Food* | 20 |
| Ruby's | *Diner* | 17 |
| Sharky's Mex. | *Mex.* | 18 |
| Sir Winston's | *Continental* | 21 |
| Sky Room | *Amer.* | 21 |
| ☑ Sunnin | *Lebanese* | 24 |
| Tracht's | *Amer.* | 23 |
| Yard Hse. | *Amer.* | 20 |
| Yen Sushi | *Japanese* | 21 |

## MANHATTAN BEACH

| | |
|---|---|
| Back Home | *Hawaiian* | 17 |
| Bora Bora | *Cal./Polynesian* | 22 |
| Café Pierre | *French* | 22 |
| Cali. Pizza Kitchen | *Pizza* | 18 |
| China Grill | *Cal./Chinese* | 19 |
| Coco Noche | *Dessert/Eclectic* | 17 |
| Corkscrew | *Eclectic* | 21 |
| NEW Darren's | *Cal.* | 26 |
| Ebizo's | *Japanese* | 22 |
| Fonz's | *Seafood/Steak* | 22 |
| ☑ Houston's | *Amer.* | 21 |
| Il Fornaio | *Italian* | 20 |
| Islands | *Amer.* | 16 |
| Joey's BBQ | *BBQ* | 18 |
| Johnny Rockets | *Burgers* | 15 |
| Koo Koo Roo | *Amer.* | 15 |
| La Creperie Cafe | *French* | 23 |
| LA Food Show | *Amer.* | 18 |
| Le Pain Quotidien | *Bakery/Belgian* | 19 |
| Lido/Manhattan | *Italian/Med.* | 19 |
| Mama D's | *Italian* | 21 |
| NEW Mucho Ultima | *Mex.* | 19 |
| Noah's NY Bagels | *Sandwiches* | 17 |
| ☑ Petros | *Greek* | 24 |
| Pomodoro | *Italian* | 18 |
| Rock'n Fish | *Seafood/Steak* | 21 |
| NEW Second Story | *Amer.* | - |
| Talia's | *Italian* | 24 |
| NEW Tapa Meze | *Mideast./Spanish* | - |
| Thai Dishes | *Thai* | 18 |
| Towne | *Cal.* | 18 |
| NEW Twelve + Highland | *Amer.* | 21 |
| Uncle Bill's | *Diner* | 21 |
| Versailles | *Cuban* | 21 |

## REDONDO BEACH

| | |
|---|---|
| ☑ Addi's Tandoor | *Indian* | 26 |
| Baleen | *Amer.* | 20 |
| Bluewater Grill | *Amer./Seafood* | 19 |
| Buca di Beppo | *Italian* | 15 |
| Buona Sera | *Italian* | 22 |
| NEW Catalina | *Amer.* | 24 |
| Chaba | *Thai* | 20 |
| Chart House | *Seafood/Steak* | 19 |

| | |
|---|---|
| ☑ Cheesecake Factory | *Amer.* | 19 |
| ☑ Chez Mélange | *Eclectic* | 25 |
| Cialuzzi's | *Italian* | 20 |
| Coyote Cantina | *SW* | 20 |
| El Torito | *Mex.* | 15 |
| ☑ Gina Lee's | *Asian/Cal.* | 26 |
| Joe's Crab | *Seafood* | 13 |
| Kincaid's | *Seafood/Steak* | 20 |
| Momoyama | *Japanese* | 19 |
| Original Pancake | *Diner* | 23 |
| NEW Ortega 120 | *Mex.* | - |
| Ruby's | *Diner* | 17 |
| W's China | *Chinese* | 21 |
| Zazou | *Med.* | 23 |

## SAN PEDRO

| | |
|---|---|
| ☑ Papadakis Tav. | *Greek* | 21 |
| 22nd St. Landing | *Seafood* | 18 |
| Whale & Ale | *Pub* | 16 |

## TORRANCE

| | |
|---|---|
| Aioli | *Med./Spanish* | 18 |
| BCD Tofu | *Korean* | 19 |
| Chabuya | *Japanese* | 19 |
| Chipotle | *Mex.* | 18 |
| ☑ Christine | *Med./Pac. Rim* | 26 |
| Claim Jumper | *Amer.* | 19 |
| Depot | *Eclectic* | 24 |
| El Pollo Inka | *Peruvian* | 19 |
| El Torito Grill | *Mex.* | 18 |
| Gyu-Kaku | *Japanese* | 20 |
| Islands | *Amer.* | 16 |
| Jody Maroni's | *Hot Dogs* | 19 |
| Lazy Dog | *Eclectic* | 19 |
| Local Pl. | *Amer./Hawaiian* | 18 |
| Loft, The | *Hawaiian* | 19 |
| Lucille's BBQ | *BBQ* | 22 |
| Mimi's Cafe | *Diner* | 17 |
| Misto Caffé | *Cal./Eclectic* | 20 |
| Musha | *Japanese* | 24 |
| O-Nami | *Japanese* | 17 |
| Outback | *Steak* | 17 |
| Pei Wei | *Pan-Asian* | 16 |
| Poquito Más | *Mex.* | 21 |
| RA Sushi | *Japanese* | 16 |
| Romano's Macaroni | *Italian* | 17 |
| Yuzu | *Japanese* | 23 |

## WESTCHESTER

| | |
|---|---|
| Alejo's | *Italian* | 19 |
| NEW Bistrotek | *Amer.* | - |
| Buggy Whip | *Seafood/Steak* | 19 |
| ☑ In-N-Out | *Burgers* | 23 |
| Kanpai | *Japanese* | 22 |
| Paco's Tacos | *Mex.* | 20 |
| Truxton's | *Amer.* | - |

# Inland Empire

## MORENO VALLEY

| | |
|---|---|
| BJ's \| *Pub* | 17 |
| **NEW** Portillo's \| *Hot Dogs* | 18 |

## ONTARIO

| | |
|---|---|
| Benihana \| *Japanese* | 18 |
| Panda Inn \| *Chinese* | 21 |
| Rainforest Cafe \| *Amer.* | 12 |

# Pasadena & Environs

## ARCADIA

| | |
|---|---|
| BJ's \| *Pub* | 17 |
| Derby \| *Steak* | 23 |
| **Z** Din Tai Fung \| *Chinese* | 25 |
| Doña Rosa \| *Bakery/Mex.* | 16 |
| Hop Li \| *Chinese* | 20 |
| Jody Maroni's \| *Hot Dogs* | 19 |
| Johnny Rockets \| *Burgers* | 15 |
| Outback \| *Steak* | 17 |
| Souplantation \| *Amer.* | 16 |
| Tokyo Table \| *Japanese* | 19 |
| Wood Ranch BBQ \| *BBQ* | 20 |

## EAGLE ROCK

| | |
|---|---|
| Auntie Em's \| *Amer.* | 23 |
| Blue Hen \| *Viet.* | 14 |
| Café Beaujolais \| *French* | 23 |
| Camilo's \| *Cal.* | 23 |
| Casa Bianca \| *Pizza* | 23 |
| Fatty's & Co. \| *Veg.* | 23 |
| Larkin's \| *Southern* | 20 |
| Mia Sushi \| *Japanese* | 18 |
| Oinkster, The \| *BBQ* | 20 |
| Spitz \| *Turkish* | 23 |

## LA CAÑADA FLINTRIDGE

| | |
|---|---|
| Dish \| *Amer.* | 16 |
| Taylor's Steak \| *Steak* | 21 |

## MONROVIA

| | |
|---|---|
| Café Mundial \| *Cal./Med.* | 21 |
| Claim Jumper \| *Amer.* | 19 |
| Devon \| *Cal./French* | 23 |
| Mimi's Cafe \| *Diner* | 17 |
| Romano's Macaroni \| *Italian* | 17 |

## PASADENA

(See map on page 280)

### TOP FOOD

| | |
|---|---|
| Derek's \| *Cal./French* \| **H2** | 27 |
| Bistro 45 \| *Cal.* \| **D5** | 26 |
| Parkway Grill \| *Cal.* \| **F2** | 26 |

| | |
|---|---|
| Langham Huntington \| *Cal.* \| **I5** | 26 |
| Ruth's Chris \| *Steak* \| **D3** | 26 |
| Maison Akira † *French/Japanese* \| **E4** | 25 |
| Yujean Kang's \| *Chinese* \| **D2** | 25 |
| Arroyo Chop \| *Steak* \| **F2** | 25 |
| Tre Venezie \| *Italian* \| **E1** | 25 |
| Raymond, The \| *Cal.* \| **H2** | 24 |
| Madeleine's \| *Cal.* \| **E4** | 24 |
| Gale's \| *Italian* \| **F2** | 24 |
| Saladang \| *Thai* \| **E2** \| **F2** | 23 |
| Roy's \| *Asian Fusion/Hawaiian* \| **D4** | 23 |
| Celestino \| *Italian* \| **E5** | 23 |

### LISTING

| | |
|---|---|
| Akbar \| *Indian* | 22 |
| All India \| *Indian* | 22 |
| Arroyo Chop \| *Steak* | 25 |
| Baja Fresh \| *Mex.* | 17 |
| Bar Celona \| *Spanish* | 16 |
| Beckham Grill \| *Amer.* | 18 |
| Big Mama's \| *BBQ/Soul Food* | 19 |
| Bistro 45 \| *Cal.* | 26 |
| Buca di Beppo \| *Italian* | 15 |
| Burger Continental \| *Mideast.* | 17 |
| **Z** Café Bizou \| *Cal./French* | 23 |
| Café Santorini \| *Med.* | 20 |
| Cali. Pizza Kitchen \| *Pizza* | 18 |
| Celestino \| *Italian* | 23 |
| Central Park \| *Amer./Cal.* | 17 |
| **Z** Cheesecake Factory \| *Amer.* | 19 |
| Chipotle \| *Mex.* | 18 |
| CrêpeVine \| *French* | 21 |
| Crocodile Cafe \| *Cal.* | 16 |
| **Z** Derek's \| *Cal./French* | 27 |
| Doña Rosa \| *Bakery/Mex.* | 16 |
| El Cholo \| *Mex.* | 18 |
| El Torito \| *Mex.* | 15 |
| Five 61 \| *Cal./French* | 22 |
| Fu-Shing \| *Chinese* | 19 |
| Gale's \| *Italian* | 24 |
| Gaucho Grill \| *Argent./Steak* | 17 |
| Gordon Biersch \| *Pub* | 16 |
| Green St. Rest. \| *Amer.* | - |
| **NEW** Green St. Tav. \| *Cal./Euro.* | 23 |
| Gyu-Kaku \| *Japanese* | 20 |
| Hamlet \| *Amer.* | 16 |
| Holly St. \| *Cal.* | 19 |
| **Z** Houston's \| *Amer.* | 21 |
| Hurry Curry \| *Japanese* | 18 |
| Il Fornaio \| *Italian* | 20 |
| Islands \| *Amer.* | 16 |
| Japon Bistro \| *Japanese* | 25 |
| JJ Steak \| *Steak* | 23 |
| Koo Koo Roo \| *Amer.* | 15 |
| **NEW** La Grande Orange \| *Amer.* | - |

| | |
|---|---|
| La Maschera | *Italian* | 22 |
| ☑ Langham Huntington | *Cal.* | 26 |
| Le Pain Quotidien | *Bakery/Belgian* | 19 |
| Louise's Tratt. | *Cal./Italian* | 17 |
| Madeleine's | *Cal.* | 24 |
| Magnolia Lounge | *Contemp. LA* | 19 |
| Maison Akira | *French/Japanese* | 25 |
| Maria's Italian | *Italian* | 17 |
| Marston's | *Amer.* | 23 |
| McCormick/Schmick | *Seafood* | 19 |
| Melting Pot | *Fondue* | 18 |
| Mijares | *Mex.* | 17 |
| Mi Piace | *Cal./Italian* | 20 |
| NEW Mojitos | *Cuban* | 24 |
| Neomeze | *Eclectic* | 23 |
| Noah's NY Bagels | *Sandwiches* | 17 |
| NEW Oba Sushi Izakaya | *Japanese* | - |
| Panda Inn | *Chinese* | 21 |
| ☑ Parkway Grill | *Cal.* | 26 |
| Pei Wei | *Pan-Asian* | 16 |
| P.F. Chang's | *Chinese* | 19 |
| Pie 'N Burger | *Diner* | 19 |
| NEW Porta Via Italian | *Italian* | 23 |
| Porto Alegre | *Brazilian/Steak* | 20 |
| Radhika's | *Indian* | 22 |
| Raymond, The | *Cal.* | 24 |
| redwhite+bluezz | *Amer.* | 22 |
| Robin's BBQ | *BBQ* | 17 |
| Roscoe's | *Soul Food* | 20 |
| Roy's | *Asian Fusion/Hawaiian* | 23 |
| Russell's Burgers | *Diner* | 19 |
| ☑ Ruth's Chris | *Steak* | 26 |
| Saladang | *Thai* | 23 |
| NEW Seoul Bros. | *Korean* | - |
| Sharky's Mex. | *Mex.* | 18 |
| NEW Siena | *Italian* | - |
| Smitty's Grill | *Amer.* | 21 |
| Souplantation | *Amer.* | 16 |
| Sushi Roku | *Japanese* | 22 |
| Thai Dishes | *Thai* | 18 |
| Tibet Nepal | *Nepalese/Tibetan* | 19 |
| Tre Venezie | *Italian* | 25 |
| Twin Palms | *Amer.* | 18 |
| Vault, The | *Amer.* | 14 |
| Vertical Wine | *Eclectic/Med.* | 23 |
| Villa Sorriso | *Italian* | 16 |
| Wokcano Cafe | *Chinese/Japanese* | 19 |
| Yang Chow | *Chinese* | 22 |
| Yard Hse. | *Amer.* | 20 |
| ☑ Yujean Kang's | *Chinese* | 25 |
| Zankou | *Med.* | 22 |

## SAN MARINO

| | |
|---|---|
| Julienne | *French* | 25 |

## SOUTH PASADENA

| | |
|---|---|
| Bistro de la Gare | *French* | 19 |
| Briganti | *Italian* | 23 |
| Firefly Bistro | *Amer.* | 18 |
| NEW Gus's BBQ | *BBQ* | - |
| Mike & Anne's | *Amer.* | 21 |
| 750 ml | *French* | 19 |
| ☑ Shiro | *French/Japanese* | 27 |

# San Fernando Valley & Burbank

## BURBANK

| | |
|---|---|
| ☑ Arnie Morton's | *Steak* | 25 |
| Baja Fresh | *Mex.* | 17 |
| Bistro Provence | *French* | 23 |
| BJ's | *Pub* | 17 |
| Cali. Pizza Kitchen | *Pizza* | 18 |
| Castaway | *Cal.* | 13 |
| Chadaka | *Thai* | 24 |
| Chili John's | *Amer.* | 17 |
| Chipotle | *Mex.* | 18 |
| Daily Grill | *Amer.* | 18 |
| El Torito | *Mex.* | 15 |
| Flavor of India | *Indian* | 22 |
| Gordon Biersch | *Pub* | 16 |
| Islands | *Amer.* | 16 |
| Johnny Rockets | *Burgers* | 15 |
| Market City | *Cal./Italian* | 17 |
| McCormick/Schmick | *Seafood* | 19 |
| Mo's | *Amer.* | 17 |
| Outback | *Steak* | 17 |
| Picanha Churr. | *Brazilian* | 21 |
| Pomodoro | *Italian* | 18 |
| Poquito Más | *Mex.* | 21 |
| ☑ Porto's | *Bakery/Cuban* | 24 |
| Ribs USA | *BBQ* | 19 |
| Sharky's Mex. | *Mex.* | 18 |
| Smoke House | *Steak* | 19 |
| South St. | *Cheese Stks.* | 18 |
| Taste Chicago | *Italian* | 16 |
| NEW Third & Olive | *Cal./French* | - |
| Tony's Bella Vista | *Italian* | 21 |
| Wokcano Cafe | *Chinese/Japanese* | 19 |
| Zankou | *Med.* | 22 |

## CALABASAS

| | |
|---|---|
| Banzai Sushi | *Japanese* | 22 |
| Calitalia | *Cal./Italian* | - |
| Fins | *Continental/Seafood* | 22 |
| King's Fish | *Seafood* | 21 |
| Marmalade Café | *Amer./Cal.* | 17 |
| Mi Piace | *Cal./Italian* | 20 |
| Riviera Rest. | *Italian* | 24 |
| ☑ Saddle Peak | *Amer.* | 26 |

Sagebrush Cantina | SW — 13
Sharky's Mex. | Mex. — 18
Spumoni | Italian — 17

## CANOGA PARK

NEW Amaranta | Mex. — 20
Coral Tree | Cal./Italian — 18
D'Amore's | Pizza — 20
Gyu-Kaku | Japanese — 20
Yang Chow | Chinese — 22

## CHATSWORTH

Z Les Sisters | Southern — 23
Mimi's Cafe | Diner — 17
Omino Sushi | Japanese — 25
Poquito Más | Mex. — 21

## ENCINO

Absolutely Pho | Viet. — 17
Benihana | Japanese — 18
Buca di Beppo | Italian — 15
Cali. Chicken | Amer. — 21
Cali. Wok | Chinese — 17
Chili My Soul | SW/Tex-Mex — 21
Coral Tree | Cal./Italian — 18
D'Amore's | Pizza — 20
Delmonico's | Seafood — 22
Fromin's Deli | Deli — 14
Hirosuke | Japanese — 19
Islands | Amer. — 16
Johnny Rockets | Burgers — 15
Z Katsu-ya | Japanese — 27
NEW Larsen's Steak | Steak — -
Maria's Italian | Italian — 17
Mulberry St. Pizzeria | Pizza — 23
Quincy's BBQ | BBQ — 16
Rosti | Italian — 16
NEW Sampa Grill | Brazilian — -
Sassi Med. | Med. — 21
Stand, The | Hot Dogs — 18
Stevie's Creole | Cajun — 19
Versailles | Cuban — 21
NEW Whisper Cafe | Eclectic — -

## GLENDALE

Carousel | Mideast. — 22
Damon's | Steak — 18
Eat Well Cafe | Amer. — 16
Far Niente | Italian — 25
Gennaro's | Italian — 20
Islands | Amer. — 16
Z Katsuya | Japanese — 24
Minx | Eclectic — 18
NEW Palate | Amer. — -
Panda Inn | Chinese — 21
Z Porto's | Bakery/Cuban — 24

NEW Richie Palmer's | Pizza — 15
Sandbag's | Sandwiches — 16
NEW Skaf's | Lebanese — 26
Zankou | Med. — 22

## GRANADA HILLS

Odyssey | Continental/Seafood — 14

## MONTROSE

NEW Bashan | Amer. — 26
La Cabanita | Mex. — 24
New Moon | Chinese — 21
Rocky Cola | Diner — 13
Zeke's Smokehse. | BBQ — 20

## NORTH HILLS

NEW Casa Don Rolando | Cuban — -

## NORTH HOLLYWOOD

Barsac Brass. | Cal./French — 21
Ca' del Sole | Italian — 22
Z In-N-Out | Burgers — 23
Poquito Más | Mex. — 21
Swinging Door | BBQ — 22

## NORTHRIDGE

Alessio | Italian — 21
Z Brent's Deli | Deli — 26
Cali. Chicken | Amer. — 21
Claim Jumper | Amer. — 19
El Torito | Mex. — 15
Emles | Cal./Med. — 19
Mandarin Deli | Chinese — 20
Maria's Italian | Italian — 17
Outback | Steak — 17
Romano's Macaroni | Italian — 17
Souplantation | Amer. — 16
Wood Ranch BBQ | BBQ — 20

## RESEDA

BCD Tofu | Korean — 19

## SHERMAN OAKS

Bamboo Cuisine | Chinese — 23
Barney's Burgers | Burgers — 20
Boneyard | BBQ/Eclectic — 21
Z Café Bizou | Cal./French — 23
Cafe 50's | Diner — 16
Carnival | Lebanese — 22
Casa Vega | Mex. — 18
Z Cheesecake Factory | Amer. — 19
D'Amore's | Pizza — 20
El Torito | Mex. — 15
El Torito Grill | Mex. — 18
Great Greek | Greek — 21
Gyu-Kaku | Japanese — 20
Hamlet | Amer. — 16

Il Tiramisù | *Italian* — 23

🆉 In-N-Out | *Burgers* — 23

Jinky's | *SW* — 19

Kung Pao | *Chinese* — 19

La Frite | *French* — 18

La Pergola | *Italian* — 22

Leaf Cuisine | *Vegan* — 17

Le Petit Rest. | *French* — 21

Maria's Italian | *Italian* — 17

Marmalade Café | *Amer./Cal.* — 17

Max | *Asian Fusion* — 24

Mel's Drive-In | *Amer.* — 15

🆉 Mistral | *French* — 25

Mr. Cecil's Ribs | *BBQ* — 18

Noah's NY Bagels | *Sandwiches* — 17

Oliva | *Italian* — 21

Panzanella | *Italian* — 22

P.F. Chang's | *Chinese* — 19

Pomodoro | *Italian* — 18

Rive Gauche | *French* — 19

Señor Fred | *Mex.* — 18

Sharky's Mex. | *Mex.* — 18

Sisley Italian | *Italian* — 17

Spazio | *Cal./Med.* — 18

Spumoni | *Italian* — 17

Stanley's | *Cal.* — 19

Sushi Mac | *Japanese* — 16

Watercress | *Cal.* — 21

## STUDIO CITY

Ahi Sushi | *Japanese* — 20

Artisan | *Cheese/Sandwiches* — 26

Art's Deli | *Deli* — 20

🆉 Asanebo | *Japanese* — 28

Baja Fresh | *Mex.* — 17

🆉 Bistro Gdn. | *Continental* — 21

Bollywood Cafe | *Indian* — 19

Caioti Pizza | *Pizza* — 22

Cali. Pizza Kitchen | *Pizza* — 18

Carney's | *Hot Dogs* — 19

Chin Chin | *Chinese* — 16

Daily Grill | *Amer.* — 18

Du-par's | *Diner* — 16

Firefly | *Amer.* — 22

Gaucho Grill | *Argent./Steak* — 17

Hugo's | *Cal.* — 21

Il Tramezzino | *Italian* — 20

🆉 In-N-Out | *Burgers* — 23

Iroha | *Japanese* — 25

Kansas City BBQ | *BBQ* — 21

🆉 Katsu-ya | *Japanese* — 27

Kung Pao | *Chinese* — 19

Lal Mirch | *Indian* — 20

La Loggia | *Italian* — 22

Le Pain Quotidien | *Bakery/Belgian* — 19

Louise's Tratt. | *Cal./Italian* — 17

Marrakesh | *Moroccan* — 19

Mexicali | *Cal./Mex.* — 15

Olé! Tapas Bar | *Spanish* — 16

Pinot Bistro | *French* — 23

Poquito Más | *Mex.* — 21

🆕 Press Panini | *Sandwiches* — -

Spark Woodfire | *Amer.* — 19

Sushi Nozawa | *Japanese* — 26

Talésai | *Thai* — 22

Tama Sushi | *Japanese* — 25

Teru Sushi | *Japanese* — 19

Vitello's | *Italian* — 14

Wine Bistro | *French* — 21

Yen Sushi | *Japanese* — 21

🆕 Yuta | *French/Japanese* — -

## TARZANA

Il Tramezzino | *Italian* — 20

India's Tandoori | *Indian* — 19

Le Sanglier | *French* — 24

Madeleine Bistro | *French/Vegan* — 24

Paul's Cafe | *Cal./French* — 17

Sharky's Mex. | *Mex.* — 18

## TOLUCA LAKE

🆕 D'Cache | *Pan-Latin* — -

Eight-18 | *Med.* — 20

Prosecco | *Italian* — 19

## UNIVERSAL CITY

Buca di Beppo | *Italian* — 15

Café/Tango | *Eclectic* — 19

Daily Grill | *Amer.* — 18

Hard Rock | *Amer.* — 14

Jody Maroni's | *Hot Dogs* — 19

Miceli's | *Italian* — 17

Saddle Ranch | *Steak* — 14

Versailles | *Cuban* — 21

Wolfgang Puck | *Cal.* — 17

## VAN NUYS

Dr. Hogly Wogly's | *BBQ* — 22

🆉 In-N-Out | *Burgers* — 23

Sam Woo | *Chinese* — 20

Zankou | *Med.* — 22

## WEST HILLS

Alessio | *Italian* — 21

Stonefire Grill | *BBQ* — 18

## WOODLAND HILLS

Adagio | *Italian* — 23

🆉 Arnie Morton's | *Steak* — 25

Baja Fresh | *Mex.* — 17

BJ's | *Pub* — 17

🆉 Brandywine | *Continental* — 27

| | |
|---|---|
| Cali. Chicken \| *Amer.* | 21 |
| 🄩 Cheesecake Factory \| *Amer.* | 19 |
| El Torito \| *Mex.* | 15 |
| Farm/Bev. Hills \| *Amer.* | 19 |
| Fleming's \| *Steak* | 25 |
| Gaucho Grill \| *Argent./Steak* | 17 |
| Gorikee \| *Cal.* | 22 |
| 🄩 In-N-Out \| *Burgers* | 23 |
| Islands \| *Amer.* | 16 |
| Kate Mantilini \| *Amer.* | 18 |
| La Frite \| *French* | 18 |
| Maggiano's \| *Italian* | 18 |
| Maria's Italian \| *Italian* | 17 |
| Monty's Steak \| *Steak* | 20 |
| Nicola's \| *Cal./Italian* | 20 |
| P.F. Chang's \| *Chinese* | 19 |
| Pomodoro \| *Italian* | 18 |
| Poquito Más \| *Mex.* | 21 |
| Rack \| *Cal.* | 16 |
| Roy's \| *Asian Fusion/Hawaiian* | 23 |
| Ruby's \| *Diner* | 17 |
| 🄩 Ruth's Chris \| *Steak* | 26 |
| Stand, The \| *Hot Dogs* | 18 |
| uWink \| *Cal.* | 13 |
| Villa Piacere \| *Eclectic* | 19 |

## San Gabriel Valley

### ALHAMBRA

| | |
|---|---|
| NEW Bistro 39 \| *French* | - |
| Cuban Bistro \| *Cuban* | 18 |
| Hop Woo \| *Chinese* | 18 |
| Johnny Rockets \| *Burgers* | 15 |
| Pho 79 \| *Viet.* | 20 |
| Sam Woo \| *Chinese* | 20 |
| Souplantation \| *Amer.* | 16 |
| Triumphal Palace \| *Chinese* | 21 |
| Wahib's Mid-East \| *Mideast.* | 21 |

### AZUSA

| | |
|---|---|
| Tulipano \| *Italian* | 24 |

### CITY OF INDUSTRY

| | |
|---|---|
| Benihana \| *Japanese* | 18 |
| Claim Jumper \| *Amer.* | 19 |
| Joe's Crab \| *Seafood* | 13 |
| Mimi's Cafe \| *Diner* | 17 |
| Outback \| *Steak* | 17 |
| NEW RED \| *Steak* | - |
| Souplantation \| *Amer.* | 16 |

### CLAREMONT

| | |
|---|---|
| Buca di Beppo \| *Italian* | 15 |
| NEW Casablanca Med. \| *Med.* | 18 |
| Heroes \| *Pub* | 17 |
| NEW Three Forks \| *Steak* | 23 |

| | |
|---|---|
| Viva Madrid \| *Spanish* | 20 |
| Walter's \| *Eclectic* | 19 |

### COVINA/WEST COVINA

| | |
|---|---|
| Green Field \| *Brazilian* | 21 |
| Hayakawa \| *Japanese* | 28 |
| Outback \| *Steak* | 17 |

### MONTEBELLO

| | |
|---|---|
| Astro Burger \| *Burgers* | 19 |
| BJ's \| *Pub* | 17 |

### MONTEREY PARK

| | |
|---|---|
| Chung King \| *Chinese* | 25 |
| Empress Harbor \| *Chinese* | 19 |
| Macau St. \| *Chinese* | 19 |
| Mandarin Deli \| *Chinese* | 20 |
| NBC Seafood \| *Chinese/Seafood* | 19 |
| Ocean Star \| *Chinese* | 21 |
| Sam Woo \| *Chinese* | 20 |

### PICO RIVERA

| | |
|---|---|
| 🄩 Dal Rae \| *Continental* | 25 |

### ROSEMEAD

| | |
|---|---|
| NEW Hunan Seafood \| *Chinese* | - |
| Sea Harbour \| *Chinese/Seafood* | 24 |

### ROWLAND HEIGHTS

| | |
|---|---|
| BCD Tofu \| *Korean* | 19 |
| Little Tokyo \| *Japanese* | 20 |

### SAN GABRIEL

| | |
|---|---|
| 🄩 Babita \| *Mex.* | 26 |
| NEW Captain Crab \| *Seafood* | - |
| Golden Deli \| *Viet.* | 23 |
| NEW Hong Yei \| *Chinese* | - |
| Mission 261 \| *Chinese* | 20 |
| Sam Woo \| *Chinese* | 20 |

### WHITTIER

| | |
|---|---|
| Mimi's Cafe \| *Diner* | 17 |
| Rocky Cola \| *Diner* | 13 |
| Ruby's \| *Diner* | 17 |

## Conejo Valley/ Simi Valley & Environs

### AGOURA HILLS/ OAK PARK

| | |
|---|---|
| Adobe Cantina \| *BBQ/Mex.* | 15 |
| Café 14 \| *Cal./Continental* | 24 |
| Chapter 8 \| *Steak* | 17 |
| 🄩 Leila's \| *Cal.* | 27 |
| Maria's Italian \| *Italian* | 17 |
| MOZ Buddha \| *Asian Fusion* | 20 |
| Padri \| *Italian* | 21 |

Sushi Ozekii | *Japanese* 17
Wood Ranch BBQ | *BBQ* 20

## CAMARILLO

Enoteca Toscana | *Italian/Spanish* 19
Jody Maroni's | *Hot Dogs* 19
Safire | *Amer.* 21
Souplantation | *Amer.* 16
Sushi Ozekii | *Japanese* 17
Wood Ranch BBQ | *BBQ* 20

## MOORPARK

Wood Ranch BBQ | *BBQ* 20

## SIMI VALLEY

Alessio | *Italian* 21
Limon Grill | *Pan-Latin* 18
NEW Red Fish | *Seafood* 21
Sharky's Mex. | *Mex.* 18

## THOUSAND OAKS

Buca di Beppo | *Italian* 15
Café Provencal | *French* 23
Z Cheesecake Factory | *Amer.* 19
D'Amore's | *Pizza* 20
Du-par's | *Diner* 16
El Torito | *Mex.* 15
Holdren's Steak | *Steak* 21
Z Mastro's Steak | *Steak* 26
Outback | *Steak* 17
Piatti | *Italian* 19
Romano's Macaroni | *Italian* 17
Sisley Italian | *Italian* 17

## WESTLAKE VILLAGE

Alessio | *Italian* 21
Bellavino | *Eclectic* 19
BJ's | *Pub* 17
Boccaccio's | *Euro./Italian* 22
Z Brent's Deli | *Deli* 26
Cantina Joannafina | *Mex.* 19
Fins | *Continental/Seafood* 22

Galletto | *Brazilian/Italian* 23
Z Hampton's | *Cal.* 23
Mandevilla | *Continental* 22
Marmalade Café | *Amer./Cal.* 17
Mediterraneo | *Med.* 17
Melting Pot | *Fondue* 18
Onyx | *Japanese* 25
P6 Rest. | *Amer.* 22
Rustico | *Italian* 23
Sharky's Mex. | *Mex.* 18
Suki 7 | *Japanese* 19
Tuscany | *Italian* 24
Vivoli Café | *Italian* 25
Zin Bistro | *Amer.* 22

# Santa Clarita Valley & Environs

## SANTA CLARITA

Mimi's Cafe | *Diner* 17
Pei Wei | *Pan-Asian* 16
Romano's Macaroni | *Italian* 17

## SAUGUS/NEWHALL

Le Chêne | *French* 23

## STEVENSON RANCH

Spumoni | *Italian* 17

## VALENCIA

BJ's | *Pub* 17
Buca di Beppo | *Italian* 15
Claim Jumper | *Amer.* 19
New Moon | *Chinese* 21
Outback | *Steak* 17
Poquito Más | *Mex.* 21
Salt Creek | *Steak* 18
Sisley Italian | *Italian* 17
Stonefire Grill | *BBQ* 18
Thai Dishes | *Thai* 18
Wood Ranch BBQ | *BBQ* 20

LOS ANGELES

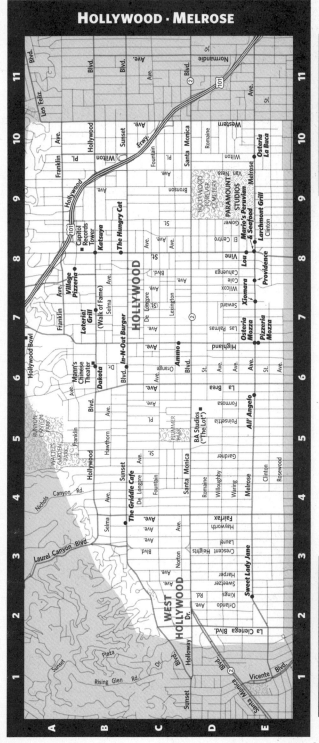

MAPS

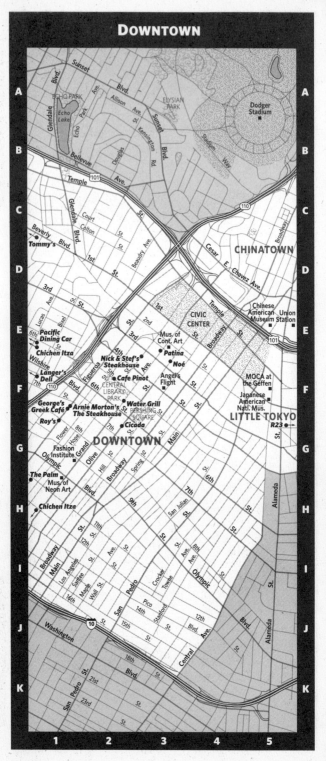

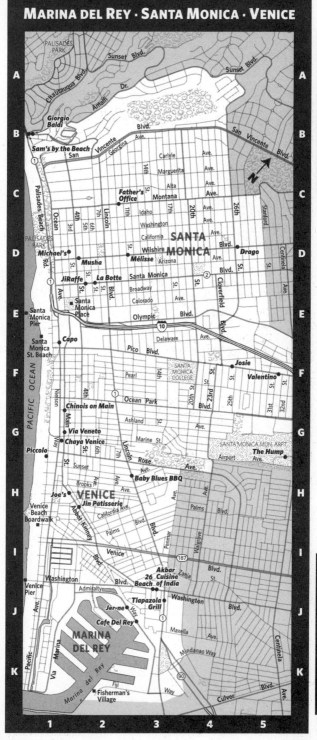

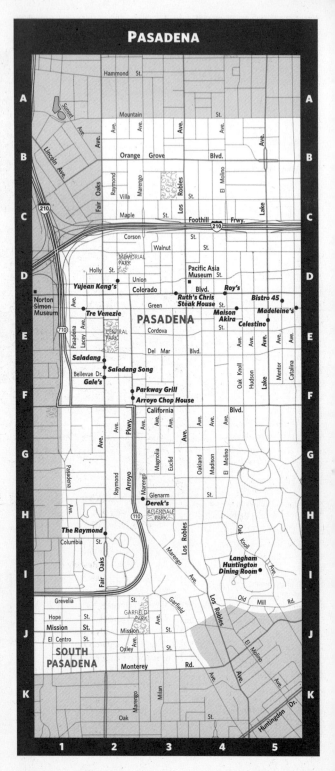

# Special Features

Listings cover the best in each category and include names, locations and Food ratings. Multi-location restaurants' features may vary by branch. ⓩ indicates places with the highest ratings, popularity and importance.

## BREAKFAST

(See also Hotel Dining)

| | |
|---|---|
| Alcove \| Los Feliz | 21 |
| Art's Deli \| Studio City | 20 |
| Auntie Em's \| Eagle Rock | 23 |
| Barney Greengrass \| Beverly Hills | 20 |
| bld \| Beverly Blvd. | 21 |
| Brighton Coffee \| Beverly Hills | 18 |
| City Bakery \| Brentwood | 19 |
| Cora's Coffee \| Santa Monica | 21 |
| Duke's Coffee \| W Hollywood | 18 |
| Du-par's \| multi. | 16 |
| Farm/Bev. Hills \| multi. | 19 |
| NEW Flake \| Venice | - |
| Fred 62 \| Los Feliz | 17 |
| Griddle Cafe \| Hollywood | 22 |
| Hugo's \| multi. | 21 |
| John O'Groats \| Rancho Pk | 21 |
| NEW JuJu \| Westwood | - |
| Lemon Moon \| West LA | 20 |
| Le Pain Quotidien \| multi. | 19 |
| Literati \| West LA | 19 |
| Lotería! \| Fairfax | 24 |
| Mäni's \| multi. | 18 |
| Marmalade Café \| multi. | 17 |
| Marston's \| Pasadena | 23 |
| Martha 22nd St. \| Hermosa Bch | 21 |
| Maxwell's Cafe \| Venice | 19 |
| Mel's Drive-In \| Hollywood | 15 |
| Mimi's Cafe \| Atwater Vill | 17 |
| Newsroom Café \| W Hollywood | 18 |
| Original Pancake \| Redondo Bch | 23 |
| Pacific Dining Car \| multi. | 22 |
| Patrick's \| Santa Monica | 17 |
| Roscoe's \| Mid-City | 20 |
| Ruby's \| multi. | 17 |
| Square One Dining \| E Hollywood | 22 |
| Susina \| La Brea | 22 |
| Sweet Lady Jane \| Melrose | 23 |
| Swingers \| Santa Monica | 17 |
| Toast \| Third St. | 19 |
| Uncle Bill's \| Manhattan Bch | 21 |
| Urth Caffé \| multi. | 20 |

## BRUNCH

| | |
|---|---|
| Abbey \| W Hollywood | 14 |
| ABC Seafood \| Chinatown | 19 |
| Axe \| Venice | 22 |
| ⓩ Belvedere \| Beverly Hills | 25 |
| Campanile \| La Brea | 26 |
| ⓩ Cliff's Edge \| Silver Lake | 21 |
| Dusty's \| Silver Lake | 18 |
| Firefly Bistro \| S Pasadena | 18 |
| Gardens \| Beverly Hills | 23 |
| ⓩ Hotel Bel-Air \| Bel-Air | 25 |
| Jer-ne \| Marina del Rey | 20 |
| ⓩ Joe's \| Venice | 26 |
| La Huasteca \| Lynwood | 26 |
| Lilly's French Cafe \| Venice | 19 |
| Massimo \| Beverly Hills | 22 |
| McCormick/Schmick \| El Segundo | 19 |
| Morels First Floor \| Fairfax | 17 |
| Napa Valley \| Westwood | 20 |
| Nine Thirty \| Westwood | 21 |
| Ocean Ave. \| Santa Monica | 23 |
| Ocean Seafood \| Chinatown | 20 |
| ⓩ One Pico \| Santa Monica | 22 |
| Polo Lounge \| Beverly Hills | 22 |
| Porta Via \| Beverly Hills | 24 |
| Prana Cafe \| W Hollywood | 18 |
| Raymond, The \| Pasadena | 24 |
| ⓩ Saddle Peak \| Calabasas | 26 |
| Spazio \| Sherman Oaks | 18 |
| 3 Square \| Venice | 20 |
| Twin Palms \| Pasadena | 18 |
| Whist \| Santa Monica | 20 |

## BUFFET

(Check availability)

| | |
|---|---|
| Akbar \| Hermosa Bch | 22 |
| Alegria \| Long Bch | 19 |
| All India \| West LA | 22 |
| Aunt Kizzy's \| Marina del Rey | 19 |
| Back Home \| Carson | 17 |
| Bombay Palace \| Beverly Hills | 21 |
| Café Pacific \| Rancho Palos Verdes | 24 |
| Castaway \| Burbank | 13 |
| Chakra \| Beverly Hills | 21 |
| Chao Krung \| Fairfax | 20 |
| Circa 55 \| Beverly Hills | 19 |
| Clay Pit \| Brentwood | 21 |
| Delmonico's \| Encino | 22 |
| El Torito \| multi. | 15 |
| El Torito Grill \| Torrance | 18 |
| Flavor of India \| multi. | 22 |
| Fogo de Chão \| Beverly Hills | 24 |
| Gate of India \| Santa Monica | 21 |
| Green Field \| multi. | 21 |
| House of Blues \| W Hollywood | 16 |

| | |
|---|---|
| i Cugini | **Santa Monica** | 21 |
| India's Tandoori | **multi.** | 19 |
| Ⓩ Inn/Seventh Ray | **Topanga** | 20 |
| Jer-ne | **Marina del Rey** | 20 |
| La Huasteca | **Lynwood** | 26 |
| Limon Grill | **Simi Valley** | 18 |
| Locanda/Lago | **Santa Monica** | 21 |
| Maison Akira | **Pasadena** | 25 |
| Mediterraneo | **Westlake Vill** | 17 |
| Mijares | **Pasadena** | 17 |
| Nawab of India | **Santa Monica** | 21 |
| Nizam | **West LA** | 18 |
| Odyssey | **Granada Hills** | 14 |
| O-Nami | **Torrance** | 17 |
| Panda Inn | **multi.** | 21 |
| Picanha Churr. | **Burbank** | 21 |
| Radhika's | **Pasadena** | 22 |
| Sagebrush Cantina | **Calabasas** | 13 |
| Salt Creek | **Valencia** | 18 |
| Smoke House | **Burbank** | 19 |
| Souplantation | **multi.** | 16 |
| Tamayo | **East LA** | 18 |
| Ⓩ Tanzore | **Beverly Hills** | 23 |
| Thousand Cranes | **Little Tokyo** | 21 |
| Tibet Nepal | **Pasadena** | 19 |
| Tra Di Noi | **Malibu** | 22 |
| Twin Palms | **Pasadena** | 18 |
| Walter's | **Claremont** | 19 |

## BUSINESS DINING

| | |
|---|---|
| Ago | **W Hollywood** | 22 |
| Alessio | **multi.** | 21 |
| NEW Anisette | **Santa Monica** | - |
| Ⓩ Arnie Morton's | **multi.** | 25 |
| Arroyo Chop | **Pasadena** | 25 |
| Barney Greengrass | **Beverly Hills** | 20 |
| Ⓩ Belvedere | **Beverly Hills** | 25 |
| Bistro 45 | **Pasadena** | 26 |
| Bistro Provence | **Burbank** | 23 |
| NEW BLT Steak | **W Hollywood** | 23 |
| Blvd | **Beverly Hills** | 20 |
| NEW Blvd 16 | **Westwood** | - |
| Breeze | **Century City** | 17 |
| Cafe Del Rey | **Marina del Rey** | 21 |
| Campanile | **La Brea** | 26 |
| Catch | **Santa Monica** | 22 |
| Celestino | **Pasadena** | 23 |
| Checkers | **Downtown** | 20 |
| Ⓩ Cicada | **Downtown** | 23 |
| Coast | **Santa Monica** | 21 |
| Craft | **Century City** | 25 |
| Ⓩ Crustacean | **Beverly Hills** | 24 |
| Ⓩ CUT | **Beverly Hills** | 26 |
| Dakota | **Hollywood** | 22 |
| Dan Tana's | **W Hollywood** | 23 |

| | |
|---|---|
| Drago | **Santa Monica** | 24 |
| eat. on sunset | **Hollywood** | 18 |
| 555 East | **Long Bch** | 24 |
| Fleming's | **Woodland Hills** | 25 |
| Fogo de Chão | **Beverly Hills** | 24 |
| Ⓩ Fraîche | **Culver City** | 24 |
| Gardens | **Beverly Hills** | 23 |
| NEW Gordon Ramsay | **W Hollywood** | - |
| Grace | **Beverly Blvd.** | 25 |
| Ⓩ Grill on Alley | **Beverly Hills** | 24 |
| Grill on Hollywood | **Hollywood** | 22 |
| Ⓩ Hampton's | **Westlake Vill** | 23 |
| Ⓩ Hatfield's | **Beverly Blvd.** | 27 |
| Il Grano | **West LA** | 26 |
| Il Moro | **West LA** | 23 |
| Jar | **Beverly Blvd.** | 25 |
| Josie | **Santa Monica** | 26 |
| Kincaid's | **Redondo Bch** | 20 |
| La Botte | **Santa Monica** | 25 |
| Ⓩ La Cachette | **Century City** | 27 |
| Ⓩ Langham Huntington | **Pasadena** | 26 |
| NEW Larsen's Steak | **Encino** | - |
| Madeo | **W Hollywood** | 24 |
| McCormick/Schmick | **multi.** | 19 |
| Ⓩ Mélisse | **Santa Monica** | 28 |
| Michael's | **Santa Monica** | 24 |
| Ⓩ Mistral | **Sherman Oaks** | 25 |
| Nick & Stef's Steak | **Downtown** | 23 |
| Nic's | **Beverly Hills** | 19 |
| NEW Nobu | **W Hollywood** | 26 |
| Ocean & Vine | **Santa Monica** | 21 |
| Ⓩ One Pico | **Santa Monica** | 22 |
| On Sunset | **Brentwood** | 22 |
| Ortolan | **Third St.** | 25 |
| NEW Paperfish | **Beverly Hills** | 23 |
| Patina | **Downtown** | 25 |
| Peppone | **Brentwood** | 23 |
| Ⓩ Petros | **Manhattan Bch** | 24 |
| Pinot Bistro | **Studio City** | 23 |
| Polo Lounge | **Beverly Hills** | 22 |
| Ⓩ Providence | **Hollywood** | 26 |
| NEW RED | **City of Industry** | - |
| Red 7 | **W Hollywood** | 24 |
| Roy's | **Downtown** | 23 |
| Rustic Canyon | **Santa Monica** | 21 |
| Ⓩ Ruth's Chris | **multi.** | 26 |
| Safire | **Camarillo** | 21 |
| Salt Creek | **El Segundo** | 18 |
| Simon LA | **W Hollywood** | 21 |
| Ⓩ Spago | **Beverly Hills** | 27 |
| NEW STK | **W Hollywood** | 21 |
| Sur | **W Hollywood** | 21 |
| Ⓩ Tanzore | **Beverly Hills** | 23 |

| | |
|---|---|
| Taylor's Steak \| **multi.** | 21 |
| Thousand Cranes \| **Little Tokyo** | 21 |
| **NEW** Three Forks \| **Claremont** | 23 |
| Tracht's \| **Long Bch** | 23 |
| **Z** Valentino \| **Santa Monica** | 26 |
| Vincenti \| **Brentwood** | 26 |
| **Z** Water Grill \| **Downtown** | 27 |
| Wilshire \| **Santa Monica** | 22 |
| **NEW** Wolfgang's Steak \| **Beverly Hills** | - |
| **Z** Yujean Kang's \| **Pasadena** | 25 |
| Zucca \| **Downtown** | 21 |

## CHEESE TRAYS

| | |
|---|---|
| **Z** Angelini Osteria \| **Beverly Blvd.** | 27 |
| **Z** A.O.C. \| **Third St.** | 26 |
| Artisan \| **Studio City** | 26 |
| **Z** Bastide \| **W Hollywood** | 27 |
| **Z** Belvedere \| **Beverly Hills** | 25 |
| **NEW** Bistro 39 \| **Alhambra** | - |
| Checkers \| **Downtown** | 20 |
| **Z** Cicada \| **Downtown** | 23 |
| Cobras/Matadors \| **La Brea** | 21 |
| **NEW** Comme Ça \| **W Hollywood** | 21 |
| cube \| **La Brea** | 22 |
| **Z** CUT \| **Beverly Hills** | 26 |
| **Z** Derek's \| **Pasadena** | 27 |
| Devon \| **Monrovia** | 23 |
| Enoteca Toscana \| **Camarillo** | 19 |
| Figaro Bistrot \| **Los Feliz** | 19 |
| Firefly \| **Studio City** | 22 |
| Firefly Bistro \| **S Pasadena** | 18 |
| Foundry, The \| **Melrose** | 23 |
| **NEW** Foxtail \| **W Hollywood** | - |
| **Z** Fraîche \| **Culver City** | 24 |
| **Z** Frenchy's Bistro \| **Long Bch** | 26 |
| Gardens \| **Beverly Hills** | 23 |
| Grace \| **Beverly Blvd.** | 25 |
| **Z** Hotel Bel-Air \| **Bel-Air** | 25 |
| Il Cielo \| **Beverly Hills** | 21 |
| Il Grano \| **West LA** | 26 |
| Kendall's Brass. \| **Downtown** | 17 |
| **Z** La Boheme \| **W Hollywood** | 22 |
| **Z** Langham Huntington \| **Pasadena** | 26 |
| La Sosta \| **Hermosa Bch** | 26 |
| **Z** Leila's \| **Oak Pk** | 27 |
| Le Marmiton \| **Marina del Rey** | 18 |
| Le Petit Bistro \| **W Hollywood** | 22 |
| Lilly's French Cafe \| **Venice** | 19 |
| **Z** Little Door \| **Third St.** | 23 |
| Lou \| **Hollywood** | 23 |
| **Z** Lucques \| **W Hollywood** | 27 |
| **Z** Madison, The \| **Long Bch** | 20 |
| Massimo \| **Beverly Hills** | 22 |
| Mediterraneo \| **Westlake Vill** | 17 |

| | |
|---|---|
| **Z** Mélisse \| **Santa Monica** | 28 |
| **NEW** Melograno \| **Hollywood** | 23 |
| Michael's \| **Santa Monica** | 24 |
| Michel Richard \| **Beverly Hills** | 23 |
| Mimosa \| **Beverly Blvd.** | 20 |
| Monsieur Marcel \| **Fairfax** | 21 |
| **Z** Murano \| **W Hollywood** | 20 |
| Napa Valley \| **Westwood** | 20 |
| Noé \| **Downtown** | 24 |
| Ortolan \| **Third St.** | 25 |
| **NEW** Palate \| **Glendale** | - |
| Pastis \| **Beverly Blvd.** | 21 |
| Patina \| **Downtown** | 25 |
| Petrossian \| **W Hollywood** | 23 |
| Polo Lounge \| **Beverly Hills** | 22 |
| Primitivo \| **Venice** | 20 |
| **Z** Providence \| **Hollywood** | 26 |
| Rustic Canyon \| **Santa Monica** | 21 |
| **Z** Saddle Peak \| **Calabasas** | 26 |
| **Z** Sona \| **W Hollywood** | 27 |
| **Z** Spago \| **Beverly Hills** | 27 |
| Taste \| **W Hollywood** | 23 |
| **NEW** Three Forks \| **Claremont** | 23 |
| Three on Fourth \| **Santa Monica** | 21 |
| **NEW** Tinto \| **W Hollywood** | 20 |
| Tre Venezie \| **Pasadena** | 25 |
| Tuscany \| **Westlake Vill** | 24 |
| Via Veneto \| **Santa Monica** | 26 |
| **NEW** Vinotéque \| **Culver City** | - |
| Whist \| **Santa Monica** | 20 |
| Wine Bistro \| **Studio City** | 21 |

## CHEF'S TABLE

| | |
|---|---|
| **Z** Bastide \| **W Hollywood** | 27 |
| blue on blue \| **Beverly Hills** | 19 |
| **Z** Chez Mélange \| **Redondo Bch** | 25 |
| **Z** ChoSun Galbee \| **Koreatown** | 23 |
| Foundry, The \| **Melrose** | 23 |
| **Z** Hampton's \| **Westlake Vill** | 23 |
| **Z** Hotel Bel-Air \| **Bel-Air** | 25 |
| Il Pastaio \| **Beverly Hills** | 25 |
| **NEW** LAMILL \| **Silver Lake** | 23 |
| Patina \| **Downtown** | 25 |
| **Z** Providence \| **Hollywood** | 26 |
| **NEW** Red Fish \| **Simi Valley** | 21 |
| Safire \| **Camarillo** | 21 |
| **NEW** Terroni \| **Beverly Blvd.** | 20 |
| **NEW** Three Forks \| **Claremont** | 23 |

## COOL LOOS

| | |
|---|---|
| Blue Velvet \| **Downtown** | 20 |
| Chapter 8 \| **Agoura Hills** | 17 |
| Firefly \| **Studio City** | 22 |
| Grace \| **Beverly Blvd.** | 25 |
| **Z** Katsuya \| **Brentwood** | 24 |
| LA Food Show \| **Manhattan Bch** | 18 |

| | |
|---|---|
| Ortolan \| **Third St.** | 25 |
| Patina \| **Downtown** | 25 |
| 🅱 Penthouse \| **Santa Monica** | 18 |
| Roy's \| **Downtown** | 23 |
| Smitty's Grill \| **Pasadena** | 21 |
| 🅱 Sona \| **W Hollywood** | 27 |
| 🅱 Spago \| **Beverly Hills** | 27 |

| | |
|---|---|
| Padri \| **Agoura Hills** | 21 |
| Saddle Ranch \| **Universal City** | 14 |
| Sky Room \| **Long Bch** | 21 |
| Smoke House \| **Burbank** | 19 |
| Taverna Tony \| **Malibu** | 20 |
| Twin Palms \| **Pasadena** | 18 |
| Villa Sorriso \| **Pasadena** | 16 |

## CRITIC-PROOF

(Gets lots of business despite so-so food)

| | |
|---|---|
| Abbey \| **W Hollywood** | 14 |
| Broadway Deli \| **Santa Monica** | 15 |
| Buca di Beppo \| **multi.** | 15 |
| Cafe 50's \| **multi.** | 16 |
| Chez Jay \| **Santa Monica** | 16 |
| Chin Chin \| **multi.** | 16 |
| Du-par's \| **multi.** | 16 |
| El Coyote \| **Beverly Blvd.** | 13 |
| El Torito \| **multi.** | 15 |
| Factor's Deli \| **Pico-Robertson** | 16 |
| Fromin's Deli \| **multi.** | 14 |
| Gladstone's \| **Pacific Palisades** | 14 |
| Gordon Biersch \| **multi.** | 16 |
| Hamlet \| **multi.** | 16 |
| Islands \| **multi.** | 16 |
| Joe's Crab \| **multi.** | 13 |
| Johnny Rockets \| **multi.** | 15 |
| Junior's \| **West LA** | 16 |
| Koo Koo Roo \| **multi.** | 15 |
| Marix Tex Mex \| **multi.** | 16 |
| Mel's Drive-In \| **multi.** | 15 |
| Original Pantry \| **Downtown** | 15 |
| Pei Wei \| **multi.** | 16 |
| Pink Taco \| **Century City** | 15 |
| Rosti \| **multi.** | 16 |
| Souplantation \| **multi.** | 16 |
| Standard, The \| **multi.** | 15 |

## DANCING

| | |
|---|---|
| Alegria \| **Long Bch** | 19 |
| Alessio \| **Westlake Vill** | 21 |
| Buffalo Club \| **Santa Monica** | 20 |
| Café/Tango \| **Universal City** | 19 |
| Chapter 8 \| **Agoura Hills** | 17 |
| Cuban Bistro \| **Alhambra** | 18 |
| 🅱 Dal Rae \| **Pico Rivera** | 25 |
| El Pollo Inka \| **Gardena** | 19 |
| 410 Boyd \| **Downtown** | 17 |
| Gardens \| **Beverly Hills** | 23 |
| Joseph's Cafe \| **Hollywood** | 18 |
| J Rest. \| **Downtown** | 16 |
| La Huasteca \| **Lynwood** | 26 |
| 🅱 Madison, The \| **Long Bch** | 20 |
| Minx \| **Glendale** | 18 |
| Monsoon Cafe \| **Santa Monica** | 18 |

## DESSERT

| | |
|---|---|
| Alessio \| **Northridge** | 21 |
| Auntie Em's \| **Eagle Rock** | 23 |
| Café 14 \| **Agoura Hills** | 24 |
| Campanile \| **La Brea** | 26 |
| 🅱 Cheesecake Factory \| **multi.** | 19 |
| City Bakery \| **Brentwood** | 19 |
| Clementine \| **Century City** | 23 |
| Coco Noche \| **Manhattan Bch** | 17 |
| Doña Rosa \| **Arcadia** | 16 |
| Farm/Bev. Hills \| **multi.** | 19 |
| Grace \| **Beverly Blvd.** | 25 |
| Jack n' Jill's \| **Santa Monica** | 19 |
| Joan's on 3rd \| **Third St.** | 23 |
| La Creperie Cafe \| **Long Bch** | 23 |
| Le Marmiton \| **Marina del Rey** | 18 |
| Magnolia \| **Hollywood** | 19 |
| Mäni's \| **multi.** | 18 |
| Max \| **Sherman Oaks** | 24 |
| Melting Pot \| **multi.** | 18 |
| Michel Richard \| **Beverly Hills** | 23 |
| 🅱 Porto's \| **multi.** | 24 |
| 🅱 Providence \| **Hollywood** | 26 |
| Simon LA \| **W Hollywood** | 21 |
| 🅱 Sona \| **W Hollywood** | 27 |
| 🅱 Spago \| **Beverly Hills** | 27 |
| Susina \| **La Brea** | 22 |
| Sweet Lady Jane \| **Melrose** | 23 |
| Tart \| **Fairfax** | 16 |

## ENTERTAINMENT

(Call for days and times of performances)

| | |
|---|---|
| Alegria \| varies \| **Long Bch** | 19 |
| Alessio \| varies \| **Westlake Vill** | 21 |
| Amalfi \| varies \| **La Brea** | 21 |
| Antonio's \| guitar \| **Melrose** | 19 |
| Arroyo Chop \| piano \| **Pasadena** | 25 |
| Auld Dubliner \| varies \| **Long Bch** | 18 |
| Bandera \| jazz \| **West LA** | 21 |
| 🅱 Brandywine \| guitar \| **Woodland Hills** | 27 |
| Buffalo Club \| varies \| **Santa Monica** | 20 |
| Buggy Whip \| piano \| **Westchester** | 19 |
| Cafe Del Rey \| guitar/piano \| **Marina del Rey** | 21 |
| Cafe des Artistes \| DJ \| **Hollywood** | 20 |
| Café/Tango \| varies \| **Universal City** | 19 |

Canal Club | DJ | **Venice** 18
Canter's | varies | **Fairfax** 18
Ⓩ Carlitos Gardel | piano/violin | **Melrose** 23
Carousel | varies | **Glendale** 22
Casablanca | guitar/Latin | **Venice** 18
Catch | varies | **Santa Monica** 22
Ciudad | flamenco | **Downtown** 21
Ⓩ Crustacean | jazz/piano | **Beverly Hills** 24
Cuban Bistro | jazz/Latin | **Alhambra** 18
Dar Maghreb | belly dancing | **Hollywood** 20
El Cholo | varies | **Pasadena** 18
Electric Lotus | DJ | **Los Feliz** 18
El Pollo Inka | varies | **multi.** 19
Fins | varies | **multi.** 22
Ⓩ Frenchy's Bistro | jazz | **Long Bch** 26
Galletto | varies | **Westlake Vill** 23
Geisha Hse. | DJ/karaoke | **Hollywood** 20
Genghis Cohen | varies | **Fairfax** 20
Great Greek | Greek | **Sherman Oaks** 21
Hal's B&G | jazz | **Venice** 20
House of Blues | varies | **W Hollywood** 16
Joseph's Cafe | DJ | **Hollywood** 18
Koutoubia | belly dancing | **Westwood** 20
Lucille's BBQ | blues | **Long Bch** 22
Ⓩ Madison, The | piano | **Long Bch** 20
Market City | strings | **Burbank** 17
Marrakesh | belly dancing | **Studio City** 19
Ⓩ Mastro's Steak | piano/vocals | **Beverly Hills** 26
Moonshadows | DJ | **Malibu** 17
Morels French Steak | jazz | **Fairfax** 18
Moun of Tunis | belly dancing | **Hollywood** 21
Nic's | bands | **Beverly Hills** 19
Ⓩ One Pico | bass/piano | **Santa Monica** 22
Padri | varies | **Agoura Hills** 21
Ⓩ Papa Cristo's | belly dancing | **Mid-City** 22
Ⓩ Papadakis Tav. | varies | **San Pedro** 21
Parker's Lighthse. | jazz | **Long Bch** 18
Ⓩ Parkway Grill | piano | **Pasadena** 26
Pig 'n Whistle | varies | **Hollywood** 13
Polo Lounge | guitar/piano | **Beverly Hills** 22
Saddle Ranch | varies | **multi.** 14
Sir Winston's | piano/vocals | **Long Bch** 21

Sky Room | varies | **Long Bch** 21
Twin Palms | varies | **Pasadena** 18
Velvet Margarita | DJ | **Hollywood** 17
Vibrato | jazz | **Bel-Air** 21
Villa Sorriso | DJ | **Pasadena** 16
Zip Fusion | karaoke | **West LA** 18

## FAMILY-STYLE

Buca di Beppo | **multi.** 15
Buddha's Belly | **Beverly Blvd.** 19
Campanile | **La Brea** 26
C & O | **Marina del Rey** 18
Carnival | **Sherman Oaks** 22
Carousel | **multi.** 22
Casa Bianca | **Eagle Rock** 23
Ⓩ Cha Cha Cha | **Silver Lake** 20
Chadaka | **Burbank** 24
Chan/Hse. of Chan | **Hollywood** 20
Chao Krung | **Fairfax** 20
Chichen Itza | **Downtown** 24
Chi Dynasty | **Los Feliz** 21
China Grill | **Manhattan Bch** 19
Chin Chin | **multi.** 16
Ⓩ Chinois | **Santa Monica** 26
Ⓩ Cholada | **Malibu** 24
Cialuzzi's | **Redondo Bch** 20
Cozymel's | **El Segundo** 16
Craft | **Century City** 25
Ⓩ Crustacean | **Beverly Hills** 24
Dominick's | **Beverly Blvd.** 21
Farm Stand | **El Segundo** 21
Ita Cho | **Beverly Blvd.** 21
Izaka-Ya | **Third St.** 25
Koo Koo Roo | **multi.** 15
Lamonica's NY Pizza | **Westwood** 21
Lucille's BBQ | **Long Bch** 22
Maggiano's | **multi.** 18
Mandarette | **W Hollywood** 18
Maria's Italian | **multi.** 17
Miceli's | **multi.** 17
Mission 261 | **San Gabriel** 20
Musha | **multi.** 24
Natalee | **Beverly Hills** 18
Ocean Seafood | **Chinatown** 20
Ocean Star | **Monterey Pk** 21
Riviera Rest. | **Calabasas** 24
Robin's BBQ | **Pasadena** 17
Romano's Macaroni | **multi.** 17
Sapori | **Marina del Rey** 20
Sea Empress | **Gardena** 19
Sisley Italian | **multi.** 17
South St. | **Burbank** 18
Stonefire Grill | **multi.** 18
Toscana | **Brentwood** 23
Truxton's | **Westchester** -

Woody's BBQ | Mid-City  23
Zeke's Smokehse. | multi.  20

## FIREPLACES

Abbey | W Hollywood  14
Admiral Risty | Rancho Palos Verdes  20
Amalfi | La Brea  21
Baleen | Redondo Bch  20
Barefoot B&G | Third St.  18
Beau Rivage | Malibu  21
Beckham Grill | Pasadena  18
Bel-Air B&G | Bel-Air  19
Z Bistro Gdn. | Studio City  21
Blue Velvet | Downtown  20
Bluewater Grill | Redondo Bch  19
boé | Beverly Hills  22
NEW Bond St. | Beverly Hills  19
Buggy Whip | Westchester  19
Ca' del Sole | N Hollywood  22
Cafe Del Rey | Marina del Rey  21
Cafe des Artistes | Hollywood  20
Café Pacific | Rancho Palos Verdes  24
Z Capo | Santa Monica  26
Catch | Santa Monica  22
Chapter 8 | Agoura Hills  17
Charcoal | Hollywood  11
Chart House | multi.  19
Checkers | Downtown  20
Chez Mimi | Santa Monica  22
Christy's | Long Bch  22
Claim Jumper | multi.  19
NEW Comme Ça | W Hollywood  21
Z Dal Rae | Pico Rivera  25
Dan Tana's | W Hollywood  23
NEW D'Cache | Toluca Lake  –
NEW Del, The | Playa del Rey  20
Derby | Arcadia  23
Z Derek's | Pasadena  27
Dish | La Cañada Flintridge  16
Dolce Enoteca | Melrose  17
Dominick's | Beverly Blvd.  21
eat. on sunset | Hollywood  18
El Cholo | multi.  18
El Coyote | Beverly Blvd.  13
El Torito | Long Bch  15
Fins | Calabasas  22
Ford's | Culver City  19
Foundry, The | Melrose  23
Gardens/Glendon | Westwood  19
Geisha Hse. | Hollywood  20
Gennaro's | Glendale  20
Guido's | West LA  19
Hamlet | Pasadena  16
Z Hotel Bel-Air | Bel-Air  25
Z Houston's | multi.  21

Il Cielo | Beverly Hills  21
Il Fornaio | multi.  20
Z Inn/Seventh Ray | Topanga  20
Ivy, The | W Hollywood  22
James' Bch. | Venice  18
Jer-ne | Marina del Rey  20
JJ Steak | Pasadena  23
Josie | Santa Monica  26
Koi | W Hollywood  24
Z La Boheme | W Hollywood  22
Larchmont Grill | Hollywood  22
La Rive Gauche | Palos Verdes  19
Lasher's | Long Bch  23
Z Lawry's Prime | Beverly Hills  24
Literati | West LA  19
Z Little Door | Third St.  23
Lodge Steak | Beverly Hills  19
Z Lucques | W Hollywood  27
Madeleine's | Pasadena  24
Marrakesh | Studio City  19
Z Mastro's Steak | Thousand Oaks  26
McCormick/Schmick | Pasadena  19
Mediterraneo | Westlake Vill  17
Z Mélisse | Santa Monica  28
NEW Melrose B&G | W Hollywood  18
Minx | Glendale  18
Mission 261 | San Gabriel  20
Monty's Steak | Woodland Hills  20
MOZ Buddha | Agoura Hills  20
Napa Valley | Westwood  20
Ocean & Vine | Santa Monica  21
Z One Pico | Santa Monica  22
Ortolan | Third St.  25
Osteria La Buca | Melrose  25
Padri | Agoura Hills  21
Panda Inn | Ontario  21
Paradise Cove | Malibu  15
Z Parkway Grill | Pasadena  26
Paul's Cafe | Tarzana  17
Z Penthouse | Santa Monica  18
Petrelli's Steak | Culver City  16
Piatti | Thousand Oaks  19
P6 Rest. | Westlake Vill  22
Raymond, The | Pasadena  24
Reel Inn | Malibu  20
Rive Gauche | Sherman Oaks  19
Z Saddle Peak | Calabasas  26
Safire | Camarillo  21
Salt Creek | El Segundo  18
Simon LA | W Hollywood  21
Smoke House | Burbank  19
Sonora Cafe | La Brea  22
Spanish Kitchen | W Hollywood  15

Stinking Rose | **Beverly Hills** 18

**NEW** STK | **W Hollywood** 21

Suki 7 | **Westlake Vill** 19

Taix | **Echo Pk** 16

Tam O'Shanter | **Atwater Vill** 21

Tanino | **Westwood** 23

Taverna Tony | **Malibu** 20

**NEW** Terra | **Malibu** 22

Tower Bar | **W Hollywood** 21

Vertical Wine | **Pasadena** 23

Vibrato | **Bel-Air** 21

Villa Piacere | **Woodland Hills** 19

Whale & Ale | **San Pedro** 16

Wilshire | **Santa Monica** 22

Zin Bistro | **Westlake Vill** 22

## HISTORIC PLACES

(Year opened; * building)

1900 | Porta Via Italian* | **Pasadena** 23

1900 | Raymond, The* | **Pasadena** 24

1900 | Saddle Peak* | **Calabasas** 26

1906 | Pete's Cafe* | **Downtown** 19

1908 | Philippe/Orig. | **Chinatown** 21

1910 | Mijares | **Pasadena** 17

1910 | Via Veneto* | **Santa Monica** 26

1910 | Warszawa* | **Santa Monica** 22

1911 | Larkin's* | **Eagle Rock** 20

1912 | Engine Co. 28* | **Downtown** 19

1912 | Polo Lounge* | **Beverly Hills** 22

1913 | Holly St.* | **Pasadena** 19

1916 | Alcove* | **Los Feliz** 21

1916 | Madison, The* | **Long Bch** 20

1919 | Musso & Frank* | **Hollywood** 18

1920 | Clafoutis* | **W Hollywood** 19

1920 | Farm/Bev. Hills* | **Beverly Hills** 19

1920 | La Paella* | **Beverly Hills** 23

1920 | Lasher's* | **Long Bch** 23

1921 | Pacific Dining Car | **Downtown** 22

1922 | Casablanca Med.* | **Claremont** 18

1922 | Derby* | **Arcadia** 23

1922 | Second City* | **El Segundo** 23

1922 | Tam O'Shanter | **Atwater Vill** 21

1923 | El Cholo | **Mid-City** 18

1923 | Farfalla Trattoria* | **Los Feliz** 22

1923 | Lobster, The | **Santa Monica** 22

1924 | Canter's | **Fairfax** 18

1924 | Edendale Grill* | **Silver Lake** 16

1924 | Grub* | **Hollywood** 19

1924 | Original Pantry | **Downtown** 15

1925 | Bay Cities Deli | **Santa Monica** -

1925 | Palm, The* | **Downtown** 23

1925 | Taste* | **W Hollywood** 23

1926 | Greenblatt's Deli | **Hollywood** 18

1926 | Sky Room* | **Long Bch** 21

1927 | Benihana* | **Santa Monica** 18

1927 | Far Niente* | **Glendale** 25

1927 | Pig 'n Whistle* | **Hollywood** 13

1927 | Taix | **Echo Pk** 16

1928 | Cafe Stella* | **Silver Lake** 21

1928 | Ciao Tratt.* | **Downtown** 20

1928 | Tamayo* | **East LA** 18

1929 | Campanile* | **La Brea** 26

1929 | Chateau Marmont* | **W Hollywood** 20

1929 | Tanino* | **Westwood** 23

1929 | Tower Bar* | **W Hollywood** 21

1930 | Brighton Coffee | **Beverly Hills** 18

1931 | El Coyote | **Beverly Blvd.** 13

1931 | Lucques* | **W Hollywood** 27

1931 | Petrelli's Steak | **Culver City** 16

1932 | Fatty's & Co.* | **Eagle Rock** 23

1934 | Galley, The* | **Santa Monica** 18

1935 | Stand, The* | **Westwood** 18

1936 | Sir Winston's* | **Long Bch** 21

1937 | Damon's | **Glendale** 18

1937 | Traxx* | **Downtown** 20

1938 | Du-par's | **Fairfax** 16

1938 | Lawry's Prime | **Beverly Hills** 24

1938 | Paul's Cafe* | **Tarzana** 17

1939 | Bistro 45* | **Pasadena** 26

1939 | Formosa Cafe | **W Hollywood** 12

1939 | Luna Park* | **La Brea** 17

1939 | Pink's Chili Dogs | **La Brea** 19

1940 | Il Cielo* | **Beverly Hills** 21

1942 | Mr. Cecil's Ribs* | **West LA** 18

1945 | Nate 'n Al | **Beverly Hills** 20

1946 | Billingsley's | **West LA** 15

1946 | Chili John's | **Burbank** 17

1946 | Fountain Coffee | **Beverly Hills** 20

1946 | Hotel Bel-Air | **Bel-Air** 25

1946 | Paradise Cove* | **Malibu** 15

1946 | Smoke House | **Burbank** 19

1946 | Tommy's* | **Downtown** 22

1946 | Uncle Bill's | **Manhattan Bch** 21

1947 | Apple Pan | **West LA** 22

1947 | Langer's Deli | **Downtown** 25

1948 | Cassell's | **Koreatown** 19

| Year | Restaurant | Location | Rating |
|---|---|---|---|
| 1948 | Dominick's | Beverly Blvd. | 21 |
| 1948 | Factor's Deli | Pico-Robertson | 16 |
| 1948 | Papa Cristo's | Mid-City | 22 |
| 1948 | Reddi Chick BBQ | Brentwood | 21 |
| 1949 | Miceli's | Hollywood | 17 |
| 1950 | Hamlet | W Hollywood | 16 |
| 1952 | Buggy Whip | Westchester | 19 |
| 1952 | Cafe 50's* | West LA | 16 |
| 1952 | Johnnie's Pastrami | Culver City | 20 |
| 1953 | Father's Office | Santa Monica | 24 |
| 1953 | Taylor's Steak | Koreatown | 21 |
| 1954 | El Torito | multi. | 15 |
| 1955 | Casa Bianca | Eagle Rock | 23 |
| 1955 | El Tepeyac | East LA | 24 |
| 1956 | Antonio's | Melrose | 19 |
| 1956 | Casa Vega | Sherman Oaks | 18 |
| 1956 | La Scala | Beverly Hills | 21 |
| 1957 | Art's Deli | Studio City | 20 |
| 1957 | Jan's | W Hollywood | 14 |
| 1957 | Walter's | Claremont | 19 |
| 1958 | Neptune's Net | Malibu | 18 |
| 1958 | Rae's | Santa Monica | 18 |

## HOLIDAY MEALS

(Special prix fixe meals offered at major holidays)

| Restaurant | Location | Rating |
|---|---|---|
| Barney Greengrass | Beverly Hills | 20 |
| Gardens | Beverly Hills | 23 |
| ☑ Hampton's | Westlake Vill | 23 |
| Jar | Beverly Blvd. | 25 |
| ☑ Joe's | Venice | 26 |
| Josie | Santa Monica | 26 |
| Kate Mantilini | Beverly Hills | 18 |
| ☑ La Cachette | Century City | 27 |
| ☑ Langham Huntington | Pasadena | 26 |
| Locanda/Lago | Santa Monica | 21 |
| Mediterraneo | Westlake Vill | 17 |
| ☑ Mélisse | Santa Monica | 28 |
| ☑ Saddle Peak | Calabasas | 26 |
| Whist | Santa Monica | 20 |

## HOTEL DINING

| Hotel / Restaurant | Location | Rating |
|---|---|---|
| **Avalon Hotel** | | |
| blue on blue | Beverly Hills | 19 |
| **Bel-Air, Hotel** | | |
| ☑ Hotel Bel-Air | Bel-Air | 25 |
| **Belamar Hotel** | | |
| NEW Second Story | Manhattan Bch | - |
| **Best Western** | | |
| Du-par's | Thousand Oaks | 16 |
| **Beverly Hills Hotel** | | |
| Fountain Coffee | Beverly Hills | 20 |
| Polo Lounge | Beverly Hills | 22 |
| **Beverly Hilton** | | |
| Circa 55 | Beverly Hills | 19 |
| **Beverly Laurel Motor Hotel** | | |
| Swingers | Beverly Blvd. | 17 |
| **Beverly Terrace Hotel** | | |
| Amici | Beverly Hills | 21 |
| **Beverly Wilshire** | | |
| Blvd | Beverly Hills | 20 |
| ☑ CUT | Beverly Hills | 26 |
| **Burbank Marriott** | | |
| Daily Grill | Burbank | 18 |
| **Casa Del Mar, Hotel** | | |
| Catch | Santa Monica | 22 |
| **Chateau Marmont** | | |
| Chateau Marmont | W Hollywood | 20 |
| **Crescent** | | |
| boé | Beverly Hills | 22 |
| **Custom Hotel** | | |
| NEW Bistrotek | Westchester | - |
| **Farmer's Daughter Hotel** | | |
| Tart | Fairfax | 16 |
| **Four Seasons Hotel** | | |
| Gardens | Beverly Hills | 23 |
| **Four Seasons Westlake Vill.** | | |
| ☑ Hampton's | Westlake Vill | 23 |
| Onyx | Westlake Vill | 25 |
| **Grafton Hotel** | | |
| Boa | W Hollywood | 23 |
| **Hilton Checkers** | | |
| Checkers | Downtown | 20 |
| **Hotel Angeleno** | | |
| West | Brentwood | 18 |
| **Hotel Palomar** | | |
| NEW Blvd 16 | Westwood | - |
| **Huntley Santa Monica Beach** | | |
| ☑ Penthouse | Santa Monica | 18 |
| **Hyatt Regency Century Plaza** | | |
| Breeze | Century City | 17 |
| **Kyoto Grand Hotel** | | |
| Thousand Cranes | Little Tokyo | 21 |
| **Langham Huntington Hotel** | | |
| ☑ Langham Huntington | Pasadena | 26 |
| **Le Merigot Hotel** | | |
| Cézanne | Santa Monica | 21 |
| **Loews Santa Monica Beach** | | |
| Ocean & Vine | Santa Monica | 21 |
| **London West Hollywood, The** | | |
| NEW Gordon Ramsay | W Hollywood | - |
| **Luxe Hotel** | | |
| On Sunset | Brentwood | 22 |

Luxe Hotel Rodeo Dr.
 Cafe Rodeo | **Beverly Hills**   18

Malibu Beach Inn
 NEW Carbon Beach | **Malibu**   13

Millennium Biltmore Hotel
 Sai Sai | **Downtown**   18

Mondrian Hotel
 Asia de Cuba | **W Hollywood**   23

Omni Los Angeles Hotel
 Noé | **Downtown**   24

Orlando Hotel
 La Terza | **Third St.**   22

Pacific Palms Resort
 NEW RED | **City of Industry**   –

Peninsula Hotel of Beverly Hills
 Z Belvedere | **Beverly Hills**   25

Portofino Hotel & Yacht Club
 Baleen | **Redondo Bch**   20

Renissance Long Beach Hotel
 Tracht's | **Long Bch**   23

Ritz-Carlton, Marina Del Rey
 Jer-ne | **Marina del Rey**   20

Roosevelt Hotel
 Dakota | **Hollywood**   22
 25 Degrees | **Hollywood**   21

Shutters on the Bch.
 Coast | **Santa Monica**   21
 Z One Pico | **Santa Monica**   22

Sofitel Los Angeles
 Simon LA | **W Hollywood**   21

Standard
 Standard, The | **multi.**   15

Sunset Tower Hotel
 Tower Bar | **W Hollywood**   21

Thompson Beverly Hills Hotel
 NEW Bond St. | **Beverly Hills**   19

Viceroy Santa Monica
 Whist | **Santa Monica**   20

Wilshire Grand
 Seoul Jung | **Downtown**   20

W Los Angeles Westwood
 Nine Thirty | **Westwood**   21

## LATE DINING

(Weekday closing hour)

Abbey | 2 AM | **W Hollywood**   14
Apple Pan | 12 AM | **West LA**   22
Astro Burger | varies | **multi.**   19
NEW Bar Pintxo | 12 AM | **Santa Monica**   19
BCD Tofu | varies | **multi.**   19
Berri's Pizza | varies | **Third St.**   16
BJ's | varies | **multi.**   17
Bossa Nova | varies | **multi.**   20
Bowery | 2 AM | **Hollywood**   20
Cafe 50's | varies | **multi.**   16

Cafe Sushi | 12 AM | **Beverly Blvd.**   20
Caffe Roma | 2 AM | **Beverly Hills**   17
Canter's | 24 hrs. | **Fairfax**   18
Carney's | varies | **W Hollywood**   19
Casa Bianca | 12 AM | **Eagle Rock**   23
Casa Vega | 1 AM | **Sherman Oaks**   18
NEW Catalina | 12 AM | **Redondo Bch**   24
Citizen Smith | 4 AM | **Hollywood**   17
Clafoutis | 12 AM | **W Hollywood**   19
Courtyard | 12 AM | **W Hollywood**   19
Dan Tana's | 1 AM | **W Hollywood**   23
NEW Delancey | 12 AM | **Hollywood**   –
Dominick's | 12:45 AM | **Beverly Blvd.**   21
Doña Rosa | varies | **Pasadena**   16
Du-par's | varies | **multi.**   16
NEW 8 oz. | 12 AM | **Melrose**   –
Electric Lotus | 12 AM | **Los Feliz**   18
Firefly | 12 AM | **Studio City**   22
NEW Foxtail | 2 AM | **W Hollywood**   –
Fred 62 | 24 hrs. | **Los Feliz**   17
Gaby's | varies | **multi.**   19
Geisha Hse. | 12 AM | **Hollywood**   20
Greenblatt's Deli | 1:30 AM | **Hollywood**   18
Hamburger Mary's | 12 AM | **W Hollywood**   15
NEW Honda-Ya | 1 AM | **Little Tokyo**   22
Hop Li | varies | **Arcadia**   20
Hop Woo | varies | **Chinatown**   18
Hungry Cat | 12 AM | **Hollywood**   24
Z In-N-Out | varies | **multi.**   23
Iroha | 12 AM | **Studio City**   25
NEW Isla | 12 AM | **W Hollywood**   –
Jan's | 2 AM | **W Hollywood**   14
NEW Joe's Pizza | 12 AM | **Santa Monica**   20
Johnnie's Pastrami | varies | **Culver City**   20
Jones | 1:30 AM | **W Hollywood**   18
Kate Mantilini | varies | **Beverly Hills**   18
Z Katsuya | varies | **multi.**   24
Ketchup | 12:30 AM | **W Hollywood**   15
Kitchen, The | 12 AM | **Silver Lake**   19
NEW Kitchen 24 | 24 hrs. | **Hollywood**   –
Lamonica's NY Pizza | varies | **Westwood**   21
Lares | 1 AM | **Santa Monica**   19
Macau St. | 12 AM | **Monterey Pk**   19
Z Madison, The | 12 AM | **Long Bch**   20

| | |
|---|---|
| Magnolia \| 3 AM \| **Hollywood** | 19 |
| Mel's Drive-In \| varies \| **multi.** | 15 |
| Mexicali \| 1 AM \| **Studio City** | 15 |
| Minotaure \| 12 AM \| **Playa del Rey** | 20 |
| Mi Piace \| varies \| **Pasadena** | 20 |
| Mirabelle \| 12:30 AM \| **W Hollywood** | 19 |
| Monte Alban \| 12 AM \| **West LA** | 21 |
| Nak Won \| 24 hrs. \| **Koreatown** | 16 |
| Nic's \| 12 AM \| **Beverly Hills** | 19 |
| One Sunset \| 2 AM \| **W Hollywood** | 20 |
| Original Pantry \| 24 hrs. \| **Downtown** | 15 |
| **Z** Osteria Mozza \| 12 AM \| **Hollywood** | 26 |
| Pacific Dining Car \| 24 hrs. \| **multi.** | 22 |
| Palms Thai \| 12 AM \| **E Hollywood** | 20 |
| Parc \| 12 AM \| **Hollywood** | 21 |
| Pete's Cafe \| 2 AM \| **Downtown** | 19 |
| Pho Café \| 12 AM \| **Silver Lake** | 21 |
| Pink's Chili Dogs \| 2 AM \| **La Brea** | 19 |
| Pizza Rustica \| varies \| **W Hollywood** | 22 |
| **Z** Pizzeria Mozza \| 12 AM \| **Hollywood** | 26 |
| Polo Lounge \| 1 AM \| **Beverly Hills** | 22 |
| Poquito Más \| varies \| **Studio City** | 21 |
| Rack \| varies \| **Woodland Hills** | 16 |
| Red Corner Asia \| 1:30 AM \| **E Hollywood** | 25 |
| Rocky Cola \| 12 AM \| **Hermosa Bch** | 13 |
| Roscoe's \| varies \| **multi.** | 20 |
| Ruen Pair \| 4 AM \| **E Hollywood** | 24 |
| Saddle Ranch \| varies \| **multi.** | 14 |
| Sam Woo \| varies \| **multi.** | 20 |
| Standard, The \| 24 hrs. \| **multi.** | 15 |
| **NEW** STK \| 2 AM \| **W Hollywood** | 21 |
| Swingers \| varies \| **multi.** | 17 |
| Tengu \| 1 AM \| **Santa Monica** | 22 |
| 3rd Stop \| 12 AM \| **W Hollywood** | 17 |
| **NEW** Tofu Villa \| 12 AM \| **West LA** | - |
| Tommy's \| 24 hrs. \| **Downtown** | 22 |
| **NEW** Tranquility Base \| 2 AM \| **Downtown** | - |
| **NEW** Twelve + Highland \| varies \| **Manhattan Bch** | 21 |
| 25 Degrees \| 1:30 AM \| **Hollywood** | 21 |
| uWink \| 12 AM \| **Hollywood** | 13 |
| Velvet Margarita \| 2 AM \| **Hollywood** | 17 |
| Village Idiot \| 12 AM \| **Melrose** | 19 |
| **NEW** Waffle, The \| 2:30 AM \| **Hollywood** | 16 |
| Wilshire \| varies \| **Santa Monica** | 22 |
| Wokcano Cafe \| varies \| **multi.** | 19 |
| York, The \| 2 AM \| **Highland Pk** | 18 |

## MICROBREWERIES

| | |
|---|---|
| Belmont Brew. \| **Long Bch** | 16 |
| BJ's \| **Burbank** | 17 |
| Gordon Biersch \| **multi.** | 16 |
| Yard Hse. \| **multi.** | 20 |

## NATURAL/ORGANIC

(These restaurants often or always use organic, local ingredients)

| | |
|---|---|
| **NEW** Akasha \| **Culver City** | 22 |
| Ammo \| **Hollywood** | 22 |
| **NEW** Andiamo \| **Silver Lake** | - |
| A Votre Sante \| **Brentwood** | 20 |
| Baleen \| **Redondo Bch** | 20 |
| Bar Hayama \| **West LA** | 24 |
| **Z** Bastide \| **W Hollywood** | 27 |
| Beechwood \| **Marina del Rey** | 18 |
| Bistro 767 \| **Rolling Hills Estates** | 22 |
| Bloom Cafe \| **Mid-City** | 22 |
| Blue Hen \| **Eagle Rock** | 14 |
| Blue Velvet \| **Downtown** | 20 |
| **NEW** Blvd 16 \| **Westwood** | - |
| Border Grill \| **Santa Monica** | 21 |
| Café 14 \| **Agoura Hills** | 24 |
| Cafe Stella \| **Silver Lake** | 21 |
| Celestino \| **Pasadena** | 23 |
| Chameau \| **Fairfax** | 22 |
| Chaya \| **W Hollywood** | 24 |
| Chaya \| **Venice** | 22 |
| Checkers \| **Downtown** | 20 |
| Cheebo \| **Hollywood** | 19 |
| Chef Melba's \| **Hermosa Bch** | 24 |
| **Z** Chez Mélange \| **Redondo Bch** | 25 |
| Chichen Itza \| **Downtown** | 24 |
| **Z** Chinois \| **Santa Monica** | 26 |
| Chipotle \| **Marina del Rey** | 18 |
| **Z** ChoSun Galbee \| **Koreatown** | 23 |
| **Z** Christine \| **Torrance** | 26 |
| Christy's \| **Long Bch** | 22 |
| **Z** Cicada \| **Downtown** | 23 |
| City Bakery \| **Brentwood** | 19 |
| Ciudad \| **Downtown** | 21 |
| Coral Tree \| **multi.** | 18 |
| Corkscrew \| **Manhattan Bch** | 21 |
| Counter, The \| **Santa Monica** | 21 |
| **Z** Crustacean \| **Beverly Hills** | 24 |
| cube \| **La Brea** | 22 |
| Cucina Paradiso \| **Palms** | 21 |
| **Z** CUT \| **Beverly Hills** | 26 |
| Dakota \| **Hollywood** | 22 |
| **Z** Derek's \| **Pasadena** | 27 |
| Divino \| **Brentwood** | 22 |
| Dusty's \| **Silver Lake** | 18 |
| eat. on sunset \| **Hollywood** | 18 |
| Eat Well Cafe \| **W Hollywood** | 16 |
| Farm/Bev. Hills \| **multi.** | 19 |

| | |
|---|---|
| Farm Stand \| **El Segundo** | 21 |
| Z **Father's Office** \| **Santa Monica** | 24 |
| Fatty's & Co. \| **Eagle Rock** | 23 |
| Figaro Bistrot \| **Los Feliz** | 19 |
| Firefly \| **Studio City** | 22 |
| Five 61 \| **Pasadena** | 22 |
| Ford's \| **Culver City** | 19 |
| NEW Foxtail \| **W Hollywood** | - |
| Gardens \| **Beverly Hills** | 23 |
| Getty Ctr. \| **Brentwood** | 22 |
| Grace \| **Beverly Blvd.** | 25 |
| Z Hotel Bel-Air \| **Bel-Air** | 25 |
| Hugo's \| **multi.** | 21 |
| Il Grano \| **West LA** | 26 |
| Il Sole \| **W Hollywood** | 24 |
| Z Inn/Seventh Ray \| **Topanga** | 20 |
| Ivy, The \| **W Hollywood** | 22 |
| Ivy at Shore \| **Santa Monica** | 22 |
| Jack Sprat's \| **West LA** | 19 |
| Jar \| **Beverly Blvd.** | 25 |
| Z Joe's \| **Venice** | 26 |
| Josie \| **Santa Monica** | 26 |
| Juliano's Raw \| **Santa Monica** | 19 |
| Kokomo Cafe \| **Beverly Blvd.** | 19 |
| Z La Boheme \| **W Hollywood** | 22 |
| La Bottega Marino \| **multi.** | 21 |
| NEW LAMILL \| **Silver Lake** | 23 |
| La Pergola \| **Sherman Oaks** | 22 |
| Leaf Cuisine \| **multi.** | 17 |
| Z Leila's \| **Oak Pk** | 27 |
| Le Pain Quotidien \| **multi.** | 19 |
| Literati \| **West LA** | 19 |
| Lou \| **Hollywood** | 23 |
| Z Lucques \| **W Hollywood** | 27 |
| Madeleine Bistro \| **Tarzana** | 24 |
| Z Mako \| **Beverly Hills** | 26 |
| Mäni's \| **multi.** | 18 |
| Marston's \| **Pasadena** | 23 |
| M Café \| **Culver City** | 21 |
| Z Mélisse \| **Santa Monica** | 28 |
| Michael's \| **Santa Monica** | 24 |
| Mike & Anne's \| **S Pasadena** | 21 |
| Mirü8691 \| **Beverly Hills** | 25 |
| Z Native Foods \| **Westwood** | 22 |
| Newsroom Café \| **W Hollywood** | 18 |
| Nic's \| **Beverly Hills** | 19 |
| Z One Pico \| **Santa Monica** | 22 |
| One Sunset \| **W Hollywood** | 20 |
| Orris \| **West LA** | 26 |
| Ortolan \| **Third St.** | 25 |
| Pace \| **Laurel Canyon** | 21 |
| NEW Palate \| **Glendale** | - |
| Z Parkway Grill \| **Pasadena** | 26 |
| Z Petros \| **Manhattan Bch** | 24 |
| NEW Porta Via Italian \| **Pasadena** | 23 |
| Prana Cafe \| **W Hollywood** | 18 |
| Z Real Food Daily \| **multi.** | 21 |
| Rose Cafe \| **Venice** | 19 |
| R23 \| **Downtown** | 26 |
| Salades/Provence \| **W Hollywood** | 20 |
| Z Sam's/Beach \| **Santa Monica** | 26 |
| NEW Second Story \| **Manhattan Bch** | - |
| 17th St. Cafe \| **Santa Monica** | 19 |
| Shima \| **Venice** | 27 |
| Z Sona \| **W Hollywood** | 27 |
| Z Spago \| **Beverly Hills** | 27 |
| Standard, The \| **W Hollywood** | 15 |
| NEW Stork, The \| **Hollywood** | - |
| Z Takami \| **Downtown** | 20 |
| Tender Greens \| **Culver City** | 23 |
| Tiara Cafe \| **Downtown** | 23 |
| NEW Tinto \| **W Hollywood** | 20 |
| Tracht's \| **Long Bch** | 23 |
| Traxx \| **Downtown** | 20 |
| Truxton's \| **Westchester** | - |
| Urth Caffé \| **multi.** | 20 |
| Vegan Glory \| **Beverly Blvd.** | 20 |
| Vertical Wine \| **Pasadena** | 23 |
| Via Veneto \| **Santa Monica** | 26 |
| NEW Vinotéque \| **Culver City** | - |
| Violet \| **Santa Monica** | 22 |
| NEW Waffle, The \| **Hollywood** | 16 |
| Watercress \| **Sherman Oaks** | 21 |
| Z Water Grill \| **Downtown** | 27 |
| Whist \| **Santa Monica** | 20 |
| Wilshire \| **Santa Monica** | 22 |
| Wilson \| **Culver City** | 22 |
| Wolfgang Puck \| **Downtown** | 17 |

## NOTEWORTHY NEWCOMERS

| | |
|---|---|
| Akasha \| **Culver City** | 22 |
| Amaranta \| **Canoga Pk** | 20 |
| Amarone \| **W Hollywood** | 27 |
| Andiamo \| **Silver Lake** | - |
| Animal \| **Fairfax** | - |
| Anisette \| **Santa Monica** | - |
| Bar Pintxo \| **Santa Monica** | 19 |
| Bashan \| **Montrose** | 26 |
| Beso \| **Hollywood** | - |
| Best Fish Taco \| **Los Feliz** | 21 |
| Bistrotek \| **Westchester** | - |
| Bistro 39 \| **Alhambra** | - |
| BLT Steak \| **W Hollywood** | 23 |
| Blvd 16 \| **Westwood** | - |
| BonChon \| **Koreatown** | - |
| Bond St. \| **Beverly Hills** | 19 |
| Brix 1601 \| **Hermosa Bch** | - |
| Brunello Trattoria \| **Culver City** | - |

| Restaurant | Location | Rating |
|---|---|---|
| Captain Crab | San Gabriel | - |
| Carbon Beach | Malibu | 13 |
| Casablanca Med. | Claremont | 18 |
| Casa Don Rolando | N Hills | - |
| Catalina | Redondo Bch | 24 |
| Chloe | Santa Monica | 18 |
| Citrus at Social | Hollywood | 21 |
| Comme Ça | W Hollywood | 21 |
| Creperie/Jack n' Jill's | Third St. | 21 |
| Crudo | W Hollywood | - |
| Darren's | Manhattan Bch | 26 |
| D'Cache | Toluca Lake | - |
| Del, The | Playa del Rey | 20 |
| Delancey | Hollywood | - |
| Dolce Isola | Pico-Robertson | 24 |
| 8 oz. | Melrose | - |
| Five Guys | Carson | - |
| Flake | Venice | - |
| FOOD | Rancho Pk | - |
| Foxtail | W Hollywood | - |
| Giggles 'n Hugs | West LA | - |
| Gjelina | Venice | - |
| Gordon Ramsay | W Hollywood | - |
| Green St. Tav. | Pasadena | 23 |
| Gus's BBQ | S Pasadena | - |
| Gyenari | Culver City | - |
| Hall, The | W Hollywood | - |
| Hidden | Santa Monica | 15 |
| Honda-Ya | Little Tokyo | 22 |
| Hong Yei | San Gabriel | - |
| Hunan Seafood | Rosemead | - |
| Il Carpaccio | Pacific Palisades | 23 |
| Isla | W Hollywood | - |
| Jian | Beverly Blvd. | - |
| Joe's Pizza | Santa Monica | 20 |
| JuJu | Westwood | - |
| Katsu Sushi | Beverly Hills | - |
| Ken/Kent's NY Deli | Hermosa Bch | - |
| Kitchen 24 | Hollywood | - |
| Kress, The | Hollywood | - |
| Kula | Century City | 15 |
| La Défence | Koreatown | - |
| La Grande Orange | Pasadena | - |
| LAMILL | Silver Lake | 23 |
| Larsen's Steak | Encino | - |
| Lawry's Carvery | Century City | 19 |
| Lemonade Cafe | multi. | - |
| Lido Grill | Venice | - |
| Little Dom's | Los Feliz | 17 |
| Lot 1 | Echo Pk | - |
| Luckyfish | Beverly Hills | 18 |
| Malibu Pier Club | Malibu | - |
| Medusa | Beverly Blvd. | - |
| Melograno | Hollywood | 23 |
| Melrose B&G | W Hollywood | 18 |
| Mes Amis | Los Feliz | 16 |
| Michael's/Naples | Long Bch | - |
| Mojitos | Pasadena | 24 |
| Mucho Ultima | Manhattan Bch | 19 |
| Nakkara | Fairfax | - |
| Nobu | W Hollywood | 26 |
| Nonna | W Hollywood | 18 |
| O!Burger | W Hollywood | - |
| Oak Room | Pacific Palisades | - |
| Oba Sushi Izakaya | Pasadena | - |
| Ortega 120 | Redondo Bch | - |
| Palate | Glendale | - |
| Paperfish | Beverly Hills | 23 |
| Park, The | Echo Pk | - |
| Point, The | Culver City | 18 |
| Porta Via Italian | Pasadena | 23 |
| Portillo's | Moreno Valley | 18 |
| Press Panini | Studio City | - |
| R+D Kitchen | Santa Monica | - |
| RED | City of Industry | - |
| Red Fish | Simi Valley | 21 |
| Rest. 15 | Echo Pk | 20 |
| Richie Palmer's | multi. | 15 |
| Robata Bar | Santa Monica | 21 |
| Röckenwagner | Santa Monica | - |
| RockSugar | Century City | - |
| Rush Street | Culver City | - |
| Sampa Grill | Encino | - |
| Second Story | Manhattan Bch | - |
| Seoul Bros. | Pasadena | - |
| Shojin | Little Tokyo | - |
| Siena | Pasadena | - |
| Sila Bistro | Silver Lake | - |
| Skaf's | Glendale | 26 |
| STK | W Hollywood | 21 |
| Stork, The | Hollywood | - |
| sugarFISH | Marina del Rey | - |
| Tapa Meze | Manhattan Bch | - |
| Terra | Malibu | 22 |
| Terroni | Beverly Blvd. | 20 |
| Third & Olive | Burbank | - |
| Three Forks | Claremont | 23 |
| Tinto | W Hollywood | 20 |
| Tofu Villa | West LA | - |
| Tranquility Base | Downtown | - |
| Twelve+Highland | Manhattan Bch | 21 |
| Veggie Grill | El Segundo | 19 |
| Village Pantry | Pacific Palisades | 14 |
| Vinotéque | Culver City | - |
| Waffle, The | Hollywood | 16 |
| Whisper Cafe | Encino | - |
| Wolfgang's Steak | Beverly Hills | - |
| Yamato | Westwood | 19 |
| Yuta | Studio City | - |
| Zane's | Hermosa Bch | - |

## OUTDOOR DINING

(G=garden; P=patio; S=sidewalk; T=terrace)

| | |
|---|---|
| Alcove \| P \| **Los Feliz** | 21 |
| Antonio's \| S \| **Melrose** | 19 |
| Asia de Cuba \| P \| **W Hollywood** | 23 |
| Babalu \| S \| **Santa Monica** | 19 |
| Barefoot B&G \| P \| **Third St.** | 18 |
| Barney Greengrass \| T \| **Beverly Hills** | 20 |
| Barney's Burgers \| P \| **Brentwood** | 20 |
| ☑ Bastide \| G, P \| **W Hollywood** | 27 |
| Beacon \| P \| **Culver City** | 22 |
| Beau Rivage \| P \| **Malibu** | 21 |
| Beechwood \| P \| **Marina del Rey** | 18 |
| Bel-Air B&G \| P \| **Bel-Air** | 19 |
| ☑ Belvedere \| G, P \| **Beverly Hills** | 25 |
| bld \| P \| **Beverly Blvd.** | 21 |
| blue on blue \| T \| **Beverly Hills** | 19 |
| BottleRock \| P \| **Culver City** | 16 |
| Bravo \| P \| **Santa Monica** | 17 |
| Breadbar \| P \| **multi.** | 18 |
| Burger Continental \| P \| **Pasadena** | 17 |
| Ca' del Sole \| P \| **N Hollywood** | 22 |
| Cafe des Artistes \| G \| **Hollywood** | 20 |
| Cafe Med \| P \| **W Hollywood** | 18 |
| Cafe Pinot \| P \| **Downtown** | 22 |
| Café Santorini \| P \| **Pasadena** | 20 |
| C & O \| P \| **Marina del Rey** | 18 |
| Cha Cha Chicken \| P \| **Santa Monica** | 21 |
| Chapter 8 \| P \| **Agoura Hills** | 17 |
| Chateau Marmont \| G \| **W Hollywood** | 20 |
| Chez Mimi \| G, P \| **Santa Monica** | 22 |
| China Grill \| P \| **Manhattan Bch** | 19 |
| Clementine \| P, S \| **Century City** | 23 |
| ☑ Cliff's Edge \| G, P \| **Silver Lake** | 21 |
| Coral Tree \| P \| **multi.** | 18 |
| Cora's Coffee \| P \| **Santa Monica** | 21 |
| Courtyard \| P \| **W Hollywood** | 19 |
| Dominick's \| G, P \| **Beverly Blvd.** | 21 |
| eat. on sunset \| P \| **Hollywood** | 18 |
| Farm/Bev. Hills \| P, S \| **multi.** | 19 |
| Fat Fish \| P \| **W Hollywood** | 20 |
| Fins \| P \| **multi.** | 22 |
| Firefly \| P \| **Studio City** | 22 |
| Firefly Bistro \| P \| **S Pasadena** | 18 |
| Ford's \| S \| **Culver City** | 19 |
| Foundry, The \| G \| **Melrose** | 23 |
| ☑ Fraîche \| P \| **Culver City** | 24 |
| Gardens \| G, T \| **Beverly Hills** | 23 |
| ☑ Geoffrey's \| G, P \| **Malibu** | 21 |
| Gladstone's \| T \| **Pacific Palisades** | 14 |
| Gumbo Pot \| P \| **Fairfax** | 19 |
| ☑ Hotel Bel-Air \| T \| **Bel-Air** | 25 |

| | |
|---|---|
| Hungry Cat \| P \| **Hollywood** | 24 |
| i Cugini \| P \| **Santa Monica** | 21 |
| Il Cielo \| G, P \| **Beverly Hills** | 21 |
| Il Moro \| P \| **West LA** | 23 |
| ☑ Inn/Seventh Ray \| G \| **Topanga** | 20 |
| Ivy, The \| G, P \| **W Hollywood** | 22 |
| Ivy at Shore \| P, T \| **Santa Monica** | 22 |
| James' Bch. \| P \| **Venice** | 18 |
| ☑ Jin Patisserie \| G \| **Venice** | 25 |
| ☑ Joe's \| P \| **Venice** | 26 |
| Katana \| P \| **W Hollywood** | 23 |
| Koi \| G, P \| **W Hollywood** | 24 |
| L.A. Farm \| G, P \| **Santa Monica** | 20 |
| ☑ Langham Huntington \| G, P \| **Pasadena** | 26 |
| Library Alehse. \| P \| **Santa Monica** | 18 |
| Lilly's French Cafe \| P \| **Venice** | 19 |
| ☑ Little Door \| G, P \| **Third St.** | 23 |
| Locanda/Lago \| P \| **Santa Monica** | 21 |
| Lotería! \| P \| **Fairfax** | 24 |
| ☑ Lucques \| P \| **W Hollywood** | 27 |
| Marix Tex Mex \| P \| **W Hollywood** | 16 |
| Martha 22nd St. \| S \| **Hermosa Bch** | 21 |
| Mediterraneo \| P \| **Hermosa Bch** | 20 |
| Mediterraneo \| T \| **Westlake Vill** | 17 |
| Michael's \| G, P \| **Santa Monica** | 24 |
| Minx \| P, T \| **Glendale** | 18 |
| Mi Piace \| P \| **multi.** | 20 |
| Moonshadows \| T \| **Malibu** | 17 |
| Morels First Floor \| P \| **Fairfax** | 17 |
| Neomeze \| P \| **Pasadena** | 23 |
| Neptune's Net \| P \| **Malibu** | 18 |
| ☑ Nobu \| P \| **Malibu** | 27 |
| Noé \| T \| **Downtown** | 24 |
| Padri \| P \| **Agoura Hills** | 21 |
| Pane e Vino \| G, P \| **Beverly Blvd.** | 21 |
| Pink's Chili Dogs \| P \| **La Brea** | 19 |
| Polo Lounge \| G, P \| **Beverly Hills** | 22 |
| Pomodoro \| P \| **multi.** | 18 |
| ☑ Porto's \| S \| **multi.** | 24 |
| P6 Rest. \| P \| **Westlake Vill** | 22 |
| Raymond, The \| G, P \| **Pasadena** | 24 |
| Reel Inn \| P \| **Malibu** | 20 |
| Rose Cafe \| P \| **Venice** | 19 |
| ☑ Saddle Peak \| P, T \| **Calabasas** | 26 |
| Safire \| P \| **Camarillo** | 21 |
| Salt Creek \| P \| **multi.** | 18 |
| Shack, The \| P \| **multi.** | 17 |
| Simon LA \| P \| **W Hollywood** | 21 |
| Sor Tino \| P \| **Brentwood** | 19 |
| ☑ Spago \| P \| **Beverly Hills** | 27 |
| Stand, The \| G, P \| **multi.** | 18 |
| Standard, The \| P, T \| **multi.** | 15 |
| Suki 7 \| P \| **Westlake Vill** | 19 |
| Taverna Tony \| P \| **Malibu** | 20 |

| | |
|---|---|
| Tony P's Dock \| P \| **Marina del Rey** | 18 |
| Tra Di Noi \| P \| **Malibu** | 22 |
| Traxx \| P \| **Downtown** | 20 |
| Twin Palms \| G, P, T \| **Pasadena** | 18 |
| Ummba Grill \| P \| **Century City** | 16 |
| Urth Caffé \| P, S \| **multi.** | 20 |
| Villa Piacere \| P \| **Woodland Hills** | 19 |
| Whist \| T \| **Santa Monica** | 20 |
| Wood Ranch BBQ \| P \| **multi.** | 20 |
| **Z** Yamashiro \| G \| **Hollywood** | 18 |
| Zin Bistro \| P \| **Westlake Vill** | 22 |

## PEOPLE-WATCHING

| | |
|---|---|
| Abbey \| **W Hollywood** | 14 |
| NEW Akasha \| **Culver City** | 22 |
| Alcove \| **Los Feliz** | 21 |
| Alessio \| **Simi Valley** | 21 |
| NEW Amaranta \| **Canoga Pk** | 20 |
| NEW Animal \| **Fairfax** | - |
| NEW Anisette \| **Santa Monica** | - |
| **Z** A.O.C. \| **Third St.** | 26 |
| Asia de Cuba \| **W Hollywood** | 23 |
| Auntie Em's \| **Eagle Rock** | 23 |
| Bar Hayama \| **West LA** | 24 |
| Barney Greengrass \| **Beverly Hills** | 20 |
| Beechwood \| **Marina del Rey** | 18 |
| Bella Cucina \| **Hollywood** | 23 |
| NEW Beso \| **Hollywood** | - |
| bld \| **Beverly Blvd.** | 21 |
| NEW BLT Steak \| **W Hollywood** | 23 |
| Blue Velvet \| **Downtown** | 20 |
| Blvd \| **Beverly Hills** | 20 |
| NEW Bond St. \| **Beverly Hills** | 19 |
| Bono's \| **Long Bch** | 20 |
| Boulevard Lounge \| **W Hollywood** | 19 |
| Bowery \| **Hollywood** | 20 |
| Café Pacific \| **Rancho Palos Verdes** | 24 |
| Caffe Primo \| **W Hollywood** | 19 |
| Caffe Roma \| **Beverly Hills** | 17 |
| Canelé \| **Atwater Vill** | 23 |
| NEW Carbon Beach \| **Malibu** | 13 |
| Chapter 8 \| **Agoura Hills** | 17 |
| Charcoal \| **Hollywood** | 11 |
| Chateau Marmont \| **W Hollywood** | 20 |
| Chaya \| **W Hollywood** | 24 |
| Chaya \| **Venice** | 22 |
| Circa 55 \| **Beverly Hills** | 19 |
| Citizen Smith \| **Hollywood** | 17 |
| NEW Citrus at Social \| **Hollywood** | 21 |
| NEW Comme Ça \| **W Hollywood** | 21 |
| Craft \| **Century City** | 25 |
| cube \| **La Brea** | 22 |
| **Z** CUT \| **Beverly Hills** | 26 |
| Dakota \| **Hollywood** | 22 |
| Danny's \| **Venice** | 17 |

| | |
|---|---|
| NEW Darren's \| **Manhattan Bch** | 26 |
| NEW Delancey \| **Hollywood** | - |
| Dolce Enoteca \| **Melrose** | 17 |
| eat. on sunset \| **Hollywood** | 18 |
| e3rd Steak \| **Downtown** | 19 |
| **Z** Father's Office \| **Culver City** | 24 |
| Ford's \| **Culver City** | 19 |
| Formosa Cafe \| **W Hollywood** | 12 |
| Foundry, The \| **Melrose** | 23 |
| NEW Foxtail \| **W Hollywood** | - |
| **Z** Fraîche \| **Culver City** | 24 |
| Fred 62 \| **Los Feliz** | 17 |
| Geisha Hse. \| **Hollywood** | 20 |
| NEW Gordon Ramsay \| **W Hollywood** | - |
| **Z** Grill on Alley \| **Beverly Hills** | 24 |
| **Z** Hatfield's \| **Beverly Blvd.** | 27 |
| NEW Hidden \| **Santa Monica** | 15 |
| Hungry Cat \| **Hollywood** | 24 |
| Il Sole \| **W Hollywood** | 24 |
| NEW Isla \| **W Hollywood** | - |
| Ivy, The \| **W Hollywood** | 22 |
| Izaka-Ya \| **Third St.** | 25 |
| Jones \| **W Hollywood** | 18 |
| J Rest. \| **Downtown** | 16 |
| Katana \| **W Hollywood** | 23 |
| **Z** Katsu-ya \| **Encino** | 27 |
| **Z** Katsuya \| **multi.** | 24 |
| Ketchup \| **W Hollywood** | 15 |
| Koi \| **W Hollywood** | 24 |
| NEW Kress, The \| **Hollywood** | - |
| NEW LAMILL \| **Silver Lake** | 23 |
| Larchmont Grill \| **Hollywood** | 22 |
| Larkin's \| **Eagle Rock** | 20 |
| **Z** Little Door \| **Third St.** | 23 |
| Locanda/Lago \| **Santa Monica** | 21 |
| Lou \| **Hollywood** | 23 |
| Magnolia \| **Hollywood** | 19 |
| Magnolia Lounge \| **Pasadena** | 19 |
| **Z** Mastro's Steak \| **Beverly Hills** | 26 |
| M Café \| **Melrose** | 21 |
| NEW Melrose B&G \| **W Hollywood** | 18 |
| Meltdown Etc. \| **Culver City** | 18 |
| Minotaure \| **Playa del Rey** | 20 |
| Minx \| **Glendale** | 18 |
| Mirü8691 \| **Beverly Hills** | 25 |
| Morels First Floor \| **Fairfax** | 17 |
| Mr. Chow \| **Beverly Hills** | 21 |
| NEW Mucho Ultima \| **Manhattan Bch** | 19 |
| Nate 'n Al \| **Beverly Hills** | 20 |
| Neomeze \| **Pasadena** | 23 |
| Nine Thirty \| **Westwood** | 21 |
| **Z** Nobu \| **Malibu** | 27 |
| O-Bar \| **W Hollywood** | 21 |

| | |
|---|---|
| On Sunset \| **Brentwood** | 22 |
| Ortolan \| **Third St.** | 25 |
| **Z** Osteria Mozza \| **Hollywood** | 26 |
| Palm, The \| **W Hollywood** | 23 |
| **NEW** Paperfish \| **Beverly Hills** | 23 |
| Parc \| **Hollywood** | 21 |
| **Z** Penthouse \| **Santa Monica** | 18 |
| **Z** Petros \| **Manhattan Bch** | 24 |
| Pink Taco \| **Century City** | 15 |
| **Z** Pizzeria Mozza \| **Hollywood** | 26 |
| P6 Rest. \| **Westlake Vill** | 22 |
| Red 7 \| **W Hollywood** | 24 |
| **NEW** RockSugar \| **Century City** | - |
| **NEW** Rush Street \| **Culver City** | - |
| Rustic Canyon \| **Santa Monica** | 21 |
| Safire \| **Camarillo** | 21 |
| Salades/Provence \| **W Hollywood** | 20 |
| Salt Creek \| **El Segundo** | 18 |
| Saluzzi \| **Rancho Palos Verdes** | 22 |
| 750 ml \| **S Pasadena** | 19 |
| SHU \| **Bel-Air** | 21 |
| Simon LA \| **W Hollywood** | 21 |
| **Z** Spago \| **Beverly Hills** | 27 |
| Square One Dining \| **E Hollywood** | 22 |
| Stand, The \| **Century City** | 18 |
| Standard, The \| **W Hollywood** | 15 |
| **NEW** STK \| **W Hollywood** | 21 |
| **NEW** Stork, The \| **Hollywood** | - |
| Sur \| **W Hollywood** | 21 |
| Sushi Roku \| **multi.** | 22 |
| Tasca Winebar \| **Third St.** | 23 |
| Three on Fourth \| **Santa Monica** | 21 |
| 3 Square \| **Venice** | 20 |
| Tower Bar \| **W Hollywood** | 21 |
| Tracht's \| **Long Bch** | 23 |
| 25 Degrees \| **Hollywood** | 21 |
| Ugo/Italian \| **Culver City** | 17 |
| Vertical Wine \| **Pasadena** | 23 |
| Village Idiot \| **Melrose** | 19 |
| Wilshire \| **Santa Monica** | 22 |
| Wilson \| **Culver City** | 22 |
| York, The \| **Highland Pk** | 18 |

## POWER SCENES

| | |
|---|---|
| Ago \| **W Hollywood** | 22 |
| **NEW** Akasha \| **Culver City** | 22 |
| **Z** Angelini Osteria \| **Beverly Blvd.** | 27 |
| **NEW** Anisette \| **Santa Monica** | - |
| **Z** A.O.C. \| **Third St.** | 26 |
| **Z** Arnie Morton's \| **multi.** | 25 |
| Arroyo Chop \| **Pasadena** | 25 |
| Baleen \| **Redondo Bch** | 20 |
| Barney Greengrass \| **Beverly Hills** | 20 |
| **Z** Bastide \| **W Hollywood** | 27 |
| **Z** Belvedere \| **Beverly Hills** | 25 |

| | |
|---|---|
| **NEW** Beso \| **Hollywood** | - |
| bld \| **Beverly Blvd.** | 21 |
| **NEW** BLT Steak \| **W Hollywood** | 23 |
| Blvd \| **Beverly Hills** | 20 |
| **NEW** Blvd 16 \| **Westwood** | - |
| Buffalo Club \| **Santa Monica** | 20 |
| **NEW** Carbon Beach \| **Malibu** | 13 |
| Chapter 8 \| **Agoura Hills** | 17 |
| **Z** Cicada \| **Downtown** | 23 |
| **NEW** Comme Ça \| **W Hollywood** | 21 |
| Craft \| **Century City** | 25 |
| **Z** CUT \| **Beverly Hills** | 26 |
| Dakota \| **Hollywood** | 22 |
| Dan Tana's \| **W Hollywood** | 23 |
| Dominick's \| **Beverly Blvd.** | 21 |
| eat. on sunset \| **Hollywood** | 18 |
| **NEW** Foxtail \| **W Hollywood** | - |
| **Z** Fraîche \| **Culver City** | 24 |
| Giorgio Baldi \| **Santa Monica** | 24 |
| **Z** Gonpachi \| **Beverly Hills** | 18 |
| **NEW** Gordon Ramsay \| **W Hollywood** | - |
| Grace \| **Beverly Blvd.** | 25 |
| **Z** Grill on Alley \| **Beverly Hills** | 24 |
| Grill on Hollywood \| **Hollywood** | 22 |
| Hamasaku \| **West LA** | 26 |
| **Z** Hatfield's \| **Beverly Blvd.** | 27 |
| **Z** Hotel Bel-Air \| **Bel-Air** | 25 |
| Il Grano \| **West LA** | 26 |
| **Z** Katsuya \| **multi.** | 24 |
| **Z** La Cachette \| **Century City** | 27 |
| **NEW** Larsen's Steak \| **Encino** | - |
| Madeo \| **W Hollywood** | 24 |
| **Z** Mastro's Steak \| **Beverly Hills** | 26 |
| **Z** Matsuhisa \| **Beverly Hills** | 27 |
| Nick & Stef's Steak \| **Downtown** | 23 |
| **NEW** Nobu \| **W Hollywood** | 26 |
| Ortolan \| **Third St.** | 25 |
| **Z** Osteria Mozza \| **Hollywood** | 26 |
| Palm, The \| **W Hollywood** | 23 |
| **NEW** Paperfish \| **Beverly Hills** | 23 |
| Patina \| **Downtown** | 25 |
| **Z** Petros \| **Manhattan Bch** | 24 |
| **Z** Pizzeria Mozza \| **Hollywood** | 26 |
| Polo Lounge \| **Beverly Hills** | 22 |
| **Z** Providence \| **Hollywood** | 26 |
| Simon LA \| **W Hollywood** | 21 |
| **Z** Sona \| **W Hollywood** | 27 |
| **Z** Spago \| **Beverly Hills** | 27 |
| **NEW** STK \| **W Hollywood** | 21 |
| **NEW** Stork, The \| **Hollywood** | - |
| Sur \| **W Hollywood** | 21 |
| **Z** Tanzore \| **Beverly Hills** | 23 |
| Taylor's Steak \| **multi.** | 21 |
| Toscana \| **Brentwood** | 23 |

| | |
|---|---|
| Tracht's \| **Long Bch** | 23 |
| Ⓩ Valentino \| **Santa Monica** | 26 |
| Vertical Wine \| **Pasadena** | 23 |
| Vincenti \| **Brentwood** | 26 |
| Ⓩ Water Grill \| **Downtown** | 27 |
| Wilshire \| **Santa Monica** | 22 |
| **NEW** Wolfgang's Steak \| **Beverly Hills** | - |

## PRIVATE ROOMS

(Restaurants charge less at off times; call for capacity)

| | |
|---|---|
| Admiral Risty \| **Rancho Palos Verdes** | 20 |
| Aioli \| **Torrance** | 18 |
| Antonio's \| **Melrose** | 19 |
| Ⓩ A.O.C. \| **Third St.** | 26 |
| Ⓩ Arnie Morton's \| **multi.** | 25 |
| Arroyo Chop \| **Pasadena** | 25 |
| Banzai Sushi \| **Calabasas** | 22 |
| Barefoot B&G \| **Third St.** | 18 |
| Beau Rivage \| **Malibu** | 21 |
| Beckham Grill \| **Pasadena** | 18 |
| Ⓩ Belvedere \| **Beverly Hills** | 25 |
| Ⓩ Bistro Gdn. \| **Studio City** | 21 |
| boé \| **Beverly Hills** | 22 |
| Bravo \| **Santa Monica** | 17 |
| Buca di Beppo \| **multi.** | 15 |
| Buffalo Club \| **Santa Monica** | 20 |
| Buggy Whip \| **Westchester** | 19 |
| Buona Sera \| **Redondo Bch** | 22 |
| Ca'Brea \| **La Brea** | 22 |
| Ca' del Sole \| **N Hollywood** | 22 |
| Ⓩ Café Bizou \| **multi.** | 23 |
| Cafe Del Rey \| **Marina del Rey** | 21 |
| Cafe Pinot \| **Downtown** | 22 |
| Café Santorini \| **Pasadena** | 20 |
| Campanile \| **La Brea** | 26 |
| Canal Club \| **Venice** | 18 |
| Castaway \| **Burbank** | 13 |
| Cézanne \| **Santa Monica** | 21 |
| Chart House \| **Redondo Bch** | 19 |
| Checkers \| **Downtown** | 20 |
| Chez Jay \| **Santa Monica** | 16 |
| Ⓩ Chez Mélange \| **Redondo Bch** | 25 |
| Chez Mimi \| **Santa Monica** | 22 |
| Ⓩ Christine \| **Torrance** | 26 |
| Ⓩ Cicada \| **Downtown** | 23 |
| Courtyard \| **W Hollywood** | 19 |
| Ⓩ Dal Rae \| **Pico Rivera** | 25 |
| Dar Maghreb \| **Hollywood** | 20 |
| Depot \| **Torrance** | 24 |
| Derby \| **Arcadia** | 23 |
| Ⓩ Derek's \| **Pasadena** | 27 |
| Devon \| **Monrovia** | 23 |
| Drago \| **Santa Monica** | 24 |

| | |
|---|---|
| Duke's \| **Malibu** | 17 |
| El Cholo \| **multi.** | 18 |
| El Torito \| **multi.** | 15 |
| Enoteca Drago \| **Beverly Hills** | 21 |
| Fleming's \| **El Segundo** | 25 |
| Gaucho Grill \| **Studio City** | 17 |
| Geisha Hse. \| **Hollywood** | 20 |
| Giorgio Baldi \| **Santa Monica** | 24 |
| Gladstone's \| **Pacific Palisades** | 14 |
| Gordon Biersch \| **multi.** | 16 |
| Grace \| **Beverly Blvd.** | 25 |
| Hal's B&G \| **Venice** | 20 |
| Il Cielo \| **Beverly Hills** | 21 |
| Il Fornaio \| **multi.** | 20 |
| Il Moro \| **West LA** | 23 |
| Il Sole \| **W Hollywood** | 24 |
| Ⓩ Inn/Seventh Ray \| **Topanga** | 20 |
| James' Bch. \| **Venice** | 18 |
| Jones \| **W Hollywood** | 18 |
| Katana \| **W Hollywood** | 23 |
| Kate Mantilini \| **Beverly Hills** | 18 |
| Kendall's Brass. \| **Downtown** | 17 |
| King's Fish \| **Long Bch** | 21 |
| Ⓩ La Cachette \| **Century City** | 27 |
| Ⓩ Langham Huntington \| **Pasadena** | 26 |
| La Terza \| **Third St.** | 22 |
| Ⓩ Lawry's Prime \| **Beverly Hills** | 24 |
| Ⓩ Little Door \| **Third St.** | 23 |
| L'Opera \| **Long Bch** | 23 |
| Ⓩ Madison, The \| **Long Bch** | 20 |
| Maggiano's \| **multi.** | 18 |
| Marino \| **Hollywood** | 21 |
| Massimo \| **Beverly Hills** | 22 |
| Ⓩ Mastro's Steak \| **Beverly Hills** | 26 |
| Ⓩ Matsuhisa \| **Beverly Hills** | 27 |
| McCormick/Schmick \| **multi.** | 19 |
| McKenna's \| **Long Bch** | 19 |
| Michael's \| **Santa Monica** | 24 |
| Monsoon Cafe \| **Santa Monica** | 18 |
| Morels French Steak \| **Fairfax** | 18 |
| Napa Valley \| **Westwood** | 20 |
| Nick & Stef's Steak \| **Downtown** | 23 |
| Ⓩ One Pico \| **Santa Monica** | 22 |
| Ortolan \| **Third St.** | 25 |
| Pacific Dining Car \| **multi.** | 22 |
| Palm, The \| **multi.** | 23 |
| Ⓩ Parkway Grill \| **Pasadena** | 26 |
| Patina \| **Downtown** | 25 |
| Pinot Bistro \| **Studio City** | 23 |
| Polo Lounge \| **Beverly Hills** | 22 |
| P6 Rest. \| **Westlake Vill** | 22 |
| R23 \| **Downtown** | 26 |
| Ⓩ Ruth's Chris \| **Beverly Hills** | 26 |
| Simon LA \| **W Hollywood** | 21 |

subscribe to ZAGAT.com

| | |
|---|---|
| Smitty's Grill \| **Pasadena** | 21 |
| **Z** Sona \| **W Hollywood** | 27 |
| Sonora Cafe \| **La Brea** | 22 |
| **Z** Spago \| **Beverly Hills** | 27 |
| Suki 7 \| **Westlake Vill** | 19 |
| Tanino \| **Westwood** | 23 |
| Tantra \| **Silver Lake** | 20 |
| Thousand Cranes \| **Little Tokyo** | 21 |
| Urasawa \| **Beverly Hills** | 28 |
| **Z** Valentino \| **Santa Monica** | 26 |
| Vibrato \| **Bel-Air** | 21 |
| Villa Sorriso \| **Pasadena** | 16 |
| Woo Lae Oak \| **Beverly Hills** | 22 |
| **Z** Yamashiro \| **Hollywood** | 18 |
| Zucca \| **Downtown** | 21 |

## QUIET CONVERSATION

| | |
|---|---|
| Asaka \| **Rancho Palos Verdes** | 18 |
| Baleen \| **Redondo Bch** | 20 |
| **Z** Bastide \| **W Hollywood** | 27 |
| Bella Roma \| **Pico-Robertson** | 23 |
| **Z** Belvedere \| **Beverly Hills** | 25 |
| Bloom Cafe \| **Mid-City** | 22 |
| Blossom \| **Downtown** | 22 |
| Blvd \| **Beverly Hills** | 20 |
| boé \| **Beverly Hills** | 22 |
| Boulevard Lounge \| **W Hollywood** | 19 |
| Breeze \| **Century City** | 17 |
| Café 14 \| **Agoura Hills** | 24 |
| Caffe Primo \| **W Hollywood** | 19 |
| Caffe Roma \| **Beverly Hills** | 17 |
| **Z** Capo \| **Santa Monica** | 26 |
| Cézanne \| **Santa Monica** | 21 |
| Chaba \| **Redondo Bch** | 20 |
| Chadaka \| **Burbank** | 24 |
| Checkers \| **Downtown** | 20 |
| Chez Mimi \| **Santa Monica** | 22 |
| Circa 55 \| **Beverly Hills** | 19 |
| Coast \| **Santa Monica** | 21 |
| Coco Noche \| **Manhattan Bch** | 17 |
| Corkscrew \| **Manhattan Bch** | 21 |
| Coupa Café \| **Beverly Hills** | 17 |
| CrêpeVine \| **Pasadena** | 21 |
| cube \| **La Brea** | 22 |
| Cucina Paradiso \| **Palms** | 21 |
| Dakota \| **Hollywood** | 22 |
| **NEW** Del, The \| **Playa del Rey** | 20 |
| **Z** Derek's \| **Pasadena** | 27 |
| Drago \| **Santa Monica** | 24 |
| Dusty's \| **Silver Lake** | 18 |
| eat. on sunset \| **Hollywood** | 18 |
| Encounter \| **LAX** | 14 |
| Enzo & Angela \| **West LA** | 22 |
| Five 61 \| **Pasadena** | 22 |
| **Z** Fraîche \| **Culver City** | 24 |

| | |
|---|---|
| Gardens \| **Beverly Hills** | 23 |
| **NEW** Gordon Ramsay \| **W Hollywood** | - |
| Grace \| **Beverly Blvd.** | 25 |
| **Z** Hampton's \| **Westlake Vill** | 23 |
| **Z** Hatfield's \| **Beverly Blvd.** | 27 |
| Holdren's Steak \| **Thousand Oaks** | 21 |
| **Z** Hotel Bel-Air \| **Bel-Air** | 25 |
| Il Grano \| **West LA** | 26 |
| JJ Steak \| **Pasadena** | 23 |
| **NEW** Kula \| **Century City** | 15 |
| La Botte \| **Santa Monica** | 25 |
| **Z** La Cachette \| **Century City** | 27 |
| La Maschera \| **Pasadena** | 22 |
| **Z** Langham Huntington \| **Pasadena** | 26 |
| Larkin's \| **Eagle Rock** | 20 |
| **NEW** Larsen's Steak \| **Encino** | - |
| La Sosta \| **Hermosa Bch** | 26 |
| Madeleine's \| **Pasadena** | 24 |
| Madeo \| **W Hollywood** | 24 |
| Magnolia Lounge \| **Pasadena** | 19 |
| Marino \| **Hollywood** | 21 |
| **Z** Mélisse \| **Santa Monica** | 28 |
| Michael's \| **Santa Monica** | 24 |
| Mirü8691 \| **Beverly Hills** | 25 |
| Neomeze \| **Pasadena** | 23 |
| **NEW** Oak Room \| **Pacific Palisades** | - |
| **NEW** Oba Sushi Izakaya \| **Pasadena** | - |
| Ocean & Vine \| **Santa Monica** | 21 |
| **Z** One Pico \| **Santa Monica** | 22 |
| One Sunset \| **W Hollywood** | 20 |
| On Sunset \| **Brentwood** | 22 |
| Ortolan \| **Third St.** | 25 |
| Polo Lounge \| **Beverly Hills** | 22 |
| Porto Alegre \| **Pasadena** | 20 |
| **Z** Providence \| **Hollywood** | 26 |
| Raymond, The \| **Pasadena** | 24 |
| Saluzzi \| **Rancho Palos Verdes** | 22 |
| 750 ml \| **S Pasadena** | 19 |
| **NEW** Siena \| **Pasadena** | - |
| **Z** Sona \| **W Hollywood** | 27 |
| Sur \| **W Hollywood** | 21 |
| Sushi Ozekii \| **Beverly Hills** | 17 |
| **Z** Tanzore \| **Beverly Hills** | 23 |
| Tasca Winebar \| **Third St.** | 23 |
| **NEW** Third & Olive \| **Burbank** | - |
| 3rd Stop \| **W Hollywood** | 17 |
| Thousand Cranes \| **Little Tokyo** | 21 |
| Three on Fourth \| **Santa Monica** | 21 |
| Tower Bar \| **W Hollywood** | 21 |
| Tracht's \| **Long Bch** | 23 |
| Trails, The \| **Los Feliz** | 16 |
| Tre Venezie \| **Pasadena** | 25 |

LOS ANGELES

SPECIAL FEATURES

Ugo/Italian | **Culver City** 17
Upstairs 2 | **West LA** 24
🅉 Valentino | **Santa Monica** 26
Vito | **Santa Monica** 20
Watercress | **Sherman Oaks** 21
Wilshire | **Santa Monica** 22
Wilson | **Culver City** 22
**NEW** Wolfgang's Steak | ‑
  **Beverly Hills**
York, The | **Highland Pk** 18

## RAW BARS

**NEW** Anisette | **Santa Monica** ‑
Bluewater Grill | **Redondo Bch** 19
Canal Club | **Venice** 18
Checkers | **Downtown** 20
Circa 55 | **Beverly Hills** 19
Coast | **Santa Monica** 21
**NEW** Comme Ça | **W Hollywood** 21
Gladstone's | **Pacific Palisades** 14
Gulfstream | **Century City** 21
Hungry Cat | **Hollywood** 24
Kendall's Brass. | **Downtown** 17
King's Fish | **multi.** 21
McKenna's | **Long Bch** 19
Neptune's Net | **Malibu** 18
Ocean Ave. | **Santa Monica** 23
🅉 Water Grill | **Downtown** 27

## ROMANTIC PLACES

Adagio | **Woodland Hills** 23
Alessio | **Simi Valley** 21
**NEW** Anisette | **Santa Monica** ‑
Baleen | **Redondo Bch** 20
🅉 Bastide | **W Hollywood** 27
Beau Rivage | **Malibu** 21
Bella Cucina | **Hollywood** 23
Bella Roma | **Pico-Robertson** 23
🅉 Belvedere | **Beverly Hills** 25
Bistro de la Gare | **S Pasadena** 19
Bistro 45 | **Pasadena** 26
Blvd | **Beverly Hills** 20
🅉 Brandywine | **Woodland Hills** 27
Brentwood, The | **Brentwood** 21
Cafe Del Rey | **Marina del Rey** 21
Cafe des Artistes | **Hollywood** 20
Caffe Roma | **Beverly Hills** 17
🅉 Capo | **Santa Monica** 26
**NEW** Carbon Beach | **Malibu** 13
Catch | **Santa Monica** 22
Cézanne | **Santa Monica** 21
Checkers | **Downtown** 20
Chez Mimi | **Santa Monica** 22
**NEW** Comme Ça | **W Hollywood** 21
Courtyard | **W Hollywood** 19
Craft | **Century City** 25

CrêpeVine | **Pasadena** 21
Cucina Paradiso | **Palms** 21
🅉 Derek's | **Pasadena** 27
Dominick's | **Beverly Blvd.** 21
Encounter | **LAX** 14
Foundry, The | **Melrose** 23
🅉 Fraîche | **Culver City** 24
Gardens | **Beverly Hills** 23
🅉 Geoffrey's | **Malibu** 21
Getty Ctr. | **Brentwood** 22
**NEW** Gordon Ramsay | ‑
  **W Hollywood**
Grace | **Beverly Blvd.** 25
🅉 Hampton's | **Westlake Vill** 23
🅉 Hatfield's | **Beverly Blvd.** 27
🅉 Hotel Bel-Air | **Bel-Air** 25
Il Cielo | **Beverly Hills** 21
Il Sole | **W Hollywood** 24
🅉 Inn/Seventh Ray | **Topanga** 20
Jer-ne | **Marina del Rey** 20
🅉 Joe's | **Venice** 26
Josie | **Santa Monica** 26
🅉 La Boheme | **W Hollywood** 22
La Botte | **Santa Monica** 25
🅉 La Cachette | **Century City** 27
L.A. Farm | **Santa Monica** 20
La Maschera | **Pasadena** 22
🅉 Langham Huntington | 26
  **Pasadena**
**NEW** Larsen's Steak | **Encino** ‑
La Sosta | **Hermosa Bch** 26
Le Chêne | **Saugus** 23
Le Marmiton | **Marina del Rey** 18
🅉 Little Door | **Third St.** 23
Lou | **Hollywood** 23
🅉 Lucques | **W Hollywood** 27
Madeleine's | **Pasadena** 24
🅉 Mélisse | **Santa Monica** 28
**NEW** Mes Amis | **Los Feliz** 16
Michael's | **Santa Monica** 24
**NEW** Michael's/Naples | ‑
  **Long Bch**
Noé | **Downtown** 24
Ortolan | **Third St.** 25
Parc | **Hollywood** 21
Patina | **Downtown** 25
🅉 Penthouse | **Santa Monica** 18
Piccolo | **Venice** 27
Pinot Bistro | **Studio City** 23
Porto Alegre | **Pasadena** 20
🅉 Providence | **Hollywood** 26
Raymond, The | **Pasadena** 24
Red 7 | **W Hollywood** 24
Rustic Canyon | **Santa Monica** 21
🅉 Saddle Peak | **Calabasas** 26
750 ml | **S Pasadena** 19

Simon LA | **W Hollywood** 21
Sir Winston's | **Long Bch** 21
Sky Room | **Long Bch** 21
🅩 Sona | **W Hollywood** 27
🅩 Spago | **Beverly Hills** 27
**NEW** Stork, The | **Hollywood** -
Sur | **W Hollywood** 21
🅩 Tanzore | **Beverly Hills** 23
Taste | **W Hollywood** 23
Tower Bar | **W Hollywood** 21
Tracht's | **Long Bch** 23
🅩 Valentino | **Santa Monica** 26
Vertical Wine | **Pasadena** 23
Vito | **Santa Monica** 20
🅩 Yamashiro | **Hollywood** 18

## SINGLES SCENES

Abbey | **W Hollywood** 14
Alessio | **Simi Valley** 21
**NEW** Amaranta | **Canoga Pk** 20
Beechwood | **Marina del Rey** 18
bld | **Beverly Blvd.** 21
Blue Velvet | **Downtown** 20
**NEW** Blvd 16 | **Westwood** -
Boa | **W Hollywood** 23
Border Grill | **Santa Monica** 21
BottleRock | **Culver City** 16
Boulevard Lounge | **W Hollywood** 19
Bowery | **Hollywood** 20
**NEW** Brix 1601 | **Hermosa Bch** -
Café Santorini | **Pasadena** 20
Caffe Roma | **Beverly Hills** 17
Canal Club | **Venice** 18
Chapter 8 | **Agoura Hills** 17
Charcoal | **Hollywood** 11
Chaya | **W Hollywood** 24
Chaya | **Venice** 22
Cheebo | **Hollywood** 19
Chez Jay | **Santa Monica** 16
Citizen Smith | **Hollywood** 17
Ciudad | **Downtown** 21
**NEW** Comme Ça | **W Hollywood** 21
Craft | **Century City** 25
Dominick's | **Beverly Blvd.** 21
El Coyote | **Beverly Blvd.** 13
Electric Lotus | **Los Feliz** 18
🅩 Father's Office | **multi.** 24
Fleming's | **multi.** 25
Ford's | **Culver City** 19
Formosa Cafe | **W Hollywood** 12
Foundry, The | **Melrose** 23
Geisha Hse. | **Hollywood** 20
Gordon Biersch | **multi.** 16
Hal's B&G | **Venice** 20
Hama Sushi | **Venice** 21
i Cugini | **Santa Monica** 21

James' Bch. | **Venice** 18
Jones | **W Hollywood** 18
🅩 Katsuya | **multi.** 24
Ketchup | **W Hollywood** 15
**NEW** Kitchen 24 | **Hollywood** -
Koi | **W Hollywood** 24
**NEW** Kress, The | **Hollywood** -
Liberty Grill | **Downtown** 18
Magnolia | **Hollywood** 19
Magnolia Lounge | **Pasadena** 19
Marty's | **Highland Pk** 18
🅩 Mastro's Steak | **Beverly Hills** 26
McCormick/Schmick | **multi.** 19
Minx | **Glendale** 18
Moonshadows | **Malibu** 17
**NEW** Mucho Ultima | **Manhattan Bch** 19
Nick & Stef's Steak | **Downtown** 23
Ocean Ave. | **Santa Monica** 23
Palm, The | **W Hollywood** 23
Parc | **Hollywood** 21
🅩 Parkway Grill | **Pasadena** 26
🅩 Penthouse | **Santa Monica** 18
🅩 Pizzeria Mozza | **Hollywood** 26
Primitivo | **Venice** 20
P6 Rest. | **Westlake Vill** 22
Rack | **Woodland Hills** 16
RA Sushi | **Torrance** 16
Rock'n Fish | **Manhattan Bch** 21
**NEW** Rush Street | **Culver City** -
Rustic Canyon | **Santa Monica** 21
Safire | **Camarillo** 21
Salt Creek | **El Segundo** 18
750 ml | **S Pasadena** 19
Simon LA | **W Hollywood** 21
Standard, The | **W Hollywood** 15
Stanley's | **Sherman Oaks** 19
Suki 7 | **Westlake Vill** 19
Sushi Roku | **multi.** 22
Swingers | **Beverly Blvd.** 17
🅩 Tanzore | **Beverly Hills** 23
Tasca Winebar | **Third St.** 23
Tengu | **Westwood** 22
**NEW** Tinto | **W Hollywood** 20
Tracht's | **Long Bch** 23
25 Degrees | **Hollywood** 21
Twin Palms | **Pasadena** 18
Urth Caffé | **W Hollywood** 20
Vault, The | **Pasadena** 14
Village Idiot | **Melrose** 19
Wabi-Sabi | **Venice** 22
Wilshire | **Santa Monica** 22
Yatai Tapas | **W Hollywood** -
Ye Olde King's | **Santa Monica** 17
York, The | **Highland Pk** 18

## SLEEPERS

(Good to excellent food, but little known)

| | |
|---|---|
| Azami \| Hollywood | 25 |
| Bella Cucina \| Hollywood | 23 |
| Bella Roma \| Pico-Robertson | 23 |
| Boss Sushi \| Beverly Hills | 25 |
| Bulan Thai \| multi. | 25 |
| Café Pacific \| Rancho Palos Verdes | 24 |
| Café Provencal \| Thousand Oaks | 23 |
| Caffe Luxxe \| Santa Monica | 24 |
| Chef Melba's \| Hermosa Bch | 24 |
| Chung King \| Monterey Pk | 25 |
| Devon \| Monrovia | 23 |
| Elf Café \| Echo Pk | 25 |
| Fatty's & Co. \| Eagle Rock | 23 |
| Galletto \| Westlake Vill | 23 |
| Harold & Belle's \| Mid-City | 24 |
| Hayakawa \| Covina | 28 |
| Japon Bistro \| Pasadena | 25 |
| La Huasteca \| Lynwood | 26 |
| La Sosta \| Hermosa Bch | 26 |
| Le Chêne \| Saugus | 23 |
| Le Sanglier \| Tarzana | 24 |
| Madeleine Bistro \| Tarzana | 24 |
| Marouch \| E Hollywood | 23 |
| Mirü8691 \| Beverly Hills | 25 |
| Nanbankan \| West LA | 24 |
| Neomeze \| Pasadena | 23 |
| Nishimura \| W Hollywood | 26 |
| Omino Sushi \| Chatsworth | 25 |
| Onyx \| Westlake Vill | 25 |
| Petrossian \| W Hollywood | 23 |
| Red Corner Asia \| E Hollywood | 25 |
| Red 7 \| W Hollywood | 24 |
| Ruen Pair \| E Hollywood | 24 |
| Rustico \| Westlake Vill | 23 |
| Saito's Sushi \| Silver Lake | 24 |
| Shima \| Venice | 27 |
| Sushi Duke \| Hermosa Bch | 23 |
| Sushi Sushi \| Beverly Hills | 24 |
| Sushi Zo \| West LA | 29 |
| Tiara Cafe \| Downtown | 23 |
| Tulipano \| Azusa | 24 |
| Wa \| W Hollywood | 25 |
| Woody's BBQ \| multi. | 23 |
| Yuzu \| Torrance | 23 |

## SPECIAL OCCASIONS

| | |
|---|---|
| NEW Anisette \| Santa Monica | – |
| Baleen \| Redondo Bch | 20 |
| Z Bastide \| W Hollywood | 27 |
| Bella Roma \| Pico-Robertson | 23 |
| Z Belvedere \| Beverly Hills | 25 |
| Bistro 45 \| Pasadena | 26 |
| NEW BLT Steak \| W Hollywood | 23 |
| Blue Velvet \| Downtown | 20 |
| Blvd \| Beverly Hills | 20 |
| Boulevard Lounge \| W Hollywood | 19 |
| Chapter 8 \| Agoura Hills | 17 |
| Z Chinois \| Santa Monica | 26 |
| Z Cicada \| Downtown | 23 |
| Circa 55 \| Beverly Hills | 19 |
| NEW Citrus at Social \| Hollywood | 21 |
| Coast \| Santa Monica | 21 |
| NEW Comme Ça \| W Hollywood | 21 |
| Craft \| Century City | 25 |
| Z CUT \| Beverly Hills | 26 |
| Drago \| Santa Monica | 24 |
| E. Baldi \| Beverly Hills | 22 |
| Fleming's \| Woodland Hills | 25 |
| Foundry, The \| Melrose | 23 |
| Z Fraîche \| Culver City | 24 |
| NEW Giggles 'n Hugs \| West LA | – |
| NEW Gordon Ramsay \| W Hollywood | – |
| Grace \| Beverly Blvd. | 25 |
| Z Hampton's \| Westlake Vill | 23 |
| Hatfield's \| Beverly Blvd. | 27 |
| Z Hotel Bel-Air \| Bel-Air | 25 |
| Jar \| Beverly Blvd. | 25 |
| Z Joe's \| Venice | 26 |
| Josie \| Santa Monica | 26 |
| Z La Boheme \| W Hollywood | 22 |
| La Botte \| Santa Monica | 25 |
| Z La Cachette \| Century City | 27 |
| La Maschera \| Pasadena | 22 |
| NEW Larsen's Steak \| Encino | – |
| Madeleine's \| Pasadena | 24 |
| Marino \| Hollywood | 21 |
| Z Mastro's Steak \| Beverly Hills | 26 |
| Z Matsuhisa \| Beverly Hills | 27 |
| Minx \| Glendale | 18 |
| NEW Nobu \| W Hollywood | 26 |
| Noé \| Downtown | 24 |
| Ocean & Vine \| Santa Monica | 21 |
| Z One Pico \| Santa Monica | 22 |
| Ortolan \| Third St. | 25 |
| Z Osteria Mozza \| Hollywood | 26 |
| Palm, The \| W Hollywood | 23 |
| Patina \| Downtown | 25 |
| Z Petros \| Manhattan Bch | 24 |
| Z Providence \| Hollywood | 26 |
| Riordan's Tav. \| Downtown | 15 |
| Roy's \| multi. | 23 |
| Z Ruth's Chris \| Pasadena | 26 |
| Z Saddle Peak \| Calabasas | 26 |
| Safire \| Camarillo | 21 |
| Z Sona \| W Hollywood | 27 |
| Z Spago \| Beverly Hills | 27 |
| NEW Stork, The \| Hollywood | – |

| | | |
|---|---|---|
| Tower Bar | **W Hollywood** | 21 |
| Tracht's | **Long Bch** | 23 |
| Tuscany | **Westlake Vill** | 24 |
| Urasawa | **Beverly Hills** | 28 |
| ☑ Valentino | **Santa Monica** | 26 |
| ☑ Water Grill | **Downtown** | 27 |
| **NEW** Wolfgang's Steak \| **Beverly Hills** | | - |

## TASTING MENUS

| | | |
|---|---|---|
| All' Angelo | **Melrose** | 25 |
| ☑ Asanebo | **Studio City** | 28 |
| Azami | **Hollywood** | 25 |
| Bar Hayama | **West LA** | 24 |
| Bella Roma | **Pico-Robertson** | 23 |
| Blue Velvet | **Downtown** | 20 |
| Boss Sushi | **Beverly Hills** | 25 |
| Brass.-Cap. | **Santa Monica** | 19 |
| Briganti | **S Pasadena** | 23 |
| ☑ Capo | **Santa Monica** | 26 |
| **NEW** Catalina | **Redondo Bch** | 24 |
| ☑ Christine | **Torrance** | 26 |
| ☑ Cicada | **Downtown** | 23 |
| Dakota | **Hollywood** | 22 |
| ☑ Derek's | **Pasadena** | 27 |
| Devon | **Monrovia** | 23 |
| e3rd Steak | **Downtown** | 19 |
| Foundry, The | **Melrose** | 23 |
| ☑ Gonpachi | **Beverly Hills** | 18 |
| **NEW** Gordon Ramsay \| **W Hollywood** | | - |
| Grace | **Beverly Blvd.** | 25 |
| ☑ Hatfield's | **Beverly Blvd.** | 27 |
| Hayakawa | **Covina** | 28 |
| Hirozen | **Beverly Blvd.** | 25 |
| Hokusai | **Beverly Hills** | 24 |
| i Cugini | **Santa Monica** | 21 |
| **NEW** Il Carpaccio \| **Pacific Palisades** | | 23 |
| Il Cielo | **Beverly Hills** | 21 |
| Il Grano | **West LA** | 26 |
| ☑ Inn/Seventh Ray | **Topanga** | 20 |
| Japon Bistro | **Pasadena** | 25 |
| ☑ Joe's | **Venice** | 26 |
| ☑ Katsuya | **multi.** | 24 |
| Koutoubia | **Westwood** | 20 |
| K-Zo | **Culver City** | 23 |
| La Botte | **Santa Monica** | 25 |
| ☑ La Cachette | **Century City** | 27 |
| **NEW** La Défence | **Koreatown** | - |
| La Maschera | **Pasadena** | 22 |
| ☑ Langham Huntington \| **Pasadena** | | 26 |
| La Terza | **Third St.** | 22 |
| ☑ Lucques | **W Hollywood** | 27 |
| Maison Akira | **Pasadena** | 25 |

| | | |
|---|---|---|
| ☑ Matsuhisa | **Beverly Hills** | 27 |
| ☑ Mélisse | **Santa Monica** | 28 |
| Michael's | **Santa Monica** | 24 |
| Napa Valley | **Westwood** | 20 |
| ☑ Nobu | **Malibu** | 27 |
| Noé | **Downtown** | 24 |
| One Sunset | **W Hollywood** | 20 |
| Ortolan | **Third St.** | 25 |
| ☑ Osteria Mozza | **Hollywood** | 26 |
| **NEW** Palate | **Glendale** | - |
| Patina | **Downtown** | 25 |
| Piccolo | **Venice** | 27 |
| Polo Lounge | **Beverly Hills** | 22 |
| ☑ Providence | **Hollywood** | 26 |
| Raymond, The | **Pasadena** | 24 |
| Red Pearl | **Hollywood** | 17 |
| redwhite+bluezz | **Pasadena** | 22 |
| ☑ Saddle Peak | **Calabasas** | 26 |
| ☑ Sona | **W Hollywood** | 27 |
| ☑ Spago | **Beverly Hills** | 27 |
| Sushi Roku | **multi.** | 22 |
| Sushi Sasabune | **West LA** | 26 |
| Sushi Sushi | **Beverly Hills** | 24 |
| Taiko | **multi.** | 20 |
| Takao | **Brentwood** | 24 |
| **NEW** Third & Olive | **Burbank** | - |
| Tiara Cafe | **Downtown** | 23 |
| Towne | **Manhattan Bch** | 18 |
| ☑ Valentino | **Santa Monica** | 26 |
| Vincenti | **Brentwood** | 26 |
| Wa | **W Hollywood** | 25 |
| ☑ Water Grill | **Downtown** | 27 |
| Wilson | **Culver City** | 22 |
| Yabu | **W Hollywood** | 23 |

## TRENDY

| | | |
|---|---|---|
| Ago | **W Hollywood** | 22 |
| **NEW** Akasha | **Culver City** | 22 |
| All' Angelo | **Melrose** | 25 |
| Ammo | **Hollywood** | 22 |
| **NEW** Animal | **Fairfax** | - |
| Asia de Cuba | **W Hollywood** | 23 |
| **NEW** Bar Pintxo | **Santa Monica** | 19 |
| Beacon | **Culver City** | 22 |
| Beechwood | **Marina del Rey** | 18 |
| **NEW** Beso | **Hollywood** | - |
| bld | **Beverly Blvd.** | 21 |
| **NEW** BLT Steak | **W Hollywood** | 23 |
| blue on blue | **Beverly Hills** | 19 |
| Blue Velvet | **Downtown** | 20 |
| **NEW** Blvd 16 | **Westwood** | - |
| **NEW** Bond St. | **Beverly Hills** | 19 |
| Boulevard Lounge | **W Hollywood** | 19 |
| Bowery | **Hollywood** | 20 |
| Canelé | **Atwater Vill** | 23 |

## VIEWS

| | | | | |
|---|---|---|---|---|
| Kincaid's \| **Redondo Bch** | 20 | Craft \| **Century City** | 25 |
| Lobster, The \| **Santa Monica** | 22 | ☑ Crustacean \| **Beverly Hills** | 24 |
| Malibu Seafood \| **Malibu** | 22 | ☑ CUT \| **Beverly Hills** | 26 |
| McKenna's \| **Long Bch** | 19 | Dakota \| **Hollywood** | 22 |
| Moonshadows \| **Malibu** | 17 | Devon \| **Monrovia** | 23 |
| Noé \| **Downtown** | 24 | Dominick's \| **Beverly Blvd.** | 21 |
| Odyssey \| **Granada Hills** | 14 | Drago \| **Santa Monica** | 24 |
| ☑ One Pico \| **Santa Monica** | 22 | E. Baldi \| **Beverly Hills** | 22 |
| Paradise Cove \| **Malibu** | 15 | Fogo de Chão \| **Beverly Hills** | 24 |
| Parker's Lighthse. \| **Long Bch** | 18 | Gardens \| **Beverly Hills** | 23 |
| Patrick's \| **Santa Monica** | 17 | Geisha Hse. \| **Hollywood** | 20 |
| ☑ Penthouse \| **Santa Monica** | 18 | ☑ Geoffrey's \| **Malibu** | 21 |
| Reel Inn \| **Malibu** | 20 | **NEW** Gordon Ramsay \| **W Hollywood** | - |
| ☑ Saddle Peak \| **Calabasas** | 26 | | |
| Saluzzi \| **Rancho Palos Verdes** | 22 | Grace \| **Beverly Blvd.** | 25 |
| Sapori \| **Marina del Rey** | 20 | Grill on Hollywood \| **Hollywood** | 22 |
| Sir Winston's \| **Long Bch** | 21 | ☑ Hampton's \| **Westlake Vill** | 23 |
| Sky Room \| **Long Bch** | 21 | ☑ Hatfield's \| **Beverly Blvd.** | 27 |
| Taverna Tony \| **Malibu** | 20 | Holdren's Steak \| **Thousand Oaks** | 21 |
| Thousand Cranes \| **Little Tokyo** | 21 | Hump, The \| **Santa Monica** | 25 |
| Tony P's Dock \| **Marina del Rey** | 18 | Ivy, The \| **W Hollywood** | 22 |
| Tower Bar \| **W Hollywood** | 21 | Ivy at Shore \| **Santa Monica** | 22 |
| 22nd St. Landing \| **San Pedro** | 18 | Jar \| **Beverly Blvd.** | 25 |
| Typhoon \| **Santa Monica** | 22 | Jer-ne \| **Marina del Rey** | 20 |
| West \| **Brentwood** | 18 | ☑ JiRaffe \| **Santa Monica** | 26 |
| ☑ Yamashiro \| **Hollywood** | 18 | ☑ Joe's \| **Venice** | 26 |
| Yard Hse. \| **Long Bch** | 20 | Josie \| **Santa Monica** | 26 |
| | | ☑ La Boheme \| **W Hollywood** | 22 |
| **VISITORS ON** | | ☑ La Cachette \| **Century City** | 27 |
| **EXPENSE ACCOUNT** | | ☑ Langham Huntington \| **Pasadena** | 26 |
| Ago \| **W Hollywood** | 22 | | |
| **NEW** Anisette \| **Santa Monica** | - | ☑ Little Door \| **Third St.** | 23 |
| ☑ A.O.C. \| **Third St.** | 26 | Lobster, The \| **Santa Monica** | 22 |
| ☑ Arnie Morton's \| **multi.** | 25 | L'Opera \| **Long Bch** | 23 |
| Arroyo Chop \| **Pasadena** | 25 | ☑ Lucques \| **W Hollywood** | 27 |
| Baleen \| **Redondo Bch** | 20 | Madeleine's \| **Pasadena** | 24 |
| ☑ Bastide \| **W Hollywood** | 27 | ☑ Mako \| **Beverly Hills** | 26 |
| ☑ Belvedere \| **Beverly Hills** | 25 | ☑ Mastro's Steak \| **Beverly Hills** | 26 |
| **NEW** Beso \| **Hollywood** | - | ☑ Matsuhisa \| **Beverly Hills** | 27 |
| **NEW** BLT Steak \| **W Hollywood** | 23 | ☑ Mélisse \| **Santa Monica** | 28 |
| Blue Velvet \| **Downtown** | 20 | Michael's \| **Santa Monica** | 24 |
| Blvd \| **Beverly Hills** | 20 | Mr. Chow \| **Beverly Hills** | 21 |
| **NEW** Blvd 16 \| **Westwood** | - | Nick & Stef's Steak \| **Downtown** | 23 |
| Boa \| **W Hollywood** | 23 | Nic's \| **Beverly Hills** | 19 |
| Buffalo Club \| **Santa Monica** | 20 | **NEW** Nobu \| **W Hollywood** | 26 |
| Campanile \| **La Brea** | 26 | ☑ Nobu \| **Malibu** | 27 |
| ☑ Capo \| **Santa Monica** | 26 | ☑ One Pico \| **Santa Monica** | 22 |
| Catch \| **Santa Monica** | 22 | One Sunset \| **W Hollywood** | 20 |
| Celestino \| **Pasadena** | 23 | Ortolan \| **Third St.** | 25 |
| Chaya \| **W Hollywood** | 24 | ☑ Osteria Mozza \| **Hollywood** | 26 |
| Checkers \| **Downtown** | 20 | Pacific Dining Car \| **multi.** | 22 |
| ☑ Chinois \| **Santa Monica** | 26 | Palm, The \| **W Hollywood** | 23 |
| ☑ Cicada \| **Downtown** | 23 | ☑ Parkway Grill \| **Pasadena** | 26 |
| **NEW** Citrus at Social \| **Hollywood** | 21 | Patina \| **Downtown** | 25 |
| **NEW** Comme Ça \| **W Hollywood** | 21 | ☑ Petros \| **Manhattan Bch** | 24 |

| | |
|---|---|
| Polo Lounge \| **Beverly Hills** | 22 |
| 🅩 Providence \| **Hollywood** | 26 |
| Raymond, The \| **Pasadena** | 24 |
| Roy's \| **multi.** | 23 |
| 🅩 Ruth's Chris \| **Pasadena** | 26 |
| 🅩 Saddle Peak \| **Calabasas** | 26 |
| 🅩 Shiro \| **S Pasadena** | 27 |
| SHU \| **Bel-Air** | 21 |
| Simon LA \| **W Hollywood** | 21 |
| 🅩 Sona \| **W Hollywood** | 27 |
| NEW STK \| **W Hollywood** | 21 |
| NEW Stork, The \| **Hollywood** | - |
| Sur \| **W Hollywood** | 21 |
| Sushi Nozawa \| **Studio City** | 26 |
| Sushi Roku \| **multi.** | 22 |
| Takao \| **Brentwood** | 24 |
| Tracht's \| **Long Bch** | 23 |
| 🅩 Valentino \| **Santa Monica** | 26 |
| Vincenti \| **Brentwood** | 26 |
| 🅩 Water Grill \| **Downtown** | 27 |
| Wilshire \| **Santa Monica** | 22 |
| NEW Wolfgang's Steak \| **Beverly Hills** | - |
| 🅩 Yujean Kang's \| **Pasadena** | 25 |

## WATERSIDE

| | |
|---|---|
| Baleen \| **Redondo Bch** | 20 |
| Belmont Brew. \| **Long Bch** | 16 |
| Bluewater Grill \| **Redondo Bch** | 19 |
| Boa \| **Santa Monica** | 23 |
| Boccaccio's \| **Westlake Vill** | 22 |
| Cafe Del Rey \| **Marina del Rey** | 21 |
| Catch \| **Santa Monica** | 22 |
| Chart House \| **multi.** | 19 |
| 🅩 Cheesecake Factory \| **Redondo Bch** | 19 |
| Duke's \| **Malibu** | 17 |
| El Torito \| **Redondo Bch** | 15 |
| Gaby's \| **Marina del Rey** | 19 |
| 🅩 Geoffrey's \| **Malibu** | 21 |
| Gladstone's \| **Pacific Palisades** | 14 |
| Guido's \| **Malibu** | 19 |
| Il Boccaccio \| **Hermosa Bch** | 22 |
| 🅩 Inn/Seventh Ray \| **Topanga** | 20 |
| Ivy at Shore \| **Santa Monica** | 22 |
| Jer-ne \| **Marina del Rey** | 20 |
| Jody Maroni's \| **Venice** | 19 |
| Joe's Crab \| **multi.** | 13 |
| Kincaid's \| **Redondo Bch** | 20 |
| Lobster, The \| **Santa Monica** | 22 |
| McKenna's \| **Long Bch** | 19 |
| Mediterraneo \| **Westlake Vill** | 17 |
| Moonshadows \| **Malibu** | 17 |
| Neptune's Net \| **Malibu** | 18 |
| 🅩 One Pico \| **Santa Monica** | 22 |
| Paradise Cove \| **Malibu** | 15 |

| | |
|---|---|
| Parker's Lighthse. \| **Long Bch** | 18 |
| Ruby's \| **Redondo Bch** | 17 |
| Saluzzi \| **Rancho Palos Verdes** | 22 |
| Sapori \| **Marina del Rey** | 20 |
| Sir Winston's \| **Long Bch** | 21 |
| Sky Room \| **Long Bch** | 21 |
| Tony P's Dock \| **Marina del Rey** | 18 |
| 22nd St. Landing \| **San Pedro** | 18 |
| Yard Hse. \| **Long Bch** | 20 |

## WINE BARS

| | |
|---|---|
| Alessio \| **Northridge** | 21 |
| NEW Amarone \| **W Hollywood** | 27 |
| 🅩 A.O.C. \| **Third St.** | 26 |
| NEW Bar Pintxo \| **Santa Monica** | 19 |
| Bellavino \| **Westlake Vill** | 19 |
| Bistro de la Gare \| **S Pasadena** | 19 |
| BottleRock \| **Culver City** | 16 |
| Broadway Deli \| **Santa Monica** | 15 |
| Cafe Stella \| **Silver Lake** | 21 |
| C & O \| **Marina del Rey** | 18 |
| Coco Noche \| **Manhattan Bch** | 17 |
| Corkscrew \| **Manhattan Bch** | 21 |
| CrêpeVine \| **Pasadena** | 21 |
| Enoteca Drago \| **Beverly Hills** | 21 |
| Enoteca Toscana \| **Camarillo** | 19 |
| Fleming's \| **multi.** | 25 |
| 🅩 Frenchy's Bistro \| **Long Bch** | 26 |
| Hungry Cat \| **Hollywood** | 24 |
| La Sosta \| **Hermosa Bch** | 26 |
| 🅩 Leila's \| **Oak Pk** | 27 |
| Lilly's French Cafe \| **Venice** | 19 |
| Lou \| **Hollywood** | 23 |
| Madeleine's \| **Pasadena** | 24 |
| Minotaure \| **Playa del Rey** | 20 |
| Monsieur Marcel \| **Fairfax** | 21 |
| Neomeze \| **Pasadena** | 23 |
| Petrossian \| **W Hollywood** | 23 |
| Primitivo \| **Venice** | 20 |
| 750 ml \| **S Pasadena** | 19 |
| Tasca Winebar \| **Third St.** | 23 |
| NEW Tinto \| **W Hollywood** | 20 |
| 25 Degrees \| **Hollywood** | 21 |
| Upstairs 2 \| **West LA** | 24 |
| 🅩 Valentino \| **Santa Monica** | 26 |
| Vertical Wine \| **Pasadena** | 23 |
| NEW Vinotéque \| **Culver City** | - |
| Violet \| **Santa Monica** | 22 |
| Wine Bistro \| **Studio City** | 21 |

## WINNING WINE LISTS

| | |
|---|---|
| Ago \| **W Hollywood** | 22 |
| NEW Akasha \| **Culver City** | 22 |
| All' Angelo \| **Melrose** | 25 |
| NEW Anisette \| **Santa Monica** | - |
| 🅩 A.O.C. \| **Third St.** | 26 |

## WORTH A TRIP

Camarillo
  Safire — 21

Conejo Valley/Simi Valley
  **Z** Leila's — 27
  Mandevilla — 22
  Padri — 21
  P6 Rest. — 22
  Suki 7 — 19
  Tuscany — 24

Long Beach
  555 East — 24
  **Z** Frenchy's Bistro — 26
  L'Opera — 23
  Sky Room — 21

Malibu
  **Z** Geoffrey's — 21
  **Z** Nobu — 27

Manhattan Beach
  **Z** Petros — 24

Monrovia
  Devon — 23

San Gabriel Valley
  **Z** Babita — 26
  Empress Harbor — 19
  Golden Deli — 23
  Hayakawa — 28
  NBC Seafood — 19
  Ocean Star — 21

San Pedro
  **Z** Papadakis Tav. — 21

Saugus
  Le Chêne — 23

South Bay
  Café Pierre — 22
  **Z** Chez Mélange — 25
  **Z** Christine — 26
  Il Boccaccio — 22
  Sea Empress — 19

Woodland Hills
  Gorikee — 22

subscribe to ZAGAT.com

# ORANGE COUNTY

# Top Food

Ratings are to the left of names.

| | | |
|---|---|---|
| 29 | Tabu Grill | *Seafood/Steak* |

| | | |
|---|---|---|
| 28 | Tradition by Pascal | *French* |
| | Napa Rose | *Californian* |

| | | |
|---|---|---|
| 27 | Stonehill Tavern | *American* |
| | Hobbit | *Cont./French* |

Marché Moderne | *French*
Bluefin | *Japanese*
Basilic | *French/Swiss*
Cafe Zoolu | *Californian*

| | | |
|---|---|---|
| 26 | Studio | *Californian/French* |

# Top Decor

| | |
|---|---|
| 29 | Stonehill Tavern |
| 28 | Studio |
| 27 | Pelican Grill |
| | Summit House |
| | Mastro's Ocean |

Napa Rose

| | |
|---|---|
| 26 | Hobbit |
| | Ritz Rest. & Gdn. |
| 25 | Splashes |
| | 162', Rest. |

# Top Service

| | |
|---|---|
| 28 | Hobbit |
| 27 | Studio |
| | Tabu Grill |
| | Napa Rose |
| 26 | Ritz Rest. & Gdn. |

Park Ave.
Tradition by Pascal
Mr. Stox
Stonehill Tavern

| | |
|---|---|
| 25 | Cat & Custard Cup |

## BY LOCATION

### ANAHEIM

| | |
|---|---|
| 28 | Napa Rose |
| 26 | Ruth's Chris |
| 25 | Morton's Steak |

### CORONA DEL MAR

| | |
|---|---|
| 24 | Five Crowns |
| 23 | Crow Bar |

### COSTA MESA

| | |
|---|---|
| 27 | Marché Moderne |
| 26 | Mastro's Steak |
| 25 | Golden Truffle |

### IRVINE

| | |
|---|---|
| 26 | Ruth's Chris |
| 25 | Wasa |
| 24 | Bistango |

### LAGUNA BEACH

| | |
|---|---|
| 29 | Tabu Grill |
| 27 | Cafe Zoolu |
| 26 | Studio |

### NEWPORT BEACH

| | |
|---|---|
| 28 | Tradition by Pascal |
| 27 | Basilic |
| 25 | Ritz Rest. & Gdn. |

| | FOOD | DECOR | SERVICE | COST |
|---|---|---|---|---|

### Abe *Japanese*
**24 | 15 | 20 | $43**

**Newport Beach** | 2900 Newport Blvd. (29th St.) | 949-675-1739
Despite a "tiny", "unimpressive" setting and a few laments that it's "not the same" since the namesake founder left, peninsula insiders insist the "superb sushi" "cures all doubts" at this Newport Beach Japanese; pricey tasting menus are available at dinner, but many rave about the "incredible omakase lunch" that's "delicious, beautifully plated" and a "great deal" to boot.

### Antonello ⊠ *Italian*
**24 | 24 | 24 | $57**

**Santa Ana** | South Coast Plaza | 3800 S. Plaza Dr. (Sunflower Ave.) | 714-751-7153 | www.antonello.com
The "grande dame of OC restaurants", this "classy" South Coast Plaza "institution" lures the expense-account elite with "first-rate" Italian cuisine and a wine cellar stocked with "scarce regional gems"; though cynics declare the food "underwhelming", the "lush" palazzo setting and "gracious" service redeems, prompting proponents to judge it among "the area's best" for a "truly pleasurable experience."

### Basilic ⊠M *French/Swiss*
**27 | 19 | 25 | $56**

**Newport Beach** | 217 Marine Ave. (Park Ave.) | 949-673-0570 | www.basilicrestaurant.com
"Tiny but mighty", this Newport Beach "hideaway" attracts "locals in-the-know" for "splendid" feasts of "top-level" Swiss-French fare crafted by chef-owner Bernard Althaus; though the "quaint" country-style quarters "border on cramped", "personable" servers keep the mood "warm", and also smooth the sting of "hefty" price tags; P.S. "be sure to make a reservation" because this "gem" seats only 24.

### Bayside *American*
**24 | 22 | 23 | $52**

**Newport Beach** | 900 Bayside Dr. (Jamboree Rd.) | 949-721-1222 | www.baysiderestaurant.com
For "business lunches" or "impressing a date", surveyors count on this "lovely" "high-end" spot on Newport Bay's southern inlet for "creative" New American fare set down by an "attentive" staff; its "beautiful" art-filled setting (look for the "unusual wine cellar tower") gets a lift from live jazz nightly, while the wraparound patio proves a more "relaxed" setting, perfect for Sunday's champagne brunch.

### Bistango ⊠ *American*
**24 | 23 | 23 | $49**

**Irvine** | Atrium | 19100 Von Karman Ave. (bet. Campus Dr. & DuPont Ave.) | 949-752-5222 | www.bistango.com
"Dependable" New American cooking with an "artistic" touch makes this "solid performer" in Irvine's "high-rise" district a "top target" for exec lunches or a "romantic" evening out; "top-notch" service adds to the appeal, while its "fantastic" setting owes its "cool, urban vibe" to rotating "gallery" exhibits and "great jazz" nightly.

### Black Sheep Bistro ⊠M *French/Spanish*
**25 | 17 | 25 | $47**

**Tustin** | 303 El Camino Real (3rd St.) | 714-544-6060 | www.blacksheepbistro.com
"Elegant yet earthy", this "cozy" Tustin bistro transports its flock to "Europe" with "authentic" and "creative" French-Spanish cooking (the "lamb dishes" are "tops") "served impeccably" by a "knowledgeable" staff; hosts Rick and Diana Bouffard "make you feel welcome" in their

homespun storefront, and if some demur on pricey tabs, wallet-watchers insist the "midweek specials" – like their "paella nights" – are a deal.

**Bluefin** *Japanese*      27 | 21 | 23 | $59

**Newport Coast** | Crystal Cove Promenade | 7952 E. PCH (Crystal Heights Dr.) | 949-715-7373 | www.bluefinbyabe.com

Acolytes of chef-owner Takashi Abe find "sheer perfection" in his "beautifully plated" sushi and "buttery sashimi" at this "tony" Japanese "gem" tucked into the Crystal Cove Promenade; the spare and "modern" digs "with a peek of the ocean" prove a pull for "yuppies" and "the wealthy kids of OC", so expect "great people-watching" along with platinum-card pricing; P.S. it's "more affordable" at lunch.

**Café Hiro** Ⓜ *Asian Fusion*      25 | 10 | 17 | $27

**Cypress** | 10509 Valley View St. (Cerritos Ave.) | 714-527-6090 | www.cafehiro.com

Connoisseurs claim this "mini-mall gem" in "unglamorous Cypress" "tingles the taste buds" with "original" French- and Italian-influenced Asian fusion dishes like sea urchin risotto at "bargain" prices that "would be double the cost in LA"; since its "tiny" digs can only accommodate "just so many diners a night", regulars suggest "reservations" or try to snag a counter seat offering a "peek at the chefs" in the open kitchen.

**Cafe Zoolu** Ⓜ *Californian*      27 | 13 | 20 | $44

**Laguna Beach** | 860 Glenneyre St. (bet. St. Anne's Dr. & Thalia St.) | 949-494-6825 | www.cafezoolu.com

A "truly Laguna crowd" fills up this "funky" "local favorite" where the "terrific" charbroiled swordfish is the standout on the "amazing" Californian menu; though the vaguely "Hawaiian" quarters can seem "cramped", the congenial staff "makes you feel at home" ensuring "everyone is in for a good time"; N.B. reservations recommended.

**Cat &**      26 | 23 | 25 | $50
**The Custard Cup, The** *American/Californian*

**La Habra** | 800 E. Whittier Blvd. (Harbor Blvd.) | 562-694-3812 | www.catandcustardcup.com

"Hidden" in "unlikely" La Habra, this "romantic" respite charms customers with its "intimate" "tavern-like" digs, flickering fireplace and hospitality that shows the "pride of family ownership"; its "delicious" Cal-New American menu earns accolades from diners, while oenophiles appreciate the "phenomenal" wine list with "half-price specials" on Monday and Tuesday nights; N.B. a jazz pianist provides accompaniment Tuesdays–Saturdays.

**Ⓩ Cheesecake Factory** *American*      19 | 18 | 18 | $27

🆕 **Anaheim** | Anaheim GardenWalk | 321 W. Katella Ave. (Clementine St.) | 714-533-7500

**Brea** | 120 Brea Mall (Imperial Hwy.) | 714-255-0115 ◑

**Irvine** | Irvine Spectrum Ctr. | 71 Fortune Dr. (Pacifica St.) | 949-788-9998

**Mission Viejo** | Shops at Mission Viejo | 42 The Shops at Mission Viejo (I-5 at Crown Valley Pkwy.) | 949-364-6200

**Newport Beach** | Fashion Island | 1141 Newport Center Dr. (Santa Barbara Dr.) | 949-720-8333

www.thecheesecakefactory.com

Additional locations throughout Southern California

See review in Los Angeles Directory.

| | FOOD | DECOR | SERVICE | COST |
|---|---|---|---|---|

### NEW Crow Bar & Kitchen  Gastropub      | 23 | 21 | 23 | $33 |

**Corona del Mar** | 2325 E. PCH (PCH & McArehur) | 949-675-0070 |
www.thecrowbarcdm.com

"Finally a gastropub for us" crow fans of this Corona del Mar newcomer
delivering "creative", "excellent" Eclectic small plates alongside a "well-
thought-out" beer and wine selection; with rustic but "modern" decor,
"good" service and "reasonable" prices, it's "justifiably popular" with
the "local 'in' crowd", and "quite the hot spot at night."

### First Cabin  American/Continental      | 24 | 22 | 25 | $66 |

**Newport Beach** | Balboa Bay Club Resort & Spa | 1221 W. PCH (east of
Newport Blvd.) | 949-645-5000 | www.balboabayclub.com

"If you're looking for old-school, this is it" affirm admirers of this
"lovely", high-end Newport venue where the waterside views of bobbing
boats are "beautiful" and the "ambitious" menu yields "excellent"
American-Continental cuisine; capping it off, the "A-plus" service evokes
a "well-run private club", though it's all a bit too "sedate" for some.

### Five Crowns  Continental      | 24 | 22 | 24 | $52 |

**Corona del Mar** | 3801 E. PCH (Poppy Ave.) | 949-760-0331 |
www.lawrysonline.com

"Beef eaters can't go wrong" at this "olde" British-style "grande
dame" in Corona del Mar, where plates of "perfectly cooked"
Lawry's prime rib and other "tasty" Continental selections are pur-
veyed by a "great" staff; while the "traditional" surroundings strike
some as "dated", the majority maintains it's "warm" and "cozy",
particularly at "Christmas with carolers at your table;" P.S. "Sunday
brunch on the patio" is also "excellent."

### Five Feet  Chinese/French      | 23 | 17 | 20 | $54 |

**Laguna Beach** | 328 Glenneyre St. (bet. Forest Ave. & Mermaid St.) |
949-497-4955 | www.fivefeetrestaurants.com

"There isn't an ordinary dish on the menu" assert advocates of this
"funky" "find" in Laguna Beach distinguished by the "inventive"
Chinese-French cuisine of chef-owner Michael Kang (his "signature
catfish" "still rocks after all these years"); while some prefer the "unusual" à la carte options and others the "grandiose" prix fixe menu,
most deem the overall experience "a taste sensation", citing "close-
together" tables as the only distraction.

### Fleming's Prime Steakhouse & Wine Bar  Steak      | 25 | 22 | 24 | $58 |

**Newport Beach** | Fashion Island | 455 Newport Center Dr. (San Miguel Dr.) |
949-720-9633 | www.flemingssteakhouse.com
See review in Los Angeles Directory.

### French 75  French      | 20 | 22 | 19 | $47 |

**Laguna Beach** | 1464 S. PCH (bet. Calliope St. & Mountain Rd.) |
949-494-8444
**Newport Beach** | Fashion Island | 327 Newport Center Dr. (McCarthur Blvd.) |
949-640-2700
www.culinaryadventures.com

After surviving a shakeup in the chain, these seductive south county
sisters by David Wilhelm still "impress dates", "a hip crowd" and
"ladies who lunch" with "rich" Gallic grub served amid "sexy de-

| | FOOD | DECOR | SERVICE | COST |

cor"; if some deem the "over-the-top" French fare on the "faux" side (and "pricey" to boot), most are appeased by the real-deal "happy-hour specials" and "terrific champagne cocktails".

### Gabbi's Mexican Kitchen  *Mexican*  25 | 21 | 20 | $31

**Orange** | 141 S. Glassell St. (Chapman Ave.) | 714-633-3038 | www.gabbimex.com

"There's no sign on the building", but this "transporting" "upscale" Mex in Old Town Orange is a "find" for its "fantastic", "creative" regional cuisine served by an "excellent" staff; its snug storefront setting tends to get "packed" by those in-the-know, but most agree it's "worth the wait" (no reservations taken).

### Golden Truffle, The  🛱 Ⓜ *Caribbean/French*  25 | 12 | 21 | $46

**Costa Mesa** | 1767 Newport Blvd. (bet. 17th & 18th Sts.) | 949-645-9858 | www.goldentruffle.com

Chef-owner Alan Greeley's Costa Mesa "sleeper" keeps wide-eyed "foodies" on the alert for "inventive" "gourmet-to-comfort" French-Caribbean fare from a daily changing menu (just ask the toque for "recommendations" – when he's there – and "you'll never go wrong"); the "tired looking" digs "leave a lot to be desired", but proponents prefer to ponder the "delightful yet unusual" edibles.

### Ⓩ Hobbit, The  Ⓜ *Continental/French*  27 | 26 | 28 | $96

**Orange** | 2932 E. Chapman Ave. (Malena St.) | 714-997-1972 | www.hobbitrestaurant.com

"Don't wait for a special occasion" to partake in this "full evening of dining enchantment" spotlighting a seven-course prix fixe "indulgence" of "phenomenal" French-Continental cuisine by chef-owner Michael Philippi in a "lovely homelike setting" in Orange; the "theatrical experience" commences with "hors d' oeuvres and champagne" in the "incredible wine cellar" and is bolstered to the end by an "impeccable" staff, earning it the No. 1 score for Service in Orange County; P.S. there's only one seating each night (Wednesday–Sunday), so "call far in advance for a reservation."

### Ⓩ In-N-Out Burger  ❶ *Burgers*  23 | 10 | 19 | $8

**Costa Mesa** | 594 W. 19th St. (bet. Anaheim & Maple Aves.)
**Huntington Beach** | 18062 Beach Blvd. (bet. Talbert Ave. & Taylor Dr.)
**Irvine** | 4115 Campus Dr. (bet. Bridge Rd. & Stanford Ct.)
**Laguna Niguel** | 27380 La Paz Rd. (Avenida Breve)
**Placentia** | 825 W. Chapman Ave. (Placentia Ave.)
**Tustin** | Tustin Mktpl. | 3020 El Camino Real (bet. East Dr. & Jamboree Rd.)
800-786-1000 | www.in-n-out.com
Additional locations throughout Southern California
See review in Los Angeles Directory.

### La Cave  🛱 *Steak*  24 | 17 | 22 | $46

**Costa Mesa** | 1695 Irvine Ave., downstairs (17th St.) | 949-646-7944 | www.lacaverestaurant.com

"An excellent martini" is "all you need to feel like one of the Rat Pack" at this Costa Mesa "retro" "underground" steakhouse/lounge where diners select among "expensive" "fresh seafood" and "thick, juicy steaks" from "rolling carts" wheeled to their booths in "old-school" style; live entertainment, including Monday night tributes to Ol' Blue Eyes himself, lends an extra kick to the "dark, mysterious" vibe.

|  | FOOD | DECOR | SERVICE | COST |
|---|---|---|---|---|

### Leatherby's Cafe Rouge ☒ *Asian/Californian* | 24 | 24 | 24 | $68 |

**Costa Mesa** | Orange County Performing Arts Ctr. | 615 Town Center Dr.
(Ave. of the Arts) | 714-429-7640 | www.patinagroup.com

A dedicated following praises the "seasonal" Cal-Asian cuisine at this
"sophisticated" Patina Group venue set within the Segerstrom Concert
Hall; the "elegant" (if "somewhat stark") glass-enclosed setting boasts a
"mercifully low noise level", so even if service swings between "professional" and "needs polishing", for most it sets a "high standard" for
"pre-theater" dining; N.B. open for dinner on performance evenings only.

### ☑ Marché Moderne *French* | 27 | 24 | 24 | $59 |

**Costa Mesa** | South Coast Plaza | 3333 Bristol St. (Anton Blvd.) |
714-434-7900

"Passionate" chef-owners Florent and Amelia Marneau are "hands-on
and it shows" at this "sophisticated" bistro in South Coast Plaza where
their "exquisite" French creations showcase "fresh, seasonal ingredients"; its "upscale" setting gets a boost from a "lovely patio" and "unfussy" service, while "low corkage fees" and a bargain "three-course
lunch prix fixe" mean "anyone can enjoy" "some of OC's best dining."

### Mastro's Ocean Club *Seafood/Steak* | 25 | 27 | 24 | $73 |

**Newport Coast** | Crystal Cove Promenade | 8112 E. PCH (Reef Point Dr.) |
949-376-6990 | www.mastrosoceanclub.com

A "heavy-hitting" Newport crowd convenes at this "posh" "see-and-
be-seen" chophouse in Crystal Cove for "oversized martinis" "bub-
bling with dry ice" and "fabulous" filets and seafood set down in a
"contemporary" yachtlike space with "fantastic views" of the Pacific;
critics sniff it's "all form and no substance", but insiders insist this total "scene" is the "place to be" in OC – "if you can afford it, go for it."

### ☑ Mastro's Steakhouse *Steak* | 26 | 23 | 24 | $73 |

**Costa Mesa** | 633 Anton Blvd. (Park Center Dr.) | 714-546-7405 |
www.mastrosoceanclub.com
See review in Los Angeles Directory.

### Morton's The Steakhouse *Steak* | 25 | 21 | 23 | $64 |

**Anaheim** | 1895 S. Harbor Blvd. (Convention Way) | 714-621-0101
**Santa Ana** | South Coast Plaza | 1641 W. Sunflower Ave. (bet. Bear &
Bristol Sts.) | 714-444-4834
www.mortons.com

"Consistency abounds" at this "can't-go-wrong" steakhouse chain
pairing "well-prepared" chops that "hang off the plate" with "seriously
powerful martinis"; "arm-and-a-leg" pricing comes with the territory,
along with a "Saran-wrapped presentation" of raw meats (accompanied by an instructional "recitation" by the waiter) – so despite "terrific" service, some "could do without the dog and pony show."

### Mr. Stox *American* | 24 | 23 | 26 | $57 |

**Anaheim** | 1105 E. Katella Ave. (bet. Lewis St. & State College Blvd.) |
714-634-2994 | www.mrstox.com

"Still standing tall" amid construction for Anaheim's booming Platinum
Triangle, this New American remains "an institution" thanks to "top-
notch service" and "superb" cuisine matched by "spectacular" wines
from their sizable cellar; prices are high, but loyalists insist it exudes an
"old-fashioned elegance" that makes any occasion feel "extra-special."

| | FOOD | DECOR | SERVICE | COST |
|---|---|---|---|---|

### ☑ Napa Rose  *Californian*  | 28 | 27 | 27 | $65 |

**Anaheim** | Disney's Grand Californian Hotel & Spa | 1600 S. Disneyland Dr. (Katella Ave.) | 714-781-3463 | www.disneyland.com

Voted Most Popular in this year's OC survey, this "deluxe" Disneyland venue is deemed "an absolute five-star experience" thanks to "innovative" Californian creations by "über-chef" Andrew Sutton bolstered by an "encyclopedic wine list" plus an "attentive", "well-trained staff" whose "knowledge" "can be indispensable"; its "extremely family-friendly" vibe accounts for a few "cranky kids in shorts" in the dining room, so those in-the-know insist you "go late" or "eat in the lounge" if you plan to "avoid the park crowd."

### Old Vine Café  *Eclectic*  | 24 | 17 | 22 | $39 |

**Costa Mesa** | The Camp | 2937 Bristol St., Ste. A-102 (Baker St.) | 714-545-1411 | www.oldvinecafe.com

"Tucked away" in Costa Mesa's "arty" retail venue The Camp, this "charming" Eclectic is a find for "leisurely breakfasts", "casual" lunches and dinners of "creative" small plates backed by wines from a "vast" list; add an "informed staff", and an appealing "San Francisco vibe" and converts conclude this "hip" little "treasure" may not be their "secret" for much longer; N.B. an on-site boutique sells vinos and other gourmet goodies.

### 162', Restaurant  *Californian*  | 25 | 25 | 25 | $61 |

**Dana Point** | Ritz-Carlton, Laguna Niguel | 1 Ritz-Carlton Dr. (PCH) | 949-240-2000 | www.ritzcarlton.com

"Outstanding views" from "162 feet above the Pacific" make up the "spectacular" setting at this clifftop destination in the Dana Point Ritz-Carlton that devotees declare a "superlative choice" for "high-class" repasts, including a noteworthy Sunday brunch; though a few find the scenery "outshines the food", most marvel in the "innovative" Californian cuisine backed by "superb" service in a blue-and-cream-hued room and agree it's "worth the tab" – just "bring lots of money."

### Onotria Wine Country Cuisine  ☒ *Eclectic*  | 25 | 18 | 21 | $50 |

**Costa Mesa** | 2831 Bristol St. (Bear St.) | 714-641-5952 | www.onotria.com

Oenophiles adore this "delightful" Costa Mesa bistro where chef-owner Massimo Navarettea's "creative" vin-focused Eclectic cuisine is bested only by the "wonderful" 500-label selection of vintages available by the glass or flight; although wallet-watchers wince over "excessive corkage fees" and "other-worldly pricing", most revel in the "attentive" service and rustic atmosphere, adding that if you "put yourself in [their] hands", you're "in for a treat."

### Park Ave.  Ⓜ *American*  | 26 | 24 | 26 | $35 |

**Stanton** | 11200 Beach Blvd. (Katella Ave.) | 714-901-4400 | www.parkavedining.com

A "surprisingly sophisticated menu" of Traditional and New American cuisine is the draw at this attractive Stanton venue, an "oasis" in "an area in need of fine dining"; "excellent" service amid "swanky" "retro" digs reminiscent of a "supper club" boost the "thoroughly delightful experience", as do "reasonable prices", leaving the "loud acoustics" as the "only negative."

| | FOOD | DECOR | SERVICE | COST |
|---|---|---|---|---|

### NEW Pelican Grill *Californian*
### (fka Pelican Hill Grill)

| 20 | 27 | 23 | $66 |

**Newport Coast** | Pelican Hill Resort | 22800 Pelican Hill Rd.
(Newport Coast Dr.) | 949-467-6800

"Spectacular" ocean views are part of the "stunning" setting at this venue inside the posh new Resort at Pelican Hill inhabiting a "spacious" high-ceilinged room; yet in spite of its "beautiful" setting, foodies find the "haute" Cal cuisine "could use more creativity" and add that the staff also needs "more training" in order to measure up to the tony prices.

### Pinot Provence *French*

| 24 | 23 | 24 | $61 |

**Costa Mesa** | Westin South Coast Plaza Hotel | 686 Anton Blvd. (Bristol St.) | 714-444-5900 | www.patinagroup.com

It's "class all the way" at this "grown-up" Costa Mesa French that's favored for "outstanding" cuisine that's "impeccably" served in a Provençal-style dining room well-suited for "clients", "special dates" and "pre-theater" meals; despite some quibbles that it's no longer as "exciting" as it once was, most insist it's "still going strong", remaining one of the "best in "OC"; P.S. the "zero corkage fee" is a bonus.

### Ramos House Café ⓜ *American*

| 25 | 20 | 22 | $34 |

**San Juan Capistrano** | 31752 Los Rios St. (Ramos St.) | 949-443-1342 | www.ramoshouse.com

"Trains roaring by very few minutes only adds to the charm" of this "delightful" daytime eatery, set in a "historic" home "in Old San Juan Capistrano", where chef-owner John Q. Humphreys whips up "fabulous" feasts of Southern-accented New American fare; "waitresses in overalls" and all-outdoor seating "under a spreading tree" evoke a "rustic" feel making this a "very special place"; P.S. "don't miss the Bloody Mary" – stuffed with crab, beans and herbs grown on site, "it's a meal in itself."

### Ritz Restaurant & Garden, The *Continental*

| 25 | 26 | 26 | $63 |

**Newport Beach** | 880 Newport Center Dr. (Santa Barbara Dr.) | 949-720-1800 | www.ritzrestaurant.com

"Newport society" types insist the "beauty never fades" from this "high-rolling" Continental "institution" catering to "cosmetically perfect blonds of all ages" with an "extensive menu" of "superb" "old-world" cuisine presented by "courteous" and "professional" tuxedo-clad servers; live piano Wednesday–Sunday adds to the "clubby" atmosphere, making this "special-occasion" standby well "worth" the "splurge."

### Roy's *Asian Fusion/Hawaiian*

| 23 | 22 | 22 | $49 |

**Anaheim** | Anaheim GardenWalk | 321 W. Katella Ave. (Clementine St.) | 714-776-7697
**Newport Beach** | Fashion Island | 453 Newport Center Dr. (San Miguel Dr.) | 949-640-7697
www.roysrestaurant.com
See review in Los Angeles Directory.

### ⓩ Ruth's Chris Steak House *Steak*

| 26 | 22 | 24 | $63 |

**Anaheim** | 2041 S. Harbor Blvd. (bet. Katella & Orangewood Aves.) | 714-750-5466
**Irvine** | Park Pl. | 2961 Michaelson Dr. (Jamboree Rd.) | 949-252-8848
www.ruthschris.com
See review in Los Angeles Directory.

| | FOOD | DECOR | SERVICE | COST |
|---|---|---|---|---|

### Sage  *American*
24 | 22 | 22 | $49

**Newport Beach** | Eastbluff Shopping Ctr. | 2531 Eastbluff Dr. (Vista del Sol) | 949-718-9650

### Sage on the Coast  *American*

**Newport Coast** | Crystal Cove Promenade | 7862 E. PCH (Crystal Heights Dr.) | 949-715-7243
www.sagerestaurant.com

Admirers of "adventurous" chef-owner Rich Mead adore his "uniquely fresh" riffs on New American classics at these "vibrant" venues in Newport Beach; "neighborhood foodies" favor the "charming" Eastbluff original while the newer Crystal Cove site pulls in a "trendier" crowd, though both offer "lovely, tranquil" outdoor seating.

### Sapphire Laguna  *Eclectic*
24 | 24 | 22 | $54

**Laguna Beach** | Old Pottery Pl. | 1200 S. PCH (Brooks St.) | 949-715-9888 | www.sapphirellc.com

"Exquisitely built in Craftsman style", Laguna Beach's latest "hot spot" offers a "smart", "Eclectic but sophisticated" lineup of dishes, either within an "arty" interior or on a "lovely patio" with a fire pit; a few fume the "food's fussy", but most say "try it" – and if the scene gets too "noisy", "the gourmet shop next door offers delicious take-home" bites.

### Splashes  *Californian*
19 | 25 | 19 | $52

**Laguna Beach** | Surf & Sand Resort | 1555 S. PCH (bet. Blue Bird Canyon Dr. & Calliope St.) | 949-376-2779 | www.surfandsandresort.com

"You feel as though the surf will hit your table" at this Laguna Californian that boosters believe boasts "the best beachside ambiance in OC"; true, critics say the somewhat "expensive" food "becomes more average every year", but the "view makes everything good", especially "at sunset."

### ☑ Stonehill Tavern  Ⓜ *American*
27 | 29 | 26 | $80

**Dana Point** | St. Regis Resort, Monarch Bch. | 1 Monarch Beach Resort (Niguel Rd.) | 949-234-3318 | www.michaelmina.net

"Michael Mina outdoes himself" in Dana Point with this resort eatery whose "beautiful location" "overlooking the ocean" earns it OC's No. 1 Decor score; almost as "glorious" is the "decadent" New American food "matched by a deep wine list" and furthered by "unobtrusive" service, so many "cast fiscal common sense aside" for a "fabulous splurge."

### ☑ Studio  *Californian/French*
26 | 28 | 27 | $88

**Laguna Beach** | Montage Laguna Bch. | 30801 S. PCH (Montage Dr.) | 949-715-6420 | www.studiolagunabeach.com

"Bring your platinum plastic" to this "pinnacle" "destination" located, appropriately, on a "fabulous clifftop on the grounds of the Montage Laguna Beach resort"; "one of the West Coast's most romantic restaurants", it's "perfect for that special date or for impressing clients" thanks to chef James Boyce's "beautifully inventive" Cal–New French cuisine, "superb service" and, of course, that "spectacular view"; just remember that by OC standards, it's "slightly formal" (no jeans).

### Summit House  *Continental*
24 | 27 | 25 | $47

**Fullerton** | 2000 E. Bastanchury Rd. (State College Blvd.) | 714-671-4111 | www.summithouse.net

For diners who "intend to impress", Fullerton's hilltop Continental "never misses" for "very traditional" "special dinners" (they're "known for their prime rib" and John Dory) underscored by an "unsurpassed view" of north county city lights from a "homey" Tudor-style manse that's "long on atmosphere" and "awesome service"; the private rooms are "especially nice for a celebration."

### S Vietnamese Fine Dining  *Vietnamese*    26 | 25 | 23 | $31

**Westminster** | 545 Westminster Mall Dr. (bet. Bolsa Ave. & Goldenwest St.) | 714-898-5092 | www.sfinedining.com

"From the moment you enter" you know you're in for a "special" meal at this "chic" "surprise" in the rather "prosaic" Westminster Mall showcasing "heavenly" "high-end" Vietnamese dishes from chef-owner Stephanie Dinh; its "elegant" decor includes "subtle lighting", "contemporary art" and a curtained patio evoking "colonial Saigon", and though pricing is "upscale" for the genre, dinner here is still a relative bargain.

### ☑ Tabu Grill  *Seafood/Steak*    29 | 22 | 27 | $61

**Laguna Beach** | 2892 S. PCH (Nyes Pl.) | 949-494-7743 | www.tabugrill.com
Plenty of things could make this Laguna Beach grill taboo: a "tinier-than-tiny room", "tough parking" and "very pricey" tabs; but the "exotic combinations" of Pacific Rim–influenced surf 'n' turf fare (e.g. rib-eye with 'forbidden rice' risotto) are so "impeccably presented", and so "flawlessly served", that this "intimate" venue proves "irresistible" – and it has OC's No. 1 Food score to prove it; reservations require "good-luck" to snag, but it's "so worth it if you succeed"; P.S. if you want "to watch the chefs, just ask for grill seating."

### TAPS Fish House & Brewery  *American/Seafood*    25 | 21 | 22 | $36

**Brea** | 101 E. Imperial Hwy. (Brea Blvd.) | 714-257-0101 | www.tapsbrea.com
Both beer boosters and fin fans tap this titanic American seafooder in Brea as a "solid choice" for "fresh seafood and great brews" (there's a ro-tating selection of drafts), served by a "polite" crew in "delightful" warehouse-style digs or on a garden patio; however, some say it's "best for happy hours" or during the "amazing Sunday brunch"; N.B. it recently spawned a sister operation, just across the county line in Corona.

### ☑ Tradition by Pascal  *French*    28 | 22 | 26 | $59
(aka Pascal)

**Newport Beach** | 1000 N. Bristol St. (Jamboree Rd.) | 949-263-9400 | www.pascalnewportbeach.com

"Mock France's politics if you must, but you can't find fault" with the "classically made", "first-class French" "masterpieces" "created by warm, caring" chef-owner Pascal Olhats at his "pretty", "intimate" bistro hidden in a strip-mall location (at least that means "tons of parking in the evening"); the "staff is very professional and attentive" as well, so while prices aren't low, they seem "reasonable, particularly for Newport Beach"; P.S. "you can also order a picnic basket or spe-cialty [foods] at their deli next door."

### 230 Forest Avenue  *Californian*    23 | 17 | 19 | $45

**Laguna Beach** | 230 Forest Ave. (PCH) | 949-494-2545 | www.230forestavenue.com

"Arty and upbeat", this "busy" village venue draws "locals and visi-tors" alike for a "true Laguna" experience rooted in "innovative" midpriced Californian cuisine, "fabulous" drinks and "excellent

| | FOOD | DECOR | SERVICE | COST |
|---|---|---|---|---|

people-watching"; considering the often "loud" and "cramped" interior, alfresco dining on the front patio is especially appealing.

### Vine ⓈⓂ *Californian/Mediterranean*  | 25 | 23 | 23 | $53 |

**San Clemente** | 211 N. El Camino Real (Avenida Cabrillo) | 949-361-2079 | www.vinesanclemente.com

"San Clemente's best" is a "friendly" "beach-town surprise" that "impresses" with "creative" Cal-Med fare "presented in style" by chef-owner Justin Monson "who seems to be there every night and it shows"; "inspired by Napa Valley", in everything from the wine-barrel tables to the Zinfandel-braised lamb, the "small place" has a "cozy atmosphere" that could become a habit – if only the "menu would change more often."

### Walt's Wharf *Seafood*  | 24 | 16 | 21 | $37 |

**Seal Beach** | 201 Main St. (Central St.) | 562-598-4433 | www.waltswharf.com
"There's always a line" at Seal Beach's pier-adjacent seafooder, nearly 40 years old but "still one of the best" for oak-grilled fish "so fresh it tastes like it just jumped out of the nearby surf", complemented by an "extensive, reasonably priced wine list" (namesake Walt also "owns Babcock Vineyards and knows his vino"); the service comes "without attitude", though "tables jammed together" make things "a bit noisy", and since there are "no reservations (except lunch)", better "get there early" or plan to "wait on the bench outside."

### Wasa *Japanese*  | 25 | 16 | 20 | $40 |

**Irvine** | The Market Pl. | 13124 Jamboree Rd. (Irvine Blvd.) | 714-665-3338
**Lake Forest** | The Orchard | 23702 El Toro Rd. (bet. Rockfield Blvd.) | 949-770-3280 ⓈⓂ
**Newport Beach** | Bluffs Shopping Ctr. | 1346 Bison Ave. (MacArthur Blvd.) | 949-760-1511
www.wasasushi.com

"When you absolutely must have great sushi", this "awesome" Japanese trio delivers a "broad menu" of "razzmatazz" rolls and fish "so fresh it wiggles"; the "imaginative fare" and "friendly chefs" who are "both masters of their craft and entertainers" "make up for the long waits, cramped seating" and "strip-mall decor" (though the Market Place branch has been "redone" after a fire).

### Wild Artichoke, The ⓈⓂ *Californian/Eclectic*  | 24 | 15 | 23 | $37 |

**Yorba Linda** | Yorba Ranch Vill. | 4973A Yorba Ranch Rd. (Yorba Linda Blvd.) | 714-777-9646 | www.thewildartichoke.com
There's "more than just artichokes"' at this "great find in Yorba Linda" offering "creative" Cal-Eclectic fare by chef-owner James d'Aquila, who's "very interactive with guests"; some "would love them to move into bigger" digs, but it's "worth a visit" now to see "how so small a place can turn out such outstanding food."

### Wildfish Seafood Grille *American/Seafood*  | 23 | 21 | 22 | $54 |

**Newport Beach** | The Bluffs | 1370 Bison Ave. (MacArthur Blvd.) | 949-720-9925 | www.wildfishseafoodgrille.com
It may be in landlocked Newport Beach, but the specialty is "superbly fresh fish" at this American "hot spot" where the local "business chic meet" and an "enthusiastic, youngish crowd" plays; if dissenters are driven wild by the "noise", most "don't seem to mind", hailing "the best happy hours ever."

# PALM SPRINGS/
# SANTA BARBARA
# RESTAURANT
# DIRECTORY

# Palm Springs & Environs

## TOP FOOD

27 Le Vallauris | *French/Med.*
26 Le St. Germain | *French/Med.*
   Ruth's Chris | *Steak*
   Jillian's | *Continental*
25 Johannes | *Eclectic*

## TOP SERVICE

28 Wally's Desert
   Le Vallauris
26 Le St. Germain
25 Copley's
   Cuistot

## TOP DECOR

27 Le Vallauris
26 Wally's Desert
   Cuistot
25 Jillian's
24 Arnold Palmer's

## BEST BUYS

1. In-N-Out
2. Original Pancake
3. Johnny Rockets
4. Ruby's
5. Souplantation

### Adobe Grill  *Mexican*

▽ 18 | 19 | 18 | $42

**La Quinta** | La Quinta Resort & Club | 49-499 Eisenhower Dr.
(Washington St.) | 760-564-5725 | www.laquintaresort.com
Resortgoers relax with an "amazing" margarita on one of
the "lovely" patios at this "upscale" hacienda on the "beautifully
landscaped" grounds of the "luxury" La Quinta Resort; though
some surveyors say the "nontraditional" Mexican food can be
"inconsistent", they still suggest it for "out-of-town guests",
especially since live mariachi and Peruvian music spices things
up most nights.

### ☑ Arnold Palmer's  *Steak*

20 | 24 | 21 | $48

**La Quinta** | 78164 Ave. 52 (Washington St.) | 760-771-4653 |
www.arnoldpalmers.net
"No bogies here" say surveyors who claim they're pleasantly "surprised" by the "solid" American "comfort food" at this La Quinta
steakhouse owned by the legendary golf pro; an "enormous collection
of memorabilia" plus a nine-hole putting green are additional pulls for
fans, while the "wonderful" staff and lively "piano bar" keep it "popular" with the non-playing set as well.

### AZUR ☒Ⓜ  *Californian/French*

- | - | - | E

**La Quinta** | La Quinta Resort & Club | 49-499 Eisenhower Dr.
(Washington St.) | 760-564-7600 | www.laquintaresort.com
Located inside the "classy" La Quinta Resort & Club, this upscale
desert entry showcases a seasonal Cal-French menu backed by an extensive list of international vintages; though the elegantly understated
interior with high ceilings and live jazz in the lounge creates a "relaxed
environment", critics claim it's ultimately "much too expensive for
what it is."

### Bellini ☒  *Italian*

▽ 21 | 19 | 24 | $57

**Palm Desert** | 73111 El Paseo (bet. Ocotillo Dr. & Sage Ln.) |
760-341-2626
"Kind" owners Carlo and Marylena Pisano "go out of their way to make
diners feel comfortable" at their "warm" Palm Desert Italian offering
"well-prepared" fare in a "cozy" setting "hidden from the street" behind a small courtyard; though it's "friendly", some say they're peeved
by "pricey" tabs; N.B. closed July–September.

| | FOOD | DECOR | SERVICE | COST |
|---|---|---|---|---|

**Billy Reed's** *American* — 17 | 15 | 19 | $24

**Palm Springs** | 1800 N. Palm Canyon Dr. (Vista Chino) | 760-325-1946

"A fixture, and rightly so", this "friendly" "old Palm Springs" coffee shop pleases families and the "early-bird" crowd with "whopping portions" of "reliable" American "comfort food" and decadent diner-style desserts like Boston cream pie; though loyalists find the Victorian interior with "lots of booths" as comfy as "an old shoe", considering it opened in 1975, a minority murmurs that a "face-lift" is in order.

**Bing Crosby's Restaurant &** — 20 | 24 | 20 | $61
**Piano Bar** *Californian*

**Rancho Mirage** | 71743 Hwy. 111 (Bob Hope Dr.) | 760-674-5764 | www.bingcrosbysrestaurant.com

Diners "dress up" for a night on the town at this "expensive" Rancho Mirage "blast from the past", where the "clubby" decor evokes old Hollywood, complete with photos of the famous crooner, deep leather booths and live piano nightly; a Californian menu with perennial "all-American" favorites like prime rib and oysters Rockefeller drive home the theme, and though some find the food "inconsistent", most maintain they "want to go back."

**BJ's** *Pub Food* — 17 | 16 | 16 | $20

**Corona** | Crossings at Corona | 2520 Tuscany St. (bet. Cajalco Rd. & Grand Oaks) | 951-271-3610 ☻

**Rancho Cucamonga** | 11520 Fourth St. (Buffalo Ave.) | 909-581-6750

**San Bernardino** | 1045 E. Harriman Pl. (Tippecanoe Ave.) | 909-380-7100 ☻

**Temecula** | 26500 Ynez Rd. (Overland Dr.) | 951-252-8370
www.bjsbrewhouse.com

Additional locations throughout Southern California

See review in Los Angeles Directory.

**Café des Beaux-Arts** *French* — 18 | 15 | 19 | $39

**Palm Desert** | 73640 El Paseo (Larkspur Ln.) | 760-346-0669 | www.cafedesbeauxarts.com

Lunchers who linger over "lovely" French fare and "aromatic" coffee amid a "noisy" peak-hour bustle say this "atmospheric" Palm Desert bistro evokes a "New Orleans cafe" and "feels European"; while the prices reflect its status as a "tourist stop" and the decor could use a "spruce-up", patrons continue to flock to the "pleasant" patio in a "perfect" location for watching passersby; N.B. closed July–August.

**California Pizza Kitchen** *Pizza* — 18 | 14 | 17 | $21

**Rancho Cucamonga** | Victoria Gdns. | 12517 N. Mainstreet (bet. Kew & Monet Aves.) | 909-899-8611

**Riverside** | Riverside Plaza | 3540 Riverside Plaza Dr., Ste. 308 (Riverside Ave.) | 951-680-9362

**Temecula** | Promenade in Temecula | 40820 Winchester Rd. (bet. Margarita & Ynez Rds.) | 951-296-0575

**Palm Desert** | El Paseo Collection | 73080 El Paseo, Ste. 8 (bet. Hwy. 74 & Ocotillo Dr.) | 760-776-5036

**Palm Springs** | Desert Fashion Plaza | 123 N. Palm Canyon Dr. (bet. Amado Rd. & Tahquitz Canyon Way) | 760-322-6075
www.cpk.com

Additional locations throughout Southern California

See review in Los Angeles Directory.

| | FOOD | DECOR | SERVICE | COST |
|---|---|---|---|---|

**Castaway** Ⓜ *Californian* — 13 | 19 | 15 | $38

**San Bernardino** | 670 Kendall Dr. (bet. 36th & 40th Sts.) | 909-881-1502 |
www.castawayrestaurant.com
See review in Los Angeles Directory.

**Castelli's** *Italian* — 22 | 17 | 22 | $52

**Palm Desert** | 73098 Hwy. 111 (Monterey Ave.) | 760-773-3365 |
www.castellis.cc
It "feels like the Rat Pack should be dining" at this "lively, loud
haunt" in Palm Desert where a "warm" (if sometimes "too
friendly") staff serves up "classic" Italian pastas and specials to
the tune of live piano music; while some find it "overpriced" and
the setting "dated", others say it only "gets better with age";
N.B. closed July–September.

**Ⓩ Cheesecake Factory** *American* — 19 | 18 | 18 | $27

**Rancho Cucamonga** | Victoria Gdns. | 12379 N. Mainstreet (bet. Monet &
Monticello Aves.) | 909-463-3011
**Rancho Mirage** | The River | 71800 Hwy. 111 (bet. Bob Hope &
Rancho Las Palmas Drs.) | 760-404-1400
www.thecheesecakefactory.com
Additional locations throughout Southern California
See review in Los Angeles Directory.

**Chez Philippe** *French* — - | - | - | M

**Palm Springs** | 245 S. Palm Canyon Dr. (bet. E. Arenas & W. Baristo Rds.) |
760-323-0772 | www.chezphilippeps.com
The date-worthy patio draped with grape vines and twinkling lights is
the centerpiece of this classic bistro in the heart of Downtown Palm
Springs; it attracts a mix of locals and tourists who tuck into moderately priced Mediterranean-influenced French dishes like bouillabaisse and Provençal pot roast with a full lineup of sweet and savory
crêpes available at breakfast and lunch.

**Chez Pierre** Ⓢ Ⓜ *French* — ▽ 22 | 17 | 20 | $45

**Palm Desert** | 44250 Town Center Way (Fred Waring Dr.) | 760-346-1818 |
www.chezpierrebistro.com
"Tucked away in a shopping center", this Palm Desert bistro serves
"seasonally changing" French fare that's "always on the mark" in
an "intimate" setting with a "nice patio"; a "friendly" staff enhances
the "enjoyable" meal, and though some say the location and "early
closing" time "diminish the ambiance", others call it a "real find"
for the money.

**Chop House** *Steak* — 21 | 18 | 20 | $59

**Palm Desert** | 74040 Hwy. 111 (Portola Ave.) | 760-779-9888
**Palm Springs** | 262 S. Palm Canyon Dr. (bet. Arenas & Baristo Rds.) |
760-320-4500
www.restaurantsofpalmsprings.com
"Now these guys know steak" nod regulars of these Palm Desert
and Palm Springs beef meccas where the "generous" cuts of meat
are often "on par" with higher-profile competitors and the service
is generally "excellent"; still, some critics call them "only fair for
desert fare", citing a "touristy" feel and bills that may equal
"your last paycheck."

| | FOOD | DECOR | SERVICE | COST |
|---|---|---|---|---|

### Citron  *Caribbean/French*
▽ 22 | 23 | 22 | $56

**Palm Springs** | Viceroy Palm Springs | 415 S. Belardo Rd. (Ramon Rd.) | 760-320-4117 | www.viceroypalmsprings.com

Attracting an "elite" clientele, this "swanky" spot in the Viceroy Palm Springs boasts "delicious", "interesting" Caribbean-French cuisine, "trendy" yellow-and-white decor and a poolside patio; while most go for the "hip" "LA vibe in the desert", it sours some guests who find it a tad "noisy", full of "attitude" and "overpriced."

### Citrus City Grille  *Californian*
19 | 17 | 20 | $29

**Riverside** | Riverside Plaza | 3555 Riverside Plaza Dr. (bet. Central & Merrill Aves.) | 951-274-9099 | www.citruscitygrille.com

This Riverside offshoot of a fruitful OC-based mini-chain keeps crowds coming with "solid" Californian eats from an "eclectic menu"; affordable tabs, "spot-on" service and a "pleasant" setting with patio seating and live jazz makes it "worth a try" even if sourpusses are "less than impressed" by fare they deem "not special in any way."

### Claim Jumper  *American*
19 | 18 | 18 | $25

**Corona** | 380 McKinley St. (Promenade Ave.) | 951-735-6567
**Rancho Cucamonga** | 12499 Foothill Blvd. (I-15) | 909-899-8022
**San Bernardino** | 1905 S. Commercenter E. (Hospitality Ln.) | 909-383-1818
www.claimjumper.com

See review in Los Angeles Directory.

### ☑ Copley's on Palm Canyon  *American*
25 | 23 | 25 | $48

**Palm Springs** | 621 N. Palm Canyon Dr. (bet. Alejo & Tamarisk Rds.) | 760-327-9555 | www.copleyspalmsprings.com

Palm Springs pleasure-hounds cheer for chef Andrew Copley's "exquisite" menu at this "must-go" New American offering "something for everyone", including "innovative" dishes prepared with "herbs grown in the garden" and desserts "too fabulous" for words; it's "expensive", but "professional" service and a "lovely" hacienda setting where you can "sit under the trees on Cary Grant's old patio" add to the experience.

### Cork Tree  *Californian*
25 | 24 | 24 | $61

**Palm Desert** | Desert Springs Mktpl. | 74950 Country Club Dr. (Cook St.) | 760-779-0123 | www.thecorktree.com

A "big-city place" that's a "pleasing" addition to Palm Desert, this newcomer offers Californian cuisine that customers call "exciting" and "uniformly excellent" with "service and ambiance to match"; despite its strip-mall setting, the "glitzy" interior and "wonderful" patio help justify a bill that's "expensive for the desert."

### NEW Counter, The  *Burgers*
21 | 13 | 16 | $17

**Corona** | Promenade Shops at Dos Lagos | 2785 Cabot Dr. (Temescal Canyon Rd.) | 951-277-1711 | www.thecounterburger.com

See review in Los Angeles Directory.

### ☑ Cuistot Ⓜ  *Californian/French*
25 | 26 | 25 | $67

**Palm Desert** | 72595 El Paseo (Hwy. 111) | 760-340-1000 | www.cuistotrestaurant.com

"French gourmet meets contemporary Californian" cuisine at this "simply outstanding" Palm Desert "special-date place" where "every-

FOOD | DECOR | SERVICE | COST

thing is pleasing to the palate", including the "superb" wines; the "large", "beautiful" space is "divided into cozy areas" overseen by "ultra-attentive" servers, making it a "must" for both visitors and locals who "don't mind paying the high prices."

### Daily Grill  *American*
18 | 17 | 18 | $31

**Palm Desert** | 73061 El Paseo (Monterey Ave.) | 760-779-9911 | www.dailygrill.com
See review in Los Angeles Directory.

### Europa Ⓜ *Continental*
- | - | - | E

**Palm Springs** | Villa Royale Inn | 1620 S. Indian Trail (E. Palm Canyon Dr.) | 760-327-2314 | www.villaroyale.com
If you had a rich grandmother with a restaurant on her estate, this pricey Palm Springs eatery from another era at the secluded Villa Royale Inn might well be it; its old-school dining room with a fireplace, pretty poolside patio, gracious service and Continental menu keep the dining experience comfortable for a fairly sedate crowd.

### Falls Prime Steakhouse  *Steak*
20 | 21 | 18 | $60

**La Quinta** | 78430 Hwy. 111 (Washington St.) | 760-777-9999 | www.thefallsprimesteakhouse.com
**Palm Springs** | Mercado Plaza | 155 S. Palm Canyon Dr., 2nd fl. (Arenas Rd.) | 760-416-8664 | www.thefallsrestaurants.com
"Popular" for their signature "smoking martinis" and breezy patio seating, these twin meateries in La Quinta and Palm Springs draw a steady stream of visitors for "high-quality" steaks enhanced by "great people-watching"; though servers "try hard", foes find the experience "not worth the price" and say they're ultimately more about the "pickup" scene than the "pedestrian" food.

### Gyu-Kaku  *Japanese*
20 | 17 | 18 | $31

**Rancho Cucamonga** | Victoria Gdns. | 7893 Monet Ave. (Foothill Blvd.) | 909-899-4748 | www.gyu-kaku.com
See review in Los Angeles Directory.

### Hog's Breath Inn  *American*
15 | 16 | 18 | $34

**La Quinta** | Old Town La Quinta | 78065 Main St. (Calle Tampico) | 760-564-5556 | www.hogsbreathinnlaquinta.com
An offshoot of the original in Carmel, this Clint Eastwood-owned eatery in La Quinta dishes out "decent tasting" American grub in environs that pay homage to the actor/director with movie memorabilia and a "lively" saloon with "great piano playing" (Wednesday-Sunday); more jaded surveyors judge it "overrated" and claim they need to "get back to quality food" if they want to be known as anything more than a "tourist trap."

### Ⓩ In-N-Out Burger ◑ *Burgers*
23 | 10 | 19 | $8

**Corona** | 2305 Compton Ave. (bet. Ontario Ave. & Taber St.)
**Corona** | 450 Auto Center Dr. (bet. Rte. 91 & Wardlow Rd.)
**Riverside** | 6634 Clay St. (bet. General Rd. & Van Buren Blvd.)
**Riverside** | 72265 Varner Rd. (bet. Manufacturing & Ramon Rds.)
**Riverside** | 7467 Indiana Ave. (bet. Madison & Washington Sts.)
800-786-1000 | www.in-n-out.com
Additional locations throughout Southern California
See review in Los Angeles Directory.

| | FOOD | DECOR | SERVICE | COST |
|---|---|---|---|---|

### Islands *American*
16 | 15 | 17 | $17

**Chino** | 3962 Grand Ave. (Spectrum East) | 909-591-8393
**Corona** | 1295 Magnolia Ave. (15 Frwy.) | 951-279-7724
**Rancho Cucamonga** | 11425 Foothill Blvd. (Milliken Ave.) | 909-944-6662
**Riverside** | Riverside Plaza | 3645 Central Ave. (bet. Magnolia & Riverside Aves.) | 951-782-8199
**Palm Desert** | 72353 Hwy. 111 (Desert Crossing) | 760-346-4007
www.islandsrestaurants.com
Additional locations throughout Southern California
See review in Los Angeles Directory.

### ☒ Jillian's ☒ *Continental*
26 | 25 | 24 | $63

**Palm Desert** | 74155 El Paseo (Hwy. 111) | 760-776-8242 | www.jilliansfinedining.com
"Always a delight", this "top-notch" Palm Desert "destination" presents "wonderful" Continental fare in an "'old California' setting" that boasts a "warm", "peaceful" interior and a "magical" courtyard; with "outstanding" service too, many guests agree it's a "special place when you want to splurge"; N.B. jacket suggested.

### Joe's Crab Shack *Seafood*
13 | 15 | 15 | $26

**Rancho Cucamonga** | 12327 Foothill Blvd. (Dry Creek Blvd.) | 909-463-6599 | www.joescrabshack.com
See review in Los Angeles Directory.

### ☒ Johannes *Eclectic*
25 | 18 | 22 | $58

**Palm Springs** | 196 S. Indian Canyon Dr. (Arenas Rd.) | 760-778-0017 | www.johannesrestaurants.com
"Smart, sophisticated" Eclectic fare with some Austrian accents by chef-owner Johannes Bacher draws Palm Springs locals to this high-end "surprise in the desert" when they're having a "city attack"; "gracious" service and "attention to detail" enhance the experience, and though some cite "spartan" digs, it has recently been renovated and "expanded to accommodate the people discovering it."

### John Henry's ☒ *Eclectic/French*
18 | 12 | 20 | $35

**Palm Springs** | 1785 E. Tahquitz Canyon Way (Sunrise Way) | 760-327-7667
A "little bit of everything" in "plentiful" portions, a "wonderful" staff and a "lovely" patio keep the "same people coming back year after year" to this "cheap and cheerful" Palm Springs Eclectic-French "standby"; while reservations are required, critics who call it "mediocre" feel that "huge" plates and "low prices" account for its "popularity"; N.B. closed June–October.

### Johnny Rebs' *BBQ*
22 | 17 | 21 | $21

**Victorville** | 15051 Seventh St. (Victor Dr.) | 760-955-3700 | www.johnnyrebs.com
See review in Los Angeles Directory.

### Johnny Rockets *Burgers*
15 | 15 | 16 | $14

**Rancho Cucamonga** | Victoria Gdns. | 7800 Kew Ave. (N. Mainstreet) | 909-463-2800 | www.johnnyrockets.com
Additional locations throughout Southern California
See review in Los Angeles Directory.

FOOD | DECOR | SERVICE | COST

### Kaiser Grille  *American*

16 | 16 | 17 | $39

**Palm Springs** | 205 S. Palm Canyon Dr. (Arenas Rd.) | 760-323-1003 |
www.kaisergrille.com

"People-watching" is the main attraction of this "touristy" Palm
Springs American in a "prime" location where tables get snapped up
for early-bird dinners and "warm evenings" "on the patio"; as for the
rest of the dining experience, many agree the food is "kinda inciden-
tal" and call the service middling too.

### King's Fish House  *Seafood*

21 | 18 | 19 | $34

**Corona** | 2530 Tuscany Rd. (Calico Rd.) | 951-284-7900
**Rancho Cucamonga** | Victoria Gdns. | 12427 N. Mainstreet (Monet Ave.) |
909-803-1280
www.kingsfishhouse.com
See review in Los Angeles Directory.

### La Quinta Cliffhouse  *American*

16 | 19 | 17 | $40

**La Quinta** | 78250 Hwy. 111 (Washington St.) | 760-360-5991 |
www.laquintacliffhouse.com

Boasting a scenic "babbling brook" and "awesome" mountain views,
this La Quinta locale impresses guests even if its "ok" American dishes
"don't live up to the setting"; still, the "happy-hour" bar menu is a "real
deal", but "get there early" or expect to be "elbowed out" by discount
diners, the "golf crowd" and others who go for the "big scene."

### Las Casuelas  *Mexican*

18 | 19 | 18 | $27

**Rancho Mirage** | 70050 Hwy. 111 (Via Florencio) | 760-328-8844 |
www.lascasuelasnuevas.com
**La Quinta** | 78480 Hwy. 111 (Washington St.) | 760-777-7715 |
www.lascasuelasquinta.com
**Palm Springs** | 222 S. Palm Canyon Dr. (Arenas Rd.) | 760-325-2794 |
www.lascasuelas.com
**Palm Springs** | 368 N. Palm Canyon Dr. (bet. Alejo & Amado Rds.) |
760-325-3213 | www.lascasuelas.com

### Casuelas Cafe  *Mexican*

**Palm Desert** | 73703 Hwy. 111 (Larkspur Ln.) | 760-568-0011 |
www.lascasuelasquinta.com

A "desert tradition", these "family-owned" cantinas ply "tourists and
snowbirds" with "plentiful", "dependable" Mexican eats and "powerful margaritas" in "upbeat" environs that turn into "party spots at
night", especially on the "attractive" patios; even if they're not as "authentic" as some "holes-in-the-wall" in the area, they're still a "value
for the dollar", and their atmospheres are a "step up."

### La Spiga Ristorante Italiano 🅱 *Italian*

▽ 24 | 21 | 20 | $64

**Palm Desert** | 72557 Hwy. 111 (El Paseo) | 760-340-9318

"Superb" Italian fare, such as homemade sausage and rack of lamb, lures
desert dwellers away from their pools to this "pricey" but "wonderful"
Palm Desert place, which relocated from El Paseo to "gorgeous" larger
digs; since it gets "crowded" as ever, "reservations are a must."

### 🅩 Le St. Germain  *French/Mediterranean*

26 | 24 | 26 | $67

**Indian Wells** | 74985 Hwy. 111 (Cook St.) | 760-773-6511 |
www.lestgermain.com

The French-Med meals "shine" at this Indian Wells "special-occasion"
place that pleases with "wonderful" fare, "excellent" service and a

"lovely setting" both inside and on the covered patio with a fire pit; a piano bar adds to its "'50s" aura, though the prices are more up to date.

**☑ Le Vallauris** *French/Mediterranean* | 27 | 27 | 28 | $70 |

**Palm Springs** | 385 W. Tahquitz Canyon Way (N. Museum Dr.) | 760-325-5059 | www.levallauris.com

"Always tops", this "amazing" French-Med, voted No. 1 for Food and Decor and the Most Popular restaurant in Palm Springs, "enchants" with "extraordinary" dishes, a "fabulous" setting featuring a "fairy-tale" patio beneath a "ficus-tree canopy" and "impeccable" service helmed by owner and "consummate host" Paul Bruggemans; such "luxury" doesn't come cheap, but it remains a "wonderful escape"; N.B. closed from mid-July to mid-September.

**LG's Prime Steakhouse** *Steak* | 23 | 20 | 21 | $61 |

**La Quinta** | 78525 Hwy. 111 (Washington St.) | 760-771-9911
**Palm Desert** | 74225 Hwy. 111 (Cabrillo Ave.) | 760-779-9799
**Palm Springs** | 255 S. Palm Canyon Dr. (bet. Arenas & Baristo Rds.) | 760-416-1779
www.lgsprimesteakhouse.com

"Life's good" for both "tourists" and locals who "splurge" at this steakhouse trio on "excellent meats" "prepared correctly" and "must-order" Caesar salads made tableside; the service is a bit less consistent than the cuisine, and the decor "could use a little livening up", but it still makes for an "enjoyable" experience with a "classic" touch.

**Lord Fletcher's** ☒ Ⓜ *Pub Food* | ▽ 17 | 19 | 19 | $51 |

**Rancho Mirage** | 70385 Hwy. 111 (Country Club Dr.) | 760-328-1161

Let the wench jokes begin at this "dependable" Brit in Rancho Mirage, the "Tam O'Shanter of the desert", where waitresses serve up platters of prime rib, steaks and other upscale "English comfort" fare in an "old-fashioned" pub room; sure, it's a "time warp", but that's part of why it's "still popular with the older generation."

**Lucille's Smokehouse Bar-B-Que** *BBQ* | 22 | 18 | 19 | $27 |

**Rancho Cucamonga** | 12624 N. Main St. (Foothill Blvd.) | 909-463-7427 | www.lucillesbbq.com
See review in Los Angeles Directory.

**Matchbox** *American/Pizza* | - | - | - | M |

**Palm Springs** | Mercado Plaza | 155 S. Palm Canyon Dr., 2nd Fl. (W. Arenas Rd.) | 760-778-6000 | www.matchboxpalmsprings.com

Just steps from the statue of former mayor Sonny Bono comes this stylish Palm Springs pizza parlor and bistro proffering a moderately priced New American menu of wood-fired pies, burgers, steaks and seafood; it boasts a patio with fire pit, handsome brick-and-stone interior and nightly happy-hour specials.

**Melting Pot** *Fondue* | 18 | 18 | 19 | $46 |

**Rancho Cucamonga** | 12469 Foothill Blvd. (bet. Day Creek Blvd. & Etiwanda Ave.) | 909-899-1922 | www.meltingpot.com
See review in Los Angeles Directory.

**Mimi's Cafe** *Diner* | 17 | 17 | 18 | $19 |

**Chino** | 3890 Grand Ave. (Rosewell Ave.) | 909-465-1595

*(continued)*

*(continued)*

## Mimi's Cafe

**Corona** | 2230 Griffin Way (McKinley St.) | 951-734-2073
**Rancho Cucamonga** | 10909 Foothill Blvd. (Spruce Ave.) | 909-948-1130
**Rancho Mirage** | 71861 State Hwy. 111 (Bob Hope Dr.) | 760-836-3905
www.mimiscafe.com
Additional locations throughout Southern California
See review in Los Angeles Directory.

## Mister Parker's Ⓜ *French*                  − | − | − | VE

**Palm Springs** | Parker Palm Springs | 4200 E. Palm Canyon Dr.
(S. Cherokee Way) | 760-321-4629 | www.misterparkers.com

The kind of place where you might expect to see Austin Powers on a date with Barbarella, this swanky, sexy hangout in the Parker Palm Springs hotel attracts a youthful but deep-pocketed set with its eccentric interior designed by Jonathan Adler, including '70s-era chandeliers, a mirrored ceiling and pop art female nudes on the walls; fancy French dishes with a classic bent, eclectic music and unstuffy service round out the rakishly rarified experience; N.B. it's open for dinner only Wednesday–Sunday.

## Morton's The Steakhouse *Steak*          25 | 21 | 23 | $64

**Palm Desert** | Desert Springs Mktpl. | 74880 Country Club Dr. (Cook St.) |
760-340-6865 | www.mortons.com
See review in Orange County Directory.

## Native Foods 🅔 *Californian/Eclectic*        22 | 11 | 16 | $17

**Palm Desert** | 73890 El Paseo (Portola Ave.) | 760-836-9396
**Palm Springs** | 1775 E. Palm Canyon Dr. (S. Sunrise Way) | 760-416-0070
www.nativefoods.com
See review in Los Angeles Directory.

## Okura Robata Grill & Sushi Bar *Japanese*  ▽ 26 | 20 | 21 | $51

**La Quinta** | Point Happy Plaza | 78370 Hwy. 111 (Washington St.) |
760-564-5820
**NEW** **Palm Springs** | 105 S. Palm Canyon Dr. (Tahquitz Canyon Way) |
760-327-1333 Ⓜ
www.okurasushi.com

An "innovative" menu featuring "superior" Japanese dishes like Kobe beef carpaccio and some of the "best sushi" in the desert distinguishes this Japanese duo with one location in La Quinta and a newer outpost in Palm Springs; though the tabs strke some as "pricey", both are ensconced in "modern settings" that feel appropriately upscale with stone walls and a fiery orange-and-black color scheme.

## Original Pancake House *Diner*              23 | 10 | 18 | $15

**Temecula** | 41377 Margarita Rd., Ste. F101 (Winchester Rd.) |
951-296-9016 | www.originalpancakehouse.com
See review in Los Angeles Directory.

## Outback Steakhouse *Steak*                  17 | 15 | 17 | $28

**San Bernardino** | 620 E. Hospitality Ln. (Waterman Ave.) | 909-890-0061
**Upland** | 530 N. Mountain Ave. (Arrow Hwy.) | 909-931-1050
**Palm Desert** | Waring Plaza | 72220 Hwy. 111 (Fred Waring Dr.) |
760-779-9068
www.outback.com
Additional locations throughout Southern California
See review in Los Angeles Directory.

| | FOOD | DECOR | SERVICE | COST |
|---|---|---|---|---|

### Pacifica Seafood Restaurant  *Seafood*    | 22 | 22 | 22 | $49 |

**Palm Desert** | The Gardens | 73505 El Paseo (San Pableo Ave.) |
760-674-8666 | www.pacificaseafoodrestaurant.com

There's a "nice buzz" around this "busy" Palm Desert seafooder presenting "excellent" fin fare alongside a 125-bottle list of vodkas and "good values" on wines; "smooth" service and a "lovely" patio affording mountain vistas complement the overall "relaxing" vibe; N.B. reservations recommended.

### NEW Picanha Churrascaria  🅂 *Brazilian*    | 21 | 16 | 21 | $40 |

**Cathedral City** | 68-510 Hwy. 111 (Country Club Dr.) | 760-328-1818 |
www.picanharestaurant.com
See review in Los Angeles Directory.

### Pomodoro Cucina Italiana  *Italian*    | 18 | 14 | 18 | $22 |

**Corona** | Hidden Valley Plaza | 510 Hidden Valley Pkwy. (off Rte. 15) |
951-808-1700 | www.pastapomodoro.com
See review in Los Angeles Directory.

### NEW Purple Palm, The  *Mediterranean*    | - | - | - | E |

**Palm Springs** | Colony Palms Hotel | 572 N. Indian Canyon Dr. (E. Via Colusa) |
760-969-1818 | www.colonypalmshotel.com

"Have a drink at the bar and enjoy the amazing view" of the pool at this Palm Springs eatery inside the Colony Palms Hotel lauded for its "beautiful" Moroccan-style interior with breezy patio seating; yet despite the appealing setting, many take issue with "attitude" from the staff as well as "overpriced" Mediterranean food they claim "underdelivers."

### NEW Rattlesnake  *American*    ▽ | 27 | 21 | 20 | $66 |

**Palm Desert** | Classic Club Golf Resort | 75200 Classic Club Blvd. (Cook St.) |
760-601-3690 | www.rattlesnakeclub.com

"Marvelous steaks" and "well-shaken" cocktails head up the Traditional American menu at this "luxe" new eatery inside Palm Desert's Classic Club Golf Resort; fine service and a "fashionable" setting overlooking the links appeal to most, though some warn that all this finery comes "at a price."

### Ristorante Mamma Gina  *Italian*    | 20 | 16 | 20 | $44 |

**Palm Desert** | 73705 El Paseo (bet. Larkspur Ln. & San Luis Rey Ave.) |
760-568-9898 | www.mammagina.com

"Classic, not trendy", this Palm Desert Northern Italian pulls in an "older crowd" of "ladies who lunch" for "consistently wonderful" fare abetted by "old-fashioned" service; though critics may find the decor "dated", others find solace in the pretty patio overlooking the El Paseo Boardwalk.

### Ristorante Tuscany  *Italian*    ▽ | 26 | 25 | 26 | $57 |

**Palm Desert** | JW Marriott Desert Springs | 74855 Country Club Dr. (Cook St.) | 760-341-1839 | www.desertspringsresort.com

"Unexpectedly sophisticated" Northern Italian cuisine headlines at this "lovely" dining room in Palm Desert's JW Marriott Desert Springs hotel; admirers avow it's "always a pleasure" thanks to a "refined" staff that "treats you like royalty" and a "romantic" setting enhanced by lake views.

| | FOOD | DECOR | SERVICE | COST |
|---|---|---|---|---|

## Rosine's  *Armenian/Mediterranean*    22 | 12 | 18 | $26

**Corona** | Crossings at Corona | 2670 Tuscany St., Ste. 101 (Cahalco Rd.) | 951-372-9484 | www.rosines.com

Regular patrons pack this "wonderful find" in Corona for "heavenly" rotisserie chicken and other "mouthwatering" Med-Armenian eats complemented by a "four-star wine list" at "giveaway prices"; though the setting is "modest", service is "attentive", so most leave "satisfied."

## Roy's  *Asian Fusion/Hawaiian*    23 | 22 | 22 | $49

**Rancho Mirage** | 71959 Hwy. 111 (Magnesia Falls Dr.) | 760-340-9044 | www.roysrestaurant.com

See review in Los Angeles Directory.

## Ruby's  *Diner*    17 | 17 | 18 | $16

**Rancho Mirage** | 71-885 Hwy. 111 (Date Palm Ave.) | 760-836-0788
**Riverside** | Tyler Galleria | 1298 Tyler St. (Magnolia Ave.) | 951-359-7829
**Palm Springs** | 155 S. Palm Canyon Dr. (W. Tahquitz Canyon Way & W. Arenas Rd.) | 760-406-7829
www.rubys.com

See review in Los Angeles Directory.

## ☑ Ruth's Chris Steak House  *Steak*    26 | 22 | 24 | $63

**Palm Desert** | 74-740 Hwy. 111 (Portola Ave.) | 760-779-1998 | www.ruthschris.com

See review in Los Angeles Directory.

## Shame on the Moon  *American*    23 | 20 | 23 | $46

**Rancho Mirage** | 69950 Frank Sinatra Dr. (Hwy. 111) | 760-324-5515 | www.shameonthemoon.com

"It's a gay old time" for people of all persuasions at this "upscale" Rancho Mirage "gem" that may be "hard to get into" ("book ahead") but is "worth it" for the "skillfully prepared, beautifully presented" American fare and "generous drinks" at "reasonable prices"; a "competent" staff lends extra "class" to the "welcoming" atmosphere.

## Sirocco  *Italian*    24 | 23 | 23 | $59

**Indian Wells** | Renaissance Esmeralda Resort & Spa | 44-400 Indian Wells Ln. (Hwy. 111) | 760-773-4444 | www.renaissanceesmeralda.com

A "diamond in the desert", this "remarkable" Indian Wells destination in the Renaissance Esmeralda Resort dazzles with "delectable" Northern Italian dishes that are "prepared with love" and "expertly served"; admirers advise the "beautiful" setting with a mountain view makes it ideal for "celebrating a special occasion", so it's a splurge "you won't regret."

## Sisley Italian Kitchen  *Italian*    17 | 16 | 17 | $27

**Rancho Cucamonga** | Victoria Gdns. | 12594 N. Mainstreet (Eden Ave.) | 909-899-2554 | www.sisleykitchen.com
See review in Los Angeles Directory.

## Souplantation  *American*    16 | 10 | 12 | $12

**Rancho Cucamonga** | 8966 Foothill Blvd. (Vineyard Ave.) | 909-980-9690
**San Bernardino** | 228 W. Hospitality Ln. (Hunts Ln.) | 909-381-4772
**Temecula** | 26420 Ynez Rd. (Winchester Rd.) | 951-296-3922
www.souplantation.com
Additional locations throughout Southern California
See review in Los Angeles Directory.

| | FOOD | DECOR | SERVICE | COST |
|---|---|---|---|---|

**Spencer's** *Eclectic* | 22 | 23 | 22 | $54 |

Palm Springs | Palm Springs Tennis Club | 701 W. Baristo Rd.
(Palm Canyon Rd.) | 760-327-3446 |
www.spencersrestaurant.com

Diners "can't decide whether [they] like the food or setting better" at this "sexy" Eclectic in the Palm Springs Tennis Club featuring "imaginative" cuisine with a Pacific Rim touch that's "beyond your typical banquet fare"; sporting a baby grand inside and an "outstanding" poolside patio with "beautiful" mountain views, it's steeped in "Hollywood glamour", so insiders recommend "reserving a cabana" for those "special occasions."

**NEW TAPS Fish House &** | 25 | 21 | 22 | $36 |
**Brewery** *American/Seafood*

Corona | 2745 Lakeshore Dr. (Temescal Canyon Rd.) | 951-277-5800 |
www.tapsbrea.com
See review in Orange County Directory.

**Tommy Bahama's Tropical Café** *Caribbean* | 20 | 22 | 20 | $41 |

Palm Desert | The Gardens | 73595 El Paseo (bet. Larkspur Ln. &
San Pablo Ave.) | 760-836-0188 | www.tommybahama.com

Beach buffs "love the tropical setting" at this "relaxing" Palm Desert Caribbean chain link where the "island"-inspired decor – complete with steel drums and a "wonderful patio" – gives some the feel that they're "dining in one of Tommy Bahama's shirt designs"; though the fare's "dependable", some call it "overpriced for what it is" and stick to "rum drinks" and browsing at the attached store.

**Z Wally's Desert Turtle** *Continental* | 25 | 26 | 28 | $76 |

Rancho Mirage | 71775 Hwy. 111 (Rancho Las Palmas Dr.) | 760-568-9321 |
www.wallys-desert-turtle.com

"An oldie but goodie", this "formal, but not fussy" Rancho Mirage destination "sets the standard" for "elegant" dining in the desert thanks to its "polished" staff (voted tops for Service in Palm Springs) and near-"flawless" Continental cuisine set down in a flower-filled interior with crystal light fixtures; though it's certainly "pricey", it remains a favorite for "special-occasion dinners" with "business clients" and "May-December couples" "packing the lovely dining room night after night."

**NEW Wood Ranch BBQ & Grill** *BBQ* | 20 | 16 | 18 | $28 |

Corona | The Promenade Shops at Dos Lagos |
2785 Lakeshore Drive (Temescal Canyon Rd.) | 951-667-4200 |
www.woodranch.com
See review in Los Angeles Directory.

**Yard House** *American* | 20 | 18 | 18 | $26 |

Rancho Cucamonga | Victoria Gdns. | 12473 N. Mainstreet (Day Creek Blvd.) |
909-646-7116 ●
Rancho Mirage | 71800 Hwy. 111 (bet. Hwy 111 & Rancho Las Palmas Dr.) |
(760) 779-1415 ●
**NEW** Riverside | 3775 Tyler Street Space 1A (bet. Tyler & Magnolia) |
(951) 688-9273
www.yardhouse.com
See review in Los Angeles Directory.

| | FOOD | DECOR | SERVICE | COST |
|---|---|---|---|---|

**Zin**  *American/French* | 24 | 16 | 22 | $47 |

**Palm Springs** | 198 S. Palm Canyon Dr. (Arenas Rd.) | 760-322-6300 | www.zinamericanbistro.com

*Beaucoup* backers sing the praises of this Palm Springs bistro that's become a "destination for foodies" (and "tourists") thanks to its "wonderful" French–New American menu and "extensive" wine list that's "priced right"; though the "storefront" setting is "rather ordinary", it gets a lift from "outstanding" servers who "really care."

**Zip Fusion**  *Japanese* | 18 | 15 | 16 | $27 |

**Corona** | Crossings at Corona | 2560 Tuscany St. (Grand Oaks) | 951-272-2177 | www.zipfusion.com
See review in Los Angeles Directory.

# Santa Barbara & Environs

### TOP FOOD
28 Ballard Inn | *French*
   Downey's | *Californian/Eclectic*
27 Westside Cellar | *Eclectic*
26 Arigato Sushi | *Japanese*
   Suzanne's | *French/Italian*

### TOP DECOR
27 Stonehouse
25 Stella Mare's
24 Ranch House
   Westside Cellar
   Coast

### TOP SERVICE
27 Downey's
26 Louie's
25 Ballard Inn
   Stonehouse
24 Ruth's Chris

### BEST BUYS
1. In-N-Out
2. Noah's NY Bagels
3. Sharky's Mexican
4. Baja Fresh Mexican
5. La Super-Rica

---

**NEW All India Café** *Indian*    22 | 13 | 17 | $22

**Santa Barbara** | 431 State St. (bet. Gutierrez & Haley Sts.) | 805-882-1000 | www.allindiacafe.com
See review in Los Angeles Directory.

---

**☑ Arigato Sushi** *Japanese*    26 | 16 | 18 | $42

**Santa Barbara** | 1225 State St. (bet. Anapamu & Victoria Sts.) | 805-965-6074
Devotees "dream about" this Santa Barbara Japanese offering up "everything you'd want in a high-end sushi" joint – from "innovative" rolls to "amazing" nigiri that tastes so "fresh", "it's like swimming in the ocean"; though "long waits", "tight seating" and "head-spinningly loud" acoustics are among the drawbacks, "if you can deal with the ambiance", you'll be rewarded with "some of the best" fish around.

---

**Austen's at the Pierpont Inn** *Californian*    ▽ 19 | 26 | 22 | $39

**Ventura** | Pierpont Inn | 550 Sanjon Rd. (Harbor Blvd.) | 805-643-6144 | www.pierpontinn.com
"Old-time charm" abounds at this historic Craftsman-style inn where "impeccable" servers set down "well-prepared" Californian feasts in a flower-filled room with white linens and a working fireplace; live music on the weekends adds to the appeal, as does its location "situated on a bluff" in Ventura affording soothing "ocean views."

---

**Baja Fresh Mexican Grill** *Mexican*    17 | 10 | 14 | $11

**Ventura** | Telephone Plaza | 4726-2 Telephone Rd. (Westinghouse St.) | 805-650-3535 | www.bajafresh.com
Additional locations throughout Southern California
See review in Los Angeles Directory.

---

**☑ Ballard Inn & Restaurant, The Ⓜ** *French*    28 | 23 | 25 | $58

**Ballard** | Ballard Inn | 2436 Baseline Ave. (bet. Alamo Pintado & Refugio Rds.) | 805-688-7770 | www.ballardinn.com
A "wine country must" attest oenophiles of this "unbelievable find" in Ballard – voted No. 1 for Food in Santa Barbara – showcasing chef-owner Budi Kazali's "talent in the kitchen" with "sophisticated" Asian-inflected New French fare crafted from "fresh" ingredients and complemented by a lengthy list of "local" vintages; the "intimate" setting with a "roaring fireplace" is elevated by "superb" service, making the entire "dining adventure" an "extremely pleasant" "getaway."

| | FOOD | DECOR | SERVICE | COST |
|---|---|---|---|---|

**Bella Vista** *Californian* ▽ 26 | 24 | 24 | $63

**Montecito** | Four Seasons Resort, The Biltmore | 1260 Channel Dr. (Hill Rd.) | 805-565-8237 | www.fourseasons.com

"In typical Four Seasons fashion" this Californian tucked inside Montecito's historic Biltmore hotel is deluxe in all respects, from the "beautifully designed" dining room with Italian stone floors and retractable glass roof to the rich and "tasty" wine country menu featuring lobster in vanilla butter sauce and a decadent prix fixe champagne and caviar brunch; service is "purposefully slow-paced", allowing guests to linger and enjoy the sweeping ocean views.

**BJ's** *Pub Food* 17 | 16 | 16 | $20

**Oxnard** | Esplanade Plaza | 461 W. Esplanade Dr. (bet. Oxnard Blvd. & Vineyard Rd.) | 805-485-1124 | www.bjsbrewhouse.com
Additional locations throughout Southern California
See review in Los Angeles Directory.

**Blue Agave** ● *Eclectic* ▽ 22 | 21 | 23 | $40

**Santa Barbara** | 20 E. Cota St. (State St.) | 805-899-4694 | www.blueagavesb.com

"Dark" candlelit rooms, cushioned private booths and a fireplace set the stage for an "excellent" meal at this bi-level Eclectic in Downtown Santa Barbara, where a cordial staff delivers "outstanding cocktails" and "interesting" signatures like pan-roasted duck breast and whiskey bread pudding all made with local and sustainable ingredients; though the bar area plays host to a "noisy" "singles scene", upstairs is quieter with cigars for sale to smoke on the balcony.

**Boccali's** ⊟ *Italian* ▽ 18 | 13 | 17 | $24

**Ojai** | 3277 Ojai-Santa Paula Rd. (Reese Rd.) | 805-646-6116 | www.boccalis.com

The "epitome of a great local hangout", this cash-only Ojai Italian draws a convivial crowd for "rustic" fare (like pastas and pizzas) made with produce grown on-site and wine from the family vineyard; red-checkered tablecloths give it an "informal" feel as do picnic tables outside where diners can "eat under huge oak trees" on "warm nights."

**Bouchon** *Californian/French* 25 | 21 | 24 | $61

**Santa Barbara** | 9 W. Victoria St. (bet. Chapala & State Sts.) | 805-730-1160 | www.bouchonsantabarbara.com

Smitten surveyors swear this "classy" Cal-French in Santa Barbara "exceeds expectations" with a seasonal menu of "wine country" cuisine backed by an "exceptional" cellar stocked with "boutique" bottles you'd be hard-pressed to "find anywhere else"; some feel the sting of "pricey" tabs, but most revel in the "intimate" French country setting with garden terrace and "knowledgeable" service that make this "delightful" place one of the "top dining experiences" in town.

**Brooks** Ⓜ *American* 25 | 20 | 24 | $46

**Ventura** | 545 E. Thompson Blvd. (S. California St.) | 805-652-7070 | www.restaurantbrooks.com

Chef-owner Andy Brooks hits "a home run" with this "wonderful" "high-end" "addition to Ventura's dining scene" showcasing an "inventive" New American menu with global influences and a focus on organic ingredients; "enthusiastic servers" oversee the "airy" "not-too-loud" "cosmopolitan" space dressed in brown and blue, so even if a few fault occasional "hit-or-miss" dishes, the majority insists it's "great to have in these parts."

**Brophy Bros. Restaurant & Clam Bar**  *Seafood*   | 20 | 16 | 18 | $29 |

**NEW** Ventura | 1559 Spinnaker Dr. (Harbor Blvd.) | 805-639-0865
**Santa Barbara** | 119 Harbor Way (Shoreline Dr.) | 805-966-4418
www.brophybros.com

Fin fans say "it's hard not to like" these "popular" harborfront twins in Santa Barbara and Ventura famed for their "stunning views" and "straightforward" menu of fish so "fresh" it tastes like it was just plucked "out of the sea"; "long waits" for a table can be "off-putting" to some, though the "cheerful" staff "really hops" to "keep things moving" once you're seated.

**Brothers Restaurant at
Mattei's Tavern**  *American*   | 25 | 24 | 24 | $46 |

**Los Olivos** | 2350 Railway Ave. (Foxen Canyon Rd.) | 805-688-4820 |
www.matteistavern.com

The "charming" "old stagecoach stop" setting "is the star" of this Los Olivos tavern that's "a favorite" after "a long day of wine-tasting"; a "fantastic" Traditional American menu featuring "tremendous" prime rib and "superb" service earn a loyal following among "visitors" and "locals" alike, and many maintain they've "never had a bad meal there."

**Bucatini**  *Italian*   | 20 | 16 | 20 | $33 |

**Santa Barbara** | 436 State St. (bet. E. Gutierrez & Haley Sts.) | 805-957-4177 |
www.bucatini.com

Families with "kids" "chow down" on "crisp" wood-fired pizzas and other "dependable, gut-filling" Italian specialties at this "reasonably priced" Santa Barbaran on busy State Street; though the "casual" interior is pleasant enough, those in-the-know choose the tree-surrounded patio that's "delightful" "on a warm evening."

**Ca' Dario**  *Italian*   | 24 | 17 | 20 | $42 |

**Santa Barbara** | 37 E. Victoria St. (Anacapa St.) | 805-884-9419 |
www.cadario.net

"Simple dishes made delicious" could be the motto of this Santa Barbara Italian that "does everything right" from the "unbelievable" pastas to the "sophisticated" atmosphere full of "old-world" charm; though it's often "packed" with a "neighborhood" crew, some feel the usually "professional" staff sometimes delivers less-than-stellar service amid all the "hustle and bustle."

**Café Bariloche**  *S American*   | 22 | 21 | 19 | $24 |

**Ventura** | 500 E. Main St. (Califnornia St.) | 805-641-2005 |
www.cafebariloche.com

Named after a small city in Argentina, this "charming, little" venue in Downtown Ventura offers "a break from the norm" with "phenomenally fresh" South American specialties (like "terrific empanadas") matched with regional wines; given the "reasonable prices" and friendly service too, it's no wonder local eaters seem to "love" it here.

| | FOOD | DECOR | SERVICE | COST |
|---|---|---|---|---|

### Cafe Buenos Aires  *Argentinean*
| 16 | 21 | 18 | $37 |

**Santa Barbara** | 1316 State St. (bet. Arlington Ave. & E. Victoria St.) | 805-963-0242 | www.cafebuenosaires.com

"A slice of Argentine heaven" sigh supporters lingering "under the stars" in the "beautiful courtyard" of this "romantic" bistro in the "heart of Downtown Santa Barbara"; though tango on Wednesdays and live Latin folk and jazz Fridays and Saturdays increase the appeal, less enamored eaters attest the "lovely" atmosphere "can't compensate" for fare they find "forgettable."

### Cafe del Sol  *Californian*
| ▽ 17 | 17 | 22 | $31 |

**Montecito** | 30 Los Patos Way (Cabrillo Blvd.) | 805-969-0448

With a patio overlooking a bird sanctuary in Montecito, it's all about "hanging out" and "watching the sunset" while sipping margaritas at this laid-back Californian, poised as a grown-up alternative to the "teenage bars" nearby; a "competent staff" that believes "the customer is always right" makes up for fare that some say is "mediocre" for the price.

### Cafe Fiore  *Italian*
| 22 | 22 | 18 | $34 |

**Ventura** | 66 S. California St. (bet. Main St. & Santa Clara St.) | 805-653-1266 | www.fiorerestaurant.net

Ventura's smart set frequents this "romantic" eatery for its "eclectic" Southern Italian dishes, "wonderful" pizza and specialty martinis (a bit "steeper" in price than some of the food); live music, an open kitchen and a fireplace make it extra "inviting", but service can be "spotty" and the room gets "loud", so "sit in the back or outside if you want to talk."

### Café Nouveau  *Californian*
| ▽ 20 | 20 | 17 | $24 |

**Ventura** | 1497 E. Thompson Blvd. (San Jon St.) | 805-648-1422

"Quaint and off the beaten path", this "cozy" Ventura cafe in a "Spanish-style home on a residential street" dishes up "casual Californian" cooking and "French cafe" charm with "people-watching" on the patio; most say go for the "great breakfast", but dinner is a little "less exciting" and service "lacks a bit."

### Cajun Kitchen  *Cajun*
| 18 | 9 | 17 | $16 |

**Goleta** | 6831 Hollister Ave. (Glen Annie Rd.) | 805-571-1517
**NEW** **Ventura** | 301 E. Main St. (Palm St.) | 805-643-7701
**Carpinteria** | 865 Linden Ave. (bet. 8th & 9th Sts.) | 805-684-6010
**Santa Barbara** | 1924 De La Vina St. (Mission St.) | 805-687-2062
**Santa Barbara** | 901 Chapala St. (Cañon Perdido St.) | 805-965-1004 Ⓢ
www.cajunkitchensb.com

"Solid" "country-style breakfasts" with a Cajun twist provide the "perfect hangover remedy" (if you can "tune out the crowds") at this daytime "greasy spoon" chain where "there's always a wait on the weekends"; sure, it's "nothing fancy", but it's "friendly" and "prompt" once you sit down, and the "big portions" are a bonus.

### California Pizza Kitchen  *Pizza*
| 18 | 14 | 17 | $21 |

**Ventura** | Pacific View Mall | 3301 E. Main St. (Mills Rd.) | 805-639-5060
**Santa Barbara** | Paseo Nuevo Mall | 719 Paseo Nuevo, on Chapala St. (De La Guerra St.) | 805-962-4648
www.cpk.com
Additional locations throughout Southern California
**See review in Los Angeles Directory.**

|  | FOOD | DECOR | SERVICE | COST |
|---|---|---|---|---|

### Cantina Joannafina y Bar La Luna  *Mexican*   ▽ 19 | 14 | 21 | $19

**Ventura** | 1127 S. Seaward Ave. (Pierpont Ave.) | 805-652-0360 |
www.cantinajoannafina.com
See review in Los Angeles Directory.

### Carlitos Café y Cantina  *Mexican*   18 | 16 | 15 | $30

**Santa Barbara** | 1324 State St. (bet. Sola & Victoria Sts.) | 805-962-7117 |
www.carlitos.com
"Fresh" Mexican fare, "fine" margaritas and a "festive", "colorful" atmosphere are the signatures of this Santa Barbara "favorite" in a "great location"; laid-back types say live music and "people-watching on the patio" help make up for mediocre service and relatively "steep prices", plus the "servings are big enough to share."

### Cava  *Pan-Latin*   18 | 18 | 18 | $37

**Montecito** | 1212 Coast Village Rd. (Olive Mill Rd.) | 805-969-8500 |
www.cavarestaurant.com
"Chimichurri heaven" cheer amigos of this Montecito "locals' place" (a sib of Carlito's Café) and its "varied" menu of "haute" Pan-Latin fare; while the service can be "spotty", the tile-floored interior and outdoor seating are "comfortable", plus the mojitos add a festive touch.

### Chad's ⓩ  *American*   21 | 18 | 18 | $36

**Santa Barbara** | 625 Chapala St. (bet. Cota & Ortega Sts.) | 805-568-1876 |
www.chadsonline.com
A "lively setting for a celebration", this Santa Barbaran rocks steady with "well-executed" New American cuisine, dependable service and a "comfy" atmosphere in a 19th-century house; a few call it "overpriced", but the martinis and live music ensure a "huge scene" on the weekends.

### Chef Karim's   ▽ 19 | 19 | 18 | $44
### Moroccan Restaurant Ⓜ  *Moroccan*

**Santa Barbara** | Victoria Ct. | 1221 State St. (Anapamu St.) | 805-899-4780 |
www.chefkarim.com
"Bring your dancing hips and join in the spirit" cry fans of this Santa Barbara Moroccan where the "b'steeya is lovely and the tagines fine"; many "go for the drapery-hung low couch seats and the belly dancing" despite critics' claims that the "music is intrusive" and means too high a markup on the meal.

### China Pavilion  *Chinese*   19 | 16 | 19 | $25

**Montecito** | 1070 Coast Village Rd. (bet. Hermosillo Dr. & Hot Springs Rd.) |
805-565-9380
**Santa Barbara** | 1202 Chapala St. (Anapamu St.) | 805-560-6028
www.china-pavilion.com
"A cut above your neighborhood Chinese", these Montecito and Santa Barbara sibs provide "updated standard fare and innovative dishes" prepared with a "light touch"; the settings are fairly refined and "cheerfully" staffed to support the "elevated" cost, though homebodies would be more enamored "if only they delivered!"

### Cholada  *Thai*   24 | 9 | 19 | $22

**Ventura** | 387 E. Main St. (bet. Oak & Palm Sts.) | 805-641-3573 |
www.choladathaicuisine.com
See review in Los Angeles Directory.

| | FOOD | DECOR | SERVICE | COST |
|---|---|---|---|---|

**Z NEW Coast** *Californian/Seafood*    21 | 24 | 22 | $43

**Santa Barbara** | Canary Hotel | 31 W. Carrillo St. (Chipala St.) | 805-884-0300 | www.canarysantabarbara.com

See review in Los Angeles Directory.

**Cold Spring Tavern** *American*    20 | 23 | 19 | $36

**Santa Barbara** | 5995 Stagecoach Rd. (Rte. 154) | 805-967-0066 | www.coldspringtavern.com

"Step back into the Old West" at this "hidden" historic stagecoach stop in the mountains above Santa Barbara featuring "rustic" "charm galore" and all-American "meat-eater" sustenance from "outstanding chili" to wild game; though it gets "touristy" and some of the fare is "nothing special", live country and bluegrass acts wow on weekends, attracting an "eclectic gathering of bikers and yuppies" alike.

**Z Downey's M** *Californian/French*    28 | 20 | 27 | $66

**Santa Barbara** | 1305 State St. (Victoria St.) | 805-966-5006 | www.downeyssb.com

"Exceptional since it opened" in 1982, this "foodie original" owned by John and Liz Downey (he cooks and she runs the front of the house) turns out "magnificent" Cal-French cuisine emphasizing "local ingredients treated with care", and boasts a "wonderful", "convivial" staff – earning it the No. 1 score for Service as well as the Most Popular title in Santa Barbara; a "quiet", "romantic" setting enhances the meal, so most agree the "expensive" tab is "worth it."

**Elements** *Californian*    18 | 23 | 20 | $44

**Santa Barbara** | 129 E. Anapamu St. (bet. Anacapa & Santa Barbara Sts.) | 805-884-9218 | www.elementsrestaurantandbar.com

Locals laud the "lovely views" of the Santa Barbara courthouse gardens afforded at this moderately priced Californian set in a "beautiful" converted "old house" divided into four elementally themed drinking and dining areas (some with "noisy acoustics"); its "creative" menu boasts a seasonal sensibility and is backed by a wine list featuring local and boutique selections.

**El Torito** *Mexican*    15 | 14 | 15 | $21

**Santa Barbara** | 29 E. Cabrillo Blvd. (State St.) | 805-963-1968 | www.eltorito.com

Additional locations throughout Southern California

See review in Los Angeles Directory.

**Emilio's** *Italian/Mediterranean*    20 | 18 | 18 | $41

**Santa Barbara** | 324 W. Cabrillo Blvd. (Bath St.) | 805-966-4426 | www.emiliosrestaurant.com

"Ocean breezes" add to the "relaxing" atmosphere of this moderately priced Santa Barbara Northern Italian–Med "located right across from the marina" where the "balanced" dishes are crafted from "fresh, local ingredients" and served up with "nicely chosen wines" in a "quaint" setting complete with "flattering lighting" and a wood-beamed ceiling; though longtimers lament "it's not as good as it used to be", it remains a "dependable" pick among the "regular visiting set"; N.B. the above Food rating may not fully reflect a 2008 chef change.

| | FOOD | DECOR | SERVICE | COST |
|---|---|---|---|---|

**Enterprise Fish Co.** *Seafood* — 19 | 17 | 18 | $34
**Santa Barbara** | 225 State St. (bet. Montecido & State Sts.) | 805-962-3313 |
www.enterprisefishco.com
See review in Los Angeles Directory.

**Hitching Post** *BBQ* — 23 | 14 | 19 | $42
**Buellton** | 406 E. Rte. 246 (½ mi. east of Rte. 101) | 805-688-0676 |
www.hitchingpost2.com
**Casmalia** | 3325 Point Sal Rd. (Santo Rd.) | 805-937-6151 |
www.hitchingpost1.com
Thanks to "sightseers" making "a post-*Sideways* pilgrimage", it's
often a "madhouse" at the Buellton branch of these "classic" Central
Coast-style BBQs searing "perfectly seasoned steaks" and serving
them with "wonderful" "well-priced" local wines – like "Pinot Noir",
natch – in "cozy" "cowboy"-style quarters; the Casmalia outpost also
offers similarly "fine", "honest" fare at a "good price", in quieter,
less "touristy" environs; P.S. don't forget to try "their own brand" of
vino, Hartley Ostini.

**Holdren's Steaks & Seafood** *Seafood/Steak* — ▽ 21 | 19 | 20 | $42
**Santa Barbara** | 512 State St. (Haley St.) | 805-965-3363 | www.holdrens.com
See review in Los Angeles Directory.

**Hungry Cat, The** ❶ *Seafood* — 24 | 16 | 20 | $43
**Santa Barbara** | 1134 Chapala St. (bet. Anapamu & Figueroa Sts.) |
805-884-4701 | www.thehungrycat.com
See review in Los Angeles Directory.

**⊠ In-N-Out Burger** ❶ *Burgers* — 23 | 10 | 19 | $8
**Goleta** | 4865 Calle Real (bet. Pebble Hill Pl. & Turnpike Rd.)
**Ventura** | 2070 Harbor Blvd. (Seaward Ave.)
**Oxnard** | Esplanade Plaza | 381 W. Esplanade Dr. (Oxnard Blvd.)
800-786-1000 | www.in-n-out.com
Additional locations throughout Southern California
See review in Los Angeles Directory.

**Jade** ⊠Ⓜ *Pacific Rim* — - | - | - | M
**Santa Barbara** | 3132 State St. (Las Positas Rd.) | 805-563-2007 |
www.jadesb.com
Husband-and-wife team Dustin and Jeannine Green conjure up a "creative" menu of "fine" Pacific Rim dishes at this Santa Barbara locale
that remains somewhat undiscovered; despite white tablecloths, the
vibe is casual and the food is "reasonably priced", making it an accessible refuge "away from the tourist crowd."

**Joe's Crab Shack** *Seafood* — 13 | 15 | 15 | $26
**Ventura** | 567 San Jon Rd. (Vista Del Mar Pl.) | 805-643-3725 |
www.joescrabshack.com
See review in Los Angeles Directory.

**Jonathan's at Peirano's** *Californian/Mediterranean* — 23 | 21 | 22 | $38
**Ventura** | Peirano | 204 E. Main St. (bet. N. Ventura Ave. & Palm St.) |
805-648-4853 | www.jonathansatpeiranos.com
Set in a landmark brick building in Ventura's historic Mission District,
this "fine" Cal-Med provides an eclectic menu of "inventive" dishes at
an "excellent value"; the "overall ambiance" is pleasing with patio ta-

bles, a "helpful" staff and live music on the weekends, plus chef/co-owner Jason Collis also serves up small bites at J's Tapas next door.

### ☑ La Super-Rica ⊅ *Mexican* | 25 | 5 | 13 | $14 |

**Santa Barbara** | 622 N. Milpas St. (Alphonse St.) | 805-963-4940

Any "favorite of Julia Child" is "way good enough for me" boast fans of this Mexican "shack" in Santa Barbara, a "one-star setting" with "five-star food" (and order-at-the-counter service) where "grilled meats", "off-the-charts *horchata*" and "tender" tortillas made right before your eyes are among the sought-after specialties; true, the lines often "snake" down the block, but that's no problem for peso-pinchers who pronounce it a "champion" of "cheap" eats.

### Los Arroyos *Mexican* | 22 | 16 | 15 | $24 |

**Montecito** | 1280 Coast Village Rd. (Olive Mill Rd.) | 805-969-9059
**Santa Barbara** | 14 W. Figueroa St. (bet. Chapala & State Sts.) | 805-962-5541
www.losarroyos.net

"Delicious" "upmarket" Mexican fare can be found at this "family-run, family-oriented" taqueria twosome turning out "fresh" seafood burritos among other "simple" specialties; samplers say "Montecito is the pretty place" with a "nice patio", while the Santa Barbara original is more "fast-foodie."

### Los Olivos Cafe *Californian/Mediterranean* | 22 | 19 | 21 | $36 |

**Los Olivos** | 2879 Grand Ave. (Alamo Pintado Ave.) | 805-688-7265 | www.losolivoscafe.com

A "fun stop on the wine trail", this "packed" Cal-Med made famous in the movie *Sideways* lures Los Olivos locals and "tourists" alike with "well-prepared" seasonal cuisine and an "excellent" 500-bottle cellar, with tastings offered during the day; a "helpful" staff, "comfortable" dining room and wisteria-covered patio all contribute to a refreshingly un-"stuffy" experience.

### ☑ Louie's *Californian* | 23 | 23 | 26 | $43 |

**Santa Barbara** | Upham Hotel | 1404 De La Vina St. (W. Sola St.) | 805-963-7003 | www.louiessb.com

"Ah, relaxing" – this Californian "sleeper" in Santa Barbara's Upham Hotel, a historic Victorian, has "style and grace", making it a "treat" before "Downtown cultural events"; a "dependable" menu of "delectable dishes", "fabulous" wines and "wonderful" service keep locals loyal.

### Lucky's *Steak* | 25 | 22 | 23 | $62 |

**Montecito** | 1279 Coast Village Rd. (Olive Mill Rd.) | 805-565-7540 | www.luckys-steakhouse.com

"Always a winner", this Montecito steakhouse attracts a "monied" "entertainment-world" crowd that goes to "see and be seen" over "superb", "juicy" porterhouse cuts and "consistently good" sides ferried by a "fabulous" staff in a "packed" mahogany-accented room; though a few critics contend that "stargazing" trumps the food and service, most agree "you'll walk away happy."

### Maravilla ⓜ *Californian* | ▽ 21 | 26 | 27 | $68 |

**Ojai** | Ojai Valley Inn & Spa | 705 Country Club Dr. (San Antonio St.) | 805-646-5511 | www.ojairesort.com

"Excellent in every respect", this Spanish-accented Californian in the Ojai Valley Inn & Spa offers "incredible" mountain views and a "phe-

|  | FOOD | DECOR | SERVICE | COST |
|--|------|-------|---------|------|

nomenal" 700-bottle wine list to accompany the seasonal, locally sourced cuisine; service is top-notch too, so "sit outside for lunch on a spring day and just try to be grouchy."

### NEW Marmalade Café *American/Californian*    17 | 17 | 18 | $26

**Santa Barbara** | La Cumbre Plaza | 3825 State St. (La Cumbra Rd.) | www.marmaladecafe.com
See review in Los Angeles Directory.

### Mimi's Cafe *Diner*    17 | 17 | 18 | $19

**Ventura** | 3375 E. Main St. (Mills Rd.) | 805-644-1388 | www.mimiscafe.com
Additional locations throughout Southern California
See review in Los Angeles Directory.

### Mimosa *French*    19 | 14 | 15 | $36

**Santa Barbara** | 2700 De La Vina St. (Alamar Ave.) | 805-682-2272
"Nothing nouvelle here", just "dependable" "old-fashioned" French fare at this midpriced Santa Barbara longtimer; some call it "middling" all around, but advocates say "if you can get past the grandma decor", it's "excellent."

### Miró ⑤Ⓜ *Spanish*    - | - | - | VE

**Santa Barbara** | Bacara Resort | 8301 Hollister Ave. (Rte. 101) | 805-968-0100 | www.bacararesort.com
A sprinkling of surveyors commends the "elegant dining" at this Santa Barbaran in the Bacara Resort & Spa, featuring Basque-Catalan cuisine made with produce "grown on the property", and an epic 1,200-bottle cellar; Miró sculptures and other original artwork provide the backdrop for ocean views, but some feel the experience is best left to the "idle rich."

### Montecito Cafe *Californian*    24 | 19 | 22 | $38

**Montecito** | Montecito Inn | 1295 Coast Village Rd. (Olive Mill Rd.) | 805-969-3392 | www.montecitocafe.com
One of the "best bargains" around, this "tried-and-true" "treasure" in the historic Montecito Inn "continues to please" with its "light, healthy" Cal dishes (including "scrumptious" salads) that are "interesting but never outrageous"; "efficient" service is another plus, and while the bright, open space can get "noisy and crowded", fans call that "part of the fun."

### Noah's New York Bagels *Sandwiches*    17 | 11 | 14 | $9

**Ventura** | Victoria Vill. | 1413 S. Victoria Ave. (bet. Ralston & Telephone Sts.) | 805-650-1413 | www.noahs.com
See review in Los Angeles Directory.

### Olio e Limone *Italian*    24 | 19 | 23 | $52

**Santa Barbara** | 11 W. Victoria St., Ste. 17 (bet. Chapala & State Sts.) | 805-899-2699 | www.olioelimone.com
"Simply delightful" coo those charmed by this Santa Barbara Italian where a "strong kitchen" turns out "earthy dishes" that show a "deft handling" of ingredients; husband-and-wife-team Alberto and Elaine Morello preside over the "lovely" ivory-walled dining room giving the operation a "personal" touch that overrides any complaints about "pricey" tabs; P.S. "reservations a necessity."

| | FOOD | DECOR | SERVICE | COST |
|---|---|---|---|---|

**Opal** *Californian/Eclectic*    22 | 18 | 22 | $39

**Santa Barbara** | 1325 State St. (Arlington Ave.) | 805-966-9676 | www.opalrestaurantandbar.com

"Jammed with locals", this "well-located" Santa Barbaran "next to the Arlington Theater" offers a "broad menu" of "inspired" Cal-Eclectic dishes like chile-crusted filet mignon plus stiff signature cocktails at prices declared an "excellent value" for the area; an "easygoing staff" keeps the mood convivial, though a few find the "noisy" acoustics at night mean that "lunch with friends" is a more civilized bet.

**Outback Steakhouse** *Steak*    17 | 15 | 17 | $28

**Goleta** | 5690 Calle Real (bet. Fairview & Patterson Aves.) | 805-964-0599
**Oxnard** | 2341 Lockwood St. (Outlet Center Dr.) | 805-988-4329
www.outback.com
Additional locations throughout Southern California
See review in Los Angeles Directory.

**Palace Grill** *Cajun/Creole*    22 | 19 | 24 | $35

**Santa Barbara** | 8 E. Cota St. (State St.) | 805-963-5000 | www.palacegrill.com

Fans of "New Orleans"–style cooking claim it "doesn't get any better" than this "boisterous" Santa Barbara "crowd-pleaser" where the "just plain good" Cajun-Creole fare gets a kick from spicy signature martinis served in "mason jars" ("a must-have"); service is "exceptionally pleasant", but "come early or late" as there's often "a line"; N.B. there's live music Tuesday, Thursday and Saturday nights.

**Pane e Vino** 🆂 *Italian*    21 | 21 | 21 | $39

**Santa Barbara** | Upper Montecito Vill. | 1482 E. Valley Rd. (bet. Santa Angela Ln. & San Ysidro Rd.) | 805-969-9274
See review in Los Angeles Directory.

**Piatti** *Italian*    19 | 19 | 19 | $36

**Montecito** | 516 San Ysidro Rd. (E. Balley Rd.) | 805-969-7520 | www.piatti.com
See review in Los Angeles Directory.

**Piranha Restaurant & Sushi** *Japanese*    - | - | - | M

**Santa Barbara** | 801 State St. (E. De La Guerra St.) | 805-965-2980
Though ensconced in new State Street digs, this "wonderful" Santa Barbara sushi specialist can still be counted on for "unusual" Japanese offerings like lobster gyoza complemented by "great cocktails"; its sleek white-and-black dining room is decorated with a "stylish" touch, but in warm weather, most angle for a seat on the patio.

**Plow & Angel** *Californian/Eclectic*    ∇ 24 | 26 | 24 | $56

**Montecito** | San Ysidro Ranch | 900 San Ysidro Ln. (E. Mountain Dr.) | 805-969-5046 | www.sanysidroranch.com

"Split a meal with your sweetie" at this "Montecito favorite" located in the "fabled San Ysidro Ranch" resort whose rustic "fireplace-lit" atmosphere conjures up a "cozy English pub"; the Californian-Eclectic menu features "classic mac 'n' cheese", "upscale hamburgers" and the like, and though it's not inexpensive, a meal here may be "the cheapest" ticket onto the "idyllic" grounds.

| | FOOD | DECOR | SERVICE | COST |

**Z Ranch House M** *Californian* — 23 | 24 | 23 | $56

**Ojai** | 500 S. Lomita Ave. (Tico Rd.) | 805-646-2360 |
www.theranchhouse.com

The picture of "country elegance", this pricey Ojai retreat makes the most of its "naturally beautiful" setting with an outside dining area surrounded by "glorious gardens" of "fragrant flowers and herbs"; seasonal Californian fare is enhanced by a 1,200-label wine list, so even if cynics call it "dated", it remains a standby for "special occasions" nonetheless.

**Z NEW Ruth's Chris Steak House** *Steak* — 26 | 22 | 24 | $63

**Santa Barbara** | La Cumbre Plaza | 3815 State St. (Hope Ave.) |
805-563-5674

See review in Los Angeles Directory.

**Sakana M** *Japanese* — - | - | - | M

**Montecito** | 1046 Coast Village Rd. (Hot Springs Rd.) | 805-565-2014

A husband-and-wife team are behind this midpriced Montecito Japanese whose simple black-and-white space is bedecked with numerous sake bottles; though diners divide on the sushi and sashimi ("fantastic" vs. "not worth a special trip"), either way, it's "popular with locals", so "be prepared for a wait."

**Savoy Truffles** *American* — - | - | - | I

**Santa Barbara** | 24 W. Figueroa St. (State St.) | 805-966-2139 |
www.savoytruffles.com

Get ready to "assemble your own meal" from "fresh and tasty" salads, soups, sandwiches and other American comestibles at this Santa Barbara gourmet shop also famed for its "homemade desserts"; "good-value" pricing makes it a popular lunch stop, but given its diminutive size, some suggest you "go early" to avoid the rush.

**NEW Seagrass** *Seafood* — - | - | - | E

**Santa Barbara** | 30 E. Ortega St. (Anacapa St.) | 805-963-1012

This upscale Santa Barbara seafooder and sib of Bouchon features a seasonally shifting menu that relies on sustainable fin fare, farmer's market produce and local wines; though its luxuriously whitewashed and wainscoted interior is reminiscent of a Cape Cod cottage, its location just off busy State Street gives it a distinctly central coast feel.

**71 Palm** *American/French* — 20 | 21 | 21 | $41

**Ventura** | 71 N. Palm St. (bet. Main & Poli Sts.) | 805-653-7222 |
www.71palm.com

Set in a "beautiful old Craftsman house" dating back to 1910, this Ventura destination doles out "sturdy" French-American "classics" – think "rich sauces", steaks and seafood – in a "delightful" country-style room with bare wood floors and lacy curtains; though the experience is heightened by "fine service", a few feel stung by "high prices."

**Sevilla** *Pan-Latin* — ▽ 20 | 24 | 16 | $57

**Santa Barbara** | 428 Chapala St. (State St.) | 805-564-8446

"Hip" and "romantic", this Santa Barbara spot "sets the mood for a special occasion" with a "loungey" atmosphere, "seductive drinks" and an "amazing" wine selection; while its pricey Pan-Latin plates "stimulate the taste buds", some find them "not particularly Spanish" and feel the service is less swanky than the surroundings.

| | FOOD | DECOR | SERVICE | COST |
|---|---|---|---|---|

**Sharky's Mexican Grill**  *Mexican*  | 18 | 11 | 15 | $12 |

**Ventura** | Gateway Ctr. | 4960 Telephone Rd. (bet. Portola Rd. & Saratoga Ave.) | 805-339-9600 | www.sharkys.com
Additional locations throughout Southern California
See review in Los Angeles Directory.

**Sidecar Restaurant** ⓜ *American*  | 25 | 22 | 22 | $38 |

**Ventura** | 3029 E. Main St. (bet. Mills & Telegraph Rds.) | 805-653-7433 | www.thesidecarrestaurant.com
"Still humming along", this Ventura American "showcases the season's best" with chef/co-owner Tim Kilcoyne's "innovative", "well-presented" dishes; "upscale" yet "relaxed", the "warm, inviting atmosphere" inside a restored Pullman train car lends itself to events like the "fun" grilled cheese and jazz night every Tuesday.

**Spice Avenue**  *Indian*  | - | - | - | I |

**Santa Barbara** | 1027 State St. (Figueroa St.) | 805-965-6004 | www.spiceavenuesb.com
"A reasonable choice", this Santa Barbara Indian on State Street turns out "satisfying" fare with a seafood focus from a "friendly", family-run team; though it's "not innovative" in its cuisine or decor, guests appreciate the "good value" of the buffet during lunch and Wednesday dinner.

**Square One** ⓜ *American*  | ▽ 24 | 18 | 21 | $49 |

**Santa Barbara** | 14 E. Cota St. (State St.) | 805-965-4565 | www.squareonesb.com
"Maturing" but still "relatively undiscovered", this casually upscale New American in Santa Barbara features a "high-quality", weekly changing menu by "creative" chef Jason Tuley; the staff enhances the "comfortable" atmosphere, though a few suggest the earthy decor "could use some oomph."

**Z Stella Mare's** ⓜ *Californian*  | 23 | 25 | 23 | $44 |

**Santa Barbara** | 50 Los Patos Way (Cabrio Blvd.) | 805-969-6705
"Exquisite" surroundings, "wonderful" wine-country fare and "excellent" service make this "fairly priced" Santa Barbara Californian inside a converted Victorian house a "delightful place to dine"; especially "gorgeous" in the "greenhouse room", it entices both "ladies who lunch" and couples out for a "romantic" evening.

**Z Stonehouse**  *American*  | 25 | 27 | 25 | $80 |

**Montecito** | San Ysidro Ranch | 900 San Ysidro Ln. (Hwy. 101) | 805-969-4100 | www.sanysidroranch.com
"Beautiful and secluded", this renovated, reopened Montecito New American in a 19th-century stone house, voted No. 1 for Decor in Santa Barbara, creates a "warm", "magical" dining experience, both inside and on the "wonderful" deck; "fresh, imaginative" cooking and "polished" service also draw "Hollywood types" to its "remote" location at the San Ysidro Ranch resort, so "be ready to park next to Bentleys and Aston Martins and pay the price."

**Sushi Ozekii** Ⓩ *Japanese*  | ▽ 17 | 16 | 20 | $30 |

**Ventura** | 1437 S. Victoria Ave., Ste. E (Ralston St.) | 805-477-9897
See review in Los Angeles Directory.

### Z Suzanne's Cuisine *French/Italian*

| | | | |
|---|---|---|---|
| 26 | 21 | 23 | $48 |

**Ojai** | 502 W. Ojai Ave. (Bristol Ave.) | 805-640-1961 |
www.suzannescuisine.com

Admirers assert "a trip to Ojai is incomplete without a visit" to this "top-notch" French-Italian owned by mother-daughter team Suzanne Roll and Sandra Moore, offering "imaginative" high-end dishes with an emphasis on "local meats, fish and produce"; the "attentive" service suits a "leisurely" meal on a "weekend getaway", whether in the "homey" interior or on the "delightfully romantic" patio "overlooking the garden."

### Taproom, The *Californian*

| | | | |
|---|---|---|---|
| ▽ 20 | 20 | 18 | $22 |

**Buellton** | Firestone Walker Brewing Co. | 620 McMurray Rd. | 805-686-1557 |
www.firestonewalker.com

Offering "more" than bar food, this Buellton watering hole at Firestone Walker Brewing Company serves Californian fare made from "local ingredients" to go with its "good beer on draft"; decked with oak tables, it provides a "friendly atmosphere" fit for "meeting friends after work."

### Tee-Off *Seafood/Steak*

| | | | |
|---|---|---|---|
| - | - | - | E |

**Santa Barbara** | Ontare Plaza | 3627 State St. (Ontare Rd.) | 805-687-1616 |
www.teeoffsb.com

A "meat-and-potatoes" kind of place, this "clubby" "1960s"-era eatery in Santa Barbara turns out "expensive" but satisfying "old-fashioned" surf 'n' turf along with "giant drinks"; decorated with golf memorabilia, it makes for a "pleasant throwback."

### Trattoria Grappolo *Italian*

| | | | |
|---|---|---|---|
| 25 | 18 | 24 | $40 |

**Santa Ynez** | 3687 Sagunto St. (Meadowvale Rd.) | 805-688-6899 |
www.trattoriagrappolo.com

"An oasis in the near-desert" that's ideal for "post-winery meals", this "welcoming" Santa Ynez Italian with a wood-burning oven ranks as a "secret favorite" thanks to its "fresh", "authentic" dishes and "reasonable" selection of local bottles served with "hospitality and enthusiasm"; as the "Old West setting" is "always packed", be sure to "go early or make a reservation."

### Trattoria Mollie M *Italian*

| | | | |
|---|---|---|---|
| 22 | 19 | 20 | $46 |

**Montecito** | 1250 Coast Village Rd. (Elizabeth Ln.) | 805-565-9381 |
www.tmollie.com

"The only thing more delightful than the food" is chef-owner Mollie Ahlstrand cheer champions of this Montecito "hangout" luring "local beautiful people" with its "fresh, tasty" Tuscan fare, including those "famous meatballs"; though critics consider the surroundings "somewhat cold" and the eats a bit "ordinary", at least they're "spiced by who might be sitting next to you."

### Tre Lune *Italian*

| | | | |
|---|---|---|---|
| 21 | 20 | 21 | $49 |

**Montecito** | 1151 Coast Village Rd. (bet. Butterfly Ln. & Middle Rd.) |
805-969-2646

"Upbeat" and "comfortable", this "unexpected place" in Montecito serves "real-deal" pastas and pizzas that make you feel "like you're in Italy again", even if it is "a little pricey"; customers say the "cute 'old Hollywood'" digs can get "noisy", but given the clientele of "local VIPs", it makes for "interesting eavesdropping"; P.S. the "opera dinners are outstanding."

**Tupelo Junction** *Southern*

20 | 18 | 20 | $35

**Santa Barbara** | 1218 State St. (bet. Anapamu & Victoria Sts.) |
805-899-3100 | www.tupelojunction.com

This Santa Barbara Southerner "excels" at "gourmet" renditions of
"comfort food" like "heavenly fried chicken" and "savory pot pies"
plus "hearty" breakfasts that are "not to be missed"; "quick" service is
appealing, as are the cheery surroundings with fruit-crate labels
adorning the walls, so even if some "dieters" demur on the "heavy"
fare, most are more than happy to consider a visit here "a vacation
from calorie counting."

**Via Vai** *Italian*

20 | 15 | 21 | $33

**Montecito** | Upper Vill. | 1483 E. Valley Rd. (San Ysidro Rd.) | 805-565-9393
"Satisfying" Italian cooking like "terrific" thin-crust pizzas and
"fine pastas" keep this "inexpensive" Montecito Italian "popular
with locals"; a "gracious" staff maintains a "family-friendly" vibe in
the "casual" beige-toned interior, while outside features a patio
affording "unbeatable" views of "the mountains" and the "old mission-
style buildings" nearby.

🔲 **Westside Cellar Cafe & Wine Store** *Eclectic*

27 | 24 | 23 | $40

**Ventura** | 222 E. Main St. (bet. Palm St. & Ventura Ave.) | 805-652-7013
"Wonderful wines" are matched with "delicious" cheese platters and
more substantial "innovative" Eclectic bistro offerings at this Ventura
"favorite" where the "fabulous" selection of global vintages is also
available for sale in the adjoining shop; seating in the narrow brick-
walled space can feel a bit "jammed", but the mood is "comfortable"
so most say they "enjoy" the overall experience.

**Wine Cask** *Californian*

24 | 23 | 22 | $57

**Santa Barbara** | 813 Anacapa St. (bet. Canon Perdido & De La Guerra Sts.) |
805-966-9463 | www.winecask.com

The "glorious" 2,000-bottle wine list is the star of this Santa Barbara
Californian that "takes its food seriously" too with a seasonal menu
yielding "distinctive" "delicious" dishes; service is "attentive" while
the dining room – housed in a historic late-19th-century building and
graced with a "beautiful" hand-stenciled ceiling – is deemed "romantic" as well, putting this "pricey" "treasure" near the "top of the list"
for a "special" evening.

# ORANGE COUNTY/ PALM SPRINGS/ SANTA BARBARA INDEXES

Restaurant locations are indicated by the following abbreviations:
Orange County=OC; Palm Springs & Environs=PS; and Santa
Barbara & Environs=SB.

vote at ZAGAT.com                                                     347

# Cuisines

Includes restaurant names, locations and Food ratings. ☑ indicates places with the highest ratings, popularity and importance.

## AMERICAN (NEW)

| | |
|---|---|
| Bayside \| **Newport Bch/OC** | 24 |
| Bistango \| **Irvine/OC** | 24 |
| Brooks \| **Ventura/SB** | 25 |
| Cat/Custard Cup \| **La Habra/OC** | 26 |
| Chad's \| **SB** | 21 |
| ☑ Copley's \| **PS** | 25 |
| La Quinta Cliffhse. \|   **La Quinta/PS** | 16 |
| Matchbox \| **PS** | - |
| Mr. Stox \| **Anaheim/OC** | 24 |
| Park Ave. \| **Stanton/OC** | 26 |
| Ramos Hse. \| **San Juan Cap/OC** | 25 |
| Sage \| **multi.** | 24 |
| Square One \| **SB** | 24 |
| ☑ Stonehill Tav. \| **Dana Pt/OC** | 27 |
| ☑ Stonehouse \| **Montecito/SB** | 25 |
| Wildfish/Grille \| **Newport Bch/OC** | 23 |
| Yard Hse. \| **multi.** | 20 |
| Zin \| **PS** | 24 |

## AMERICAN (TRADITIONAL)

| | |
|---|---|
| ☑ Arnold Palmer's \| **La Quinta/PS** | 20 |
| Billy Reed's \| **PS** | 17 |
| BJ's \| **multi.** | 17 |
| Brothers Rest. \| **Los Olivos/SB** | 25 |
| ☑ Cheesecake Factory \| **multi.** | 19 |
| Claim Jumper \| **multi.** | 19 |
| Cold Spring \| **SB** | 20 |
| Daily Grill \| **Palm Desert/PS** | 18 |
| First Cabin \| **Newport Bch/OC** | 24 |
| Hog's Breath Inn \| **La Quinta/PS** | 15 |
| Islands \| **multi.** | 16 |
| Johnny Rockets \| **Rancho Cuca/PS** | 15 |
| Kaiser Grille \| **PS** | 16 |
| Mimi's Cafe \| **multi.** | 17 |
| Original Pancake \|   **Temecula/PS** | 23 |
| Park Ave. \| **Stanton/OC** | 26 |
| **NEW** Rattlesnake \|   **Palm Desert/PS** | 27 |
| Ruby's \| **Riverside/PS** | 17 |
| Savoy Truffles \| **SB** | - |
| Shame on Moon \|   **Rancho Mirage/PS** | 23 |
| Sidecar Rest. \| **Ventura/SB** | 25 |
| Souplantation \| **multi.** | 16 |
| TAPS \| **Brea/OC** | 25 |

## ARGENTINEAN

| | |
|---|---|
| Cafe Buenos Aires \| **SB** | 16 |

## ARMENIAN

| | |
|---|---|
| Rosine's \| **Corona/PS** | 22 |

## ASIAN FUSION

| | |
|---|---|
| Café Hiro \| **Cypress/OC** | 25 |
| Roy's \| **multi.** | 23 |

## BARBECUE

| | |
|---|---|
| Hitching Post \| **multi.** | 23 |
| Johnny Rebs' \| **Victorville/PS** | 22 |
| Lucille's BBQ \| **Rancho Cuca/PS** | 22 |
| Wood Ranch BBQ \| **Corona/PS** | 20 |

## BRAZILIAN

| | |
|---|---|
| Picanha Churrascaria \|   **Cathedral City/PS** | 21 |

## BRITISH

| | |
|---|---|
| Lord Fletcher's \|   **Rancho Mirage/PS** | 17 |

## BURGERS

| | |
|---|---|
| ☑ In-N-Out \| **multi.** | 23 |
| Islands \| **multi.** | 16 |
| Johnny Rockets \| **Rancho Cuca/PS** | 15 |
| Ruby's \| **Riverside/PS** | 17 |

## CAJUN

| | |
|---|---|
| Cajun Kitchen \| **multi.** | 18 |
| Palace Grill \| **SB** | 22 |

## CALIFORNIAN

| | |
|---|---|
| Austen's \| **Ventura/SB** | 19 |
| AZUR \| **La Quinta/PS** | - |
| Bella Vista \| **Montecito/SB** | 26 |
| Bing Crosby's \| **Rancho Mirage/PS** | 20 |
| Bouchon \| **SB** | 25 |
| Cafe del Sol \| **Montecito/SB** | 17 |
| Café Nouveau \| **Ventura/SB** | 20 |
| Cafe Zoolu \| **Laguna Bch/OC** | 27 |
| Castaway \| **San Bern/PS** | 13 |
| Cat/Custard Cup \| **La Habra/OC** | 26 |
| Citrus \| **Riverside/PS** | 19 |
| ☑ Coast \| **SB** | 21 |
| Cork Tree \| **Palm Desert/PS** | 25 |
| ☑ Cuistot \| **Palm Desert/PS** | 25 |
| ☑ Downey's \| **SB** | 28 |
| Elements \| **SB** | 18 |
| Jonathan's/Peirano \| **Ventura/SB** | 23 |

Leatherby's | **Costa Mesa/OC** 24
Los Olivos Cafe | **Los Olivos/SB** 22
**Z** Louie's | **SB** 23
Maravilla | **Ojai/SB** 21
Marmalade Café | **SB** 17
Montecito Cafe | **Montecito/SB** 24
**Z** Napa Rose | **Anaheim/OC** 28
Native Foods | **multi.** 22
162' | **Dana Pt/OC** 25
Opal | **SB** 22
**NEW** Pelican Grill | 20
  **Newport Coast/OC**
Plow & Angel | **Montecito/SB** 24
**Z** Ranch Hse. | **Ojai/SB** 23
Splashes | **Laguna Bch/OC** 19
**Z** Stella Mare's | **SB** 23
**Z** Studio | **Laguna Bch/OC** 26
Taproom, The | **Buellton/SB** 20
230 Forest Ave. | **Laguna Bch/OC** 23
Vine | **San Clemente/OC** 25
Wild Artichoke | **Yorba Linda/OC** 24
Wine Cask | **SB** 24

## CARIBBEAN

Citron | **PS** 22
Golden Truffle | **Costa Mesa/OC** 25
Tommy Bahama's | 20
  **Palm Desert/PS**

## CHINESE

China Pavilion | **multi.** 19
Five Feet | **Laguna Bch/OC** 23

## COFFEE SHOPS/DINERS

Billy Reed's | **PS** 17
Mimi's Cafe | **multi.** 17
Original Pancake | **Temecula/PS** 23
Ruby's | **Riverside/PS** 17

## CONTINENTAL

Europa | **PS** -
First Cabin | **Newport Bch/OC** 24
Five Crowns | **Corona del Mar/OC** 24
**Z** Hobbit | **Orange/OC** 27
**Z** Jillian's | **Palm Desert/PS** 26
Ritz Rest./Gdn. | **Newport Bch/OC** 25
Summit Hse. | **Fullerton/OC** 24
**Z** Wally's Desert | 25
  **Rancho Mirage/PS**

## CREOLE

Palace Grill | **SB** 22

## ECLECTIC

Blue Agave | **SB** 22
**Z** Johannes | **PS** 25

John Henry's | **PS** 18
Native Foods | **multi.** 22
Old Vine Café | **Costa Mesa/OC** 24
Onotria | **Costa Mesa/OC** 25
Opal | **SB** 22
Plow & Angel | **Montecito/SB** 24
Sapphire Laguna | **Laguna Bch/OC** 24
Spencer's | **PS** 22
**Z** Westside Cellar | **Ventura/SB** 27
Wild Artichoke | **Yorba Linda/OC** 24

## FONDUE

Melting Pot | **Rancho Cuca/PS** 18

## FRENCH

AZUR | **La Quinta/PS** -
**Z** Ballard Inn | **Ballard/SB** 28
Basilic | **Newport Bch/OC** 27
Bouchon | **SB** 25
Citron | **PS** 22
**Z** Cuistot | **Palm Desert/PS** 25
**Z** Downey's | **SB** 28
Five Feet | **Laguna Bch/OC** 23
Golden Truffle | **Costa Mesa/OC** 25
**Z** Hobbit | **Orange/OC** 27
John Henry's | **PS** 18
**Z** Le St. Germain | 26
  **Indian Wells/PS**
**Z** Le Vallauris | **PS** 27
**Z** Marché Moderne | 27
  **Costa Mesa/OC**
Mimosa | **SB** 19
Mister Parker's | **PS** -
Pinot Provence | **Costa Mesa/OC** 24
71 Palm | **Ventura/SB** 20
**Z** Studio | **Laguna Bch/OC** 26
**Z** Suzanne's | **Ojai/SB** 26
**Z** Tradition/Pascal | 28
  **Newport Bch/OC**

## FRENCH (BISTRO)

Black Sheep | **Tustin/OC** 25
Café des Beaux-Arts | 18
  **Palm Desert/PS**
Chez Philippe | **PS** -
Chez Pierre | **Palm Desert/PS** 22
French 75 | **multi.** 20
Zin | **PS** 24

## GASTROPUB

**NEW** Crow Bar | Eclectic | 23
  **Corona del Mar/OC**

## HAWAIIAN

Roy's | **multi.** 23

## INDIAN

| | |
|---|---|
| All India \| **SB** | 22 |
| Spice Ave. \| **SB** | - |

## ITALIAN

(N=Northern; S=Southern)

| | |
|---|---|
| Antonello \| **Santa Ana/OC** | 24 |
| Bellini \| **Palm Desert/PS** | 21 |
| Boccali's \| **Ojai/SB** | 18 |
| Bucatini \| N \| **SB** | 20 |
| Ca' Dario \| **SB** | 24 |
| Cafe Fiore \| S \| **Ventura/SB** | 22 |
| Castelli's \| **Palm Desert/PS** | 22 |
| Emilio's \| N \| **SB** | 20 |
| La Spiga \| **Palm Desert/PS** | 24 |
| Olio e Limone \| **SB** | 24 |
| Pane e Vino \| N \| **SB** | 21 |
| Piatti \| **Montecito/SB** | 19 |
| Pomodoro \| **Corona/PS** | 18 |
| Rist. Mamma Gina \| N \| **Palm Desert/PS** | 20 |
| Rist. Tuscany \| N \| **Palm Desert/PS** | 26 |
| Sirocco \| **Indian Wells/PS** | 24 |
| Sisley Italian \| **Rancho Cuca/PS** | 17 |
| ☑ Suzanne's \| **Ojai/SB** | 26 |
| Tratt. Grappolo \| **Santa Ynez/SB** | 25 |
| Tratt. Mollie \| N \| **Montecito/SB** | 22 |
| Tre Lune \| **Montecito/SB** | 21 |
| Via Vai \| **Montecito/SB** | 20 |

## JAPANESE

(* sushi specialist)

| | |
|---|---|
| Abe* \| **Newport Bch/OC** | 24 |
| ☑ Arigato Sushi* \| **SB** | 26 |
| Bluefin* \| **Newport Coast/OC** | 27 |
| Gyu-Kaku \| **Rancho Cuca/PS** | 20 |
| Okura Robata \| **multi.** | 26 |
| Piranha* \| **SB** | - |
| Sakana* \| **Montecito/SB** | - |
| Sushi Ozekii* \| **Ventura/SB** | 17 |
| Wasa* \| **multi.** | 25 |
| Zip Fusion* \| **Corona/PS** | 18 |

## MEDITERRANEAN

| | |
|---|---|
| Emilio's \| **SB** | 20 |
| Jonathan's/Peirano \| **Ventura/SB** | 23 |
| ☑ Le St. Germain \| **Indian Wells/PS** | 26 |
| ☑ Le Vallauris \| **PS** | 27 |
| Los Olivos Cafe \| **Los Olivos/SB** | 22 |
| NEW Purple Palm \| **PS** | - |
| Vine \| **San Clemente/OC** | 25 |

## MEXICAN

| | |
|---|---|
| Adobe Grill \| **La Quinta/PS** | 18 |
| Baja Fresh \| **Ventura/SB** | 17 |
| Cantina Joannafina \| **Ventura/SB** | 19 |
| Carlitos Café \| **SB** | 18 |
| El Torito \| **SB** | 15 |
| Gabbi's Mex. \| **Orange/OC** | 25 |
| Las Casuelas \| **multi.** | 18 |
| La Super-Rica \| **SB** | 25 |
| Los Arroyos \| **multi.** | 22 |
| Sharky's Mex. \| **Ventura/SB** | 18 |

## MOROCCAN

| | |
|---|---|
| Chef Karim's \| **SB** | 19 |

## PACIFIC RIM

| | |
|---|---|
| Jade \| **SB** | - |

## PAN-LATIN

| | |
|---|---|
| Cava \| **Montecito/SB** | 18 |
| Sevilla \| **SB** | 20 |

## PIZZA

| | |
|---|---|
| BJ's \| **multi.** | 17 |
| Cali. Pizza Kitchen \| **multi.** | 18 |
| Matchbox \| **PS** | - |

## PUB FOOD

| | |
|---|---|
| BJ's \| **multi.** | 17 |
| Lord Fletcher's \| **Rancho Mirage/PS** | 17 |

## SANDWICHES

| | |
|---|---|
| Noah's NY Bagels \| **Ventura/SB** | 17 |

## SEAFOOD

| | |
|---|---|
| Brophy Bros. \| **multi.** | 20 |
| Enterprise Fish \| **SB** | 19 |
| Holdren's Steak \| **SB** | 21 |
| Hungry Cat \| **SB** | 24 |
| Joe's Crab \| **multi.** | 13 |
| King's Fish \| **multi.** | 21 |
| Mastro's Ocean \| **Newport Coast/OC** | 25 |
| Pacifica Seafood \| **Palm Desert/PS** | 22 |
| NEW Seagrass \| **SB** | - |
| ☑ Tabu Grill \| **Laguna Bch/OC** | 29 |
| TAPS \| **Brea/OC** | 25 |
| Tee-Off \| **SB** | - |
| Walt's Wharf \| **Seal Bch/OC** | 24 |
| Wildfish/Grille \| **Newport Bch/OC** | 23 |

## SMALL PLATES

| | |
|---|---|
| NEW Crow Bar \| Eclectic \| **Corona del Mar/OC** | 23 |
| ☑ Marché Moderne \| French \| **Costa Mesa/OC** | 27 |
| Old Vine Café \| Eclectic \| **Costa Mesa/OC** | 24 |
| Sage \| Amer. \| **multi.** | 24 |

## SOUL FOOD

Lucille's BBQ | **Rancho Cuca/PS**  22

## SOUTH AMERICAN

Café Bariloche | **Ventura/SB**  22

## SOUTHERN

Johnny Rebs' | **Victorville/PS**  22
Tupelo Junction | **SB**  20

## SPANISH

Black Sheep | **Tustin/OC**  25
Maravilla | **Ojai/SB**  21
Miró | **SB**  -

## STEAKHOUSES

Z Arnold Palmer's | **La Quinta/PS**  20
Chop Hse. | **multi.**  21
Falls Steak | **multi.**  20
Fleming's | **Newport Bch/OC**  25
Holdren's Steak | **SB**  21
La Cave | **Costa Mesa/OC**  24
LG's Steak | **multi.**  23

Lucky's | **Montecito/SB**  25
Mastro's Ocean |
  **Newport Coast/OC**  25
Z Mastro's Steak |
  **Costa Mesa/OC**  26
Morton's Steak | **multi.**  25
Outback | **multi.**  17
Z Ruth's Chris | **multi.**  26
Z Tabu Grill | **Laguna Bch/OC**  29
Tee-Off | **SB**  -

## SWISS

Basilic | **Newport Bch/OC**  27

## THAI

Cholada | **Ventura/SB**  24

## VEGETARIAN

(* vegan)
Native Foods* | **multi.**  22

## VIETNAMESE

S Vietnamese | **Westminster/OC**  26

OC/PS/SB

CUISINES

# Locations

Includes restaurant names, cuisines and Food ratings. ☑ indicates places with the highest ratings, popularity and importance.

## Orange County

### ANAHEIM/ ANAHEIM HILLS

| | |
|---|---|
| ☑ Cheesecake Factory | *Amer.* | 19 |
| Morton's Steak | *Steak* | 25 |
| Mr. Stox | *Amer.* | 24 |
| ☑ Napa Rose | *Cal.* | 28 |
| Roy's | *Asian Fusion/Hawaiian* | 23 |
| ☑ Ruth's Chris | *Steak* | 26 |

### BREA

| | |
|---|---|
| ☑ Cheesecake Factory | *Amer.* | 19 |
| TAPS | *Amer./Seafood* | 25 |

### CORONA DEL MAR

| | |
|---|---|
| NEW Crow Bar | *Gastropub* | 23 |
| Five Crowns | *Continental* | 24 |

### COSTA MESA

| | |
|---|---|
| Golden Truffle | *Carib./French* | 25 |
| ☑ In-N-Out | *Burgers* | 23 |
| La Cave | *Steak* | 24 |
| Leatherby's | *Asian/Cal.* | 24 |
| ☑ Marché Moderne | *French* | 27 |
| ☑ Mastro's Steak | *Steak* | 26 |
| Old Vine Café | *Eclectic* | 24 |
| Onotria | *Eclectic* | 25 |
| Pinot Provence | *French* | 24 |

### CYPRESS

| | |
|---|---|
| Café Hiro | *Asian Fusion* | 25 |

### DANA POINT

| | |
|---|---|
| 162' | *Cal.* | 25 |
| ☑ Stonehill Tav. | *Amer.* | 27 |

### FULLERTON

| | |
|---|---|
| Summit Hse. | *Continental* | 24 |

### HUNTINGTON BEACH

| | |
|---|---|
| ☑ In-N-Out | *Burgers* | 23 |

### IRVINE

| | |
|---|---|
| Bistango | *Amer.* | 24 |
| ☑ Cheesecake Factory | *Amer.* | 19 |
| ☑ In-N-Out | *Burgers* | 23 |
| ☑ Ruth's Chris | *Steak* | 26 |
| Wasa | *Japanese* | 25 |

### LAGUNA BEACH/ S. LAGUNA BEACH

| | |
|---|---|
| Cafe Zoolu | *Cal.* | 27 |
| Five Feet | *Chinese/French* | 23 |
| French 75 | *French* | 20 |
| Sapphire Laguna | *Eclectic* | 24 |
| Splashes | *Cal.* | 19 |
| ☑ Studio | *Cal./French* | 26 |
| ☑ Tabu Grill | *Seafood/Steak* | 29 |
| 230 Forest Ave. | *Cal.* | 23 |

### LAGUNA NIGUEL

| | |
|---|---|
| ☑ In-N-Out | *Burgers* | 23 |

### LA HABRA

| | |
|---|---|
| Cat/Custard Cup | *Amer./Cal.* | 26 |

### LAKE FOREST

| | |
|---|---|
| Wasa | *Japanese* | 25 |

### MISSION VIEJO

| | |
|---|---|
| ☑ Cheesecake Factory | *Amer.* | 19 |

### NEWPORT BEACH

| | |
|---|---|
| Abe | *Japanese* | 24 |
| Basilic | *French/Swiss* | 27 |
| Bayside | *Amer.* | 24 |
| ☑ Cheesecake Factory | *Amer.* | 19 |
| First Cabin | *Amer./Continental* | 24 |
| Fleming's | *Steak* | 25 |
| French 75 | *French* | 20 |
| Ritz Rest./Gdn. | *Continental* | 25 |
| Roy's | *Asian Fusion/Hawaiian* | 23 |
| Sage | *Amer.* | 24 |
| ☑ Tradition/Pascal | *French* | 28 |
| Wasa | *Japanese* | 25 |
| Wildfish/Grille | *Amer./Seafood* | 23 |

### NEWPORT COAST

| | |
|---|---|
| Bluefin | *Japanese* | 27 |
| Mastro's Ocean | *Seafood/Steak* | 25 |
| NEW Pelican Grill | *Cal.* | 20 |
| Sage | *Amer.* | 24 |

### ORANGE

| | |
|---|---|
| Gabbi's Mex. | *Mex.* | 25 |
| ☑ Hobbit | *Continental/French* | 27 |

### PLACENTIA

| | |
|---|---|
| ☑ In-N-Out | *Burgers* | 23 |

subscribe to ZAGAT.com

## SAN CLEMENTE

Vine | *Cal./Med.*  25

## SAN JUAN CAPISTRANO

Ramos Hse. | *Amer.*  25

## SANTA ANA

Antonello | *Italian*  24
Morton's Steak | *Steak*  25

## SEAL BEACH

Walt's Wharf | *Seafood*  24

## STANTON

Park Ave. | *Amer.*  26

## TUSTIN

Black Sheep | *French/Spanish*  25
Z In-N-Out | *Burgers*  23

## WESTMINSTER

S Vietnamese | *Viet.*  26

## YORBA LINDA

Wild Artichoke | *Cal./Eclectic*  24

# Palm Springs & Environs

## CATHEDRAL CITY

Picanha Churrascaria | *Brazilian*  21

## CHINO

Islands | *Amer.*  16
Mimi's Cafe | *Diner*  17

## CORONA

BJ's | *Pub*  17
Claim Jumper | *Amer.*  19
Counter, The | *Burgers*  21
Z In-N-Out | *Burgers*  23
Islands | *Amer.*  16
King's Fish | *Seafood*  21
Mimi's Cafe | *Diner*  17
Pomodoro | *Italian*  18
Rosine's | *Armenian/Med.*  22
TAPS | *Amer./Seafood*  25
Wood Ranch BBQ | *BBQ*  20
Zip Fusion | *Japanese*  18

## INDIAN WELLS

Z Le St. Germain | *French/Med.*  26
Sirocco | *Italian*  24

## LA QUINTA

Adobe Grill | *Mex.*  18
Z Arnold Palmer's | *Steak*  20

AZUR | *Cal./French*  -
Falls Steak | *Steak*  20
Hog's Breath Inn | *Amer.*  15
La Quinta Cliffhse. | *Amer.*  16
Las Casuelas | *Mex.*  18
LG's Steak | *Steak*  23
Okura Robata | *Japanese*  26

## PALM DESERT

Bellini | *Italian*  21
Café des Beaux-Arts | *French*  18
Cali. Pizza Kitchen | *Pizza*  18
Castelli's | *Italian*  22
Chez Pierre | *French*  22
Chop Hse. | *Steak*  21
Cork Tree | *Cal.*  25
Z Cuistot | *Cal./French*  25
Daily Grill | *Amer.*  18
Islands | *Amer.*  16
Z Jillian's | *Continental*  26
Las Casuelas | *Mex.*  18
La Spiga | *Italian*  24
LG's Steak | *Steak*  23
Morton's Steak | *Steak*  25
Native Foods | *Cal./Eclectic*  22
Outback | *Steak*  17
Pacifica Seafood | *Seafood*  22
NEW Rattlesnake | *Amer.*  27
Rist. Mamma Gina | *Italian*  20
Rist. Tuscany | *Italian*  26
Z Ruth's Chris | *Steak*  26
Tommy Bahama's | *Carib.*  20

## PALM SPRINGS

Billy Reed's | *Amer.*  17
Cali. Pizza Kitchen | *Pizza*  18
Chez Philippe | *French*  -
Chop Hse. | *Steak*  21
Citron | *Carib./French*  22
Z Copley's | *Amer.*  25
Europa | *Continental*  -
Falls Steak | *Steak*  20
Z Johannes | *Eclectic*  25
John Henry's | *Eclectic/French*  18
Kaiser Grille | *Amer.*  16
Las Casuelas | *Mex.*  18
Z Le Vallauris | *French/Med.*  27
LG's Steak | *Steak*  23
Matchbox | *Amer./Pizza*  -
Mister Parker's | *French*  -
Native Foods | *Cal./Eclectic*  22
Okura Robata | *Japanese*  26
NEW Purple Palm | *Med.*  -

Ruby's | *Diner* 17
Spencer's | *Eclectic* 22
Zin | *Amer./French* 24

## RANCHO CUCAMONGA

BJ's | *Pub* 17
Cali. Pizza Kitchen | *Pizza* 18
🄩 Cheesecake Factory | *Amer.* 19
Claim Jumper | *Amer.* 19
Gyu-Kaku | *Japanese* 20
Islands | *Amer.* 16
Joe's Crab | *Seafood* 13
Johnny Rockets | *Burgers* 15
King's Fish | *Seafood* 21
Lucille's BBQ | *BBQ* 22
Melting Pot | *Fondue* 18
Mimi's Cafe | *Diner* 17
Sisley Italian | *Italian* 17
Souplantation | *Amer.* 16
Yard Hse. | *Amer.* 20

## RANCHO MIRAGE

Bing Crosby's | *Cal.* 20
🄩 Cheesecake Factory | *Amer.* 19
Las Casuelas | *Mex.* 18
Lord Fletcher's | *Pub* 17
Mimi's Cafe | *Diner* 17
Roy's | *Asian Fusion/Hawaiian* 23
Ruby's | *Diner* 17
Shame on Moon | *Amer.* 23
🄩 Wally's Desert | *Continental* 25
Yard Hse. | *Amer.* 20

## RIVERSIDE

Cali. Pizza Kitchen | *Pizza* 18
Citrus | *Cal.* 19
🄩 In-N-Out | *Burgers* 23
Islands | *Amer.* 16
Ruby's | *Diner* 17
Yard Hse. | *Amer.* 20

## SAN BERNARDINO

BJ's | *Pub* 17
Castaway | *Cal.* 13
Claim Jumper | *Amer.* 19
Outback | *Steak* 17
Souplantation | *Amer.* 16

## TEMECULA

BJ's | *Pub* 17
Cali. Pizza Kitchen | *Pizza* 18
Original Pancake | *Diner* 23
Souplantation | *Amer.* 16

## UPLAND

Outback | *Steak* 17

## VICTORVILLE

Johnny Rebs' | *BBQ* 22

# Santa Barbara & Environs

## BALLARD

🄩 Ballard Inn | *French* 28

## BUELLTON

Hitching Post | *BBQ* 23
Taproom, The | *Cal.* 20

## CARPINTERIA

Cajun Kitchen | *Cajun* 18

## CASMALIA

Hitching Post | *BBQ* 23

## GOLETA

Cajun Kitchen | *Cajun* 18
🄩 In-N-Out | *Burgers* 23
Outback | *Steak* 17

## LOS OLIVOS

Brothers Rest. | *Amer.* 25
Los Olivos Cafe | *Cal./Med.* 22

## MONTECITO

Bella Vista | *Cal.* 26
Cafe del Sol | *Cal.* 17
Cava | *Pan-Latin* 18
China Pavilion | *Chinese* 19
Los Arroyos | *Mex.* 22
Lucky's | *Steak* 25
Montecito Cafe | *Cal.* 24
Piatti | *Italian* 19
Plow & Angel | *Cal./Eclectic* 24
Sakana | *Japanese* -
🄩 Stonehouse | *Amer.* 25
Tratt. Mollie | *Italian* 22
Tre Lune | *Italian* 21
Via Vai | *Italian* 20

## OJAI

Boccali's | *Italian* 18
Maravilla | *Cal.* 21
🄩 Ranch Hse. | *Cal.* 23
🄩 Suzanne's | *French/Italian* 26

## OXNARD

BJ's | *Pub* 17
🄩 In-N-Out | *Burgers* 23
Outback | *Steak* 17

## SANTA BARBARA

All India | *Indian* 22
🄩 Arigato Sushi | *Japanese* 26
Blue Agave | *Eclectic* 22

Bouchon | *Cal./French* 25
Brophy Bros. | *Seafood* 20
Bucatini | *Italian* 20
Ca' Dario | *Italian* 24
Cafe Buenos Aires | *Argent.* 16
Cajun Kitchen | *Cajun* 18
Cali. Pizza Kitchen | *Pizza* 18
Carlitos Café | *Mex.* 18
Chad's | *Amer.* 21
Chef Karim's | *Moroccan* 19
China Pavilion | *Chinese* 19
🅩 Coast | *Cal./Seafood* 21
Cold Spring | *Amer.* 20
🅩 Downey's | *Cal./French* 28
Elements | *Cal.* 18
El Torito | *Mex.* 15
Emilio's | *Italian/Med.* 20
Enterprise Fish | *Seafood* 19
Holdren's Steak | *Seafood/Steak* 21
Hungry Cat | *Seafood* 24
Jade | *Pac. Rim* -
La Super-Rica | *Mex.* 25
Los Arroyos | *Mex.* 22
🅩 Louie's | *Cal.* 23
Marmalade Café | *Amer./Cal.* 17
Mimosa | *French* 19
Miró | *Spanish* -
Olio e Limone | *Italian* 24
Opal | *Cal./Eclectic* 22
Palace Grill | *Cajun/Creole* 22
Pane e Vino | *Italian* 21
Piranha | *Japanese* -
🅩 Ruth's Chris | *Steak* 26
Savoy Truffles | *Amer.* -

**NEW** Seagrass | *Seafood* -
Sevilla | *Pan-Latin* 20
Spice Ave. | *Indian* -
Square One | *Amer.* 24
🅩 Stella Mare's | *Cal.* 23
Tee-Off | *Seafood/Steak* -
Tupelo Junction | *Southern* 20
Wine Cask | *Cal.* 24

## SANTA YNEZ

Tratt. Grappolo | *Italian* 25

## VENTURA

Austen's | *Cal.* 19
Baja Fresh | *Mex.* 17
Brooks | *Amer.* 25
Brophy Bros. | *Seafood* 20
Café Bariloche | *S Amer.* 22
Cafe Fiore | *Italian* 22
Café Nouveau | *Cal.* 20
Cajun Kitchen | *Cajun* 18
Cali. Pizza Kitchen | *Pizza* 18
Cantina Joannafina | *Mex.* 19
Cholada | *Thai* 24
🅩 In-N-Out | *Burgers* 23
Joe's Crab | *Seafood* 13
Jonathan's/Peirano | *Cal./Med.* 23
Mimi's Cafe | *Diner* 17
Noah's NY Bagels | *Sandwiches* 17
71 Palm | *Amer./French* 20
Sharky's Mex. | *Mex.* 18
Sidecar Rest. | *Amer.* 25
Sushi Ozekii | *Japanese* 17
🅩 Westside Cellar | *Eclectic* 27

# Special Features

Listings cover the best in each category and include names, locations and Food ratings. Multi-location restaurants' features may vary by branch.
**Z** indicates places with the highest ratings, popularity and importance.

## BREAKFAST

(See also Hotel Dining)

| | |
|---|---|
| Billy Reed's \| **PS** | 17 |
| Cajun Kitchen \| **multi.** | 18 |
| Old Vine Café \| **Costa Mesa/OC** | 24 |
| Original Pancake \| **Temecula/PS** | 23 |
| Ramos Hse. \| **San Juan Cap/OC** | 25 |
| Ruby's \| **Riverside/PS** | 17 |
| Tupelo Junction \| **SB** | 20 |

## BRUNCH

| | |
|---|---|
| Bayside \| **Newport Bch/OC** | 24 |
| **NEW** Crow Bar \| **Corona del Mar/OC** | 23 |
| Five Crowns \| **Corona del Mar/OC** | 24 |
| French 75 \| **Newport Bch/OC** | 20 |
| 162' \| **Dana Pt/OC** | 25 |
| Pinot Provence \| **Costa Mesa/OC** | 24 |
| Ramos Hse. \| **San Juan Cap/OC** | 25 |
| Sapphire Laguna \| **Laguna Bch/OC** | 24 |
| TAPS \| **Brea/OC** | 25 |

## BUSINESS DINING

| | |
|---|---|
| Antonello \| **Santa Ana/OC** | 24 |
| **Z** Arnold Palmer's \| **La Quinta/PS** | 20 |
| Bayside \| **Newport Bch/OC** | 24 |
| Bistango \| **Irvine/OC** | 24 |
| Brooks \| **Ventura/SB** | 25 |
| Bucatini \| **SB** | 20 |
| Cat/Custard Cup \| **La Habra/OC** | 26 |
| China Pavilion \| **SB** | 19 |
| First Cabin \| **Newport Bch/OC** | 24 |
| Fleming's \| **Newport Bch/OC** | 25 |
| Leatherby's \| **Costa Mesa/OC** | 24 |
| Mastro's Ocean \| **Newport Coast/OC** | 25 |
| **Z** Mastro's Steak \| **Costa Mesa/OC** | 26 |
| Morton's Steak \| **multi.** | 25 |
| Mr. Stox \| **Anaheim/OC** | 24 |
| 162' \| **Dana Pt/OC** | 25 |
| Park Ave. \| **Stanton/OC** | 26 |
| Pinot Provence \| **Costa Mesa/OC** | 24 |
| **NEW** Rattlesnake \| **Palm Desert/PS** | 27 |
| Ritz Rest./Gdn. \| **Newport Bch/OC** | 25 |
| Roy's \| **Newport Bch/OC** | 23 |
| **Z** Ruth's Chris \| **Irvine/OC** | 26 |

| | |
|---|---|
| Sevilla \| **SB** | 20 |
| **Z** Stonehill Tav. \| **Dana Pt/OC** | 27 |
| **Z** Stonehouse \| **Montecito/SB** | 25 |
| Summit Hse. \| **Fullerton/OC** | 24 |
| S Vietnamese \| **Westminster/OC** | 26 |
| **Z** Tradition/Pascal \| **Newport Bch/OC** | 28 |

## CHEESE TRAYS

| | |
|---|---|
| Basilic \| **Newport Bch/OC** | 27 |
| Black Sheep \| **Tustin/OC** | 25 |
| **Z** Cuistot \| **Palm Desert/PS** | 25 |
| **Z** Downey's \| **SB** | 28 |
| Elements \| **SB** | 18 |
| Five Crowns \| **Corona del Mar/OC** | 24 |
| French 75 \| **Laguna Bch/OC** | 20 |
| Golden Truffle \| **Costa Mesa/OC** | 25 |
| **Z** Johannes \| **PS** | 25 |
| Jonathan's/Peirano \| **Ventura/SB** | 23 |
| Leatherby's \| **Costa Mesa/OC** | 24 |
| Los Olivos Cafe \| **Los Olivos/SB** | 22 |
| Maravilla \| **Ojai/SB** | 21 |
| **Z** Marché Moderne \| **Costa Mesa/OC** | 27 |
| Mr. Stox \| **Anaheim/OC** | 24 |
| **Z** Napa Rose \| **Anaheim/OC** | 28 |
| Old Vine Café \| **Costa Mesa/OC** | 24 |
| Onotria \| **Costa Mesa/OC** | 25 |
| Pinot Provence \| **Costa Mesa/OC** | 24 |
| Sage \| **Newport Bch/OC** | 24 |
| Sapphire Laguna \| **Laguna Bch/OC** | 24 |
| Square One \| **SB** | 24 |
| **Z** Stonehill Tav. \| **Dana Pt/OC** | 27 |
| **Z** Tradition/Pascal \| **Newport Bch/OC** | 28 |
| **Z** Wally's Desert \| **Rancho Mirage/PS** | 25 |
| **Z** Westside Cellar \| **Ventura/SB** | 27 |
| Zin \| **PS** | 24 |

## CHEF'S TABLE

| | |
|---|---|
| Cork Tree \| **Palm Desert/PS** | 25 |
| **Z** Cuistot \| **Palm Desert/PS** | 25 |
| Five Feet \| **Laguna Bch/OC** | 23 |
| **Z** Napa Rose \| **Anaheim/OC** | 28 |
| Rist. Tuscany \| **Palm Desert/PS** | 26 |
| **Z** Studio \| **Laguna Bch/OC** | 26 |

subscribe to ZAGAT.com

## DANCING

☑ Arnold Palmer's | **La Quinta/PS** 20
Bistango | **Irvine/OC** 24
Cafe Buenos Aires | **SB** 16
Cafe Fiore | **Ventura/SB** 22
First Cabin | **Newport Bch/OC** 24
Las Casuelas | **multi.** 18

## ENTERTAINMENT

(Call for days and times of performances)
Bayside | jazz | **Newport Bch/OC** 24
Bistango | varies | **Irvine/OC** 24
Cat/Custard Cup | piano | 26
  **La Habra/OC**
La Cave | jazz/rock | 24
  **Costa Mesa/OC**
Lucille's BBQ | blues | 22
  **Rancho Cuca/PS**

## FIREPLACES

Adobe Grill | **La Quinta/PS** 18
☑ Arnold Palmer's | **La Quinta/PS** 20
Austen's | **Ventura/SB** 19
☑ Ballard Inn | **Ballard/SB** 28
Bella Vista | **Montecito/SB** 26
Blue Agave | **SB** 22
Brothers Rest. | **Los Olivos/SB** 25
Cafe del Sol | **Montecito/SB** 17
Cafe Fiore | **Ventura/SB** 22
Cafe Zoolu | **Laguna Bch/OC** 27
Cat/Custard Cup | **La Habra/OC** 26
Cava | **Montecito/SB** 18
Chad's | **SB** 21
Citron | **PS** 22
Claim Jumper | **multi.** 19
Cold Spring | **SB** 20
☑ Cuistot | **Palm Desert/PS** 25
Falls Steak | **multi.** 20
Five Crowns | **Corona del Mar/OC** 24
French 75 | **Laguna Bch/OC** 20
Hitching Post | **Buellton/SB** 23
Hog's Breath Inn | **La Quinta/PS** 15
☑ Le Vallauris | **PS** 27
LG's Steak | **La Quinta/PS** 23
Lord Fletcher's | 17
  **Rancho Mirage/PS**
Los Olivos Cafe | **Los Olivos/SB** 22
Lucky's | **Montecito/SB** 25
Maravilla | **Ojai/SB** 21
Matchbox | **PS** -
Miró | **SB** -
Mr. Stox | **Anaheim/OC** 24
☑ Napa Rose | **Anaheim/OC** 28

162' | **Dana Pt/OC** 25
Park Ave. | **Stanton/OC** 26
NEW Pelican Grill | 20
  **Newport Coast/OC**
Piatti | **Montecito/SB** 19
Pinot Provence | **Costa Mesa/OC** 24
Plow & Angel | **Montecito/SB** 24
Sage | **Newport Coast/OC** 24
71 Palm | **Ventura/SB** 20
Splashes | **Laguna Bch/OC** 19
☑ Stella Mare's | **SB** 23
☑ Stonehill Tav. | **Dana Pt/OC** 27
☑ Studio | **Laguna Bch/OC** 26
Summit Hse. | **Fullerton/OC** 24
☑ Suzanne's | **Ojai/SB** 26
Vine | **San Clemente/OC** 25
☑ Westside Cellar | 27
  **Ventura/SB**
Wine Cask | **SB** 24

## HISTORIC PLACES

(Year opened; * building)
1800 | Tupelo Junction* | **SB** 20
1876 | Chad's* | **SB** 21
1877 | Jonathan's/Peirano* | 23
  **Ventura/SB**
1881 | Ramos Hse.* | 25
  **San Juan Cap/OC**
1886 | Brothers Rest.* | 25
  **Los Olivos/SB**
1886 | Cold Spring* | **SB** 20
1890 | Wine Cask* | **SB** 24
1893 | Plow & Angel* | 24
  **Montecito/SB**
1895 | Stonehouse* | 25
  **Montecito/SB**
1910 | Austen's* | **Ventura/SB** 19
1910 | 71 Palm* | **Ventura/SB** 20
1910 | Sidecar Rest.* | 25
  **Ventura/SB**
1923 | Maravilla | **Ojai/SB** 21
1926 | AZUR* | **La Quinta/PS** -
1927 | Bella Vista* | 26
  **Montecito/SB**
1930 | Elements* | **SB** 18
1930 | Hobbit* | **Orange/OC** 27
1930 | Las Casuelas* | **PS** 18
1933 | Citron* | **PS** 22
1934 | Five Crowns* | 24
  **Corona del Mar/OC**
1952 | Hitching Post | 23
  **Casmalia/SB**
1953 | Ranch Hse.* | **Ojai/SB** 23
1956 | Tee-Off | **SB** -
1958 | Las Casuelas | **PS** 18

OC/PS/SB

SPECIAL FEATURES

## HOTEL DINING

Bacara Resort
  Miró | SB | –

Balboa Bay Club Resort & Spa
  First Cabin | **Newport Bch/OC** | 24

Ballard Inn
  🆉 Ballard Inn | **Ballard/SB** | 28

Canary Hotel
  🆉 Coast | **SB** | 21

Classic Club Golf Resort
  **NEW** Rattlesnake |
    **Palm Desert/PS** | 27

Colony Palms Hotel
  **NEW** Purple Palm | **PS** | –

Disney's Grand Californian
  🆉 Napa Rose | **Anaheim/OC** | 28

Four Seasons Biltmore
  Bella Vista | **Montecito/SB** | 26

JW Marriott Desert Springs
  Rist. Tuscany |
    **Palm Desert/PS** | 26

La Quinta Resort & Club
  Adobe Grill | **La Quinta/PS** | 18
  AZUR | **La Quinta/PS** | –

Montage Laguna Bch.
  🆉 Studio | **Laguna Bch/OC** | 26

Montecito Inn
  Montecito Cafe | **Montecito/SB** | 24

Ojai Valley Inn & Spa
  Maravilla | **Ojai/SB** | 21

Parker Palm Springs
  Mister Parker's | **PS** | –

Pelican Hill Resort
  **NEW** Pelican Grill |
    **Newport Coast/OC** | 20

Pierpont Inn
  Austen's | **Ventura/SB** | 19

Renaissance Esmeralda Resort
  Sirocco | **Indian Wells/PS** | 24

Ritz-Carlton Laguna Niguel
  162' | **Dana Pt/OC** | 25

San Ysidro Ranch
  Plow & Angel | **Montecito/SB** | 24
  🆉 Stonehouse |
    **Montecito/SB** | 25

St. Regis Resort, Monarch Bch.
  🆉 Stonehill Tav. | **Dana Pt/OC** | 27

Surf & Sand Resort
  Splashes | **Laguna Bch/OC** | 19

Upham Hotel
  🆉 Louie's | **SB** | 23

Viceroy Palm Springs
  Citron | **PS** | 22

Villa Royale Inn
  Europa | **PS** | –

Westin South Coast Plaza Hotel
  Pinot Provence |
    **Costa Mesa/OC** | 24

## LATE DINING

(Weekday closing hour)

Hungry Cat | 12 AM | **SB** | 24
🆉 In-N-Out | varies | **multi.** | 23

## NATURAL/ORGANIC

(These restaurants often or always use organic, local ingredients)

Austen's | **Ventura/SB** | 19
AZUR | **La Quinta/PS** | –
🆉 Ballard Inn | **Ballard/SB** | 28
Bellini | **Palm Desert/PS** | 21
Blue Agave | **SB** | 22
Brooks | **Ventura/SB** | 25
Bucatini | **SB** | 20
Ca' Dario | **SB** | 24
Cafe Buenos Aires | **SB** | 16
Cafe del Sol | **Montecito/SB** | 17
Café des Beaux-Arts |
  **Palm Desert/PS** | 18
Cafe Fiore | **Ventura/SB** | 22
Carlitos Café | **SB** | 18
Cava | **Montecito/SB** | 18
Chef Karim's | **SB** | 19
Chez Pierre | **Palm Desert/PS** | 22
China Pavilion | **Montecito/SB** | 19
Citron | **PS** | 22
Cold Spring | **SB** | 20
🆉 Copley's | **PS** | 25
**NEW** Crow Bar |
  **Corona del Mar/OC** | 23
🆉 Downey's | **SB** | 28
Elements | **SB** | 18
Falls Steak | **multi.** | 20
Five Feet | **Laguna Bch/OC** | 23
Jade | **SB** | –
🆉 Jillian's | **Palm Desert/PS** | 26
John Henry's | **PS** | 18
Jonathan's/Peirano | **Ventura/SB** | 23
Los Olivos Cafe | **Los Olivos/SB** | 22
🆉 Louie's | **SB** | 23
Maravilla | **Ojai/SB** | 21
🆉 Marché Moderne |
  **Costa Mesa/OC** | 27
Mimosa | **SB** | 19
Miró | **SB** | –
Native Foods | **multi.** | 22
Old Vine Café | **Costa Mesa/OC** | 24
Onotria | **Costa Mesa/OC** | 25

OC/PS/SB

SPECIAL FEATURES

Ballard Inn | **Ballard/SB** 28

Basilic | **Newport Bch/OC** 27

Black Sheep | **Tustin/OC** 25

Bluefin | **Newport Coast/OC** 27

Brooks | **Ventura/SB** 25

Bucatini | **SB** 20

Cafe Fiore | **Ventura/SB** 22

First Cabin | **Newport Bch/OC** 24

Five Crowns | **Corona del Mar/OC** 24

Jade | **SB** -

Marché Moderne | **Costa Mesa/OC** 27

Mastro's Steak | **Costa Mesa/OC** 26

Morton's Steak | **Anaheim/OC** 25

Mr. Stox | **Anaheim/OC** 24

Napa Rose | **Anaheim/OC** 28

162' | **Dana Pt/OC** 25

Ritz Rest./Gdn. | **Newport Bch/OC** 25

71 Palm | **Ventura/SB** 20

Sidecar Rest. | **Ventura/SB** 25

Square One | **SB** 24

Stonehill Tav. | **Dana Pt/OC** 27

Stonehouse | **Montecito/SB** 25

Studio | **Laguna Bch/OC** 26

Summit Hse. | **Fullerton/OC** 24

S Vietnamese | **Westminster/OC** 26

Tradition/Pascal | **Newport Bch/OC** 28

## RAW BARS

Coast | **SB** 21

Enterprise Fish | **SB** 19

Hungry Cat | **SB** 24

King's Fish | **multi.** 21

TAPS | **Brea/OC** 25

Wildfish/Grille | **Newport Bch/OC** 23

## ROMANTIC PLACES

Antonello | **Santa Ana/OC** 24

Arnold Palmer's | **La Quinta/PS** 20

Ballard Inn | **Ballard/SB** 28

Basilic | **Newport Bch/OC** 27

Brooks | **Ventura/SB** 25

Bucatini | **SB** 20

Cafe Fiore | **Ventura/SB** 22

Cat/Custard Cup | **La Habra/OC** 26

Elements | **SB** 18

Europa | **PS** -

French 75 | **Laguna Bch/OC** 20

Hobbit | **Orange/OC** 27

La Cave | **Costa Mesa/OC** 24

Leatherby's | **Costa Mesa/OC** 24

Le Vallauris | **PS** 27

Marché Moderne | **Costa Mesa/OC** 27

Mastro's Steak | **Costa Mesa/OC** 26

Mr. Stox | **Anaheim/OC** 24

162' | **Dana Pt/OC** 25

Pinot Provence | **Costa Mesa/OC** 24

Plow & Angel | **Montecito/SB** 24

Ritz Rest./Gdn. | **Newport Bch/OC** 25

71 Palm | **Ventura/SB** 20

Sevilla | **SB** 20

Splashes | **Laguna Bch/OC** 19

Stonehill Tav. | **Dana Pt/OC** 27

Stonehouse | **Montecito/SB** 25

Studio | **Laguna Bch/OC** 26

Tradition/Pascal | **Newport Bch/OC** 28

## SINGLES SCENES

Bayside | **Newport Bch/OC** 24

Bistango | **Irvine/OC** 24

Brooks | **Ventura/SB** 25

Brophy Bros. | **Ventura/SB** 20

NEW Crow Bar | **Corona del Mar/OC** 23

Elements | **SB** 18

Fleming's | **Newport Bch/OC** 25

Mastro's Ocean | **Newport Coast/OC** 25

Mastro's Steak | **Costa Mesa/OC** 26

Plow & Angel | **Montecito/SB** 24

Shame on Moon | **Rancho Mirage/PS** 23

## SLEEPERS

(Good to excellent food, but little known)

Abe | **Newport Bch/OC** 24

Bella Vista | **Montecito/SB** 26

Blue Agave | **SB** 22

Café Bariloche | **Ventura/SB** 22

Café Hiro | **Cypress/OC** 25

Chez Pierre | **Palm Desert/PS** 22

Citron | **PS** 22

First Cabin | **Newport Bch/OC** 24

Jonathan's/Peirano | **Ventura/SB** 23

La Cave | **Costa Mesa/OC** 24

La Spiga | **Palm Desert/PS** 24

Okura Robata | **multi.** 26

Plow & Angel | **Montecito/SB** 24

Rist. Tuscany | **Palm Desert/PS** 26

Sidecar Rest. | **Ventura/SB** 25

Square One | **SB** 24

S Vietnamese | **Westminster/OC** 26

Tratt. Mollie | **Montecito/SB** 22

Vine | **San Clemente/OC** 25

Wild Artichoke | **Yorba Linda/OC** 24

## SPECIAL OCCASIONS

Antonello | **Santa Ana/OC** 24

🔲 Arnold Palmer's | **La Quinta/PS** 20

Bayside | **Newport Bch/OC** 24

Bistango | **Irvine/OC** 24

Brooks | **Ventura/SB** 25

🔲 Cuistot | **Palm Desert/PS** 25

🔲 Downey's | **SB** 28

Elements | **SB** 18

Five Crowns | **Corona del Mar/OC** 24

Fleming's | **Newport Bch/OC** 25

French 75 | **Laguna Bch/OC** 20

🔲 Hobbit | **Orange/OC** 27

🔲 Johannes | **PS** 25

Leatherby's | **Costa Mesa/OC** 24

🔲 Le St. Germain |
**Indian Wells/PS** 26

🔲 Le Vallauris | **PS** 27

🔲 Marché Moderne |
**Costa Mesa/OC** 27

Mastro's Ocean |
**Newport Coast/OC** 25

🔲 Mastro's Steak |
**Costa Mesa/OC** 26

Miró | **SB** -

Morton's Steak | **multi.** 25

🔲 Napa Rose | **Anaheim/OC** 28

162' | **Dana Pt/OC** 25

Pinot Provence | **Costa Mesa/OC** 24

🔲 Ranch Hse. | **Ojai/SB** 23

Roy's | **multi.** 23

Sapphire Laguna | **Laguna Bch/OC** 24

71 Palm | **Ventura/SB** 20

Splashes | **Laguna Bch/OC** 19

Square One | **SB** 24

🔲 Stonehill Tav. | **Dana Pt/OC** 27

🔲 Stonehouse | **Montecito/SB** 25

🔲 Studio | **Laguna Bch/OC** 26

🔲 Tradition/Pascal |
**Newport Bch/OC** 28

🔲 Wally's Desert |
**Rancho Mirage/PS** 25

## TASTING MENUS

Abe | **Newport Bch/OC** 24

🔲 Ballard Inn | **Ballard/SB** 28

Basilic | **Newport Bch/OC** 27

Bluefin | **Newport Coast/OC** 27

Bouchon | **SB** 25

Brooks | **Ventura/SB** 25

Five Feet | **Laguna Bch/OC** 23

Leatherby's | **Costa Mesa/OC** 24

Miró | **SB** -

Old Vine Café | **Costa Mesa/OC** 24

Rist. Tuscany | **Palm Desert/PS** 26

**NEW** Seagrass | **SB** -

Square One | **SB** 24

🔲 Stella Mare's | **SB** 23

🔲 Stonehill Tav. | **Dana Pt/OC** 27

🔲 Studio | **Laguna Bch/OC** 26

Wild Artichoke | **Yorba Linda/OC** 24

## TRENDY

Bistango | **Irvine/OC** 24

Bluefin | **Newport Coast/OC** 27

Brooks | **Ventura/SB** 25

Citron | **PS** 22

**NEW** Crow Bar |
**Corona del Mar/OC** 23

Fleming's | **Newport Bch/OC** 25

Hungry Cat | **SB** 24

La Cave | **Costa Mesa/OC** 24

🔲 Marché Moderne |
**Costa Mesa/OC** 27

Mastro's Ocean |
**Newport Coast/OC** 25

🔲 Mastro's Steak |
**Costa Mesa/OC** 26

Mister Parker's | **PS** -

Sapphire Laguna | **Laguna Bch/OC** 24

Shame on Moon |
**Rancho Mirage/PS** 23

🔲 Stonehill Tav. | **Dana Pt/OC** 27

🔲 Stonehouse | **Montecito/SB** 25

## VIEWS

Adobe Grill | **La Quinta/PS** 18

🔲 Arnold Palmer's | **La Quinta/PS** 20

Austen's | **Ventura/SB** 19

AZUR | **La Quinta/PS** -

🔲 Ballard Inn | **Ballard/SB** 28

Bella Vista | **Montecito/SB** 26

Bellini | **Palm Desert/PS** 21

Bouchon | **SB** 25

Cafe Buenos Aires | **SB** 16

Cafe del Sol | **Montecito/SB** 17

Café des Beaux-Arts |
**Palm Desert/PS** 18

Carlitos Café | **SB** 18

Cava | **Montecito/SB** 18

China Pavilion | **SB** 19

🔲 Cuistot | **Palm Desert/PS** 25

Elements | **SB** 18

Emilio's | **SB** 20

Falls Steak | **PS** 20

First Cabin | **Newport Bch/OC** 24

**Z** Johannes | **PS** 25

Jonathan's/Peirano | **Ventura/SB** 23

La Quinta Cliffhse. | **La Quinta/PS** 16

Mastro's Ocean |
**Newport Coast/OC** 25

Miró | **SB** –

162' | **Dana Pt/OC** 25

Pacifica Seafood | **Palm Desert/PS** 22

**NEW** Pelican Grill |
**Newport Coast/OC** 20

**Z** Ranch Hse. | **Ojai/SB** 23

**NEW** Rattlesnake |
**Palm Desert/PS** 27

Rist. Mamma Gina |
**Palm Desert/PS** 20

Rist. Tuscany | **Palm Desert/PS** 26

Sirocco | **Indian Wells/PS** 24

Splashes | **Laguna Bch/OC** 19

**Z** Stella Mare's | **SB** 23

**Z** Stonehill Tav. | **Dana Pt/OC** 27

**Z** Studio | **Laguna Bch/OC** 26

Summit Hse. | **Fullerton/OC** 24

## VISITORS ON EXPENSE ACCOUNT

Antonello | **Santa Ana/OC** 24

**Z** Arnold Palmer's |
**La Quinta/PS** 20

Bayside | **Newport Bch/OC** 24

Bistango | **Irvine/OC** 24

Bluefin | **Newport Coast/OC** 27

Brooks | **Ventura/SB** 25

**Z** Cuistot | **Palm Desert/PS** 25

**Z** Downey's | **SB** 28

Five Crowns |
**Corona del Mar/OC** 24

Five Feet | **Laguna Bch/OC** 23

Fleming's | **Newport Bch/OC** 25

**Z** Hobbit | **Orange/OC** 27

**Z** Johannes | **PS** 25

Leatherby's | **Costa Mesa/OC** 24

**Z** Le St. Germain |
**Indian Wells/PS** 26

**Z** Le Vallauris | **PS** 27

**Z** Marché Moderne |
**Costa Mesa/OC** 27

Mastro's Ocean |
**Newport Coast/OC** 25

**Z** Mastro's Steak |
**Costa Mesa/OC** 26

Miró | **SB** –

Morton's Steak | **multi.** 25

Mr. Stox | **Anaheim/OC** 24

**Z** Napa Rose | **Anaheim/OC** 28

162' | **Dana Pt/OC** 25

Onotria | **Costa Mesa/OC** 25

Pinot Provence | **Costa Mesa/OC** 24

**Z** Ranch Hse. | **Ojai/SB** 23

Ritz Rest./Gdn. | **Newport Bch/OC** 25

Roy's | **multi.** 23

**Z** Ruth's Chris | **Irvine/OC** 26

Sapphire Laguna | **Laguna Bch/OC** 24

Splashes | **Laguna Bch/OC** 19

Square One | **SB** 24

**Z** Stonehill Tav. | **Dana Pt/OC** 27

**Z** Stonehouse | **Montecito/SB** 25

**Z** Studio | **Laguna Bch/OC** 26

Summit Hse. | **Fullerton/OC** 24

**Z** Tradition/Pascal |
**Newport Bch/OC** 28

**Z** Wally's Desert |
**Rancho Mirage/PS** 25

## WATERSIDE

Bella Vista | **Montecito/SB** 26

Cava | **Montecito/SB** 18

**Z** Cheesecake Factory |
**Rancho Mirage/PS** 19

Citron | **PS** 22

Emilio's | **SB** 20

First Cabin | **Newport Bch/OC** 24

Miró | **SB** –

**Z** Stella Mare's | **SB** 23

**Z** Studio | **Laguna Bch/OC** 26

## WINNING WINE LISTS

Antonello | **Santa Ana/OC** 24

Bayside | **Newport Bch/OC** 24

Bistango | **Irvine/OC** 24

Black Sheep | **Tustin/OC** 25

Brooks | **Ventura/SB** 25

Cold Spring | **SB** 20

**Z** Cuistot | **Palm Desert/PS** 25

Elements | **SB** 18

Five Crowns |
**Corona del Mar/OC** 24

Fleming's | **Newport Bch/OC** 25

Golden Truffle | **Costa Mesa/OC** 25

**Z** Hobbit | **Orange/OC** 27

**Z** Le St. Germain |
**Indian Wells/PS** 26

**Z** Le Vallauris | **PS** 27

**Z** Marché Moderne |
**Costa Mesa/OC** 27

**Z** Mastro's Steak |
**Costa Mesa/OC** 26

| | |
|---|---|
| Miró \| **SB** | - |
| Mr. Stox \| **Anaheim/OC** | 24 |
| **Z** Napa Rose \| **Anaheim/OC** | 28 |
| Old Vine Café \| **Costa Mesa/OC** | 24 |
| Onotria \| **Costa Mesa/OC** | 25 |
| Pinot Provence \| **Costa Mesa/OC** | 24 |
| Plow & Angel \| **Montecito/SB** | 24 |
| Ritz Rest./Gdn. \| **Newport Bch/OC** | 25 |
| Rosine's \| **Corona/PS** | 22 |
| Roy's \| **Newport Bch/OC** | 23 |
| Sapphire Laguna \| **Laguna Bch/OC** | 24 |
| **Z** Stonehill Tav. \| **Dana Pt/OC** | 27 |
| **Z** Stonehouse \| **Montecito/SB** | 25 |
| **Z** Studio \| **Laguna Bch/OC** | 26 |
| **Z** Tradition/Pascal \| **Newport Bch/OC** | 28 |
| **Z** Wally's Desert \| **Rancho Mirage/PS** | 25 |
| Walt's Wharf \| **Seal Bch/OC** | 24 |
| Wildfish/Grille \| **Newport Bch/OC** | 23 |

## WORTH A TRIP

| | |
|---|---|
| Anaheim | |
|   **Z** Napa Rose | 28 |
| Costa Mesa | |
|   **Z** Marché Moderne | 27 |
|   Pinot Provence | 24 |
| Dana Point | |
|   **Z** Stonehill Tav. | 27 |
| Laguna Beach | |
|   Five Feet | 23 |
|   French 75 | 20 |
|   Sapphire Laguna | 24 |
|   Splashes | 19 |
|   **Z** Studio | 26 |
| Newport Beach | |
|   Ritz Rest./Gdn. | 25 |
|   **Z** Tradition/Pascal | 28 |
| Orange | |
|   **Z** Hobbit | 27 |
| Santa Ana | |
|   Antonello | 24 |

**OC/PS/SB**

**SPECIAL FEATURES**

# Wine Vintage Chart

This chart, based on our 0 to 30 scale, is designed to help you select wine. The ratings (by **Howard Stravitz**, a law professor at the University of South Carolina) reflect the vintage quality and the wine's readiness to drink. We exclude the 1991–1993 vintages because they are not that good. A dash indicates the wine is either past its peak or too young to rate. Loire ratings are for dry white wines.

| Whites | 88 | 89 | 90 | 94 | 95 | 96 | 97 | 98 | 99 | 00 | 01 | 02 | 03 | 04 | 05 | 06 |
|---|---|---|---|---|---|---|---|---|---|---|---|---|---|---|---|---|
| **French:** | | | | | | | | | | | | | | | | |
| Alsace | – | 25 | 25 | 24 | 23 | 23 | 22 | 25 | 23 | 25 | 27 | 25 | 22 | 24 | 25 | – |
| Burgundy | – | 23 | 22 | – | 28 | 27 | 24 | 22 | 26 | 25 | 24 | 27 | 23 | 27 | 26 | 24 |
| Loire Valley | – | – | – | – | – | – | – | – | – | 24 | 25 | 26 | 23 | 24 | 27 | 24 |
| Champagne | 24 | 26 | 29 | – | 26 | 27 | 24 | 23 | 24 | 24 | 22 | 26 | – | – | – | – |
| Sauternes | 29 | 25 | 28 | – | 21 | 23 | 25 | 23 | 24 | 24 | 28 | 25 | 26 | 21 | 26 | 23 |
| **California:** | | | | | | | | | | | | | | | | |
| Chardonnay | – | – | – | – | – | – | – | 24 | 23 | 26 | 26 | 25 | 27 | 29 | 25 | |
| Sauvignon Blanc | – | – | – | – | – | – | – | – | – | – | 27 | 28 | 26 | 27 | 26 | 27 |
| **Austrian:** | | | | | | | | | | | | | | | | |
| Grüner Velt./ Riesling | – | – | – | – | 25 | 21 | 26 | 26 | 25 | 22 | 23 | 25 | 26 | 25 | 26 | – |
| **German:** | 25 | 26 | 27 | 24 | 23 | 26 | 25 | 26 | 23 | 21 | 29 | 27 | 24 | 26 | 28 | |

| Reds | 88 | 89 | 90 | 94 | 95 | 96 | 97 | 98 | 99 | 00 | 01 | 02 | 03 | 04 | 05 | 06 |
|---|---|---|---|---|---|---|---|---|---|---|---|---|---|---|---|---|
| **French:** | | | | | | | | | | | | | | | | |
| Bordeaux | 23 | 25 | 29 | 22 | 26 | 25 | 23 | 25 | 24 | 29 | 26 | 24 | 25 | 24 | 27 | 25 |
| Burgundy | – | 24 | 26 | – | 26 | 27 | 25 | 22 | 27 | 22 | 24 | 27 | 25 | 25 | 27 | 25 |
| Rhône | 26 | 28 | 28 | 24 | 26 | 22 | 25 | 27 | 26 | 27 | 26 | – | 25 | 24 | 25 | – |
| Beaujolais | – | – | – | – | – | – | – | – | – | 24 | – | 23 | 25 | 22 | 28 | 26 |
| **California:** | | | | | | | | | | | | | | | | |
| Cab./Merlot | – | – | 28 | 29 | 27 | 25 | 28 | 23 | 26 | 22 | 27 | 26 | 25 | 24 | 24 | 23 |
| Pinot Noir | – | – | – | – | – | – | 24 | 23 | 24 | 23 | 27 | 28 | 26 | 25 | 24 | – |
| Zinfandel | – | – | – | – | – | – | – | – | – | – | 25 | 23 | 27 | 24 | 23 | – |
| **Oregon:** | | | | | | | | | | | | | | | | |
| Pinot Noir | – | – | – | – | – | – | – | – | – | – | – | 27 | 25 | 26 | 27 | – |
| **Italian:** | | | | | | | | | | | | | | | | |
| Tuscany | – | – | 25 | 22 | 24 | 20 | 29 | 24 | 27 | 24 | 27 | 20 | 25 | 25 | 22 | 24 |
| Piedmont | – | 27 | 27 | – | 23 | 26 | 27 | 26 | 25 | 28 | 27 | 20 | 24 | 25 | 26 | – |
| **Spanish:** | | | | | | | | | | | | | | | | |
| Rioja | – | – | – | 26 | 26 | 24 | 25 | 22 | 25 | 24 | 27 | 20 | 24 | 25 | 26 | 24 |
| Ribera del Duero/Priorat | – | – | – | 26 | 26 | 27 | 25 | 24 | 25 | 24 | 27 | 20 | 24 | 26 | 26 | 24 |
| **Australian:** | | | | | | | | | | | | | | | | |
| Shiraz/Cab. | – | – | – | 24 | 26 | 23 | 26 | 28 | 24 | 24 | 27 | 27 | 25 | 26 | 24 | – |
| **Chilean:** | – | – | – | – | – | – | 24 | – | 25 | 23 | 26 | 24 | 25 | 24 | 26 | – |

subscribe to ZAGAT.com

# ON THE GO.
## IN THE KNOW.

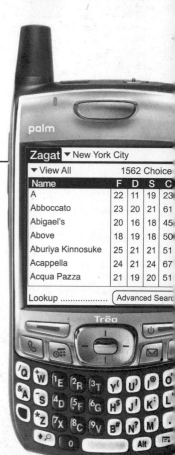

**ZAGAT** TO GO℠

Unlimited access
to Zagat dining &
travel content
in hundreds of
major cities.

Search by name,
location, ratings,
cuisine, special
features & Top Lists.

BlackBerry,® Palm,®
Windows Mobile®
and mobile phones.

Get it now at **mobile.zagat.com**
or text* **ZAGAT** to **78247**

# Zagat Products

Available wherever books are sold or at ZAGAT.com. To customize
Zagat guides as gifts or marketing tools, call 800-540-9609.

## RESTAURANTS & MAPS

America's Top Restaurants
Atlanta
Beijing
Boston
Brooklyn
California Wine Country
Cape Cod & The Islands
Chicago
Connecticut
Europe's Top Restaurants
Hamptons (incl. wineries)
Hong Kong
Las Vegas
London
Long Island (incl. wineries)
Los Angeles I So. California
(guide & map)
Miami Beach
Miami I So. Florida
Montréal
New Jersey
New Jersey Shore
New Orleans
New York City (guide & map)
Palm Beach
Paris
Philadelphia
San Diego
San Francisco (guide & map)
Seattle
Shanghai
Texas
Tokyo
Toronto
Vancouver
Washington, DC I Baltimore
Westchester I Hudson Valley
World's Top Restaurants

## LIFESTYLE GUIDES

America's Top Golf Courses
Movie Guide
Music Guide
NYC Gourmet Shop./Entertaining
NYC Shopping

## NIGHTLIFE GUIDES

Los Angeles
New York City
San Francisco

## HOTEL & TRAVEL GUIDES

Beijing
Hong Kong
Las Vegas
London
New Orleans
Montréal
Shanghai
Top U.S. Hotels, Resorts & Spas
Toronto
U.S. Family Travel
Vancouver
Walt Disney World Insider's Guide
World's Top Hotels, Resorts & Spas

## WEB & WIRELESS SERVICES

ZAGAT TO GO℠ for handhelds
ZAGAT.com℠ • ZAGAT.mobi℠